Retailing Principles

Retailing

A Global Outlook

Principles

Lynda Gamans Poloian

SOUTHERN NEW HAMPSHIRE UNIVERSITY

Fairchild Publications, Inc., New York

Executive Editor: Olga T. Kontzias
Assistant Acquisitions Editor: Carolyn Purcell
Development Editor: Sylvia Weber
Associate Production Editor: Amy Zarkos
Art Director: Adam B. Bohannon
Production Manager: Priscilla Taguer
Editorial Assistant: Suzette Lam
Copy Editor: Fran Marino
Interior Design: Charles B. Hames
Cover Design: Adam B. Bohannon

Library of Congress Catalog Card Number: 2002104012

ISBN: 1-56367-192-1

GST R 133004424

Printed in the United States of America

To Rosie, the Wolf,

and all members of Phantom Wolf Farm

Special Tribute

The undertaking of a vast body of work such as this text stems from ideas old and new and is never solely the domain of the present author. The first edition of this text was due to the vision and indefatigable efforts of Dorothy S. Rogers. She has been my mentor, co-author on other projects, business partner, and always, very good friend.

She and colleague Mercia M.T. Grassi laid the groundwork for this edition when they wrote the first edition of *Retailing: New Perspectives* in 1987. The second edition was written by Dorothy and me in 1992.

The retail industry has changed profoundly since the first edition, but the heart of a readable, valid compendium of ideas has not. The author gratefully acknowledges her co-author's contribution to retail education and to her personal and professional development.

Contents

Extended Contents

Preface

What is retailing? Where has it come from? Where is it going? Who are the players? How do they operate? These are just some of the questions that students should be asking in a principles of retailing course and that are answered in *Retailing Principles: A Global Outlook*, known as *Retailing: New Perspectives* in two previous editions. This new text confirms the reality that retailers, suppliers, and consumers participate in a global economy. Students also must look beyond their immediate domains, for many will live and build careers in the international marketplace. These reasons justify the title change and expanded coverage that reflects the strategic imperative of globalization. Eighty-five percent of the text material and 95 percent of the more than 200 photographs, figures, and tables are new to this edition.

This book is written for students taking their first course in retailing who possess a rudimentary knowledge of marketing and who may be preparing for a career in retailing or related fields. Other constituents include students in marketing, business management, international business, fashion merchandising, and vocational/technological programs. The text delivers solid information in a straightforward manner and is an equally useful reference for training directors and managers of retail organizations.

Organization and Scope

Current information, comprehensive coverage of important retail issues and institutions, and exposure to strategic planning and operational nuance is presented in a pragmatic way. Unit One, "The State of the Industry" covers the past, present, and future status of the retail industry. Chapter 1, "Roots and Rudiments," lays the groundwork with basic facts, terminology, a discussion of retailing's role in the supply chain, and concludes with a discussion of retail strategic planning. Chapter 2, "Planning and Predicting," leads off with a section on strategic planning followed by futurists' predictions and a survey of ten critical areas of change affecting retailers and customers this decade. Key retail institutions and the ways they are adapting to change are introduced here and woven throughout the text. Chapter 3, "The Retail Environment," gives special consideration to events in the economic, political, legal, social, and competitive realms that affect retail planning, and the impact of September 11, 2001 on retailing is also included.

Unit Two, *Retail Structures and Strategies*, devotes two chapters to retail stores and ownership and three chapters to important growth strategies. Chapter 4, "Brick-and-Mortar Retailers," identifies and defines retailers that operate from traditional stores. Chapter 5, "Ownership Dynamics," categorizes types of retail ownership and discusses merger, acquisition, and divestiture activity. It presents the reasons why retailing has changed substantially in the last 15 years. Strategies used by retailers as they compete through multiple marketing channels are included in Chapters 6,7, and 8. "Direct Marketing and Selling" examines catalog selling, telemarketing, direct mail tactics, and many nonstore retail formats. The "Electronic Retailing" chapter contains useful information about a subject that evolves at breathtaking speed. "Global Retailing" features reasons for global expansion, qualities of successful global retailers, and two comparative country studies.

Unit Three, "The Human Factor," consists of chapters on "Human Resource Management" and "Customer Behavior." Retailing is and always will be a people business. Chapter 9 addresses recruiting, training, and retaining personnel. Basic theories of consumer behavior and the changing roles and status of today's customers around the world are covered in Chapter 10.

Unit Four, "Store Location and Planning," comprises three chapters that deal with physical structures where retailing occurs. Chapter 11, "Site Selection," discusses the importance of selecting an appropriate store location and criteria involved in the selection process. Advanced geospatial research methods and a discussion of emerging retail sites, such as airports, are new to this edition. Chapter 12, "Shopping Centers and Malls," is a new chapter devoted entirely to venues from freestanding boutiques to megamalls. Challenges faced by mall developers and managers are included. Subjects treated separately in the previous edition are combined in Chapter 13, "Store Design and Visual Merchandising." Topics including store image, atmosphere, traffic flow, design principles, and displays are elucidated. A section on safety and security completes the chapter.

Unit Five, "Marketing the Merchandise," applies key marketing concepts—product, price, distribution, and promotion—to retailing. Chapter 14, "Merchandise Planning and Buying," looks at dollar and unit planning and discusses the role retail buyers play in the process. Contemporary pricing strategies and tactics are covered in Chapter 15, "Pricing for Profit." Chapter 16, "Supply Chain Management," examines logistics, physical distribution, and inventory control practices, including the ways technology helps create operational efficiencies. Chapter 17, "Retail Promotion,"combines essential aspects of advertising, sales promotion, and personal selling, culminating in a discussion of customer service.

Appendix A, "Retail Career Directions," presents career planning strategies and suggests avenues for career search, including Internet references. In addition, Appendix B, "Focus on Small Business," examines a career in retailing from the perspective of an entrepreneur.

Highlights of this Edition

Retailing Principles: A Global Outlook takes a more rigorous approach than did its predecessors to the fundamental principles upon which all successful retail institutions operate. This manifests in several new ways:

1. Global retail profiles at the end of each unit integrate chapter themes and challenge students to think critically and explore topics through further research.
2. Enhanced coverage of the retail environment includes timely information from leading trade associations such as the National Retail Federation and others.
3. Direct marketing is introduced in Chapter 6 for the first time as an important strategy.
4. Ethical issues are woven into text material in several pertinent areas including the sections on consumerism in Chapter 2 and global sourcing in Chapter 14.
5. Technology as an agent of change underlies the development of every chapter. In the last edition coverage was important; in this edition, it is imperative.

Pedagogical Features

Throughout this text the author has made every attempt not only to include international references, profiles, and examples but also to encourage students to think less ethnocentrically. Although some students may not be familiar with all retailers mentioned, the author has been careful to use international examples in contexts where knowledge of a specific retailer is not as important as the concept being discussed.

The end-of-unit Global retail profiles are about actual retail companies that operate internationally or globally or have the potential to do so.

These profiles are followed by study questions to encourage thoughtful analysis of the material. Sources used to compile the profiles include professional field trips, interviews, and personal discussions with retail executives, as well as the author's own international teaching and business experiences.

Two new features in this edition are Did You Know? and Cyberscoop. The first feature spotlights retail trivia that illuminates a point or example, breaks up the tedium of reading, and fosters interest in retailing. Cyberscoops are used in much the same way and encourage students to use the Internet. As this text went to press, all Web sites mentioned in the Cyberscoops were accessible. Because of constant upgrading, redesigning, and natural attrition, some may not be available as you read this. The author regrets any inconvenience this may cause students and instructors.

Pedagogical features carried over from previous editions, but updated and improved for this book, include From the Field vignettes in each chapter. They bring a strong dose of reality to the reader in brief bursts of information. Meaningful, and occasionally humorous, industry incidents from leading trade and consumer publications link to concepts presented in the chapter.

Other special learning features include concise learning objectives at the beginning of each chapter and a summary at the end of each chapter, followed by a selection of questions for review and discussion. Throughout the text key terms are set in bold type at their first occurrence and then highlighted in the margin along with a definition.

Many of the photos throughout the text are the author's own and present a unique perspective. Full-color inserts illustrate mannequin as conveyers of store image, visual merchandising techniques, and site selection mapping tools.

An Instructor's Guide featuring course outlines, suggestions for projects and activities, and a test bank is available for use in conjunction with the text. A PowerPoint presentation provides chapter highlights and illustrations not found in the text.

Acknowledgments

Numerous colleagues, retailers, and trade associations supported my efforts to complete this book. Thanks go to present and past members of the Southern New Hampshire University library staff including Pat Beaton, Ed Daniels, Judy Romein, and Carol West. Many other members of the SNHU community deserve mention. Bob Doucette, at the time Academic Dean of the Undergraduate School, granted release time and preferred scheduling. Karen Stone, Chair of the Marketing Department, provided ongoing enthusiasm and support. Donna Marshall and Kevin Degnan, graphics and Web gurus respectively, are responsible for any computer literacy I may possess. Tony Pizur contributed photography and his inimitable perspective on the world economy. Secretaries Linda Owens, Norma Comeau, and Karla Lamphere eased me through computer glitches and impending deadlines. Maggie Bourgeois, retired Associate Director of the Career Development Center, suggested significant additions to the retail careers section. Akanit Bijaphala is responsible for the virtual reality toy store that supplements material in Chapter 13. He was assisted by Xin Xu, Rio Rumawas, and Allison Costa, all graduates of SNHU. The Brothers of Zeta Beta Tau fraternity bestowed many acts of kindness. When it was difficult for me to participate fully as their faculty advisor, they understood and always asked, "Is it finished yet?" Sara Bilodeau served as research assistant until she graduated and accepted a management training position in retailing that she has written about in Appendix A.

Colleagues from other universities have also played a major roll in the preparation of this work. Tony Hernandez of Ryerson University in Toronto made significant contributions to the Site Selection chapter. Professor Emerita Eleanor May fine-tuned the section on the wheel of retailing. Marilyn Lavin, University of Wisconsin-Whitewater, contributed her photography and cross-cultural insight. Allison Young, University of Tennessee, and members of the University of Arizona community, Sherry Lotz, Mary Ann Eastlick, Ken Gertz, and Soyeon Shim also deserve special thanks.

Many retailers and trade organizations have provided material for this edition. At Global Retail Symposiums held annually at the Southwest Retail Center at the University of Arizona, I have had the opportunity to meet and learn from many global retailers. Study tours sponsored by the American Collegiate Retailing Association have also made me privy to retail information not accessible in any other way. Executives from Carrefour, Tesco, Saks, Selfridges, Gap, Gymboree, Spiegel, Wal-Mart, and Kmart are among those who have contributed extensively to my research. Celia MacKay and Mike Loveless reviewed several drafts of their Costco profile and have hosted countless field trips for students. Roland Hearns and Lisa Rainis deserve special mention for spearheading the inclusion of several Saks references. Nancy Adam of Greenwood Partners and Colleen Schelde of Environmental Systems Research Institute were eminently helpful in securing special site selection materials. Susan Bates, owner of the Cooperage in Townsend Harbor, MA, spoke with me on several occasions to be sure the perspective of the entrepreneur was accurately reflected in the "Focus on Small Business." Also a special thanks to Miranda Latimer of Monitor, Keith Fishman of ClipArt, David Bellman, Bellman Jewelers, and Isabel DiGregorio of Georgiou for special photos and content. The resources of the National Retail Federation, the Direct Marketing Educational Foundation, the Direct Selling Association, and the International Council of Shopping Centers also have been of great help during the preparation of this text.

This text is better because of the diversity of comments made by the reviewers of this edition. The author would particularly like to thank Ellen Flotman, Professor Emerita of the University of North Texas, whose detailed comments contributed greatly to the validity of this text. The reviewers selected by the publisher include: James H. Glenn, Jr., Owensboro Community College; Debi Forse, Holland College; Sharon T. Wagner, Missouri Western State University; P. Renee Foster, Delta State College; Jane T. Walker, North Carolina Agricultural and Technical State University; Deborah C. Fowler, University of South Carolina; Harvey Shoemack, International Academy of Merchandising and Design, Oaktown Community College, and Illinois Instittute of Art; Debra K. Weninger, Allentown Business School; and Diane Minger, Cedar Valley College.

Many authors enjoy having written their own books but find that the process itself can often be grueling, frustrating, and laborious. For me, the process was made easier by the staff of Fairchild Books. From Sylvia Weber, my development editor, I have learned more about writing and managing what she once called a "daunting task" than I have at any other stage of my career. Thank you, Sylvia. I am also grateful to Olga Kontzias, executive editor, for her fair and compassionate treatment over the four years of this project. Mary McGarry, the acquiring editor during the early stages of manuscript development, provided valuable guidance in organizing the text. For their roles in transforming the manuscript into a printed book, I thank Amy Zarkos, my production editor, art director Adam Bohannon, and production manager Priscilla Taguer.

Retailing Principles

The State of

the Industry

Chapter 1

Roots and Rudiments

Learning Objectives

After completing this chapter you should be able to:

- Define basic retailing and marketing terms.
- Apply popular theories to the evolution of retail businesses.
- List the six functional areas in retailing.
- Identify retail marketing channels and members of the supply chain.
- Describe how history has affected the formation of contemporary retail organizations.
- Delineate basic types of retail stores and nonstore operations.

Figure 1.1 Build-a-Bear combines the best of all retail worlds for customers of all ages. Time, place, and possession utility are considered by this experiential retailer (See p 17).

gross domestic product(GDP)
Total retail value of all goods and services produced by a country during a specific time period.

CYBERSCOOP

Many statistics on the size, scope, and classifications of retailing are available from the United States government. Visit www.census.gov and click on "R" for retail. What volume of retail sales was recorded in your state last quarter? What category of merchandise generates higher sales: apparel or home electronics?

Retailing is all around us. It is as old as ancient trade routes and outdoor markets and as new as the World Wide Web. It includes elegant Tiffany's and eclectic garage sales. Retailing is small town and big city, local and regional, national, international, and global. It is the most important link in the journey from producer to consumer, since much of a country's wealth—its gross domestic product—is accrued through some form of retailing. The **gross domestic product(GDP)** is the total value of all goods and services produced by a country during a specific time period. Retail sales are a significant contributor to the GDP. In 2001, retail sales in the United States were expected to reach $3.5 trillion.[1]

Understanding the origins of the industry means a deeper appreciation for the state of the industry today. Retailers in the 21st century search for excellence in every phase of their operations. Challenges abound and encompass people, communications, technology, information, distribution, competition, pressure to perform, and much more. Retailing is above all a *people* business. Success depends on understanding customers' needs, motivations, and lifestyles no matter what retailing venue is employed. Automobile salespeople who do not understand why one person wants a green BMW Z-3 convertible while another prefers a blue Ford Taurus sedan can not succeed at their jobs.

Retail employees need excellent written and oral communication skills. A misunderstood directive, memo, e-mail, or sales presentation can result in decreased good will or financial loss. Every loss, no matter how small, affects sales and profits. A loyal customer, who is verbally assaulted when making a return can easily find another store in which to shop. Improperly written retail Web sites do not hold the surfer's interest. Skills in dealing with people at all levels are among the most valued in the industry. Retailers that prosper in a highly competitive, technological world are those that nurture effective communication.

High performing retailers cannot exist without technology. Retailing demands state-of-the-art equipment and the expertise to use it to full capacity. Retailers must do more than utilize terminals that supply information on sales, inventory, and commission earnings. They must develop programs that efficiently monitor customer behavior and provide information that makes serving customers more efficient. The goal of this textbook is to present a myriad of topics to welcome you to the world of retailing.

Definitions and Dynamics

Every discipline and industry has its own terminology and retailing is no exception. Because retailing is such an important part of business and rests under the big umbrella of marketing, the language reflects an integration of marketing terms. This section serves as a review of marketing terminology for those that have taken a basic marketing course and as an introduction to key terms for those who have not. In addition to a marketing orientation, classifications of retail businesses, size and scope of the industry, and the educational benefits of retailing also are included.

Retailing in a Marketing Context

Marketing is at the heart of every business function. **Marketing** is a set of business activities that includes product, price, promotion, and distribution. Most marketers also include people. Doing so underscores their importance to the success of any marketing endeavor. **Marketing mix** is the unique blend of product, price, promotion, people, and distribution practices that is intended to reach and satisfy a **target market**, that is, a group of people with similar characteristics and needs who a company wishes to reach. The **marketing concept** is the philosophy that guides a company in creating its marketing mix so as to satisfy its customers and, as a result, make a profit.

The process of tracing the existence of a product in the marketplace by examining the stages through which it passes and the time it spends in each stage is called the **product life cycle**. The cycle consists of four stages: introduction, growth, maturity, and decline. Knowing which stage a product occupies helps retailers determine the appropriate steps to take to ensure a long life in the marketplace.

Without knowledge of marketing channels, it is difficult to understand the role played by retailing in the distribution process. A **marketing channel** is the route taken by a product as it travels from producer to final consumer. This is also called the channel of distribution or the supply chain, a more contemporary term. The **supply chain** refers to the various participants in the marketing channel including manufacturers, suppliers, distributors, and retailers. Manufacturers, suppliers, and distributors are also called vendors. **Vendors** are manufacturers, distributors, and other members of the supply chain that provide goods and services to the retailer. The term *resource* also is used interchangeably with vendor. Efficient distribution is one of the most crucial competitive elements for retailers. Fine-tuning relationships with vendors, managing inventory, streamlining transportation

marketing A set of business activities that includes product, price, promotion, and distribution. Most marketers also include people.

marketing mix The unique blend of product, price, promotion, people, and distribution practices that is intended to reach and satisfy a target market.

target market A group of people with similar characteristics and needs that a company wishes to reach.

marketing concept The philosophy that guides a company in creating its marketing mix so as to satisfy its customers and, as result, make a profit.

product life cycle The process of tracing the existence of a product in the marketplace by examining the stages through which it passes and the time spent in each stage.

marketing channel The route taken by a product as it travels from producer to final consumer.

supply chain Various participants in the marketing channel including manufacturers, suppliers, distributors, and retailers.

vendor Manufacturers, distributors, or other members of the supply chain that provide goods and services to the retailer.

Figure 1.2 Tommy Bahama produces a line of sporty men's apparel that is a top seller at the Parisian department store in Birmingham, Alabama.

retailing The selling of goods or services directly to the final customer.

retailers Businesses or individuals that sell more than 50 percent of their goods and/or services to final customers.

retail mix Various activities in which retailers are engaged as they attempt to satisfy customers.

merchandise assortment All the goods in a store, defined in terms of breadth and depth of stock.

product line Group of closely related items produced by a manufacturer.

classification Group of related merchandise carried by a retailer.

modes, and refining technology are ways retailers become more competitive.

Retailing Defined

When marketing is conducted at the level of the final consumer it is considered retailing. **Retailing** is the selling of goods or services directly to the customer for personal, nonbusiness use. It is implied that retail transactions involve individual units or small quantities of merchandise or limited use of a service. **Retailers** are businesses or individuals who sell more than 50 percent of their goods and/or services to final customers. Similar to the marketing mix, the retail mix specifically pertains to store, service, and nonstore settings. **Retail mix** describes the various activities in which retailers are engaged as they attempt to satisfy customers. Physical facilities, planning, merchandising, pricing, promoting, and distributing are important aspects of the mix. Applications to retailing are vast and cited throughout the text.

A variety of merchandising terms are helpful to know since they appear frequently as retailers are described. One way that retailers differentiate themselves is through merchandise assortment. A **merchandise assortment** consists of all the goods in a store, defined in terms of its breadth and depth of stock. Breadth refers to the number of different product lines carried in a store. Depth measures the number of different styles or models in each line. A **product line** is a group of closely related items produced by a manufacturer. For example, Calvin Klein jeans and Nokia cell phones are each product lines. In Figure 1.2, the Tommy Bahama line of men's casual apparel is illustrated. Different categories of merchandise are referred to as merchandise classifications. A **classification** is a group of related merchandise in a store. For example all brands of jeans, shirts, or cell phones carried by a retailer.

Definitions help us organize the parlance of a discipline, but they do not necessarily make a topic come alive. The many dimensions of retailing will become clearer, the industry more vibrant, and the message more personal as chapters unfold.

Retail Classifications

This textbook concentrates on firms that are classified as retailers rather than on manufacturers or wholesalers with retail operations. This term is not to be confused with merchandise classifications described in the previous section. Some former manufacturers and wholesalers are now considered retailers, because once a company begins to realize more than 50 percent of its sales at retail it officially changes channel position from manufacturing or wholesaling to retailing.

According to the National Retail Federation, each type of retailer falls into one of the following eight major classifications, based on merchandise carried:

1. Food stores.
2. General merchandise.
3. Apparel and accessories.
4. Building materials and gardening supplies.
5. Furniture and home furnishings.
6. Automotive dealers and service stations.
7. Eating and drinking places.
8. Miscellaneous retailers, which include drug stores, gift shops, book stores, catalog retailers, and many other varieties.[2]

Each is vitally important to the economy as a whole. The various types of traditional retail operations are discussed in depth in Chapter 4; nonstore and electronic formats are discussed in Chapters 6 and 7.

Scope of Retailing

Think for a moment about what you're wearing on your feet today. Where did you purchase your sneakers? Maybe at a specialty store like Footlocker? **Specialty stores** are retail outlets that maintain large selections of limited lines of merchandise. If you wanted to pick up some running gear, a fishing pole, and a sports watch in addition to your shoes, you might have shopped at a category killer, like Sports Authority. **Category killers** are specialty superstores that focus on limited merchandise classifications and a great breadth and depth of assortments. If you are very brand conscious, maybe a Nike superstore was your choice. **Superstores** are huge retail stores, usually over 150,000 square feet, combining general merchandise and often food under one roof. The term also applies to category killers, even though these stores do not usually carry food, and discounters. Virgin Records, a category killer specializing in music, is illustrated in Figure 1.3. If you are on a tight budget this semester you might have visited Wal-Mart, a discounter. **Discounters** are stores that buy and sell at low prices and depend on high volume and low overhead to be profitable. With little time to shop, you may have ordered your new outdoor boots through a catalog like

specialty stores Retail outlets that maintain large selections of limited lines of merchandise.

category killers Specialty superstores that focus on limited merchandise classifications and great breadth and depth of assortments.

superstores Huge retail stores, usually over 150,000-square-feet, that combine general merchandise, and often food, under one roof.

discounters Retailers that buy and sell at low prices and depend on high volume and low overhead to be profitable.

Figure 1.3 The Virgin Megastore is classified as a category killer because the company provides great breadth and depth of music and video products. © *2000 Copyright. Designed by Development Design Group, Inc. Photo by Walter Larimore*

L.L.Bean. If you're into something very hip, the Skecher's Web site may have been your destination.

Assume that you have decided to shop at Sports Authority. As you enter the store you will be tempted by the efforts of store planners and visual merchandisers. Their goal is to catch your attention: "Look here, touch me, walk this way!" If you thought you were making a relatively simple purchase, guess again. The situation is probably more complicated, for you realize that your next decision involves the type of shoe you want from among a myriad of sport styles. What will it be—tennis, running, aerobics, walking, cross trainers?

Now consider why you chose Sports Authority. Was it convenient to home, work, or school? Were you at the shopping center anyway and just happened to see the store sign? Maybe a friend told you about a great sale the store was having. Possibly the newest Air Jordan's were out of stock at another store you visited.

Why did you decide to buy footwear in the first place? Your old pair might have worn out, or perhaps you were bored with your existing shoe wardrobe. For most products and services, the choice of retail outlets is vast, and your decision is often based on a complex network of factors. If you are looking for a broad selection of styles, you will probably go to a specialty store. If you need to be educated on the suitability of athletic footwear styles for various sports, you may choose a sporting goods store, where salespeople have the expertise to assist you. If you do not own a car, but can get to a nearby mall by bus, then location and accessibility may determine your choice of retailer. Personal finances may override all other factors involving your purchase decision. You may choose not to buy at all, to postpone your purchase, or, to shop at a secondhand consignment shop.

Consider this scenario further and you will probably come up with dozens of places you have shopped or could shop for new shoes. This exercise has demonstrated the omnipresence of retailing, the importance of accessibility, and the many factors that affect purchasing decisions. If you can apply any of these incidents or questions to your own shopping behavior, then you are beginning to *think retailing*.

Educational Dimension

You probably never thought of your local retail store as a school. If not, observe young children riding in supermarket baskets, their inquisitive eyes darting from shelf to shelf, and you will understand the educational dimension of retailing. Through such questions as "What is that?" and "Can I eat this?" children learn. Product knowledge is often followed by a lesson in simple economics. "No, it's too much money" may be said in reference to brightly packaged but more expensive cereals.

A retail store is often the place where a child learns social patterns. As examples, a 10-year-old accompanying Mom to the supermarket in 1960 soon learned that she was the decision maker when it involved selecting groceries and fresh vegetables. In 1980, a 5-year-old may have watched Dad make the selections, reflecting an increase in single parent families. In 1990, it may have been a teenage son or daughter who shopped for the whole family and made independent product choices because Mom and Dad were both working full-time. For families of all types in the early 21st century it may be the responsibility of whoever gets home first to dial up or log on to the Internet and order groceries or prepared foods for delivery.

Many of us routinely have been introduced to new products or new uses for existing ones through point-of-purchase displays in stores. **Point-of-purchase(POP) displays** are fixtures, or special racks and printed materials positioned close to customer interface areas in a store. Display devices are often furnished by manufacturers. POP displays communicate to a shopper that an old brand of frozen pizza has been improved or a new piece of software that recognizes the human voice has been released. They are often located on end caps in self-service stores. **End caps** are display areas located at the ends of shopping aisles. They are often used in superstores, discount, and other large format stores. An end cap featuring wine is illustrated in Figure 1.4.

Electronic media provide other forms of retail education. The Internet takes us to places only dreamed of a decade ago. If we are looking for a new laptop we can search many sites to comparison shop, enter chat rooms to learn about other shoppers' experiences, or we can easily access consumer reports in order to make a more informed decision.

Through programmed 30-minute commercials we may know more about exercise equipment than any previous generation, but the equipment still might hold laundry rather than be used to keep us fit once purchased. Some aspects of consumer behavior may not change despite the temptations of technology.

Basic economics, psychology, and sociology can be added to the list of lessons learned in almost all retail stores. Education is an inherent part of retailing, and it is not only for the very young.

Figure 1.4 End cap display featuring fine wines spills over into the aisle to gain even more attention from Carrefour customers. Carrefour of France is the second largest retail company in the world.

point-of-purchase(POP) displays Fixtures or special racks and printed materials positioned close to customer interface areas in stores.

end caps Display areas located at the ends of shopping aisles.

The Process of Change

Constant motion and change are other characteristics of retailing that are explained by various theories whose very names evoke action: wheel of retailing, methods of retail dissemination, and geographic movement.

Wheel of Retailing

wheel of retailing Theory that describes a cyclical pattern of retail evolution consisting of three phases: entry, trading-up, and vulnerability.

The **wheel of retailing** theory describes a cyclical pattern of retail evolution consisting of three phases: entry, trading up, and vulnerability. According to this theory, retailers enter the marketplace as low-price, low-margin, and low-service operators and over time mature into more elaborate, and higher-cost establishments. As they do so, they become increasingly vulnerable to new, lower-priced, lower-margin, lower-service competitors, that in turn may go through the same process.[3] In many ways the wheel of retailing is similar to marketing's product life cycle. In that, products, services, and even retail stores go through four stages of the cycle in varying lengths of time. Along the way many forces, including competition, affect the pace. The wheel of retailing theory describes the dynamic nature of the retailing industry. Its connotation of constant motion and competition are conveyed through an historical example.

Evolution of a Specific Retail Store The wheel of retailing theory is explained using the former discount retailer, Zayre. The Zayre Corporation was at one time a multibillion-dollar operation with more than 300 discount department stores in the United States plus a number of subsidiaries.

In phase one, entry, Zayre opened two experimental discount stores in 1956, in Massachusetts. These stores were immediately successful in part because they were highway accessible, had plentiful parking, and were modern, well-lighted, and air-conditioned—in contrast to the mill-outlet stores that were popular at the time. Mill-outlets were retail stores located in manufacturing facilities.

Its crisp image helped Zayre move the entire industry up from its humble beginnings. Discount retailing entered phase two, trading-up. Strong consumer acceptance caused other retailers to want to compete for a share of the lucrative discount business.

Other discounters such as Kmart and mass merchandisers like JC Penney eventually were able to surpass Zayre. **Mass merchandisers** are large format chain stores with broad geographic coverage that carry large assortments of general merchandise. Large discount stores with broad distribution networks also are referred to as mass merchandisers. Volume buying, competi-

mass merchandisers Large format chain stores with broad geographic coverage that carry large assortments of general merchandise.

tive pricing, aggressive expansion, and forward-thinking management became their tools of competition. Stores were made more appealing to customers as decor and customer services were improved. Eventually older discounters like Zayre became vulnerable to the strengths and strategies of the new breed of discounters.

Zayre was bought by Ames Department Stores in 1988. Ames targets budget conscious consumers. Most Zayre stores changed their name to Ames at that time. The aftermath of the merger and acquisition activity, discussed in Chapter 5, was one reason why Ames declared bankruptcy in 1990, forcing the once strong Zayre stores virtually out of existence. Ames gradually improved its financial position but was forced to liquidate in 2002. **Department stores** are retail stores organized into separate departments for purposes of selling a wide variety of soft goods such as apparel for men, women, and children, and hard goods such as home electronics and furniture. In the mid-80s, JC Penney shifted from mass merchandiser to full-fledged department store status. Typically department stores are considered more attractive places in which to shop than mass merchandisers.

Figure 1.5 Selfridges department store dominates an entire city block in London and has been trading from its Oxford Street address since 1909.

department stores Retail stores organized into separate departments for purposes of selling a wide variety of soft goods such as apparel for men, women, and children and hard goods, such as furniture.

Competitive Nature of Retailing In some instances the development of entirely new types of retail institutions has kept the wheel turning. This occurrence addresses the competitive nature of retailing throughout history.

In the early 1800s, simple provisioners were the norm in the United States. By 1850, able to offer greater variety, better service, and stable prices all under one—usually very elegant—roof, department stores opened in large cities. An impressive structure, Selfridges department store in London is illustrated in Figure 1.5. Department stores forced smaller stores to reassess their formats and priorities.

By the late 1950s, department stores had become complacent, top heavy with excess management, and open to competition. Enterprising retailers responded to the demand for easy access, ample parking, and more aggressive pricing by growing numbers of post-World War II customers. Their market share eroded as discount stores advanced.

The 1980s witnessed another milestone as off-price specialty discount retailers developed. **Off-price retailers** are specialty discount stores that sell branded products at 20 to 60 percent less than traditional specialty or

off-price retailers Specialty discount stores that sell branded products at 20 to 60 percent less than traditional specialty or department stores.

department stores. Apparel retailers like T.J.Maxx and Marshalls intensified the competition. T.J. Maxx was once part of the Zayre organization, and Marshalls was acquired in 1995 by TJX Corp., the parent company of T.J.Maxx. Off-price stores maintained a soft goods focus, applied enterprising merchandise procurement practices, and offered discount pricing on popular brand-name goods. At the time more unbranded, generic merchandise was offered by the discount department stores. Feel the motion of the wheel in action.

The longevity of some retail institutions cannot be explained by the wheel of retailing. Apparently some have withstood the test of time and seem immune to competition. The vending machine industry is an example and catalog retailing may be another. It remains to be seen if electronic retailing will eventually join this category or if it will be displaced by newer retail formats. As retailing professor emerita, Eleanor May said, "specialty catalogs are showing some maturity problems and electronic retailing some immaturity problems."[4] Perhaps both will create further activity on the wheel.

The wheel theory is one explanation of the dynamic nature of retailing. Possible drivers of change called the trickle theories are another.

Trickle Theories of Retail Dissemination

Originally used to describe how fashion trends disseminate across consumer markets, trickle theories also explain retail movement. They acknowledge the importance of trend innovation and acceptance as well as economic impact. Three types are trickle-down, trickle-up, and trickle-across:

1. *Trickle-down.* Some retailers initially target high income markets. They eventually face competition from merchants who copy their strategies to appeal to lower income groups. To generate more sales, these upmarket retailers trade down to appeal to a lower income market. This new market was not originally their chosen segment. Designer fashion retailers such as Armani, Versace, Donna Karan, and Ralph Lauren give credence to the trickle-down process. In addition to their higher-priced merchandise lines, they all produce fashion and stores with prices more customers can afford.

2. *Trickle-up.* The trickle-up process occurs when a lower class trend is identified by customers and retailers and filters up to a supposed higher economic strata—or perhaps taste level—of society. This could be a plausible explanation for the tactics of highly focused specialty stores. Retailers that take ordinary products, such as coffee and candles, and el-

evate them to elite experiences illustrate the trickle-up process. Gourmet coffee retailer Starbucks and Yankee Candle Company have accomplished this. Denim jeans, once the wardrobe of farmers and other laborers, have risen to designer fashion status. They also command higher prices than when jeans were considered utilitarian apparel. Jeans now are virtually a commodity in mass markets, perhaps diluting the credibility of this theory.

3. *Trickle-across.* The trickle-across process occurs when trends are observed happening across all economic and taste levels at about the same time and speed. In this circumstance products at varying price and quality levels are available from many types of retailers at approximately the same time. Try to find a Furbee™ or Tickle Me Elmo™ in a department, specialty, or discount store; in a catalog, on a Web site, or on a home shopping channel; in San Diego, Santiago, or Singapore, and you probably can.

Retail stores that provide a broad range of merchandise to an equally diverse customer base need to identify trends and interpret them expediently for their markets. Because many retailers carry essentially the same merchandise, knowledge of the trickle-across process is essential. Another indication of the dynamic nature of retailing is geographic movement.

Geographic Movement

Retailers have always followed consumers in order to meet their changing needs. At other times gentrification of residential and shopping areas has precipitated change. Several examples illustrate these points. Sometimes retail development has been influenced by the media. Melrose Avenue in Los Angeles has been a funky shopping street for decades, although it did not attain its popularity until the TV show bearing its name brought throngs of shoppers and new retailers to the area. Extensive developments by luxury goods retailers on Sloane and Bond Streets in London in the last decade exemplify the increase in upwardly mobile professionals in these areas. An equally major movement by retailers into new urban malls in New York City's Harlem shows what happens when old economic structures begin to erode, making way for redevelopment of areas previously considered undesirable by retailers.

Planned communities also play a part in geographic movement. Los Colinos outside Dallas, Texas, encouraged people to move to the suburbs. The gated community is totally self-contained and appears to spring out of nowhere on the plains of Texas, yet has created a customer base by its very existence. The development first drew major employers, then housing, people, transportation systems, and of course, retailing.

The presence of ATM machines in previously unexpected locations and minibanks in supermarkets not only indicates changes in retail banking services but shows how innovative service providers meet the immediate needs of customers by overcoming the limits of geography. A mobile ATM van at the famous Brimfield Antique Market in Massachusetts is shown in Figure 1.6. If your customers can't easily get to your bank, bring the bank to your customers.

Figure 1.6 Total convenience is the sentiment behind this mobile ATM van parked in the hubbub of a famous antique market in Brimfield, Massachusetts.

sourcing The identification and utilization of resources for the manufacture of goods.

Retail Store Functions

The five universal functions of all retail businesses are merchandising, operations, promotion, finance, and human resource management. Advances in technology have created another important area, information technology.

- *Merchandising* includes all sourcing, buying, and, in some smaller stores, selling activities. **Sourcing** is the identification and utilization of resources for the manufacture of goods. Product development, assortment planning, purchasing, educating sales staff, and making the product available for sale are a few of the responsibilities in this sector.
- *Operations* involves all aspects of managing the physical plant. Operations staff oversee maintenance, scheduling, customer services, shipping and receiving, warehousing, inventory control, and store security. Facilities development is part of operations, but in most large companies, separate real estate divisions handle this aspect of business. In many chains, selling is an aspect of operations.
- *Promotion* includes advertising, visual merchandising, public relations, personal selling, and sales promotion events.
- *Finance* involves controlling the company's assets and includes accounting, record keeping, forecasting, budgeting, taxation, and deriving capital.
- *Human resource management* involves the recruiting, hiring, training, and evaluation of personnel. The administration of benefits, liaising with unions, and general employee welfare are included.
- *Information technology* crosses all functional areas and is of particular importance in planning, control, management, merchandising, and customer service.

Functional areas do not exist in isolation. Without constant communication between areas no retail operation can work efficiently no matter how strong each part may be individually. The six functional areas are illustrated in Figure 1.7.

Retail Marketing Channels

Success stems from selecting the appropriate channel that will fulfill customers needs most efficiently. Understanding the concept of economic utility is crucial to this task.

Economic Utility

There would be little satisfaction for customers if manufacturers created new items but did not consider customers' wants and needs. This is the core of the marketing concept. It stresses that consumer satisfaction should be the basis for all retail planning. Economic utility further explains this concept. **Utility** is the ability of a product to satisfy consumers' needs and wants. The four basic utilities are time, place, form, and possession. In an industrial world, where people are no longer self-sufficient, the key to success is having the right goods in the right place at the right time. If a marketing system works well, it provides for the four basic utilities isolated by economists that are explained in a retailing context:

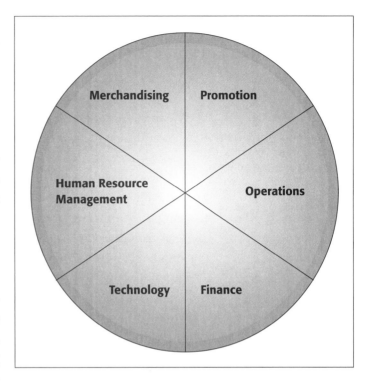

Figure 1.7 Functional Areas in Retailing

utility Ability of a product to satisfy consumers' needs and wants. The four basic utilities are time, place, form, and possession.

- *Time utility* occurs when retailers have merchandise that customers want exactly when they want it.
- *Place utility* occurs when retailers locate their stores—or Web sites—with easy access for their customers.
- *Form utility* refers to the power of retailers to create a satisfying merchandise assortment within their stores or places of business.
- *Possession utility* happens when merchandise is sold to the customer.

Build-a-Bear is a specialty retailer that has been unusually successful at providing all four types of economic utility. The growing chain locates its stores in high-traffic, family-oriented shopping centers. The opportunity to design, stuff, dress, and name your personalized bear provides a unique entertainment and ownership experience. As illustrated in Figure 1.1, a satisfied customer expresses the joy of possession as she emerges from Build-a-Bear.

Typical Retail Channels

Where does retailing belong in the vast marketing channel that brings New Zealand Kiwi fruit to Harrod's food hall in London and hand-painted silk scarves from Malaysia to fashion retailers in Colombia? Are retailers always involved as goods move from manufacturer to user? There is no single answer to these questions because the distinction between retailers and wholesalers, and others in the supply chain, has blurred in recent years.

A firm does not have to be a retailer by definition in order to engage in retailing. Even though the largest percentage of consumer goods is marketed through the retail sector, many other firms throughout the channel engage in the functions traditionally performed by retailers. Warehouse clubs such as Costco Wholesale or Sam's Club are examples of firms that sell to more than one member of the supply chain. **Warehouse clubs** are large format, bare-bones retail stores that sell a broad assortment of merchandise to small businesses as well as families and individuals.

warehouse clubs Large format, bare-bones retail stores that sell a broad assortment of merchandise to small businesses as well as families and individuals.

Direct, indirect, dual, and multiple marketing channels used to reach the customer are now addressed. Figure 1.8 illustrates contemporary retail marketing channels.

Manufacturer to Consumer Manufacturers can play a number of retail roles—supplier, partner, inventory control specialist, shipping agent, promotion consultant, to name a few. The more functions they undertake, the more control they can exert over the channel and ultimately the more profits they can generate.

Manufacturer to customer is the shortest, most direct channel. No intermediaries such as wholesalers are used. Some nonstore retailers that reach the customers through catalogs or the Internet also belong to this category. **Nonstore retailers** are those that sell through means other than traditional storefronts. Included in this channel are diverse types of retailers such as the following:

nonstore retailers Retailers that sell through means other than traditional storefronts.

- *Direct sellers.* Retailers that sell to customers one-on-one are included in this category. As examples, Mary Kay Cosmetics sells through party plans and Cutco Cutlery via in-home consultations.
- *Direct marketers.* Retailers that manufacture some or all of their own products and reach many of their customers through catalogs, direct-mail pieces, telemarketing, or the Internet are included in this category. Omaha Steaks is an example.

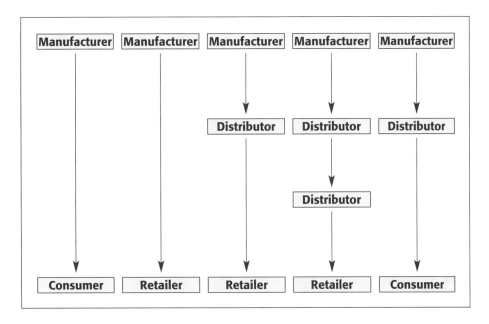

Figure 1.8 Contemporary View of Retail Marketing Channels

- *Factory outlet stores.* Stores that are owned by the manufacturer belong to this group. **Factory outlets** are company-owned stores that sell manufacturers' overruns, seconds, irregulars, and sample products. Bugle Boy apparel, Mikasa china, and Hanes hosiery and underwear are all examples.
- *Craft artisans.* Individuals that design and produce goods and sell to customers operate through direct channels. Independent furniture and pottery makers as well as artists who sell their own works belong in this category.
- *Couture fashion designers.* Company figureheads who create one-of-a-kind garments at extremely high prices and deal directly with a limited number of high income customers also use this channel. Yves St. Laurent and Christian La Croix are examples.

factory outlets Company-owned stores that sell manufacturers' overruns, seconds, irregulars, and sample products.

The marketing strategies of manufacturers that sell direct are very customer oriented, because they are not selling to middlemen. In some situations the name brand or reputation is extremely important. In other instances, such as shoes sold in factory outlets, the emphasis is on price, and brand may be of less importance.

Promotion strategies also vary. Television may be the catalyst for inducing Victoria's Secret catalog sales; personal selling the promotion tool for a fine watercolor painting; and print media the boon of the factory outlet store. All components of the retail mix are selected with the target market in mind.

Manufacturer to Retailer A longer route, and one in which the retailer is the only middleman, is the one from manufacturer directly to retailer, and then to customer. Retailers are a very important link in the distribution chain because most goods are marketed through some type of retail outlet.

Industry dominant retailers, such as Wal-Mart, generally buy directly from producers because of the vast quantities of goods that they purchase. In this instance Wal-Mart is considered a channel captain because of the power it has to influence the flow of goods within its marketing channel.

This channel is often selected for fads and fashion items that have a relatively short life. Middlemen were not used extensively by retailers that sold periwinkle-blue nail polish or summer tube-tops in their respective strong seasons.

Manufacturer to Distributor to Retailer The longest channel travels from manufacturer to distributor to retailer before it reaches the consumer. Today it is not the most important one in the United States, but under certain circumstances may be the only way for the retailer to obtain certain goods.

When retailers were located in city centers and the nation's transportation network was controlled by railroads, wholesale distributors dominated the marketing channel. They brought goods from manufacturing centers to trade centers where retailers from all over a region could converge and view many products from a variety of resources. The rapid expansion of retailing into the suburbs, plus the development of a nationwide highway network by the mid-20th century, made buying through more direct channels a logical choice. Retailers who needed merchandise for their branch stores were buying in large quantities from manufacturers, who shipped to retailer-owned central distribution centers. **Branch stores** are satellite stores within a department store group. They are usually located in the suburbs or cities remote from the main store. When retailers began taking over the distribution functions formerly performed by wholesalers, most wholesalers lost their dominant position in the channel.

Even now, certain circumstances call for the use of a long channel. In home electronics, more than 80 percent of all wholesale transactions go through a manufacturer's representative. A **manufacturer's representative** is an independent business person who works in a specific territory selling related but noncompeting products to more than one account.

Some firms also sell directly to consumers in small quantities. A typical example is a sporting goods distributor that sells to a select group of consumers who are acquainted with someone in management. Another example is a fashion wholesaler who occasionally opens its doors to the public and sells merchandise at or slightly above wholesale prices.

branch stores Satellite stores within a department store group; usually located in the suburbs or cities remote from the main store.

manufacturer's representative Independent business person who works in a specific territory selling related but noncompeting products to more than one account.

Convenience goods that are bought frequently in small quantities and are available from a variety of different types of retailers often pass through longer channels. Beauty products that are sold to customers via hair salons may have been purchased from specialty wholesalers that purchased them from other distributors.

The length of distribution channels varies by country. The Japanese distribution system is known for having multiple middlemen, although this practice is changing. Intricate, time-honored marketing channels contribute to higher retail prices.

At every point in the marketing channel, supply chain members—large or small, manufacturer, distributor, or retailer—are willing to serve the customer directly if it means added dollars. New distribution techniques are changing the definition of retailing.

Dual Channels Increasingly, manufacturers are becoming retailers and retailers are becoming manufacturers while continuing their dominance in both marketplaces. Verizon, one of the largest telephone and wireless communications providers in the United States, opened retail stores and kiosks to sell cellular phones and accessories. The industry is ripe with retailers that have become manufacturers. Organizations like Liz Claiborne, the Gap, and the Limited are examples. This practice also is called vertical integration. **Vertical integration** occurs when two or more supply chain members are owned by the same company. It is done in order to gain control and dominance in a marketing channel.

vertical integration When two or more supply chain members are owned by the same company.

Multichannels Multichannel retailing has become paramount to retailers whose goals are to provide customer convenience, compete effectively, grow, and achieve profitability. The practice of trading through two or more methods of distribution concurrently is known as **multichannel retailing**. The inception of Internet commerce was a precipitating factor in the upsurge of interest in this approach. Coldwater Creek, Victoria's Secret, Land's End, and J.Crew each sell through stores, catalogs, and the Internet and are prime examples of practitioners. Questions raised by multichannel retailing are discussed in From the Field in Box 1.3.

multichannel retailing The practice of trading through two or more methods of distribution concurrently.

Retailing History

No attempt is made to do a comprehensive chronology of retailing in this chapter. Instead an anecdotal approach is used to bring the history of retailing to the reader. This section emphasizes retailing in the United States;

From the Field: Retailers Must Use Cross-Channel Strategies
By Michelle Ballauf

The retail playing field has changed significantly and will most likely continue to do so. As the dot-coms initially took their positions on the competitor list, consumers responded to the ease of purchasing with, in some cases, deep price discounts. As competition among dot-coms began to get heated, many traditional retailers entered the online sales field, some with strategies, some without.

With the demise of many pure Internet retailers, traditional retailers now are securing their positions. In the beginning, pure Internet retailers had the advantage of deep pockets for advertising and promotions that set the groundwork. However, the rules have changed, and traditional retailers are setting them. Retailers and manufacturers are entering the playing field in droves, but are cautiously entering for the long term. As the playing field changed, retailers were challenged with offering an additional tier of distribution. Three important questions deserve reflection:

Does being multichanneled result in cannibalization among the channels? Not necessarily. Research shows that a large percentage of new and repeat customers use all channels. This is not a sign of cannibalization, but a sign of customer service. It is being available to your customers when and where they want you to be.

Each channel should complement the others, but function in a manner that optimizes that channel. Each channel should provide customers with a unique shopping experience.

Competition is no longer among the dot-coms, but with established traditional retailers competing for customers' share of wallet. The playing field has stabilized with the same set of competitors, but in a new medium.

Do customer expectations differ among channels? Customer expectations not only vary by channel, but also by product type and brand. Though brand images should remain consistent among channels, each channel provides unique benefits to enrich the consumer experience.

The Internet provided a quick and relatively inexpensive platform in which to test new promotions, products and concepts, while in-store still provides the customer with touch and feel experience.

For many traditional retailers, especially catalogers, entering the online marketplace is a logical expansion of their business. However, just building an online store does not ensure success.

Unlike many of the dot-coms, traditional retailers have current processes such as merchandising, branding and fulfillment, that can be leveraged. And some need to be modified or adjusted to meet the demands of the online marketplace.

In a world of vendor overload, what does the consumer really expect and does the experience need to be the same across channels? The business model and long-term online strategy would be the key drivers in deciding whether to implement a certain solution. It is not about having tons of bells and whistles on a site, but what your consumers actually expect from your brand and their shopping experiences. Consumers want a shopping experience that allows them to find the product they are looking for in a quick and efficient manner with assistance when needed. However, additional functionality and systems may be distracting and frustrating for the consumer.

Now that the playing field has become level, it is imperative that retailers continue their strategy and continue to find ways to distinguish themselves from other retailers whether it be online, in-store, or via catalog. Long-term, this must be through distinctive product offerings, image, and customer service—not price. Though online price promotions have been effective— and will most likely continue to be—retailers will have to provide special product offerings to continue to capitalize on all channels.

Traditional retailers will be best served by capitalizing on the strengths of each channel and market accordingly. If consumer expectations differ among channels, why shouldn't their experiences?

Source: *iMarketing News.* May 21, 2001: 11,17. © Courtenay Communications. (Ms. Ballauf is Internet director at The Bombay Company, Inc., Fort Worth, TX.)

however, the establishment of major institutions was similar in many industrialized societies, and several international examples are included.

The Marketplace

Visit an outdoor market and you will witness the essence of retail trade. Markets are as old as time and predate recorded history. In anthropological writings "potsherd talk" refers to the study of migratory patterns of peoples based on types of pottery remnants found near trade routes. Six thousand years ago in Mesopotamia, pottery designs varied from village to village, showing us that tastes and preferences were as important to consumers then as they are now.

To trade profitably, surplus stock is necessary. This is the basis for the exchange process which is fundamental to all marketing. As nations evolved from agrarian to industrial economies and food consumption was no longer tied to the cycles of nature, there was less need for traditional marketplaces. However many exist despite the availability of more modern retail facilities. For example, the grand Bazaar in Istanbul and some of the souks in Morocco and the Middle East are centuries old and still in use.

Figure 1.9 Outdoor markets like this one in Alor Setar, Malaysia operate much the same as they have for hundreds of years, fulfilling the basic needs of consumers.

By studying present day outdoor markets in developing countries of Africa or Asia, one can get an inkling as to what earlier trade arenas must have looked like. Everything from fresh fish to peanut butter is available, but customers may have to bring their own containers. Even chicken—dressed or still alive—makes its way to the dinner table from the outdoor market. Fresh seafood for sale at a market in Malaysia is illustrated in Figure 1.9.

In the United States and other fully developed countries, the marketplace may have waned in popularity, but the fascination still exists. Many people frequent flea markets or swap meets and others prefer to buy their produce at farm stands or collaboratives. Farmers' markets are staging a resurgence in major American cities from Portland, Oregon, to Portland, Maine. A major indoor fruit and vegetable facility is located on the lower level of Grand Central Station in New York City.

London markets have never waned in popularity. However they have become specialists. On weekends, Petticoat Lane is the place to go for apparel and general household goods, but if antique lithograph prints are sought, Brick Mill Lane market is a better choice. It is said in partial jest that you can find your grandmother's lost silverware for sale in stalls on Portobello

Road. The marketplace has played an important part in retailing through the centuries, around the world.

Pre-Industrial Evolution

More formal retail formats evolved in the 17th and 18th centuries, although they were not as sophisticated as they would become later. Trading posts, seaports, roving peddlers, and general stores paved the way for contemporary retail stores and nonstore operations.

Trading Posts The first North American retailers were probably Native Americans. They sold to the early settlers skins from animals they had trapped and killed. Although settlers were mostly self-sufficient, the ability to buy fur skins gave them more time for other chores and to look for other material goods. Trading posts in what is now the United States and Canada were central places where furs could be bartered for products imported from Europe. One contemporary Canadian retailer traces its roots to the Hudson Bay Trading Company. Founded in the late 1600s, the department store company now is called, simply, The Bay.

Trading posts were located along navigable waterways or at intersections of trails, areas that were also natural locations for villages. When settlers arrived, the trappers who had preceded them served customers in what could be called—with a stretch of the imagination—retail stores.

Port City Retail Centers The shipping industry practiced global trade long before it was a popular concept. Ports from London to New York, Cartegena in Colombia to Cadiz (now Seville) in Spain were important centers of trade where markets served the growing population. Some merchants imported finished furniture, cloth, and clothing from Europe or spices and silks from Asia. Carpenters made and sold products for the home, and tailors offered custom-made garments to the wealthy.

Yankee Peddlers Called Yankee peddlers because their original homes were in New England, these early retailers purchased a variety of goods from importers, auctioneers, and at fairs. They traveled the countryside, first with packs on their backs, and later with horses and wagons. They sold everything from needles and pins to groceries, housewares, patent medicines, and magic elixirs—usually derived from a strong alcohol base—to their country customers. As the colonists moved inland, so did the Yankee peddler. Success depended on his strength, size of wagon, ability to traverse terrible terrain, demand for his products, and ability of customers to pay.

The appearance of the traveling merchant was a highlight in settlers' lives. He brought not only needed goods but also news of events in the cities. Certainly not exclusive to the United States, itinerant merchants have long played an important role in the dissemination of products and information in villages remote from bustling cities.

General Stores Life was hard on the road, and eventually peddlers settled down often joining forces with settlers who ran local trading posts. At other times peddlers opened their own small stores in growing communities. The result was the birth of the general store, which was to be the most important retail institution of the latter part of the 17th century and most of the 18th century. Figure 1.10 depicts a restored general store in Old Town San Diego, California, a popular tourist stop. The development is centered around a town green and depicts retailing as it was in centuries past.

Figure 1.10 The general store served consumers in the United States for much of the nineteenth century. Restored buildings in Old Town San Diego approximate what a general store would have looked like in that era.

Shopkeepers, as they were called, carried groceries, dry goods, medicines, and other household goods. They also traded for or bought products produced in the geographic areas where they were located. Their assortments came from trips to wholesale centers, wholesale merchants, and local farms or producers.

Consumers of this era benefited from international trade. In the second half of the 19th century, fresh citrus fruit was regularly shipped from the Mediterranean to Scandinavia. Most people today expect that exotic foods and fruits were not widely distributed until modern times.

Shopkeepers did not operate on a one-price policy. Instead, they bargained with their customers for the optimum price. They also started the first charge account systems, often giving credit to farmers for as long as a year. When the crops came in or the sheep were shorn, payment was made.

The Industrial Revolution

When economies were dominated by agriculture, the general store was able to address the few needs that could not be met by farmers themselves. As countries became industrialized, people began to work away from their homes. The growth of the textile industry in the United States contributed significantly to this shift, and also to the production of fabric that eventually would fuel the ready-to-wear market. Amoskeag Manufacturing Company in Manchester, New Hampshire, was once the largest textile mill in the world.

Did You Know?

One reason JC Penney's first retail venture failed was because the owner offered too much credit. Ironically, the founder's full name is James Cash Penney.
Source: *Corporate Viewbook*. JC Penney. Plano, Texas

Two of the company's biggest accounts were Marshall Field and JC Penney. Both companies purchased great quantities of fabric for their stores.[5]

Growing affluence increased demand for a broader assortment of goods in all categories. Families could now purchase goods in stores, rather than rely on home production. As life in industrialized cities changed, so did the nature of retail stores. Two important retail concepts flourished: specialty shops and department stores.

Predominance of Specialty Stores Single-line stores such as shoe and millinery(hat) shops developed at this time. Home production could not keep up with demand so factories that specialized in popular merchandise lines were established in cities in Europe and the United States. Early specialty stores were small shops owned and operated by one merchant in much the same manner as many of today's boutiques. They were clustered together in easily accessible city locations.

Industrialization created urban areas that became hubs where railroads and ships imported and exported goods from around the world. Central business districts in these cities attracted residents from every part of town, and public transportation facilitated trips to larger retail venues.

Birth of Department Stores The first true department stores, including Chicago's Marshall Field and New York's R. H. Macy, opened during the 1850's. London's Harrods, considered the largest department store in the world, was founded by Henry Charles Harrod on Brompton Road in 1849—although trade had been conducted there since the early 1600s. Through gradual acquisition of the space surrounding the original modest grocery shop, Harrods now encompasses an entire city block. Surviving various fires, several owners, and other challenges, the company has been held by the Al Fayed family since 1985.[6] A translation of Harrod's Latin Motto: "omnia, omnibus, ubique," tells us that the store carries all things, for all people, everywhere. This sentiment adequately reflects the extensive merchandise assortment and array of services offered to Harrods' customers.

Another early retailer was James C. Penney, who began his career in the waning days of the 19th century in Kemmerer, Wyoming, a mining and sheep ranching town. His first venture, a butcher shop, was not successful because Penney extended too much credit to his customers. His second attempt at retailing, a general merchandise store called *The Golden Rule,* was successful due to his intense customer service orientation and probably because experience had taught him to operate on a cash-only basis. He provided a large assortment of quality goods in one location and stayed open long hours. Penney kept his doors open until the last sheep rancher or miner was off the streets of Kemmerer. Penney's first year's sales were

$28,898, not a small sum at that time in a town with a population of 1,000.[7] With over 1,100 department stores in the United States, Puerto Rico, Mexico, and Brazil, the company plans further international expansion. Based in Plano, Texas, J.C. Penney had revenues of $32 billion in 2001.[8] Department stores have withstood many ups and downs in the last 150 years.

Approaching the 20th Century

Chain stores were a product of the late 19th and early 20th centuries. Some of the early ventures, such as Walgreen's drug stores, are still with us today. Founded in 1901, the stores featured soda fountains—a requisite part of drug stores until the 1960s. Now the top volume drugstore chain, Walgreen Company recorded sales of $21.2 billion in 2000, and expects to have 6,000 stores by 2010.[9]

General merchandise chains and variety stores also formed in this era and included companies like Kresge and Woolworth. Kresge evolved into today's Kmart. Woolworth continues in the United States and abroad but changed its name to Venator Group in 1998, Footlocker in 2002, and no longer operates any U.S. stores under its original name. The strategy behind these name changes is discussed in Chapter 5.

Montgomery Ward and Sears, Roebuck Company, in 1872 and 1888, respectively, are credited with creating the first catalogs, though they were not as substantial as what would follow. Ward's version was only a single page and featured 163 items.[10] Sears', larger at 80 pages, featured only watches and jewelry.[11] Both evolved into wish books made up of hundreds of pages containing everything a person could hope to possess. Early catalogs were directed to a rural population that could not get to market as easily as their city counterparts.

In the United States, grocery chains were also a product of the late 19th century, although they were not of the size and scope of today's supermarkets. **Supermarkets** are self-service food and grocery stores of under 100,000-square-feet that may carry some nonfood items, but do not have extensive specialty departments. As early as 1880, the Great Atlantic and Pacific Tea Company, better known as A&P, had 95 stores that stretched from Boston to Milwaukee. Single unit mom and pop grocery stores, like the one illustrated in Figure 1.11, were predominant in this era. Larger units did not evolve until the 1930s. Stores were located on the periphery of cities and towns where parking was more plentiful, rents were less expensive, and more square footage was available. The advent of the automobile allowed growing ranks of mobile consumers to shop less frequently but purchase more products on their shopping junkets. Better refrigeration

CYBERSCOOP

Find out more about Walgreen's history. Go to www .walgreens.com/about/history/defalt.jhtml and discover what famous taste-treat Walgreen's invented. What strategic move in 1933 helped position the drug store as an innovator?

supermarkets Self-service food and grocery stores of under 100,000-square-feet that carry some nonfood items, but do not have extensive specialty departments.

Figure 1.11 The neighborhood grocery store was a staple in the retail community in the early 20th century. This store owner in Massachusetts posed for a promotional postcard that was used to announce his twentieth anniversary in business in 1932.

and more attention to product development and packaging also aided the growth of the supermarket.

It is interesting to contrast the development of supermarkets in the industrial world to one in a less developed area. In Banjul, The Gambia, located on the west coast of Africa, the first supermarket opened in the mid-1980s in the downtown area. At that time the main street was still unpaved and retail stores were rudimentary, servicing basic needs. Proud of the new retail institution, a stop at Chellaram's was on the city tour itinerary for tourists. Campbell soup was displayed next to fine French champagne not far from insect repellent. In the rear of the store one could purchase cotton beach towels or a boom box. The two check-out aisles equipped with new cash registers were certainly a far cry from the outdoor market nearby. Progress had come to Banjul.

Retail growth remained at a standstill during much of the 1930s because of the severe depression in the United States. Rationing of consumer products during World War II also slowed progress. It was not until after 1945, that retailers were again able to move forward.

Post-World War II Retail Growth

The second and largest spurt in retail growth took place immediately after World War II. With the war finally over, people in Europe, the United States and Asia could go home to growing economies and increased consumption. Retailers were eager and willing to help in both instances. Those in Europe and Asia were in the process of rebuilding their countries, including their commercial districts that were often in ruins from devastating bombings.

During this period in the United States, the right place to live was in the suburbs. People poured out of cities to areas where new ranch houses, Chevy station wagons, and backyard barbecue equipment rapidly were becoming a way of life. Real estate developers and highway systems linked city jobs to suburban living.

Instead of refurbishing their old downtown stores, department store owners followed the newly moneyed populace to the burgeoning suburban communities. Between 1950 and 1970, suburban shopping centers became community landmarks. Almost no suburb was without a center, and one-stop shopping became the norm.

In their rush to follow the affluent customer to the suburbs, department stores made one major mistake—they forgot the blue-collar market. These families, with almost as much money to spend as their white-collar neighbors, maintained the shopping patterns of their less affluent parents. They did not feel at home in the early suburban branch stores of department stores. To them, that portrayed a high-price image. To fulfill the household needs of blue-collar families discount stores evolved.

Approaching the 21st Century

While the suburbs flourished, urban blight also prevailed. Years of war and neglect, followed by another 20 years of suburban growth, left many central city districts looking like ghost towns.

Department stores suffered most, and the decades that followed saw the demise of many significant downtown retailers. To compete with changes that began more than 50 years ago, some adopted store-within-a-store concepts to break up their cavernous spaces and bring more intimate shopping experiences to customers. Industry consolidation closed many department store doors. Shopping center development in suburban areas posed other challenges as department stores were forced to contend with increased competition from specialty stores and discounters. To this day, department stores that have survived practice promotional pricing techniques much like their discount store counterparts.

Beginning in the 1970s and continuing to this day, urban renewal became a national goal. With funding from both government and private sources, some city centers once again began to look clean, fresh, and exciting. Many middle class and upper class suburbanites slowly started to move back from the suburbs. By the early 1980s, cities from coast to coast were again places where people lived, shopped, and worked. Smaller cities also benefited from the surge in revitalization. Some have re-created their historic pasts through architecture. The movement continues.

Western Europe has traditionally maintained a different perspective on redevelopment. The past is revered, and it is customary to rebuild centuries-old establishments. In England, historical preservation orders ensure that old buildings are not torn down but are restored. This has not always been the attitude in the United States, but fortunately as times change, so does public sentiment. Progress no longer means that an older structure must be torn down in order to put in a parking lot.

The last 20 years also witnessed the establishment of new management tools that transgressed existing technologies and became precursors to modern systems. At the time electronic data interchange systems were electronic data interchange(EDI) **Computer-guided communications network between retailer, manufacturer, and other supply chain members.**

considered innovative. **Electronic data interchange(EDI)** is a computer-guided communication network between retailer, manufacturer, and other supply chain members. Today EDI is being surpassed by more advanced computer and wireless technologies as history continues to be made.

Retailing unquestionably has become more complex since its inception when growth seemed limitless, world economies were fairly stable, and competitive battles revolved around the question of who could get to the next hot spot first. Retailing in the 21st century demands as much science as art if the goals of customer satisfaction, productivity, growth, and profit are to be met. The rules, players, locus of exchange, methods, and customers are changing. In the future, challenges will be met differently. Lessons from history are valuable as retailers make informed decisions faster than the competition. Welcome to the world of retailing.

Summary

Retailing exists everywhere people gather. It is always changing in order to continue to meet the needs of the final consumer. Product knowledge that we learn is largely due to the marketing efforts of retailers.

Retailing is presented throughout this book in a marketing context. In order to be classified as a retailer, a company must sell more than 50 percent of its goods or services directly to individual consumers. Many manufacturers and wholesalers also engage in retailing.

The cyclical pattern of retail evolution, according to the wheel of retailing theory, consists of three stages: entry, trading-up, and vulnerability. The wheel theory is the only one that explains the element of change in retailing. Trickle-up, trickle-down, and trickle-across processes are also offered as explanations. Finally, geographic movement is a precursor of change, as retailers follow customers, or customers follow retailers, to new locations.

The six functional areas of retailing are: merchandising, operations, promotion, finance, human resources, and information technology. Each must work with the other to assure smooth operations.

Having the right goods in the right place at the right time is imperative. To do this, retailers carefully select one or more marketing channels through which they expedite the flow of goods and satisfy the customer.

From outdoor markets and trading posts to central business districts and shopping centers, retail stores throughout the world have changed along with the societies they serve. The lessons of history are the starting point for understanding and appreciating the status of retailing today.

Questions for Review and Discussion

1. How does the educational dimension of retailing affect children and adults?

2. Does a company have to be a retailer by definition in order to engage in retailing? Give examples of nonretailers that sell to ultimate consumers.

3. How does the wheel of retailing theory explain the evolution of retail organizations? What other dynamics help explain the movement of retailing?

4. Describe the areas of responsibility that fall under each of the six functional areas in retail organizations.

5. How do retailers select marketing channels? Give examples of channels most frequently used by retailers of convenience goods, fashion apparel, and home electronics?

6. What factors precipitated interest in multichannel retailing? How widespread is this practice?

7. How did retail organizations in the United States evolve as compared to those in other countries?

Endnotes

1. www.census.gov/mrts/www/data/pdf/annpub01.pdf Available: May 30, 2002.
2. Retail Industry Indicators. NRF Foundation. Washington, DC. August, 2001: v.
3. McNair, Malcome P. "Significant Trends and Developments in the Postwar Period." *Competitive Distribution in a Free, High-Level Economy and Its Implications for the University.* Edited by A.B. Smith. University of Pittsburgh Press. Pittsburgh. 1958:1–25.
4. May, Eleanor. Interview. October 24, 2001.
5. Hareven, Tamara K. and Langenbach, Randolph. *Amoskeag: Life and Work in an American Factory City.* Pantheon Books. New York. 1978:335.
6. www.harrods.com/about_us.asp?contents=historydetail. Online June, 2001.
7. "The Illustrated JC Penney." Edited by Robert Pasch and Cynthia McGrath. JC Penney. Plano, Texas. Undated.
8. www.jcpenney.net/company/finance/archives/annual/2001/web31-34pdf. Accessed: May 30, 2002.
9. Walgreens.com/about/press/anreport2000.html. June, 2001.
10. www.mward.com/html/history/html. October, 2000.
11. Sun, Douglas. "Sears." *International Directory of Company Histories.* Volume 18. 1997:475

Chapter 2

Planning and Predicting

Learning Objectives

After completing this chapter you should be able to:

- Apply the important components of strategic planning to retailing.

- Identify ten crucial aspects of change and determine how they affect retailers.

- List several ways classic and nonstore retailers are adapting to change.

Figure 2.1 Laptop computers, small TV cameras, and in-line skates used by "Webcamers" make customer service easier at Printemps department store in Paris (See p. 43). *Courtesy of Fairchild Publications, Inc.*

If anyone had told us five years ago that My Virtual Model™ technology would enable us to log in our body type, facial structure, and hair style and color to ensure better fitting apparel from many online retailers, we would have laughed. Although we have been using our ATM cards forever, we marvel at the chip technology that allows us to load monetary funds in our choice of currencies onto a smart card. **Smart cards** are plastic cards with advanced microchip technologies that permit more sophisticated financial and nonfinancial services to be rendered. We are approaching a cashless society.

smart cards Plastic cards with advanced microchip technologies that permit more sophisticated financial and nonfinancial services to be rendered.

The word *smart* takes on new meaning as we contemplate living in smart houses where rooms vacuum themselves, assisted by a mouse-controlled personal robot. Telephones that simultaneously translate speech into foreign languages may well be a part of our smart household.

Talking and interactive window displays seemed beyond our comprehension, yet passers-by were treated to an electronic display at Macy's Herald Square store in New York City. Motion detection of people on the sidewalk triggered action within the display window that captured the attention of shoppers.

Change is apparent in all of our lives; the retail sphere is not exempt. Mergers and acquisitions have caused some time-tested retailers to disappear. Global expansion has made other retailers highly visible. **Mergers** involve the pooling of resources by two or more companies so as to become one. **Acquisition** describes the buying of one company by another in either a friendly or hostile manner. This practice is also called a buyout or a takeover.

merger The pooling of resources by two or more companies so as to become one.

acquisition The buying of one company by another, in either a friendly or hostile manner; this practice also is called a buyout or takeover.

Forecasters agree that successful retailers will be those that understand how to operate in the information age. Many believe that we live in an era that is as important to the future direction of the world as the industrial revolution was 150 years ago. The basic principles of retailing may not change, but the methods used to reach the customer certainly will. Because of the profound importance of the topics presented in this chapter, all appear again as either a whole chapter, major sections of chapters, or themes throughout this text.

Retail objectives can be reached with less risk if thoughtful plans are put forth. Past history, present status, and future direction of a company should be considered in the strategic planning process. **Strategic planning** is the

strategic planning Process of gathering and analyzing information from a variety of internal and external sources for the purpose of reducing risk before specific business plans are executed.

process of gathering and analyzing information from a variety of internal and external sources for the purpose of reducing risk before special business plans are executed. This process is now considered.

Retail Strategy Development

Advance planning requires collecting information that may be crucial to decision making. The strategic planning process requires constant assessment of strengths and weaknesses, which change over time. Maintaining a delicate balance while the world is constantly changing is not easy. Planning has become a science, practiced by all businesses that are concerned with growth. Strategic planning involves five fundamental steps:

1. Performing a **situation analysis** to determine the strengths and weaknesses of a company, specific business plan, or proposed strategy.
2. Determining a **differential advantage,** which involves pinpointing the unique characteristics of a business or product that may give it a superior position in the marketplace**.**
3. Developing a **mission statement,** usually a brief paragraph that concisely describes a business and its reason for existence**.**
4. Preparing company goals and objectives. **Goals** are statements that indicate general company aims or end results. **Objectives** are more specific intentions stated by a company.
5. Planning detailed **strategies,** action plans that prescribe tactics used by a company to reach common goals and objectives.

Details regarding these five steps are provided along with examples of the ways retailers are using strategic planning to develop their businesses.

Step 1: Performing a Situation Analysis

Assessing the strengths and weaknesses of a retail company is the starting point for strategic planning. Completing a situation analysis involves surveying the environment in which the retail organization operates, and identifying the opportunities and threats that the company faces. This is often accomplished by the use of S.W.O.T. analysis. **S.W.O.T. analysis** lists a company's strengths, weaknesses, opportunities, and threats and is used to determine future direction.

For example, a retailer intending to sell herbal supplements such as ginseng or St. John's wort may view past success selling traditional vitamins as a strength. Costco Wholesale clubs added herbal supplements to its shelves

situation analysis The process of determining the strengths and weaknesses of a company, specific business plan, or proposed strategy.

differential advantage Unique characteristics of a business that may give it a superior position in the marketplace.

mission statement A brief paragraph that concisely describes a business and its reason for existence.

goals Statements that indicate general company aims or end results.

objectives Specific intentions stated by a company.

strategies Action plans that prescribe tactics used by a company to reach common goals and objectives.

S.W.O.T. analysis Lists a company's strengths, weaknesses, opportunities, and threats and is used to help determine future direction.

Figure 2.2 Previous success with traditional vitamins paved the way for herbal remedies such as St. John's wort at Costco Wholesale clubs.

positioning The perception a customer has of a store (or product) in relation to others.

adjacent to other health and beauty aids. The company's St. John's wort end cap display is illustrated in Figure 2.2. Employees' lack of knowledge about herbal remedies may be considered a weakness. The trend toward using alternative medicines may be perceived as an opportunity, but the presence of General Nutrition Center—a strong vitamin and herbal supplement retailer—in its trading area would be seen as a threat. A retailer may find ways to develop its strengths by focusing on its established channel of distribution, thereby shortening the learning curve as it launches similar products. It can deal with the weakness of employees' lack of product knowledge by sending employees to herbal medicine seminars or by taking advantage of vendor training sessions. The threat of being in a location where an established retailer of herbal medicines is already trading need not change the company's plans. Although it could seek another site, it could also provide higher quality products, outstanding customer service, competitive pricing, or a combination of these incentives.

Step 2: Determining a Differential Advantage

The strategic planning process cannot go forth without articulating a differential advantage, which is closely related to positioning. **Positioning** is the perception a customer has of a store (or product) in relation to others. Retailers work hard to instill this perception in the minds of customers. For example, Nordstrom's is positioned as an extremely customer service-oriented store. Wal-Mart is known for its everyday low pricing policies. These qualities constitute a differential advantage when they distinguish a seller or product as better than the competition. Customers have a clear image and can easily identify the intentions of each retailer.

Step 3: Developing a Mission Statement

Building a mission statement involves succinctly focusing on a retailer's core business, its reason for existence and its differential advantage. What business are we in? What customers do we want to serve? What image do we want to portray? Retailers should ask all these questions as they prepare to draft their mission statements.

Eastern Mountain Sports (EMS) is a retailer of products for serious outdoor enthusiasts. The company has stores in a dozen states in the United States.

The EMS mission is to provide the highest level of customer satisfaction by selling and servicing quality, functional outdoor equipment and clothing through stores that uniquely convey the outdoor experience.[1]

Whether simple or detailed, the mission statement should be the foundation for all the goals and objectives of a company.

Step 4: Preparing Company Goals and Objectives

Company goals are usually general, although stated with a clear focus. They may take several forms. An established discount store may be most concerned with achieving a high sales volume. A new specialty retailer selling only digital videodisks may be more interested in establishing itself as an expert in DVD technology.

Objectives are more specific and should be written so that end results are easy to measure. For example, a retail company might state this objective: "To increase profit by two percent next year." This is a measurable objective, but too broad. It would be better to state it this way: "To increase profit by two percent in the next fiscal year by implementing a new control procedure that will reduce inventory shrinkage." Tying the objective to a concrete plan of action is more meaningful and easier to measure.

Once objectives have been carefully constructed, the next step is to devise tactics that will bring the objectives to fruition.

Step 5: Planning Detailed Strategies

Developing strategies involves seeing the big picture. Retailers may make decisions involving location, management, operations, pricing policies, product and service offerings, store image, and/or promotional efforts. These examples are known as controllable elements and must be properly blended into the retail mix. Retailers have little or no control over competition, government laws, customers, or technology. Equally uncontrollable are economic, political, social, and environmental conditions. These factors also are considered during the strategic planning process and are discussed in Chapter 3.

Every retailer, regardless of size, must develop its own plan for satisfying its customers and earning a profit. Highlights of Sears, Roebuck & Company's strategic plan developed in 1999 includes five key points:

1. To focus business in areas where Sears has strengths. This involves working to build stronger relationships with customers by identifying relevant programs for them.

2. To position Sears as an exciting place to shop by redefining its notion of customer service. The company is prepared to serve the customer via the Internet if that is what the customer wants.

3. To concentrate on local markets. The company anticipates creating special merchandise assortments to serve customers in different markets. It expects to use its database to reach this objective.

4. To practice sound financial and human resource management. Sears intends to take a long term approach to costs and increase productivity in all areas.

5. To develop a winning corporate culture. The company wants to build morale within the company, encourage entrepreneurial thinking, and decrease employee turnover.[2]

In preparing these strategies, Sears followed the steps in the planning process. The company acknowledged its strengths and weaknesses and surveyed the opportunities and threats that will guide the company's course of action in the next century. Stating these strategies is not the end of the planning process for Sears, but the beginning of new directions for the company. Two years later, the company announced plans to divest its Homelife furniture store division. Later in 2001, Sears announced that it would change its image from department store to discounter. More space would be given to electronic goods and appliances, but less emphasis would be placed on personal service. As a result 4,900 jobs were cut.[3] In mid-2002, the company's decision to buy Lands' End added another dimension to its business. Sears hopes to upgrade its apparel offerings and thereby attract a more upscale consumer as a result of this acquisition.[4] All are major tactics as the company continues to redefine its strategic direction (Figure 2.3).

Critical Aspects of Change

The following ten critical areas of change present deeper insight into the forces that compel retailers to plan strategically. Suggestions regarding how these aspects will affect retailers and customers in the decade ahead are given.

Technological Advancement

We live in a time when technology reinvents itself as frequently as we change our clothes. This revolution will continue to leave its stamp on retailing. Technology now makes it possible to distribute goods through marketing channels faster and more efficiently than ever before. It also helps customers shop in more convenient and well-informed ways and have fun through electronic marketing. Through technology, retailers assess customer needs more effectively.

A Look at the Future Thom Blischok, president of MindMeld, is a thought leader and futurist who speaks on "Reimagineering Retail"(TM) at conferences around the globe. Some of his most entertaining and thought provoking predictions involve new technologies that will change the way people fulfill their needs. His many examples address the importance of serving the customer rather than simply selling to the customer. His general premise is that we are moving

Figure 2.3 Sears is the ninth largest retailer in the world and maintains that distinction by careful strategic planning and implementation of well-conceived business tactics. *Courtesy of Fairchild Publications, Inc.*

from an information economy to a network economy. With information doubling every 18 months in what he defines as a "quantum explosion," what may seem fanciful as this is being written may be reality when you read it.

Blischok envisions Lifescapes,™ holographic display windows that activate through customers' hand prints and verbal directives. Imagine seeing a new rock climbing outfit in an outdoor gear display and be able to say, "I like that brown one, but I'd really like to see it in blue," and have it happen. One of the first Lifescapes™ to appear in Macy's windows is illustrated in Figure 2.4.

Blischok also sees personal shopping achieving new heights by combining customer database information with other electronic wizardry. Conjure up an electric mirror so that you can use it to see whether the blue outfit looks best or whether it is the right size. This ability would certainly save time in the fitting room.

He also anticipates updated electronic kiosks for the ultimate touch-and-feel based shopping experience. Picture yourself seated on a Harley, making equipment and color choices for your custom wheels via an electronic console integrated into the bike. You would have appropriate music playing in the background to enhance your decision-making process.

Fantasy? Not entirely, although most of us have yet to experience these advanced customer services. The technology

Figure 2.4 Macy's interactive store windows are a product of The Decisioneering Group. Called Lifescapes™, these windows combine virtual technologies, computer animation, and sound. *Courtesy of Fairchild Publications, Inc.*

exists though it is not yet fully adapted to these applications. What is important to recognize is that many of these predicted forms of retailing are designed to reach us in our homes. This fact alone is enough to jog our minds into a new way of thinking about how we will live, work, and shop in the future.[5]

Electronic Banking Electronic banking includes the use of automatic teller machines (ATMs) and the instant processing of retail purchases through a variety of technologies including EFT and debit cards. **Electronic fund transfers (EFT)** are computerized systems that process financial transactions, exchanges, or information. **Debit cards** are plastic cards with electronic capabilities that allow purchase prices to be instantly deducted from customers' bank accounts. The number of people that use these technologies and conduct personal banking business and financial planning via personal computers is increasing.

Companies that produce products for the anticipated cashless society are important to consumers and the retail industry. Mondex, a London-based company owned by MasterCard, franchises its electronic cash cards and related products to financial institutions and is building a network of retailers amenable to card use. **Electronic cash (e-cash) cards** are smart cards that load and hold cash values in any currency via an ATM or telephone. Balances are checked easily via a handy key chain device, or through more detailed transaction information reviewed by way of an electronic wallet that can be locked as a security precaution. Not a credit, debit, nor an ATM card, the Mondex card is used instead of money for buying lunch or admission to a movie. With additional smart card capabilities, it can also be used as an access card to one's apartment complex, as was shown in a test of the device in England. Smart card technology is also the basis for prepaid phone cards and store loyalty cards that emerged in the late twentieth century. After completing extensive market research and development throughout the world, Mondex expects that retailers will encourage cash card use. In the late 1990s, about 80 percent of all retail transactions were still done in cash. Because of this the company sees much growth potential for its products. It has also noted that the rate of acceptance of cash cards will vary by country and by the types of consumers that will be comfortable using this technology.[6] The From the Field box in this chapter gives a unique and humorous perspective of cash cards as seen through the eyes of a Mondex card.

Electronic banking will not replace credit options and old-fashioned money. Even so, paperless and cashless transactions are expected to increase in importance.

electronic fund transfers (EFT) Computerized systems that process financial transactions, exchanges, or information.

debit cards Plastic cards with electronic capabilities that allow purchase prices to be instantly deducted from customers' bank accounts.

electronic cash (e-cash) cards Smart cards that load and hold cash values in any currency via an ATM or telephone.

From the Field: Fit for Purpose: The Life of a Mondex Card

My back is killing me, my chip feels like it is about to pop out, and I just heard that my poor old mate, Daniel, got melted down in a washing machine. Let me assure you, life as a Mondex card is all stress and strain, Sturm and Drang. And do not let anyone tell you otherwise.

The problem is ISO testing specifications. I am not sure what it stands for, but it all comes down to plenty of grief for us cards. And what's worse, Mondex insists on testing us over and above what these ISO people require, so life for us cards gets really tough. For instance, this morning, I did a couple of hours in the stress machines—2,000 bends in the dynamic flexer, followed by 2,000 twists in the dynamic torsion

machine. Round here they call it aerobics, but it's not because it hurts more and you don't get to wear a leotard and listen to Madonna.

Anyway, it seems I passed the test, as my chip stayed tucked safely in its housing. So I was feeling quite good...

This afternoon it was time for mental gymnastics. First, I had my transaction test. I am supposed to be able to do up to 1,000,000 payments before I peg out, so it is good to keep in practice. Then I had my language lesson. I am going to be carrying Euros as well as good old Sterling, so I have to learn plenty of useful phrases. I can already order *dos cervezas* in Spanish, and *un kilo de beurre* in French, so I am well on the

way. But I am struggling with the Smorgasbord.

The rumour in the testing lab is that things are going to get even more mentally trying for us Mondex cards. Apparently we are going to have to be able to memorize loyalty points every time someone buys something in a shop. And we will even have to keep a personal audit for expenses. It will mean doing at least two things at once. But then I really am a computer, and I have got plenty of brainpower I am not using yet, so I suppose I will be up to it.

Anyway, that is my life as a Mondex card.

Source: *Mondex Magazine.* Summer, 1996:42. Copyright © 1996 by Mondex International Ltd.

Information Technology (IT) Computer-based decision support systems that are used to provide more efficiencies in retail operations fall under the umbrella term **information technology (IT).** Retailers review past performance, analyze alternatives, plan inventories, and facilitate interaction between retailers and vendors using IT. Other applications include human resources scheduling, predictive modeling, store location and design planning, logistics management, security, and customer service programs. In the customer service area, database development and mining have become crucial to the success of large and small retail organizations. Retailers have long been aware that 80 percent of their sales come from 20 percent of their customers. Tapping information stored in databases can help stores tailor offers to core shoppers and also to those they hope to elevate to select client status. Tom Gordon, Senior Vice President and General Manager for Equifax Retail Solutions, believes that the best data gathering systems go beyond basic demographic information. Information about special life events, personal favorites, and significant dates are equally important to collect at the point of impulse. **Point of impulse (POI)** is an updated version of point of sale (POS) that more accurately reflects customer behavior when it occurs.[7]

Quick response technology represents another way retailers are making their operations more efficient. **Quick Response (QR)** is the umbrella term for integrated supply chain distribution systems that allow rapid replenishment of merchandise. In some instances, QR systems have

information technology (IT) The umbrella term for computer based decision support systems that are used to provide more efficiency in retail operations.

point of impulse (POI) Updated version of point of sale (POS) that more accurately records consumer behavior where and when it occurs.

Quick Response (QR) The umbrella term for integrated supply chain distribution systems that allow rapid replenishment of merchandise.

very small aperture terminal (VSAT) Satellite communication system that is linked to a computer network without using telephone lines.

shortened product concept-to-delivery times from months to weeks. Integrated with electronic data interchange systems, retailers and vendors can communicate crucial information faster and more accurately. As a result participants may gain a competitive advantage.

Wal-Mart, Target, and Frederick's of Hollywood are examples of retailers that use VSAT technology. **VSAT** stands for very small aperture terminal and is a satellite communication system that is linked to a computer network without using telephone lines. As existing technologies are perfected, wireless Internet access systems also will enhance IT capabilities.

Electronic Retailing Electronic retailing grew by leaps and bounds in the 1990s, and continues to shape our shopping behavior. Included in this sector are Web technology, television home shopping channels, and other electronic means. Because of the impact of emerging technology on retailing, this topic is covered fully in Chapter 7. Here are three examples to pique your interest:

- *Internet Shopping.* As you read this, everyone in your classroom will have surfed the Web and used it to do research. Most will have shopped online. Some will have ordered a pair of khakis from Landsend.com, precisely to their pant length requirements. Others may have ordered a digital picture frame from Photoworks.com. Using its special online subscription service, family photos can be updated daily via a digital window. Online malls, like fashionmall.com, are reached through all major service providers and are shopped regularly. Books, music, and computer products may top the lists of products most frequently sold on the Web today, but the potential for products presently under-represented is vast.
- *Direct Access TV.* A host of other electronic innovations are changing the way products are presented to the public. Prolific product placement is now observed in films and on TV. Soon viewers may see a hot outfit worn by a favorite *Sex in the City* character, immediately call up product information by remote access, and place their orders.
- *Internet Cafes.* Retail stores where customers can enjoy a cup of their favorite coffee while they log on to the Internet are becoming popular. Many are located in areas that are heavily populated with tourists. They have become the contemporary equivalent of a place where travelers can phone home. One such place, the international chain, easyEverything is illustrated in Figure 2.5.

Technology is making possible shopping experiences we once only dreamed about. Small computer stations called electronic kiosks are used for delivering extended customer services. For example, designing your own greeting cards, ordering a pizza, printing a movie ticket, or ordering related music based on harmonic qualities of a favorite artist are all kiosk options. Figure 2.1 shows a new breed of customer service representative at Printemps department store in Paris. During a test, "Webcamers" on in-line skates communicated with customers via laptop computers and small TV cameras. Shoppers accessed their personal shoppers through Printemps' special Web site and were able to see store departments and actual merchandise before making their selections.[8] Using Webcamers could make it possible for customers to shop during hours that the store is normally closed. Many of these innovations are becoming available to individuals in small towns and major metropolitan areas.

Global Retail Expansion

The movement toward global retailing is not quite as new as some would have us think. McDonald's has operated units all over the globe for several decades. However, most experts feel that the proliferation of global retailers will grow dramatically in the early 21st century and that all retailers must at least address the possibility of globalization as they prepare their strategic plans. At a Global Retail Symposium, Daniel Sweeney, Vice President of IBM Consulting Group said, "In the early 21st century global expansion will create vast changes that will forever change all players." In explaining why retailers would choose to expand globally he added, "Because they must and because they can."[9] The top 20 global retailers are listed in Table 2.1.

There are several reasons why global expansion is occurring, although the following list refers primarily to mature retail companies. Large, well-developed retailers that have the financial and managerial expertise to consider global expansion are called **mature retail companies**. There is some evidence that smaller companies are also expanding internationally.

Many retailers are extending their reach through Web sites that are capable of being accessed anywhere in the world. There were close to 500 million Internet users worldwide by the end of 2001. Users in Western Europe constituted 29.8 percent compared to 29.2 in the United States. In contrast, the United States accounted for 47.7 percent of the more than $600 billion in e-commerce revenue in 2001, compared to 25.7 percent for users in Western Europe.[10] This shows strong potential for future retail development in this vital and volatile sector.

The main reasons for international expansion include:

Figure 2.5 Easy Everything in Amsterdam provides products, services, and coffee for the Internet devotee.

CYBERSCOOP

If you want to send flowers to a friend overseas, you might want to research international floral etiquette at **www.ftd.com** before you do. To find out how to say, "I love you," in many languages click on Gift Advisor and then on Quotable Sentiments.

mature retail companies Large, well-developed retailers that have the financial and managerial expertise to consider global expansion.

Table 2.1 Top 20 Global Retailers

DT Ranking	Country of Origin	Name of Company	Formats	1998 Total Revenue* (US$ mil)	1998 Retail Revenue (US$ mil)	1998 Income/ (Loss)* (US$mil)	Countries of Operation
1	US	Wal-Mart	Discount, Warehouse	193,295	191,329	6,295	Argentina, Brazil, Canada, China, Germany, Mexico, Puerto Rico, South Korea, UK, US
2	France	Carrefour	Cash & Carry, Convenience, Discount, Hypermarket, Supermarket	67,369	59,703	967	Argentina, Belgium, Brazil, Chile, China, Colombia, Czech Rep., France, Greece, Indonesia, Italy, Japan, Malaysia, Mexico, Poland, Portugal, Singapore, Slovakia, Spain, S. Korea, Switzerland, Taiwan, Thailand, Turkey
3	US	Kroger	Convenience, Department, Drug, Specialty, Supermarket	49,000	49,000	877	US
4	US	Home Depot	DIY, Specialty	45,738	45,738	2,581	Argentina, Canada, Chile, Puerto Rico, US
5	Germany	Metro	Department, DIY, Hypermarket, Mail Order, Specialty, Supermarket, Warehouse	42,636	42,439E	388	Austria, Belgium, Bulgaria, China, Czech Rep., Denmark, France, Germany, Greece, Hungary, Italy, Luxembourg, Morocco, Netherlands, Poland, Portugal, Romania, Slovakia, Spain, Switzerland, Turkey, UK
6	Netherlands	Ahold	Cash & Carry, Convenience, Discount, Drug, Hypermarket, Speciality, Supermarket	48,592	41,539	1,034	Argentina, Brazil, Chile, Czech Rep., Denmark, Ecuador, El Salvador, Estonia, Guatemala, Honduras, Indonesia, Latvia, Lithuania, Malaysia, Morocco, Netherlands, Norway, Paraguay, Peru, Poland, Portugal, Spain, Sweden, Thailand, US
7	US	Kmart	Discount	37,028	37,028	(244)	Guam, Puerto Rico, US, Virgin Islands
8	US	Albertson's	Drug, Supermarket	36,762	36,762	765	US

(Table 2.1 continued on page 45.)

■ *Saturated home markets.* When expansion is complete in retailers' existing markets or there is limited geographic area for further growth, some retailers look beyond their home borders.

■ *Increased competition.* In strong economies, stiff competition may propel a retailer to enter less fit countries if they see growth potential.

Table 2.1 Top 20 Global Retailers *(Table 2.1 continued from page 44.)*

DT Ranking	Country of Origin	Name of Company	Formats	2000 Total Revenue* (US$ mil)	2000 Retail Revenue (US$ mil)	2000 Income/ (Loss)* (US$mil)	Countries of Operation
9	US	Sears	Department, Mail Order, Specialty	40,937	36,548	1,343	Canada, Puerto Rico, US
10	US	Target (Dayton Hudson)	Department, Discount	36,903	36,362	1,264	US
11	US	Safeway	Supermarket	31,977	31,977	1,092	Canada, US
12	US	JCPenney	Department, Drug, Mail Order	31,846	31,846	(705)	Brazil, Mexico, Puerto Rico, US
13	UK	Tesco	Convenience, Hypermarket, Supermarket	31,757	31,751	1,162	Czech Rep., France, Hungary, Poland, Rep. of Ireland, S. Korea, Slovakia, Taiwan, Thailand, UK
14	US	Costco	Warehouse	32,164	31,621	631	Canada, Japan, Korea, Mexico, Taiwan, UK, US
15	Germany	Rewe	Cash & Carry, Convenience, Department, Discount, DIY, Hypermarket, Specialty, Supermarket	34,694	31,100E	N/A	Austria, Bulgaria, Czech Rep., France, Germany, Hungary, Italy, Poland, Romania, Slovakia, Ukraine
16	France	Intermarche	Convenience, Discount, DIY, Hypermarket, Restaurant, Specialty, Supermarket	30,698e	30,698E	423	Belgium, Bosnia, France, Germany, Italy, Poland, Portugal, Spain
17	France	Auchan	Convenience, DIY, Hypermarket, Restaurant, Specialty, Supermarket	29,134	29,134	282	Argentina, China, France, Hungary, Italy, Luxembourg, Mexico, Morocco, Poland, Portugal, Spain, Taiwan, Thailand, US
18	Germany	Edeka/AVA	Convenience, Discount, DIY, Supermarket, Hypermarket	28,782	28,782	N/A	Austria, Czech Rep., Denmark, France, Germany, Luxembourg, Poland
19	Japan	Ito-Yokado	Convenience, Department, Discount, Hypermarket, Restaurant, Specialty, Supermarket	28,307	25,381	446	Canada, China, Denmark, Japan, Malaysia, Mexico, Norway, Philippines, Singapore, South Korea, Sweden, Taiwan, Thailand, Turkey, US
20	UK	J Sainsbury	Convenience, Hypermarket, Supermarket	25,486	25,266	393	France, UK, US

E = Estimate
* = Includes nonretail
Source: *Stores*, "Top 200 Global Retailers," Deloitte & Touche, January 2002: G8, G9

■ *Attractive new markets.* Developing countries present opportunities for certain established retailers to find multitudes of similarly minded international consumers. Countries moving out of third world or emerging nation status are considered **developing countries**. Usually developing countries are in transition from an agricultural economy to an industrialized one.

developing countries Countries moving out of third world or emerging nation status.

import snobbery The tendency for people to believe that better, more desirable products come from other countries.

Did You Know?

"Overstimulation means things that got a wow 10 years ago, get a yawn today."
Source: Wynn, Steve. Chairman of the Board and CEO, Mirage Resorts, Inc. Presentation. "The World of Entertainment." International Council of Shopping Centers Leasing Conference. Las Vegas. May 16, 1995.

■ *Demanding investors.* In some situations pressures from stockholders for sustained high growth cause retailers to seek opportunities abroad.

■ *Customer sophistication.* Because of worldwide media efforts, increased travel, and better education many people have developed global brand awareness as well as import snobbery. The tendency for people to believe that better, more desirable products come from other countries is called **import snobbery**. Internet access has also contributed to this phenomenon.

■ *Reduced trade restrictions.* Trade agreements and a general lessening of bureaucracy in many parts of the world are making global expansion easier.

The size and scope of mature global players have made expansion not only possible, but also much easier than it would have been a decade ago. Tremendous capabilities in technology, distribution, and product sourcing have expedited the global moves of such companies as Wal-Mart in the United States, and Carrefour, the French hypermarket company. Both are profiled at the end of Unit One. Extended coverage of global retailing is presented in Chapter 8.

Links Between Retailing and Entertainment

Since the mid-1990s, a recurring theme in retail stores and shopping centers is *entertainment.* Sometimes called *retailtainment,* this combination of retailing and entertainment also extends to online shopping. Tour a virtual store on the Web and you will agree. Other forms of nonstore retailing such as home parties also fit the category. Let us explore why this trend has occurred.

Customers are jaded. How many malls can they visit before those malls become dull and loose their ability to lure, persuade, and impress? Perhaps not many. This is one reason retailers continue to create a sense of excitement and awe to renew the magic. They also hope their efforts will generate profits. Disney and Build-a-Bear stores certainly excel in their ability to recapture the child in all of us. The Forum Shops at Caesar's Palace in Las Vegas, illustrated in Figure 2.6, is typical of shopping center developments that have gone beyond the norm to create a compelling environment. The center combines historically influenced architecture, luxury retailing, fine dining, pageants, animatronic sculptures, an aquarium, and the glamour of a casino—in other words, entertainment. Atmosphere and ambiance, discussed further in Chapter 13, play a big role in this phenomenon. The hand-painted sky ceiling at The Forum is so realistic that you forget you are in a building. The lighting system is programmed to portray dawn to dusk every hour. This is no chance occurrence since once hooked on the imagery, most customers will stay in the facility to experience all possible stages, and shop as they stroll in the mall. Entertainment may take grand or modest forms, but novelty and excitement are as important to shoppers in Fargo, North Dakota, as they are in Las Vegas, Nevada.

Direct Marketing Growth

Selling directly to customers is not a new retail method. Direct selling companies like Tupperware and Mary Kay Cosmetics have been in business for decades. **Direct selling** is the practice of selling to consumers through one-on-one situations or parties usually held in homes or work places. **Direct marketing** is defined as any direct communication to a consumer or business recipient that is designed to generate a response in the form of an order, new lead, or store traffic. Offers to participate in direct marketing reach us by catalogs, direct mail pieces, telephone, or the Internet. All these ways of reaching consumers fall into the category known as nonstore retailing. Some experts believe that nonstore sales will outpace conventional store sales this decade. In a study conducted by Wharton Econometrics Forecasting Associates for the Direct Marketing Association, shopping by computer or catalog is expected to grow by 81 percent by 2004. Direct marketing sales will then account for 6.25 percent of all retail sales in the United States.[11]

Direct marketing can be extremely customer focused using personalized messages, fine-honed data collection and storage capabilities, creative media messages, and persistent customer contact methods. More on this topic is presented in Chapter 6.

Shorter Supply Chains

The term direct marketing can be taken more literally as companies use vertical integration to shorten their marketing channels, thus making them more efficient. The many specialty divisions of The Limited and The Gap are not simply retail chains. They have learned that control of the manufacturing process can create higher profits. Gap Body, one of the newest Gap divisions, carries private label intimate apparel. Its exclusive products for men and women are produced less expensively in company-owned factories than if purchased from outside vendors (See Figure 2.7).

Figure 2.6 The Forum Shops at Caesar's Palace in Las Vegas is a mall dedicated to retail entertainment.

direct selling The practice of selling to consumers through one-on-one situations or parties usually held in homes or work places.

direct marketing Any direct communication to a consumer or business recipient that is designed to generate a response in the form of an order, new lead, or store traffic.

Figure 2.7 The Gap practices vertical integration by controlling the manufacturing and retailing functions for several of its chains including Gap Body. *Courtesy of Fairchild Publications, Inc.*

divestiture The selling of one retail company to another.

bankruptcy Legal declaration to inform the public of financial insolvency of a company.

Discounters such as Wal-Mart have effectively shortened their supply chains. They have accomplished this through extensive private label manufacturing programs, strict vendor selection criteria, and the elimination of most wholesalers. This is one of the factors that have brought Wal-Mart to the stellar position it now holds. The company does more than two times the business of its nearest competitor, Carrefour.

Continued Industry Consolidation

Mergers and acquisitions of retail companies have been chosen tactics for decades. The latest ripple of activity began in the mid-1980s. Similarly, divestiture and bankruptcy proceedings are not new but escalated in the late twentieth century. **Divestiture** is the selling of one business to another company. **Bankruptcy** is a legal declaration to inform the public of the financial insolvency of a company. Both practices became strategic devices wielded by some retailers seeking to sustain their failing businesses. Some retailers used divestiture to refocus their operations and remain solvent in the face of increased competition. For example, some department store groups sold off discount divisions rather than buy or establish their own discount stores. May Company sold its Venture and Caldor discount chains in order to concentrate on its department store business. This was a good strategic move for May Co., a financially sound retailer. Venture and Caldor both declared bankruptcy and went out of business in the late 1990s.

Consolidation is still occurring in banking, health care, insurance, telecommunications, and manufacturing. The trend will continue in retailing as companies seek arrangements in which they can continue to perform well. More on this topic is covered in Chapter 5.

Customer-Centric Relationships

Focus on customer service was the industry creed in the 1980s, but many of the earlier efforts were lip service compared to the lofty ideas of contemporary retailers. A distinct shift has occurred. Reaching greater numbers of customers may not be as important as serving existing customers better. Cultivating more customers is necessary, but not at the expense of alienating loyal clientele. The many ways retailers are embracing customer-centric relationships are observed in a variety of settings.

Borrowing from airline frequent flyer programs, retailers of all kinds are developing frequent shopper programs, incentives, and exclusive services. Customers are at the center, but retailers also anticipate increased market share, sales, and/or profitability as a result of strong customer service programs. Increased technological capabilities are crucial to the execution of some new customer services.

Neiman Marcus' Inner Circle program offers incentive points for dollars spent in its stores. Awards ranging from designer chocolates to European trips are enticing. Customers must spend thousands of dollars in a calendar year in order to be eligible for the larger gifts. JC Penney has added a similar program, but with significantly lower annual purchase requirements and less lavish rewards.

Personal shopping programs are another way retailers have maintained and nurtured relationships with customers. Formerly the domain of department and specialty stores like Macy's and Nordstrom's, this more intimate involvement with customers is demonstrating its benefits even to home improvement centers.

On the selling floor, easy access to merchandise, appropriate fixtures, and user-friendly electronic kiosks are other ways customer service will be delivered. Cross-merchandising will be used as goods are positioned where they better match customers' shopping patterns. **Cross-merchandising** is the practice of allocating the same merchandise to two or more areas of the store instead of one. During a Christmas selling season, Bloomingdales featured Godiva candy displays in several store locations. The retailer even positioned individual bars and small-boxed candies along with cashmere sweaters, making the suggested multiple purchase almost irresistible. These are all examples of the changing relationship between retailers and customers.

cross-merchandising The practice of allocating the same merchandise to two or more areas of the store instead of one.

Emphasis on Branding

The importance of branding in retailing should not be underestimated. **Branding** is the process of developing, building, and maintaining a name in the marketplace. High recognition and demand for a product or store by consumers are goals of companies that use branding as a strategy. Branding is used to reach customers in several ways. Emphasis in a store might be on nationally or globally recognized labels. Retailers can chose to combine national or global brands with private label merchandise. When the brand is the store itself, emphasis is usually placed on private label merchandise. The store as brand was one of the key concepts to emerge in the 1990s that will persist in the 21st century. The significance of this shift from product to store is profound. The building of a retail brand takes time, effort, investment, and consumer acceptance. It is crucial to the success of most retailers

branding The process of developing, building, and maintaining a name in the marketplace.

Figure 2.8 Co-branding strategies are popular globally. Wendy's and Kentucky Fried Chicken (KFC) share signage and square footage in Taipei, Taiwan.

co-branding Retail partnership that is formed when two separate retailers (brands) join forces to reach more customers more effectively thus increasing sales for both parties.

today. Hanes, Levi's, and Victoria's Secret are among the top 10 most recognized brand names in fashion as identified in the *WWD 100*.[12] Although these companies manufacturer the products they sell, all have built their brands through their own retail store chains. Their logos speak clearly and loudly wherever in the world they are noticed. Other brand-related techniques attest to the power of branding.

Co-branding strategies are used to create new partnerships. The intention is that the union of two is stronger than the individual companies. When two separate retailers (brands) join forces for the purpose of reaching customers more effectively and increasing sales for both parties this partnership is called **co-branding**. Two examples stress this point. Two fast food operators Wendy's and Kentucky Fried Chicken (KFC) share a sign and quarters in Taipei, Taiwan, where space is expensive and at a premium. Co-branding of Wendy's and KFC is illustrated in Figure 2.8. Starbucks cafes in Barnes & Noble superstores may keep customers in the stores longer, buying more books, but the partnership also addresses psychological needs. For some, a stop at Barnes & Noble and a sip of cappuccino is a pleasant respite from an otherwise harried existence. Starbucks' presence suggests a subtle, but perhaps important reason why consumers will visit Barnes & Noble time and time again.

Resurgence of Entrepreneurship

Revitalization of the entrepreneurial spirit is expected to continue as more individuals choose to strike out on their own as retailers. For some, the opportunity has come because of downsizing at the corporate level. For others it is fulfillment of a lifelong dream to own and operate a store and control one's own destiny. Despite the long hours, stress, and financial uncertainty this entails, many are drawn to small business ownership. Sole proprietors are particularly drawn to specialty store retailing, often in smaller shopping centers, peripheral downtown locations, and resort sites, where rents are sometimes more affordable. Shoppers looking for unusual merchandise and personal service often are target markets for sole proprietors. Over 93 percent of all retail firms in the United States are comprised of only one store.[13] This statistic supports the fact that retail entrepreneurism is strong.

A study done by Babson College in the United States and London Business School in the United Kingdom, showed that the number of people involved in new business start-ups varies by country. For example, there is a higher percentage of entrepreneurs in the United States than in many

Table 2.2 Rates of Entrepreneurship

Country	Percentage of Adults Involved in Start-ups
United States	8.4
Canada	6.8
Israel	5.4
France	1.8
Japan	1.6
Finland	1.4

Source: Babson College, Wellesley, Mass., and London Business School as reported in the *Wall Street Journal*, Business Bulletin, June 24, 1999:A1

other countries. These statistics are shown in Table 2.2. The number of women in the workforce and the proportion of corporate employment in a country also affect the rate of entrepreneurism. In Finland, there are fewer females working and the country depends on one significant employer for more than one-third of its domestic growth.[14] These facts explain the low rate of entrepreneurism in that country.

The number of women and ethnic minority business owners in the United States has grown in the last decade. Innovation in retailing often comes from these sectors. As developing countries move toward industrialization, more women enter the workforce, and more people recognize the benefits of small business ownership, these numbers will continue to increase.

The Internet has become an entrepreneurial stronghold. There, almost anyone with something to sell can at least set up a home page. For some the opportunity to be able to work from home is the principal reason for taking this route. For others it is the excitement of being on the cusp of retail change.

Concern for Safety

As they have changed the way we view the world and our place in it, the tragic events of September 11, 2001, also affected retailing. People, who were emotionally ready to fly by the holiday season that year, packed lightly. They either traveled with unwrapped holiday gifts or postponed their purchases until they reached their destinations, unsure what increased airline security procedures would entail. Consumer sentiment also lagged and some consumers bought fewer or less expensive presents because they chose to focus less on materialistic pleasures and more on the quality of our sometimes short, fragile lives. The economic downturn had less to do with low spending that year than did quality of life factors. Increased concerns for privacy paralleled those of personal safety. Families became wary of accepting direct mail pieces and packages as biological warfare scares made us fearful. Because of the profound impact terrorist attacks have had on the world, policies that affect the safety and security of individuals, businesses, governments, and other organizations will forever change the way we think and act.

These ten critical aspects of change herald adaptation by consumers and businesses. Ways that retailers are addressing and managing change are now addressed.

Retail Adaptation

brand equity The level of consumer recognition a brand, label, or store has in the marketplace.

The future will belong to retailers that present a strong identity, improve customer service, establish loyalty programs, sharpen their marketing skills, remain attuned to customer safety and privacy, and expand globally. Some retailers will reduce their store numbers or sizes while others will expand their formats or reallocate space. Thinking more in terms of profit than of volume is another possibility. Many will target customers more specifically and take more risks. Most will adopt enlightened attitudes toward developing management talent. Mature retailers may chose to strengthen their brand equity by opening new chains. **Brand equity** is the level of consumer recognition a brand, label, or store has in the marketplace. All retailers will integrate technology to the fullest and embrace and adapt to the changing world as we know it. Dynamics of key institutions including specialty, department, and discount stores, and food retailers are highlighted next.

Specialty Stores

Characterized by their limited lines of merchandise, specialty stores will change in several ways. Some apparel retailers will remain strong by narrowing their customer focus and their merchandise assortments. Others will tighten their bonds with customers by creating environments or providing customer services that cannot be easily duplicated. Three important directions are considered.

Market Segmentation Market segmentation will continue to be one of the most important strategies of the 21st century as specialty retailers become more precise in their selection of markets. For example, Toronto-based Club Monaco segments its market by fashion attitude. The retailer targets men and women aged 18 to 45 who appreciate designer clothing but cannot afford high prices. The attributes of good quality and fit are in high demand, and the company provides these for customers. The chain uses age and lifestyle to determine its market. Club Monaco also has stores in the United States and Asia and is considering opening units in the United Kingdom.[15]

Concept Shops Areas that are dedicated to highly specialized merchandise or that which has high brand recognition can bring new profit centers to traditional retailers. **Concept shops** are select in-store areas that allow retailers to expand on a broad scale without the high overhead of chain store expansion. For example, Fauchon, the French retailer of exquisite gourmet foods, expanded internationally by locating approximately 400 Fauchon shops in department stores and airports. Figure 2.9 illustrates the Fauchon concept shop in Selfridge's department store in London.

Destination Stores The future will also include more **destination stores**, stores that have drawing power because they offer unique merchandise or strong brand identification. Many specialty stores offer goods that customers will go out of their way to purchase. Well-known retailers such as Tiffany and L.L.Bean hold this distinction. Diesel, the Italian specialty store chain, is a popular destination for fashion-conscious youth with urban attitudes. Lesser-known small retailers that cultivate customers who refuse to accept substitutes for the products carried or the ambiance of the store also are considered destination stores.

Department Stores

In the past, department stores endured many pressures including competition, changing consumer attitudes, and redundant merchandise. They weathered moves from urban to suburban locations and many image reassessments. Department stores addressed these issues and adapted to change admirably. They continue to be a venue of choice for many shoppers. Evidence of several new strategies has already appeared and is expected to escalate this decade.

New and Revived Selling Formats Major retailers will turn departments into stores, experiment with new distribution techniques, and revive former formats. Strategies include:

Figure 2.9 Fauchon, the French gourmet food retailer, has opened concept shops in many retail stores around the world, including this one in Selfridges department store in London.

CYBERSCOOP

Check out Diesel's Web site at www.diesel.com/contact_diesel /downloads/press. Find out what percentage of business is done outside Italy, the company's homebase. Where does the innovative apparel company produce its jeans?

concept shops Select in-store areas featuring merchandise that has high brand recognition. A format used by retailers to expand on a broad scale without the high overhead costs of chain expansion.

destination stores Stores that have drawing power because they offer unique merchandise or strong brand identification.

- *Department spin-offs.* Some retailers will take entire departments out of existing stores and open freestanding stores. JC Penney did this with its Home Stores.

- *Alternative sales channels.* Expecting to supplement in-store sales, most department stores have opened Web stores. Sears began selling appliances online in 1999. Prior to this move, customers who purchased Craftsman tools online were studied. Results showed that after making an online purchase, customers spent 27 percent more when shopping in Sears' stores.[16]

- *Temporary locations.* Through satellite centers some stores will provide products and services for time-sensitive events such as the Olympics.

- *Leased departments.* In the past leased departments have often been the provenance of gift-wrapping, jewelry, cosmetics, and shoe departments. **Leased departments** are owned and operated by a company other than the host store. This trend will escalate as more manufacturers take on merchandising responsibilities and create stronger partnerships with retailers. Leased departments are discussed further in Chapter 5.

- *In-store restaurant revival.* Phased out in the last decade, food service operations in many department stores are being relaunched.

leased departments Departments that are owned and operated by a company other than the host store.

Customer Service Improvements Concentration on customer services will intensify in department stores and include the following directions:

- *Enhanced amenities.* Some department stores will have a concierge on duty, much like those in better hotels. Convenient play areas for children and seating sections for seniors also are being added. Other stores plan to introduce unique customer services to help alleviate redundancies that contribute to a meaningless shopping experience for many people. Many shoppers report boredom and disinterest when they shop. They are experiencing the **sameness syndrome,** the tendency of some retailers to offer the same or similar merchandise or services as their competitors.

- *International customer focus.* Many stores have added multilingual signs in addition to bilingual associates, since department stores around the globe attract a cross-section of foreign tourists. Some stores already employ associates that collectively speak 50 different languages.

- *Social responsibility emphasis.* Some retailers are taking a proactive stance on health and social responsibility issues when introducing services. Nordstrom opened a mammography center in one of its stores and anticipated more openings if the first was well received.[17]

sameness syndrome The tendency of some retailers to offer the same or similar merchandise or services as their competitors.

Discount Stores

Discounters are known collectively as big box retailers because of their tendency to operate from huge buildings. The term **big box** identifies a broad spectrum of discount and discount-like retailers that operate out of large, utilitarian stores. Discounters will continue to seek competitive advantages as intensely as specialty and department stores. General merchandise discounters will flourish in the United States, with continued domination by the top three: Wal-Mart, Kmart, and Target. Intense competition in this sector is underscored by the filing for bankruptcy protection by Kmart in early 2002. Other probable causes for the company's weakened position included poor holiday sales, problems with supply chain partners, and difficulties securing necessary financing. The heart of the problem may be an image one. Kmart has neither the aggressive pricing, distribution expertise, nor the buying power of Wal-Mart. Target attracts a more affluent clientele than the other discounters. Being caught in the nebulous middle may have contributed to Kmart's woes. Some retailers have successfully changed their images in order to carve out a more precise market niche. Progressive retailers will develop new formats and locations while Kmart attempts to recover. The assimilation of traits typical of department and specialty stores is also expected to occur in the discount sector.

big box stores Term used to identify a broad spectrum of discount and discount-like retailers that operate out of large, utilitarian stores.

New Formats and Locations Giant specialty discounters such as Home Depot, Toys"R"Us, and Staples are big box stores that are called category killers. They sell limited and deep assortments of products in home improvement, toy, and office products categories, respectively. The 1990s saw other types of category killers emerge including book, pet, and auto supply stores. Health care and wedding stores are expected to draw attention early in the 21st century as they too adopt big box formats.

Some category killers are opening smaller format stores. Home Depot moved into home decor and housewares with the introduction of its Village Hardware stores in 1999. At 40,000 square feet, the new stores are much smaller than the company's home improvement centers. Village Hardware carries many of the same power tools, electrical and plumbing supplies, and paints but has enhanced home storage, window and wall fashions, and kitchenware sections. The new concept targets more female and older customers, and provides more extensive customer services.[18] Circuit City and Staples each use smaller, express stores to reach customers in transportation terminals and other high traffic locations such as malls. More discounters will create smaller, express-type units and focus on specific market segments.

Figure 2.10 Electronic price checkers provide convenient service for Toys"R"Us customers on the selling floor.

Trait Assimilation Many characteristics of specialty and department stores will be adopted by discounters. Development of private label programs, re-design of selling floors to encourage more lifestyle departments, and cross-merchandising are three areas in which change will occur. Expect decor to be less utilitarian as discounters recreate space, refurbish their stores, and add amenities. The following examples describe tactics already in progress:

■ *Enhanced services.* Kmart superstores incorporate do-it-yourself (DIY) departments with services equivalent to those expected of a home improvement specialty retailer. For example, computer devices match colors from a swatch of wallpaper or fabric so that custom paints can then be mixed for customers. Many retailers provide electronic price check devices for customer convenience (See Figure 2.10).

■ *Urbanization.* Site selection strategies are also changing. Some discounters, including Kmart and Wal-Mart, have left traditional suburban community shopping center sites and moved to inner-city locations.

■ *Changing service policies.* Warehouse clubs like Costco and Sam's Club will continue to serve customers on a members-only basis. Clubs serve both wholesale and retail customers but have seen a shift in the proportion of sales attributed to each type. Originally, the industry served mostly small businesses; now, more families shop the clubs. Operating from pared-down formats, some are adding new services. Costco operates travel, pharmacy, and optical centers, and offers free delivery service to some of its wholesale clients.

■ *Off-price retrenchment.* As competition intensifies, consolidation in the off-price sector is expected. T.J. Maxx gained momentum by purchasing rival Marshall's and is expected to dominate this specialty discount niche. Other retailers, such as Filene's Basement and Loehmann's, found it difficult to compete with large general merchandise discounters, outlet stores, and stronger off-price stores. Both retailers have survived bankruptcy filings and continue to refine their merchandise offerings and create efficiencies operationally. Value City, a discount and liquidation specialist purchased Filene's Basement. Off-price stores are discussed in more detail in Chapter 4.

Food Retailers

Retailers of food products are also subject to change as time constraints continue to perplex consumers who adapt their lifestyles accordingly. Developments in supermarkets, superstores, hypermarkets, and convenience stores are highlighted in this section.

Supermarkets and Superstores For decades, supermarkets were the soul of the food industry. These stores gave way to the superstores of the 1990s. Superstores are much larger than conventional supermarkets and most have bakeries, delis, fish markets, liquor stores, flower shops, pharmacies, and restaurants on the premises. In some of them as much as half of the inventory is nonfood items and may even include music and jewelry. Certain trends are expected to continue:

- *Longer hours of operation.* At some stores the doors never close; the hours are 24 a day, 7 days a week. Extended hours will become the norm in many high-traffic areas.
- *Changing formats.* Some supermarkets will expand into superstores, or purchase them. Certain supermarkets and superstores will develop smaller grocery store formats.
- *Increased competition.* General merchandise discounters will continue to add grocery and food products to their traditional apparel, home electronics and furnishings, increasing competition for supermarkets.
- *More customer service technologies.* Technological devices will assist food retailers as they continue to experience a high turnover of employees. In some supermarket checkout areas, a computerized voice states the prices as customers scan their own purchases. In others, a recorded video of a clerk is programmed to give messages and information when customers ask for help via a touch sensitive screen. Electronic kiosks also are used to order deli products.

Hypermarkets **Hypermarkets** are stores of 150,000 square feet or more—70 percent of which is devoted to general merchandise and 30 percent to food products. Hypermarkets go beyond the size and scope of superstores in several ways:

hypermarkets Stores of over 150,000 square feet, 70 percent of which is devoted to general merchandise and 30 percent to food products.

- *Extended services.* Insurance and travel agencies, ticket kiosks, and even a marriage bureau may be part of a hypermarket as they are at Carrefour.
- *Retailtainment.* Hypermarkets create their own brand of entertainment. Employees wear colorful uniforms, balloons and banners sway above cash registers or hang from ceilings. In almost every aisle a demonstrator is cooking

or serving everything from chocolate chip cookies to chicken-to-go, as seen in Figure 2.11.

■ *Unique merchandise mix.* Hypermarkets carry fewer products than conventional supermarkets, but great quantities of those products they do carry.

In Europe, Asia, and South America, the hypermarket is a way of life for most people, but it has not achieved the same status in the United States despite attempts by Wal-Mart and Carrefour. Whether these industry leaders will revisit the introduction of the hypermarket in the United States is yet to be determined.

Convenience Stores Years ago, customers marveled when convenience stores began to stay open 24 hours a day. In the 1980s, they added gas stations and coffee for customers on the run. In this century convenience stores will continue to innovate in several ways:

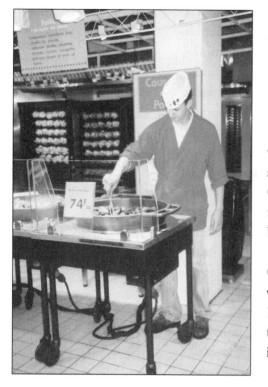

Figure 2.11 Excitement prevails in Carrefour hypermarkets where in-store product demonstrations and food preparation are part of the draw.

■ *Expanded products and services.* Some chains will add selling space, and new products and services but remain primarily a people-run business. Banking, dry cleaning, and shoe repair services will be commonplace. Prepared food concessions—even some with in-store seating—will grow in popularity.

■ *Robotic units.* Others will take technology to new heights and open robotic units that will employ no humans but will continue to provide ample products and services. One can only speculate: will robot gas pumpers take the place of the human touch? This would bring back an era when full service meant customers did not pump their own gas.

■ *Delivery services.* Home delivery of convenience goods may keep pace with food and grocery home delivery services.

■ *Time-saving technology.* Technology will be used to provide better customer service. At several self-serve Shell gas stations in California, customers can place orders for convenience items on the same touchscreen used to select gas, saving a separate transaction. Purchases can either be delivered to the car or picked up at a drive-up window.[19]

In the future—which, in many cases, is now—customers will be able to shop where and when they please. While visiting the Smithsonian Museum in Washington, DC, they can stop into one of its many gift shops. If waiting for a flight at an airport, they can check out Victoria's Secret or The Body Shop before they pick up their TCBY yogurt cones. People will still be dialing 800 numbers or using their car computers to catalog shop while stuck in freeway traffic. Perhaps college students will still gather in dorm rooms for Party Lite candle parties and consider a weekend visit to a flea market a good time.

Despite predictions of a cashless society, our need to socialize and examine products before we purchase them is a hard habit to break. Considering human nature, we might not want to change anyway. It would probably take genetic alteration for many people to give up the mall experience!

Not all of the many changes in retailing that have been predicted will come true, but many will. Innovative products and services will enhance the quality of life. Some will simply provide fun. The rewards that many of these futuristic formats furnish will far outweigh the risks of change.

Summary

Today's merchants must plan ahead if their businesses are to grow. Strategic planning involves five key steps: (1) performing a situation analysis, (2) determining a differential advantage, (3) developing a mission statement, (4) formulating company objectives, and (5) planning company and marketing strategies. To achieve customer satisfaction and earn a profit retailers everywhere must acknowledge this important process, implement it and monitor it on an ongoing basis.

Change is occurring in several critical areas. Technology will offer more choices of where to shop including the Internet. Retailers that use information technology effectively may gain a competitive edge.

Global expansion by mature retail companies will continue to occur for several reasons: saturated home markets, increased competition, availability of new markets, demands of investors, increased customer sophistication, and reduced trade restrictions.

Retailing and entertainment will merge as consumers seek to fulfill more than basic shopping needs in the retail marketplace. Direct marketing and direct selling will be important alternatives to classic retail stores. The sophisticated databases of direct marketers will allow them to reach customers more effectively, often over the Internet.

Shorter supply chains will develop throughout the industry as retailers seek to cut their costs of doing business. Mergers, acquisitions, divestitures, and bankruptcies will continue as further consolidation occurs across all retail institutions. Fewer moderate and large size companies will exist, but those that do will be more powerful.

Retailers of all types and sizes will continue to seek closer relationships with their customers through a variety of well-tailored programs.

Branding is an important concept for retailers in the 21st century. Selling national, global, or private label brands may provide impetus for retailers to serve customers and operate profitably. Some retailers position their stores as brands.

There always will be a place for small retailers that offer distinct specialties and personal service in classic or electronic locations. Rates of entrepreneurism vary by country.

Terrorist attacks throughout the world have indelibly left their mark on our way of life and the way we do business. Consumers increased need for privacy and personal security will create new challenges and perhaps new opportunities for retailers.

Institutional change will occur in many ways. Some retailers will reduce selling space while others will grow larger or re-allocate the space they have. All retailers will use technology to the fullest extent and focus on their customers as they seek competitive niches. The many changes that seem somewhat futuristic at this moment may very well become commonplace as we learn new ways to cope in a troubled world.

Questions for Review and Discussion

1. Why is strategic planning important to retailers? Discuss the kinds of information that may surface while conducting a situation analysis.

2. Discuss three changes in retailing that are occurring or are expected to occur early this century. How will these changes affect customers and retailers?

3. Why is it necessary to anticipate changes in nonstore retailing, particularly in the direct marketing area?

4. Why will there always be a place in retailing for entrepreneurs? What demographic and business climate issues affect new retail start-ups?

5. Why is the concept of retail branding an important one? Explain several ways branding strategies may be implemented.

6. Discuss some expected changes in specialty, department, discount, and food stores.

Endnotes

1. www.emsonline.com/EMSdirect/ES/index.html. December 26, 2001.
2. Martinez, Arthur C. "Sears' Strategy for Renewal." *Chain Store Age.* July, 1999:64-74.
3. "Sears Will Cut 4,900 Jobs." *Boston Globe.* October 25, 2001:C2.
4. "Sears to Buy Lands' End for $1.9 Billion." *The New York Times.* May 13, 2002 Available: www.nytimes.com/reuters/business/business-retail-landsend.html
5. Blischok, Thomas. "Reimagineering(Global Retailing." Presentation. Global Retail Symposium. Southwest Retail Center. University of Arizona. Tucson. March 7, 1997.
6. Masters, Chris. "Mondex: Product and Brand Development." Presentation. Mondex International. London. July 10, 1997.

7. Gordon, Tom. "Global Implications of Point of Impulse Marketing." Presentation. Global Retail Symposium. Southwest Retail Center. University of Arizona. Tucson. March 6, 1998.

8. "Printemps Offers Skating Cyberclerks." *Women's Wear Daily*. April 23, 1999:8.

9. Sweeney, Daniel. "Global Expansion: An Update." Global Retail Symposium. Southwest Retail Center. University of Arizona. Tucson. March 16, 1997.

10. "Western Europe Pulls Ahead of United States." *IDC Newsletter*-eBusiness Trends. January 3, 2002. Available online January 4, 2002.

11. "Economic Impact: US Direct Marketing Today." Annual Study. Wharton Econometrics Forecasting Associates. Commissioned by the Direct Marketing Association, New York. 2001.

12. "The WWD 100." *Women's Wear Daily*. A WWD Special Report. December, 2001:7-8.

13. *1997 Census of Retail Trade*. US Department of Commerce, Bureau of the Census, Available: www.census.gov.

14. "New Entrepreneurs Appear Vital to Healthy Economic Growth." *Wall Street Journal*. Business Bulletin. June 24, 1999:A1.

15. Club Monaco Presentation. American Collegiate Retailing Association. Toronto, Canada. May, 2000.

16. Coleman, Calmetta Y. "Sears to Begin Online Sale of Appliances." *Wall Street Journal*. May 13, 1999.

17. "Service and Solutions Invite Success." *Chain Store Age*. State of the Industry. August 1997:21A.

18. Duff, Mike. "Home Depot Debuts New Format." *Discount Store News*. July 12, 1999:1,80.

19. "Customers Feed on Convenience." *Chain Store Age*. State of the Industry. August 1997:16A.

Chapter 3

The Retail Environment

Learning Objectives

After completing this chapter you should be able to:

- Discuss how the economy, political events, and legislation affect retailing.
- Describe several ways demographic and social changes influence retailing.
- Discuss how retailers and consumers deal with environmental issues.
- Describe several competitive strategies used by retailers.
- Explain how retailers react to unpredictable events.

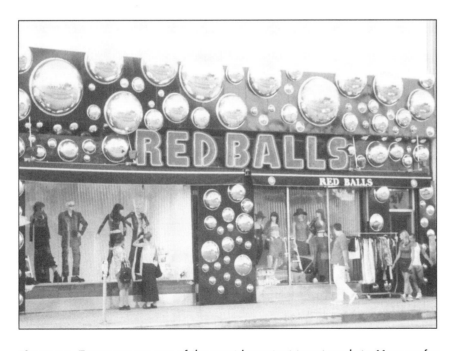

Figure 3.1 Teenagers are one of the most important target markets. Many prefer to shop trendy streets like Melrose Avenue in Los Angeles (See p. 81).

geocentric Viewing the world as a whole—the locus for ideas and decision making.

ethnocentric Viewing individual countries in narrow focus; the attitude that one's own country or culture is superior.

Retailers must be trend watchers in every sense of the word. Changes in the economy, political movements, legislation, demographics, society, environmental consciousness, competition, and technology all affect business. Individuals do not have control over these components of the retail environment, nor do retail companies to any great extent. Using information from this world laboratory to predict customer behavior and the types of retail strategies that will succeed is not an easy task or an exact science. It is important to adopt a geocentric rather than an ethnocentric view when analyzing the retail environment, since all nations and economies are dependent on one another. A **geocentric** perspective is one that views the world as a whole—the locus for ideas and decision making. An **ethnocentric** perspective views individual countries in narrow focus and perpetuates the attitude that one's own country or culture is superior. Retailers run their businesses effectively today and plan for the future by acknowledging uncontrollable forces and dealing with them in ethical ways.

This chapter tracks dynamics in several areas of the retail environment. Many statistics on the United States market are given and, where appropriate, several international examples are included. The goal is to demonstrate that the same environmental factors affect retailing around the world.

Retailing and the Economy

Feel the pulse of the economy and you will feel the pulse of retailing. Inflation, recession, war, peace, and prosperity are all reflected at the point of sale. Retail sales and strategies change in response to events such as tax increases or reductions, stock market fluctuations, or currency crises. Layoffs in major industries or openings of new businesses also affect retail planning.

How does the manager of a department store cope during a recession? What happens to a local hardware store owner when wholesale prices increase along with direct competition from large chains? Can the costly service orientation of specialty stores allow them to survive the onslaught of discount fashion merchants? These are the kinds of questions that retailers routinely ask. Although specific problems may change from year to year, the need to work within an ever-changing economy remains constant. Retailers must be attuned to current world, national, regional, and local economic indicators if they expect to create profitable operations.

The economy is the first blamed when retail sales are down. Retail analysts recognize that this is both the truth and an oversimplification, since the mechanics of the economy are complex. Knowledge of how interest rates, inflation, recession, and currency devaluation affect business is important to retailers. Monitoring of key economic indicators such as buying power and gross domestic product is equally imperative.

Interest Rates

Carefully watched in the United States by the Federal Reserve, interest rates affect retail sales and development. Fluctuations in the prime rate affect many sectors of the economy. The **prime rate** is the interest rate charged by the Federal Reserve Bank to commercial lending institutions. Using furniture as an example, changes in the prime rate may affect consumers and business in the following ways:

prime rate The interest rate charged by the Federal Reserve bank to commercial lending institutions.

- Lower interest rates usually precede a rise in new home construction.
- More housing sales may mean that homeowners will purchase more furniture.
- Furniture purchases may be charged, because lack of cash is frequently the plight of new homeowners.
- If credit card interest rates are high, homeowners may put off purchases and make do with what they already have.
- If interest rates are low, customers may use credit cards and not defer their purchases.
- Some individuals curtail spending irrespective of the interest rates and choose either to pay cash or not purchase at all.

When a nation as a whole carries high credit card balances, the outlook for retail sales is usually not a healthy one. A furniture retailer like IKEA needs to analyze interest rates because the company's existence depends on the housing market.

Inflation

Currency inflation is another economic phenomenon that is watched and addressed. **Inflation** is the abnormal increase in the volume of money and credit in a country resulting in a substantial and continuing rise in price levels. To understand how inflation affects retail pricing, track the price of the same item over time. For example, in 1950, a pound of hamburger cost

inflation The abnormal increase in the volume of money and credit in a country resulting in a substantial and continuing rise in price levels.

Figure 3.2 To better understand how inflation affects pricing, notice how the price of hamburger and other items on this sales slip from 1949 compares with prices today.

consumer price index (CPI) Economic indicator that measures changes in the cost of living due to inflation.

generic goods Products that do not bear highly recognizable manufacturers' or retailers' labels.

recession Period of time in which there is less money in the economy than there previously was.

approximately 59 cents. This price is documented on the vintage grocery receipt illustrated in Figure 3.2. In 1980, the same amount of meat cost about $1.69. In 2002, the average rate per pound was $2.99.

The **consumer price index (CPI)** is an economic indicator that measures changes in the cost of living due to inflation. The figure is released monthly by the U.S. government and is based on price fluctuations in a group of retail products tracked over time. When the index increases, individuals are able to purchase less for their money. The worry of most people is that wages won't keep up with increases in prices. This is why many receive cost-of-living increases annually when their salaries are reviewed. Inflation causes wholesale prices to increase as well. Retailers must pass along price increases to their customers or expect lower profits.

The rate of inflation also changes with time and is affected by other economic factors. In the United States, inflation was considered very low in 2002, at approximately 2.5 percent. Two decades earlier, the rate was almost 5 percent.

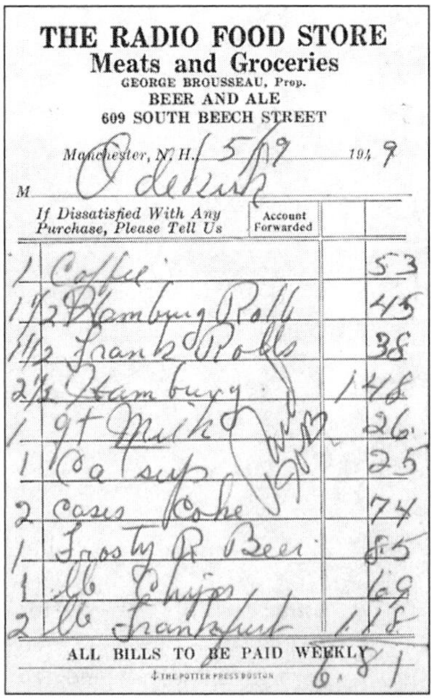

Inflation affects the importation of goods and consumer spending. Without imports coming into a country from foreign markets, there is no incentive for domestic firms to moderate prices. If there are no imports, prices are set at what the market will bear, which is generally higher than in a competitive marketplace. Retail profit declines because the basic costs of doing business increase along with vendors' prices. To cover their costs, retailers increase prices and customers pay more for some products, perhaps more than they are intrinsically worth. Because many retailers depend upon imports as a large percentage of their inventories, the rate of inflation is considered during the merchandise planning process.

Customers often change their buying patterns during periods of inflation. People eat at Taco Bell more often than at Red Lobster and shop at discounters more frequently than department stores. As the cost of living increases, so does the sale of **generic goods**—products that do not bear manufacturers' or retailers' labels and are cheaper than comparable brand name goods. Most generic products feature simple packaging with nondescript labels.

Recession

A **recession** is a period in which there is less money in the economy than there previously was. Consumers generally spend less on goods and services during a recession than in prosperous times. In the manufacturing sector, recession is anticipated when wholesale orders for products slow down appreciably. This hurts retailers, because sales may be down but the basic costs of doing business (wages, energy, credit) remain at prerecession levels. Countries such as Japan, the United States, Germany, and the United Kingdom coped with recession in the 1990s. The United States experienced further economic downturn when many e-commerce companies failed in 2000–2001. This situation was made worse by the terrorist attacks and subsequent turmoil in financial markets. In periods of recession, retailers generate low or no business growth, and bankruptcies increase.

People expect bigger markdowns on merchandise during periods of recession. Because retailers carry less inventory at these times, customers find less selection in stores. Recession also affects human resources. Layoffs may occur as retailers cut payroll costs. If retailers attempt to keep employees working while sales are sluggish, eventually profits are affected. Fewer services for customers and less promotional advertising also are part of general retrenchment during a recession.

Economic Indicators

Retailers closely watch many economic indicators. These include buying power, gross domestic product, consumer confidence levels, and unemployment trends. Two examples illustrate the use and importance of economic indicators.

The amount of money a family has available for purchases after taxes is called **buying power**. It indicates ability and inclination to spend at retail. Wal-Mart looks for buying power of at least the equivalent of $18,000 per household as the company surveys potential locations for new stores in Asia.[1] This figure would be substantially higher in the United States and other developed markets.

buying power The amount of money a family has available for purchases after taxes.

Another key economic indicator, the gross domestic product measures the total value of goods and services produced in a country annually. Retail companies that are considering global expansion use this information.

Currency Devaluation

The worth of most world currencies is linked to the U.S. dollar that is considered less volatile than foreign currencies. This is due to the size of the U.S. economy, stability of its currency, and the solid performance of its stock and financial markets over time. When a currency becomes hardly worth the paper it is printed on, devaluation has occurred. **Devaluation** is a reduction in the international exchange value of a currency. This condition happens for many reasons including bank failures, stock market crashes, unrestricted foreign investments, poor financial management, and panic. A dramatic example of the effects of devaluation is the Asian currency crisis

devaluation Reduction in the international exchange value of a currency.

that began in 1997. It affected not only several Pacific Rim countries but also the nations with which they do business. Understanding the factors that converged to create this financial crisis teaches an important lesson in global economics.

The problem began in Thailand then mushroomed throughout the Pacific Rim. Most severely affected were Thailand and Indonesia, with the economies of Malaysia, the Philippines, Hong Kong, Korea, and Japan also tainted. Poor bank management was one reason for the Thai problems. The country's banks had been borrowing money at lower interest rates abroad than could be obtained domestically and were flagrantly granting loans to businesses. Transactions were often in dollars, not baht, the local currency. When loan repayment time came and the local currency had lost strength, companies had to come up with more baht to pay their debts. Many could not and defaulted on their loans. The baht declined further against the dollar despite efforts to strengthen the currency. Panic spread as international agencies were called upon to help the situation. Several additional reasons for declines in currency values are listed in Table 3.1.

A crisis of this magnitude affects retailing. Consumer buying power was diminished, therefore retail sales were curtailed. Retailers and shopping center developers responded in several ways. Stores lowered prices to invigorate declining sales. Some landlords put holds on retail lease payments, others issued outright lease cutbacks. For example, in Hong Kong, 30 to 40 percent reductions in rents were reported.[2]

Tourism decreased throughout the Pacific Rim affecting hotels, restaurants, and stores. Retailers in Hawaii and those on the West Coast of the United States also experienced declining sales. In Hawaii, Asian tourists represent 50 to 90 percent of sales for luxury goods retailers like Louis Vuitton, Charles Jourdan, and Prada. Liberty House, a Hawaiian department store chain, declared bankruptcy in early 1998, citing the Asian currency crisis as one contributing factor.[3] In 2002, Liberty House was acquired by Federated Department Stores.

By 1999, economic recovery began in many parts of the globe. Many experts believed that repairing the financial devastation in Asia would require two to five years. Economists predicted declines of 4 percent to 8 percent in the GDP of most Asian countries affected.[4] It is important to recognize that although the 1997 crisis began in Asia, reverberations were felt in many countries. Other circumstances could converge to create economic unrest elsewhere in the world. Successful retailers recognize that changes in the economy affect large and small companies; so do political influences.

Table 3.1 Reasons for Declines in Currency Values
■ Increased and unchecked foreign borrowing and investment
■ Increased interest rates
■ Excessive bad debts
■ Foreign exchange gambles
■ Trade imbalances
■ Improper bank management
■ Bank failures
■ Stock market declines

Political Influences

Political events often bring about enormous changes that affect the day-to-day operations of all businesses. During a presidential election year, many companies take a wait-and-see attitude, expecting that a new U.S. President will revisit economic and social policies. The emergence of new world powers and trade alliances between nations calls for new legal parameters. Leadership changes in remote parts of the world also may affect global trade. This occurred in Indonesia in the late 1990s. Domestic politics affect consumer behavior at the local level also. Presence of state sales taxes cause customers to shop in neighboring states where taxes are lower or nonexistent. **Outshopping** is the practice of purchasing goods from retailers that are located outside of a customer's usual shopping territory.

Volatile political regimes, trade alliances, and preferred-member status in global trade organizations all herald change in the retail environment. A look at the ways political turmoil affects retail trade illustrates this point.

outshopping The practice of purchasing goods from retailers that are located outside a customer's usual shopping territory.

Political Regimes

Not only did the Asian currency crisis affect Indonesia's economy, so did leadership change. In 1998, President Suharto, the military-backed leader for over 30 years, was blamed for many of the country's financial problems and for unbridled favoritism. His family and friends had enjoyed special privileges for decades. They controlled many sectors of business, creating monopolies in everything from cars to cloves.

Student riots, stemming from escalating discontent, occurred in many areas of the country, causing some deaths and many injuries. Currency devaluation, massive unemployment, the unstable government, and internal racial unrest fueled the protests. As a result, Suharto resigned. The ensuing presidential election was billed as the first democratic election in decades, but accusations of ballot tampering, unjustified time lapses between the election and vote counting, and other indiscretions were rampant. Later a conservative religious leader was chosen to lead the country, but he was deposed in favor of Megawati Sukarnoputri, the daughter of another former president.

The combined political and financial turmoil wreaked havoc in the retail community. This manifested in several ways:

- Rampages of crime caused looting and burning of businesses.
- Stores that weren't ravaged experienced shortages of goods due to crippled trade channels.
- Stores that did have merchandise had few customers because few had any money after severe devaluation.
- Tourism declined significantly.

Price comparisons further illustrate the affects on the retail community. Luxury hotels that charged $120 per night before the currency devaluation later charged $20 for the same room. To have a copy made of a favorite Orvis shirt that was purchased for $55 in the United States, a customer paid $5.65.[5]

The International Monetary Fund (IMF) provided billions of dollars in aid to Indonesia with the understanding that economic reforms would be instituted by the new political regime. This monumental task will take years but shows how political duress increases economic problems.

Trade Alliances

North American Free Trade Agreement (NAFTA) Trade alliance that promotes free trade between the United States, Canada, and Mexico.

Political motivations frequently are the basis for establishing trade alliances between countries. Many such partnerships exist throughout the world. One is the **North American Free Trade Agreement (NAFTA)**, a trade alliance that promotes trade among the United States, Canada, and Mexico. Others, including the European Union (EU) are discussed in Chapter 8. Delicate maneuverings and years of talks between the participating governments preceded NAFTA, which went into effect in 1993. Essentials of the agreement included:

tariff A duty or tax imposed by a government on an import.

quota Limitations imposed on the quantities of products imported from other countries.

- Elimination of tariffs on most products crossing the borders of the three countries. A **tariff** is a duty or tax imposed by a government on an import.
- Elimination of quota requirements on most apparel made from yarn and fabric from any of the three countries. **Quota** is a limitation imposed on the quantities of product imported from other countries.

■ Elimination of duties on yarn made in Mexico used in items involved in 807 programs. **807 programs** are Caribbean initiative programs offering low taxation on goods, among other incentives, to encourage manufacturing in selected countries.

NAFTA provides several advantages to retailers in member countries. In Mexico, retailers can purchase more U.S. goods for their stores because of relaxed import regulations. Mexicans had long practiced cross-border shopping, but with more imports from the United States available, this is no longer necessary. Merchandise deliveries to Mexico are quicker, and delays at the border are minimized.

Since the inception of the agreement, trade between the United States and Mexico has more than doubled. Approximately 85 percent of Canadian exports were shipped to the United States by 1999.[6] From 1994 to 1996, approximately 311,000 jobs were created in the United States as a result of NAFTA.[7] In Mexico, 600,000 were created since NAFTA went into effect.[8]

Not all observers view NAFTA in a positive light. Detractors say that the mechanisms for intercountry trade were in place long before NAFTA was implemented. Some believe that the impact on all parties has been minimal and that the number of jobs gained or lost has been equalized. On the local level, some communities where factories have closed as firms have moved their manufacturing facilities to Mexico do not regard NAFTA as having a neutral effect.

Protectionism Another aspect of consumer concern focuses on the initiatives of manufacturers and retailers to support domestic manufacturing programs. **Protectionism** is a government policy that protects domestic manufacturers by placing restrictions on foreign producers of the same goods. The verdict on whether customers truly care about purchasing only products made in their home countries is still to be determined. Most people realize that the best prices and values may be had on goods that are produced in low labor rate countries, despite their patriotic feelings. The events of September 11, 2001 evoked new expressions of dedication to the United States by many citizens and businesses. It remains to be seen to what extent these sentiments will affect product selection. Protectionist policies are expected to decline as retailers and manufacturers become more committed to international partnerships, free trade agreements, and the resulting cost savings.

807 programs Caribbean initiative programs offering low taxation on goods and other incentives that encourage manufacturing in selected countries.

protectionism Government policy that protects domestic manufacturers by placing restrictions on foreign producers of the same goods.

Preferred Trading Partners

preferred trading partner (PTP) Countries that engage in trade freely with all other countries once approved by the World Trade Organization. Formerly referred to as "most favored nations."

World Trade Organization (WTO) International governing body composed of representatives from 140 countries that grants PTP status, regulates trade, and settles disputes among members.

A country that engages in trade freely with other countries once it has been approved by the World Trade Association is considered a **preferred trading partner (PTP)**. The **World Trade Organization (WTO)** is an international governing body made up of representatives from approximately 140 countries that grants PTP status, regulates trade, and settles disputes among members. Whether China would be granted preferred trading partner status by the WTO was an issue that was hotly debated. The situation became political when financial and ethical issues converged. China is America's second largest source of imported apparel and textile products. Many government and industry leaders in the United States and other sympathetic countries objected to sweatshop and other human rights violations that have occurred in China. Yet most wholesalers and retailers know that cost savings gained by purchasing goods made in China are substantial for their companies and consumers. There were many sides to this preferred trading partner issue, but China was granted full status in the WTO late in 2001.

These are only three of the many ways political change affects retailing. Certain mechanisms are used to curtail the movement of goods and selection of trading partners. A **trade embargo** is a restriction on the importation of goods set by a government. Many trade embargoes are politically motivated. For example, the United States does not trade with Cuba because it is ruled by a communist government which is in direct opposition to our capitalistic way of doing business.

trade embargo Restriction on the importation of goods set by a government.

Globalization has created sources of power that fall outside political and governmental interests. Huge companies that operate on many continents wield great influence. Many U.S. retailers and manufacturers doing business in foreign countries and, conversely, foreign companies doing business in the United States fall into this category. Consumer and human rights activists, industry trade associations, and retailers themselves have influenced current federal laws affecting retailers.

Retailing and the Law

When retailers make decisions, they pay close attention to local, state, federal, and, increasingly, international laws. Wholesaling, importing or exporting, hiring help, advertising practices, and credit policies are regulated by government agencies. Consumers are becoming more knowledgeable about retail law and are quick to identify their rights. The penalties for violations of laws can be severe monetarily to retailers, and infractions can affect store image. Fortunately for both parties, most retailers recognize that doing business legally and ethically is best. The legal power of the individual is viewed in historical and contemporary ways through the consumerism movement.

Consumerism

Consumer advocacy can be traced to medieval England, when an edict required certain products to be imprinted with an identification hallmark (early trademark) so that producers would bear the responsibility for defects. After World War II, consumerism became the term used to describe the growing concerns of individuals regarding their interaction with merchants of all kinds. The movement became a significant social force in the United States. Consumers no longer accepted a **caveat emptor** attitude from retailers. Translated from Latin, caveat emptor means "let the buyer beware." The expression is applied to merchandise sold without a warranty or return option. As consumer rights legislators worked to gain support, politicians who would hold manufacturers and retailers accountable for faulty merchandise won votes. The 1960s and 1970s saw many changes as the marketing concept took on new meaning for industry, and customer satisfaction became a long-term retail goal.

Impact on Retailing Evidence of the impact of the consumer movement is seen in informative labels, advertising that warns people of potential health hazards, and increased product quality safety standards. Privacy, especially as it affects Internet commerce, is growing in importance. Many laws directly regulate retailing operations and functions. How credit is given, how customers are billed, taxation of goods purchased on the Internet, and how sales are run are all of concern.

Global Ethical Orientation American consumerism has shifted from a self-centered orientation to a more global one. Customers are no longer interested only in fair practices regarding consumer rights. They are concerned that workers around the world are treated ethically.

Sweatshop and fair wage issues permeated the discussions of ethical issues in the 1990s. Several companies were cited for underpaying factory workers, illegally withholding wages, physically abusing workers, employing children, and running unsafe operations. The following examples illustrate this point.

In 1998, a group of demonstrators representing the Campaign for Labor Rights protested Nike's alleged involvement in human rights violations abroad. Buses full of primarily young people converged on a sidewalk in the

CYBERSCOOP

Visit the Warner Brothers online store at **www.wbstore.com.** What are "cookies"? How do they help Warner Brothers provide better customer service? Is your privacy protected when you accept a "cookie"? Does this seem legal?

caveat emptor "Let the buyer beware." This is applied to merchandise sold without a warranty or return option.

Figure 3.3 Human rights activists on the sidewalk in the Georgetown section of Washington, DC, protest Nike's alleged involvement in sweatshop issues in Asia and the Middle East.

bribe Payment made to an individual, company, or government in order to secure special business privileges.

Georgetown section of Washington, DC, to hand out literature and drum up media and consumer support. The photo in Figure 3.3 shows demonstrators preparing to state their case publicly.

A class-action suit filed by several Asian garment workers illustrates growing sentiments against retailers and manufacturers in the United States. Many well-known companies including Nordstrom, J. Crew, and Gymboree were accused of violating international human rights laws. The alleged violations occurred on the island of Saipan and included forced labor, inhumane hours, inadequate or withheld compensation, safety hazards, poor living conditions, and conspiracy with factory owners. Employees in the factories were mostly females from nearby countries. Companies involved initially either denied allegations or refused comment on the issues, but later settled the case and agreed to set up a $1.25 million fund to finance monitoring of their Saipan contractors by an independent organization.[9]

No ethical individuals support grievous conditions in any country. However, an awareness of cultural norms, local standards of living, and work ethics are important to acknowledge. For example, in some Southeast Asian countries, semiskilled workers are paid the United States equivalent of 50 cents an hour for their work. However, a good breakfast can be had for 40 cents. Companies may provide transportation and other amenities for their employees, and working conditions are quite comfortable, though perhaps not ideal by U.S. standards. One must be careful not to judge too quickly and to have all the facts before sides are taken in a protest situation.

Bribery is another issue that straddles legal and ethical grounds. A **bribe** is a payment made to an individual, company, or government in order to secure special business privileges. These might include contracts, favorable pricing, legal oversights, or any number of incentives. Attitudes toward giving and receiving bribes differ radically by country. Bribes are expected in some countries and rarely used in others. They are illegal in some and overlooked in others, even though laws prohibiting them may exist. A study was done at a German university examining who pays bribes in business. Results showed that American and Swedish companies were the least likely to pay bribes. Businesses in Belgium, France, and Italy were the most likely to pay bribes.[10] Cultural values, choice of trading partners, presence of laws, degree of punishment for violating laws, size of bribe, and ethical orientations of participants are only some of the factors that affect the decision to pay or receive bribes.

Federal Laws

In every business situation, the law imposes limits beyond which retailers cannot venture. Retailers often complain that there are too many legal constraints in business. However, consumerism is strong and people want protection from unfair and unscrupulous practices. Examples of laws affecting retail trade that are presently in use and those that are pending follow.

Antitrust Laws Several laws enacted in the United States regulate mergers and restrain trade activity. These include the Sherman, Clayton, and Antimerger Acts. Called antitrust laws, they are administered by the Federal Trade Commission (FTC). Occasionally the FTC invokes antitrust laws in order to disallow monopolies from forming. A case in point is the 1997 U.S. federal court order requiring Staples to cease and desist its merger plans with Office Depot, another office supply chain.[11] The FTC determined that the proposed merger would result in unfair competition in certain markets.

In another application of the laws, Toys "R" Us allegedly pressured manufacturers, including Mattel and Little Tikes, to not sell to discount stores. According to the plaintiffs, Toys "R" Us unfairly used its size and power in its supply chain to force toy manufacturers to stop selling to other retailers, thereby removing competition and raising prices. Toys "R" Us was found guilty and was required by the court to pay a large settlement involving cash and toys in 1999.[12] The public's right to competitive prices and choice sometimes must be upheld legally.

Americans With Disabilities Act (ADA) The ADA took effect in 1992, and prohibits discrimination against people with disabilities in all areas of employment. The law affects retailers in several ways. It calls for accommodations to be made in the workplace allowing all persons equal access to merchandise, services, and the store itself. Special provisions made by retailers might include ramps, wide doorways, and specially designed restroom stalls to meet the needs of customers and employees who are confined to wheelchairs, or special computers that project enlarged images for sight-impaired individuals.

A chronology including these and other federal laws that are important to the retail industry in the United States is listed in Table 3.2. The need to assimilate vast amounts of legal information intensifies as retailers expand globally.

Pending Legislation The National Retail Federation monitors legislation that affects retailers and lobbies in Washington on behalf of its members. The objectives of the trade association are to keep Congress informed of the impact laws have on retailing and to be aware of retailers' positions on key issues. Legislative issues followed by the NRF in 2002, included economic stimulus initiatives, taxes, bankruptcy reform, health insurance, and trade stimulus. Examples of selected bills and proposals include:

- *Economic stimulus package.* Aspects of President Bush's proposal included several proposals to help small businesses. An accelerated depreciation program would allow firms with new investments of up to $325,000 to deduct the first $40,000, rather than to depreciate the entire amount. Another item in the stimulus package would speed tax rate reductions. This provision was expected to help boost consumer spending.
- *Health insurance.* The formation of Association Health Plans was another area of reform supported by the NRF. Special programs would allow small businesses and trade organizations to pool health care benefits with similar organizations in order to provide affordable health insurance for their employees.
- *Pension reform bills.* After the collapse of the Enron Corporation in 2002, several federal bills were under consideration that would allow employees more control over their 401(k) and other pension accounts.
- *USA Patriot Act.* The Uniting and Strengthening America by Providing Appropriate Tools Required to Intercept and Obstruct Terrorism Act of 2001—otherwise known as the USA Patriot Act—was passed in October of 2001. The main thrust of the act addresses the need for money-laundering detection devices to help stop the flow of money to terrorist groups. One aspect directly affects retailers that deal in large cash transactions. Retailers must report cash transactions of over $10,000 to the Financial Crimes Enforcement Network. This provision could affect jewelers, high-end carpet stores, furniture, and automobile retailers.[13]

Laws enacted in the United States are not the only ones that affect retailers. Regulations proposed by the European Union could negatively affect direct marketers including retailers doing catalog and online business in Europe. The European Commission's Directive on Data Privacy went into effect in late 1998, and enforcement began in early 2002. Attitudes regarding the use of customer data vary greatly by country. The United States has less restrictive attitudes toward the collection and sharing of data than does its European counterparts.[14]

Aspects of the legal environment challenge retailers at every turn. Changes in the characteristics of a market also indicate new opportunities for retailers or the need to modify tactics.

Demographic Changes

Statistics on human populations, including age, gender, ethnic origin, education, income, occupation, type of housing, and other descriptors are called **demographics**.

Population Trends

Population numbers, growth, and density are statistics retailers utilize when seeking new markets whether in Chicago or China. Companies like Circuit City and Toys "R" Us generally look at areas with high population growth when planning new stores. Large companies like these depend on present numbers and future growth to sustain business. However, size alone may not indicate a viable market. Growth rates and population density may be more important measures. **Population density** indicates the number of people per square mile or kilometer in a specific geographic area. Population density may indicate great opportunity for retailers if the area under scrutiny is understored. For example, Hong Kong has the world's most dense population with 6,768 people per square kilometer. The United States has 30 people per square kilometer.[15] In this case Hong Kong is a small geographic area and the United States a large one, but both markets are relatively overstored. Understanding the comparative worth of this kind of information is important. Table 3.3 shows population data on several countries.

Factors such as birth and death dynamics, immigration figures, health standards, and marriage and divorce rates also help retailers understand a population. Other significant statistics include the number of households in the retailer's market, composition of those households, and number of dual-career households. The traditional American family became a myth years ago, as a mixture of family types became reality. Census data shows that in only 7 percent of U.S. households, fathers work and mothers stay at home with children.[16]

Age Mix

To understand the significance of the newest age shifts in the United States, we need to look at them in relation to the baby boomers. The 76 million people born between 1946 and 1964 are considered **baby boomers**. They have dominated consumer behavior discussions for the past two decades.

Children of early baby boomers, usually those born between 1965 and 1976, are identified as **Generation X**. This time span was a period of slow

demographics Statistics on human populations including age, gender, ethnic origin, education, income, occupation, type of housing, etc.

population density The number of people per square kilometer in a specific geographic area.

baby boomers The 76 million Americans born between 1946 and 1964.

Generation X Children of early baby boomers, usually those born between 1965 and the late 70s.

TABLE 3.2 Selected U.S. Legislation Important to the Retail Industry

Date	Act	Description
1890	Sherman Act	Prohibited monopoly or conspiracy in restraint of trade unlawful.
1914	Clayton Act	Made specific acts in restraint of trade unlawful.
1914	Federal Trade Commission Act	Established the enforcing agency for governing unfair methods of competition.
1931	Resale Price	Agreement legalized resale price maintenance between manufacturers and retailers.
1935	Unfair Practices Acts	Prohibited sales below cost.
1936	Robinson-Patman Act	Prohibited unlawful price discrimination.
1937	Miller-Tydings Act	Legalized certain resale price maintenance contracts.
1938	Food, Drug, and Cosmetic Act	Expanded the responsibility of the Food and Drug Administration to include cosmetics and therapeutic devices by amending an earlier act.
1938	Wheeler-Lea Act	Expanded the FTC's responsibility to include unfair or deceptive acts or practices and gave it the power to take action whenever it is in the public interest, even when there is no proof of competitive injury.
1938	Fair Labor Standards Act	Established minimum wages.
1939	Wool Products Labeling Act	Required that products containing wool carry labels showing the fiber content.
1950	Antimerger Act	Regulated mergers that might substantially lessen competition.
1951	Fur Products Labeling Act	Required that all fur products carry labels correctly describing the fur composition.
1953	Flammable Fabrics Acts	Prohibited the manufacture or sale of fabrics or wearing apparel that were dangerously flammable.
1958	Food Additives Amendment (Delaney Act)	As an amendment to the Food, Drug, and Cosmetic Act of 1938, it required that food additives be limited to those that do not cause cancer in humans or animals.
1960	Hazardous Substances Labeling Act	Required proper labeling on packages of hazardous household products.
1960	Textile Fiber Identification Act	Required fiber content identification on all apparel.
1962	Kefauver-Harris Amendment to Food, Drug and Cosmetic Act (1938)	Required that all drugs be tested for safety and efficacy.
1963	Equal Pay Act	Required compliance with regulations on child labor and employee health and safety.
1964	Civil Rights Act, Title VII	Required equal pay for similar work, regardless of sex, race, color, religion, or national origin.
1966	Fair Packaging and Labeling Act	Permitted the voluntary adoption of industry-accepted uniform packaging standards and required clearer labeling of consumer goods.
1966	Child Protection Act of 1966	Amended the Hazardous Substances Labeling Act (1960) to ban all hazardous substances and prohibit sales of potentially harmful toys and other articles used by children.
1967	Flammable Fabrics Act	Amended the 1953 act and expanded textile legislation to include the Department of Commerce Flammability Standards for additional products.

TABLE 3.2 Selected U.S. Legislation Important to the Retail Industry

Date	Act	Description
1968	Consumer Credit Protection Act	(Truth in Lending) Required full disclosure of the terms and rates charged for loans and credit.
1968	Age Discrimination in Employment Act	Prevented discrimination against employing anyone on basis of age; extended retirement age to 70.
1970	Fair Credit Reporting Act	Regulated credit information reporting and use.
1970	Poison Prevention Packaging	Provided standards for child-resistant packaging of hazardous substances.
1971	Care Labeling Act	Stated that all apparel selling for over $3 carry labels with washing or dry-cleaning instructions.
1972	Consumer Product Safety Act	Established the Consumer Product Safety Commission and empowered it to set safety standards for a broad range of consumer products.
1974	Equal Credit Opportunity Act	Ensured that the various financial institutions and other firms engaged in the extension of credit make credit available without discrimination on the basis of sex or marital status.
1975	Magnuson-Moss Act	Established disclosure requirements and minimum federal standards for written warranties.
1975	Consumer Goods Price Act	Outlawed legalized resale price setting.
1977	Foreign Corrupt Practices Act	Prohibits U.S. companies from making payments (bribes) to high ranking foreign government officials.
1980	Federal Trade Commission (FTC)	Improvement Act limited the power of the FTC to set and enforce trade regulations.
1984	Toy Safety Act	Granted power to the government to recall dangerous toys from the market.
1986	Tax Reform Act	Eliminated deductions for sales tax and for interest payments on revolving or installment credit; also plugged many former tax loopholes for corporations as well as consumers.
1989	Omnibus Trade Bill	Included the switch to a harmonized system of tariff codes, reduction of licensing requirements for exports to U.S. allies, and strengthening of U.S. import restrictions.
1990	Nutrition Labeling and Education Act	Provided for detailed nutritional information on food product labels.
1992	American Disabilities Act (ADA)	Required that employers make provisions for disabled people in the workplace.
1996	Family and Medical Leave Act (FMLA)	Granted workers 12 weeks unpaid leave to deal with personal or family health needs.
1999	Fairness in Musical Licensing Act	Expanded law to allow for all forms of performance broadcast incidental to main purpose of an establishment. Exempts sellers of audio or visual equipment from having to pay music royalties.
2001	Intercept and Obstruct Terrorism Act	Limitations on cash transactions to help stop the flow of money to terrorist groups
2001	Internet Tax Freedom Act	Extends limitations on collection of taxes based on internet sales

Table 3.3 Population Statistics for Selected Countries, 2000 (In Millions)*

China	1,262	Canada	31
India	1,014	Venezuela	24
United States	276	Malaysia	22
Indonesia	225	Australia	19
Brazil	173	Netherlands	16
Russia	147	Chile	15
Japan	127	Greece	11
Mexico	100	Czech Republic	10
Germany	83	Belgium	10
Philippines	81	Hungary	10
Egypt	68	Portugal	10
Turkey	66	Sweden	9
Thailand	61	Austria	8
United Kingdom	60	Switzerland	7
France	59	Hong Kong	7
Italy	58	Israel	6
South Korea	47	Denmark	5
South Africa	43	Finland	5
Spain	40	Norway	4
Poland	39	Singapore	3
Argentina	328		

*US Census Bureau, International Data Base
Source: *Stores.* 2002 Global Powers of Retailing. "Economic and Social Indicators," Deloitte & Touche. Section 2. January, 2002:G26

population growth called the *baby-bust years.* Now in their twenties and thirties, this group is also known as the Sesame Street generation, having been the first generation to grow up with great media influences.

Persons born between 1977 and 1994, who include contemporary young adults, teens, and younger school-age children are members of **Generation Y**. They will influence retail sales for decades to come. Figure 3.4 shows the number of young people in the United States projected to 2025.

The youngest Generation Y children are also called *techno-tots* or *cyber-boomers* since they are the first generation to grow up with electronic wizardry for companions. They are very media savvy. The first generation to have a majority of their mothers working outside the home, they have attended pre-school in record numbers. One-third of them are Black or Hispanic. Many live in single parent families and one-fourth live in poverty.[17]

What does Generation Y mean to retailers? More clothes, toys, electronic games, computers, educational necessities, and books will be sold for use by the younger children. Barnes & Noble, shown in Figure 3.5, has already

Generation Y Persons born between the late 70s and 1994 that include contemporary young adults, teens, and techno-tots.

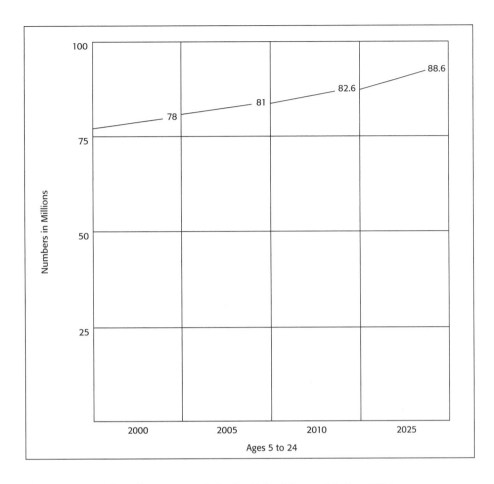

Figure 3.4 **Number of Young People in the United States, 2000 to 2025**
Source: US Census Bureau Current Population Reports, p. 25–1130.

added "Junior" departments complete with story-telling areas, small stages for performances, and child-oriented decor and merchandising.

Stores like Gadzooks, Arden B., Wet Seal, and Delia's target the young teen customer. Many teenage young women find Internet retailers speak their language. All have Web sites. Teens have money earned through part-time jobs or given as allowances, and they are spending it. With its trendy shops, Melrose Avenue in Los Angeles, shown in Figure 3.1, is an example of a street that attracts teens. Retailers that know how to talk and market to young consumers create teenage heaven.

The oldest of the baby boomers turned 56 in 2002. The youngest of the group will be 50 in 2014—almost senior citizens! They will defy whatever previous generations thought old age meant. Walk through any department store and you will see mature shoppers buying tennis, golf, or ski clothes. They will want health care products, books on meditation, menopause, and the joys of Viagra as they age. They'll buy vitamins, perhaps some ginseng, retinol for cosmetic purposes, and progressive-vision

Figure 3.5 The Barnes & Noble, Jr. department reflects the importance retailers are placing on the younger generations.

eyewear. The term *elderly* hardly applies to this burgeoning group, who are active, vigorous, and full of unique wants and needs.

Groups of senior citizens in the United States are growing. Between 2000 and 2025, the number of people 75 to 84 years old will increase by one-third; the number of individuals aged 85 and over will almost double.[18] People now approaching their senior years are affluent and are big spenders. No wonder retailers are interested.

Ethnic Mix

Retailers also look at changes in the ethnic composition of markets. Almost half of the U.S. population will be non-Caucasian by 2020. Ethnic markets are viable segments with specific needs and retailers are seeking new minority markets as well as African-American, Asian, and Hispanic. This trend is expected to grow as more people learn to value and display pride in their ethnic heritage. At the same time, some ethnic products have acquired a great deal of mainstream appeal. For example, ethnic restaurants are widely accepted. Chinese and Italian restaurants have been part of most communities in the United States for a century or more. Japanese, Thai, and Mexican restaurants gained popularity in the 1980s. The 1990s brought an upsurge in popularity of lesser-known Asian cuisine including Vietnamese and Malaysian. A rebirth of interest in Greek, Polish, Russian, and other foods is also apparent and will provide new opportunities for forward thinking retailers this century.

Ethnic marketing is evident in supermarkets that allocate considerable square footage to products that appeal to specific groups that reside in the neighborhood. In areas where Asians are the predominant ethnic group, apparel shops carry sizes that fit the typically smaller build of Asian men and women.

Gender Issues

The huge increase in the number of working women over the past few decades means greater need for one-stop shopping, fast food, time saving devices, clothing for work, and child care services. The availability of child care for working parents is an important issue. Many single parents, who have the potential to make up much of the retail workforce, have a problem finding appropriate child care. Some retailers have addressed this issue and offer partial reimbursement for day care expenses. Others set up day care consortiums with other businesses in the area. Staples runs an on-site child care facility at its Massachusetts headquarters.

Significant discrepancies in weekly salaries earned by females representing several ethnic groups were found in a study of women in management. Results showed that Asian women in the United States earned the highest median weekly pay, $593. White women earned $528, Black women $514, and Hispanic women $423. The same study found that for every dollar white male managers earned, minority male managers earned 73 cents. White female managers earned 59 cents and minority females 57 cents.[19] There is still room for work on racial and gender equity issues.

Occupational and Educational Outlook

Growth in the computer and health care fields indicates many job prospects. According to the U.S. Bureau of Labor Statistics, the retail area is predicted to generate approximately three million new jobs by 2008. Many of these jobs will be in the retail service sector. Restaurants, auto dealers, furniture, and home furnishings stores added the most jobs in 2000. Retailing employs almost one out of five persons in the United States.[20]

The trend toward attaining higher education levels is expected to continue. Goal attainment continues to rise across all educational levels in the United States. High school graduates; individuals possessing some college education but no degree; associate, bachelor, postgraduate, and professional degree holders all showed significant growth from the 1990 to the 2000 census.[21] Many Generation Y members will reach college age in 2007. After a slowdown in the 1990s, interest in the business disciplines is expected to grow. This is of special note to retailers and marketers seeking qualified management trainees. Possessing a college degree affects future income and expenditure habits. College educated individuals in well-paying positions have more discretionary income to spend on retail products.

Income Dynamics

In the United States, family income varies greatly from state to state. There also is a great disparity between rich and poor. Approximately 19 million households in the United States had incomes under $15,000 in 2000. Almost 48 million households had incomes between $15,000 and $50,000. Almost 30 million households were in the $50,000 to $100,000 range, and only 6.5 million earned over $100,000.[22]

Economists speculate that in periods of economic boom, the disparity between the rich and the poor decreases, but in actuality this is not true. Personal and household income varies widely, depending on the part of the world being studied.

Did You Know?

In a study done for the American Orthopedic Foot and Ankle Society, researchers found that heel heights worn by women are negatively correlated to education level. The study showed that higher the heel, the lower the education level, and the lower the heel the more formal education women possessed.
Source: *Los Angeles Times.* "High Heels, Low Education." LA Life Section. March 1, 1999:2.

disposable income The amount of money available for purchases after taxes are deducted.

discretionary income The amount of money available for nonessential purchases after taxes and basic expenses for food, clothing, and shelter have been paid.

Customers' decisions to buy or not to buy affects a retailer's survival. Customers' purchase decisions reflect changes in their disposable and discretionary incomes. **Disposable income** is the amount of money available for purchases and savings after taxes have been deducted. **Discretionary income** is the amount of money available for nonessential purchases after taxes and basic food, clothing, and shelter expenses have been paid. Retailers are interested particularly in discretionary income for it allows luxury and impulse goods to be purchased.

A hypothetical example of a family that lives in a thriving, upper-middle class community further explains discretionary income. Both parents are employed and have been able to provide a good standard of living and many extras for their family. However, times have changed since their son is attending an expensive private college and their daughter a state university. Suddenly the family's substantial discretionary income decreases. Like many families with college-age children, this family can no longer buy all of the things they did before children went to college. Choices must be made. Will it be a new car or a European trip, a condo at a ski resort or tuition? Chances are you know the answer. As family expenses increase, retailers selling goods purchased from discretionary income notice sales to this group dropping. Although based on personal rather than environmental factors, this change in shopping behavior deserves attention from retailers in the community where families with college-bound children are typical of the population.

Several circumstances contributed to the rising standard of living in the late 20th to early 21st century:

- Increasing numbers of dual income families.
- Rising level of sophistication among the educated.
- Higher paying jobs in technological fields.
- Increasing wealth due to stock market growth.

Exclusive shops in such communities as Beverly Hills, California; Scottsdale, Arizona; and Palm Beach, Florida respond to the needs of upmarket people who share one or more of these attributes. Similar shopping districts that target high-income customers exist in major cities around the world. Posh Worth Avenue in Palm Beach, Florida, is illustrated in Figure 3.6.

At the other extreme are retailers who have perceived opportunities among middle-income and lower-income families. Some have responded with deep discount stores and consignment shops. Play It Again Sports is a retail chain that sells new merchandise as well as used sporting goods on a consignment basis. Outfitting a fledgling hockey player was never easier or less expensive. In this example, income is not the only component considered. Equally important are customers' values and attitudes.

Income data alone do not identify potential customers. They do not indicate buying power or whether an individual has interest in purchasing from a retailer. The relationship between income and social class is discussed in Chapter 10, Customer Behavior.

Social Changes

Changes in lifestyle are molded by the behavior, attitudes, and values of society. These in turn become the guideposts that retailers follow in order to meet the needs and preferences of their customers. Several changes in the social fiber of the United States affect retailing.

Figure 3.6 Upper-income consumers find a plethora of luxury retailers on Worth Avenue in Palm Beach, Florida. *Courtesy of Fairchild Publications, Inc.*

Simplified Lifestyles

The inclination to live a more basic existence is manifest in several ways. Choosing to purchase clothing made from natural fabrics may be closely related to environmental consciousness as well as a more earthy approach to life. Some psychologists call this mindset "ecopsychology" and consider it part of our need to bond with the universe and identify our roots. For many, it is a return to organic fruits and vegetables, herbal medicines, and marketplace shopping.

Time Deprivation

Most people, regardless of vocation, complain of having no free time. As jobs became careers and consumed more of a day, productivity became paramount. Many people are trying to find ways to live in societies that operate on warp drive. Multi-task individuals altered the meaning of busy, as it became commonplace to speak on cellular phones in cars and while walking through airports. Feet tapped impatiently in front of the counter if Big Macs were not ready in 30 seconds. The raft of retail products and services demanded by time-starved families is fascinating to consider. After-school programs for children and pet sitter and grocery delivery services are common. Specialists that sort through boxes of old photos and high school memorabilia and create scrapbooks are in demand. Time management and

Figure 3.7 Pizza Hut delivery vehicles may take a different form in Taipei, Taiwan, but they serve busy customers just as well as automobiles do in the United States.

stress reduction seminars are no longer directed only to busy executives. Hectic lives are as common in many other countries as they are in the United States. Time constraints, in addition to traffic congestion, and dense population in Taipei, Taiwan, call for Pizza Hut to deliver via motor scooter rather than automobile, as illustrated in Figure 3.7.

Value Consciousness

Many people have adopted a more value-conscious way of shopping, even if they can afford more. Consumers want products that have more inherent quality for the prices they are willing to pay. Retailers that consistently offer well-made products at fair prices attract value-conscious customers. The growth of secondhand, vintage, and consignment shops has fueled this thrifty philosophy. Children's used clothing shops, once-worn designer apparel boutiques, and previously-owned furniture stores have all become popular. Flea markets and auctions also attract people concerned with value. The movement became mainstream during the major recession in the late 1980s and early 1990s. Whatever stigma previously existed regarding purchasing other peoples' cast-offs has been removed as shoppers find their dollars go further on good quality used clothing and furniture than on new products.

Professional Dressing

If sales are up or down in men's and women's careerwear, the economy probably has less to do with the decline than professional-dress trends in corporate America. The casual Friday's trend of the late 1990s, reflected the loosening of strict dress codes that had been popular in decades past. Defining people and their worth to a company less in terms of physical appearance and more in terms of competencies could be perceived as positive change. However, the relaxed attitude toward dress took a strange twist. New status looks emerged as casual clothing was selected for the workplace. J. Crew polo shirts and chinos became acceptable in many corporate offices. Tee shirts and jeans probably never will be, yet all are considered casual attire by someone's standards.

A resurgence of interest in dressing more traditionally in suits, rather than more casual separates, occurred at about the same time as the economic downturn and the events of September 11, 2001. This new conservatism might be born of patriotic sentiment, the need to cope with a troubled economy, and a desire to maintain a degree of dignity in the face of chaos.

Despite the tendency toward wearing more professional or more casual apparel on the job, dressing down has become more accepted for social and personal occasions as well. Notice this when attending a wedding or dining in a fine restaurant.

Changing Aspirations

Data from pollsters Yankelovich, Skelly, and White indicate five ways that the American character will change in the 21st century. People are expected to:

1. Be more tolerant of alternative lifestyles and cultures.
2. Be more focused on international issues.
3. Place more importance on marriage and children.
4. Place more emphasis on giving back to the community.
5. Be more religious.[23]

All of these points address ways that individuals look beyond their immediate needs and focus on the needs of others. Altruistic causes are gaining momentum in families, nations, and the world. Retail companies also seek higher goals in socially responsible ways. Many sponsor fund raisers for charity, form philanthropic partnerships, and contribute to those in need. **Cause marketing** is the practice of staging promotions that benefit charitable organizations or communities and also build positive public relations for the sponsoring retailer. More companies are becoming involved in positive social change. AIDS awareness, breast cancer research, and other important causes are gaining momentum. Many programs might not have developed if retailers had not been open to cause marketing. Environmental causes also benefit from media attention.

cause marketing The practice of staging promotions that benefit charitable organizations or communities and also secure positive public relations for the sponsoring retailer.

Environmental Consciousness

The fervor attached to the environmental movement in the United States seems to ebb and wane every decade. This movement evolves at a slower pace in developing countries as compared to those that are fully industrialized and have the money and resources to devote to the cause. Concern for the environment also varies by country. Retailers have responded to the concern for the world's ecosystems and demonstrate their responsibility to the movement in many ways.

CYBERSCOOP

Wal-Mart prides itself on its community involvement. Go to the company's Web site at **www.wal-mart.com** and discover what it is doing locally and nationally to foster social responsibility.

Eco-Friendly Products

Many retailers stock recyclable and biodegradable products. Some retail chains have been founded on the premise of providing only goods that are environmentally safe and that are tested without cruelty to animals. The Body Shop created an entire image and social responsibility platform around environmental issues. Its positions against product testing on animals and for rain forest preservation have received much publicity worldwide.

Harmony is a catalog dedicated to the retailing of earth-sensitive products. Customers can choose cotton sheets that are free of dyes, bleaches, and other harmful chemicals and an alarm clock that awakens the sleeper with Zen rhythms. Recycled metal magazine racks are also available. The catalog targets shoppers who believe that every individual has an impact on the environment and that every individual makes a difference. As part of its philanthropy program, the U.S. catalog company is involved with The National Arbor Day Foundation and plants seedlings in national forests to demonstrate its concern.

Waste and Conservation Issues

In many states, hazardous waste disposal issues are being addressed by legislatures. Retailers are concerned because many items that they sell have come under scrutiny. Some of the products include automobile tires and batteries, oil, and appliances. Retailers are expected to take a proactive approach to the education of customers by providing brochures and signs outlining proper disposal procedures. Bottle bills—legislation having to do with disposal of bottles—are also priorities. Some states are passing bills that alleviate tax on beverage containers that can be refilled, thus encouraging recycling.[24]

Retailers practice energy conservation through improvements in lighting and heating, ventilation, and air-conditioning (HVAC) systems. Customers are not always aware that efficiencies in these areas are part of retailers' commitment to the environment.

Competition is another aspect of the retail environment that cannot be changed. To cope with encroaching competition, retailers have devised many tactics.

Retail Competition

Department stores compete with other department stores but also with specialty stores, off-price discount stores, catalogs, and Internet retailers. Every retailer is eager to increase sales, none hesitates to invade another's domain. Competition is horizontal (retailer against retailer) and vertical (retailer against wholesaler or manufacturer who engages in retailing). Vertical competition is more obvious since Internet shopping began. Competition comes from outside the industry also, as people decide whether to spend their annual bonuses on a Palladian window to improve their family rooms or deposit money into their bank accounts. Retail competition occurs domestically and internationally.

In an attempt to find a competitive advantage, retailers use many different strategies. Some combat the competition head on while others differentiate their operations in unique ways. Internally, retailers may use merchandising and store location techniques. Externally, aggressive acquisition or marketshare growth strategies may be implemented.

Internal Techniques

Selling unique or unexpected merchandise, providing incomparable service, or trading from an architecturally interesting building may help retailers stand out from the crowd. Several examples illustrate these techniques:

- *Scrambled merchandising.* Carrying products unrelated to a store's traditional or expected merchandise mix is called **scrambled merchandising**. For example, a supermarket adds a rack of L'eggs pantyhose, Hartz Mountain pet supplies, or pots and pans to its regular stock of meat, produce, and groceries. A drugstore adds gifts and bottled soft drinks to its expected health and beauty aids. These retailers are practicing scrambled merchandising to gain or maintain a competitive edge and to increase sales.

- *Product differentiation.* Retailers add name brands, limited merchandise lines, or new departments in order to differentiate their operations. As examples, Kmart sells moderately priced sheets designed by Martha Stewart in its stores. Replacements, Ltd. is a store that sells only odd china cups and saucers to collectors or people who have broken favorite sets. Hair salons are departing from their traditional service focus and are adding holistic beauty product boutiques in order to gain a competitive advantage.

- *Location strategies.* Seeking a competitive advantage by locating where throngs of people gather in an historic landmark gives some retailers an opportunity to stand out in a crowd. B. Dalton bookstores operates a store in

scrambled merchandising
Carrying products unrelated to a store's traditional or expected merchandise mix.

Figure 3.8 B. Dalton seeks a competitive niche by locating in busy Union Station in Washington, DC. The railroad hub for the area features a shopping mall and many other consumer enticements.

market share The proportion of industry-wide product sales earned by one company.

Union Station in Washington, DC. This restored building is not only the Amtrak hub for the area, but also houses a shopping mall, metro stop, cinema complex, and more than 25 eating establishments. B. Dalton's store is illustrated in Figure 3.8.

External Techniques

Outside of the store, retailers practice aggressive, sometimes predatory tactics by acquiring competing firms or staging market share battles.

■ *Acquisitions.* Retailers may attempt to control competition by purchasing rival firms, believing that if they own their competition, profits can be funneled into one corporate pocket. Carrefour, profiled at the end of this unit, acquired Promodes, a major competitor in 2000. Many turn their attention off-shore to markets that may be less saturated and may have a population prepared economically, demographically, and psychographically to receive foreign retailers.

■ *Market share growth.* Seeking dominance by gaining market share at the expense of fellow retailers is a strategy used by some retailers. **Market share** is the proportion of industry-wide product sales earned by one company. Hollywood Video gave Blockbuster serious competition by boldly opening stores very near Blockbuster—sometimes directly across the street. The company challenged the domination of Blockbuster as the country's only national video rental superstore. Blockbuster had more than 5,000 stores and held a 25 percent share of the market at the turn of the century. Contrast this figure with upstart Hollywood Video's 5 percent share, and the strategies identified by Hollywood may seem inadequate to overtake Blockbuster. Hollywood's founder Mark Wattles' decision to open new stores in the best possible locations, no matter what the competition was doing, was an aggressive one. Location may be the key to success if customers do not care from which video store they rent. To the customer, brand name may not be as important as convenience.[25] Oregon-based Hollywood Video operated 1,800 stores in 47 states in 2002.[26]

Competitive battles will escalate this century, and will exist as long as free enterprise exists. As the world becomes smaller and communication improves, competition will come from distant shores and from within our own countries. Retailers that recognize the need for constant environmental monitoring, the development of coping strategies, and the scientific study of competition will succeed. They must also be able to adapt to change, have high ethical standards, and deal with unexpected events.

Unpredictable Events

In addition to demographic and social changes, environmental concerns, and knowledge of competition, other unexpected events affect customers and retailers. From riots to raging storms, accidents to earthquakes, disease to terrorism—all are uncontrollable aspects of the world in which we live and do business.

For example, the 1994 earthquake in Los Angeles brought out the best and the worst in people. Businesses suffered short term and long term as mother nature ravaged the city. In the aftermath, many small businesses in the service sector resisted the temptation to engage in **price gouging,** the tactic of marking up prices on retail products unreasonably high. Some retailers did resort to price gouging, although most did not. One convenience store was criticized for charging $16 for two small bottles of water, but Safeway Supermarkets was praised for giving water away.

price gouging The tactic of marking up retail products unreasonably high.

Street maps became popular commodities since people needed help to find new routes around the devastated areas of the city. Carpet cleaning and other similar services also recorded sales increases.[27] Natural disasters influence retailing in positive and negative ways.

Public displays of concern over the death of international celebrities can paralyze some retailers yet still provoke extraordinary sales for others. After the untimely death of Britain's Princess Diana in 1997, the outpouring of sympathy was mind-boggling as people the world over dealt with their grief. Florists in London and its environs were inundated with business shortly after the tragedy. The Kensington Palace home of the Princess was strewn with bouquets as retailers' stocks were totally depleted. No flowers remained for usual customer purchases. (Figure 3.9 illustrates the impact of Princess Diana's death on the florist trade in London.) However, most other kinds of stores were closed for several days after the event and consequently had no sales at all. Within two weeks of her death, record and book stores experienced dramatic sales increases. A year later, sales of commemorative merchandise was still strong. If they could be found at all, "Princess" Beanie Babies were known to sell for $300 or more in the United States. Elton John's remake of "Candle in the Wind" became one of the top selling CDs of all time. Interest in Diana resurfaces every time a new retrospective is published and placed in bookstores around the world.

Perhaps the most profoundly unsettling event of many generations was the attack on America on September 11, 2001. The events that occurred on

Figure 3.9 After the death of Princess Diana in 1997, thousands of floral bouquets and cards were sold. Sympathizers placed mementos at the gates of Kensington Palace, Diana's home in London. *Courtesy of Miranda Latimer*

that day and in successive months in the United States and other countries have had and will continue to affect our lives and business practices and are discussed in this chapter's From the Field.

The Impact of Technology

All elements of the retail environment described so far are of considerable importance to retailers, but no other aspect is having such a profound affect on business as the technological revolution. It has given retailers the means for instant sales and inventory updates, accurate and speedy credit and check approvals, video conferencing and training capabilities, and countless other tools that help retailers make better decisions and operate more efficiently. Technological advancement has made Internet retailing and other home-based electronic shopping methods possible. Because of its supreme importance, electronic retailing is the focus of Chapter 7.

Elements of the retail environment do not operate in isolation. Retailers must be sociologists, economists, demographers, ecologists, and perhaps philosophers if they are to understand and benefit from the changes in the retail environment.

Summary

Uncontrollable variables in the world guide retailing policy. Economic factors, political events, legal actions, changing demographics, social change, environmental concerns, competition, unpredictable events, and technology all affect retailing. Taken collectively, these elements make up the retail environment, which is constantly changing.

Inflation, recession, and other economic factors influence retail planning. Changes in political regimes, formation of new trade alliances or laws, and attainment of preferred trading partner status affect retailing around the world.

Retailers follow demographic changes in household composition, age mix, population size, ethnic groups, and family income statistics. Information on gender issues, occupational and educational trends is also helpful to know. Strategies developed by retailers reflect behaviors, values, and attitudes of their target markets. As examples, sales of ethnic products grow

As with all mind-boggling and devastating events, we remember where we were, what we were doing, what we were wearing, and whom we called first when we heard about the World Trade Center and Pentagon tragedies on September 11, 2001. Contemplating how the events affected lives and our nation was paramount in our minds. To consider otherwise would have been disrespectful to all those lost and to their families.

However, acts of terrorism and war also affect the economy in general and retail business specifically. On September 13, consumer confidence levels reached their lowest point in eight years. The country experienced a $100 billion dollar economic jolt, and that figure did not include property or human life losses.[1] Several premises set the tone for deeper understanding of the affects of the terrorist attacks:

1. There would be short-term and long-term economic impact on retail businesses.
2. The area closest to the terrorist incidents would be more deeply affected than those that were further removed.
3. There would be negative and positive impact on retail sales.
4. The events would change business practices and consumer behavior domestically and globally.

Airline, hotel, and tourism related businesses were some of the first hurt. Grounded almost immediately after the attacks, airline sales stagnated. Restaurant sales plummeted as families stayed home out of fear and out of concern to monitor every possible newscast. While networks and cable channels broadcast news 24 hours per day advertising revenues declined by $700 million during the first week after September 11.[2] An estimated 114,700 workers were laid off between September 15 and December 29, as a direct or indirect result of 9/11.[3] Despite the efforts of multiple service agencies, many people from New York and its environs were still without jobs six months later. Retail workers in lower Manhattan and food service workers in airports near and far away, suddenly joined the ranks of the unemployed.

The direct marketing sector was paralyzed as postal services curtailed deliveries. The Direct Marketing Association reported that catalog retailers suffered declines of 50 percent or more immediately after the attacks. In October, the anthrax scare opened new wounds, as the public became fearful of receiving mail. Later reflection showed that the need for increased security, insurance, transportation safeguards, and new privacy measures would further compromise the ability of direct marketing firms to fulfill orders. Prices on products were expected to rise as a result.[4]

Reactions to the disasters shed light on the local and global impact of the events. Positive and negative response is highlighted in several examples culled from news media reports:

■ The 75-store shopping mall located beneath the World Trade Center ceased to exist. Fortunately, no mall employees or customers were known to have been lost.
■ Riding as cargo on one of the doomed flights, 2000 pounds of live Maine lobster, worth $2.85 per pound wholesale, plus shipping and handling charges, never reached its destination. Sea urchins, a delicacy in Japan, could not be shipped as airlines ceased flying. The famous Fulton Fish Market in New York temporarily shut down operations.[5]
■ Cell phone sales at Radio Shack were up 20 percent; Wal-Mart reported record sales of American flags and emergency supplies, and sales of sympathy cards at American Greetings increased immediately following the crisis.[6]
■ Sales at Macy's and Bloomingdale's in New York City fell 40 percent two weeks after the attacks.[7]
■ Sales of tanzanite jewelry were curtailed at Zales and Tiffany's and on QVC as information linking financing of El Quaeda to mines in Tanzania was made public.[8]

The global outpouring of sympathy was manifest in unbridled generosity and desire to display a strong pro-American statement. Citizens were encouraged to buy in order to build the economy and not give terrorist

Figure 3.10 Sales of patriotic merchandise soared immediately following the terrorist attacks of September 11, 2001 and again as individuals commemorated the first anniversary of the disasters. *AP/Worldwide Photos.*

organizations an inkling that their evil agendas had succeeded.

Merchandising opportunities abounded for manufacturers and designers to produce patriotic products. Gowns, shoes, sweaters, tee shirts, pajamas, jewelry, and even diapers quickly found their way into the marketplace. Many companies donated all or part of their proceeds from the sale of goods to appropriate charities.

Seven months after the attacks, most of the physical evidence had been removed from the site. Mental and spiritual healing takes much longer. It is a sad commentary on our world today that anguish of this magnitude should serve as an explicit example of the uncontrollable environment in which business is done.

1. Hilsenrath, Jon E. "Terror's Toll on the Economy." *Wall Street Journal.* October 9, 2001: B1.
2. Ibid.
3. Tejada, Carlos. "Terror Effects." Work Week. *Wall Street Journal.* February 19, 2002.
4. Turner, Michael A. "DMA Perspective: Economic Impact of the Attack on America on US Direct Marketing." *The DMA Interactive,* Available: www.thedma.org/library/whitepapers/attackonamerica.shtml Retrieved: September 18, 2001.
5. *The Working Waterfront.* "Tremors from New York, Washington Felt in Maine." Volume 14, No. 9, October 2001:1,2.
6. Hilsenrath: B1
7. Hilsenrath: B4.
8. Markon, Jerry. "Gemstone Dealers Named in Suit Over Sept. 11." *Wall Street Journal.* February 15, 2002: B1.

because of changes in the composition of a population and people's changing values. Internet retailing evolves because the technology is available and some individuals prefer to shop from home or work.

Social trends this decade include: (1) simplified lifestyles, (2) time deprivation, (3) value consciousness, (4) professional dressing, and (5) changing aspirations. Environmental concerns affect retailers and consumers. Development of ecologically safe products is a concern as are hazardous waste disposal and energy conservation.

Competition for the consumer's dollar has never been greater or come from so many directions. Internal techniques designed to beat the competition include merchandising and store planning techniques. External techniques include acquisition of competing stores or the use of market share growth strategies.

Unpredictable events such as natural disasters, death of celebrities, and acts of terrorism also affect retail sales. In the 21st century the most important element in the retail environment is technology.

Questions for Review and Discussion

1. How do fluctuating interest rates affect homeowners and retailers?
2. What affect do international political events have on retailing?
3. What types of legislation are of concern to retailers this decade?
4. How do demographic and social changes bring about changes in retailing? Discuss several examples.
5. What is the difference between disposable income and discretionary income? Are luxury goods retailers more interested in disposable or discretionary income? Why?
6. How do retailers respond to the environmental consciousness of consumers?
7. What are several ways retailers differentiate their stores from the competition?
8. How do unpredictable events challenge retailers and provide new opportunities for sales?

Endnotes

1. Martin, Bob L. "Global Retailing: A Revolution in the Making." Presentation. Global Retail Symposium. Southwest Retail Center. University of Arizona. Tucson. March, 1996.

2. Furukawa, Tsukasa. "Retail's Building Blocks." *Women's Wear Daily.* Global Supplement. February 1998:18.

3. MacDonald, Laurie. "Hawaii Stores Are Hit by Asian Woes." *Women's Wear Daily.* April 7, 1998:2,19.

4. Rohwer, Jim. "Asia's Meltdown." *Fortune.* February 16,1998:85.

5. Sterba, James P. "Puppet Regime: Or the Art of Traveling Cheaply in Indonesia." *Wall Street Journal.* June 24, 1998:1, A10.

6. *Wall Street Journal*. "U.S. Trade Gap's New Culprits: Canada, Mexico." July 20, 1999:A16.

7. Ostroff, Jim. "Report: NAFTA Helped Both US and Mexico." *Women's Wear Daily*. July 14, 1997:24.

8. Millman, Joel. "Is the Mexican Model Worth the Pain?" *Wall Street Journal*. March 8, 1999:A1.

9. Lewis, Diane E. "Four Retailers Settle Sweatshop Allegations." *Boston Globe*. August 10, 1999:D6

10. Steinmetz, Greg. "U.S. Firms Appear Among Least Likely to Bribe Overseas." *Wall Street Journal*. August 25, 1997:A9B.

11. Wilke, John R. and Pereira, Joseph. "Office Depot, Staples Deal Is Blocked." *Wall Street Journal*. July 1, 1997:1, A3.

12. *Boston Globe*. "Toys R Us Settles Antitrust Suit." May 26, 1999:C2.

13. *Washington Retail Insight*. National Retail Federation. Volume 7, No.6, March 1, 2002 and No. 8, March 22, 2002. Available: www.nfr.com. Accessed, April 13, 2002

14. Seideman, Tony. "Threat of Sanctions Heats Up Debate Over European Privacy Rules." *Stores*. June, 2001: 92.

15. "Global Powers of Retailing." *Stores*. January, 2002:G26..

16. Butler, David, Long, John, and Yemma, John. "America 2000: Measuring the Nation." *Boston Sunday Globe*. November 21, 1999:A22 (Source: Ameristat, 1998)

17. Beck, Melinda. "Next Population Bulge Shows Its Might." *Wall Street Journal*. February 3, 1997:B1.

18. U.S. Census Bureau. *Statistical Abstract of the United States: 1999*. "No. 24, Projections of Resident Population by Age, Sex, and Race: 2000 to 2025." 119th edition. Washington, DC. 1999.

19. Wynter, Leon E. "Study Measures Status of Female Managers." *Wall Street Journal*. December 3, 1997:B1.

20. *Retail Industry Indicators*. NRF Foundation. Washington, DC. August, 2001: 17-20.

21. www.census.gov

22. Ibid.

23. "The American Character." *Wall Street Journal*. March 5, 1998:A14.

24. "Statesupdate." National Retail Federation. March 1998:41.

25. Garrett, Diane. "Video Renter Fights Store by Store." *Los Angeles Times*. August 20, 1997:D4.

26. www.hollywoodvideo.com/company/company.htm Available: May 31, 2002

27. Holden, Benjamin. "Quake Price-Gouging Is Tempting But Shortsighted." *Wall Street Journal*. January 27, 1994:B2.

Global Retail Profile

Wal-Mart, USA

It seems only fitting that the largest retailer in the United States should be the subject of the first company profile, but Wal-Mart holds other distinctions. Not only is it the largest retailer in the world, but second only to ExxonMobil as the largest corporation in the world. With headquarters in Bentonville, Arkansas, the company operates over 4,400 stores worldwide and sales reached almost $218 billion for the year ending January 31, 2002.[1] In its home market and abroad, the company is aggressive and innovative, always looking for the next competitive advantage, It never rests on past triumphs and faces change with alacrity. Wal-Mart's strengths in operations, merchandising, and distribution in the United States are considered first in order to understand the impact of its current position internationally.

Wal-Mart USA

Founded in 1962 by flamboyant Sam Walton, the company has become the top discount retailer despite the fact that its full presence was not known in the United States until the 1990s when it expanded coast-to-coast. Some of the reasons why Wal-Mart has attained its lofty position are illuminated.

Wal-Mart's ability to source merchandise domestically and internationally in an efficient manner is one of its distinguishing characteristics. The company's relationships with vendors large and small are important and tightly controlled. Its state of the art distribution systems in terms of lo-

gistics, communications, and computer support are legendary. On the consumer level, Wal-Mart was one of the first retailers to bring service with a smile to the discount sector. Wal-Mart associates from all levels of the organization are involved in store decision making processes. The company's strong stand on environmental issues, social responsibility, and concern for customers brought forth considerable publicity. For example, Wal-Mart welcomes tourists arriving in their RVs and encourages them to spend a night in the parking lot. In some locations Wal-Mart greeters have knocked on doors to let travelers know that the store is open and coffee is brewing. In others, welcoming notes are placed under windshield wipers.[2]

Its location strategy has always been a maverick one compared to other retailers. Long an advocate of the large-frog-small-pond theory, the company chose to locate its stores in Familyville, USA—smaller cities and towns located on the fringes of metropolitan areas. Also, it saturated each regional market before moving into a new territory, ensuring more cost effective delivery and stock replenishment systems. Wal-Mart operates approximately 1,650 discount stores, 1,000 supercenters, 500 Sam's Warehouse Clubs, and 30 neighborhood market stores in the United States. Wal-Mart opened its 1,000th superstore in August, 2001. To celebrate the event in Missouri, $50,000 was donated to local community programs by Wal-Mart associates and suppliers.[3] New location tactics and selling formats—particularly in food retailing, and Walmart.com—highlight the company's plans.

Departing from past location strategies, the company gradually has opened stores in highly populated urban areas. Wal-Mart opened its first inner-city store on the outskirts of Los Angeles in 1998, followed by a store in the middle of that city in 2001. The latter is located in a three story building that previously housed a Macy's department store.[4] The company's plans to open a 220,000-square-foot supercenter in Dallas were curtailed in mid-2002 when the local planning commission deemed the project too large for the area.[5] Once Wal-Mart dominates rural markets, it looks to alternative sites for continued growth.

Another departure from standard practices, Wal-Mart test-marketed supermarkets in Arkansas in 1998. This did not come as a surprise to most retail analysts. Wal-Mart had extensive experience in food retailing through its supercenters for more than a decade. Called Wal-Mart Neighborhood Markets, stores are less than half the size of customary 100,000-square-foot supermarkets. More convenience for the customer is the principal reason for the new format, but saturation of the market is another. The company intends to find a niche between convenience stores and its own superstores. Small-Marts, as the company calls them, feature drugstores, seasonal merchandise, food, and groceries. Neighborhood markets carry approximately 20,000 different items compared to 100,000 items in a supercenter. Store designs are more personalized, with murals depicting local scenes, rather then the stark decor of Wal-Mart superstores and discount units.[6]

Latte is served at some Wal-Marts. The company introduced Cafe Tostino coffee bars in the United States in 1999, bringing gourmet coffee to Wal-Mart's customers. New ideas usually are tested in the United States before they are launched internationally. In this case, the test-marketing was done in Mexico. Tostino Coffee Roasters, Inc., a wholesale supplier of coffee, rents space for the cafe operation from Wal-Mart. True to its competitive pricing policies, at $2.25, Wal-Mart's latte is slightly less expensive than Starbucks'. The company expects to locate cafes in locations where Starbucks does not have a strong presence.[7]

Surviving several reincarnations since launching its Web site in 1996, Wal-Mart's efforts at online selling had been considered lackluster by many industry experts and customers. The company's presentation of merchandise changed radically with each revamp as the company continues to perfect its Web presence. Poor sales in apparel necessitated removing this merchandise category from the Web site in 2001. Gifts, jewelry, and electronics fare well by comparison.[8] The main goals of the Web site are to communicate more product information, expand customer relationships, and heighten awareness of Wal-Mart.[9]

International Operations

Wal-Mart's aggressive international expansion occurred for several reasons: the company's saturation of the American market, increased competition stateside, available capital, and a forward-thinking posture that the company prides itself on.

As of 2002, Wal-Mart owned 551 stores in Mexico, 250 in the United Kingdom, 196 in Canada, 17 in Puerto Rico, 22 in Brazil, 11 in Argentina, 95 in Germany, 9 in South Korea, and 19 in China with more planned there and elsewhere. For the fiscal year that ended in January 2002, Wal-Mart recorded international sales of $35.5 billion.[10] Highlights of operations in key countries include:

- *Mexico.* In 1991, Wal-Mart opened its first Sam's Club in Mexico as a joint venture with Cifra SA, a supermarket, convenience store, and general merchandise retailer. Despite the devaluation of the peso and general economic unrest, challenging bureaucracies, and NAFTA implementation issues, Wal-Mart de Mexico continues to be a front runner in the retail sector. According to Bob L. Martin, former President of Wal-Mart International, when the peso devalued, Wal-Mart's position remained firm: the company takes a long-term view, knowing there will be ups and downs in business cycles. In early 1998, the company purchased controlling shares of Cifra, increasing its ownership stake in the Mexican venture and changing its relationship with its partner.[11]

■ *Canada.* Wal-Mart entered the Canadian market in 1994 with its acquisition of 122 Woolco stores, purchased from Woolworth, Canada, Inc. The company holds a significant share of the Canadian discount market. Canadian customers were not familiar with pricing strategies practiced by Wal-Mart in its stateside stores and needed to be educated. It took several years to accomplish this and bring the stores to profitability.

■ *Brazil.* Wal-Mart opened in Sao Paulo, Brazil, with an abbreviated Sam's Club format in 1995. Featuring fewer frills than its U.S. warehouse club stores, the operation initially was plagued by intense competition and price wars. Wal-Mart owns 60% of the operation; Lojas Americanas, Brazil's largest discount chain, owns the remainder. Major competition comes from French hypermarket, Carrefour, and local retailer, Pao de Acucar. Carrefour has several stores in Brazil including one right next to Wal-Mart's Sao Paulo store. Wal-Mart opened its first Todo Dia store and a distribution center outside Sao Paulo in 2001. Todo Dia means *everyday* in Portuguese. The stores are smaller than typical Wal-Mart supercenters, and Wal-Mart sells products that appeal to local tastes, including black beans in bulk from large barrels.[12]

■ *Argentina.* Examples of how Wal-Mart caters to different consumer needs internationally are apparent in its stores in Argentina. Consumers in Argentina are big beef eaters and prefer to select their cuts from huge hanging sides of beef which Wal-Mart provides along side less obtrusive packaged meats like those found in U.S. supermarkets. Another difference, families tend to turn grocery shopping into an outing for the whole family and do not as routinely send one purchasing agent to make selections. This tendency opens up merchandising and sales promotion possibilities for the stores. When the first store opened, free apples and beverages were offered to customers as part of the promotional activities. Most Argentineans were not used to this type of special touch, yet "freebies" are expected at U.S. grand openings.[13]

■ *China.* In 1994 Wal-Mart operated three Value Clubs in China in Joint venture with Ek Chor Distribution Systems, a Hong Kong subsidiary of Bangkok-based C.P.Pokphard Company. They were not high performers for the company and by 1997, the partnership was ended. However, the venture did serve as a springboard to future expansion in China. In 1996, the company opened its first Sam's Club in Shenzhen, China, followed by several more units.[14] Wal-Mart is counting on the rising standard of living there and in other Asian countries to sustain its growth.

■ *Germany.* Wal-Mart departed from its customary joint venture entry strategy when it acquired Germany retailer Wertkauf in 1998. Prior to this transaction its only other acquisition had been its Canadian stores. Wertkauf operated 21 hypermarkets and gave Wal-Mart its introduction to retailing in Europe.[15] The company acquired 74 Interspar stores from Metro, another major German retailer, in 1999. It faced many challenges including merging Interspar and Werkauf offices, revitalizing stores, and extending its distribution system in Germany.[16] Wal-Mart learned that customer behavior and expectations are different in Germany than they are in other countries. It has adopted a conservative stance regarding its growth plans until the company becomes more familiar with the market.

- *United Kingdom.* Competitive retailing in the United Kingdom accelerated when Wal-Mart's purchase of Asda Group occurred in 1999. At the time, Tesco, J. Sainsbury, Safeway, and Asda dominated British food retailing. Asda operated on a pricing strategy similar to Wal-Mart's, and also employed customer greeters. Admittedly, this idea was stolen from Wal-Mart, according to an Asda executive.[17]

- *Japan.* In 2002, Wal-Mart announced that it would buy a small stake in the Seiyu supermarket chain, eventually increasing its ownership to 66.7 percent by 2007. The company expects to utilize lessons learned from an earlier, failed joint venture with Ito-Yokado in the mid-1990s and to benefit from growing positive reactions from consumers toward discounters.[18]

Many retail analysts questioned whether the company would thrive after the death of Sam Walton, a dominant, colorful, and charismatic figure. If the company's current growth rate continues, annual sales could easily reach $300 billion by 2005. It appears Walton's legacy will live on, and Wal-Mart's quest for dominance of the world market will continue unabated.

Discussion Questions

1. What tactics is Wal-Mart using to maintain its position as the world's largest retail company?

2. What gives Wal-Mart a competitive advantage? Utilizing situation analysis, examine the strengths and weaknesses of the company.

3. What are the main reasons Wal-Mart decided to open stores outside the United States?

4. When is it more advantageous for Wal-Mart to purchase an existing retail company in another country rather than open new stores?

5. What kinds of cultural differences does Wal-Mart face when it opens stores outside the United States?

6. If Wal-Mart reaches its goal of $250 billion in sales by 2005, what will be the main reasons for its success?

Profile Notes

1. http://www.walmartstores.com Annual Report Available: June 11, 2002.

2. Cart, Julie. "Finding Shelter on the Open Road." *Boston Globe.* March 15, 2001:A2.

3. http://www.walmartstores.com Annual Report Available June 11, 2002.

4. Moin, David "Wal-Mart Set to Open Its First LA Store. *Women's Wear Daily.* February 14, 2000:2,16.

5. "Report: Wal-Mart's Plan for Dallas Urban Supercenter Rejected." homeworldbusiness.com and ICDnet.com. Available: www.homeworldbusiness.com/news/news_brief.asp?brief_ID=4442 . June 11,2002

6. Nelson, Emily. "Wal-Mart's 'Small-Marts' Make It Biggest Grocer." *Wall Street Journal.* June 21, 1999:B4.

7. Nelson, Emily. "Wal-Mart Puts Coffee to Test in Indiana Stores." *Wall Street Journal.* April 2, 1999:B1,6.

8. Clark, Evan and Seckler, Valerie. "Wal-Mart Pulls Apparel from Its Web Site." *Women's Wear Daily.* May 18, 2001:13.

9. Young, Kristin. "Walmart.com Relaunch Set for Holiday Season." *Women's Wear Daily.* October 23, 2000:2,16.

10. http://www.walmartstores.com Annual Report Available: June 11, 2002.

11. Martin, Bob L. Presentation. "Global Retailing: A Revolution in the Making." Global Retailing Symposium. Southwest Retail Center. University of Arizona. Tucson. March 28, 1996.

12. Jordan, Miriam. "Wal-Mart Gets Aggressive About Brazil." *Wall Street Journal.* May 25, 2001:A8,12.

13. Martin, 1996.

14. "Retailer Expects to Open Six New Stores in China.' *Wall Street Journal.* June 4, 1998:B10.

15. Lee, Louise and Rohwedder, Cacilie. "Wal-Mart to Acquire German Retailer, Moving into Europe for First Time." *Wall Street Journal.* December 19, 1997:A2.

16. Troy, Mike. "Wal-Mart Goes Shopping for Next Acquisition." *Discount Store News.* June 7, 1999:90,127.

17. Nelson, Emily and Beck, Ernest. "Wal-Mart Seeks UK Supermarket Firm." *Wall Street Journal.* June 15, 1999:A3,4.

18. Ono, Yumiko and Zimmerman, Ann. "Wal-Mart Enters Japan with Seiyu Stake." *Wall Street Journal.* March 15, 2002: B5.

Global Retail Profile

Carrefour, France

Considered the "inventor" of the hypermarket, Carrefour operates huge format stores that carry a unique mix of food and general merchandise. When the company merged with Promodes, a competitor, it became the second largest retailer in the world. The company expected sales to reach $73 billion in 2002. With more than 9,200 stores in 30 countries and aggressive expansion plans, Carrefour is a formidable global retailer. Carrefour was founded in 1959, by Marcel Fournier and Louis Defforey in Annecy, an industrial city in eastern France. The store originally was located in the basement of what was then Fournier's department store, but soon was moved to its own site. It was an immediate success.[1]

Carrefour considers Auchan its chief competitor in France. It believes Auchan offers a broader merchandise assortment and may generate more fun, and encourage better traffic flow. Compared to Carrefour, Auchan competes on the basis of price. Carrefour also believes that its stores are exceptionally clean compared to Auchan and that its customers recognize and appreciate this attribute. Globally, Carrefour recognizes Wal-Mart, Metro of Germany, and Ahold of The Netherlands as competitors.

Annual market research studies are done to update Carrefour's customer profile. The customer base is broad according to most key demographics, but the company reveals that it does target a more upscale customer than rival Auchan. Research has shown three reasons why customers shop at Carrefour:

- Stores are large and comfortable to shop in.
- Stores are clean.
- Produce is top quality.

Approximately 98 percent of the customers at Villabe arrive at the store by car indicating a wide draw and the transportation preference of the clientele.[2]

Merchandising Policies and Profit Goals

The basic merchandise assortment is similar in all Carrefour stores in France. Key merchandise areas include electronics; textiles(soft goods such as apparel and home furnishings); produce, meat and groceries; and bazaar, which features toys and seasonal items. The company individualizes the merchandise mix for local tastes. For example, in its Chinatown store in Paris, more Asian products are stocked.

Stores carry shallow merchandise assortments by supermarket standards, but do substantial volume in the products they carry. Carrefour sells approximately 3,000 different produce items and 6,000 to 7,000 grocery items. Food sales account for approximately 70 percent of the business with general merchandise making up the remaining 30 percent.

Carrefour features low prices. The company operates on a 16 to 20 percent gross margin and looks for a 2 percent net profit. Losses due to theft is less than 1 percent. The range of profit on items is staggering with low profits generated by groceries and high profits recorded on bakery goods. The latter is considered a high volume, high turn, high profit department for Carrefour. Merchandise turnover, called *turn of stock* in France, averages 10–12 days for grocery products and about 30 days for non food items.[3]

Store Design and Promotion

Although its typical hypermarket is 100,000 square feet, Carrefour operates stores as small as 50,000 square feet and as large as 240,000-square-feet. The French government places legal restrictions on the opening of extremely large stores on new sites in France. In addition, French law prohibits retail stores from opening on Sunday any more than four times per year. These policies have limited retail expansion in France.

A wealth of auxiliary services is often housed in retail space adjacent to the hypermarket. This creates a mall-within-a-mall appearance and adds to the store's definitive presence. Several kiosks and shops complement the main store at the 100,000-square-foot Villabe site on the outskirts of Paris. A pharmacy, optical shop, travel and insurance agency, photo and print shop, ticket bureau, and even a marriage license counter are conveniently located for one-stop shoppers. At this particular location, Carrefour is the principal anchor and also owns the mall. It leases space to global retailers such as McDonald's, Toys "R" Us, and Pier Imports, plus a host of local and regional specialty stores and chains. Ninety percent of the stores are in shopping malls and 10 percent are free standing. Extensive free parking areas also typify hypermarkets.

Light and bright decor, scrupulously clean environment, and wide aisles are noticeable in the store. A strict grid floor plan is used. A few merchandise kiosks add interest to the spacious, customer-friendly store. Visually, a "pile 'em high and watch 'em buy" strategy is utilized. The bottled water section covers at least 50 feet of linear shelf space that reaches nearly to the ceiling, creating impact if not easy reach.

Carrefour uses nonaggressive promotion techniques. Information of an educational nature is made available at convenient sites throughout the store. Signage is ubiquitous as well as clear, concise, and compelling. The company encourages store loyalty with a variety of customer-oriented programs including their own "Pass" credit card.

Distribution

France is not considered as advanced logistically as some other European countries or the United States. This is due to a long history of regional retailing, necessitating less emphasis on physical distribution. As more chains expand nationally and internationally, technologically advanced systems are becoming the norm. Under Daniel Bernard, chairman of Carrefour, the company has instituted one central ordering and distribution center with satellite distribution points in each major region of France. Bernard came to Carrefour from German retailer, Metro, bringing experience from another top food retailer in Europe.

Some direct delivery of merchandise from vendors to individual stores is done, not much is anticipated in the future. All soft goods classifications are automated, as the company moves toward more integration of technology.

Global Expansion

Carrefour is more internationalized than most retail companies in the world. It has stores in Spain, Portugal, Italy, Turkey, Greece, Poland, Hungary, Switzerland, and the Czech Republic. It also operates in Mexico, Brazil, Argentina, Chile, and Colombia. Stores in Taiwan, Malaysia, China, Hong Kong, Thailand, Indonesia, South Korea, and Japan comprise its Asian holdings. Stores are owned solely or with partners.[4] The company eventually expects to have 65 stores in Japan. Expansion began when real estate prices in Japan were low due to the recession in the 1990s.[5]

The company articulated in its mission statement, "Le Dessein de Carrefour," its goals for operating world-wide:

- To satisfy clients.
- To motivate its people.
- To maintain clear and simple concepts.
- To be international.
- To create synergy with partners.[6]

Carrefour intends to reach these goals through development of new markets and acquisition. Carrefour is ready to expand further since it has acclimated to the international scene and is a strong company financially.

After trying in vain to convince customers to shop at its hypermarkets, Carrefour exited the U.S. market. The company opened a 330,000-square-foot store outside Philadelphia and a smaller one in New Jersey in 1988. Carrefour learned that it would have to adapt its ways of doing business to those preferred by U.S. shoppers. For example, Carrefour initially merchandised the store French-style by placing paper goods in housewares departments rather than in grocery areas as is the common practice in U.S. supermarkets. Newspaper advertising was used, which Carrefour rarely does in France. Ironically, later research showed that 60 percent of customers learned of the stores by word-of-mouth. Customers complained that Carrefour carried too few items which meant they could not do their entire weekly food shopping in the store. Management responded by adding more merchandise to the assortment.

The organizational structure was different from typical U.S. mass merchandisers. There is no central buying office. At Carrefour, each department manager is responsible for buying and pricing merchandise, settling personnel issues, planning profit, and setting its own gross margins.

The Philadelphia store eventually reached a million dollars per week sales volume, missing the target of 5 million per week. After predicting 21 stores by 1992, the company pulled out of the United States in late 1993. Several reasons for the departure were:

- The format was too large for U.S. customers.
- The stores were not well run.
- The competition was too intense.
- The shopping experience was too time consuming for customers.
- Customers were not used to shopping for food and general merchandise in the same place.
- The company experienced union boycotts and zoning problems in the Philadelphia area.
- The company spent too much money to build stores.[7]

Carrefour learned from its mistakes. It has wisely shopped its global competition, especially Wal-Mart and Metro. Carrefour launched its on-line grocery store, Ooshop, in 2000, and expected its home delivery service to reach seven countries by 2003.[8] Carrefour is a seasoned global retailer.

The company also formed GlobalNetXchange (GNX), with several partners including Sears and Kroger of the United States, J. Sainsbury of the United Kingdom, and Metro of Germany. The business-to-business electronic marketplace is expected to create efficiencies through group purchasing and reduced costs of administration, according to Jeremy Hollows, chief information officer for Carrefour. According to Hollows, to be successful in business, four things matter: "people, process, partners, and the power of technology."[9] These sentiments and ventures like Ooshop and GNX leave Carrefour well poised to continue its global quest and eventually re-enter the U.S. market. Carrefour owns a minority share in U.S. retailer Petsmart. This might indicate that a comeback is likely.

Profile Discussion Questions

1. What makes Carrefour different from typical supermarkets or superstores?
2. What are the three main reasons why customers like shopping at Carrefour? Would you like to shop there?
3. Explain the advantages and disadvantages of a "pile'em high and watch 'em buy" visual merchandising technique.
4. What do you believe were the three main reasons for the demise of Carrefour in the United States? Do you think Carrefour would succeed if it opened stores in the United States in the future?
5. How do Carrefour's global expansion plans compare to Wal-Mart's?

Profile Notes

1. http://www.carrefour.com/english/homepage/index.jsp Available: June 12, 2002.
2. Excerpted from presentation made to members of the American Collegiate Retailing Association by Carrefour management. Villabe, France. July, 1997.
3. Ibid.
4. http://carrefour.com/english/homepage/index.jsp Available: June 12, 2002.
5. Woodruff, David. "Carrefour Pushes to Expand Into Japan, Counting on Appeal of Hypermarkets." *Wall Street Journal*. June 15, 1999:B7C.
6. Carrefour management presentation, 1997.
7. Zweibach, Elliot. "Carrefour Closing U.S. Stores: Two Hypermarkets in Northeast to Shut Within Two Months." *Supermarket News*. September 13, 1993:1.
8. "Carrefour: Major Growth in Retail, E-Commerce." Women's Wear Daily. March 31, 2000:2.
9. Hollows, Jeremy. "The Rise of eMarkets—Revolutionizing the Retailer/Supplier Relationship." Presentation. National Retail Federation 90th Convention and Expo. New York. January 17, 2001.

Retail Structures

and Strategies

Chapter 4

Brick-and-Mortar Retailers

Learning Objectives

After completing this chapter you should be able to:

- Identify key characteristics of retail stores including size, target market, merchandise, image, turnover, gross margin, and other pertinent descriptors.

- Contrast department, specialty, and discount stores.

- Compare supermarkets, superstores, and hypermarkets and speculate on the future of these institutions in the United States and other countries.

- Summarize changes in convenience store, restaurant, and fast food retailing.

Figure 4.1 Parisian is a multi-unit department store based in Birmingham, Alabama, with stores throughout the southeast and midwest (See p. 110).

The retail industry is in a state of flux. Stores that did not exist a decade ago are now commonplace; those that supposedly withstood the tests of time are no longer with us. A stroll through any shopping mall or downtown area confirms this fact. Gone are Jordan Marsh, Woolworth's, Lechter's, Montgomery Ward, and Merry-Go-Round; here today are Best Buy, Gadzooks, Zara, and Starbucks. Similar changes are occurring in many other countries.

Every retail store serves certain target markets and has its own personality, but the same or similar functions are performed in each. The universal functions of all retail businesses—merchandising, operations, promotion, finance, human resource management, and information technology—were introduced in Chapter 1. Because of similarities in organization, product orientation, and customer focus, retailers can be classified into a few major types. In this chapter we consider how these categories apply to classic, brick-and-mortar stores that have four walls and a roof. Nonstore operations, such as catalog and electronic retailers, are discussed in Chapters 6 and 7.

Brick-and-mortar stores can be categorized as department stores, specialty stores, general merchandise chains, discount retailers, and food retailers. For each kind of store we will consider typical characteristics, including size, target market, merchandise, image, pricing policy, turnover, and gross margin. Tracking how fast merchandise sells, and how much it costs a company to sell goods are aspects that are commonly discussed by comparing turnover and gross margins. **Turnover** is the number of times inventory is sold and replenished in a year. It is also referred to as turn or stock turn. **Gross margin** is the difference between net sales and the cost of merchandise sold, expressed as a percentage. Where appropriate we will also consider such characteristics as organizational structure, site selection policies, and operational procedures. Retailers within each category put their own stamp of identity on functional areas as they compete with each other and with other types of stores to maintain and increase market share.

turnover The number of times inventory is sold and replenished in a year. Also referred to as *turn* or *stock turn*. (Note: Some European retailers use the word *turnover* to refer to annual sales volume.)

gross margin The difference between net sales and the cost of merchandise sold, expressed as a percentage.

Department Stores

Department stores are large-scale operations that carry broad assortments of goods and offer depth in most merchandise classifications and wide varieties of services. From an organizational standpoint, each department is operated as a separate unit, and merchandise is grouped according to similarity. Full-line department stores carry both hard and soft lines of merchandise. **Hard lines** refer to products such as furniture, home electronics, computers, home improvement goods, housewares, books, and automotive supplies. **Soft lines** are products such as apparel, accessories, linens, and bedding. Macy's is an example of a full-line department store.

Limited-line department stores that usually focus on upmarket soft lines are called **department/specialty stores**. These stores share many merchandising and operating characteristics with full-line department stores. In addition to emphasizing soft goods, department/specialty stores operate on high gross margins and carry branded merchandise in stores large enough to be shopping center anchors. They include limited-line retailers such as Lord & Taylor, Saks Fifth Avenue, and Neiman Marcus. The opulent interior of the Neiman Marcus store in downtown Dallas is shown in Figure 4.2. The company went a step further in refining its specialty when it opened NM Galleries, units much smaller than its limited-line department stores. International examples of department/specialty stores include Holt Renfrew, which operates in six cities in Canada, and Dickins and Jones in London.

Target markets of limited-line stores are more narrowly defined and price levels typically are higher than for full-line department stores. Department/specialty stores are considered more fashion-forward in their apparel merchandising.

Figure 4.2 The first floor of the Neiman Marcus flagship store in Dallas, Texas, features rich wood showcases, opulent lighting fixtures, and plush seating.

Target Market and Pricing Strategies

Department stores provide merchandise for consumers from newborn to centenarians, but that does not mean their target markets are that broad. Demographics, especially age, income, and ethnic background, play a large role. Geographic locations and customer lifestyles are also important. For example, Bloomingdale's flagship store in New York City caters to somewhat older customers, whose average age is 49. A **flagship store** is the main store in a retail group, usually located in a city and often on the site of the original store. More women than men shop in Bloomingdale's. Forty-four percent of customers are not employed outside the home and their average household income is $110,000.[1] All of these factors combine to influence merchandise and service choices made by Bloomingdale's. Price points are

hard lines Products such as furniture, home electronics, computers, home improvement goods, toys, housewares, books, and automotive supplies.

soft lines Products such as apparel, accessories, linens, and bedding.

department/specialty store Limited-line department store that usually focuses on upmarket soft lines.

flagship store The main store in a retail group, usually located in a city and often on the site of the original store.

higher than one would expect in a less cosmopolitan area, where the taste level is not as rarefied. The customer profile varies somewhat in its other stores throughout the United States.

In contrast, JC Penney directs its merchandising efforts to a middle class market. Customers want name brands and fashion as much as their Bloomingdale's counterparts, but the average household income of the Penney shopper is significantly lower. Prices at JC Penney are lower, and merchandise selections are made for less sophisticated and less cosmopolitan customers.

Physical Facilities

Department stores are the showplaces of retailing. A visit to Macy's Herald Square store in New York or Marshall Field in Chicago will substantiate this statement. Some of the grandest department stores in the world are in Asia and Europe. Japanese department stores like Takashimaya and Mitsukoshi are famous for their lavish surroundings and extensive services. Many department stores in Europe operate in buildings of historical significance. Magazin du Nord's flagship is an impressive Beaux-Arts building in Copenhagen, Denmark. Harrods in London has many special features within its one million square feet of selling space. One of its food halls features a ceiling mosaic that is protected by a historical preservation order. Even if Harrods wanted to change the ceiling, it could not, under British law. The ceiling is featured in Figure 4.3. Department stores of this stature are called *grand magasins*, derived from the French word for storehouse.

Flagship and Multi-Unit Stores

Flagship stores are generally larger and have more character than other units in a department store company. Suburban stores may be somewhat smaller and frequently more contemporary in design. As more accouterments are added to new locations and renovated sites, many satellite stores seem as embellished as their flagships.

The flagship store is the hub of activity as it oversees the merchandising, promotion, operational, financial planning, and information technology needs of its branches. The functions are the same in large multi-unit department stores and smaller single-unit department stores. A department store organization consisting of a flagship store and two or more stores is considered a **multi-unit department store**. The difference is that in large, multi-unit organizations like Parisian or Proffitt's, each function is performed by a team of specialists. Both stores are part of Saks, Inc. Department Store Group. A Parisian department store is illustrated in Figure 4.1.

multi-unit department store
Department store organization consisting of a flagship store and two or more stores.

In small, family-owned department stores, a few people perform all functions.

More complex retail systems necessitate the separation of buying and selling. Buyers in the main store purchase merchandise for the entire company and work closely with vendors, store managers, and department sales managers, who are responsible for selling. This method allows **economies of scale,** savings achieved through producing or purchasing large quantities of goods, to be realized and makes for a more efficient and profitable organization. Because selling floor space is so valuable, some retailers have moved their buying staffs to corporate headquarters or other locations off the store premises, but usually close to the flagship.

Department Store Challenges

Department store business in the past 20 years gradually faded for many reasons including:

- increased competition
- clichéd merchandise
- industry consolidation
- altered images
- excessive promotion
- adjusted pricing
- decreased customer service

Figure 4.3 Harrods' food halls are legendary, carrying all manner of worldly goods. Because of its historical importance, the ceiling on this hall is preserved by British law.

economies of scale Savings achieved through producing or purchasing large quantities of goods.

These problems contributed to declines in department store market share in the last decade. A deeper look at some of these reasons will clarify this complex issue.

Increased Competition Department stores initially were successful in making the shift from cities to suburbs in the 1950s. They dominated shopping centers as they had downtowns. Competition primarily came from other department stores. A series of social changes, performance pressures, and perhaps poor decisions changed the nature of department store retailing. Efforts to provide everything customers wanted, maintain merchandising leadership, and remain profitable could not be sustained. Determined to survive, some department stores concentrated on higher-margin apparel and dropped merchandise such as furniture, major appliances, home electronics, music, and sporting goods. Restaurants were scaled-down or discontinued in many department stores. These decisions left retailers vulnerable because they were no longer providing all the merchandise and services that customers expected.

Customers also changed. Value rather than status become their chief objective. Famous brands that formed the bulk of department store business were still important, but some customers preferred to sacrifice the wide choice of branded merchandise for lower prices.

While department stores were busy competing against one another and adjusting their merchandise mixes, specialty and discount stores quickly filled the void. Specialty stores bring a narrow variety of merchandise to their more highly defined markets and are very focused. This directly opposes department store policy. Discounters offered hard lines that department stores were dropping as well as lower priced soft goods. Later, off-price discounters, category killers, catalogs, and eventually electronic retailers added competitive pressure.

Clichéd Merchandise In an attempt to keep stockholders happy in the face of declining stock values, department store buyers were directed to be more conservative in their selection of merchandise. As a result merchandise became staid and redundant. Innovation had been the lifeblood of department stores. Now, merchants seemed paralyzed and were unwilling to take risks on exciting but unproved merchandise. Customers who looked for fashion-forward merchandise were disappointed and shopped elsewhere.

Competitive pressures also contributed to ultra-conservative attitudes toward merchandise buying. For example, most department stores purchase the bulk of their merchandise from a few big vendors that have proved satisfactory in the past. One reason this procedure is followed is to mimic the competition, but it also contributes to uninspired merchandising. Many buyers are unable to seek out smaller vendors for unique merchandise that could bring new life to their stores because they are instructed to purchase goods only from approved companies. **Preferred vendor lists** are comprised of prescreened manufacturers that are chosen to do business with large retail companies. The practice often closes out smaller vendors. This problem exists in most other large retailing organizations as well as department stores.

preferred vendor lists Pre-screened manufacturers that are chosen to do business with large retail companies. The practice often closes out smaller vendors.

Industry consolidation may also encourage conservative, mundane merchandising. Larger organizations are able to achieve economies of scale in the quantities of merchandise they purchase, but this benefit does not spark creative merchandise planning. Some retailers believe that effective merchants are not being developed at the store level as they once were. The disruption in human resources that comes with consolidation, job-hopping within the industry, the luring of talented merchandisers into other fields, and poor training are possible reasons for this problem.

Altered Images The nature of department stores is to bring a wide variety of goods to an expanded market. Some stores, trying to be all things to all people, diluted their merchandise mixes and lost focus. Customers began to complain of boring merchandise and sameness. Stores that cut lower margin hard lines found they lost customers who valued one-stop shopping. In order to compete, department stores cut prices and promoted sales incessantly. Most analysts agree that the combination of these factors contributed to the image erosion experienced by department stores. No longer perceived as leaders, they had become members of the retail pack.

Department stores have been described as being about as agile and timely as a tyrannosaurus rex. Cumbersome merchandise procurement methods contributed to this perception. Other types of retailers were able to turn merchandise faster, replace stock faster, and identify hot new resources more rapidly than department stores. Sluggish response times have greatly improved, but old impressions die hard.

Forced to develop a stronger image, many department stores re-evaluated their management styles and strategic policies rather than lose out to competitors. The May Company and Federated Department Stores are good examples of retailers that have faced the challenges of the decade and are not only surviving, but are flourishing. Retailers have invoked many tactics to return their companies to their former glory. Department stores continue to win back market share in several ways. Some combine the best aspects of specialty store retailing and branded merchandise by adding concept shops (see Chapter 3). **Branded concept shops** refer specifically to store-within-a-store formats featuring internationally known mega-brand merchandise such as Nautica, Tommy Hilfiger, or Liz Claiborne. Other retailers focus on private label or market development.

branded concept shops Store-within-a-store formats featuring internationally known mega-brand merchandise such as Nautica, Tommy Hilfiger, or Liz Claiborne.

- ■ *Branded concept shops.* In an effort to create more sales, higher margins, and increased focus, most department stores welcome branded concept shops. Many carve out small specialty areas for the sale of apparel, brand-name linens and bedding, or lifestyle merchandise. Internationally recognized manufacturers dominate prime department store square footage. In-store shops are important revenue drivers, but pressure to maintain growth affects both retailers and manufacturers. For example, if Nautica has lackluster merchandise for more than one season, it could loose valuable department store space. On the other hand, if Tommy Hilfiger opens more company stores, and they are more profitable than in-store shops, it could

Figure 4.4 Tommy Hilfiger maintains close to 2,000 branded concept shops in department and specialty stores. *Courtesy of Fairchild Publications, Inc.*

private label Merchandise that is manufactured to store specifications and bears the retailer's name or other names created by the retailer.

result in loss of revenue for department stores.[2] A typical Hilfiger branded concept shop is shown in Figure 4.4.

■ *Private labeling.* Department stores are achieving higher margins through private label programs. **Private label** merchandise is manufactured to store specifications and bears the retailer's name or other names created by the retailer. Private labeling helps build brand awareness and consumer loyalty. JC Penney's *Arizona* brand jeans and sportswear have become well known and sell better than some manufacturers' brands. *Relativity, Cezani,* and *URit* are popular brands sold in several of the Saks. Inc. Department Store Group stores. Macy's success with its *INC* apparel private label precipitated the opening of an *INC* specialty store in Tokyo.[3]

■ *Market development.* Department stores are also reaching out to underserved markets. They are bringing in new brands such as *Fubu, XOXO,* and *Mudd* to attract teenagers. Some are bringing back concepts that had been previously discarded. Restaurants are once again appearing in department stores that are trying to reconnect with shoppers.

One of the most important issues department stores face is the gap between customers' perceptions of them and stores' perception of themselves. These inconsistencies surfaced in a study done by *Women's Wear Daily Infotracs.* When asked why they avoid department stores, customers surveyed mentioned "too expensive" 84 percent of the time. When asked the same question, department store merchants cited that factor only 53 percent of the time.[4]

Department stores will continue to face intense competition. They will also contend with price adjustments, overdependence on promotion, and further consolidation within the industry. Despite the special problems they face, many have risen to the challenge admirably and will continue to be recognized as truly exciting places to shop. Some are experimenting with centralized, rather than departmentalized, check out options that are intended to quell growing impatience on the part of time-starved consumers. Saks, Inc. was successful in testing centralized registers and will use this technique in most of its department stores.[5]

Writer David Moin sums up the ideal department store: "What's the ultimate vision? Department stores as huge upscale carnivals with demonstrations, technology, interactive displays, parades, fashion shows, music, celebrities, and great restaurants. A little bit of what they have now, what they used to have, and more."[6]

Specialty Stores

Specialty stores zero in on one particular market instead of trying to create broad acceptance. Their markets may be defined by age, interest, gender, income level, ethnic origin—in fact, most any demographic or behavioral dimension. Specialty stores may be as small as a single unit sole proprietorship or a large as a several thousand unit corporate chain. In general, to be considered a chain, a company must operate more than 10 stores. Specialists are known for being on top of trends, delivering excellent customer service, turning merchandise faster, and adapting to change more quickly than department stores.

The "Age of McFashion," as it has sometimes been called, refers to the retail practice of taking the same exact format and imprinting it a thousand times over in malls across an entire trading area. Cookie-cutter retailers like these are probably a thing of the past as even the largest specialty chains seek to differentiate individual units.

Differences Between Specialty and Department Stores

In department stores, there are specialists in each functional area. In specialty stores, a few generalists within the store usually perform all the major functions. Of course this arrangement depends upon the size of the operation and whether it is part of an independently held small business or a chain. For example, in a small boutique, buyers—who are often owners—spend more time on the selling floor than do buyers in department stores like Bloomingdale's or specialty store chains like H&M and Old Navy. Department and specialty store buyers purchase merchandise to be sold in multiple locations and do not have the time to supervise the selling floor.

A difference between specialty chain stores and most department stores is the centralization of all major specialty store functions in a headquarters, rather than a flagship store. Policies and procedures are determined centrally and one buying staff purchases merchandise. The responsibility for selling and servicing the chain's customers remains with local store management. This structure is typical of the Limited Brand's various specialty store divisions that are housed in central headquarters in Columbus, Ohio. The Burton Group in London operates its several specialty store chains similarly.

Did You Know?

Encouraged by the fondness of customers for Magic, the company's canine mascot, Old Navy launched a "canine couture" business. Dog beds, bandannas, rubber bones, and collars are available in stores or online.
Source: *Wall Street Journal.* "Gap's Old Navy Sets Sail with Items for Dogs." March 2, 2001: B5.

Table 4.1 Top 20 Specialty Stores

Rank	Company	Headquarters	2000 Volume (In Billions)
1	Best Buy	Minneapolis, MN	$19,597,000
2	Gap	San Francisco, CA	13,847,873
3	Office Depot	Delray Beach, FL	11,154,081
4	Toys "R" Us	Paramus, NJ	11,019,000
5	Staples	Framingham, MA	10,744,373
6	TJX	Framingham, MA	10,708,998
7	Circuit City Group	Richmond, VA	9,589,803
8	Limited Brands Inc.	Columbus, OH	9,363,018
9	CompUSA	Dallas, TX	6,100,00
10	Intimate Brands	Columbus, OH	5,020,953
11	Barnes & Noble	New York	4,870,390
12	AutoZone	Memphis, TN	4,818,185
13	RadioShack	Fort Worth, TX	4,775,700
14	OfficeMax	Cleveland, OH	4,636,024
15	Foot Locker	New York	4,379,000
16	Big Lots	Columbus, OH	3,433,321
17	Borders Group	Ann Arbor, MI	3,387,900
18	Spiegel	Downers Grove, IL	3,078,912
19	Ross Stores	Newark, CA	2,986,596
20	Bed Bath & Beyond	Union, NJ	2,927,962

Source: Excerpted from *Stores* ""Top 100 Specialty Stores," an Ernst&Young Special Report. August, 2002:S5

Scope of Specialty Retailers

There are specialty stores for all merchandise categories—clothing, shoes, accessories, food, appliances, automotive supplies, home electronics equipment, furniture, toys, home furnishings, jewelry, and pharmaceuticals. Hundreds of used golf carts are the primary products for sale at an outdoor lot near Hampton, New Hampshire. The smallest specialty store in London is Twinings whose store in Fulham sells only tea. These examples give dimension to the term single-line specialty store. Table 4.1 lists the top 20 specialty store chains in the United States.

Hard lines specialists include electronics, toy, housewares, sporting goods, and furniture retailers. The service sector also has its share of retailers. Dry cleaners, repair shops, photo finishers, hair salons, and video rental stores are technically all specialty retailers.

Specialty chains come in all shapes and sizes, and cater to many different whims. Health care stores like Relax The Back and General Nutrition contrast sharply with Marlboro shops and Godiva Chocolates. Names like Victoria's Secret, Brooks Brothers, Brookstone, and Mrs. Fields are familiar throughout the United States. Specialty stores such as Guess and the Gap are as popular in Europe and Asia as they are in America. Ask any teenager what Sunglass Hut means. Whether in New Orleans or Paris, the answer will be new shades!

Other trends in specialty stores combine one or more service businesses with product sales. One company which provides Internet service, use of related computer and media equipment, and coffee is profiled in this chapter's From the Field.

Designer Boutiques

Boutiques in department stores or stand-alone specialty stores which feature top-of-the-line merchandise by international designers such as Prada or Georgio Armani are called **collection shops**. They are closely related to branded concept shops, but are driven primarily by European designers turned retailers, rather than mass marketed brands. Collections by Versace are higher priced, more fashion-forward, and more exclusive than the mass-merchandised goods produced by Liz Claiborne. Perhaps a bit of import snobbery is at work when the likes of Max Mara, Ferragamo, or Chanel move into a city. An in-store Chanel boutique is illustrated in Figure 4.5. American designer/retailers such as Donna Karan, Calvin Klein, and Ralph Lauren also fit this category and thrive in foreign markets.

The designer connotation is the defining element in the expansion of collection shops. Price points and taste levels also play roles in shoppers' ability to discern differences between designer and nondesigner fashions. Some individuals do perceive higher quality levels in designer apparel. Others do not see or care if there are differences.

Most designers produce merchandise in two or more price categories and sell their apparel in separate stores. Designer collections exemplify higher-priced merchandise. **Diffusion lines** are groups of merchandise that are produced and sold at lower prices than designer collections. Armani has collection as well as diffusion stores. Armani A/X and Armani Jeans Stores offer lower prices than the collection stores.

Many designers are building flagship stores that acknowledge their importance in the retailing community. Twenty-thousand-square-foot monuments are being built in most major world cities such as London, Paris, Tokyo, and New York. Some feel that this is an indication that power has shifted from department to specialty stores.

CYBERSCOOP

Brookstone was forced to buy back the rights to its domain name, **www.Brookstone.com,** when the company discovered the site address was already taken. Visit Brookstone on the Web and find out what products it sells. How do you classify this retailer?

collection shops Boutiques in department stores or stand-alone specialty stores that feature top-of-the-line merchandise by international designers such as Prada or Georgio Armani.

diffusion lines Groups of merchandise that are produced and sold at lower prices than designer collections.

Figure 4.5 A Chanel boutique within a department store offers an intimate setting for the sale of luxury goods.

Drug Stores

Traditional drug stores are also specialists that adapt to changing market conditions. The 1980s saw many small, independent pharmacies close as national chains like Walgreen's, Rite Aid, and CVS expanded. In the 1990s, price wars, location maneuvering, and industry consolidation changed drug store retailing.

Drug store chains added services such as drive-up prescription windows and scrambled merchandising to remain solvent in the face of strong competition from supermarkets and superstores. It is not unusual to enter a drug store expecting to find a new lounge chair, pet food, greeting cards, and a snack before picking up a prescription.

Location strategy has changed as drug stores grow to accommodate their broader merchandise selections. Freestanding locations more frequently are selected for new construction. Corner sites are favored by Rite Aid, for example.

A host of mergers and acquisitions occurred in the 1990s and early 2000s. For example, JC Penney departed from its usual department store business and acquired Eckerds in 1996. Florida-based Eckerds is one of the top drug store retailers in the United States. Brooks and Osco merged in 2001.

By concentrating on one kind of customer and one or a few types of products, specialty chains reduce risk. It is easier to merchandise stores if the targeted customers have the same tastes and buying power, even if the stores are geographically dispersed. High visibility that accompanies intense saturation of the marketplace is another major reason for the success of specialty stores.

General Merchandise Chains

Retailers like Sears and Montgomery Ward have been, or were, in business for well over a century. Sears has survived ups and downs of many business cycles. The company had considered itself a department store, but in late 2001, announced that it was changing its image and no longer wished to be classified as one. Operating more like a discounter may position Sears more favorably in what had become troubled economic times for many department stores. Sears is considered a general merchandise chain in this text because of its size, wide geographic range, and merchandise and service mix. Montgomery Ward emerged from two years in bankruptcy protection in 1999. Although it sold nonperforming divisions and returned to its original general merchandise business, this was not enough to sustain the chain and it ceased operations in 2001. Discount stores like Wal-Mart, Kmart, and Target also have the general merchandiser and mass merchandiser designations. In addition to national and international general merchandise stores, regional chains are popular in most countries.

Did You Know?

Montgomery Ward's advertising copywriter, Robert L. May, devised the character and wrote the poem, "Rudolph the Red-Nosed Reindeer." Originally intended as a handout for children visiting Santa in the store during the Christmas season, the poem became a classic around the world.
Source:
www.mward.com/html/history/html

Characteristics

Merchants to millions, general merchandise stores sell a wide variety of hard and soft goods. They deal in widely accepted styles, mid-level prices, and average sizes. Unusual merchandise is not part of their identity. The middle-of-the-road approach describes general merchandise stores and their customers.

Like discounters, stores are large and modest in terms of decor. Unlike discounters, general merchandise stores usually are anchors of large shopping malls, rather than located in freestanding locations or smaller shopping centers.

Pricing policy and stock turns tend to be more like those of department stores than discounters. However, Sears was one of the first to introduce everyday low pricing, which presently is perceived as a discount pricing technique.

Merchandise focus is on a combination of national and private label brands. Sears carries its popular Kenmore line of appliances, but also carries national brands like Maytag. Automotive shops, garden centers, and other extended services are a part of general merchandise stores.

General merchandise chains are successful because they appeal to a broad spectrum of customers. Sometimes shoppers defy income, educational, and social status and housing statistics. For example, a female customer may never shop at Sears for apparel, but she may buy a new lawnmower there. General merchandise stores have experienced demise due to the influx of discount department stores and category killers but are redefining their roles in the marketplace.

Repositioning Strategies

For decades JC Penney also was known as a general merchandise chain, similar to Sears. In the mid-1980s, the company attempted to adopt a more upscale, department store image. Penney stores underwent extensive re-modeling to keep up with the times and the changing needs of its customers. Working hard to overcome its old paint-and-hardware image, it added more branded merchandise and embarked on an extensive private label business. In spite of major changes, Penney continues to attract middle income shoppers. It is a top volume department store in the United States, a significant catalog retailer, and an international retailer. However, Penney has been hurt by increased competition and image problems. Competition comes from other department stores, specialty stores, and discounters like Target. Ironically, Target rose from a lower to more upscale discount image and appears headed towards mid-market department store status.

Penney has implemented strategies to revive its image. The company created its Home Store division to showcase its furniture and domestics business, and grant more selling space to lucrative apparel lines. The spin-off made it easier for Penney to compete with off-price retailers such as TJX's Home Goods stores in the home furnishings area. Penney decentralized its buying function in the 1980s, but in early 2000 once again took control of purchasing at its Texas headquarters. Customers may not see Penney in the same league as other department stores, but the company's new concepts and procedures may change perceptions.

The continued attempts of JC Penney and Sears to reposition their stores and the failure of Montgomery Ward pose a question. Is it time for general merchandisers to develop new concepts or should they just move on? Kohl's is a general merchandise retailer that is attempting to bridge the gap between department and discount retailing. The company features quality brand names, offers shopping carts in the manner of discount stores, and follows an aggressive expansion strategy. Its unique format may be the missing link that will sustain shoppers and answer the question.

Discount Retailers

Discount stores multiplied quickly during the 1960s and 1970s. As their numbers increased, so did the income levels and sophistication of their customers. Fashion departments were added to meet changing demands. Customers began to think of discount stores as places to buy more than household gadgets and small appliances. Attracting customers with low prices, discount stores are the top choice across many consumer groups in the United States. Kmart indicates that 180 million people each year shop in its stores.[7] Prices in discount stores are usually lower than in the general merchandise chains and are almost always lower than in department and specialty stores. This distinction palls in comparison to deep discounters like warehouse clubs that work on low prices and even leaner gross margins. A **deep discounter** is a discount store that operates on much lower markups and gross margins than conventional or other discount retailers. At the other extreme are luxury goods specialty stores that may operate on disproportionately high prices.

Discount Department Stores

Discounters differ more radically from traditional department stores than from other mass merchandisers. Decor is minimal in Kmart compared to Macy's, but none the less effective for its purposes. Huge format discounters tend to do business on only one floor; department stores are frequently multifloored buildings. Lighting in discount stores tends to be bold rather than subtle, materials are more utilitarian than aesthetic, floor plans are more structured in appearance, and every square foot is taken up with merchandise. However, as the format evolves, more discount department stores are raising their ceilings, widening aisles, and adding numerous amenities for their customers. National fast food restaurants now take the place of old hot dog counters and celebrity endorsed lines supplant no-name products in discount stores.

Operating practices of discount department stores have become more like those of traditional department and specialty chain stores. Wal-Mart is an excellent example of an astutely managed, highly profitable, and well-positioned retail operation. It dominates large rural communities of 25,000 or fewer people in an ever-widening tier of stores throughout the world. Wal-Mart is known for its ability to maintain low prices, motivate store personnel, and create merchandising excitement within the store. Using a satellite network to keep in touch with its stores, it is said to be a decade ahead of many retailers in its use of technology.

Both Kmart and Wal-Mart operate stores internationally. Target reaches for total market coverage in the United States but has not announced international expansion plans. Regional chains in this category include Ames and ShopKo.

Discount department stores usually seek locations in community shopping centers or in freestanding locations on the periphery of cities. This tendency is changing as key players look to urban sites and anchor positions in regional malls. Discount department stores are becoming more like other retailers.

Did You Know?

Kmart stores sell 83,000 tons of potting soil each year—the equivalent weight of 342 blue whales.
Source: "Kmart Fun Facts." Kmart. Troy, Michigan.

deep discounter Discount store that operates on much lower gross margins than conventional or other discount retailers.

Category Killers

Category killers, introduced in Chapter 1, are overgrown specialty stores with discount overtones. The Sports Authority and Oshmans are strong in sales of sporting goods. Home centers and do-it-yourself (DIY) stores are represented by Home Depot, Lowe's, and Payless Cashways. A large DIY store in the United Kingdom ironically is named Texas. Office Depot, OfficeMax, and Staples provide office supply products to businesses and individuals. All three operate globally. Borders Books and Barnes & Noble dominate the book market, and Circuit City and Best Buy, the home electronics trade. Even household pets are not ignored and can shop with their families at Petco or PetsMart. Tower Records, HMV, and Virgin Megastores dominate the music industry internationally. Category killers share the superstore descriptor.

These giants are experimenting with new strategies as the market dictates. Home Depot entered the high-end of the home improvement market by adding expensive appliances and lighting fixtures to merchandise assortments in its Expo stores. Staples, Office Depot, and OfficeMax expanded to smaller towns in sharp contrast to the larger markets they once sought. Some of these rural markets are underserved, but in other instances, the arrival of category killers effectively eradicates small independent competitors.

Off-Price Discounters

Off-price fashion discounters emerged in the 1970s, bringing famous brand goods to shoppers at much lower prices than conventional department and specialty stores. Off-price stores have had a great impact on both customers and other retailers.

Early Off-Price Stores Although the term off-price was not yet in use, Filene's Basement in Boston was one of the first to open in 1909. Originally, Filene's department store intended to sell slow moving items from its upstairs store, but later added closeouts from manufacturers or other retailers to its automatic bargain basement. Filene's Basement is not to be confused with Filene's department store that is now owned by May Co. The Basement store underwent a management buyout in 1988, but was forced to file for bankruptcy protection in 1999. It subsequently closed many of its underperforming suburban stores. Filene's Basement uses a time-sensitive markdown method in its Boston flagship store. Goods are reduced in price in proportion to the amount of time they have spent on the selling floor. The store and its automatic markdown policy are illustrated in Figure 4.6.

Inventory Turnover The philosophy of off-price fashion discounting is based on high volume gained through lower markup and faster inventory turnover—12 or 13 times a year. Many traditional retailers, especially department stores, are trying to emulate this off-price tactic. Considering that department store gross margins are higher, and merchandise turns only 4 or 5 times a year, it is not an easy task.

Competition Other off-price companies include T.J. Maxx and Marshall's (both owned by TJX), Syms, Ross, and The Dress Barn. T.J. Maxx is the only U.S. chain that presently runs international off-price stores. The company operates in Canada, Europe, and as T.K. Maxx in the United Kingdom.

New competition emerged when a French company, Tati, opened its first store in New York City in 1998. Counting on customers who appreciate bargains, Tati sells everything from inexpensive wedding dresses and pantyhose to school supplies and bulk candy. The stores' target market is different from typical off-price discount stores. Tati draws "left-wing intellectuals, streetwise youth and other pop-culture devotees."[8] The company has stores in Germany, Belgium, and Switzerland as well as units in less traditional locations including Lebanon, Poland, Turkey, and the Ivory Coast. Within a few years, Tati expects to have 50 to 60 stores outside France. This example stresses the point that competition comes from domestic as well as foreign retailers.

It is essential for off-price retailers to attain high sales per square foot. Yet with every new element of competition, this becomes more difficult. Competition is now coming from all sides: department, specialty and discount stores, catalogs, and Internet retailers. Some sort of shakedown is almost inevitable.

Figure 4.6a Filene's basement flagship store in Boston is a bare-bones facility bringing off-price merchandise to the multitudes.

4.6b An automatic markdown system keeps bargain hunting customers coming back for more.

Warehouse Clubs

The mission of warehouse clubs is to merge wholesale and retail audiences and bring a diverse product mix in bulk quantities at competitive prices to their members. Warehouse clubs operate on very low gross margins and markups average 8 to 10 percent on most products. Volume is the key to profitability as it is in all discount operations. Individuals and businesses pay nominal annual membership fees to shop at stores like Costco Wholesale and Sam's Club. Warehouse clubs specialize in high-volume merchandise, generate higher stock turns than other discounters, and also are considered deep discounters. Usually located on the fringes of cities, they are rapidly working their way into high traffic urban locations.

stock keeping unit (SKU) Individual inventory control numbers, indicated by bar codes, that distinguish one product from another.

Few stock keeping units are represented in most warehouse clubs. **Stock keeping units (SKUs)** are the individual inventory control numbers—indicated on bar codes—which distinguish one product from another. Despite having fewer choices within merchandise categories, customers are treated to an array of merchandise such as fresh meat, bakery goods, fine wines, canned goods, apparel for the family, health and beauty aids, books, computers, and car tires. Also available are sporting goods, office supplies, jewelry, tools, and the occasional hot tub or Oriental rug. Many goods are displayed in shipping cartons on wooden pallets as shown in Figure 4.7. During peak traffic periods, product demonstrators hand out samples of new foods or beverages and create excitement in an otherwise stark environment.

Costco Wholesale, based in Issaquah, Washington, merged with Price Club in 1993, and operates more than 500 stores in the United States and abroad. Approximately 60 percent of sales is generated by individuals and 40 percent by local businesses in the average Costco store. Well-known brands offered at approximately 20 percent less than conventional retailers intermingle with Costco's own Kirkland brand. Its private label extends to everything from soda to shampoo to socks. This technique also is practiced in other warehouse clubs. More information on Costco Wholesale is presented in the Global Retail Profile following Unit Four.

Catalog Showrooms

In catalog showrooms, shoppers select discounted merchandise from catalogs that have either been delivered to them or are on display in the store. Either way, customers write selections on a sales order form that is processed by warehouse clerks. Catalog showrooms purchase in large quantities, secure favorable terms, and need very little display space. Because of this, branded hard goods such as cameras, jewelry, and small kitchen appliances are generally priced lower than in competing stores.

Competition from category killers and discount depart-ment stores has closed all but a few operations. Service Mer-chandise, based in Tennessee, attempted to shed its catalog image in favor of a more classic format. At one time the com-pany operated about 350 stores in the United States. Due to declining revenues, Service Merchandise filed for bank-ruptcy protection in 2000, and ceased operating in 2002.

Argos, the leading catalog showroom merchant in Eng-land, operates 400 small storefronts. Owned by Great Univer-sal Stores (GUS), Argos sells hard goods and some domestic soft lines. Because of GUS's strength in mail-order retailing, Argos is expected to be the vehicle of choice for the com-pany's home shopping venture.[9] These examples show that competition and evolution create change in the catalog showroom industry.

Factory Outlets

Manufacturers sell closeouts, seconds, and discontinued items through their factory outlet stores. In the past they were located very near production facilities and were called mill or company stores. This image is deceiving since today's factory outlet stores have become chains themselves. They no

Figure 4.7 Specially designed cardboard car-tons are displayed on wooden pallets in ware-house clubs like Costco Wholesale.

longer possess a down-home image and most are not located near a manu-facturing facility. Factory outlets are clustered together in outlet malls that are destinations for countless shoppers.

Pricing in outlet stores has come under close scrutiny. Prices on compa-rable merchandise may be less than those in department or specialty stores. However, customers have to work hard and be knowledgeable to find the rock-bottom prices that were customary in early, authentic factory stores. Freeport, Maine—the home of L.L.Bean—has many factory outlets. Outlet stores *are* the main street of Freeport. Outlet malls in Rehobeth, Delaware, are attractive to shoppers from New Jersey and Maryland, and to beach va-cationers, because Delaware has no sales tax. Expect pared-down decor, fa-cilities, and prices in true outlet stores. As outlet shopping strips and malls add amenities, prices ultimately increase.

Outlet stores and malls are becoming more popular throughout the world. Levi Strauss is a universally recognized brand that successfully brought its outlet concept to the United Kingdom. The Levi Company Store in London is illustrated in Figure 4.8. Outlet malls now exist in Japan, a country that did not easily embrace the discount concept. Read about a Japanese discount mall in Chapter 12.

Figure 4.8 The Levi's store in London shows that the company has taken its outlet concept international.

Food Retailers

Traditional categories of food retailers—convenience stores, supermarkets, and restaurants—no longer adequately describe this aspect of retailing. Distinctions are less clear as grocery retailers add general merchandise and general merchandisers become grocery retailers in return. Hypermarkets, a European innovation, may be the inspiration for superstores. Hypermarkets combine the best of grocery retailing with the sale of hard and soft goods. Food superstores were one of the fastest growing retail formats in the late 1990s.

Convenience Stores

Convenience stores are characterized by their location—close to residential areas, places of business, or on commuting paths. Long hours, often 24 hours a day, also are typical of convenience stores. Limited food and non-food items, from motor oil to milk comprise their merchandise mix. Shoppers looking for fill-in or emergency items are the target market. Convenience stores generally carry a variety of recognizable national brands but a limited selection of products. Fast food or deli components and extensive services, are newer additions to these stores. Prices are higher than in supermarkets but customers accept this because the stores are in the right place at the right time with the right products.

C-stores, as they are often called, are small in size when compared to other food retailers. They use only 1,000 to 4,000 square feet. This evolution of the corner mom-and-pop grocery store and neighborhood superette offers plenty of parking and often a gas pump on the premises. A **superette** is a small grocery store that is larger than a mom-and-pop store but smaller than a supermarket.

With more than 5,700 stores, the leading convenience store chain is 7-Eleven, operated by Southland Corporation and owned by Japan's Ito Yokado. Circle K, owned by Kroger supermarkets, is the next largest chain in the United States. Its c-stores are mostly in the South and Southwest.[10] Many supermarkets are responding to competition from convenience stores and are staying open 24 hours a day. Using lower prices, express checkouts, electronic self-checkouts, and special entrances for time-pres-

superette Small grocery store that is larger than a mom-and-pop store but smaller than a supermarket.

From the Field: Logging on With Lattes
by Dan Scheraga

The London-based company easyEverything has been ambitiously expanding its chain of Internet cafes across Europe. In 2000, easyEverything opened its first café in New York's Times Square. The company is looking at nationwide expansion.

EasyEverything could face tough competition stateside. Starbucks is piloting paid customer Internet access in 70 coffee shops and may expand the program chainwide. And both Kinko's and Mail Boxes Etc. offer such services, albeit at much higher fees and sans the lattes. Critics add the U.S. market may be less receptive to easyEverything's offer as many more Americans than Europeans can access the Web at home.

The Times Square location is impressive, occupying 18,300-square-feet across two levels. Lined up in banks are 800 Hewlett-Packard computers equipped with web cameras, Internet phones, and flat-screen monitors. A snack bar on the ground floor sells coffee, bagels, and other sustenance.

The café draws solid traffic—about 5,000 customers per day—estimates easyEverything's U.S. marketing manager, Stephanie Engelsen. Nevertheless, easyEverything's grand entrance into the U.S. market has skeptics scratching their heads. Its flagship store occupies a large piece of real estate. And it couldn't have been cheap to equip the store with 800 computers.

But if easyEverything has a lot to recoup, you would not know by its prices. Internet fees vary depending on the time of day, but during its peak period—around 5:00 P.M. to 8:00 P.M.—$4 buys an hour of access. At other times, a user can get an hour of computer time for as little as $2.

With prices like these, some question whether the retailer can turn a profit. But the merchant has revenue streams other than Internet access, such as its snack bar. easyEverything also earns money through in-store ad placements on its walls and idle monitors.

The company locates most of its stores in areas with heavy tourist traffic, including young backpackers and others. A weekday morning visit finds several dozen customers e-mailing, some in foreign languages. But there are also customers web-surfing, reading online news, chatting, even playing chess. Not all the clientele is young. More then a few silver coiffures and bifocals are evident.

Clearly, lots of consumers have reason to like easyEverything. Time will tell if there are enough of them to support the chain's American expansion.

Source: Reprinted by permission from *Chain Store Age*, ("May 2001"). Copyright Lebher-Friedman, Inc. 425 Park Avenue, NY, NY 10022.

sured customers, supermarkets will no doubt continue to keep pace with convenience stores.

Supermarkets

Introduced in Chapter 2, supermarkets are self-service food stores with grocery, meat, and produce departments, and usually an element of scrambled merchandising. Supermarkets operate on very low profit margins. In an attempt to increase their margins, many sell generic and private label brands. This helps keep customers interested and also increases sales and profits. With headquarters in Cincinnati, Kroger is the second largest food retailer in the United States, and the world's third largest retail company.[11] In the summer of 1998, Albertson's, headquartered in Idaho, acquired American Stores. This transaction brought the company almost 2,500 stores and $10 billion more sales annually than Kroger.[12] Kroger retaliated with its purchase of Fred Meyer supermarkets shortly thereafter. This boosted Kroger back to second position in the United States. Consolidation has affected the

---

Table 4.2 Top 20 U.S. Supermarket Companies

Rank	Company	Headquarters	2001–02 Est. Volume (In Billions)
1	Wal-Mart Supercenters	Bentonville, AK	67.0
2	Kroger Co.	Cincinnati, OH	50.7
3	Albertson's	Boise, ID	38.3
4	Safeway	Pleasanton, CA	34.4
5	Ahold USA Retail	Chantilly, VA	23.0
6	Supervalu	Minneapolis, MN	21.3
7	Costco Wholesale Corp.	Issaquah, WA	20.5
8	Sam's Clubs	Bentonville, AK	18.4
9	Fleming	Dallas, TX	15.8
10	Delhaize America	Salisbury, NC	15.2
11	Publix Super Markets	Lakeland, FL	15.1
12	Loblaw Cos	Toronto, Ontario	14.6
13	Winn-Dixie Stores	Jacksonville, FL	13.0
14	A&P	Montvale, NJ	11.0
15	Meijer, Inc.	Grand Rapids, MI	10.6
16	H.E. Butt Grocery Co	San Antonio, TX	9.0
17	7-Eleven	Dallas, TX	9.0
18	C&S Wholesale Grocers	Brattleboro, VT	8.5
19	Sobeys	Stellarton, Nova Scotia	7.6
20	Wakefern Food Corp.	Elizabeth, NJ	5.9

Source: Excerpted from *Supermarket News*. "SN's Top 75." January 14, 2002:20. Courtesy of Fairchild Publications, Inc.

supermarket industry as it has all others. The top 20 U.S. supermarket companies are listed in Table 4.2.

Companies seeking stronger, sometimes international stature have consumed other regional chains. J. Sainsbury of the United Kingdom and Royal Ahold of the Netherlands are aggressive supermarket retailers that are acquiring strong regional companies in other countries. Some of the largest supermarket companies in the world are based in countries other than the United States.

Superstores

Some retailing experts point to superstores as American versions of European hypermarkets, although true hypermarkets can be even larger stores. Perhaps the real differences between them are in the merchandise mix, the proportions of food and general merchandise, and consumer habits and perceptions.

Superstores have a much broader profit base than smaller supermarkets. Although they require a substantial investment, superstores permeate the retail scene, especially in heavily populated urban and suburban areas.

When superstores enter a new market, they put some small food stores out of business. Other retailers retaliate by refining their marketing strategies and continuing to compete. There will always be a place for large and small food retailers. When you are in a hurry to go from school to work wouldn't you rather shop at a 7-Eleven than a 150,000-square-foot superstore?

Hypermarkets

Hypermarkets are a European mainstay, and they are becoming popular in Asia. Retail history of the past 20 years is littered with the attempts of hypermarkets to find their niche in American markets. Wal-Mart's Hypermart USA, Kmart's American Fare, and French-owned Carrefour all attempted to do business in the United States in the last decade. None remain today. The Wal-Mart and Kmart ventures evolved into superstore formats. Reasons for Carrefour's demise in the United States are included in the Global Retail Profile at the end of Unit One.

Hypermarkets, like superstores, offer many store-within-a-store concepts. Dry cleaners, shoe repair shops, and pharmacies are expected in most large format stores. Extended services, such as travel and ticket agencies, make hypermarkets special. Hypermarkets need great population density—more than one million people within a 30-minute radius—to make the concept work. The challenge is to sell enough higher-margin general merchandise in addition to food to make a profit. In countries like the United States, where habits differ, people need convincing that hypermarkets are viable shopping alternatives.

The current global leaders are Carrefour and Auchan of France, and Makro of Germany. The attractions at stores like these include innovative atmospheres and prices that are 10 percent below market prices for peak demand merchandise. Where else would stock clerks zip around on in-line skates to fill shelves or service the needs of consumers? The employee in Figure 4.9 was photographed after delivering a bicycle to a customer at the front of a Carrefour store in France.

Throughout the world, the competitive threat of hypermarket expansion is apparent. The Indonesian Retailers Association in Jakarta expressed concern over the proposed opening of French hypermarkets. The association believes that the huge hypermarkets bring a level of competition that

Did You Know?

Carrefour means, "Happiness for the whole family" in Chinese.

Figure 4.9 When stock clerks need in-line skates to navigate the selling floor, we know a hypermarket must be huge.

is unfair to small retailers in the city. It is expected that retail laws will be rewritten to protect local retailers. This example shows that hypermarkets are no more immune to legal issues than other retailers but also illustrates the power large organizations wield.

Superstores may continue to fill the needs of American consumers or they may not. Since hypermarkets are popular in other areas of the world, they may again find a place in the United States.

Restaurants and Quickserve Operations

Restaurants, including quickserve, otherwise known as fast food, operations are part of the general retail scene. Sales from all types of food service business in the United States were expected to top $400 billion in 2002. Included in this figure are sales from eating and drinking establishments, restaurants in hotels and retail stores, vending machine food sales, sales of food at recreational sites like football stadiums, and mobile retailers such as ice cream trucks. Sales from cafeterias, hospital and school restaurants, and military establishments are also included.[13]

Many food service operators are also merchandisers and entertainers. Companies like Planet Hollywood, Hard Rock Cafe, and the Fashion Cafe illustrate this point. Signature merchandise may comprise one-third of sales in theme restaurants like these. Logo jackets, tee shirts, key rings, and posters add to the excitement for the consumer and to profits for the businesses. Fast food is an intensely competitive segment of retailing. Where one restaurant locates, others follow. It is not at all unusual to find four or five fast food operations within a few yards of each other. Many U.S. fast food restaurants are well known worldwide. Fast food retailers were among the first to expand internationally and adapt their menus accordingly. Figure 4.10 shows the omnipresent Ronald McDonald flanked by a banner advertising samurai burgers in front of a McDonald's in Kuala Lumpur, Malaysia.

These low-priced, convenient family eateries have survived buy-outs, spin-offs, and global expansion. Tricon Global Restaurants owns Pizza Hut, Taco Bell, and Kentucky Fried Chicken (KFC). The company was formed when PepsiCo divested the businesses in 1997. Because of saturated home markets, all restaurant divisions have expanded globally. Tricon had worldwide sales of $22 billion in 2001. The company planned to acquire Long John Silver's seafood restaurants and A&W All American Food Restaurants in

2002, when it also announced its name change to Yum! Brands, Inc. The name was chosen to reflect growing consumer desire to have fun-filled dining experiences.[14] Fast food chains inside and outside the United States usually are owned through joint ventures or franchise agreements. A **franchise** is a contractual agreement in which an independent franchisee agrees to purchase and operate a business according to the franchisor's specifications. In return for paying a fee and ongoing percentage of sales, the franchisee agrees to adopt a common store front and management procedures, and to purchase product from the host company. Franchises are a form of ownership and are discussed further in Chapter 5.

Figure 4.10 McDonald's, king of the fast food industry, tempers its menu to suit local tastes. The presence of Ronald is important whether the restaurant is in Kalamazoo or, in this case, Kuala Lumpur.

In order to remain competitive, many fast food restaurants are upgrading aging facilities. Burger King, divested by Britain's Diageo in 2002, changed its neutral decor to a more vibrant red and yellow color scheme and designed a new logo. Interior reconfiguration now allows customers a view of the busy kitchen. Faster food delivery systems also have been implemented. Electronic kiosks with interactive games were added along with video conferencing centers that enable youngsters to talk with their friends at other Burger King units. Burger King holds a 21.9 percent share of the U.S. burger market. After years of poor performance abroad, its European sales have improved.[15]

Price cutting, new product development, public relations, and promotional campaigns typify the strategies of fast food chains. These tactics are designed to encourage frequent repeat business. Most chains try to reduce operating expenses and improve productivity as they continue their quests for market share.

Changes in the National Retail Federation membership parallel many of the general retail trends presented in this chapter. The trade organization has noticed more small stores and fewer mid-sized stores joining their ranks. It has also observed that department store membership has declined because of massive consolidation in that sector. More hard line retailers have joined NRF as have distinct specialty operations like Starbucks, 1-800-FLOWERS, and airport mall retailers. Global retailers are also well represented.[16]

If you experienced a degree of confusion in categorizing retailers, you are not alone. Defining classic retail stores is not an exact science. Even

franchise A contractual arrangement in which an independent franchisee agrees to purchase and operate a business according to the franchisor's specifications.

CYBERSCOOP

Visit the National Restaurant Association Web site at **www.restaurant.org.** Find out what are the most popular day and month to dine in a restaurant. Also determine the increase in the number of African-American-owned and female-owned restaurants in the last decade.

people in the industry blur distinctions as retailing theory and practice are rewritten. It is important to recognize the nuances that make retailing a most dynamic and fascinating industry.

Summary

There are different categories of brick-and-mortar retail stores, but the basic functions carried out in each are similar. The view from the executive suite, whether hidden behind the stairs to the stockroom or located on the top floor of a skyscraper, is therefore much the same. Profit is the universal motivator and varies by type of retailer.

There are department stores, specialty stores, discount stores, and food retailers of all descriptions. Stores and retail services may operate as small single unit businesses or large multi-unit chains. Department stores usually have a flagship store in a city and stores in other cities and suburbs. Locating branded concept shops within department stores is one way popular manufacturers extend their reach.

General merchandise retailers include companies that provide a wide selection of goods and services for diverse population. Also included in this category are discount retailers. Discount department stores, category killers, off-price retailers, warehouse clubs, catalog showrooms, and factory outlets comprise the discount sector.

Supermarkets are becoming superstores, while discount stores are emulating department stores or opening supermarkets themselves. Hypermarkets are strong in Europe and other parts of the world. Although unsuccessful in the past, attempts to bring European concepts in food and general merchandise retailing to the United States may occur in the future. Theme restaurants are also soft goods retailers and entertainment specialists. Fast food operations continue to answer the general public's need for immediate gratification and an inexpensive meal.

Some retailers break free of their original categories only to find their way back to their original formats as time passes. Others struggle with clear identities as distinctions between categories blur in consumers' eyes.

Questions for Review and Discussion

1. Discuss two major strengths and two major weaknesses of department stores. What must department stores do to maintain or regain competitive advantages?

2. Why are specialty stores considered experts at target marketing? Give examples of stores in your area that support your answer.

3. How are off-price discounters different from other discounters? What new directions are off-price stores taking?

4. How do general merchandise stores, such as Sears, differ from discount stores like Kmart?

5. What are the differences between a superstore and a hypermarket? In what circumstances do hypermarkets flourish? Will hypermarkets ever become popular in the United States?

6. Why do restaurants like the Hard Rock Cafe combine merchandise and entertainment with food?

7. To what degree are fast food restaurants global retailers? Give several examples to support your answer.

Endnotes

1. Harvey, Susan J. Presentation. Direct Marketing Educational Foundation. New York City. June, 1996.

2. Silverman, Dick. "Sparring for Space: Big Labels Brandish Their Clout at Retail." *Women's Wear Daily.* Strategic Information Systems Division of Fairchild Publications. February 5, 1998:1,4-5.

3. Lundgren, Terry. "The Economic Outlook for the Retail and Consumer Products Sector for 2002." Presentation. National Retail Federation Annual conference and Expo. New York. January 14, 2002.

4. Infotracs. *Women's Wear Daily.* June, 1997.

5. "Department Stores Fight an Uphill Battle Just to Stay Relevant." *Wall Street Journal.* March 12, 2002: A17.

6. Moin, David. "The Department Store Saga." Infotracs. *Women's Wear Daily.* June, 1997:10.

7. "Kmart Fun Facts." Kmart News Release. Troy, Michigan. Undated.

8. Barrett, Amy. "French Discounter Takes Cheap Chic World-Wide." *Wall Street Journal.* May 27, 1998:B1.

9. GUS, Burberry's Parent, Bids for Argos." *Women's Wear Daily.* February 4, 1998:4.

10. "Top 100 Retailers." *Chain Store Age.* State of the Industry Supplement. Section Two. August 1999

11. *Supermarket News.* "SN's Top 75." January 14, 2002: 20. and Top 200 Global Retailers." *Stores.* 2002 Global Powers of Retailing. Section 2. January, 2002:G8.

12. Coleman, Calmetta. "Albertson's Plans to Buy American Stores." *Wall Street Journal.* August 4, 1998:A3.

13. "Restaurant Industry Food-and-Drink Sales Projections Through 2002." *2002 Restaurant Industry Forecast Preview.* Accessed: http://www.restaurant.org. April 19, 2002.

14. "Tricon Global Restaurants to Acquire Long John Silver's and A&W All American Food Restaurants to Drive Multibranding Leadership." Press Release. March 12, 2002. http://www.triconglobal.com. Accessed: April 19, 2002.

15. Gibson, Richard. "Burger King Seeks New Sizzle." *Wall Street Journal.* April 14, 1999:B1.

16. VanKleek, Bruce. Presentation to the American Collegiate Retailing Association. National Retail Federation. Washington, DC. April, 1998.

Chapter 5

Ownership Dynamics

Learning Objectives

After completing this chapter you should be able to:

- Describe seven major forms of retail ownership.
- Relate the role independent, small business ownership plays in the economy.
- Note the causes and effects of merger, acquisition, diversification, and divestiture activity in retailing.
- Identify some of the major retail holding companies.

Figure 5.1 When the long-established Jordan Marsh department store changed its name to Macy's, reflecting its new ownership status, not all Boston shoppers were pleased. Ownership change has become a constant in retailing (See p.145). *Courtesy of Fairchild Publications, Inc.*

Keeping up with retail ownership changes is like charting a complex family genealogy. It is one of the most intriguing aspects of retailing. This chapter examines different types of retail ownership and incidents that change the structure of retailing including mergers, acquisitions, divestitures, and bankruptcy filings—often precursors to acquisition activity. Ownership turmoil began in earnest in the 1980s and has not yet subsided. Some major retail conglomerates have emerged in the United States and abroad as a result of this activity.

Seven Forms of Ownership

Seven major forms of retail store ownership include: independent retailers, corporate chains, franchised operations, leased departments, government-owned stores, and consumer cooperatives. Several nontraditional forms of ownership add to the variety.

Independent Retailers

independent retailer Single stores, multi-unit operations, or service businesses that are owned by an individual, partnership, or family.

Single stores, multi-unit operations, and service businesses owned by an individual, a partnership, or a family are called **independent retailers**. Retail stores owned by only one person are also called sole proprietorships. Independent retail stores can be incorporated under a variety of legal arrangements. About 80 percent of individual stores in the United States are independently owned, forming the largest ownership group in the United States. However, they only account for about 20 percent of total retail revenue. Many mom-and-pop operations and single-unit boutiques fall into this category. According to U.S. Census figures, there are more than 1 million small retail businesses in the United States.[1] There are untold millions worldwide.

Complicating the definition, many large regional or national retailers are also considered independents. Using a census of business approach, when the majority of the company stock rests with a few key individuals or within a family, the company is defined as independent. Nordstrom, in Seattle, Washington, and L.L. Bean in Freeport, Maine, are retailers that fit

Table 5.1 Key Statistics Regarding Minority-Owned Businesses

Ownership	Hispanic	Black	Asian
Number of Businesses*	1,401,531	881,646	1,055,641
Annual Receipts*	$183.8 billion	$59.3 billion	$275.1 billion
Number of Employees*	1,492,773	583,752	1,917,244
Percent of Total U.S. Self employed+	6.4%	5.2%	4.5%

Source: U.S. Small Business Administration, Office of Advocacy, based on data from the U.S. Department of Commerce, Bureau of the Censes, Survey of Minority-Owned Business Enterprises. Excerpted for summary purposes.
* Data estimated for 1997
+ Actual data for 1998

this definition. Limited Brands, one of the largest retail companies, with many divisions, is also considered independently owned. Size may not have a bearing on independent ownership status, but gender and ethnicity might.

According to the United States Small Business Administration (SBA), women are starting new businesses at twice the rate of all others, and own almost 40 percent of all firms in the United States. There were 8.5 million female-owned businesses in 1997.[2] Many in this number are independent retailers. Women who enter the field include:

- Minority women who feel the only way they can get a fair shake is to start their own business.
- Women with strong entrepreneurial interests and skills.
- Older women who left work to raise a family and find they are unable to get back into the labor force and find a job at their level of competence.
- Women who may have lost financial support due to the loss of a spouse through death, separation, or divorce.
- Younger women who are single heads of households and have to support and raise children without outside help.
- Employed women who cannot reach the level within their companies that their talents warrant in what they consider an acceptable time frame.

Between 1987 and 1997 minority-owned businesses grew 168 percent in the United States. The 3.25 million minority-owned businesses earned $495 billion in revenue in 1997. Hispanic-owned businesses accounted for the greatest share of growth, but Asian-American-owned firms generated 56 percent of the total revenue.[3] Statistics regarding minority-owned businesses are charted in Table 5.1.

From this brief look at the growth of female-owned and minority-owned firms, it is evident that the face of business is changing. Demographic and lifestyle changes affect ownership patterns in retailing.

Corporate Chains

Usually, 80 to 95 percent of the stores in any regional mall belong to large corporate chains. A string of 25 or more stores with identical or similar formats under central ownership is classified as a **corporate chain**. Normally, these chains are centrally managed and merchandise buying is done through central headquarters. In this text, a corporate chain will be considered any chain of more than 25 units of which no more than 50 percent of the stock is held by more than one person, family, or partnership. Four types of corporate chains include unified, segmented, manufacturer-based, and holding company formats.

Unified Format Sears, JC Penney, and Kmart are examples of retailers that own and operate the majority of their stores under the name of the parent company. These companies have central headquarters—Sears in Chicago Illinois; JC Penney in Plano, Texas; and Kmart in Troy, Michigan—where most strategic decisions are made. There are always exceptions. JC Penney operates all of its department stores under its name but also acquired the Eckerd drugstore chain, which continues to do business under that name. It also spun off its hard goods business and opened its Home Store division. The broad scope of unified format companies assures that each name has high customer recognition.

Segmented Format Many corporate chains have grown by purchasing other chains or establishing their own. The stores may not all adopt the name of the parent company as several examples show. Venator, originally the F.W. Woolworth company, operated no stores under its corporate name but owned chains such as Champ Sports and Foot Locker. Footwear sales drove the company's business so in 2001, Venator changed the name of its holding company to Footlocker. The Gap acquired Banana Republic, but has developed several other chains. Some names, such as GapKids and Baby-Gap, bear a strong resemblance to the parent company's. In 1998, the company created GapBody in an effort to draw market share away from Victoria's Secret, which dominated the intimate apparel market at that time. True to Gap tradition, styles are pared-down, not like the romantic

corporate chain A string of 25 or more stores with identical or similar formats under central ownership.

looks favored by Victoria's Secret.[4] Other holdings, such as Old Navy, are meant to stand on their own merits. Some acquired chains maintain independent headquarters; others are managed centrally.

Manufacturer-Based Format In several instances, manufacturers have evolved into retailers, shifting emphasis from one part of the marketing channel to another. Many apparel manufacturers including Liz Claiborne, Calvin Klein, and Donna Karan run factory outlet or other specialty store divisions. Liz Claiborne acquired Mexx, the Netherlands-based apparel retailer in 2001. Donna Karan is owned by the French Luxury Goods company, Louis Vuitton Moet Hennesy, a holding company.

Holding Company Format Huge conglomerates called **retail holding companies** are composed of many individual companies doing business under a variety of names. Retailing may or may not be the primary focus of a holding company. Many multinational holding companies are extremely large and powerful and do business across many related and unrelated product categories. **Multinational companies** conduct manufacturing, service and/or retail businesses in their home countries as well as many other countries. As examples, the French company Louis Vuitton Moet Hennessy (LVMH) owns several couture fashion houses including Christian Lacroix, John Galliano, Alexander McQueen, and its signature Louis Vuitton leather goods company, through its Louis Vuitton division. The company also owns Sephora fragrance and cosmetics stores, Thomas Pink shirtmakers, the DFS chain of duty free shops, and Synchrony watch stores, along with several timepiece manufacturers. Through its Moet Hennessy division it owns major wine and spirits companies. All divisions operate internationally.

Large conglomerates with no direct or obvious retail focus also own retail chains. Sara Lee Corporation, the multinational company known best for its packaged foods, also owns Coach as well as Hanes, Bali, Playtex, and Champion brands.

May Department Stores and Federated Department Stores are examples of U.S. holding companies whose chief interest is retailing. In both cases, department stores are the companies' chief holdings.

As retail emphasis shifts, so do corporate names. Dayton Hudson Company changed its name to Target in 2000 to better reflect the contributions of its discount store division to corporate profits. Target also owns Marshall Field, Dayton Hudson Department Stores, and Mervyn's, a mid-market department store division, that is shown in Figure 5.2.

Royal Ahold, the Dutch retailer, owns several U.S. supermarkets along with its global holdings. In Japan, Isetan owns not only a department store

Did You Know?
Venator means "sportsman" or "hunter" in Latin.

retail holding company Huge conglomerate composed of many individual companies doing business under a variety of names.

multinational company Company that conducts manufacturing, service and/or retail businesses in its home country as well as in many other countries.

Figure 5.2 Mervyns, the mid-market department store division of Target, is one of the anchors at Horton Center in downtown San Diego, California.

turnkey operation A methodically planned retail store or service that is completely ready to begin operation.

group but also many supermarkets and other retail establishments. It is also the major real estate investor in Barneys New York, an apparel retailer. These examples illustrate the complexity of holding company structure in the United States and the presence of strong multinational involvement.

Franchise Operations

Franchises are one means by which retailers expand globally. Estimates show that nearly half of all retail sales in the United States come from franchised locations.[5]

Retailers that purchase franchises are called *franchisees*. These retailers assume less risk than those that open businesses independently. Companies that sell franchise rights are called *franchisors*. Franchisors offer franchisees time-tested formats, strong brand recognition, management training, business plans, and many corporate support services. Accounting, hiring, training, site selection, advertising, and marketing assistance are available as well as trade name rights. However, franchisees also need adequate capital and managerial experience to run a successful operation.

Usually, for a flat fee and an ongoing percentage of sales paid by the franchisee, the franchisor will provide a methodically planned retail store or service that is completely ready to begin operation. Such an outlet is called a **turnkey operation**. Franchise fees can run from a low of a few thousand dollars for a lesser-known name to approximately $30,000 for a Dunkin' Donuts to several hundred thousand dollars for a McDonald's. Allied Domecq PLC, the British owner of Dunkin' Donuts, Baskin-Robbins ice cream, and Togo's sandwich shops, expects to open 5,000 *trombos* in the United States. A *trombo* is a combination store housing all three Allied Domecq franchises.[6] In 2002, Allied Domecq announced its intention to spin off Dunkin' Donuts.

One of the first franchises was sold in 1863, when the Singer Sewing Machine Company offered small stores the right to use its trade name and buy products from Singer. Times have changed. Almost all products or services—from hair salons to car washes, bagel to camera shops—are franchised. Service franchises such as Jazzercise and Century 21 real estate firms are also popular. Fast food franchises are making inroads in unconventional locations. Subway, Taco Bell, and Domino's Pizza have all established franchise agreements with high schools. Ayamas, an extension of the KFC franchise in Malaysia, is illustrated in Figure 5.3.

As a result of intensified franchising activity in the past three decades, franchise marketing firms have emerged as middlemen that link franchisor with franchisee. These firms help package a franchise for sale and then scour the market for qualified prospects as they aid the development of a retail empire.

Leased Departments

A unique form of ownership that is rarely apparent to customers, leased departments exist in most major department stores and in increasing numbers of discount and specialty stores. Introduced in Chapter 2, leased departments are often chains themselves. Some examples of departments that frequently are leased include jewelry, shoes,

Figure 5.3 Although KFC and White Castle are American franchises, Ayamas restaurants were developed to appeal more to Malay tastes. In downtown Alor Setar in northern Malaysia, it is a close neighbor to its parent company, KFC.

gift-wrapping, florist, beauty or eye-care shops, and restaurants. Meldisco, a division of Footstar, is an example of a leased shoe department chain. The company operates footwear departments in Kmart stores. Retailers welcome the diversity that leased departments bring to their merchandise mix, particularly in areas that are difficult to stock, manage, or service.

Most customers do not realize the department is not the store's own, which is the intent. Problems could surface if leased departments did not meld or if managerial inconsistencies were apparent. Leased departments usually pay a per-square-foot fee and a percentage of profits to the host store.

They are similar to concessions but differ in intent. **Concessions** are independently owned and operated departments that cross all product and service lines and are less dependent on special levels of management expertise than leased departments. Leased departments are used when products need special managerial or merchandising skills or are provided as auxiliary services. In some countries an entire retail store, or floor, may be comprised of concessions or leased departments. Nordiska Kompaniet (NK) is a Swedish department store that is made up entirely of leased departments. In the early 1990s, it converted from a traditional department store format because of increased competition and operating costs, and declining profits. Sweden is sparsely populated which makes it more difficult for retailers to sustain sales in the face of competition. NK had a well-established name

CYBERSCOOP

Visit Swedish retailer Hennes and Mauritz online at www.hm.com. Determine the company's ownership status. In how many countries does H&M operate? How long has it been an international retailer? Check out the merchandise. Would you like to shop at H&M?

concession Independently owned and operated departments that cross all product and service lines, and are less dependent on special levels of management expertise than leased departments.

CYBERSCOOP

Visit Postmark America®, the U.S. Postal Service retail store at www.usps.com/postmark. See what products you can find that appeal to new parents. Who is Eagie™?

government-owned store A store owned and operated by local, state, or federal government.

and high traffic in its eight stores. When the transition was made, many buyers and department managers became entrepreneurs, taking ownership in the departments where they were once employed. Many merchandise areas in Japanese department stores are also set up as concessions.

Government-Owned Stores

Though individual examples are few, government-owned stores are a significant contributor to the retail economy. **Government-owned stores** are those that are owned and operated by local, state, or federal governments. Examples cover a broad spectrum of store types and locales. Military families are the consumers at base exchanges or post exchanges, that are government-owned facilities where food and general merchandise can be purchased at lower prices than at comparable civilian stores.

The U.S. Postal Service, a quasi-governmental agency, owns Postmark America, a retail store at The Mall of America in Bloomington, Minnesota. The 33,000 post office outlets in the United States carry many retail products including stamps, packaging supplies, stationery, and even T-shirts and neck ties. Postmark America expanded the merchandise mix to include apparel, historical memorabilia, and gifts. Flight jackets like those worn by early air carriers are included in the Pony Express collection. Art work inspired by postage stamps and the stamps themselves are part of the Postmark Gallery group of merchandise. Japanese stamp collectors historically have been good customers of the U.S. Postal Service. Its "Import Boutique" catalogs and electronic kiosks make it possible for customers to place orders for merchandise in Japan.[7]

As other examples, in some states, including New Hampshire, liquor stores are state owned, and all proceeds on wines and spirits go into the state coffers. In Singapore, some general merchandise and food stores are government owned. In China, the government is a partner in every business venture proposed by foreigners, therefore also a retail owner.

Consumer Cooperatives

consumer cooperative Stores in which consumers own a stake, receive lower prices on merchandise, and may participate in profit sharing.

Although not a widespread phenomenon in the United States, consumer cooperatives are another form of retail ownership. **Consumer cooperatives** are stores in which customers own a stake, receive lower prices on merchandise, and may participate in profit sharing. Cooperatives are analogous to credit unions. Through a board of directors, members approve management to run the operation. For a token membership fee, consumers join and are then able to use financial services, receive preferred rates on personal loans, and vote for credit union directors. Consumer cooperatives usually sell general merchandise and food and are operated similarly.

Lower prices, profit sharing, and ready access are the motivations for belonging to a cooperative. The format is most prevalent in Scandinavia and Western Europe. Migros in Switzerland is an example of a consumer cooperative with a large membership and multiple-unit format. Approximately 80 percent of all Swiss consumers belong to Migros.

Membership in a cooperative should not be confused with membership in a warehouse club. Members of warehouse clubs do not own shares or participate in profit sharing, although both warehouse club and cooperative members enjoy the benefit of low pricing.

Nontraditional Owners

The quest for increased sales, profits, and growth has drawn nontraditional owners into retailing. Nonprofit organizations such as churches, hospitals, art galleries, and museums are prime examples. One of the most interesting is Smithsonian Retail, which operates shops in 16 of its museums in Washington, DC, and also at Reagan National and Baltimore-Washington airports. The company has been a direct marketer since 1977, offering a wealth of products—most inspired by the artwork and exhibits found in the museums' collections—through its catalogs and Web site. Between store and catalog annual sales, the Smithsonian is almost a $70 million retailer.[8]

Other examples illustrate profit-oriented firms from other industries that have become retail owners. The presence of an NBC Television Network store in New York City shows us that even media giants are exploring new methods of brand building and revenue generation. At the NBC Experience Store in Rockefeller Center, customers can browse interactive displays and purchase items inspired by their favorite sitcoms such as *Frasier* or *Friends*.

Club Med, a resort operator with high brand recognition, owns boutiques in its 130 vacation sites around the world. The company took a different approach to retail expansion when it developed apparel and accessories lines. The company sells its new lines not only through its existing boutiques, but also through new Club Med World sports centers and a European catalog. The company expects the strategies will increase retail presence and brand awareness.[9]

Health and fitness centers and dance studios are examples of service retailers that have added merchandise to their businesses. The large numbers of members and students that these businesses draw make it feasible to provide exercise-related merchandise on the premises. Business revenues grow

Did You Know?

Among the more popular items in the Smithsonian Museum's mail-order catalog is a Galileo Thermometer, adapted from weather instruments on display at the National Air and Space Museum.
Source: *Smithsonian Institution News.* "Smithsonian Retail Fact Sheet." Press Release. January 1998:3.

hostile takeover Ownership change that occurs when one company purchases large quantities of outstanding stock in another company giving controlling interest to the acquiring company.

because of retail expansion. Nontraditional ownership is expected to increase as more businesses explore the benefits of retail ownership.

Ownership Strategies

In order to continue on a growth pattern, many retailers must acquire other retailers, merge with existing companies, or create new formats. Acquisitions can be hostile or friendly, although hostile takeovers receive more public attention than innocuous mergers. An ownership change that occurs when one company purchases large quantities of outstanding stock in another company giving controlling interest to the acquiring company is called a **hostile takeover**. Developing entirely new formats is another way retailers remain competitive and expand their holdings. All strategies are important to retailers that are in the mature phase of their existence.

Mergers and Acquisitions

Throughout the last two decades, merger and acquisition activity has been occurring in all business sectors. Banking, insurance, real estate, and manufacturing companies have been touched deeply by consolidation. The retail industry is no exception. Department, specialty, drug, auto, grocery, and many other stores have experienced significant restructuring. It has been estimated that 10 companies now control half of all apparel sales in the United States.[10] Many newly formed retail entities have been successful; others have not. A look at the causes and effects of mergers and acquisitions will help clarify these business practices.

Causes and Effects Mergers and acquisitions have several basic causes:

- Companies may be less expensive to purchase because of stock market declines, currency fluctuations, or political unrest.
- Retailers with available capital in stable and thriving economies must find investments that will generate returns.
- Aggressive retail companies may need to acquire other companies in order to grow their businesses and remain competitive in a mature market.

There are several negative effects of mergers and acquisitions:

- Long-standing customers may be reticent to shop at what they perceive as a new store.

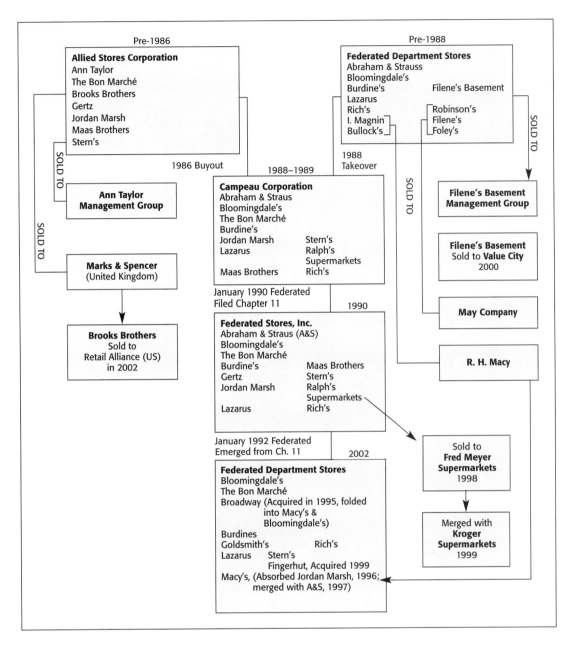

Figure 5.4 Evolution of Federated Department Stores (Selected Major Holdings) *Compiled from various trade news reports and www.federated-ads.com/companyhis*

- Changes of ownership causing changes in policies and procedures may be unsettling to employees.
- Long-standing retail chains may be gobbled up in the proceedings. History was made when Federated Department stores decided to fold many of its regional chains into its nationally recognized Macy's division. Jordan Marsh, a venerable Northeast regional chain became Macy's as illustrated in Figure 5.1. The evolution of Federated Department Stores is shown in Figure 5.4.

- When mergers abound, human resource cutbacks are inevitable.
- Takeover activity may bring nonretailers as retail partners. For example, Chemical Banking Corporation formed Chemical Venture Partners, a general partnership that now owns Parklane Hosiery, Gymboree (infants and children's wear), Domain Inc. (home furnishings), Art Mart (arts and crafts supplies), and Office Depot (discount office supplies). This company later merged with Chase Manhattan Bank.

On the other hand, mergers and acquisitions benefit retailers in many ways:

- Mergers bring an opportunity to capitalize on the strengths of both companies.
- The increased base of retail knowledge created when two companies join forces may make the organization more competitive.
- Economies of scale may be realized in many functional and managerial areas.
- Companies may significantly increase market share.
- Choice retail locations may be gained.

A merger or acquisition can also benefit an acquired company that may be too small to grow itself. The merger or acquisition could:

- Strengthen the company's retail position in the marketplace.
- Eliminate the threat of bankruptcy due to too rapid growth or lack of attention to changing consumer needs.
- Bring investment partners during periods of poor performance or economic downturn.
- Eliminate partnership conflicts.
- Expand a business for long-range investment potential.

As expected, when top retail executives were asked about the mergers or buyouts in their organizations, the majority viewed them negatively. Many felt that more government regulations against hostile takeovers should be enacted and that many takeovers could have been avoided if management had acted wisely. Not surprisingly, the majority felt that all retail companies are vulnerable and that takeovers have reduced the opportunities for young people entering the field.

The feelings of top retail executives were mixed regarding the effects of mergers on customers. Many who were surveyed felt that mergers ultimately raise prices, since new owners need to pay off excessive debts; others felt that a merger could strengthen a weak company.[11]

From the Field: Chronology of a Takeover: The Campeau Saga

December 1986 Company owned by Canadian real estate developer Robert Campeau bought the department store group, Allied Stores, for approximately $4 billion.

August 1987 Campeau considered Federated Stores for another possible takeover.

October 1987 The stock market crash dropped Federated stock to a low of $28 per share.

December 1987 Campeau began buying small amounts of Federated stock.

February 1988 Federated officially announced that it was negotiating a buyout with Campeau. Federated was negotiating with Macy's as well.

April 1988 Campeau agreed to buy Federated for more than $8 billion. As part of the agreement, Macy's would buy Bullock's and I. Magnin for $1.1 billion.

September 1989 All 17 units of the Bloomingdale's division were put up for sale. Marvin Traub, chairman and CEO of Bloomingdale's, considered a leveraged buyout of the store.

November 1989 The decision to sell Bloomingdale's was announced one week before the deadline for Campeau to obtain a commitment to repay a $400 million bridge loan or turn over 7 percent of the equity in Federated to the lenders, First Boston, Paine Webber, and Dillon Reed.

Campeau needed financing to buy Christmas stock for most of his stores and asked Olympia & York

Developments Ltd., of Toronto, for a $250 million loan. In exchange, Olympia & York gained 11 percent of Campeau Corporation.

In order for the Olympia & York loan to be approved, Campeau had to release his control of his organization to a senior executive management group, who would oversee the refinancing and restructuring of the company. Bloomingdale's was not sold.

January 1990 In Cincinnati on January 15, Federated Department Stores and Allied Stores Corporation filed petitions for Chapter 11 reorganization. Three days before the filing, Campeau paid out $100 million to creditors in checks that would bounce unless already cleared by the banks.

October 1990 Campeau was officially ousted as chairman and controlling shareholder of his own company. Campeau Corporation then officially became known as Federated Department Stores. Campeau had been the parent company of Federated Department Stores and Allied Stores Corporation.

January 1992 Macy's filed for Chapter 11 due to its large debts, the major recession, and declining sales over the previous two years.

February 1992 Federated emerged from bankruptcy.

March 1992 Federated units Abraham and Straus (A&S) and Jordan Marsh merged.

January 1994 Federated bought a 50 percent stake of the secured claim of Macy's largest creditor, Prudential Insurance Company of America. Macy's insisted that it would not be bought by Federated.

July 1994 Macy's merged with Federated Department Stores, giving Federated a 350 department store organization.

August 1994 Federated bought the 82 unit, California-based Broadway stores.

January 1995 A&S store in Manhattan became Sterns. The shopping center bearing the A&S name was renamed the Manhattan Mall.

April 1995 A&S flagship store in Brooklyn was renamed Macy's.

March 1996 Federated changed the name of Jordan Marsh to Macy's.

September 1996 Robert Campeau resurfaced in Germany where he was working as a residential housing developer in a small community outside Berlin.*

April 2002 Federated operated 457 department stores in 34 states, Guam, and Puerto Rico, and reported more than $15 billion in sales in 2001.+

Source: Rogers, Dorothy S. and Gamans, Lynda R. *Retailing: New Perspectives.* Harcourt Brace. 1992:125-126. Updates compiled from various trade sources.
* Steinmetz, Greg and Greenberg, Larry M. "Campeau Resurfaces, Not as a Store Owner But a German Builder." *Wall Street Journal.* September 16, 1996: A1.
+ http://www.federated-fds.com. Accessed: April 25, 2002.

Acquisition Parameters Retailers attempting to acquire other companies do so with care. They must be able to negotiate well and not pay too much for a company. Attention must be paid to locations, leasing arrangements, financial details, and the competition. Retailers must prepare in-depth evaluations before a merger or acquisition can occur. This process is called **due diligence**.

due diligence In-depth evaluation of financial and other details before a merger or acquisition can occur.

Figure 5.5 The purchase of Parisian department stores by Proffitt's was part of its master plan to become a national retailer. The interior of its Phipps Plaza store in Atlanta is artful and sophisticated.

leveraged buyout Purchases in which the acquiring company borrows large sums of money, using the yet-to-be-owned assets as collateral, in order to finance the deal.

Sound and sensible business decisions are the best reasons for undertaking mergers or acquisitions. However, some merger participants have been accused of greed and ego gratification—perhaps the most negative attributes of capitalist economy. No socially responsible business organization should condone selling assets to cover excessive debt, and therefore causing the loss of thousands of jobs in the process.

Leveraged Buyouts The most complicated and controversial takeovers are **leveraged buyouts.** These are purchases in which the acquiring company borrows large sums of money, using the yet-to-be-owned assets as collateral, in order to finance the deal. A classic case involved Canadian real estate developer Robert Campeau. It started with his acquisition of Allied Stores in 1986, and continued until his final disposition in 1990 as head of the multibillion dollar empire. His actions affected many retail institutions and individuals, and reverberations continued into the 1990s.

A chronology of selected events documenting the Campeau case appears in this chapter's From the Field. This saga involved Campeau, Allied, Federated, Macy's, and scores of others. This timeline and Figure 5.4 document one of the most embroiled ownership transitions in retail history.

The deep recession in the early 1990s increased frenetic merger and acquisition activity and made retailers more vulnerable to take over. The core reasons for the disruption within the industry remain clear. All retailers were coping with a maturing industry, an oversaturated retail market, increased competition, bankruptcy proceedings, and changing public sentiments.

Ownership Changes

The bubbling brew of merger and acquisition activity cooled only marginally by the new millenium. New patterns have emerged as retailers vie for position in the industry. Several pertinent examples illustrate recent trends in ownership changes. The acquisition activities of Proffitt's and Dillard's show many dimensions of strategic planning.

Proffitt's Purchase of Saks Fifth Avenue When Proffitt's purchased Saks Fifth Avenue for $2.14 billion in 1998, some viewed this as the action of an upstart. Proffitt's, however, had been preparing for the acquisition for some time. The Birmingham, Alabama, retailer had already purchased several strong regional department stores including McRae's in 1994; Parks-Belk in 1995; Parisian, Younkers, and Herberger's in 1996; and merged with Chicago retailer Carson Pirie Scott in 1997. Investcorp, a Bahrain company, had operated Saks Fifth Avenue since 1990. Prior to that, the company was owned by B.A.T. Industries of the United Kingdom and went public in 1996. With intentions of becoming a national powerhouse, the Saks Fifth Avenue acquisition propelled Proffitt's to its goal of attracting a more upscale market. Because of the high recognition and regard for the Saks brand, Proffitt's officially changed its name to Saks, Inc. The company operates approximately 360 stores in the United States and one in Saudi Arabia.[12] The company's Parisian store is illustrated in Figure 5.5. This example demonstrates the intricacies of acquisition strategy and the complexities of ownership from a historical perspective.

Dillard's Acquisition Strategies

Arkansas retailer Dillard's added to its department store holdings over the years, purchasing regional chains such as Joske's, Maison Blanche, and Stix Baer & Fuller. In a joint venture with mall developer DeBartolo, Dillard's bought 50 percent of Ohio-based Higbee's in 1988.

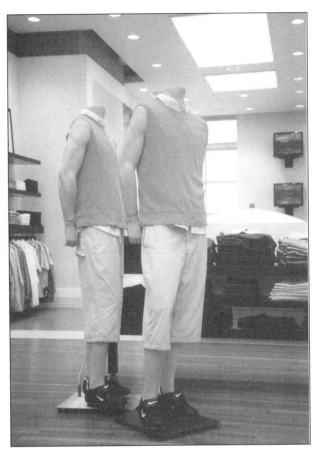

Figure 5.6 When Club Monaco was acquired by Ralph Lauren it was considered a good match since both companies focus on tasteful, minimalist design. The sleek imagery of the menswear department in the Club Monaco store on Bloor Street in Toronto reinforces that point.

A holdout independent retailer, Dillard's did not add a nonfamily shareholder until 1991, when, Vendamerica BV, a division of Vendex International located in the Netherlands, became part of the organization. Analysts were not surprised when the company purchased Mercantile Stores for 2.9 billion in 1998.[13] Mercantile stores served a similar clientele. The acquisition added 120 stores to Dillard's holdings. Some were later sold to May Company and Saks to avoid duplication within markets. The company operated approximately 400 department stores as of 2000.

When Dillard's, acquires two locations in the same mall, it frequently keeps both. One is converted to a women's, children's, and home furnishings store, and the other becomes a men's and junior's operation. Dillard's has considerable presence in malls where it has two anchors.[14] This practice

Figure 5.7 Barneys presents New York chic merchandise in its Madison Avenue facility and survived three years of ownership conflagration with Japan's Isetan.

illustrates another successful tactic born of changes in ownership.

Ralph Lauren's Acquisition of Club Monaco Ralph Lauren made an unprecedented move when it acquired a Canadian specialty retailer in 1999. Lauren was aware of the growth potential of Club Monaco and felt an affinity with the company since both cater to customers with refined taste levels. Club Monaco carries understated, contemporary merchandise that is stylish, yet ageless. Through its lifestyle concept formats, it sells men's and women's apparel, accessories, and cosmetics. The company operates several outlet stores and maintains an e-commerce site. With an influx of Ralph Lauren capital, the company is expected to add 200 stores in the United States (See Figure 5.6).[15]

The Demise of Merry-Go-Round Frenzied growth and acquisition activity gone awry epitomizes the demise of Merry-Go-Round. Established in the late 1960s, the Maryland-based apparel retailer blossomed in the late 1980s and early 1990s, filed for bankruptcy protection in 1994, and by early 1996, ceased operations entirely.[16]

At its height, the retailer owned approximately 1,450 stores. They included Merry-Go-Round, which carried unisex apparel; Cignal, Dejaiz, Attivo, Chess King, and Fashion Outlets, which were predominantly menswear chains; and Boogies Diners.[17]

Much of the company's expansion was due to aggressive store openings of its signature division and opportunistic purchases of regional chains. In its prime the company was highly rated for several reasons:

- Its merchandise mix, consisting of 75 percent national brands and 25 percent private label goods.
- Its experienced merchandising staff and state of the art information technology systems.
- Its adeptness at spotting trends for its 14-year-old to 25-year-old target market.[18]

Paralleling the shift from rock and roll to alternative music, Merry-Go-Round's market also changed. The deep recession brought a reduction in teen spending coupled with less interest in dressy merchandise. Overinventoried and over-extended, the company unsuccessfully attempted to right itself. The one time high-flyer crashed and become another retail statistic.

The drama continued as Merry-Go-Round filed suit against a major consulting firm that the company had hired to help avert bankruptcy. Merry-Go-Round accused the consulting firm of ineptness and unethical behavior. The retailer contended that the consultants had not moved fast enough to improve Merry-Go-Round's position and had conflicts of interest. The consulting firm had not disclosed that it had prior business dealings with the law firm that recommended the consulting firm to Merry-Go-Round. The retailer also alleged that the consulting firm had done business with the landlord of some of its stores. Had the bankruptcy proceedings been handled more expediently, the stores would have been closed, and the landlord would have lost business. The case was settled in favor of Merry-Go-Round for $135 million in 1999.[19] The ramifications of bankruptcy dealings sometimes continue long after the fact.

The Barneys-Isetan Conflict The resolution of a bitter ownership conflict between Barneys and Isetan Ltd., a key investor in Barneys, dragged on for over three years. Barneys began as a New York City menswear retailer in 1923, and became a purveyor of fine merchandise for men, women, children, and the home in its select sites in the United States and Japan. Isetan is a Japanese holding company, owner of department stores in Japan, Singapore, China, Taiwan, Thailand, and Malaysia. Barneys New York store is featured in Figure 5.7.

The dispute centered on allegations of fraud and conflicts regarding the partnership that was established in 1989, between the Pressman family—owners of Barneys—and Isetan. The Japanese company had extended loans and conveyed real estate to Barneys as part of the agreement. These factors plus cash flow problems forced Barneys to file for bankruptcy protection in 1996. The company turned a profit the following year and emerged from bankruptcy proceedings in 1999. At one point in the conflict, Dickson Concepts, another holding company from Hong Kong, extended an offer to purchase Barneys but was rejected.

The closing of the company's original flagship store in lower Manhattan and the establishment of its new headquarters in midtown were also products of the tumultuous 1990s. Other sites were closed as the company worked to strengthen its position.

Under the terms of the agreement to settle the dispute, Isetan became the owner of Barneys stores in Chicago, Beverly Hills, and New York City. Creditor debt was converted into 93.5 percent equity in Barneys and Isetan received $25.6 million in cash.[20] Other terms of the agreement changed the ownership proportions in other holdings of the partnership. The arrangement may appear one-sided, but at least Barneys remains a retailer.

In a move that surprised many industry insiders, Allen Questrom was named chairman and CEO of Barneys New York in 1999. The well-respected Questrom is the retired head of Federated Department Stores, which he was instrumental in bringing out of bankruptcy after the Campeau issue in 1993. He was a director of Barneys prior to his appointment.[21] Later Questrom left Barneys to head J.C. Penney.

As these examples have shown, acquisitions, bankruptcies, and ownership conflicts are propelled by a variety of factors. These dynamics are expected to continue in the early 21st century.

Diversification and Divestiture

diversification Acquiring or developing stores that are not directly related to a company's core business.

The practice of acquiring or developing stores that are not directly related to a company's core business is called **diversification**. Some department store groups have added specialty store chains; mass merchandisers followed suit, adding stores and retail services. Specialty store chains that built their businesses selling apparel, later acquired accessory, lingerie, and bath product shops. They also added sporting goods chains and catalogs. Diversification strategy works best when the economy is strong and competition is low.

As competition gets stiffer, some large companies sell off portions of their businesses so that the end result is more manageable units. Specialty store businesses often divest companies that are underperformers or out of character with other holdings. Some retail companies form entire new divisions, grouping similar chains together. Two examples illuminate these points.

When it formed its Intimate Brands division in the mid-1990s, The Limited created an environment where Victoria's Secret and Bath & Body Works could flourish. The Limited also sold its Brylane catalog businesses to the French company Redoute to concentrate on its store business. In 2002, however, The Limited bought back its outstanding stock in Intimate Brands and changed its corporate name to Limited Brands.

Melville, originally a shoe manufacturer, formed Footstar to consolidate its retail footwear enterprises into one company. It divested most of its non-shoe and drugstore holdings, including Wilson's: The Leather Experts and CVS Corporation, and now operates under the Footstar name.

Diversification and divestiture remain tools retailers use to gain or re-acquire a competitive edge. Timing, company goals, and conditions in the retail environment dictate which technique should be used.

Retail failure rates are growing in the United States. In 1997, slightly more than 15,000 retail companies of all sizes went out of business. This figure represents a failure rate of 79 businesses per 10,000 companies.[22] Examples used throughout this chapter indicate that the reasons for retail demise are complex. However, superficial indications of a retailer's impending failure often include the following:

■ changes in a store's regular ordering or routine.

■ irregular or slow payments to vendors.

■ sparse inventories.

These conditions may be apparent whether the retailer is a huge corporation or a single unit store.

After all of the mergers, acquisitions, diversification, divestitures, and bankruptcies, one fact remains: retailing will never be the same. Stores that survive these changes will become larger, stronger, more powerful, and more profitable operations. Undoubtedly there will be more surprises for retailers and customers this century.

Summary

The seven major forms of retail ownership are independent retailers, corporate chains, franchised operations, leased departments, government-owned stores, consumer cooperatives, and nontraditional owners.

Although there are more independent retailers than any other group, more volume is done in the corporate sector. Major retail holding companies are often multinational firms, doing business in many countries. More women and ethnic minorities in the United States are buying or developing retail stores.

Franchising is an important form of retail ownership. Risks of doing business are somewhat less than in other forms of ownership because franchisees purchase time-tested formats. Almost all retail products and services can be franchised.

The reasons for mergers and acquisitions have been basically economic. Retailers must sell nonperforming units and purchase those that will give them a competitive advantage. In saturated markets, these strategies help retailers continue to grow their businesses.

Corporate ownership is complex and ever changing. In the future, fewer holding companies will exist, and those that withstand merger and acquisition procedures probably will be stronger as a result. It is expected that ownership changes will continue in the 21st century.

Questions for Review and Discussion

1. What are seven major forms of retail ownership? Why are there so many options available to retailers?

2. What are leased departments, and what purposes do they serve? How do they differ from concessions?

3. Assume you are interested in purchasing a franchise. What are the advantages and disadvantages of franchising as a form of retail ownership?

4. What types of nontraditional organizations are buying or developing retail stores? Why?

5. Select a major retail company and update its holdings. How have they changed in the past five years?

6. Why has extensive merger and acquisition activity in retailing taken place in recent years? What are effects of this activity on retailers and consumers?

7. How did changes in ownership status affect Proffitt's, Dillard's, Club Monaco, Merry-Go-Round, and Barneys?

Endnotes

1. Retail Industry Indicators. "Number of Retail and Food Service and Drinking Establishments Per Firm." The Trade Partnership for the NRF Foundation. Washington, D.C. August, 2001: 33.

2. www.sba.gov/womeninbusiness. "Changing the Face of America's Economy." U.S. Small Business Administration. January, 2000.

3. "New Report on Growth of Minority-Owned Businesses." U.S. Small Business Administration. Office of Advocacy. http://www.sba.gov/advo/press/99-16.html. January, 2000.

4. Coleman, Calmetta Y. "The Gap Plans Panty Raid on Victoria's Secret." *Wall Street Journal.* October 1, 1998:B1.

5. *Franchise Annual Directory.* Info Franchise News, Inc. 1998.

6. Gobson, Richard. "Franchising. Make Sure to Read Between the Web Lines." *Wall Street Journal.* May 14, 2001: R12.

7. DeShields, Kay. Presentation to the American Collegiate Retailing Association. U.S. Postal Service. Washington, D.C. April, 1998.

8. Smithsonian Institution News. "Smithsonian Retail Fact Sheet." Press Release. January 1998.

9. Weisman, Katherine. "Club Med Shops to Showcase Own Brand." *Women's Wear Daily.* November 18, 1999:10.

10. Alsop, Ronald. "Business Bulletin." *Wall Street Journal.* April 29, 1999:A1.

11. Neisner, Lewis J. "Mergers and Acquisitions in Retailing as Viewed by Retailing Executives." Paper presented to the American Collegiate Retailing Association. Key Biscayne, Florida. April 1990.

12. *Saks Incorporated History.* Corporate Fact Sheet. Birmingham, Alabama, March, 2001.

13. "Dillard's Beats Estimates with Increase of 8% in 2nd-Quarter Profit." *Wall Street Journal.* August 13, 1998: B9.

14. *Hoover's Company Profile Database.* "Dillard's Inc." 1998. http://web.lexis-nexis.com.univers. November, 1998.

15. Club Monaco. Presentation by management team. American Collegiate Retailing Association Spring Conference. Toronto. May 4, 2000.

16. "Retailer to Stop Operating Due to Lack of Financing." *Wall Street Journal.* February 5, 1996:B5.

17. Emert, Carol. "375 More MGR Stores, Scheduled to Be Closed." *Women's Wear Daily.* November 14, 1995.

18. D'Innocenzio, Anne. "Merry-Go-Round's Rollercoaster." *Women's Wear Daily.* August 5, 1992:10-11.

19. MacDonald, Elizabeth and Paltrow, Scot J. "Merry-Go-Round, Ernst & Young Advised the Client, but Not About Everything." *Wall Street Journal.* August 10, 1999:A1,12.

20. Moin, David and Young, Vicki M. "End of Ch.11? Barneys, Isetan Reach Accord." *Women's Wear Daily.* May 21, 1998:1,14.

21. Quick. Rebecca. "Barneys New York Names Questrom, A Retailing Veteran, as Chairman, CEO." *Wall Street Journal.* May 6, 1999:B11.

22. *Retail Industry Indicators.* National Retail Institute. National Retail Federation. Washington DC. May 1999: 22.

Chapter 6

Direct Marketing and Selling

Learning Objectives

After completing this chapter you should be able to:

- Summarize why many customers choose to shop in nonstore environments.

- Differentiate between direct marketing and direct selling.

- List the advantages and disadvantages of catalog retailing and telemarketing from both retail and customer perspectives.

- Explain some of the alternative methods of nonstore retailing including vending, auctions, flea markets, mobile retailing, and temporary site retailing.

- Deduce the scope and importance of the retailing services sector.

Figure 6.1
In addition to the quintessential L.L. Bean catalog, the company has several specialty versions including L.L. Bean Home. All are characterized by distinctive, appealing photos and artwork and are distributed around the world (See p. 166).

Previous chapters stressed how brick-and-mortar retail stores have changed along with the customers they serve. This chapter looks at retailers that do business through nonstore formats. There are many nonstore alternatives including direct marketing and direct selling. Both reach the customer through direct-to-home techniques. Direct marketing uses nonpersonal means involving the Internet, telephones, fax, mail, magazines, newspapers, radio, and television. Direct selling uses personal methods such as one-on-one or group situations.

Retailing of services is important in our time-pressured society. Many service businesses do not operate out of traditional storefronts. Flea markets and swap meets, auctions, mobile retailers, marketplace carts, and the vending industry are other aspects of nonstore retailing that are considered in this chapter.

Although the terms were introduced in Chapter 2, the distinction between direct marketing and direct selling needs further explanation. The Direct Marketing Association defines direct marketing as: "any direct communication to a consumer or business recipient designed to generate a response in the form of an order (direct order), a request for further information (lead generation), or a visit to a store or other place of business for the purchase of specific products or services (traffic generation)."[1] Direct marketing advertising pieces are characterized by the sense of immediacy that they convey to the customer. Many brick-and-mortar retailers use direct marketing techniques to reach their customers.

Direct selling, in contrast to direct marketing, is a personal form of selling that involves meeting with the customer face-to-face. The Direct Selling Association provides this definition: "Direct selling is the sale of a consumer product or service, person-to-person, away from a fixed retail location."[2] Depending on the company, the salespeople may be called distributors, representatives, consultants, or various other titles. Products are sold primarily through in-home product demonstrations, parties, and one-on-one selling. Direct selling also occurs in the workplace as representatives set up displays during coffee or lunch breaks or after work.

Reasons for Nonstore Retailing Growth

Many factors have influenced the growth of nonstore retailing, and impressive predictions affirm its importance in the future. The need for convenience, reduced stress, safety, and the desire for lifestyle enhancement all contribute to nonstore retailing growth. Advanced technology plays a big role in the expansion of direct marketing and selling formats.

Customer Convenience

Whether an individual is looking for an epicurean selection of frozen foods or automobile insurance, the physical process of shopping is made easier by the direct marketing process. If customers want to experiment with new cosmetics in the privacy of their homes, direct selling may be the answer. Sometimes, salespeople in retail stores are not helpful or knowledgeable. Stores may not be open at the moment a person perceives the need to buy. In stores, the retail process influences and somewhat controls the customer. This is also true of direct selling. In direct marketing, however, the customer controls the process to a large degree. For some, the flexibility of direct marketing is an attractive alternative to the relatively inflexible process of retail shopping. Examples illustrating these nuances appear in this chapter.

Nonstore shopping is more convenient for elderly or disabled shoppers, who may not be able to access traditional stores. Families living in rural areas also benefit from direct marketing and selling. Most people think twice about taking extra hours out of a normally hectic day to drive to the nearest shopping center if it is 50 miles away. For most customers, saved time is worth money.

Reduced Stress and Increased Safety

Some customers are finding that patronizing direct marketing and selling firms diminishes stress in their lives. Not all individuals were born to shop, and for those that do not find mall shopping exciting or therapeutic, nonstore methods are enticing. Parents who do not find carting children on extensive shopping expeditions particularly fulfilling also embrace direct marketing and selling.

Many cities of the world experience intense traffic congestion. Customers who experience gridlock on highways benefit from nonstore retailing. They do not have to sit on a freeway for hours waiting to go five miles to their local mall. Environmentalists also concur on this point. They per-

CYBERSCOOP

Retail services are provided online as well as through traditional channels. Visit **www.reflect.com** to see how this Proctor & Gamble beauty site will customize makeup and skin care products for you. How would you design your signature fragrance?

ceive that some forms of direct marketing and selling contribute less to transportation emission pollution and wasted energy.

In parts of some cities crime retards retail patronage. Direct marketing in particular is attractive to customers who are not comfortable on the streets or in a mall at night. For consumers who feel threatened by terrorist activity, direct marketing is a viable alternative to large, heavily populated shopping centers.

New Communications Technology

Several important developments were catalysts for the growth of direct marketing. The U.S. Postal Service introduced ZIP codes in the 1960s. ZIP codes enable direct marketers to reach target markets residing in specific geographic areas more easily. Universal credit cards also were developed in the sixties, and the mailing lists of credit card companies made the first large-scale database marketing possible. **Database marketing** is the process of gathering, maintaining, and using demographic, psychographic, and behavioral data on customers. Computer technology has made possible sophisticated data collection and **data mining**, which involves probing a database for pertinent information that can be used to target future offers to customers. Advanced systems greatly help direct marketers reach, understand, and satisfy their customers.

database marketing The process of gathering, maintaining, and using demographic, psychographic, and behavioral data on customers.

data mining Probing a database for pertinent information that can be used to target future offers to customers.

More television channels are available through cable, satellite, and fiber optic technology, bringing more opportunity for electronic retailers. E-retailing is providing new avenues for retailers that choose to sell direct. Because of its importance as a direct marketing medium, this nonstore format is discussed in the next chapter. As more retailers use direct marketing and direct selling, they are finding that the methods are not competitive with retail stores but complementary to them.

Direct Marketing

Direct marketing reflects the social and economic fiber of a society together with the lifestyles of its members. The following facts lay the groundwork for the discussion of direct marketing and its significance to retailers:

◼ Women make up more than 50 percent of the U.S. labor force. They are the primary family purchasing agents.
◼ Bankcards provide people with a universal credit system. Electronic banking and cashless systems mentioned in Chapter 2 make direct marketing easier.

Table 6.1 Value of U.S. Direct Marketing Driven Sales Compared to Total U.S. Sales (Billions of Dollars)

	2000	2001	2005	Compound Annual Growth 95-00	00-05
Consumer DM Sales	$937.7	$1019.2	$1396.8	9.1%	8.3%
Direct Order	306.6	332.4	450.8	8.8	8.0
Lead Generation	452.8	492.9	685.6	9.4	8.1
Traffic Generation	178.3	194.4	265.0	9.2	8.2
Total U.S. Consumer Sales	$7,195.7	$7,554.4	$9,040.6	6.5%	4.7%
DM Consumer Sales Percent of Total Sales	13%	13.5%	15.4%		

Source: Direct Marketing Association. Economic Impact: *U.S. Direct & Interactive Marketing Today.* New York, 2002.

- ■ Specialty catalogs now account for the bulk of mail-order volume. Mail order is not the exclusive domain of generalists like JC Penney and Spiegel as it once was.
- ■ More than half of the U.S. population orders merchandise or services by mail or telephone.
- ■ Direct marketing provides a means for small businesses to enter the marketplace.
- ■ Sales generated by direct marketers in the United States and abroad are vast and are expected to grow.

Consumer-driven direct marketing sales in the United States reached $937.7 billion in 2000. That number was expected to exceed $1.3 trillion by 2005.[3] Growth in direct marketing sales attributed to consumers outpaces total U.S. retail sales. Figures documenting this fact, broken down into direct order, lead generation, and traffic generation sales, are shown in Table 6.1. Of items ordered by mail, phone, or Internet the greatest number of sales tend to be in clothing and music.

Catalogs, direct mail pieces, coupons, and sweepstakes offers have been used by direct marketers for some time. In the past, these tactics were used mainly by firms that concentrated exclusively on mail order as a method of selling. They were often looked down on by retailers, manufacturers, and even by some individuals. Now retailers set up Web sites, issue all manner of specialty catalogs, use telemarketing, and send out complex and effective direct mail pieces. The best synchronize these activities as they fulfill the needs of customers who prefer to shop at home or work.

CYBERSCOOP

A challenge to all direct marketers is to keep track of customers, who are constantly on the move. Go to **www.cleanlist.com** to see what this Canadian company can do to refine mailing lists for its customers. What does *cleaning* mean?

Direct Marketing Mechanics

Like all specialized business areas, direct marketing comes with its own vocabulary and ways of operating. Practitioners speak of prospecting, mailing lists, and fulfillment. Other terms, such as lifetime value and customer resource management, extend to broader business usage. Some specialized terms include:

- *Prospecting.* Seeking qualified potential customers through screening and analysis of database information is called prospecting. Most direct marketers indicate that future customers are very much like present customers. They follow a birds-of-a-feather-flock-together philosophy when identifying new prospects.
- *Mailing lists.* Collections of names and addresses of present or potential customers comprise mailing lists. Lists can be compiled in-house through use of retail charge account holders, developed through secondary sources such as club memberships or census information, rented from list brokers, or even bartered between two companies.
- *Merge/Purge.* The practice of updating lists or removing duplicate or non-performing names from a list is called merge/purge.
- *Predictive modeling.* Examining data involving recency, frequency, and monetary value (RFM) of past sales in order to identify key prospects is a special form of predictive modeling.
- *Fulfillment.* The practice of using physical distribution systems efficiently to deliver products to consumers in a timely manner is called fulfillment.
- *Lifetime value.* Direct marketers acknowledge that the true worth of a customer to a company is not based on one large or a few occasional sales, but on sales generated over a long period of time called the lifetime value of the customer.
- *Customer relationship management (CRM).* The total company effort to satisfy the needs of all customers forms the core of CRM.

These terms provide a framework for understanding the unique operations that are performed in the industry. They also introduce many attributes that form the core of direct marketing.

Global Direct Marketing

Direct marketing is practiced worldwide. In fact, some of the largest direct mail companies are European. The ease with which customers can be reached, their response rates, and their attitudes toward privacy differ dramatically.

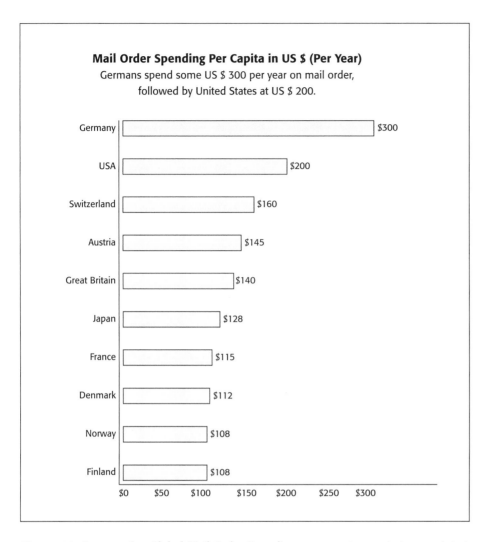

Figure 6.2 **Comparative Global Mail-Order Spending** *Source: Direct Marketing Association's Statistical Fact Book, 2001, and Deutsch Post Global Mail, 2000. (Used with permission.)*

According to the Direct Marketing Association, other than the United States, the five markets that generated the most direct marketing revenue are Japan, Germany, United Kingdom, Italy, and France.[4] Mail-order customers in Germany spend more per capita than individuals in the United States.[5] Comparative mail-order spending in several countries is shown in Figure 6.2. Fascinating contrasts are apparent when examining global direct marketing practices. Four examples illustrate different challenges that direct mail companies face:

■ *Personal mailbox use.* In Australia, private companies can use personal mailboxes for independently delivered direct mail pieces. The practice is prohibited in the United States and many other countries.

- *Postal rate increases.* Postal rate increases affect direct mailings worldwide. Authorities in Mexico implemented an average 30 percent postal rate increase in 1999.[6] Increases of this magnitude are bound to negatively influence direct mail and catalog companies.

- *Availability of workers.* In some areas, envelope sorters and stuffers are difficult to hire. Occasionally in Costa Rica, Boy Scouts and high school bands have been hired for the task.[7]

- *Receptiveness to unsolicited mail.* In Germany, customers are not as receptive to unsolicited mail as in the United States. Direct mail companies face challenges as they expand their networks internationally.

- *Response rate differences.* Direct marketing companies receive a very high response rate from customers in certain parts of the world. Households in developing countries have not been deluged with direct mail pieces and therefore view mailings as a novelty and take an interest in them.

- *Creative adaptation.* The writing of copy for direct marketing pieces also varies by country. For example, writing an advertising piece in which the word *color* is used necessitates different spellings. For Malaysia or Hong Kong, British form is suitable so the word is spelled *colour.* If creating the piece for Japan or the Philippines, an American form is proper, so *color* would be used. Despite higher costs, many direct marketing firms use local copywriters to translate copy into appropriate languages and print separate versions of a catalog.

There are many benefits to using direct marketing internationally. For retailers it may be an ideal way to introduce their products into a new territory. By cutting out middlemen and increasing gross margins, they may find a competitive edge and have more money to invest in sales promotion and advertising. The key to international direct marketing lies in the ability of practitioners to learn how to find the information and resources they need, use them effectively, and adapt to local business practices.

Catalog Retailing

Sears was one of the first retailers in the United States to sell through catalogs—launching its first in the late 1800s. Sears later discontinued its large format catalogs, but instead launched a small gift version in 1999. JC Penney's catalog business became stronger as a result.

Major stores like Bloomingdale's, Lord & Taylor, and Neiman Marcus have established thriving mail-order operations. Abercrombie and Fitch publishes a **magalog,** which is a combination magazine and catalog published by a retailer and distributed in stores or by direct mail. Magalogs include product pitch and editorial content. Otto Versand, a German catalog

magalog Combination magazine and catalog published by a retailer and distributed in stores or by direct mail.

Table 6.2 Top 20 United States Catalog Companies

Rank	Companies	Headquarters	2000 Sales (In Millions)
1	Dell Computer Corp.	Round Rock, TX	$31,890.0
2	International Business Machines Corp.	White Plains, NY	7,500.0
3	W.W. Grainger	Lincolnshire, IL	4,977.0
4	Corporate Express North America	Broomfield, CO	4,054.3
5	JC Penney Co.	Piano, TX	3,834.0
6	CDW Computer Centers	Vernon Hills, IL	3,800.0
7	Office Depot	Delray Beach, FL	3,600.0
8	Staples	Westborough, MA	2,955.0
9	Micro Warehouse	Norwalk, CT	2,564.8
10	Henry Schein	Melville, NY	2,381.7
11	Fisher Science	Burr Ridge, IL	2,164.0
12	Insight Enterprises	Tempe, AZ	2,041.1
13	Federated Department Stores	New York, NY	1,940.0
14	Spiegel	Downers Grove, IL	1,711.2
15	Systemax	Port Washington, NY	1,686.0
16	VWR Scientific Products	West Chester, PA	1,531.0
17	PC Connection	Merrimack, NH	1,450.0
18	Brylane	New York, NY	1,400.0
19	Lands' End	Dodgeville, WI	1,355.0
20	L.L. Bean	Freeport, ME	1,110.0

Source: *Catalog Age Magazine* "The Catalog Age 100 . . ." August, 2001 Issue

company, purchased Spiegel in 1982. In turn, Spiegel owns Eddie Bauer and Newport News, bringing a dimension of grand scale retailing to the industry. Spiegel is profiled at the end of this unit.

There were 16.6 million catalogs mailed in the United States in 2000.[8] Never before have catalog shoppers had so many kinds of merchandise from which to choose. Catalog companies are offering everything from expensive writing instruments to environmentally safe vacuum cleaners, apparel for tall men and petite women, beds for dogs, and paraphernalia for cat lovers. Table 6.2 lists the top 15 U.S. catalog companies. This listing includes business-to-business companies so that readers can see where consumer catalog companies rank industrywide. Some, like Gateway, serve both consumer and business markets.

Categories of Catalog Retailers Three distinct categories in catalog retailing exist:

- ■ *Pure catalog companies.* Businesses that operate no (or very few) stores, only catalog businesses. Examples include Lillian Vernon and Hanover Direct.
- ■ *Multichannel retailers.* Brick-and-mortar retail stores that have catalog operations, sometimes run as separate divisions. Examples include department

carryover The amount of time between a person's receipt of a catalog or advertisement and the actual sale.

and specialty store retailers such as Bloomingdale's, Macy's, Neiman-Marcus, Brookstone, Victoria's Secret, Disney Stores, Delia's, Wet Seal, and L.L. Bean. All of these retailers also operate Web sites. Several L.L. Bean specialty catalogs are illustrated in Figure 6.1.

■ *Nonretail companies.* Businesses that previously did not operate retail ventures that have entered the catalog field. Airlines and tobacco manufacturers are prime examples.

Catalog and Store Comparisons A major difference between brick-and-mortar stores and catalog retailing is that carryover time is longer from catalogs than from item advertising done by stores. **Carryover** is the period of time between a person's receipt of a catalog or advertisement and the actual sale.

Another difference is that catalogs create mood through design, layout, photography, and paper quality, while retail stores rely on lighting, carpeting, music, and other elements to create ambiance. Different sensory stimulation is used.

Stores depend on foot traffic while catalog retailers aim for repeat sales from a captive audience in their homes. Stores rely on a continuous influx of new merchandise, while catalogs are able to present a significant percentage of repeat items. Some companies send the exact same catalog under two different covers at close time intervals to different customers. Subtle changes like this are often made to test the strength of cover merchandise.

In terms of inventory management, a store can sell comparable items or suggest a switch to another item when something is out of stock. Direct marketers must backorder or cancel the order. In stores, inventory levels are planned in relation to overall sales and stock turn desired, while in direct marketing, commitments are made to fulfill each item's projected demand. If catalog sales expectations are not met, merchants may choose to sell overstocked items to off-price stores and clearance specialists, or might publish sale catalogs themselves.

Finally, measures of productivity differ. Many catalog retailers analyze sales per square inch of catalog page, while most stores measure sales per square foot of floor space.

Multichannel Implications Strategies designed to integrate store, catalog, and Internet retailing are producing interesting consequences. In a study done for a major leather goods company, a consultant reached the following conclusions:

■ An average Web order is 12 percent lower than a brick-and-mortar retail store order, but similar to an average catalog order.

From the Field: E-tailers Click and Flip to Attract More Shoppers
By Sal Ferraro

Brick-and-mortar, Internet-only, click-and-mortar—now there is a new category of retailer emerging: click-and-flip, or companies that market via the Internet and catalogs.

Catalogers were quick to build online stores as Internet-only start-ups were encroaching on their business. Now, many companies that started as Internet-only retailers have joined the ranks of click-and-flip by launching a print counterpart to their Web sites.

Why are these new economy organizations embracing a channel that some feared would be extinct? The goals of catalog programs certainly vary by company. However, there are some common objectives across most organizations.

Identify remote shoppers. There are some unique characteristics of both online and catalog shoppers, or "remote shoppers." They are comfortable providing credit card information over the phone or online and feel secure about the transaction. There is not a great need for this segment to touch and feel the product before the purchase, provided that product presentation is clear and the customers trust the brand. They can obtain shipment of products either at home or work. They enjoy the exploration for new and unique products and enjoy shopping at their own convenience around-the-clock. Online buyers tend to buy from catalogs more often than the average U.S. household.

Internet-only retailers are finding that by launching a catalog, they are able to find buyers who purchase similar products remotely. They also benefit from the targeting tools the direct marketing industry has developed, such as cooperative databases like Abacus.

Drive traffic. Companies have invested significant amounts of money on their e-commerce infrastructures, and they now need to drive traffic to their sites and deliver results. E-tailers look at their catalog efforts differently than traditional catalogers; their objective is not necessarily to make the sale via the catalog but rather to inspire a person to purchase online. E-tailers generally use their catalog to feature a sampling of the broader product offering available on their site. They also use the catalog to communicate all of the added benefits of shopping online such as special offers, detailed product information, lifestyle content and tools available on the site, all of which are likely to appeal to their target customers.

Build brand. Many e-tailers are competing in segments with well-established national brands. In most cases, these brands have a huge advantage in the marketplace because they have had the benefit of time and exposure to capture the minds and hearts of consumers.

Internet-only retailers are catching on. Millions of dollars are spent on brand awareness advertising, and several Internet-only companies have built strong brand recognition in a remarkably short period of time. Even Web-based companies, such as Amazon.com and RedEnvelope.com, with huge advertising budgets are choosing to launch catalogs as a key component of their branding strategy.

Sell e-channel-resistant consumers. Despite what many of us want to believe, there is still a large segment of consumers that is either not Web-enabled or not receptive to buying through this channel. Many Internet-only retailers have recognized this problem and, in response, have used a catalog program to reach this customer segment, which has considerable buying potential.

The number of click-and-flips is on the rise as catalogs offer great potential for Internet-only retailers to increase their customer base and revenues. Analysis of some of the early entrants into the click-and-flip arena leads us to believe that expertise is required on "the flip side." This is good news for direct marketers.

Source: April 24, 2000. Issue of DM News © Mill Hollow Corp., 2000.

- When a household receives a catalog, an average Web order made by that household doubles.
- Previous purchases through retail store and catalog increased Web response by 30 percent.[9]

These findings show that there is much to be learned by integrating direct marketing techniques. This chapter's From the Field box discusses some of the common objectives of catalog companies that have developed

Internet sites, and pure Internet retailers that have added print catalogs to their repertoires. The topic is covered in more detail in Chapter 7.

Drawbacks of Catalog Retailing Customers state several reasons why they may not order twice from the same company:

■ Disappointment with product fit, color, or quality.
■ Damaged goods.
■ Motivation to purchase limited to a one-time sale or free offer.
■ Slow service, backorders, or being offered rain checks.
■ Late or unreasonably expensive shipping.
■ Rude or poorly skilled telemarketers.
■ Infringement of privacy.

Uncertainties of a correct fit and not being able to feel the material have been two of the major drawbacks of catalog selling. These abilities are of particular importance to customers intending to purchase apparel and other soft goods. Some catalog retailers have attempted to counter both problems by providing liberal return policies, fabric swatches, and/or postage-paid return mailing labels.

Catalog retailers have also seen production and paper costs and postage rates rise, increasing their costs of doing business. Despite the costs of setting up appropriate Web sites, many sell their wares on the Internet as a supplement to their printed catalogs.

The Direct Marketing Association has taken a pro-active stance on the privacy issue. Direct marketing companies, by subscribing to the DMA Mail Preference Service and maintaining in-house name removal lists, ensure that the public does not receive unwanted materials.

Telemarketing

The telephone can provide retailers with a cost-effective means of generating incremental revenue and expanding market penetration. Consumer telemarketing in the United States was expected to grow 7.8 percent between 2000 and 2005. Sales of almost $375 billion by 2005 were predicted.[10]

Major Strengths of the Medium The telephone is a unique medium. A summary of its major strengths illustrates its effectiveness:

■ *Person-to-person.* Although the medium is not a face-to-face means of contact, well-trained telemarketers can achieve high sales rates and can recoup the missing personal touch through knowledgeable, friendly telephone service.

- *Immediately responsive.* Telemarketing, when properly structured and controlled, permits immediate statistical feedback as well as meaningful market information from customers.

- *Incremental.* The phone can be used alone, but when used in tandem with other media, it increases the overall effectiveness of both media. Emphasizing toll-free, 800 numbers and Web site addresses in sales literature may further improve mail response. The immediacy of response is attractive to many retailers as a means of order taking, encouraging multiple purchases, upgrading initial selections, cross-selling, and supporting Internet sales.

- *Cost accountable.* Like mail, the telephone is a totally cost accountable medium, enabling the user to track multiple performance variables such as cost per name, cost per call, cost per lead, and cost per order.

- *Carefully targeted.* Prospective customers can be selected on the basis of special interests, past sales behavior, and geography with relative ease via the telephone.

- *Inbound and outbound capabilities.* Retailers utilizing telephone communications have flexibility. Inbound calls from customers primed to order can be handled efficiently and provide opportunity to encourage multiple sales. Outbound calls allow the retailer to solicit new business, follow-up on orders, and provide caring customer service and positive public relations.

Challenges to Retailers Like all other types of business, telemarketing poses its own challenges and opportunities. Many customers simply do not want their schedules interrupted with unsolicited calls. Effective training of telemarketers can overcome this obstacle. Omaha Steaks customer service representatives are skilled at relationship building and use the information on their databases to encourage repeat purchases.

Using the telephone to reach consumers poses other problems as companies extend their reach globally. For example, in some Asian countries, up-to-date directories are virtually nonexistent, making telemarketing difficult. In more remote parts of the world telephones are not prevalent, much less directories.

Advantages to Customers Convenience is the prime reason individuals prefer to shop by phone. Calls are usually toll free and can be placed any time of the day or night. Deliveries are made faster because orders usually are processed immediately. Working people who have little free time have spurred the growth of teleshopping and catalog shopping.

Protection for Customers The Telephone Consumer Protection Act of 1991 includes guidelines for telemarketing companies to follow regarding socially acceptable hours during which calls can be made. It also prohibits the use of fax machines for unsolicited advertising and artificial voice and automatic dialing systems. These bans further protect individuals' privacy. Customers who find unsolicited calls intrusive can buy Caller ID systems with a blocking feature that screens out calls from telemarketers.

Although the Direct Marketing Association opposes the plan, the Federal Trade Commission announced in early 2002, that it was considering implementing a *do-not-call* registry. Using this system, consumers could call a toll-free number and place their names on a list indicating that they do not want to be called by telemarketers. The DMA believes the initiative is redundant, since for almost 20 years it has sponsored the Telephone Preference Service by which consumers can sign on to their national *do-not-call* list.[11] These are examples of the many ways concerns of the public are considered and how trade associations and national agencies may differ in opinion.

Multichannel Integration

Retailers recognize that customers who often shop at their stores sometimes will want to shop by mail, phone, or computer. All retailers have gained a new respect for direct marketing methods and have integrated them into their promotional mix because they do increase sales. Direct mail once dominated direct marketing methods, but the use of telephone and Internet marketing is increasing dramatically. Retailers who fail to notice the changes occurring between buyers and sellers will lose market share.

Direct Selling

Home and family care products lead the field in direct selling, followed closely by personal care products. There were more than 11 million salespeople involved in direct selling in the United States in 2000. Although most of them are women, many men and couples are also involved. Worldwide sales in 2000, reached $82 billion.[12]

Direct Selling Methods

The two basic types of direct selling situations are person-to-person and group. Person-to-person selling occurs when a salesperson calls on a customer at home or at the customer's place of business. Contact is made by

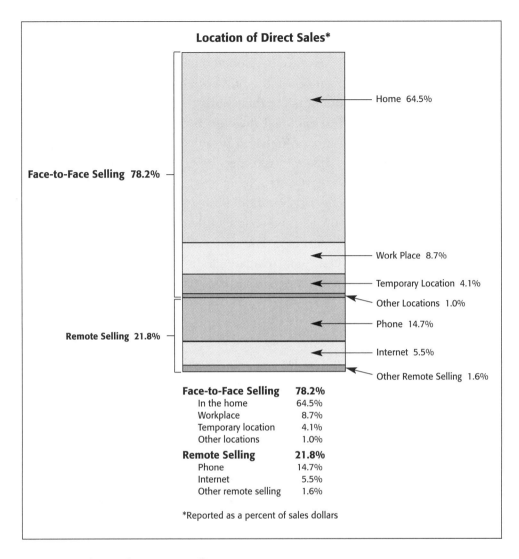

Location of Direct Sales*

Face-to-Face Selling 78.2%

Home 64.5%

Work Place 8.7%

Temporary Location 4.1%

Other Locations 1.0%

Phone 14.7%

Remote Selling 21.8%

Internet 5.5%

Other Remote Selling 1.6%

Face-to-Face Selling	**78.2%**
In the home	64.5%
Workplace	8.7%
Temporary location	4.1%
Other locations	1.0%
Remote Selling	**21.8%**
Phone	14.7%
Internet	5.5%
Other remote selling	1.6%

*Reported as a percent of sales dollars

Figure 6.3 Places Where Direct Selling Occurs *Source: Direct Selling Association. Fact Sheet. Washington, D.C. 1998. Provided courtesy of Direct Selling Association, www.dsa.org.*

appointment or through random door-to-door contact. Figure 6.3 shows places where direct selling transactions typically occur. A form of person-to-person selling, consultative selling puts the customer in a position of greater power than in many store environments, although the salesperson still controls the direction of interaction. **Consultative selling** is in-home or in-office selling by specialists whose expertise is valued by the customer. Consultants who work for home furnishing businesses as well as shop-at-home apparel, kitchen tool, and cosmetics companies use this method. A look at Cutco Cutlery illustrates how direct sellers operate.

A division of Alcas Corporation of Olean, New York, Cutco sells high-quality knives and utensils through its wholly owned global marketing arm, Vector Marketing Corporation. Vector promotes Cutco sales in the United

consultative selling In-home or in-office selling by specialists whose expertise is valued by the customer.

States and Canada. College students make up about 90 percent of Vector's independent contractor sales force in North America. Through initial family and friend contacts, sales are developed on a referral basis. An extensive support network and high-spirited motivational programs keep these commission salespeople committed to their work.

Cutco formed an international division in 1994. It entered the global market with the same mix of high-end products but gradually changed its marketing strategies to serve customers from different cultures better. When the company entered Korea, it assumed that college students would form the core of the sales organization as they did in North America. However, the company soon learned that slightly older females had a better affinity for the Korean customer and switched to that pool when seeking sales representatives. The ability to adapt has been a major factor in Cutco's success. By 2000, company sales had surpassed $100 million.

Multi-Level Marketing Companies

Many direct selling companies are also considered multi-level marketing companies. **Multi-level marketing** refers to direct selling by firms that are set up in a pyramid-style hierarchy. Salespeople pay commission on sales they generate to the leader who has recruited them. Amway, Nu Skin, and Mary Kay Cosmetics are examples of companies that are organized in this manner. Independent contractors, also referred to as pyramid leaders, recruit friends, relatives, and acquaintances to work for them. Recruits, in turn, recruit their own friends, relatives, and acquaintances. Recruiters earn commission on sales generated by each of their recruits, and pyramid leaders' commissions are based on sales from all levels of the pyramid. Monetary returns to the leader are significant if the sales organization is large and very well-motivated. Amway, the world's largest multi-level marketer, sells everything from its signature household cleaning products to cars and telephone service.

Critics of this form of direct selling argue that only a few top producers make a good living. For most salespeople, incomes are not excessive. Some people object to the near-religious fervor that is part of the corporate culture. Others complain of unscrupulous recruitment techniques and pressure placed on recruits to purchase large inventories.

Advocates stress the unlimited opportunities for independent contractors to run a small business, the strong work ethic that many multi-level sellers develop, and the many business contacts sellers are able to generate as positive reasons to join these organizations. For many it is the essence of free enterprise.

> **multi-level marketing** Direct selling by firms that are set up in a pyramid-style hierarchy. Salespeople pay commission on sales they generate to the leader who has recruited them.

Party Plan Direct Selling

The party plan salesperson enlists the aid of one customer to assist in selling to others within a community. The **party plan** method encourages in-home or in-office selling to groups hosted by a customer. Usually individuals working from homes or offices become sales representatives for party plan retailers. They invite friends or co-workers to a gathering for demonstrations of the products. Since so many women work, party plan dealers more frequently bring their wares to places of business. The shop-at-home format is expected to persist since for many people it serves the needs for social interaction as well as shopping. Tupperware, Mary Kay Cosmetics, Party Lite, and Magic Chef are direct selling firms that use the party plan as their primary means of reaching their customers.

The Direct Selling Association in Washington, D.C., is the leading trade organization for the industry and not only serves the interests of the manufacturers and distributors of products but also acts as a consumer advocate agency by enforcing high standards of ethics. Direct sellers are not limited to traditional products. In Japan, for example, a large percentage of all automobiles are sold in homes.

party plan In-home or in-office selling to groups hosted by a customer.

CYBERSCOOP

Customers will always be able to enjoy an at-home Tupperware party. Go to www.tupperware.com/party/profile and take a quiz that will tell you what kind of partier you really are. The company is also selling on the Internet, through mall kiosks, and television infomercials. Tupperware reaches customers in 100 countries.

Other Methods of Nonstore Retailing

Many other areas of nonstore retailing, although not as frequently discussed, bring a certain flavor to the industry. Vending machines, flea markets and swap meets, auctions, carts, various forms of mobile retailing, and temporary retail sites are all institutions that do not need four walls in order to do business. Some provide opportunities for entrepreneurs to gain a foothold in retailing.

The Vending Industry

Today vending machines sell a variety of products from pantyhose to photocopying, coffee to condoms. It was not always the case. A brief look at the history of the vending industry, its current status, the advantages and disadvantages of the business, and sales trends follows.

History and Present Status Early in their history, vending machines dispensed small quantities of nuts, candy, or gum that sold for a penny. The devices were placed close to cashiers so that customers could easily get change. Vending machines helped retailers minimize the problem of collecting money and recording transactions for many impulse items purchased at the point of sale. Enterprising retailers in tourist areas took advantage of developing technology and installed binoculars and pay telescopes. Advances in refrigeration soon made it possible to dispense cold soft drinks in bottles.

As the technology expanded, so did the lines of products sold in vending machines and locations for machines. Installations now exist in stores, airports, entertainment centers, hospitals, schools, offices, industrial plants, and highway rest areas.

Advantages and Disadvantages Vending machines are often accessible around the clock, eliminate the need for sales personnel, and may be located indoors or outdoors. The advantages, however, are offset by some disadvantages. Among the most important are theft, vandalism, high costs of equipment, breakdown of machines, stockouts, and a low-quality image.

Differences Between Vending and Store Retailing In traditional stores, if customers have a complaint or need service, they can ask a sales associate or go to the customer service desk for assistance. This is obviously not possible when dealing with a machine. Vending companies cope with the "psychology of dealing with the nonperson" in several ways. In a large, in-plant location, a full-service assortment of vending machines may take the place of a manually operated cafeteria. Vending companies may choose to have an attendant on the premises to greet customers, service machines, and make change. Even though change-making machines are readily available, the personal touch goes a long way in establishing good customer relations and preventing damage to machines. If a product has not been dispensed after money has been inserted, a customer might be provoked enough to abuse a machine physically. One would hope a customer would not respond in a similar fashion to a human sales associate.

The vending industry tries to restore the personal touch in humorous ways. Joe Boxer, the intimate apparel manufacturer, planned to introduce vending machines that resemble soda machines, which would dispense boxer shorts packaged in aluminum cans. What a surprise if the machine should ask, "Have you changed your underwear lately?"[13]

Sales Trends Traditionally, cold drinks, candy, coffee, and cigarettes (the 4Cs) have been the biggest sellers from vending machines. Food and beverages still garner the most sales but change in other areas is apparent. Cigarette sales declined, reflecting a growing concern for physical well-being and laws banning sales to minors, but sales of products reflecting leisure pursuits increased. When trends shift, the vending industry responds accordingly. One company has more than 700 live bait machines that are accessible in the wee hours of morning. The Iowa firm knows when most fishermen shop for supplies and provides a convenient way to purchase them.[14]

Other trends illustrate the flexibility of this nonstore medium and also its links to advanced technology. Companies in the United Kingdom created a cashless vending machine that dispenses alcohol. Utilizing smart card capabilities, these machines may eventually replace hotel mini-bars. If you are curious, yes, cards can be programmed to prohibit underage drinkers.[15]

Advanced technology, vending, and convenience store retailing meet in the creation of "roboshops." The Japanese version of an unmanned convenience store is called Super 24s MiniRobo and is equipped with a shopping basket robot that picks items customers have selected. These units are located outside regular convenience stores and CD and video shops and are accessible 24 hours a day.[16] The underlying principle illustrated by these examples is: if it can be sold, it can be vended—at any hour of the day.

Figure 6.4 Flea markets provide nonstore distribution for a myriad of products in rural or urban settings. This one is in the heart of New York City. © *Gail Mooney/CORBIS*

Indoor and Outdoor Nonstore Retailers

Looking for a Pokemon or a Yu-Gi-Oh card? Visit a flea market. A quick cup of espresso? Try a marketplace cart in a shopping center. Opportunities for nonstore retailing abound and take many different forms.

- *Flea markets.* Visit a flea market and you will find everything from great-grandmother's silverware to pre-packs of athletic socks, fine furniture to "junque." Flea markets are called *swap meets* on the West Coast of the United States. Both are usually open only on weekends and are held indoors or outdoors. A good example of an urban flea market is illustrated in Figure 6.4. Here anything from off-beat to designer fashions can be found. Flea markets are popular throughout Europe and much of the world.

- *Mobile retailing.* The chimes of an ice cream truck bring back fond childhood memories to most of us. Other foods, jewelry, imported leather goods—virtually anything—are sold legitimately from the back of a truck or van. Equipped to go where the action is, catering trucks routinely bring food service to smaller factories and businesses whose employees do not have immediate access to restaurants and stores. Taco trucks spotted on the streets of greater Los Angeles indicate that some mobile food service retailers have developed specialties.

■ *Auctions.* Indoors or outdoors, attending an auction is a fine way to observe supply and demand in action. Everything from livestock to cars, simple household items to fine paintings and expensive antiques are sold at auction. Sometimes the contents of an entire house goes up on the auction block. Called estate sales, these auctions are fun, educational, and sometimes scary. The auctioneer in charge of selling goods rattles off information and solicits bids from spectators in rapid succession. It's easy to get caught up in the excitement and bid far more money than an item is worth. Despite this inclination, often good values can be found. Auctions serve both retail and wholesale needs. Bidders can be antique dealers who are purchasing goods for resale in their antique shops. Many travel thousands of miles annually to get the best buys. Others are individuals purchasing items for their own homes or for gifts. Others never give up the hope of finding that 50-cent piece of pottery that is really worth $500.

■ *Marketplace carts.* Popular in shopping malls, downtown sites, and tourist areas, as seen in Figure 6.5, cart retailing has become a less-risky way for many entrepreneurs to gain a foothold in the retail industry. After a few seasons exposure, some cart retailers expand their businesses into stores. Some retailers operate carts on a large scale and form chains. Having carts in 20 or more shopping centers is not unusual. Cart leasing can be expensive, especially during holiday seasons, when a premium is placed on all available space. In a typical regional mall, during off-season time periods, a simple mall cart leases for approximately $1,500 per month. Cart retailers tend to offer trendy products such as crafts, jewelry, souvenir items, snack foods, accessories, and T-shirts. Special interest groups like cat lovers, musicians, or candle devotees are easily reached through marketplace carts.

■ *Temporary retail sites.* Enterprising retailers are known for setting up shop in temporary sites where the "store" may be a makeshift booth, a patch of grass, or an available table. Craft shows, harvest fairs, carnivals, and community events create opportunities to sell products and services in abbreviated time periods to people who are often primed to have fun and spend money. Some retailers make it their business to move with the events and actually spend months on the road each year offering customers their wares.

Whether nonstore retailing occurs indoors or outdoors, is permanent or temporary, operates part-time or full-time, one truth is evident: retailing occurs most anywhere products and consumers meet.

Service Retailing

Although many service retailers operate from storefronts, many do not. Some services involve physical products, but many are intangible. For this reason, service retailers are included in the nonstore discussion.

Classification of Services

Service retailers are categorized in several ways. They are considered pure service retailers if transactions do not involve merchandise. If retail services involve merchandise, they are considered owned or rented services. Services can be businesses in their own right or exist as marketing strategies for other retail businesses. Some retail services are also customer services because they enhance purchases of tangible products in classic stores. These include gift wrapping, delivery, and credit services, for example, and are discussed in more detail in Chapter 17. Several examples illustrate the distinctions between the various types of service retailers.

Pure Services Banking institutions, hotels and restaurants, hair and skin care salons, and pet care agencies are pure services. Many also have added retail product lines to their venues and some are chains. Service businesses present different challenges to retailers from those experienced in conventional store retailing, as shown by the following example.

Coin-operated laundries are moving into a new wave of customer focus and are joining the ranks of national franchise chains. Spin Cycle, based in Scottsdale, Arizona, is trying to become the Blockbuster of laundromats. The company's goal is to become a national presence by acquiring former mom-and-pop operations. The problems associated with running a retail service business are somewhat different from conventional retailing. For example, laundromats usually operate with cash-based, coin-operated systems. This works well when operations are small and localized. With national expansion, management must be prepared to supplant the personal touch lost when companies move out of mom-and-pop status. They also must plan for better security. Spin Cycle has done this by providing on-site customer service managers and by making the store environment an appealing one. Television sets have been added along with better lighting and ambiance.

Figure 6.5 Marketplace carts pop up in malls, outdoor festival marketplaces, and popular tourist destinations like this one in Old Town, San Diego.

CYBERSCOOP

Go to www.itsjustlunch.com and find out facts and figures about this dating service. If you are looking for a date in Cheyenne, Wyoming, or Sydney, Australia, can this site help you? Did you know that 38 percent of men have considered ending a relationship before Valentine's Day?

Wash-and-fold services allow customers to drop off and pick up their laundry at their convenience. Most likely, Spin Cycle will add ironing and home delivery services if customers demand, and are willing to pay for, these services. The company is considering accepting debit cards but is aware that adding this convenience would be costly. Spin Cycle planned to open approximately 150 stores a year well into the 21st century.[17]

This example shows that acquisition is a growth strategy practiced by retail services as it is by classic retail stores. It also illustrates that the human touch lacking in some service business needs to be compensated for in creative ways. Service companies also must provide excellent customer service.

Owned-Goods Services Services such as appliance, watch, or car repair are in this category. These are services that are performed on products previously purchased by individuals. Changing customer attitudes have inspired improvements in some retail service industries. For example, auto body repair shops are upgrading their images and forming chains. For many people, customer service at auto repair shops is sporadic at best and nonexistent at worst. Forward-thinking companies are training employees in customer service skills, providing clean, attractive waiting areas, and helping customers with insurance claims.

Rented-Goods Services When people need party tents, cars for vacations in Europe, or rototillers, they usually rent them rather than outlay a substantial amount of money. Sales of rented goods correlate positively to periods of economic growth. The better the economy, the more likely it is that a Mazda Miata instead of a Chevy Cavalier will be rented for a California vacation. Retailers who provide rental merchandise are particularly concerned with equipment maintenance, timely delivery, and the training of courteous customer service representatives.

Service Marketing Strategies

Many classic retailers add services when they explore ways to serve their customers better and find competitive advantages.

Category killer Home Depot tested a home repair service program for people who do not embrace the do-it-yourself philosophy. Initially offering roofing, siding, and window replacement services, the company expected to move into other areas of home improvement. The company acknowledged that cannibalization could be a problem since many independent contractors offering these services are wholesale customers of Home Depot and might choose to purchase their supplies elsewhere if Home Depot entered the service sector extensively.[18]

If current trends continue, retail services will continue to develop, expand, and form national and international chains. Many people who live time-impacted lives are willing to pay for the opportunity to make better use of the free moments they have available. Customers also are demanding more services from all retailers. Rising standards of living in many parts of the globe and the growth of the Internet mean more opportunities for service retailers and more satisfaction for customers.

Never underestimate the power of nonstore retailing. It is limited only by the degree of inventiveness of retailers and entrepreneurs. Industry consultant Lois Geller proposes this rule of thumb for the success of direct marketing programs: Forty percent is due to the offer—the product itself. Another 40 percent is due to the adequacy of the customer list. The final 20 percent is a result of the creative strategy used to reach the consumer.[19]

Traditional direct marketing channels—excluding the Internet—were responsible for about 95 percent of revenues in 2000.[20] This figure will change as companies redefine nonstore retailing and embrace e-retailing.

Summary

Because of dramatic breakthroughs in communications and technology, more and more retailers are choosing to sell directly to consumers. Because consumers have less time for shopping, seek more time for leisure activities, have more disposable income, and demand better service, they are responding to direct marketing and direct selling methods. They are shopping in their homes and workplaces by mail, telephone, the Internet and through personal consultants and party plans. Direct marketing and selling are ways many companies expanding their retail business internationally. These methods also provide the means for small retailers to enter the marketplace. Although the bulk of sales attributed to direct marketing now come from traditional media such as direct mail, catalogs, and telemarketing, this will change as more companies include the Internet in their direct marketing plans.

Brick-and-mortar retailers and other businesses are entering the nonstore arena as a supplement to their existing distribution strategies and also as a future survival tactic. The nonstore selling experience is generating excitement for both the consumer and the businessperson.

In the vending industry, technology and convenience merge to bring many interesting new options to customers. Auctions, flea markets, carts, mobile retailing, and temporary sites round out the nonstore retailing sector.

Service retailing is an important aspect of the industry. Some retailers operate pure service businesses; others run owned-goods or rental-goods establishments. Some combine service retailing with classic store retailing, and many use services as marketing strategies. Service retailers are forming national and international chains.

Questions for Review and Discussion

1. Why is nonstore retailing growing? What types of people prefer this type of retailing?

2. What are the differences between direct marketing and direct selling? What methods are used by each to reach customers?

3. Why have many brick-and-mortar retailers gone into the catalog business?

4. How did the vending industry begin and what is its status today? Discuss the problems associated with the "psychology of dealing with the nonperson."

5. What role do flea markets, auctions, and other mobile or temporary site retailers play in the world of retailing?

6. Describe some retail service businesses. Why are they important to the industry? What specific challenges do they face?

Endnotes

1. Direct Marketing Association. *Economic Impact, Executive Summary.* New York. 1999:5.

2. www.sda.org/selling . Direct Selling Association. Accessed: May 3, 2002

3. *DMA Statistical Fact Book 2001.* "Value of U.S. DM Driven Sales Compared to Total U.S. Sales." Direct Marketing Association: 299. (Source: The DMA Report: Economic Impact—U.S. Direct Marketing Today, 2000.)

4. *DMA Statistical Fact Book 2001.* "International Direct Marketing Revenue in All Markets." Direct Marketing Association: 260. (Source: The DMA Report: Economic Impact—U.S. Direct Marketing Today, 2000.)

5. *DMA Statistical Fact Book 2001.* "Mail Order Spending Per Capita in U.S. $ (Per Year)" Direct Marketing Association: 256. (Source: Deutsche Post Global Mail, 2000.)

6. Darko, Kendra L. "Market Updates." *CM/Circulation Management.* May, 1999: 56.

7. Nash, Ed. "International Direct Marketing." Presentation. Direct Marketing Educational Foundation. New York. June, 1996.

8. *DMA Statistical Fact Book 2001.* "Catalogs Mailed Per Year: 1990-2000." Direct Marketing Association: 96. (Source: DMA/USPS Revenue, Pieces and Weight by Classes of Mail Report for Fiscal Year 2000.)

9. Napolillo, Lissa. "The Retail Store, the Catalog, and the Internet." Presentation. Advanced Direct/Interactive Marketing Institute. Direct Marketing Educational Foundation. New York. June 6, 2000.

10. *DMA Statistical Fact Book 2001.* "Value of U.S. DM Driven Sales by Medium and Market." Direct Marketing Association: 300. (Source: The DMA Report: Economic Impact – U.S. Direct & Interactive Marketing Today, 2000.)

11. *3D-DMA Digest.* "The FTC Proposes to Create a National 'Do-Not-Call' Registry; DMA Says Proposal is Unnecessary." E-mail Newsletter. The Direct Marketing Association. Accessed: January 22, 2002.

12. www.sda.org/selling . Direct Selling Association. Accessed: May 3, 2002

13. Ho, Rodney. "Vending Machines Make Change." *Wall Street Journal.* July 7, 1999:B1.

14. "From Smokes to Worms: The Vending-Machine Industry Finds New Life in Bait." *Wall Street Journal.* Business Bulletin. June 19, 1998:A1.

15. Fletcher, Mike. "VSP to Launch First Cashless Alcohol Vending Machine in U.K." *Leisure Week.* July 31, 1998:9. http://web.lexis-nexis.com/univers.

16. *Asia Pulse.* "Japan's Super 24 Marketing Unmanned 24-hour Store System." May 14, 1998. http://web. lexis-nexis.com/univers.

17. http://www.spin-cycle.com/corporate/news/journaltwo/ Accessed: September, 1999.

18. Hagerty, James R. "Home Depot Tests Expanded Home Services." *Wall Street Journal.* July 27, 1998:A4.

19. Geller, Lois. "Branding." Presentation. Advanced Direct/Interactive Marketing Institute. Direct Marketing Educational Foundation. New York June 6, 2000.

20. Roman, Ernan. "Integrating Media to Build a Profitable Business." Presentation. Advanced Direct/Interactive Marketing Institute. Direct Marketing Educational Foundation. New York. June 5, 2000.

Chapter 7

Electronic Retailing

Learning Objectives

- To evaluate the impact of electronic retailing.
- To compare the advantages and disadvantages of electronic retailing from both the retailer's and customer's perspectives.
- To discern what constitutes an effective Web site.
- To profile typical Internet shoppers.
- To detect ways Internet retailers are providing service while protecting customers' privacy.
- To distinguish alternative methods of electronic retailing.

Figure 7.1 Do you Yahoo? Innovative billboards build brand awareness for major Internet service provider Yahoo. The company uses a multimedia approach to advertise its services (See p. 187).

It's getting harder to impress us. What was fantasy a decade ago has become reality. Not long ago we found it fascinating to call friends on a cell phone or to download music from the Internet. Today, if we choose, we can purchase a jacket with cell phone, MP3 player, headset, and remote control built in. If we don't feel like going out to party, we can tune-in to a live video and audio Webcast from a favorite night spot. A small bed and breakfast in Oregon can put its image and rates on the Internet and a family in Italy can book a holiday stay at the property. Drive through a highway toll booth and a microchip imbedded in the car window records our toll payment. Visit the *Wall Street Journal* Web site at www.wsj.com and see and hear the newsclip we missed on the news. When confronted with a slide projector in class, a retailing student—accustomed to PowerPoint and Web-based presentations—quipped, "I didn't think they made those anymore." Reflect on these examples for a moment. Not long ago these technologies were dreams for the future. The fact is we are living the future today as technology takes turns most people never imagined. Is it any surprise that anything written in this chapter will probably be out-of-date by the time you read it?

We have all become part of the cyber generation. Some accepted this transition easily while others fought hard to avoid the inevitable. Retailers and consumers share some of these proclivities. All must acknowledge that the industry is poised at a pivotal point as all parties explore new ways to communicate with each other.

Internet Computer lines and linkages that provide world access to information and commerce.

Web site Specific location of a business, organization, or person on the World Wide Web.

World Wide Web Totally integrated informational and commercial electronic services accessible via global computer links and wireless technology.

infomercials Television commercials that combine detailed product information, demonstration, and excitement with a sales pitch.

Although imbedded in our vernacular, definitions of frequently used terms bear clarification. The **Internet** is computer lines and linkages that provide world access to information and commerce. A **Web site** is a specific location of a business, organization, or person on the World Wide Web. The **World Wide Web**, or the Web, refers to the totally integrated informational and commercial electronic services accessible via global computer links and wireless technology.

The World Wide Web is still in its childhood, but has already become an important marketing channel for retailers. Television home shopping, in both broadcast and interactive forms, provides an alternative method of shopping for many people. Infomercials both entertain and educate, often softening the impact before a serious sales pitch occurs. **Infomercials** are television commercials that combine detailed product information, demonstration, and excitement with a sales pitch. Thiry-minute infomercials are common.

Electronic kiosks supplement the marketing efforts of some retailers. **Electronic kiosks** are small display units in stores or other locations that use computers or other devices to generate sales or provide extended customer services. A listening kiosk is illustrated in Figure 7.2.

Smart card technology has its place in the world of electronic retailing as it does in the traditional sphere. Advanced Internet options are also helping manufacturers and retailers find new ways to do business more expediently. Privacy and security issues are important to all participants using electronic retailing and also are discussed in this chapter.

Figure 7.2 Prominantly placed listening kiosks at FNAC, a European electronics store, encourage customers to sample CDs before they buy them.

It is difficult to keep abreast of all aspects of technological change, much less embrace them. Retailers must do both in order to stay competitive. Multichannel retailers, introduced in Chapter 1, invariably will have a presence on the Web in addition to doing business in more traditional formats. Electronic retailing is one of the easier ways to create a global presence.

Retailing on the World Wide Web

The Web is at the forefront of discussions involving electronic commerce. Several abbreviated terms are used to describe the various dimensions of business conducted online. **E-commerce** is the all encompassing term for business conducted on the Web. **E-retailing** is the practice of performing retail activities on the Web. **M-commerce** is business conducted on the Web using wireless devices such as cell phones or palm-held personal digital assistants(PDAs). The factors that have brought the industry to this point are covered before addressing retail implications.

electronic kiosks Small display units in stores or other locations that use computers and other devices to generate sales or provide extended customer services.

e-commerce All-encompassing term for business conducted on the Web.

e-retailing The practice of performing retail activities on the Web.

m-commerce Business conducted on the Web using wireless devices such as cell phones or palm-held personal digital assistants.

History of the Internet

Although the Internet is now used by everyone from tots to tourists and social activists to social butterflies, this was not always the case. In the late 1960s, developmental work was done by the United States government's Advanced Research Projects Agency (ARPA) in order to create a secure communications system in the event of a nuclear, or other, disaster. Computers at major universities involved in government contract work were connected. Early in the 1970s, the first e-mail message was sent by the early network, dubbed the ARPANET. At that time fewer than 100 sites were linked to the system. In the late 1970s and early 1980s the ARPANET evolved into the Internet as more users joined the network.

It was not until the early 1990s that the World Wide Web was invented in Switzerland, allowing users to communicate with graphics, sound, and video which opened the door to serious commercial applications. Although the Web is actually only a part of the Internet, most people use the terms interchangeably. The first exploration tool, Mosaic, was developed in the United States during this period. Netscape Communications used the underpinnings of Mosaic to produce Netscape Navigator, its Web-browsing software.

Internet service provider(ISP) National or regional companies that provide access to the Internet.

Commercial Internet service providers, such as America Online (AOL), CompuServe, and Prodigy, took control of the former scientific network in the mid-90s. **Internet service providers (ISPs)** are national or regional companies that provide access to the Internet. Most charge users a flat monthly fee for their services. Both Prodigy and CompuServe started as modem-based home shopping services for personal computer owners, then entered the ISP domain in the 1990s. Prodigy began in 1984 as a joint venture between Sears and IBM but is presently owned by International Wireless. CompuServe initiated operations in 1985, and in 1997, was acquired by AOL.[1] The largest American Internet service provider, AOL acquired Netscape in 1999, greatly expanding its Web presence. AOL merged with entertainment and media giant, Time Warner in 2000. By 2001 the company had 29 million subscribers world-wide.[2] Because the industry is still new, more mergers and acquisitions are expected.

search engines Companies that provide the mode of transportation to specific Web sites on the Internet through complex electronic directories.

portal sites Digital doorways to information stored in cyberspace.

Search engines, including Yahoo and Lycos, rapidly developed their services enabling users to find the way through the complexities of the Web. **Search engines** are companies that provide the mode of transportation to specific Web sites on the Internet through complex directories. Companies such as Ask Jeeves, Google, and Northern Light fall into this category. **Portal sites** are digital doorways to information stored in cyberspace. They make it easier to find what you are looking for in the millions of Web pages that exist. Yahoo and Lycos, along with Internet providers MSN and AOL, are also portals because they provide extended services. Lycos, for example, offers e-mail, chat rooms, and games the way Internet service providers do. Most ISPs and search engines aspire to become portal sites, and most have global presence. Some reached portal status so that they would be considered more valuable by investors during the Internet stock craze of the late 1990s.

Since companies are turning up in more than one category, confusion is expected. The following example may help to clarify this point. Yahoo and Infoseek are both considered search engines but have different strengths. Yahoo is a true directory with subject categories and sub-categories conveniently set up branch-style on its site. If you know the name of a specific retailer, such as Amazon, Yahoo will immediately bring up its universal resource locator. A **universal resource locator(URL)** is the unique address, called a domain name, given to each Web site. If you attempt to find the same information on Infoseek, you may find the site address but you will also bring up all other references to Amazon—including the South American river and mythological females bearing the same name. Therefore Yahoo works fast, but Infoseek may be more thorough. Yahoo.com is one of the largest portal sites and advertises extensively through conventional as well as electronic media, as illustrated in Figure 7.1.

Browsers allow users to turn-on and tune-in to the Internet. **Browsers** are software that allow users to travel through cyberspace, search for information, or go directly to a site. Microsoft's Internet Explorer and AOL's Netscape Navigator are the two leading browsers. They are preset so the first Web sites to appear when users turn on their computers are theirs.

E-commerce boomed and the numbers of retail and business-to-business users mushroomed in the late 1990s. Communication networks called Intranets are commonplace. **Intranets** are internal computer communication systems within a business or institution. The information superhighway is rapidly becoming wholesale and retail superstores in cyberspace.

universal resource locator(URL) The unique address, called a domain name, given to each Web site.

browser Software that allows users to travel through cyberspace to search for information or go directly to a site.

intranets Internal computer communication systems within a business or institution.

Advantages and Disadvantages of Web Retailing

As with all other forms of retailing, it is important to examine the advantages and disadvantages of Web retailing.

Advantages to Retailers Selling on the Web offers retailers several advantages including:

1. The Internet is always open. Web stores and malls are open around the clock, every day—24/7/365 as the current jargon reads.
2. The Web offers a broad potential market, but niche markets also can be easily accessed.
3. The great potential of this medium offers businesses new opportunities for growth.
4. The Web can help extend brand awareness nationally and globally.
5. Traditional store or nonstore distribution can be enhanced.

Did You Know?

There were approximately 7,000 registered domain names in the United States in 1993. By 2001, there were more than 28 million registered with VeriSign, the company that maintains the master list of Internet addresses. Seventy-five percent of all bear the .com suffix.
Source: *Wall Street Journal.* "Web Sites Await Word on Handling of Domain Names." April 2, 2001:B6.

6. Data mining and management, now possible with advanced technology, creates a new intimacy with customers.

7. Cost reductions in store leasing, staffing, operations, and data collection are possible.

8. Setting up a Web site is less expensive than setting up a store—especially for small retailers.

9. A Web site can greatly expand geographic and demographic markets for large or small retailers.

10. E-mail can serve as an excellent promotional and customer service vehicle.

Disadvantages to Retailers Despite all the positive aspects, Web retailing is not without its disadvantages, including:

1. Channel conflicts can occur as manufacturers and suppliers set up their own sites and bypass retailers.

2. The technology is still relatively new and customers may be resistant to change.

3. The possibility of copyright infringements may be higher.

4. Product misrepresentation due to poor or inconsistent graphics is possible.

5. Without an efficient search engine or hyperlinks, consumers may have difficulty finding retailers' sites. **Hyperlinks** are programmed devices that allow a user to go from one site to another with the click of a mouse.

6. Currency exchange, taxes, tariffs, and shipping may be a problem, especially in international markets.

hyperlinks Web facilitators that allow a user to go from one site to another with a click of the mouse.

Advantages to Customers Shopping on the Web provides customers with many advantages, including:

1. The convenience of shopping from home or office.
2. Time and money savings.
3. The ability to research products, compare prices, and perks.
4. Web stores are always open.
5. Fewer hassles dealing with traffic, crowds, and street crime.
6. There is increased access to a broad array of products and services.
7. The ability to shop internationally.

Disadvantages to Customers There are several reasons why customers might avoid shopping via the Internet, including:

1. Relinquished privacy regarding personal and financial status information.
2. The possibility of credit card fraud or number theft.
3. The inability to authenticate Internet retailers since any company or person can set up a site.
4. Problems with technology including slow or sporadic transmission and viruses.
5. Distribution hassles including untimely delivery and inconvenient return policies.
6. The inability to physically examine products.
7. Vast time commitment when searching sites; might take less time to drive to a mall!

Web site Usage

There were almost 500 million Internet users worldwide in 2000, up from 44 million in 1995, generating more than $600 billion in e-commerce revenue. Web users in the United States comprise 29.2 percent of global Web users, slightly less than Western Europe with 29.8 percent. Asian/Pacific countries follow with 18.9 percent, and next Japan with 9.6 percent of total users.[3] As the availability of Internet technology spreads, usage percentages will change radically.

Services Available on Retail Web sites

From company information to marketing pitches to authentic online shopping, services available on retail Web sites run the gamut from basic to sublime. In that progression, the following are examples of what customers can expect to find:

1. Basic store information including address, store hours, and company history.
2. Corporate reports and press releases.
3. Employment opportunities.
4. Franchise information.
5. Store locator service.
6. Marketing materials including graphic ads, coupons, catalog request information, and surveys.
7. Special services such as helpful hints, menu planners, gift ideas, and new product information.
8. Entertainment.

CYBERSCOOP

Ben & Jerry's in Vermont receives thousands of calls from students seeking information about the company each year. Go ahead, visit www.benjerry.com and see what you can learn. Can you order a 6-pack of pints of Cherry Garcia® online? What's new in the *Chunkmail* newsletter this month?

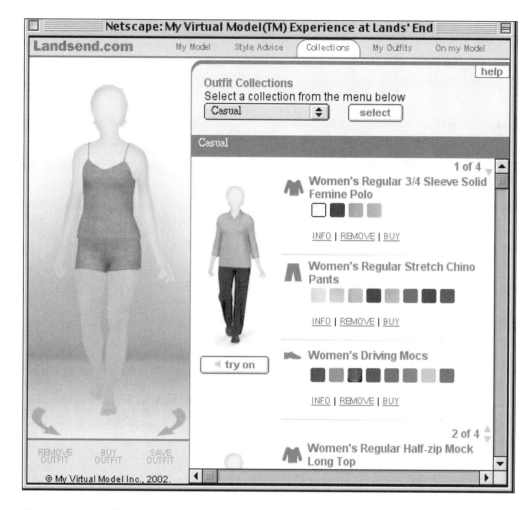

Figure 7.3 Using the Lands' End Virtual Model feature helps ensure a perfect fit every time you shop the site. Elaborate services like this help build brand equity for Lands' End. © 2002 Land's End®, Inc. and My Virtual Model™. Used with permission.

9. Free Internet access.
10. Online shopping.
11. Services such as chat groups, free software to download, online auctions, gift registries, and even eye examinations.
12. Ability to capture visitor information.
13. Secured transmissions.
14. Credit and smart card acceptance.
15. Advanced sound and video technology including media clips, interactive Java, virtual reality, and MP3.

The Lands' End interactive Web site is an example of what the more sophisticated retailers are doing online. As well as displaying a complete assortment of store products in a logical, captivating way, the site offers several marketing gimmicks to keep users interested. Shoppers can use the self-reporting virtual model (see Figure 7.3). Or, if so inclined, have their bodies scanned in special chambers, so that a model with measurements identical to their own can be created. Garments suitable for a specific body type or size can be requested. Models can be rotated so that garments can be viewed from all angles. By zooming in, details on a shirt collar can be examined to see if the top-stitching meets expectations.

Online Sales Trends

Research indicates that there are several retail product and service categories that are the most widely sought on the Web. At the top are books, computers, and CDs in the United States, but purchasing habits vary elsewhere in the world.[4]

Apparel has been slower to move on the Internet with some exceptions. According to Ernst & Young, categories including apparel, accessories, and toys are expected to comprise 10 to 12 percent of industry-wide sales by 2005.[5]

Online shopping appears to work best when customers know specifically what they want or when there is no need to judge product quality. A book purchased at the Barnes & Noble Web site is the same quality as one purchased in its superstores. When a customer has a problem or craves the human attention of a sales associate, electronic shopping venues are challenged. E-retailing may be most appealing to individuals who view traditional shopping as torturous. Table 7.1 depicts which products sell best online in the United States and selected foreign countries.

Web Customer Profiles

The American Web shopper is middle class, approximately 42 years old and female. Female cyber-shoppers, outnumbered males by approximately 60 percent to 40 percent in 2000—the reverse of what was recorded only two years previously. In comparison, 85 percent of German Internet users are male.[6] Although these statistics do not indicate the Internet shopping habits of the Germans, they do alert us to cultural differences. Men appeared to have had more access to the Internet in its early stages, though this gap has closed. Feminists may disagree, but the incentive for women to work in technological fields, thus making them more comfortable with Internet technology, was not apparent until recent times.

Web shoppers are more likely than non-Web shoppers to shop by phone, from catalogs, and via television. They are also more likely to shop at classic retail stores than non-Web consumers. When shoppers frequent more than

Table 7.1 Top Selling Products Online

	U.S.	Australia	Brazil	Canada	France
1	Books	Books	CDs	Computers	Books
2	Computers	Computers	Books	Books	Computers
3	CDs	CDs	Computers	CDs	Tickets/ Reserv.
4	Apparel	Tickets/Reserv.	Electronic Products	Tickets/ Reserv.	CDs
5	Tickets/Reserv.	Apparel	Videos	Apparel	Videos

(Table 7.1 continued on page 193.)

one marketing channel, they are also likely to spend more money annually. For example, Eddie Bauer reported that customers who shop one channel spend $200 to $300 per year. Customers who shop two channels spend up to $500 per year, and those who shop three channels tend to spend up to $1,000 per year.[7]

It is reasonable to assume that younger shoppers who have grown up with Internet technology are more likely to purchase products online. There is tremendous potential for market development after the much heralded techno-tots reach financial and social maturity. The cyber customer is more open to new technology, innovation, and change. These inclinations seem to cut across all other demographic and psychographic characteristics. Several demographic comparisons are indicated in Table 7.2.

Customer Complaints About Web sites

Online shoppers are not always pleased with what they find and voice several complaints about retail Web sites, including:

1. Sparse product offerings that are heavily promoted.
2. Illogical cross-referencing, lack of straightforward approach.
3. Inability to touch or try on products.
4. Inconvenience of making returns.
5. Too many matches on searches which can be overwhelming and discouraging.
6. Difficulty in determining quality through graphic images.
7. Unwelcome surprises, such as nudity, on a supposedly family-oriented Web site.

Some of these same complaints are voiced by shoppers who frequent traditional retail establishments. For example, "too much to choose from" is cited by reluctant mall shoppers as one reason why they do not like to shop online. Having difficulty picturing oneself in a graphically rendered Web

Table 7.1 Top Selling Products Online *(Table 7.1 continued from page 192.)*

	Germany	Israel	Netherlands	Spain	Switzerland	UK
1	Books	Books	Books	Books	Books	CDs
2	Computers	CDs	CDs	Computers	Computers	Books
3	CDs	Electronic Products	Computers	CDs	Tickets/ Reserv.	Computers
4	Tickets/ Reserv	Computers	Tickets/Reserv	Tickets/Reserv	CDs	Tickets/Reserv.
5	Videos	Household Goods	Electronic Products	Electronic Products	Financial Services	Videos

Source: *Stores*. Global Online Retailing, an Ernst&Young Special Report. January, 2001:7

page illustration is similar to reports by catalog shoppers who cite dissatisfaction with goods ordered from catalog photographs.

Types of Retailers on the Web

As of 2002, almost all major retailers were selling or expected to sell via the Internet. Web retailers fall into five of the following categories:

1. *Pure-play retailers.* Companies that have never operated retail stores or engaged in other nonstore distribution and do business exclusively online. Amazon.com is an example of a pure-play retailer.
2. *Dual-channel retailers.* Companies that operate primarily from classic stores but also engage in business online. Companies like Wal-Mart and Sears fit this description.
3. *Multichannel retailers.* Retail companies that sell through more than two marketing channels. Examples in this category include Lands' End, J.C.Penney, and Eddie Bauer which each had retail stores and/or catalog divisions before they developed Web sites.
4. *Electronic spin-offs.* Retailers that originally traded through means other than the Web. The television shopping network, QVC, also sells online, for example.
5. *Nontransactional sites.* Retailers that maintain Web sites and provide company information but do not sell online. Many small retailers, like Bellman's Jewelers, have nontransactional sites. Visit www.bellmans.com to see how a single-unit retailer can provide useful diamond selection information to its customers.

As momentum builds, expect that many nontransactional sites will add online shopping services. Many pure-play sites have failed. Others have taken a proactive approach and added catalogs and Web sites, becoming multichannel retailers. Two examples are RedEnvelope.com and Alloy.com.

Table 7.2 Demographics of Online Buyers

	U.S.	Australia	Brazil	Canada	France	Germany
Average age	42	41	34	42	36	32
Average annual household income in $US	52,300	43,700	40,000	43,600	42,700	46,000
Gender						
%Male	40%	53%	75%	51%	81%	84%
%Female	60%	47%	25%	49%	19%	16%
Marital Status						
%Married	59%	60%	40%	56%	36%	28%
4-Yr College	35%	40%	67%	39%	54%	27%

(Table 7.2 continued on page 195.)

Setting Up Cyber Shop

Although retailers large and small can set up simple Web sites for modest costs, the picture changes as exclusive arrangements with portals and search engines are broached. For example, Amazon.com paid AOL $19 million for the privilege of securing an exclusive promotion on AOL's home page. The company also obtained a prime spot with Excite's search service in exchange for paying advertising fees and a percentage of sales revenue to Excite.[8] As retailing changes, so does the demand for prime locations, whether it is in a shopping mall or the Internet.

Many challenges face fledgling Web retailers including image issues, financing the operation, choosing workable strategies, designing an appealing graphic format, and convincing customers to shop electronically.

Challenges to Retail Startups

Starting a retail business on the Internet poses some unique challenges. It's not easy to design a store when that store is in cyberspace. The element of image transfer is an important one as retailers look to re-create their successful formats without the help of common physical elements such as walls, windows, and floor plans. Retailers must create not only user-friendly Web sites, but those that have the ability to become user-familiar sites. If you are a regular L.L.Bean shopper, the L.L.Bean online store should exude the same product quality, selection, and superior customer service as store and catalog operations.

Financing a Web site

There are two principal ways to set up a Web site—own or rent. If these options sound similar to owning or renting a conventional store, they are.

Table 7.2 Demographics of Online Buyers *(Table 7.2 continued from page 194.)*

	Israel	Netherlands	South Africa	Spain	Switz.	UK
Average age	33	37	34	34	37	35
Average annual household income in $US	51,300	36,600	41,300	61,000	49,200	49,200
Gender						
%Male	74%	78%	69%	85%	80%	62%
%Female	26%	22%	31%	15%	20%	38%
Marital Status						
%Married	47%	44%	55%	36%	41%	45%
4-Yr College	70%	56%	61%	47%	30%	45%

Source: *Stores*. Global Online Retailing, an Ernst&Young Special Report. January, 2001:5.

Large retailers may prefer setting up dedicated sites, called nodes, which can cost several hundred thousand to over a million dollars. Special software, design services, and connection fees become part of set-up costs and frequent updates increase maintenance costs. Smaller retailers prefer to rent a Web page, called a hosted site, from a service provider. Thirty dollars a month and a modest outlay for design and updates are all that is necessary to open a cyber shop.

Online Strategies

The e-retailing industry is too new for totally accurate performance appraisals. The volatility of the economy early in the 21st century and the resultant failure of many e-retail and other technology-driven businesses compromized progress. Early warnings that electronic commerce would soon overtake classic stores as the major form of retailing soon abated. Retailers that will remain strong in the face of economic downturn are those tht practice multichannel retailing. E-retailing will become another option for consumers, not the ultimate answer to their shopping needs. However, reports indicate that Internet retailing works best for certain types of retailers including those that:

- Carry narrow and deep assortments
- Target highly defined specialty markets
- Use vast creativity to sell
- Sell products that do not require close inspection or handling

800flowers.com carries a narrow and deep assortment since it specializes in one product category but offers many choices in its principal merchandise area. Individuals interested in purchasing reptile skin motorcycle seats, gothic tattoo patterns, or shoes made from vegetable products can

Table 7.3 Top 25 Internet Retailers

Company	Monthly Visitors
Amazon.com	70.7 million (worldwide)
American Eagle	2 million
Jos. A. Bank.com	N/A
Bluefly.com	467 thousand
CircuitCity.com	2.3 million
Drugstore.com	1.9 million
D'Elias	1.3 million
eBay.com	42.8 million (worldwide)
EddieBauer.com	1.4 million
IBM.com	20 million
Hallmark	3.5 million
KBToys.com	1.05 million
LandsEnd.com	760 thousand
OfficeDepot.com	3.49 million
LLBean.com	2.1 million
Orvis.com	800 thousand
Overstock.com	7 million
Replacements.com	500 thousand
Polo.com	500 thousand
RitzCamera.com	1 million
Sears.com	3.4 million
VacuumBags.com	3 thousand
Uncommongoods.com	82 thousand
WilliamsSonoma.com	167 thousand
Wine.com	1.5 million

Source: *Internet Retailer.* "Best of the Web Top 25." January/February, 2002: 20-36

find specialty sites. Retail formats that lend themselves to high creativity also attract attention. Formats that delight the masses, such as Disney and Warner Bros., or specialty sites such as the Gap's, provide significant extensions to brand appeal and retail sales. The top 25 online retailers as determined by *Internet Retailer* magazine are listed in Table 7.3. Inclusion on the list reflects the magazine's judgment as the site's ease of access and use, graphics, merchandising, how well the site meets the corporate objectives of the parent company and not sales revenue or profitability.

Other e-retailing strategies include several models that parallel existing institutions in the real, rather than cyber, world. They include online malls, shopping robots, and auction sites.

Online Shopping Malls Major providers present numerous opportunities for customers to visit scores of retailers by a simple click of the mouse. "Marketplace" on AOL and "My Shopping" on Yahoo are online malls dedicated to marathon shopping. On some, shoppers can access recipient preferences through gift or bridal registries before purchasing merchandise.

nternational shopping experiences can be cultivated by visiting a myriad of malls emanating from other countries. Luxury goods retailers find online homes at eluxury.com, a subsidiary of Louis Vuitton Moet Hennessy (LVMH), the French conglomerate. These sites bring extensive exposure to many designer retailers and defy the common thought that customers do not like to shop for posh merchandise online.

Shopping Robots Web sites that encourage product comparisons add to the layers of electronic wizardry available to shoppers. By typing in pertinent information such as brand, price range, and delivery date, robots take the time to perform, thus taking agitation out of a difficult personal search. Amazon's "Shop the Web" service helps customers comparison shop almost anything. Books and music are off limits, however, since comparisons in those areas might inadvertently help the competition.[9]

Online Auctions Electronic auctions are opportunities for customers to be entertained and perhaps obtain a great buy in a reasonably secure environment. Most auction sites charge sellers a listing fee and percentage of the selling price. Ebay.com operates in this way, specializing in collectibles such as Elvis or sports memorabilia and products that appeal to special interest groups. During the rise in popularity of Latin pop singer Ricky Martin, eBay sold a wealth of merchandise. On one day, 325 Martin items came up for bid, including sheet music for his hit "Livin' La Vida Loca" for $4 and an autographed microphone for $75.01.[10] In 2002, eBay was considered one of the top e-commerce sites in terms of sales and profits.

Online auctions face many problems such as bogus bids that drive up prices, product misrepresentation, negated deliveries, and other fraud. To ensure safe transactions, ebay.com has developed rules for online buyers and sellers. Money management systems, called escrow accounts have been replaced now that major credit cards are accepted. Sellers are prohibited from bidding on their own merchandise. Buyers are given free insurance against fraud or mislabeled goods by eBay.[11] These safeguards greatly improve the image of online auctions.

Integrated Promotional Strategies

Retailers actively seeking Internet shoppers go to great lengths to dramatize the pleasures of Web retailing. Web shopping is often positioned as a supplement or alternative to conventional store shopping. For example, store retailers are using point-of-purchase(POP) counter cards to advertise their Web site addresses and offer giveaways or gift-with-purchase promotions to lure first-time users. Some retailers outfit store personnel in T-shirts bearing the Web site address or use the shirts as giveaways. Other tactics include cross-promotion and push/pull methods.

Did You Know?

A survey on the music listening habits of young people done by Yankelovich Partners determined that 66 percent of those surveyed said that at least once, listening to a song online encouraged them to purchase the CD in a store later. Do you fall into this category?
Source: Mathews, Anna Wilds. "Music Samplers on Web Buy CDs in Stores." *Wall Street Journal.* June 15, 2000:A3.

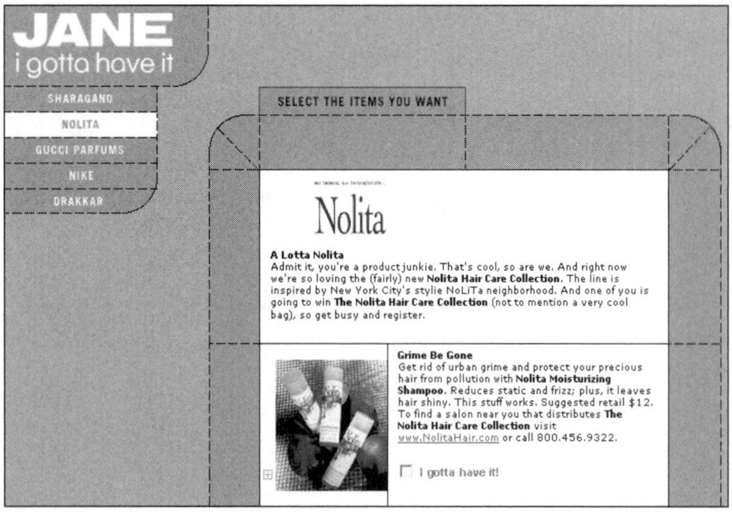

Figure 7.4 Nolita, a hair product manufacturer, uses cross promotion techniques such as setting up a link to their company's Web-site from the "Gotta Have It" page of *Jane* magazine's Web site. *Courtesy of Fairchild Publications, Inc.*

cross-promotion Practice of using multimedia to promote retail Web sites.

CYBERSCOOP

If you are dying for a Big Mac™ but aren't sure where the nearest McDonald's is, fear not. Visit www.mcdonalds.com and access its trip planner. It also will tell you how long it takes to get to the next pair of golden arches. Is this a push or pull strategy?

Cross-Promotion Businesses intending to grow sales in the electronic sector often use cross-promotion. **Cross-promotion** is the practice of using multi-media to promote retail Web sites. Retailers hope that sales in their traditional distribution channels will not be cannibalized as a result of online growth. Retailers send press kits and press releases to editorial departments of magazines to generate publicity for their Web sites. Fashion retailers in particular set up Web links between their Web sites and those of fashion magazines such as *Jane*, *Elle*, or *Seventeen*. Some companies run small classified or larger display advertisements in newspapers to keep their Web site addresses in the public eye.

Television and Internet cross-promotions also allow Web surfers with retail and sitcom interests to participate in online chats with their favorite TV show characters and order logo emblazoned merchandise.

Much product placement advertising is already seen on TV and in the cinema. The next breakthrough in interactive technology will allow items seen on TV shows to be purchased online. Imagine ordering an outfit worn by your favorite *Dawson's Creek* character from American Eagle Outfitters while the show is still in progress.

The Push and Pull Effect In its earlier stages, Web retailing tended to push information on to the viewer rather than to let the customer pull information from the site. Similar to the distribution concept discussed in Chapter 16, push strategies involve retailers sending promotional messages to a broad spectrum of potential customers. Pull strategies indicate that the customer activates the selling process, perhaps by requesting further information from a retailer. The push strategy still serves a function as retailers test new products on their Web sites. However most retailers discovered the benefits of letting customers extract information based on their specific interests and needs. The shotgun approach that a push strategy implies is less effective than a pull strategy. The implications for merchandising, sales promotion, and customer service strategies are vast. Some retailers include gift directories through which customers visiting a toy site can retrieve information on what a four-year-old boy might like for a birthday gift. Cosmetic companies elicit detailed information regarding skin types and product preferences so that shoppers can benefit from specific product counseling. Customers make better product choices and perhaps purchase more products when a pull strategy is used rather than a push strategy.

Turning Surfers into Shurfers

Web surfers may browse to their hearts' content, but converting them to serious shurfers,[12] is a challenge. **Shurfers** is the name coined to designate surfers on the Internet who choose to shop. There are several ways in which Web sites can connect with shurfers.

The homepage must convey retail image graphically in such a way that potential customers are encouraged to peruse the site. The **homepage** is the first screen image that appears when a user enters a Web site. It is the cyberspace equivalent of a store window. Banners are used to attract users' attention. Advertising graphics that appear on Web site homepages are called **banners**. As with most forms of advertising, banner ads do not necessarily precipitate immediate sales. However, in time they do build brand awareness.

Retailers that sell online encourage customers to share pertinent personal information so that they can build data bases and update them regularly. Strong graphics, top-notch copy writing, and electronic tools should lead a prospective customer through the site logically and expediently. These elements become the fixtures in Internet retailing. Merchandise must be presented with great care graphically in order to compensate for the inability of customers to touch and feel. In addition to these rudiments, shopping cart features and payment options must be clearly identified and easily accessed. **Shopping carts** are special software features that allow online shoppers to collect several products and park them electronically until they are ready to purchase the items. Customer services and opportunities to communicate with the retailer should be fully integrated so that visitors will become customers.

Privacy and Security Issues

Moving from a cash-based society, where a degree of anonymity is experienced, to one where personal details must be divulged in order to do business can be upsetting. Many people are apprehensive about the type and amount of personal information that is available to anyone on the Internet. Many of us do not realize that a record of everything from our birth to the last box of cereal we purchased may be available to outside sources. Because the World Wide Web is sometimes thought of as the Wild Wacky Web, and

shurfers Name coined to designate surfers on the Internet who choose to shop.

homepage The first screen image that comes up when users enter a Web site.

banners Advertising graphics that appear on Web site homepages.

shopping carts Special software features that allow online shoppers to collect several products and park them electronically until they are ready to purchase the items.

because industry self-regulation and governmental legislation is continually being developed, privacy issues are in a state of flux.

Protecting Privacy

There is a fine line between that which is private and proprietary and that which people are willing to share. One person may not think twice about giving name, address, telephone and credit card numbers over the phone to a catalog retailer. Another may give more thought to putting that information out on the Internet. Yet in both circumstances the possibility exists that this information will be sold or bartered to other businesses, or even stolen by unscrupulous individuals. Other people, curious about from where the next great offer will come, do not hesitate to divulge basic personal data as well as more sensitive information. For most people, the greater the perceived gain, the more personal information they will share. Those that volunteer information may also be more susceptible to spam. **Spam** is unsolicited e-mail or advertisements received on the Internet.

spam Unsolicited mail and advertisements on the Web.

Public and Private Information It is easy for anyone to find out matters of public record including births, deaths, marriages, divorces, mortgage transfers, bankruptcies, corporate acquisitions, and initial public stock offerings(IPOs). It may be a bit more difficult, but not impossible, to dig up past employment and medical records and personal behavior information. Commercial data bases such as Dun and Bradstreet and Coles Directory contain a wealth of information and can be purchased by subscribers. Coles operates like a reverse telephone directory, giving phone numbers that cross-reference addresses. Other names and addresses in a specific block or building can be found through this service that is available on CD-ROM. Credit card use, telephone calling activity, and the number of hits on a Web site are all pieces of information that are readily available to the professional marketer and the talented amateur detective.

Adopting Privacy Measures Some Internet providers do not sell the telephone numbers of its subscribers to telephone marketers, although they may use them to do telemarketing on behalf of the companies with which they partner. With retailer and provider partnerships on an upswing, this decision is a mixed blessing for shoppers.

encryption codes Computer programs that prevent hackers from committing crimes such as fraud and unauthorized access of personal information.

hackers Individuals who break into computer systems with criminal intent.

Pin codes and passwords set up by providers for customers help maintain privacy and security standards. Encryption codes prevent hackers from breaking into systems and stealing sensitive data. **Encryption codes** are computer programs that prevent unauthorized users from committing crimes such as fraud and access of personal information. **Hackers** are individuals who break into computer systems with criminal intent. They represent the dark side of computer savvy specialists. Some companies are developing devices that scan the irises of eyes in order to tighten security at ATM machines. Voice, face, and fingerprint scanners that verify identification at the point of sale involve technologies that are expected to transfer well to the Internet.

Government Regulation of the Internet   Upholders of the U.S. Constitution's First Amendment are at odds with parents and others who prefer to see provisions in place guarding against indecent materials being seen by or sold to children on the Internet. Struck down by legislators in 1997, the Communications Decency Act would have been a provision of the 1996 Telecommunication Act, making it a crime to transmit indecent material to minors on the Internet. The industry responded with software blocking systems to make discretion a parental responsibility.

By 2001, there were scores of bills passed or pending in congress that could restrict Internet use. Many of these have serious implications for retailers and other practitioners of e-commerce. For example, the deluge of printed privacy policies delivered along with credit card bills during mid-2001, was a direct consequence of the Gramm-Leach-Bliley Act of 1999. The ways companies might use customers' private information was explicitly stated. In addition, account holders were given the option of sharing—or not sharing—their personal information with third party companies.[13]

Businesses using the Internet contend that a light hand concerning government regulation will allow the Internet to grow. Most e-commerce participants advocate self-regulation as a way to monitor Internet activity that may compromise customer privacy and security. In that way, the industry—not government—will control the medium and protect its ability to generate sales.

Reducing Fraud

As in all other forms of commerce where currency—hard or electronic—is concerned, misuse and fraud are omnipresent. However, it is expected that innovations such as secure electronic transaction protocol will help guard Internet transactions. **Secure electronic transmission protocol(SET)** is software that makes transactions between buyers and sellers more safe. It was developed by major credit card companies Visa and Mastercard. Industry support, garnered from other credit card companies, banks, and computer software companies, has given momentum to the cause. As systems such as SET become more sophisticated and widespread, it is expected that risk to retailers and customers will be reduced.

Did You Know?
We all know that *cookies* are small files put on our computers by online companies that want to track content preferences and traffic patterns. In a study done by NPD Group, 61 percent of respondents who understood the cyber definition said they didn't mind cookies being placed on their hard drive. Two of those surveyed thought a *cookie* was edible! Do you believe cookies are an invasion of your privacy?
Source: *Wall Street Journal.* "These 'Cookies' Aren't Monsters." September 9, 1999:B6.

secure electronic transmission protocol(SET)   Software that makes transmission between buyers and sellers safer.

Online Marketing Communications

The Internet has spawned new ways of communicating with customers and supply chain members. Technology has made it possible for vendors and retailers to operate faster and more efficiently. Standardization in electronic payment options make it easier for consumers to do business on the Web. Customer service has become more personal and effective. These important areas are now covered.

Supply Chain Use of Internet Technology

Manufacturers and retailers seeking to make supply chain management more efficient have also tapped into Internet technology. Apparel manufacturer Liz Claiborne, using Intranet and Extranet communication tools, keeps in touch with 250 mills, factories, and offices in Asia. Secured computer links between business partners such as retailers and suppliers are called **extranets**. In many parts of the globe, telecommunication systems may be more advanced than highway systems, making the extranet a logical alternative to tedious business travel.

extranet Secured computer links between business partners such as retailers and suppliers.

Microsoft has developed a program called Value Chain Initiative that brings together scores of software, hardware, and logistics companies. The group's main objective is to develop a set of international standards to aid communication between retailers, manufacturers, and suppliers. Better communication will allow supply chain members to track merchandise shipments globally. All stages of the production process will be monitored more accurately and time savings will be realized.[14] More on the use of Internet technologies in logistics management is covered in Chapter 16, Supply Chain Management.

Smart Card Technology

Anticipating that use of credit and smart card technology will accelerate on the Web, many companies are taking a proactive stance. Some are collaborating on technologies that will standardize systems used to accept credit card payments online. Others are perfecting smart card use as an accepted payment system for small ticket online transactions. Many customers will not or can not choose to pay for smaller items by credit card, but might prefer a cash-loaded smart card. Customers and retailers benefit from smart card technology when loyalty programs are brought online. Smart cards can be reloaded with currency via telephone, making cyber stores more alluring. Many retail stores, malls, and restaurants offer smart card gift certificates.

Online Customer Service

Deciding how to serve customers better is important to all retailers, particularly those on the Internet. The results of one research study showed that 49 percent of online users felt multichannel retailers provided better customer service than pure-play retailers.[15] Whatever the format, innovative software can help provide the personal touch to online customer service.

Most sites have e-mail communications, but in the past customer queries on some sites have not been answered for several days. E-mail used in conjunction with other marketing is more meaningful to customers and effective for retailers. Promotional offers work best for merchants that reach loyal customers regularly.

Special software provides access to customer service dialog. On some sites customers can ask questions about products or delivery and receive answers in real time. Some companies have developed multimedia software that allows customers to use text, graphics, audio, and video to answer questions about their orders. Some media sites feature avatars that entertain and sometimes take visitors shopping. An **avatar** is an animated graphic form that portrays a person. Some are able to interact with customers as described in From the Field.

Customer-tracking software alerts retailers as to why some customers avoid certain Web pages. It can also determine why customers, after loading their shopping carts, exit a site before selecting a payment option. Information like this is used by retailers to upgrade their sites, re-merchandise their online stores, and bring better value to their online customers.

The Internet is the most ubiquitous form of e-retailing, but it is not the only one. The next section explores more technologically based nonstore retailing options.

avatar An animated graphic form that portrays a human.

CYBERSCOOP

Ananova is a British newscaster who is a cyber-woman. She has been developed to put a face to daily newscasts. Special text-to-speech software gives credence to this virtual news anchor, called an *avatar*. Visit her at www.ananova.com. Have you met any other avatars?

Electronic Retailing Options

Electronic kiosks, CD-ROM, and television retailing are other ways in which retailers are reaching customers through technology. Each aspect is considered in turn.

Electronic Kiosks

Not a new innovation, kiosks have been in use for as long as ATMs. Robotic music units in malls sell CDs, floral kiosks in airports dispense products without human intervention, and information units provide store and local area highlights, and sometimes Internet access to customers. Kiosks take up

From the Field: Riot G-urls
by Peter Braunstein

In the never-ending quest for a more personalized experience, avatars—animated personalities who serve as wisecracking guides to various fashion and content Web sites—are coming into their own. These walking, talking, occasionally brooding creations are becoming more and more complex. Some of the newest avatars are even capable of interacting with human visitors to the url's they call home.

Case in point: Vivian Livingston, the avatar which inhabits the eponymous Vivian-Lives.com, a site that mixes Reality TV-style voyeurism with links to hip fashion e-tail Web sites. Sherrie Krantz, the founder and chief executive officer of Forever After Inc., the corporate parent of Vivian-Lives.com, perceived Vivian as a kind of online best friend, style guru and fashionista living in Manhattan's trendy Nolita neighborhood. Those accessing the site can follow 24-year-old Vivian from room to room in her small, hopefully rent-controlled apartment, listening to her advice on fashion dos and don'ts. Clicking on enticing items in her wardrobe transports users to

such e-tailers as StyleShop.com, where they can buy the selected merchandise.

Vivian epitomizes what can be called the "warts-and-all" avatar. She's not there simply to entertain online audiences, but to draw them into her world, where they share the highs, lows, and mundane interludes of her life. A casual visit to the site might expose visitors to Vivian's reaction to a fashion trend, a potential romantic interest, or even a film.

The idea of the "avatar with attitude" seems to be catching on. Seventeen.com, the online kid sister of the world-famous teen magazine, has staked its place in the avatar wars through a new incarnation, Samantha Seventeen. A Seventeen.com spokesperson described Samantha as follows: "She looks like Leslie Bibb from "Popular," has a personality like Rachel on "Friends," and dresses like Gwyneth Paltrow." Indeed, shame on the aspiring avatar who *doesn't* dress like Gwynnie. Desktop users equipped with speakers and microphone input can interact with the voice-activated Samantha, who not only helps users log onto the Seven-

teen.com site, but also opens programs, takes users shopping, and points the way to other interesting, primarily fashion and entertainment Web sites.

Like Vivian, Samantha has a life, and being 17, has very little patience for technology-challenged, non-virtual friends. Perched behind, and occasionally slurping her omnipresent latte, Samantha does hair-flips, makes cell-phone calls when she's bored and greets users with a casual "Hey, girl." If she asks you which Web site you'd like to visit, and you take too long to respond, Samantha will snap,"Which one, I'm not psychic!" or "C'mon, my latte's getting cold."

"Samantha puts a face on our Web site and is the ultimate branding tool," said the Seventeen.com spokesperson. "And if I do a good job, she'll be one of the most in-demand costumes come next Halloween." Like, totally.

Source: *Women's Wear Daily.Internet.* "Nothing But Net." December, 2000:14-15. Courtesy or Fairchild Publications, Inc.

little space and are located anywhere people are in transit, shopping, or seeking services at odd hours.

Electronic kiosks are extensions to conventional businesses. Some retailers use the technology to provide better customer service. Customers can swipe their loyalty cards at a kiosk to update or redeem points when the conventional store is closed. Other retailers use kiosks to extend their store inventories. These are three applications that indicate the great potential of kiosk retailing. Other examples illustrate the options open to creative retailers that use kiosks:

■ American Greetings uses CreataCard kiosks at which customers can design their own cards.

- Ski America Enterprises sells ski lift tickets for major resorts in select retail stores.
- Kodak developed its Picture Maker that allows customers to do their own enlarging of prints. Kiosks are located in supermarkets, drug stores, mass merchandisers as well as photo shops. The company reports a 95 percent customer return rate.[16]
- In-store kiosks are to supplement sales of hard-to-stock items. A kiosk used to educate customers and sell lawn and garden products in Carrefour is illustrated in Figure 7.5.
- Borders installed its Title Sleuth kiosk in its bookstores. Customers can search for any book, video, or music title in the store.[17]
- Currency-accepting kiosks let cutomers pay for products and services at unattended retail locations safely and expediently.

In 2001, there were approximately 150,000 kiosks in the field. That number is expected to increase to 450,000 units by 2006. Volume generated by kiosks is expected to top $3 billion by that time.[18] As momentum builds, kiosks will bring more options to customers and more sales to retailers.

Figure 7.5 An electronic kiosk at a Carrefour hypermarket in France lets customers order lawn and garden equipment that is not on display in the store.

CD-ROM Support

A multimedia presentation format, CD-ROMS offer video, animation, photos, voice, music, graphics, and text material on a single disk. Catalog and store retailers with strong brand equity that use CD-ROM formats find that the atmosphere may be less charged with competition and offer shoppers fewer distractions than a mall Web site. Retailers and manufacturers might also find the medium appropriate to use for product support functions. "How-to" supplements that often accompany products may be distributed on CD-ROM, supplanting video tapes.

A Japanese CD-ROM educational game combines fun with experimential learning. Titled "Conveni," the game simulates setting up and running a retail convenience store. Users make store location, layout and product placement decisions, and also select employees, juggle sales and gross margins. Hints on how to be more successful are included and operational challenges are inserted at opportune moments in the game. This curious product opens many doors for future retail training and development products that could be CD-ROM based.

Television Retailing

There you are, sitting in front of the tube, zapping. You pause for a moment and view a sleek model in spandex, demonstrating the latest exercise techniques on sparkling equipment. You become more intrigued as you learn how to combat flabby glutei, and before you know it, a half hour has passed. Is this the 21st century version of Richard Simmons? Not quite, but you are experiencing a 30-minute infomercial. Then comes the call to action, "Dial our 800 number, operators are standing by." Zap again and see what HSN or QVC have to offer. It might be jewelry, apparel, cosmetics, or exercise equipment. What could be better retail selling tools than big screen presentation, stereo sound, excellent visuals, brilliant color, and action? In this section home shopping channels, infomercials, and interactive TV are discussed.

Home Shopping Channels Once considered the principal pastime of senior citizens and kooky collectors, home shopping channels have crossed geographic, demographic, and psychographic thresholds as more people shop electronically. Two major channels compete in the United States. The first to enter the interactive electronic market was Home Shopping Network(HSN), with ordering and fulfillment centers located in St. Petersburg, Florida. The second was QVC, headquartered in West Chester, Pennsylvania. Its acronym stands for "Quality, Value, and Convenience." In contrast Home Order Television(HOT), a German shopping channel, serves customers with distinctly different tastes than those of Americans.

HSN carries $20 jeans to $200 handbags and built a business using celebrities such as Ivana Trump and Susan Lucci. HSN is part of USA Networks. The shopping channel also has international television shopping ventures in Japan and Germany. According to Paul Guyardo, executive vice president of Marketing, "Interactive commerce started with us 23 years ago."[19]

HSN has partnered with Excite@Home to create a customer shopping experience that can be accessed through the cable television channel and Excite.com. Continuing the interactive focus, HSN expects to offer simultaneous online shopping so that family and friends can enjoy the experience together.[20]

Founded in 1986, QVC is considered the more sophisticated of the two, and has partnered with retailers such as Saks Fifth Avenue and designers such as Diane von Furstenberg to sell fashion items. In joint venture with BSkyB, QVC operates globally. The company leads cable shopping channels in sales volume and viewers.

Employing a cross-promotion strategy, QVC maintains a Web site, qvc.com. To be able to order online rather than endure an hour's TV slot is appealing to many contemporary shoppers.

When Home Order Television (HOT) went on the air in Germany in 1995, those involved learned that it was not easy to transfer an American concept to Europe. Initially the programming was not as exciting and fast paced as U.S. shopping channels. The German shopper perceived TV shopping as tacky and also displayed different product tastes. For example, customers liked to shop for wine via TV and also looked for more expensive jewelry than their American counterparts. On the positive side, HOT is owned by one of the largest direct marketing houses in the world, Quelle Schickedanz AG, which brings expertise and capital to the venture. Germans are known for being the most aggressive mail-order and catalog shoppers in the world, and their tendency to shop nonstore retailers was expected to carry over to the e-retailing sector.[21]

Certain product classifications sell better than others on television. Jewelry, dolls, and other collectibles have fared well. Apparel sales have not met expectations of television retailers for two main reasons. Customers do not find that fashions are adequately portrayed on TV, and items cannot be touched or tried-on. Lower ticket apparel sells well because of a lower perceived risk to consumers. These are, of course, the same complaints Web and print catalog shoppers voice. Scheduling television segments according to audience preferences is also a challenge.

Infomercials Thirty-minute messages that entertain as well as sell are another form of e-commerce that are used by manufacturers and retailers to reach consumers. It is easy to become hooked by the energetic, but always sincere sounding pitch of the host. With 30 minutes in which to sell, much detail can be given about a product. Companies that choose this format have all the tools of professional delivery at their disposal. No wonder many of us do not realize we are watching an infomercial until well into the presentation. For the retailer, production and air time costs can be prohibitive. The format works well for companies that are able to reach their target markets during the odd, and often late, hours that infomercials are usually aired. Exercise equipment targeted to young fitness buffs at midnight may find the appropriate audience but vitamins geared to senior citizens will not make an impact at that hour. As technology advances, it will be possible to combine infomercials with real-time ordering options.

Interactive Television The backbone of what will ultimately enable people to participate in true interactive retailing is called video datacasting. **Video datacasting** is a technology that uses TV airwaves to send Internet data. WebTV, developed by Microsoft, is a video datacasting system that provides access to the Web by combining the best aspects of Internet technology and television. With Internet connection and a TV tuner card, viewers can

video datacasting Technology that uses television airwaves to send Internet data.

watch regular TV, cable, or satellite broadcasts on their computer screen. Individuals can receive data from any of these sources 24 hours a day and store them for future use if desired. Using e-mail is possible and the potential for retail opportunities seems limitless.

When cable providers begin to carry more interactive portions of programming, and broadband high-speed connections become more prevalent, users will be able to participate in other activities. For example, students could access a special reading list while watching a program on a history channel. By using a handheld device linked to the TV, cable consumers will be able to order merchandise seen on programs. In 1998, Microsoft entered into an agreement with major cable company TCI to allow the marriage of cable and Internet technology to take place.[22] This direction will also change the face of retailing.

Watching a sitcom is one thing, serious shopping is another. However, the potential of this medium may be compelling to retailers. Other benefits include being able to reach exclusive target markets when people may be more relaxed at home. It is also a pull system since viewers initiate programming and ultimately product choices.

This chapter has explored many new electronic options for retailers. The implosion of the dotcom industry early this century provided a wake-up call to many participants in e-commerce. The next wave of development will provide slower, but more stable paths to profitablilty. Methods of evaluating sales, promotion effectiveness, and customer response are works in progress. At the end of 2000, there were 400 million Internet users worldwide. By 2005, the number of Internet users worldwide is expected to grow to 977 million.[23] With statistics of this magnitude, one fact can be stated with surety: this is only the beginning.

Summary

E-retailing is perhaps the most exciting form of nonstore retailing. Doing business on the Web, via electronic kiosks, television shopping channels, interactive television, and other forms of e-commerce will challenge retailers and tempt consumers. Web retailing is expected to grow, perhaps transcend some classic types of retailing, but more likely become a part of multichannel approaches to commerce.

There are many advantages and disadvantages to retailers and customers who choose to participate in online retailing. The principal advantage to retailers is the opportunity to target attractive demographic groups. Retailers can also develop markets further and reach customers more conveniently in their homes. The key customer advantages of Internet retailing are convenience and time savings. Major disadvantages are the inability to physically examine products, privacy and security breaches. Whether the rewards will outnumber the risks is yet to be determined. Internet users tend to be well-educated females of moderate financial means who shop for books, computers, and music online. Profiles vary greatly by country and are changing rapidly as people from diverse geographic, demographic, and psychographic backgrounds gain access to the Internet.

Retail Web sites fall into five categories: pure-play, dual-channel, multi-channel, electronic spin-offs, and nontransactional sites. Multichannel retailers that utilize several ways to reach customers are those that will prosper.

Designing Web sites that sell is both art and science. Effective sites must capture the customer's attention on the homepage and present exciting graphics, copy writing, and merchandise in a user-friendly environment. Customer service can be greatly enhanced by technologically advanced marketing communication methods.

The use of electronic kiosks is growing. Television shopping has a place in e-retailing but may be eclipsed by or integrated into Web technology as it grows. Interactive TV is on the next wave of technological advancement. No matter what the format, e-retailing is here to stay and will provide a framework for growth, study, compromise, and promise for retailers and customers in the 21st century.

Questions for Review and Discussion

1. How and when did the Internet evolve?
2. What is the status of e-retailing today? How does it impact classic retailers and other forms of nonstore retailing?
3. Who is the typical Web shopper? Why are demographics and psychographics of the typical shopper changing? How do shoppers' profiles vary globally?
4. What are two disadvantages to retailers who do business on the Web? How can these obstacles be overcome?
5. What are two advantages to customers who shop on the Web? How can Web retailers use these advantages to provide better customer service?
6. What constitutes an effective retail Web site? Of those that you have visited, which do you believe are the most compelling? Why?
7. How can electronic kiosks help retailers expand their businesses? Do you believe they can replace customer service representatives?
8. What is the status of credit and smart card use online?

9. What types of shoppers do home shopping channels attract? How do they differ from Web shoppers?

Endnotes

1. Kaplan, Karen. "Deal Divides a Fallen CompuServe; Telecom: The Industry Pioneer's Customer Base Will Go to Rival AOL and It's Network Services to Worldcom in $1.27 Billion Accord." *Los Angeles Times.* September 9, 1997: D1.

2. Angwin, Julia. "America Online Boosts Price for Flagship Service." *Wall Street Journal.* May 23, 2001:A3.

3. *eBusiness Trends.* "Western Europe Pulls Ahead of United States." IDC's ICMM version 7.3, 2002. January 03, 2002-No89 Accessed: January 4, 2002. www.idc.com/newsletters/

4. Global Online Retailing, an Ernst&Young Special Report. *Stores.* January 2001:7

5. Shern, Stephanie. "Executive Summary.' Global Online Retailing, an Ernst & Young Special Report. *Stores.* January, 2001:3..

6. Global Online Retailing, an Ernst&Young Special Report. *Stores.* January, 2001:5.

7. Hyde, Linda. PricewaterhouseCoopers Presentation. AMS/ACRA Triennial Conference. Columbus, Ohio, November 5, 2000.

8. *Wall Street Journal.* July 8, 1997: B1.

9. Quick, Rebecca. "'Find Anything' at Junglee.com—Well Almost." *Wall Street Journal.* March 29, 1999:B1.

10. Kulish, Nicholas. "Everybody's Biddin' La Vida Loca As Ricky Products Overrun eBay." *Wall Street Journal.* June 9, 1999:B1.

11. Anders, George. "How eBay Will Battle Sham Bids, Mislabeling." *Wall Street Journal.* January 15, 1999:B1.

12. Belsky, Gary. "Get it quick—and pay less—by shopping on the Web." *Money.* September, 1997: 174.

13. Schwartz, John. "Privacy Policy Notices Are Called Too Common and Too confusing." *The New York Times.* Online Edition. WWW.nytimes.com/2001/05/07business/07PRIV.html.

14. Zimmermann, Kim Ann. "Internet: The Vital Link in Global Supply Management." *Women's Wear Daily.* Global Supplement. July, 1997: 78-79.

15. Surmacz, Jon. "Customers Know Best." Darwin Online. WWW2.darwinmag.com/learn/numbers/report_041701.cfm April 17, 2001.

16. Yogachandra, Nat. Kodak Picture Maker: Bigger Pictures in Minutes." April, 2001:21.

17. "Borders Group Inc. Title Sleuth." *Kiosk Magazine.* April, 2001:31.

18. Connell, Rufus. "State of the Market." *Kiosk Magazine.* March, 2001:16.

19. Vranica, Suzanne. "Home Shopping Network to Run TV Ads." *Wall Street Journal.* October 3, 2000:B12.

20. Seckler, Valerie. "HSN, Excite Hook Up in Shopping Deal." *Women's Wear Daily.* July 27, 2000:13.

21. Pentz, Michelle. "Teleshopping Gets a Tryout in Europe." *Wall Street Journal.* September 9, 1996: B10A.

22. Fixmer, Rob. "Personal Computers; Windows 98 Feature Combines TV, Terminal and the Internet." *New York Times* 18, 1998:5. http. August://web.lexis-nexis.com/univers, November 1998.

23. Nua Internet Surveys: "CNET: Global B2C Revenues to Grow Six-fold by 2005." IDC Data. Online: www.nua.ie/surveys/index. April 25, 2001.

Chapter 8

Global Retailing

Learning Objectives

After completing this chapter you should be able to:

- Summarize the dynamics of global expansion and the reasons why it is occurring.

- Identify critical success factors of global retailers.

- Discern the advantages and disadvantages of the many types of global retail involvement.

- Explain the impact that the balance of trade has on the global economy.

- Relate how culture affects retailing practices in various countries.

- Determine the differences and similarities of retail trade as practiced in other countries.

Figure 8.1 Global brand awareness paved the way for retail expansion. This Coke bearing Chinese characters awaits its consumer at a Malaysian outdoor restaurant. The brand is recognizable in any language (See p. 216).

We live in what may prove to be a rare moment in retail history. Never before have so many factors converged with such vigor that all but the most pessimistic see the opportunities for retailers to expand globally. On one hand volatility in the Middle East may retard international retail development, but on the other the admission of China to the World Trade Organization may hasten it. Changes in technology, trade laws, competition, product sourcing, brand recognition, and customers affect global expansion. The changing economies of both **industrialized countries**—those that have reached full production capabilities and have well-developed infrastructures and technologies—and countries that are still developing offer retailers the chance to expand operations in foreign lands.

Retailers may operate domestically on two levels beyond their own national borders. **Domestic retailers** are organizations that are doing business only in their home countries. **International retailers** include those that operate in their home countries and in countries within their own or one other trading bloc. **Global retailers** are those that do business in their home countries and in more than one other trading bloc. A **trading bloc** is a major geographic trading area such as Europe, North America, or the Pacific Rim countries in Asia. Wal-Mart, for example, is based in the United States and also does business in the Pacific rim, North and South America, and Europe.

The ownership of some global retailers is apparent to customers. In other cases this is not clear because many do not operate under the names of their parent companies. Retailers that the average person would insist are domestically owned are not. For example, European powerhouses own some of the largest U.S. supermarket chains. In an effort to dominate East Coast supermarket retailing, Netherlands-based Royal Ahold has purchased several strong companies including Finast, Giant Food, and Stop and Shop.

An analysis of the top 200 global retailers shows that 39 percent are headquartered in the United States. Japan ranks second with 15 percent. Taken collectively, European countries and the United Kingdom account for 37.5 percent of sales generated by the top 200 global retail companies. Not surprising, the larger the company in terms of sales volume, the more likely it is to be a global retailer. Number one Wal-Mart is a prime example.[1] Other top global retailers are listed in Chapter 2.

---

industrialized countries Countries that have reached full production capabilities and have well-developed infrastructures and technologies.

domestic retailers Retail organizations that do business only in their home countries.

international retailers Retail organizations that operate in their home countries and within their own trading bloc or one other trading bloc.

global retailers Retail organizations that do business in their home countries and in more than one other trading bloc.

trading bloc Major geographic trading area such as Europe, North America, or the Pacific Rim countries in Asia.

CYBERSCOOP

For a list of U.S. retailers with international operations visit the National Retail Federation site. Find out what's new by going to www.nrf.com. Click on "Retail Information" and find your way to "Retailers with International Operations." Does Saks have a store in Japan?

This chapter examines the reasons for global expansion, critical success factors, comparative retail practices in other countries, the intricacies of global trade, and the importance of acknowledging cultural differences.

Dynamics of Global Expansion

To fully understand the dynamics of global retailing, it is necessary to identify the environmental factors introduced in Chapter 3 that affect expansion. Changes in consumer behavior that accelerate expansion also should be considered. This information provides insight into the optimal conditions under which expansion occurs.

Changes in the Global Environment

Economic indicators, emerging markets, global brand awareness, technological advances, global sourcing, trade alliances, and available capital all contribute significantly to changes in the global environment:

- *Economic indicators.* Retailers in many industrialized countries are experiencing the pains of sustained growth in saturated markets. Many developing economies are ripe for retail expansion, and growing numbers of middle-class people with new-found discretionary incomes are ready to purchase retail products. Individuals in newly industrialized countries, including many in Asia, are faced with the dilemma of having money but not enough stores in which to spend it or products on which to spend it. Opportunities abound.
- *Emerging markets.* Several geographic areas have been identified as prime for retail development. Criteria used to determine these countries or regions include gross domestic product (GDP), population statistics, household income data, retail sales per capita, stage of industrial development, and degree of political stability. The general consensus is that the following parts of the world are key emerging markets: Asia including Taiwan, India, China, Korea, and Malaysia; Eastern Europe especially the Czech Republic and Slovakia; Mexico and Central America; sub-Saharan Africa; and South America, including, Brazil, Chile, and Peru.
- *Global brand recognition.* The ease of global travel, improved communications, and better marketing have all contributed to brand awareness. In many universities around the globe, significant numbers of students are from distant shores. Employees of global corporations are often assigned an overseas tour of duty, and trips abroad are a popular form of vacation travel. Its no wonder that Gap jeans find a home in Bangkok, Chanel handbags in

Figure 8.2 Bata, based in Toronto, Canada, maintains shoe factories in developing countries and retail stores around the world, including a Bata store in France and a more modest version on the island of Nevis in the Caribbean.

Japan, or Fortnum and Mason tea in the United States. To many U.S. travelers who are a bit homesick, spotting a Dunkin' Donuts in Kuala Lumpur or a TCBY in Taiwan is a thrill. The same could be said for non-U.S. travelers who are fans of U.S. goods and services.

■ *Technological advances.* As stressed throughout this text, technology is changing the way business is done domestically and globally. Retailers and customers can have what they want, where and when they want it. Integrated computer networks are a necessary component of global retailing. They facilitate the movement of goods from a factory in Slovakia, to a warehouse in London, and then to stores in the United States.

■ *Global sourcing.* Companies that have the ability to purchase raw product, manufacture goods, maintain sound quality control, and ship merchandise to their intended end users efficiently have long held dominant positions in the marketplace. Retailers that have these capabilities are well positioned to expand globally. When a company seeks global dominance, it goes where labor rates are favorable, well-trained workforces are available, local governments are open to foreign investment, and products can be procured at good value. In their respective ways, Wal-Mart, Pier 1, and Bata are masters of these techniques. Two Bata shoe stores are illustrated in Figure 8.2.

■ *Trade alliances.* EU, NAFTA, ASEAN, MERCOSUR, and WTO are acronyms familiar to the international business community. NAFTA and WTO were introduced in Chapter 3. The **European Union (EU)** is one of the largest trading blocs in the world with 15 member nations. Details on the EU and its common currency appear later in this chapter. The **Association of Southeast Asian Nations (ASEAN)** is a trade alliance set up in 1967 with U.S. backing to benefit countries including Brunei, Indonesia, Malaysia, the Philippines, Singapore, Thailand, and later, Vietnam. **MERCOSUR** is a trade agreement to promote free trade among several South American countries, including Argentina, Brazil, Paraguay, and Uruguay. Associate members are Chile and Bolivia. The end of the twentieth century saw a lessening of trade barriers and bureaucratic turmoil although there is still much room for improvement. **Free trade,** the conduct of business without boundaries or taxation, is emerging as the global norm. The outcome of this trend will be better products and prices and greater selection.

■ *Availability of capital.* As in other vital areas of business, global expansion demands that capital and credit be readily available. Development of truly global banking institutions, investment firms, and currency markets have made this possible.

Changes in Customers

Brand recognition plays a big role in customer awareness globally. Exposure to new cultures, ideas, and products increases the likelihood that existing tastes will change. This applies to Americans' taste for foreign goods and the tastes of people elsewhere for products from the United States. Certain countries are known for producing top quality in one or more product categories. For example, a fine-tooled leather bag from Japan might not be prized, but one from Italy would be highly valued. Conversely, one would not expect to find sophisticated electronic items in Italy, but would in Japan. Taste levels and value consciousness are particularly important dimensions of consumer behavior.

■ *Taste levels.* Taste in products varies greatly by country—particularly those attributes of taste involving style, color, packaging, and dietary preference. However, one constant remains. Throughout the world, taste levels are becoming more homogeneous, more alike than different from one global neighbor to the other. This phenomenon is caused by a variety of factors including intensive exposure to world media, growing use of the Internet, increased frequency of global business and personal travel, and preference for imported goods. Import snobbery is related to the personal need to feel special or different. Certain individuals perceive a higher value in imported products and revel in saying, "My hosiery comes from Fogal in Switzerland," or "I purchased that hand-tooled leather trunk in Ecuador." Actually, don't

European Union (EU) One of the largest trading blocs in the world, its 15 member nations include Austria, Belgium, Denmark, Finland, France, Germany, Greece, Ireland, Italy, Luxembourg, the Netherlands, Portugal, Spain, Sweden, and the United Kingdom.

Association of Southeast Asian Nations (ASEAN) Trade alliance set up in 1967, with U.S. backing to benefit countries including Brunei, Indonesia, Malaysia, the Philippines, Singapore, Thailand, and later, Vietnam.

MERCOSUR Trade agreement to promote free trade among several South American countries, including Argentina, Brazil, Paraguay, and Uruguay. Associate members are Chile and Bolivia.

free trade The conduct of business without boundaries or taxation.

Figure 8.3 Switzerland's Fogal stores bring high-quality, high-price hosiery and intimate apparel to customers in elite shopping areas like Bond Street in London.

we all sometimes share these sentiments? A Fogal store targeting customers with high taste levels is illustrated in Figure 8.3.

■ *Value consciousness.* The quest for value for money spent was the catch phrase of the 1990s and may well serve as a slogan for this century as well. Attaining higher levels of education in both an academic and a consumer sense makes people more sophisticated and wary. Periods of recession and other economic unrest make individuals more cautious about how, where, or whether their money is to be spent. Changes in spiritual values make some people question whether as many "things" are needed in the first place. Such caution is a common and important part of the consumer experience.

Well-educated consumers demand better products. Wariness challenges retailers to become more conscious of consumers wants and needs and more creative in developing marketing strategies. Living well, providing more for one's children, and desiring a safe, comfortable home are universal values. No doubt they will continue to bolster retail sales.

In addition to monitoring changes in the global retail environment and in consumers, it is imperative for retailers to explore the many reasons why global expansion is occurring so that they might be better poised to open stores abroad. Many analysts believe that global retailing is as important a growth strategy as e-retailing.

Reasons for Global Expansion

Although it may appear that global retailing is a contemporary movement, the seeds for expansion were sown long ago. Fast food chains such as Kentucky Fried Chicken (KFC) were among the first to identify global opportunities. Producers of consumer goods like Coca Cola, Pepsi, and Levi Strauss have been trading internationally for decades. Many pluses and minuses are considered when expanding globally (See Figure 8.1).

Facilitating Factors

There are many reasons why retailers look to other shores for expansion.

- Many retailers have saturated or nearly saturated domestic markets. For continued growth, those operating in mature markets must look to fresh turf. This is why U.S. retailers are aggressive internationally. McDonald's, a prime example, is featured in Figure 8.4.

- Mergers and acquisitions since the 1980s created huge retail companies, contributing to saturation.

Figure 8.4 McDonald's in Belgium serves an international clientele and extends a global outlook in its promotions.

- Higher returns may be experienced globally. Some retailers report higher growth rates in their international divisions than they do in their domestic holdings.

- High labor costs in fully industrialized, mature markets cause many manufacturers to produce goods offshore. The logical extension is to retail goods in foreign countries where they are being manufactured.

- Profits for labor-intensive retailers may be higher in countries where the cost of labor is low.

- Fewer trade restrictions in many areas of the globe pave the way for easier entry and operations.

- Improved communication systems, infrastructures, and logistics promote world trade.

- Lower costs of space in foreign markets—especially those in developing countries—are attractive to retailers.

- Market potential may be greater in fully industrialized countries where demographics are more favorable. This is one reason why many foreign companies expand to the United States, where the standard of living is high.

- Capital for investment is available to eligible retailers.

Potential Problems

Expansion abroad also presents potential problems including the following:

- International transactions can involve much red tape. Receiving governmental approval in some foreign countries is often difficult and time consuming.

- Finding adequate retail space for large format stores is often difficult or too expensive in countries with limited landmass.
- The possibility of devaluation of domestic against foreign currencies makes investment outside a retailer's home country more risky.
- Many retailers who are struggling to be profitable in their home markets are reluctant to take on the responsibilities of foreign expansion.
- Qualified employees may be difficult to find in some foreign countries.
- Political instability, including wars and terrorist acts, in certain foreign countries may deter retail expansion.
- Infrastructures may not be sufficiently developed to support retail expansion in some areas.

Related Trade Issues

It is becoming easier to do business most everywhere in the world. Fewer tariffs and quotas mean freer movement of goods. Bureaucracies in the past have made starting a business time consuming and paper intensive. As governments recognize the value of increased trade, they have removed barriers to business openings. Antiquated laws, protectionist policies, and cultural biases also retard development. Progressive nations of all sizes in all stages of industrial development agree that in order to promote a workable global economy, all parties involved must be flexible. Local governments, ministries of trade, chambers of commerce, financial institutions, and trade associations work as facilitators with retailers to expedite global expansion. **Ministries of trade** are government offices able to assist businesses with importing and exporting activities. The common goals of these organizations are job creation, sales, and profits.

ministries of trade Government offices able to assist businesses with importing and exporting activities.

Criteria for Global Success

Global and international retailers face the same challenges domestic retailers face, and then some. The need for quality management, prime locations, adequate financing, astute merchandising, and good customer service does not change substantially by country. However, the desire to go global presents a whole new frame of reference for retailers that thought they could use their domestic "how-to" books. Strategies for global success vary greatly depending on the type of retailer, country of expansion, and other factors.

Ten Critical Decision Areas

Companies contemplating international expansion examine several criteria before doing so. Ten critical decision areas include:

1. *Type of ownership.* Should the operation stand alone or be part of a joint venture, partnership, licensing, or franchise arrangement? In most cases it is advantageous—and sometimes mandatory—to set up some type of local partnership.

2. *Management logistics.* Decisions on whether the company will be run from the home country, using expatriates or local management, must be developed.

3. *Degree of cultural integration.* Retailers need to fully acclimate to the countries and local communities in which they operate. A successful global retailer is one that can walk the fine line between adapting totally to a culture and encouraging change within that culture in a nonthreatening way.

4. *Strategic planning direction.* Improper planning and marketing does not work internationally any more than it would domestically. All retail projects require a long-term approach, keen insight regarding the strengths and weaknesses of a situation, and the ability to anticipate the unexpected. Being alert to new opportunities as they unfold is another crucial element, as is thinking globally on all levels of an organization.

5. *Operational flexibility.* Learning how business and social practices differ from those in the home country is crucial. Functioning in a region where technology may be archaic but goods still have to be moved efficiently can be exasperating. For example, operating a business in a country where the Sabbath is on Friday rather than Saturday or Sunday requires adaptability.

6. *Research orientation.* Retailers need to do research before deciding to move into new markets. Identifying population trends and buying habits are two examples of areas that need to be researched. Awareness of the developmental stage of countries seriously affects expansion plans. Fully industrialized countries such as Germany require different types of stores than countries like Malaysia that will not reach full industrialization until well into the 21st century. Per capita retail sales figures help retailers determine consumer spending levels. For example, retail sales per capita figures in Switzerland are the third highest in the world, but retail prices there are higher than in most other countries. In contrast, Venezuela's per capita figures are one-fifth of Switzerland's, reflecting lower prices and a less robust economy.[2] Per capita retail sales for these and many other countries are listed in Table 8.1.

Table 8.1 Per Capita Retail Sales (In US Dollars, 2000)

Japan	$8,578	Poland	2,028
United States	8,135	South Korea	1,908
Switzerland	6,792	Saudi Arabia	1,894
Norway	6,495	Czech Republic	1,727
Denmark	5,712	Argentina	1,561
Germany	5,448	Venezuela	1,527
United Kingdom	5,268	Chile	1,176
France	4,833	Hungary	1,147
Finland	4,627	Mexico	962
Sweden	4,624	Portugal	837
Italy	4,484	Turkey	825
Belgium	4,382	South Africa	580
Canada	4,278	Brazil	533
Australia	4,219	Malaysia	521
Netherlands	3,894	Russia	456
Israel	3,794	Thailand	426
Ireland	3,532	Philippines	405
Hong Kong	3,434	Egypt	271
Austria	3,279	China	307
Singapore	3,061	India	220
Greece	2,499	Indonesia	119
Spain	2,409		

Source: Euromonitor as published in *Stores*. "Economic & Social Indicators." 2002 Global Powers of Retailing. January, 2002:G28/Global Retailing Database, Euromonitor International—Chicago.

7. *Product sourcing efficiencies.* The ability to source products globally is another facet of the success formula. Setting up efficient supply chains and trusting partnerships with vendors are paramount.

8. *Technological expertise.* Using state-of-the-art technology that streamlines manufacturing, movement of goods, merchandise management, and database development is essential to retailers with global outlooks.

9. *Clear business focus.* "Know yourself and to your own self be true" may be the overriding theme of global retailers. They must know what business they are in and see themselves as their customers see them.

10. *Swift decision making.* Researching, planning, and acting within a reasonable period of time also is important. Timing is important to the success of any business, but moving into a city where competition is weak or retail space is underutilized requires immediate action. Sluggish decision making means lost opportunities. Speed also transcends other areas. Decision making is hastened by proper use of technology. Customer service is improved by timely training of employees. Entry into a new market may take less time if the right partnership is formed in the first place.

Other Success Factors

Other success factors are worth noting at this juncture. Retailers considering expansion should first try to do business in countries that speak the same language. For example, retailers in Spain are wise to enter other Spanish speaking countries first. In this case, cultural proximity may be more important than geographic closeness. This concept is particularly important for companies contemplating direct investment. For Spanish companies entering non-Spanish-speaking countries, at first it may be best to wholesale goods. Using local people to manage the distribution operation and then gradually moving into retail sales is less risky than direct investment.

In other cases, it may be more sensible, and ultimately more cost effective, for a retailer to expand within its own trading bloc. For example, Japanese department stores expanded first to Hong Kong, Singapore, and other Southeast Asian countries before making significant strides elsewhere. Keeping a low initial investment is key to a retailer's staying power in a marketplace, to future growth plans, and to eventual profitability. On a similar note, when conducting business in another country, discussions may begin in English but soon lapse into the local vernacular. Key points, innuendo, and basic understanding are frequently lost. It is wise to use translators in these situations.

Acknowledging all sides of the expansion issue, some analysts believe that a backlash movement could occur. More retail expansion could cause national boundaries to diminish in importance, taste levels to become interwoven, and philosophies to merge. If so, some customers caught in these cross-currents may choose to focus again on national pride and buy products only from their own countries. Global retailing requires executives to carefully study and adapt to the cultural climate in the area in which they intend to do business.

Types of Involvement for Global Retailers

Each of the several entry strategies retailers use to do business globally has advantages and disadvantages. The type of involvement selected depends on the objectives of the retailer, degree of control desired, availability of management, intercultural expertise, and budget. Several types of involvement are as follows:

1. *Wholly Owned operations.* Retail ownership, control, and fiscal responsibility remain solely in the hands of the single proprietor, partnership, or corporation involved in global expansion. No local venture partners are sought although local management might be employed. Disney Stores operates on this basis.

2. *Joint venture.* Commonly called a JV, this type of involvement is a partnership between the retail company doing the expansion and a compatible

company in the host country. Under this arrangement, the partners agree upon some portion of actual ownership, control, and fiscal responsibility. Companies such as Wal-Mart, Calvin Klein, and Pier 1 have operated on this basis.

3. *Franchising.* Expansion is less risky when dealing with a proven name and format. Setting up effective master franchise systems is essential when working internationally. A **master franchise** is an ownership arrangement in which one company buys the rights to a large region of a country, setting up scores of individual stores.

4. *Licensing.* This arrangement occurs when a manufacturer or retailer agrees to pay for the right to use a brand or store name to gain entry and awareness for a product or service in a foreign marketplace.

5. *Consignment.* Merchandise from a manufacturer or distributor is placed in a retail store, but revenue is not remitted to the vendor until the goods are actually sold. The risk is clearly on the manufacturer or distributor under this arrangement. Many Japanese department stores work on this basis with their vendors.

6. *Concession.* This is similar to a leased department within a retail store, in-store shop, or mall site. The manufacturer or distributor pays rent for square footage in a store directly to the retailer. In some cases, concessionaires also pay a percentage of sales or profits to the retailer.

7. *Agents and consultants.* Companies interested in starting international operations often seek agents in the countries they wish to explore. These individuals or firms are familiar with their local markets and have experience marketing similar products. They operate on a commission basis.

8. *Exporters.* Exporting products from one country to another is less risky than other types of involvement. A manufacturer's or retailer's responsibility for selling and shipping the products usually ends once the goods have been received by the retailer. Since many retailers now manufacture the goods they sell, this has become an early mode of entry for some companies.

On a high-risk to low-risk spectrum, it is much more difficult to stand alone in a global marketplace. However, it is at this level that the most control over an operation can be exercised in terms of direction, store image, operations, and financial planning.

Often it is necessary to trade off some control in order to minimize risk. This is the main reason many joint ventures are solidified around the world. Local expertise provides better security and business perspective. Learning ways to do business in the community, circumvent red tape, motivate employees, and understand local laws and customers can be accomplished best

master franchise Ownership arrangement in which one company buys the rights to operate in a large region of a country, setting up scores of stores.

Table 8.2

Type of Involvement	Adavantages	Disadavantages
Wholly Owned Acquisitions	■ Distribution channel access ■ Local management utilization ■ Existing infrastructure ■ Immediate knowledge of market ■ Maximum control	■ High cost initially ■ Difficulty finding and integrating compatible stores ■ High financial risk
Joint Ventures	■ Strengths of two partners ■ Local presence in the market ■ Local contacts ■ Local management ■ Less financial risk	■ Difficulty finding the right partner ■ Communication problems between partners ■ Possible erosion of store image
Franchising	■ Consistent image ■ High brand recognition ■ Established operational procedures	■ Risk of too rapid growth ■ Risk of oversaturation
Licensing	■ Immediate access to market ■ Opportunity to build brand equity ■ Lower risk	■ Lack of control over brand quality ■ Communications problems with licensees

with the aid of a well-chosen partner. The advantages and disadvantages of selected types of involvement are summarized in Table 8.2.

International Trade Issues

In the arena of international trade, many factors encourage or retard the movement of goods. The balance of trade is affected by trade alliances, agreements, and disputes. The **balance of trade** is the difference between a country's imports and exports over a period of time, such as a year. When trading partners do not agree on import or export practices, restrictions on trade may occur. **Trade sanctions** are penalties imposed on one country by another in an attempt to curb unfair trade practices. Governing bodies, such as the WTO, administer import and export laws and mediate disputes.

balance of trade The difference between a country's imports and exports over a period of time, such as a year.

trade sanctions Penalties imposed on one country by another in an attempt to curb unfair trade practices.

Trade Development Factors

Currently, many industrialized countries receive more products from foreign countries than they market to them. To restore a favorable balance of trade, countries in this predicament need to export more domestic products. Factors that encourage trade include the following:

- When currency is overvalued in the international exchange markets, (depending on the country), each currency unit may buy more overseas than at home. For example, during the Asian currency crisis of the late 1990s, some U.S. retailers intensified product development. Kmart used the opportunity to upgrade the quality of apparel it manufactured in Asia.[3]

- Manufacturers in many areas of the globe have become savvier and have learned marketing skills that were once known primarily by marketers in the United States and other fully developed countries.

- More efficient, less expensive transportation has lessened logistics problems in many parts of the world.

- Lower wage scales in some parts of the world—particularly Asia—allow lower prices to be placed on products from those areas than on domestic products.

- In the past, a lessening of quality control standards caused products from some countries to loose market share. This situation paved the way for higher-quality goods to be imported from other areas. Quality control tends to be more of an issue in developing countries. As retailers and manufacturers become more experienced in training employees, this problem will be less apparent.

- Regional trade alliances in several parts of the world have made importing easier and more cost effective.

- Less stringent protectionist policies are apparent once nations embrace the benefits of free trade.

Importing can be risky because of changes in international politics. Retailers must be in constant search of sources abroad that can produce quality goods at a low price and in countries where manufacturers have ample quotas. Organizations like Kmart and Limited Brands are masters at foreign sourcing.

Trade Sanctions

Imposing tariffs or placing bans on the importation of products are examples of trade sanctions. The "banana dispute" between the European Union and the United States began when bananas marketed by U.S. companies were shunned in favor of fruit imported from Africa and the Caribbean. Products from these areas generally are preferred in the EU because tariffs are lower and quotas are higher. The EU contended that they had abided by guidelines that were designed to encourage fair trade imposed in 1997, by the World Trade Organization.[4] When the problem escalated in 1999, the United States imposed trade sanctions on the EU which were approved

Figure 8.5 Fifteen Countries of the European Union

by the WTO. Included on the list of products that would be taxed at 100 percent tariff rates were designer handbags, electric coffee makers, bed linens, and bath salts.[5] Trade sanctions can drive up retail prices considerably in large and small stores, placing products out of reach for many individuals.

Impact of the European Union

Many organizations, countries, trading blocs, and individuals create the mechanisms that foster and regulate international trade. Over a period of almost 50 years, Europe has tried to create an integrated economy. Incorporating elements of free trade, harmonization, and standardization has not come easily for the European Economic Community (EEC), which officially became the European Union (EU) in 1992.

Harmonization occurs when tax rates across several countries are brought into equilibrium. **Standardization** refers to the establishment of uniform operational, environmental, and monetary systems across several

harmonization Bringing tax rates across several countries into equilibrium.

standardization Establishment of uniform and monetary systems across several countries.

countries. The 15 countries that make up the EU are Austria, Belgium, Denmark, Finland, France, Germany, Greece, Ireland, Italy, Luxembourg, the Netherlands, Portugal, Spain, Sweden, and the United Kingdom. They are indicated in Figure 8.5. The European market is made up of approximately 380 million people who, under the guidelines of the EU, can be reached across geographic borders without trade restrictions. Citizens are free to travel or work in any of the EU countries. The objectives of the EU include economic growth and increased job opportunities. Savings in the areas of central purchasing, administration, transportation and advertising costs, and time also are anticipated.

Background As early as 1952, six countries banded together to do less-restrictive business in the coal and steel industries. The countries were Belgium, France, Italy, Luxembourg, the Netherlands, and the Federal Republic of Germany. In 1958, the Treaty of Rome established the EEC. The Single European Act of 1986 initiated the drive to reach unity by 1993. By this time, the United Kingdom, Ireland, Denmark, Greece, Spain, and Portugal had become members. On the last day of 1992, the Maastrict Treaty ensured that the 12 member countries would work together to create economic and institutional efficiencies.[6] Later, Finland, Sweden, and Austria joined.

Provisions of the Agreement Operational and policy changes in several areas were implemented. Reverberations are still being felt in the EU and around the world as a result. These changes include:

- *Free trade.* Previous bilateral trade agreements between European countries were terminated, opening the borders to the free flow of goods and services. Tariffs were eliminated.
- *Harmonization.* The leveling off of value-added taxes in member nations is expected to eventually be achieved. A **value-added tax (VAT)** is a tax levied at each stage of processing for a raw material or of production and distribution for a commodity or retail product. VAT is used in EU countries and is similar to a sales tax in the United States. VATs vary greatly by country. For example 15 percent is the established rate in Luxembourg, but in Sweden, the rate is 25 percent. Harmonization will make it easier to conduct business between EU countries and less confusing for customers.
- *Standardization.* Uniform quality controls, health and safety standards, weights and measures were introduced. Standardization does not come easily to some EU countries. Changing the unit of measure for many super-

value-added tax (VAT) Tax on the value levied at each stage of processing for a raw material or of production and distribution for a commodity or retail product. The tax is used in EU countries, and is similar to U.S. sales tax.

market products from pounds to kilograms was a challenge for many retailers in the United Kingdom.

Common Currency Another provision of the Maastrict Treaty was the setting up of the European Central Bank (ECB). The **European Central Bank (ECB)** is the financial institution that administers currency policy for the EU. One of the objectives of the ECB is to encourage intra-European trade. The common currency used by the EU is called the **euro**. The system set up to facilitate the adoption and use of the euro for participating members is the **Economic and Monetary Union (EMU)**. Individual country currencies remained in effect along side the euro until the official euro adoption date, January 1, 2002. The debate over the new currency was heated. The United Kingdom chose not to participate in the economic monetary union; Sweden and Denmark also have not adopted the euro.

Influence on Retailers and Consumers Several advantages as well as some challenges to retailers and consumers were anticipated as the euro became fully integrated. The euro will make it easier for customers to comparison shop, and it should tighten competition within the EU.

With the euro in effect, international bargain hunters have been deterred from playing the exchange rates. Before the introduction of the euro, it was not unusual for American tourists to have purchases made at designer boutiques in London shipped to a Paris branch where the exchange rate was more favorable. This option will not be necessary or possible with the common currency.

During the transition period, adaptation by businesses was necessary. Catalog companies were required to adjust pricing on merchandise, reprint catalogs, and alter packaging. Computer systems needed to be reconfigured to accept decimals in prices written in euros in Italy and Spain. In the local currencies of these countries, decimals are not used. Some consumers were concerned when ATMs needed to be refitted and vending machines required new euro coins.

The EU levied a new tax on products and services ordered over the Internet by customers in the EU. Scheduled to take effect in July 2003, this could greatly affect U.S. suppliers of music, videos, software, and computer games delivered over the Web. For example, if a customer in the Netherlands orders an MP3 file from an online music site in the United States, the retailer will charge the customer the current VAT rate in effect in the Netherlands. Intra-European transactions will also be taxed.[7]

Agreements make world trade easier, but knowledge of cultural differences is equally important. Retailers smooth their entries into countries

European Central Bank (ECB) Financial institution that administers the euro currency policy for the EU.

euro Common currency used by EU countries.

Economic and Monetary Union (EMU) System set up to facilitate the adoption and use of the euro for participating EU members.

CYBERSCOOP

McDonalds's operates more than 30,000 units in 121 countries. How did Asian-Pacific sales fare this quarter? How many McDonald's are now operating in India? Does the menu there differ from the menu in your home country? Find out at www.mcdonalds.com.

where ideologies are different from those at home by learning about the society, its values, and its habits.

Cultural Issues

Customer perspectives on frequency of shopping visits, gift giving, store loyalty, customer service, perceptions of status goods, and responsiveness to sales promotion differ around the globe. Days of operation and merchandise for sale may be affected by the religious beliefs of the prevailing culture. Examples of cultural differences that affect retailing are presented in this section.

Religious Factors

The day a store closes to observe a Sabbath depends on the country and the prevailing adherence to religious tenants. In the United States, stores usually are open seven days a week. If they are closed at all, shorter hours may be in effect on Sundays in this predominantly Christian nation. In Hassidic neighborhoods of New York City, stores are closed on Friday night and Saturday—the Jewish Sabbath.

Friday is the day for Sabbath store closings in Malaysia, where the majority of people are Muslim. Sundays are simply another business day. Even in that staunchly Islamic country, attitudes are changing. Although stores in small cities and towns adhere to custom, stores in large metropolitan areas tend to straddle the issue. Shopping malls in Kuala Lumpur are open every day, much like those in cities around the world, but smaller retail stores are more likely to be closed on Fridays.

Food and beverage consumption is also affected by religious beliefs. Muslims do not eat pork or consume alcohol. Since Hindus consider cattle sacred they do not eat beef. Local ordinances called *blue laws* in some U.S. cities forbid the sale of alcoholic beverages on Sundays. These examples illustrate how taboos affect retail selling.

Shopping Frequency

Cultural inclinations and infrastructure combine to influence consumer behavior. People in London tend to shop more frequently than their U.S. counterparts. This situation is due largely to habit, but the transportation system also plays a role. Automobile traffic is very congested in the city and many residents do not own cars. The public bus and underground systems are convenient and well used but not meant for the transport of a week's worth of groceries. Rather than one main grocery expedition per week, as many families in the United States experience, British shoppers make two or three trips, purchasing only what they can carry home easily.

Attitudes Toward Gift Giving

Customs related to gift giving also differ in different parts of the world. Scholars from the University of Arizona studied the practice of gift giving in Japan. They found the rituals surrounding gifts of fruit during special holiday periods quite fascinating. Fruits such as oranges and grapefruit are considered luxuries in Japanese households, not part of the regular diet as they are in the United States. Therefore, they are well received as gifts in a country where gift giving is an art. The process is governed by complex cultural parameters. The source of the product—in this case the retail store—and packaging are as important as the fruit itself. Only perfect fruit, first individually wrapped then gift wrapped in carefully chosen, fine paper are appropriate. Price is not a major consideration since a small box of fruit can cost about $100 and a large basket around $600.[8] This tradition affects many types of retailers, because fruits are sold at specialty and department stores as well as food stores during the holiday season.

Figure 8.6 Metrojaya department store staged an American Southwest promotion in its Kuala Lumpur store. Malaysian customers, like many others, show preference for products that come from 10,000 miles away.

Responsiveness to Promotions

International differences in customer responsiveness to sales promotion events are significant. Figure 8.6 illustrates a promotion on the American Southwest staged by the Metrojaya department store at the Sungai Wang Plaza in Kuala Lumpur, Malaysia. The monthlong promotion featured a variety of western style merchandise—shirts, cowboy hats, denim apparel, and giftware—displayed in fixtures inspired by covered wagons. Part of the extravaganza included a performance by clog dancers from an American university. What was most impressive was the support and enthusiasm shown by spectators. Crowds began forming more than an hour before each scheduled performance, the display floor was swarming, and cash registers were ringing. Although advertising for the promotion was intense, most U.S. malls would have to work twice as hard to bring in as many motivated shoppers. Customers in the United States have become blinded by the number of promotions staged in countless, easily accessed malls. For the Malaysian

CYBERSCOOP

Can you buy your latte in Japan? Sure you can! Find out when Starbucks opened its 300th store in Japan by going to www.starbucks.com/aboutus/timeline.asp.

shopper, the events were more of a novelty and appealed to their sense of entertainment.

Wal-Mart experiences the same sentiment at many of its grand openings in South America. Customers there seem to be intrigued by giveaways and festivities and frequently bring their entire families to store celebrations.

Status and Brand Consciousness

The acquisition of products—materialism—is not limited to "western" cultures. Status-oriented products and brands are received with different degrees of enthusiasm around the world. For example, young Japanese women are particularly fond of designer brands and spend huge sums supporting their habits. Chanel handbags and Prada sportswear are much more important to them than they are to most women of the same age in the United States.

Joe Camel may be dead in the United States, but he is alive and well in Asia. Although cigarette advertising is banned on TV in some Asian countries, tobacco companies find ways around that restriction. Camel and Dunhill produced lines of upmarket men's apparel in order to increase visibility of their brands in Asia. A greater percentage of the Asian population smokes compared to the U.S. population. Another cigarette company, Peter Styvesant, runs a travel agency that advertises vacation packages on TV—with no mention of its tobacco product. Using a subtle approach keeps the brand name fresh in the eyes of the customers. Labels and merchandise are valued differently, and cultures have a strong influence on the formations of those values.

There is no aspect of life, shopping behavior included, that is untouched by culture. Business decisions that intrude upon religious beliefs, gender issues, deep-rooted customs, and habits of all types must be approached with sensitivity.

Comparative International Retailing

Retailers who chose to operate globally face unfamiliar environments. Glimpses at retailing in Japan and the United Kingdom point out the vast cultural differences and sometimes conflicting business practices that exist.

Japan

Japan is approximately the size of California with a population equal to about half that of the United States. The density greatly affects lifestyles, availability of retail space, and shopping habits in Japan. Estimated retail sales for the country were $1.1 trillion in 2000.[9]

Impact of Recession The powerhouse of the Asian world was set back by deep recession in the late 1990s. The government increased the consumption tax from 3 percent to 5 percent, adding to the economic woes. In 1998, Yoahan, a major supermarket and general merchandise retailer, became the largest bankruptcy in Japanese retail history. Bank failures and poor performance by other retailers in food and department store sectors contributed to the distress.[10]

Despite the recession, consumer spending remained relatively strong. Japanese customers typically have high levels of disposable income as well as high rates of personal savings. To stimulate retail sales during the low point of the recession, the Japanese government issued vouchers worth approximately $200 to all citizens.

However, by 2001, the situation had further eroded. At 5.3 percent, unemployment rates were the highest they had been since World War II, and economic growth has averaged only 1 percent for the last decade.[11] Newscasts in 2002, indicated that savings habits of Japanese consumers had changed. At zero percent interest rates, people were taking their money out of the banks and putting it into gold bouillon.

Store Location and Format Issues Space is at a premium in Tokyo, where 10 million people live in close quarters. Prior to the recession, rent for prime retail space on the Ginza, Tokyo's main retail street, had been the equivalent of $700 per square foot. The economic downturn put a crimp in the developers' ability to rent expensive space. Eventually, rates came down and the same $700-per-square-foot site might cost $200 in 2002.

Some Tokyo service businesses have gone to the rooftops of skyscrapers to find locations. Health clubs, a golf course, or tennis facilities may occupy what would be penthouse locations in less-congested cities. Several Japanese department stores have their bargain "basements" on the top floor. Retailers are aware that customers will see several floors of merchandise before they reach the lower-priced goods.

In the suburbs, U.S. superstores such as Office Depot and Sports Authority were not well received by Japanese consumers who did not like to shop in big box stores. Because the huge stores in Japan were twice as expensive to rent as comparable sites in the United States, retailers switched to smaller formats.[12]

Distribution and Pricing Japan's distribution system is complex and multitiered when compared to that of the United States and other nations.

Figure 8.7 Customers in Japanese department stores experience the ultimate in customer service. *AP/Worldwide Photos*

Although progress is being made, informal protectionist policies hinder trade. Deregulation in some business sectors has opened doors to imported goods. In 1998, restrictions involving cosmetics imports and laws prohibiting discounting were relaxed. Top-notch customer service skills are expected in Japan as evidenced by the presentation manner of the sales associate shown in Figure 8.7.

Shoppers have benefited from increased imports and now enjoy more access to products of all types, some of which were rarely enjoyed before Japan's efforts to create a better balance of trade. French wine, American broccoli, and, ironically, Sony electronic items imported from Korea are available at affordable prices.[13]

Retail prices for comparable products in Japan are often more than twice the U.S. price. For example, a Cannon "Snappy" camera selling for $90 in the United States will cost about $180 in Japan. A tube of Revlon lipstick selling for $7 to $8 in the United States will retail for about $20 in Tokyo. Discrepancies are expected to lessen as free trade continues and supply chains become shorter.

Traditionally, Japanese people believed price reductions denoted low-quality goods. The demand for luxury goods in Japan is notorious, and for decades discounting was simply not the way goods were retailed. Fewer discount or warehouse-type stores are found in Japan but this distinction is changing. Because of the recession and layoffs in the workplace, many people adopted a more conservative attitude toward shopping. In addition, the Japanese are world travelers and bring home new products and shopping preferences. Discount chains are making inroads in most all product classifications including electronic goods, furniture, and apparel. This chapter's From the Field looks at Japanese consumers' growing interest in bargain retailers.

Brand Consciousness Retailers with strong brand equity do well in Japan, where status and prestige are important commodities. American brand names are not quite as prestigious as European ones but American style and culture do exert great influence. For example, the Gap and Ralph Lauren apparel and recordings by American rock groups all are particularly well received.

Tiffany, the U.S. jewelry store, achieved impressive sales growth from 1996 to 1999, despite the sluggish economy. It promoted classic jewelry, such as engagement rings, that is considered recession proof. The company has almost 50 shops in Japan.[14]

From the Field: Placing High Value on Low Prices.
By Sharon Moshavi

Tokyo—Kimiko Mori is doing something few Japanese would have dreamed of just a few years ago. She's buying $1 underwear. She is also buying sports bras, batteries, earrings, instant soup, and a bath brush, each for 100 yen, or slightly less than $1. "I can't believe they have so many things for only 100 yen," she said, waving her hands over the aisles before heading for the checkout line with two brimming baskets.

It's a long line. The five floors of Daiso Industries' 100 Yen Plaza are crowded most days of the week with Japanese shoppers enamored with the cheap prices for everything from soup bowls to nail polish to panda-shaped sponges. Thousands of similar stores have sprouted across the country, many of them in some of Japan's trendiest neighborhoods.

In the land of a $100 melon and $10 cup of coffee, the 100-yen shops are at the forefront of a discounting trend that is changing the pricing habits of Japanese consumers.

With Japan's economy still floundering and corporate profits tumbling, many retailers have no choice but to lower prices in order to lure shoppers. Clothing prices alone have dropped about 15 percent in the last 6 to 9 months.

Until recently, low prices were never the way to attract Japanese consumers, who tend to care more about quality than price. But now even fashion magazines are offering advice on achieving what's being called "cheap chic."

None of this means, however, that Japan has abandoned its love affair with high-priced brands. Louis Vuitton and Hermes, for instance, are both enjoying record sales; one-third of all Louis Vuitton's products is sold in Japan.

As one young Japanese consumer stated, "If it has no brand name, I want it to be cheap. That leaves more money for me to spend on the expensive things I like."

Source: *Boston Globe* by Sharon Moshavi. Copyright 2002 by Globe Newspaper CO (MA). Reproduced with permission of Globe Newspaper CO (MA) in the format Textbook via Copyright Clearance Center.

Department Store Retailing Japanese department stores are famous the world over for their extensive product and service array. They are patterned after the great western department stores like Harrods, for example, but have taken the institution to even higher planes. Basements are filled with fancy foods and bakery items, pet shops, soda fountains, and restaurants. Upper floors are devoted to exotic silks; kimonos and obi materials; beauty salons; travel and concert ticket agencies; and florists. Customers can also order cars, buy prefabricated houses, take courses in flower arranging, attend live theater performances, learn how to perform a tea ceremony, arrange special services in connection with the birth of a child, order their own Shinto tombstone, and even arrange loans. Invariably, customers entering the famous Isetan, Takashimaya, or Mitsukoshi department stores are greeted with bows from the store managers and ample numbers of sales associates who are very likely dressed in uniforms. Elevator operators and ultra-fancy gift wrapping services are commonplace. Respect for the customer permeates the selling environment.

Mitsukoshi has 12 stores in Japan, and others in Germany and the United States, but few are profitable. From humble origins as a single-unit kimono store to the largest department store chain in Japan, the 300-year-old company has closed some of its poorer performers as it re-evaluates its business. Some cite outmoded business practices, loosing touch with younger consumers, and the failing economy as reasons for the slowdown.[15] Other Japanese department stores have faced similar hard times during the prolonged recession.

Merchandising Practices   Retailers in Japan use different display techniques and place importance on merchandise that may not be as popular in other parts of the world. As Internet use grows, products sold over the Web will affect merchandising practices in traditional retail stores in Japan as they have in the United States.

For example, restaurants—including fast-food types—display wax food samples in the windows or in special display cases located in front of their buildings. Potential customers are totally aware of the menu before they enter. This technique also is used by food operations in Europe.

Beauty products appear to enjoy as much popularity with males as they do with females. Many men tweeze their eyebrows and have facials. Skin care products are becoming an important part of men's daily grooming rituals. Some are showing an interest in using foundation makeup, once the exclusive domain of women and actors. Cosmetic retailers and aesthetic salon services should benefit from these changes in gender roles.[16]

A cartoon cat, popular in Japan for 20 years, became a top merchandise licensing character. The Hello Kitty logo appears on products ranging from automobiles to guitars, boxer shorts, and credit cards. A karaoke hall on the Ginza also sports the theme. The graphic rendering of Hello Kitty, though childishly cute, appeals to adults as well as children. Hello Kitty drives sales for many retailers in Japan.[17] The cartoon character appears to cross cultures easily. Hello Kitty stationery items for children have been available in U.S. Hallmark stores for years and T-shirts and other items are available from the Sanrio Company.

The Japanese convenience store retailer, 7-Eleven, departed from its conventional merchandise mix when it formed a partnership with an Internet company to sell books online. Customers are able to pay for their Web site purchases at 7-Eleven stores. E-tailing has been slower to interest Japanese customers, but efforts to integrate Web shopping with established retailers may pay off for 7-Eleven.[18]

Japan is a highly sophisticated retail market in the throes of change and adaptation. As its distribution systems become more streamlined and its economic problems subside, it will be considered one of the most important global retailing venues in the world.

United Kingdom

Over 300,000 stores employing 2.3 million people make up the British retail arena. Approximately 90 percent of UK retailers belong to the British
Retail Consortium (BRC), the leading trade association. Between 1995 and
2000, the group concerned itself with several key issues that will affect retailing in the 21st century:

- EU currency implementation
- consumer rights
- product labeling standards
- social trends affecting retailing
- minimum wage adjustments
- city and town planning[19]

The British retailing industry is approaching mature market status. Competition is more apparent than in the 1980s, although retailers operate with
higher margins compared to those in other well-developed global markets.
Because of the dominance of publicly held, large retail companies, the
leaders in all types of retailing have high market shares.

General Trends Television home shopping has not yet lived up to expectations. Sales of sporting goods and apparel are strong and more retail outlets
featuring these classifications are opening. More scrambled merchandising
is seen as nontraditional products such as toys find their way into supermarket aisles. Still undeveloped are office supply category killers, although Staples from the United States and Officeworld from Switzerland have made
an appearance. BRC maintains that the United Kingdom is not yet overstored.[20]

Status of Shopping Centers Shopping malls are not fully developed, but in
busy cities, arcades are popular. These mini-malls often run through city
blocks, street to street, and feature specialty retailers. The famed Covent
Garden is London's answer to Faneuil Hall in Boston and South Street Seaport in New York. It provides the city with a festival marketplace in the hub
of the theater district.

Shopping areas in major cities are on high streets that are the equivalent
of downtown areas. Brompton Road, Kensington High Street, Regent
Street, Oxford Street, and Bond Street are some of the more popular high
streets in London, where retailers service the needs of Londoners and
tourists.

Increased competition, parking issues, and high real estate prices combine to make planning and management of retail locations challenging. Town centers have become more service-oriented, and smaller neighborhood shopping areas are fading into history. The low per capita spending power of the typical UK individual exacerbated this trend.[21]

Comparisons to Other Countries Retailing in Britain differs from retailing in the United States in several ways. The United Kingdom has more publicly traded companies than the United States and more national chains, called *multiples*. It is estimated that England has far higher real estate costs than the United States, due to limited available land. In comparison, the United States has more factory outlet centers and more mass merchandisers.

Disposable income is lower in the United Kingdom than in the United States. Distribution in the United Kingdom is more cost-effective than in France or Germany, but not as low as in the United States. Advanced EDI category management systems are not as developed in Britain.[22]

Private label merchandise is very popular in the United Kingdom. Strong retail brands, such as Marks and Spencer's, St. Michael, and Sainsbury's food and grocery products, have global recognition. Others, such as Selfridges department store, have global potential. Harrod's extends its reach through online retailing.

As in many other European countries, the chief sale periods in the United Kingdom tend to occur in January and July—compared to the United States where every week a new promotion is presented. However, in the United Kingdom, there are no legal restrictions as to when sales can occur as there are in France. In Germany once product prices have been determined, they cannot be changed. Also, if an item is priced at a discount, it is legislated not to exceed a certain percentage. This is not the practice in the United States and many other countries.

Visual merchandising practices also differ. Physical display of prices on all merchandise in store windows is expected by the UK customer and is the practice throughout most of Europe and Scandinavia. It is not a routine part of visual merchandising practices in the United States.

The hypermarket, popular elsewhere in Europe, is not a major force in the United Kingdom, nor is it expected to be. French retailer Carrefour, with its huge format food and general merchandise stores pulled out of the United Kingdom, as it did in the United States. Although both Tesco and Sainsbury have opened supercenters, none compare to the size, merchandise, and service mix offered by true hypermarkets.

Impact of Social Trends The Body Shop has gained global attention for its socially responsible stance on environmental issues. Yet detractors have accused the company of not being as pure as its public relations and sales promotion campaigns imply. Tesco campaigns ardently for the humane treatment of animals, as discussed in the Global Retail Profile following Unit Four. Parades conducted by animal rights activists are held on major London high streets. It is possible that sentiment regarding interest and involvement in these issues is in the eye of the beholder.

Global Expansion With markets becoming more mature, more international expansion is predicted. The store Next, known for its moderately priced, well-made apparel and home furnishings, has already opened in the United States. A notable independent retailer, Jigsaw, has a fresh approach to design and color in women's and men's apparel and could also find a niche in other international markets. Jigsaw's minimalist approach to store decor is illustrated in Figure 8.8.

Boots, a health and beauty aid retailer that is called a chemist in the United Kingdom, did not perform well in Canada more than a decade ago. The company looks to Europe and Southeast Asia for continued growth. Burberry, a unit of Great Universal Stores, is already strong in wholesaling, concessions, and retail specialty store formats worldwide. It still has room to grow in the United Kingdom. W.H. Smith, the music retailer, has stores in hotels and airports internationally and will continue with this strategy.

Retailing in the United Kingdom shares many similarities with retailing in other western countries. It is the differences that give the industry a unique complexion. Conservative stores co-exist with motley, innovative shops. Shopping centers take on a flavor of their own. Shoppers in the United Kingdom include not only the British, but people from all over the world.

Global retailing is a significant trend, worthy of its own chapter in this text. The time will come when it will no longer be necessary to isolate this aspect of retailing because it will become an everyday occurrence. To this end, major retailers in the United States and Europe have banded together to form Internet supply chain services. Many prominent retailers belong to one called the WorldWide Retail Exchange. Members include Kmart, CVS, and Safeway from the United States; Royal Ahold from the Netherlands; Auchan from France; and Tesco and Marks & Spencer from the United Kingdom.[23] When competitors join forces to reduce costs of

Figure 8.8 Jigsaw in London is a progressive apparel retailer with strong international potential. The company specializes in well-made, fashion-forward merchandise for women and men, displayed with an eye for artful color and fine design.

doing business, we can be sure we are in a world where we are all global customers.

Summary

It is important for all retailers to think globally. There are many advantages as well as disadvantages to retail expansion abroad, most stemming from economic and cultural factors. Oversaturation of domestic markets is one principal reason why retailers seek alternative markets.

Better communications, increased international travel, more educated customers, and the higher perceived value of foreign goods contribute to changes in consumer behavior. These factors precipitate interest in global retailing.

To be successful, international retailers must adapt to the countries in which they do business. This is not always easy. Cultural disparity and differing business practices pose the major concerns for retailers.

The role of importing and exporting in a world economy is complex and prone to change with economic fluctuations. In order to counter trade imbalances, imports and exports must be carefully monitored. Trade organizations and agreements benefit countries engaged in international trade. The formation of the European Union in 1992, changed trade opportunities within and without the 15-country area.

Retailing practices differ by country. Shopping center and location strategies, sale periods, display techniques, and stores themselves may vary, but retailers serve customers to the best of their ability universally.

Questions for Review and Discussion

1. What are the distinctions between domestic, international, and global retailers?
2. What are some of the key reasons for the increase in global retail expansion?
3. What are the advantages and disadvantages to retailers that choose to expand abroad?
4. Discuss three critical success factors for global retailers. Which factor do you believe is most important?
5. Identify one high risk and one low risk type of global retail involvement. What are the advantages of each?
6. Why should countries maintain a favorable balance of trade? What factors affect trade positively and negatively?

7. In what ways should global retailers be alert to cultural differences? Discuss several examples.

8. Compare retailing in your home country with retailing in England and Japan. What are the similarities and differences?

Endnotes

1. "Global 200 Highlights." 2002 Global Powers of Retailing. *Stores.* Section 2. January, 2002: G7.

2. "Economic and Social Indicators." 2002 Global Powers of Retailing. *Stores.* January, 2002: G28.

3. Seckler, Valerie. "Retail's Share Master: The Discounter." *Women's Wear Daily.* September 22, 1999:11.

4. Wolf, Julie. "Banana Dispute With US, EU Hits New Stage." *Wall Street Journal.* December 14, 1999:B7A.

5. Simons, John. "Handbags, Bed Linens Included in List of Goods Covered by Trade Sanctions." *Wall Street Journal.* April, 12, 1999:A24.

6. Commission of the European Communities. Brochures. European File. "The European Single Act: Countdown to December 1992." and "The European Community." Directorate-General for Information, Communication and Culture. Brussels, Belgium. October 1990.

7. "European Union to Tax Internet Sales." Associated Press. April 7, 2002. www.msnbc.com./news. Accessed: May 9, 2002.

8. Shim, Soyeon and Gehrt, Ken "Japanese Gift Giving." Presentation. Global Retail Symposium. University of Arizona. March 1997.

9. "Economic and Social Indicators." 2002 Global Powers of Retailing. *Stores.* January, 2002: G26, 28.

10. Inoue, Junichi and Strause, Charles. "Japan." Global Powers of Retailing. *Stores.* January, 1998:S45.

11. "Retail Industry Profiles." 2002 Global Powers of Retailing. *Stores.* Section 2. January, 2002:G39.

12. "Mitsukoshi, Ltd. Available: www.hoovers.com. Accessed: May 9, 2002.

13. Hamilton, David P., "New Imports: One Tokyo Family Loves Its Italian Shoes and American Broccoli." *Wall Street Journal.* March 14, 1997:A14.

14. Ono, Yumiko. "Tiffany Glitters, Even in Gloomy Japan." *Wall Street Journal.* July 21,1998:B1.

15. "Japanese Retailer May Close Stores." *Wall Street Journal.* July 21, 1998:A9.

16. Ono, Yumiko. "Beautifying the Japanese Male." *Wall Street Journal.* March 11, 1999:B1,8.

17. Ono, Yumiko. "Kitty-Mania Grips Grown-Ups in Japan." *Wall Street Journal.* December 15, 1998:B1.

18. Landers, Peter. "Softbank, 7-Eleven Japan Go Online To Sell Books as E-Commerce Expands." *Wall Street Journal.* June 4, 1999:A12.

19. British Retail Consortium. Presentation. American Collegiate Retailing Association. London, July, 1997.

20. Ibid.

21. Ibid.

22. Ibid.

23. Coleman, Calmetta Y., and Beck, Ernest. "Big Retailers in U.S., Europe Form Exchange." *Wall Street Journal.* April 3, 2000:B19.

Global Retail Profile

Spiegel, A Subsidiary of the Otto Trading Group, Germany

The Otto Trading Group is a huge network of catalog companies reaching from Europe and North America to Asia. The company boasts the highest market share and the highest degree of globalization across all catalog retailers. Through The Spiegel Group, Otto owns Spiegel, Eddie Bauer, and Newport News catalogs, 560 specialty and outlet stores, and several e-commerce sites.[1] Spiegel is the fifth largest retail catalog company in the United States, ranking behind JC Penney, Office Depot, Staples, and the Federated Department Stores. The company also owns a majority share in Crate and Barrel.

Spiegel generated a $3.7 billion sales volume in 2000.[2] Facing losses in the late 1990s, Spiegel developed new approaches to its catalog business that are chronicled in this profile. First, the history of Spiegel and its German parent company is highlighted.

History of Spiegel and Otto Trading Company

Based in Hamburg, Germany, Otto Versand was founded in 1949, and is still controlled by the Otto family. The company's first, hand-bound, 14-page shoe catalog was distributed in 1950. The goal of the company was to bring convenience and stability to families ravaged by World War II. Twenty-four-hour ordering capabilities were introduced and appreciated after the chaos of the war years. Although the first run was only 300 copies, the company was on its way to becoming a retail power. Otto Versand became global in 1974, with the purchase of 3 Suisses, a French mail-order company. In 1982, the company acquired Chicago-based Spiegel and in 1988, added Eddie Bauer to its roster.[3] As the company grew, it evolved into the Otto Trading Company.

Joseph Spiegel founded a home furnishings retail store in Chicago after his release in 1865, from a Confederate prison where he had been a prisoner of war. By 1905 the growth of railroads made it feasible to offer mail-order merchandise to customers in rural areas. The Spiegel catalog was added in response. Spiegel was in and out of traditional store retailing over a period of more than 100 years. During the Great Depression in the 1930s, he closed the Chicago store, but reopened the operation during World War II. He again closed his stores in 1953. Spiegel did not return to classic retailing until catalog outlet stores were opened in the 1980s.

Joseph Spiegel was an innovator on several scores. He was the first to use photographs in catalogs and to offer special Christmas editions. Also, he was the first to offer credit services to his catalog customers. In the 1960s, the company shifted to more upscale, designer merchandise than the mass-merchandised goods being sold by competitors JC Penney and Sears. Spiegel went online in 1995.[4]

Divisions of Spiegel

Eddie Bauer has over 500 stores featuring casual men's and women's apparel, accessories, and home furnishings. Eddie Bauer also sells through in-store concept shops. Called EB Sport Shops, these units present apparel and equipment for hunting and fishing enthusiasts. Newport News catalog specializes in women's moderately priced apparel. Spiegel targets a predominantly female market with its big book and specialty formats.[5]

Eddie Bauer has a rich history. While on a fishing trip, Eddie Bauer had been ill-equipped and developed hypothermia as a result. Necessity being the mother of invention, he founded his company in 1928, and developed the "Skyline" goose-down filled jacket. The U.S. Air Force contracted Bauer to produce down-filled flight suits for flyers during World War II. Mail order for retail customers began in 1946, with stores following.[6]

The first new venture launched online in 2000 was Eddiebauerkids.com. The Web store was immediately successful and the line, geared to children aged 5 to 12, was introduced in Eddie Bauer stores.[7]

Faced with the same threats as many other retailers in the late 1990s—oversaturation, sameness, and the Internet—Spiegel developed several organizational and market segmentation strategies. It formulated five business units including:

- style-driven catalogs
- value-driven catalogs
- European-inspired catalogs
- outlet catalog and stores
- product sourcing and concept development[8]

Known as the "big book," the 500-page Spiegel catalog is mailed twice per year to 5 million customers. It is organized and merchandised by lifestyle. An 8-page section in one of the "big books" called *4You* featured clothing designed for various body types.[9] The company also developed spin-off catalogs, targeting special markets. *Onview* features many European labels and attracts women who prefer more ornate fashion apparel.

Global Strategies

Jon Coble, vice president of corporate business development for Spiegel, considers the company a global pioneer in the catalog industry. He cites several advantages of being a front-runner:

- ability to utilize scarce resources first
- gain a head start on learning
- create heightened customer awareness
- set industry standards
- gain an 8 to 9 percent market share advantage

On the downside, he lists two disadvantages:

- experience a greater chance for mistakes
- become vulnerable to later entrants

Levels of involvement and ownership used by Otto Trading Group differ depending on the country and circumstance. For example, in Japan, joint ventures are necessary because of relationship-based business structures and the intricacy of the local bureaucracy. In Canada and Brazil, the company uses more informal networks to do business in those countries. In Europe, it has found fewer desirable partners and therefore uses acquisition as a common means of growth.

According to Coble, the company uses two distinct approaches when addressing global expansion: multinational or national. When taking a multinational approach, Spiegel selects existing inventory from its U.S. catalogs for use in new catalogs in foreign countries. It may use some translation in its catalogs, but not all. When favoring a national approach, the entire catalog is translated and all products are re-assorted and may be priced differently. Order fulfillment is done in the host country when a national strategy is used.

Spiegel seeks significant numbers of customers currently doing business through its catalogs before it considers starting operations in specific countries. It followed this path before launching Eddie Bauer stores and catalogs in Japan. It is interesting to note that L.L. Bean followed a similar strategy when it expanded in Japan. Although Spiegel does not yet have catalog operations in Panama or Iceland, orders come from these areas.

Coble cited several merchandise categories that sell well internationally for Spiegel. In South America, for example, home textiles and draperies are popular, and more petite women's apparel is sold than in the U.S. market. In Japan and Europe, high fashion lines such as the company's *Together* private label generate high sales.

Coble believes that catalogs should look international and that changing established formats is necessary. For example, when Newport News entered the Brazilian market, apparel styles were changed substantially to suit different color and taste preferences of women.

Spiegel uses different methods when dealing in international markets including the following international cross-selling (ICS) formats:

1. International Runner Multiplication (IRM)—Single items or exact pages from one catalog are used without changes in other catalogs.
2. International Concept Multiplication (ICOM)—Whole concept or merchandise categories are transferred from one country to another. The *Eddie Bauer* catalog is distributed in this manner.
3. International Catalog Multiplication (ICAM)—Catalog development is entirely

new. For example *The World's Best catalog* was developed from scratch.

State-of-the-art technology provides the base for accurate decision making at Spiegel. It's Database for International Catalog Policy (DACAPO), links 20 companies within the Otto Trading Group. Through DACAPO, Spiegel can determine if a best seller in Japan will also be a best seller in Brazil or Canada.

Coble believes free trade is the engine of global growth. Spiegel's position on this issue is summarized as "TINA"—There Is No Alternative. Opportunities must be seized quickly since global expansion will evolve as all business does.[10]

Through Spiegel-Hermes General Service, the company is offering its extensive distribution expertise to outside businesses. Formed in 2001, the new group provides fulfillment, returns processing, call center support, database management, and product sourcing services. It is expected to generate significant revenues for Spiegel.[11]

For the first time in its history, more than half of Otto Versand's sales emanated from outside Germany in 1999.[12] Since the company does business throughout Europe, North America, China, Korea, and Taiwan, this trend is expected to continue.

Profile Discussion Questions

1. What is the relationship between Spiegel and the Otto Trading Group? Discuss the roots of the relationship. What other catalog retailers belong to the companies?
2. Relate some of the differences between catalog retailing in the United States and South America. How might Spiegel use this information to better serve its customers?

3. What kinds of cross-selling does Spiegel consider when starting operations in a new country?

4. According to Jon Coble, what are the advantages of being a global pioneer?

5. How is Spiegel using technology to enhance its traditional catalog sales?

Profile Endnotes

1. http://www.thespiegelgroup.com Available: June 12, 2002.

2. *Stores.* 2002 Global Powers of Retailing. "Top 200 Global Retailers." January, 2002: G15.

3. *International Directory of Company Histories.* Otto Versand GmbH & Co. 2000.

4. *Hoover's Company Profile Database.* "Spiegel, Inc." American Public Companies. Hoovers, Inc. Austin, Texas. 2000. Available http://web.lexis-nexis.com/univers. September, 2000.

5. "Spiegel, Inc." *Standard & Poors Corporate Descriptions Plus News.* McGraw-Hill Companies, Inc. 2000. Available: http://web.lexis-nexis.com/univers. September, 2000.

6. Hoover's.

7. http://www.thespiegelgroup.com. Available: August 23, 2001.

8. Edelson, Sharon. "Spiegel Realigning and Streamlining." *Women's Wear Daily.* June 12, 1997:15.

9. Hines, Janet A. "Spiegel Shifts to Stay in Tune With Customers." July 20, 2001 *iMarketing News.* Available: http://www.iMarketingNews.com. August 2, 2001.

10. Coble, John. "Global Catalog Marketing: The New Frontier." Presentation. Global Retail Symposium. University of Arizona. March, 1997.

11. Donnelly, Harrison. "Spiegel Brings Century-Plus Experience to Logistics Outsourcing Market." *Stores.* August, 2001:60.

12. "Otto Sales Outside Germany Top 50 Percent for First Time." *DM News.* Wednesday, June 14, 2000. Available: http://www.dmnews.com, June 23, 2000.

Global Retail Profile

Amazon.com

One of the best-known pure-play retailers on the Internet is Amazon.com, Inc., purveyor of books, audiotapes, DVDs, electronics, computer games, toys, music, housewares, tools and hardware, and more to customers worldwide. Based in Seattle, Washington, the company opened its e-retailing doors in 1995, under the direction of founder Jeff Bezos. By 2001, sales were $3.12 billion. That year, international sales grew 74 percent, comprising 25 percent of sales.[1] Despite high start-up and marketing costs, a downturn in the technology-driven economy, and difficulties reaching profitability, Amazon became a pathfinder in a new industry.

Amazon's initial Internet bookstore fit all of the criteria deemed appropriate for Web retailers. Its narrow and deep merchandise assortment boasted 3 million titles, rivaling most conventional book retailers. Shipments reached customers in 24 to 48 hours. Its Web site encouraged exploration. Detailed descriptions of books, a wealth of information about authors, book reviews, and other amenities reached a broad audience of readers. The company actively sought customer input as it planned future marketing strategies. Greeting repeat customers by name, the site offered recommendations based on customer preferences. Amazon's best sellers list rank-ordered more than a million titles, should users need this wealth of information. Having successfully built brand equity in a short period of time: all it seemed to lack was a cup of Starbucks coffee, which was available in competitor Barnes & Noble superstores.

Amazon still provides these services and much more for its customers. The company serves millions of people in 220 countries and offers what it terms as the "Earth's Biggest Selection." It also links to several global sites and provides auctions, used book sales, browsable pages, and an e-mail book review delivery system.[2] The focus changed from being a book seller to a purveyor of all things seen and unseen. Various partnerships and alliances fuel the growth of a most unique retailer.

Aggressive Diversification

Amazon first expanded its product lines by introducing videos, DVDs, and music to its product mix. Numerous opportunities for synergistic merchandising and promotional strategies were introduced once sales of a video or book could be linked to a movie soundtrack, for example.

Amazon purchased PlanetAll in August 1998, giving access to 1.5 million people who use this provider of personal agenda organization services. Access to this kind of information provides an increased customer base, but also opportunities to use cross-promotion strategies. Amazon can use PlanetAll to offer customers book or music gift suggestions based on data in their personal organizers.

Amazon added toys, home electronics, and an auction site. The company also made significant investments in several online retailers including Drugstore.com, Ashford.com, a jewelry site, and eZiba.com, a seller of global handicrafts.[3]

The most notable partnership occurred when Amazon.com and Toysrus.com merged their strengths and toy stores online. In 2000, Amazon signed a 10-year agreement for the co-branded arrangement. According to the terms, Amazon provides fulfillment, customer service, and warehousing; Toys "R" Us provides purchasing and inventory management.[4] The next year the companies announced the opening of Imaginarium.com, an educational toy specialty store.[5] Late in 2001, Amazon became partners with Target. This move increased the online retailer's ability to offer apparel, home furnishings, and jewelry.

Competition

Amazon's chief competition comes from multi-channel retailers like Barnes & Noble that sell through stores and also maintain Web sites. Amazon leads online book sales, but Barnes & Noble has approximately 900 stores and its total volume is greater at almost $4.9 billion for the fiscal year that ended in February, 2002.[6]

The failure of many Web-based businesses in the early 21st century, prompted consolidation within the e-commerce sector and the formation of new and sometimes unexpected partnerships. Amazon assumed responsibility for Borders online operations in 2001. In exchange for providing inventory, customer service and other fulfillment functions, Borders will turn over revenues from its sales to Amazon. Amazon in turn will pay Borders a commission on all online sales.[7] Book publishers such as Random House in the United States and Bertelsmann of Germany also provide competitive pressure.

Barnes & Noble originally partnered with AOL, and more recently with Lycos, in an attempt to compete on more equal footing with Amazon. Amazon works with Yahoo and Excite. In 2001, AOL purchased 2 percent of Amazon, sparking speculation that an acquisition was eminent. The arrangement would make Amazon privy to 350 AOL merchants and all of its subscribers. AOL would become Amazon.com's exclusive Internet Service Provider.[8]

In the music sector, Amazon competes with store retailers such as Record Town, Sam Goody, and Coconuts. Online retailers CDnow.com and N2K.com merged in 1998, in part to counter the thrust of competition from Amazon.[9]

Distribution Strategies

Utilizing an innovative distribution technique that brings potential competitors into the fold, entrepreneurs can join the Amazon Affiliate family. Participants use the Amazon logo on their own Web sites and sell highly specialized books to select target markets. Working in this way, affiliates get a deeper discount on Amazon products which allows them the opportunity to resell books at a profit.

Global Strategies

With customers around the world. the company's acquisition of three companies in 1998 supported its long-range global plans. Included were two United Kingdom companies, Bookpages, Ltd., one of the country's largest booksellers, and Internet Movie Database, a movie and television information company. Also acquired was Telebook, a German online book service.[10] Amazon launched Web sites in Germany and the United Kingdom, and imdb.com as a direct result of these acquisitions.

Amazon operates the Web site of Waterstone's, a bookseller based in the United Kingdom, under an arrangement similar to the Border's and Toys "R" Us online partnerships.[11] Business dealings of this nature are necessary when companies need to build sales but have maximized book sales in their home countries as Amazon had. Buying market share rather than starting new Web sites became a strategic imperative for Amazon.

Challenges and Future Strategies

As Amazon strives to remain the top online bookseller and erode market share of conventional stores, it faces several obstacles. Intense competition, pricing issues, and the need to turn a profit all place pressure on the company.

The ease of competitive shopping is a customer advantage of Web retailing. Comparative shopping services make finding the lowest price on most products even more simple. Because of this fact, exacerbated by intense competition, Amazon discounts its retail prices on books over $20 by 30 percent. The discount pricing policy forces Amazon to work on lower margins than conventional retailers. Despite the supposed cost savings derived by doing business in cyberspace rather than through traditional storefronts, Amazon must work hard to achieve its goal of becoming a profitable operation.

Attempting to build sales, Amazon experimented with a free shipping promotion. When customers purchased two or more books, CDs, or videos, they were entitled to the discount. Some customers discovered that prices on some items had been raised, so that the free shipping incentive was less enticing. Many shoppers terminate their online sessions when they learn the high price of shipping. One of Amazon's reasons for staging the promotion was to alleviate the need for customers to add another step to the purchasing process by calculating shipping charges.[12] Presently the company offers free shipping on orders over $99.

Public stock offerings, junk bond sales, acquisitions, and stock splits attest to activity and growth plans in a business that has no tangible assets. Retailing in cyberspace poses different challenges when charting the value a business. Retailers that have no actual stores, hold no traditional real estate, and have no salespeople need to be judged by different criteria than conventional stores.

As Amazon added product categories, it faced the challenge of diluting its original focus, book retailing. The company also became more vulnerable to competition as it tried to become all things to all people.

During the eight week Christmas holiday season of 2000, the Amazon.com/Toys "R" Us online partnership accrued more shopping visits than any other shopping site.[13] Sensing the future direction of Internet shopping, Amazon developed global alliances with 12 mobile phone carriers. Called Amazon Anywhere, the technology allows customers to access any of Amazon's online stores via their wireless telephones. By 2001, the service reached 500,000 customers in the United States and Europe.[14] Because the technology did not move as rapidly as initially expected, Amazon scaled back staff that supports its wireless program. Ultimately, innovations such as this are crucial to Amazon's quest to become an online presence with longevity.

Most pure-play Web retailers have either ceased to exist or evolved into multichannel retailers. Amazon.com may yet prove to be the exception to the rule. It has no plans to open traditional storefronts, but will instead work on establishing new partnerships with other online companies and suppliers.[15] Brilliant leadership, a futuristic outlook, and an aggressive stance toward competition should serve Amazon well as it strives for industry dominance and profitability.

Profile Study Questions

1. What characteristics have made Amazon an admirable Web retailer?

2. In what ways is Amazon trying to increase its market share? Do you believe the company's strategies will be effective? Why or why not?

3. How does Amazon.com compete with classic retailers like Barnes & Noble and Borders bookstores?

4. What kinds of customer services does Amazon provide on its Web site?

5. What are the advantages and disadvantages of the discount pricing strategy used by Amazon?

6. How should Amazon.com continue to battle competition and reach profitability?

Profile Endnotes

1. http: media.corporate-ir.net/media_files/nsd/amzn/reports/2001AnnualReport.pdf. Available: June 12, 2002.

2. http://www.amazon.com/exec/obidos/subst/misc/company-info.html Available: June 12, 2002.

3. Ibid.

4. Wingfield, Nick and Bulkeley, William M. "Amazon.com, Toys R Us Agree to Combine Online Toy Stores." *Wall Street Journal.* August 11, 2000:B2.

5. "Toysrus.com and Amazon.com Tackle the Specialty-learning Toy Category." July 30, 2001. "Vertical Web Media. Available: http://www.internetretailer,com/dailyNews. August 2, 2001.

6. http://www.barnesandnoble.com. Available: June 12, 2002.

7. Wingfield, Nick and White, Erin. "Borders Deal Bolsters Amazon's Strategy." *Wall Street Journal.* April 12, 2001:B13.

8. Macaluso, Nora. "Amazon 'Leaves Door Open' for Buyout by AOL - Reports." July 25, 2001. "NewsFactor Network. Available: http://www.ecommercetimes.com. August 2, 2001.

9. *Wall Street Journal.* "Amazon.com to Sell Videos on the Internet Along With Books." November 17, 1998:B10.

10. Carlton, Jim. "Amazon Posts Smaller Loss Than Forecast." *Women's Wear Daily.* April 28, 1998:B4.

11. "Amazon Agrees to Operate Waterstone's UK-based Web Site." July 25, 2001. Vertical Web Media. Available: www.internetretailer.com. August 2, 2001.

12. Wingfield, Nick. "Amazon.com's Free-Shipping Promotion Has Customers Crying, 'Price Increase.'" *Wall Street Journal.* June 27, 2001:A3.

13. Stoughton, Stephanie. "All 'e's are on Amazon." *Boston Globe.* January 7, 2001:E9. (Statistical source: Nielsen//NetRatings, December 2000)

14. "Amazon Offers Wireless Access Through New Deal with AT&T Wireless." July 20, 2001. "Vertical Web Media. Available: internetretailer.com.

15. *Women's Wear Daily.* "Amazon Reportedly Staying Out of Retail." May 3, 2001:12.

The Human

Factor

Chapter 9

Human Resource Management

Learning Objectives

After completing this chapter you should be able to:

- Discuss the challenges human resource management faces this decade.

- List the primary methods of hiring retail staff and management.

- Describe what types of training programs are used by contemporary retailers.

- Document the ways technology assists retail recruitment and training.

- Differentiate the responsibilities of human resource managers in large and small stores.

Figure 9.1 Store manager, left, and sales associate at Max Studio in Beverly Hills, California, confer over training goals. On-the-job training is important in all specialty store chains (See p. 265).

Did You Know?

Criteria including the company culture and opportunity for advancement were used to determine the Top 100 Companies for working mothers. On the list were several retail companies such as Target, Sears, McDonald's, and Patagonia. Source: *Working Mother.* "The 100 Best Companies for Working Mothers." October, 2001 Available: www.workingwoman.com/oct_2001_best. Accessed: June 4, 2002.

The success of all retail organizations depends on the ability to recruit, train, and retain talented people at every level. Carefully chosen merchandise, exciting promotions, tight financial controls, or select locations cannot guarantee success unless there are also good people to perform every function. With more than 23 million retail jobs in the United States alone this is no small task.[1] This chapter examines personnel planning and the components of human resource management. Challenges retailers routinely face regarding the changing labor pool including fluctuating unemployment rates in the United States, part-time workers, shrinkage, motivation, and dealing with diversity in the workplace are covered in this chapter. The retail industry as a desirable place to build a career is viewed from different perspectives.

Retail Employment Trends

Industry statistics show that growth in the retail job sector in the United States is expected to continue well into the new millennium. Between 1998 and 2008, a gain of 3 million jobs is anticipated.[2] Most jobs are in the sales and service sectors with managerial positions comprising 8.6 percent.[3] The United States experienced one of the lowest unemployment rates in thirty years at the turn of the millenium. Many retailers were hard pressed to find suitable employees, necessitating creative recruitment tactics.

Retailing continues to be a young person's business. Approximately 33 percent of all retail employees in the United States were between 16 and 24 years of age in 2000. Another 20.8 percent were in the 25- to 34-year age range. Only 10.6 percent were over 55 years of age, despite the current trend of employing senior citizens in many retail venues.[4]

Gender differences in the retail job market are apparent. Women made up 52.4 percent of the total workforce in 2000, but held a disproportionate share of positions in specific types of retailing. Women were overrepresented in department, general merchandise, drug, book, apparel, accessory and jewelry stores and underrepresented in auto dealers and service stations building materials, furniture and sporting goods stores.[5] Apparently old stereotypes die hard.

Retailing relies heavily on part-time employees. One study showed that part-time workers will comprise as much as 80 percent of the workforce in some stores.[6] These issues all are current trends and contribute to the challenges and opportunities retailers face this decade.

Human Resource Planning and Budgeting

Like goods and services, human resources must be planned and budgeted. To be productive, employees need to understand the missions and customers of the retailers that they serve. Orientation and training should not only help people acquire skills, but also balance their professional and personal lives. Management should support and reinforce what employees are taught.

The facts and figures in the previous section lay the groundwork for some of the monumental tasks faced by human resource planners.

Challenges to Human Resource Planning

Supplying properly trained people at the right time, in the right place to implement company objectives is at the core of human resource planning. This is difficult to coordinate for several reasons:

1. *Irregular employee demand.* Retail employment in the United States fluctuates monthly as illustrated in Figure 9.2. It is easy to understand that if the majority of sales are generated in December, extra personnel must be on the floor during that period. It is more difficult to anticipate if layoffs are necessary during an economic downturn. Both scenarios pose challenges to retailers as they schedule personnel.

2. *Small employment pool.* When unemployment rates are low, as they had been in the United States prior to the economic downtrend in 2001, there are fewer eligible people to hire. Retailers must become creative in their recruitment techniques. Incentives, signing bonuses, and outright piracy become common. **Piracy** is the luring of personnel from other firms.

   piracy The luring personnel from other firms.

3. *Lower wages.* Remuneration may not be competitive with other industries, particularly at the sales associate and lower operational levels. Wage rates also vary depending on the type of retail business.

4. *Competition for qualified people.* Within the retail industry, competition for good people increased in the 1990s and shows no decline in this decade. Companies outside the industry lure potential retail employees to other fields.

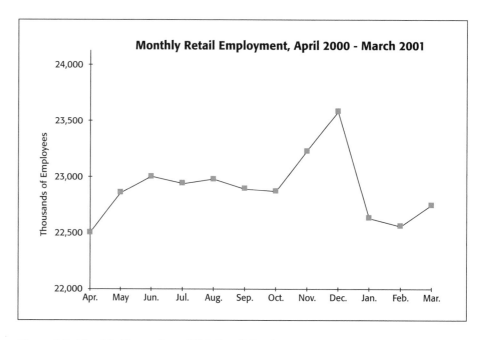

Figure 9.2 Monthly Fluctuation of U.S. Retail Employment *Source: Derived from U.S. Department of Labor, Bureau of Labor Statistics data. "Retail Industry Indicators," © NRF Foundation, August 2002.*

5. *Government standards.* Minimum wage, working conditions, and equal treatment continue to be pressing issues, not only in the United States, but in many global markets.

6. *Unionized labor issues.* Organized labor plays a role in human resource planning and management since certain retailers—notably those in the food industry—operate under union contracts. Unions are also partners in training programs designed to teach basic retail skills to people that might otherwise be unemployable.

7. *Retail image perceptions.* Long hours, weekend work, and comparatively lower wages are the main factors that turn prospective employees away from careers in retailing.

8. *Shrinkage.* The amount that an inventory is reduced due to internal theft, shoplifting, and other factors is not only an inventory management issue, but also a human resource problem. Through improved testing and interviewing techniques, retailers try to increase the honesty quotient and decrease the criminal aspirations of their new employees.

9. *Diversity.* As emigration continues and families relocate, they assimilate to new cultures. Racial and ethnic diversity present new challenges to employers around the globe.

10. *Quality of life* Quality of life issues may be the biggest factors against recruitment. People are focusing more on their families, and are looking for more satisfaction in the ways they live. As a result, job sharing and flexible scheduling are becoming more popular.

Details of what retailers are doing to cope with these challenges, change the image of retailing, and provide a better environment for workers are presented here and throughout this chapter.

Union Involvement After World War II, when retailers and all service industries were growing at a tremendous rate, they became perfect targets for union organizers. There were then (and now) many low-paid, unskilled workers in large stores who wanted and needed bargaining power. Unions seemed the perfect answer, yet did not make in-roads in retailing at that time.

Since the 1950s, the union movement has progressed more slowly in retailing than most labor organizers expected for three reasons:

■ Retail management has over time recognized the important role human resources play in the struggle for profit. As compensation plans and enrichment programs increase, there is less need for employees to organize.

■ Attitude of employees is pro-management because the possibility of promotion from within exists.

■ Part-timers make up the bulk of the employees in most retail organizations.

The three significant retail unions are the United Food and Commercial Workers International Union (UF&CWIU), an affiliate of the UFL-CIO; the United Store Workers, an affiliate of the Retail, Wholesale Distributive Services Union; and the Retail, Wholesale, and Department Store Workers Union. The UF&CWIU has been fighting Wal-Mart's advances into the freestanding supermarket business. Wal-Mart has traditionally abstained from union intervention in any of its stores. However, more than half of all supermarkets in the United States employ unionized workers. As Wal-Mart's expansion escalates, the play between this strong retailer and the unions may intensify.

In a dedicated attempt to develop national skill standards and certification for retail workers, the National Retail Federation, partnered with the UF&CWIU and DECA, a student marketing association, to provide training for retail sales and service personnel. DECA originally stood for Distributive Education Clubs of America, but the educational program is now known by its acronym.

The first retail skills center opened at the King of Prussia Mall outside Philadelphia. Using guidelines established by the National Skill Standards Board (NSSB), the program is a voluntary partnership involving companies engaged in retailing and wholesaling and other public interest groups.[7]

The center targets students, transitional workers, part-time workers, and current employees interested in upgrading their skills. Many are from lower-income, ethnically diverse families. Participants learn basic sales and customer service skills. Counseling, internships, placement services, and language development are all options in the program. At-risk students can earn high school diplomas and others can receive college credit for their work.[8] The use of technology enhanced education at the skill centers is the subject of this chapter's From the Field.

Shrinkage Issue Employee theft is a problem for retailers. Depending on the type of retail store, shrinkage as a percentage of sales varies from less than 1 percent to about 3 percent. Some types of merchandise are more susceptible to theft than others. For example, employee theft rates ran from a low of 33.1 percent in homecenters, hardware, and garden to a high of 80 percent in optical stores in 1999.[9]

Better employee screening methods may reduce the numbers of dishonest employees. Retailers also use advanced surveillance systems that monitor employees as well as customers to curb theft. Some implemented 24-hour hot lines on which employees can report infractions to proper authorities without fear of disclosure. Losses incurred through employee theft greatly affect profit and must be addressed during the hiring process.

Low Unemployment Incentives increase and alternative labor pools are tapped when low unemployment rates exist. Some retailers have gone to extreme measures offering monetary rewards to new hires and bonuses to current employees who recommend them. During the tight labor market that existed in the United States in the late 20th century, restaurants in summer resort areas offered various incentives to prospective employees.

From the Field: NRF Moves to Web-Based Training
By Jeanette Hye

The National Retail Federation in Washington, DC, is migrating to Web-based training technology at its retail skills centers.

The trade association uses Performance TRAC software on the networks at its skills center in King of Prussia, Pennsylvania, and in Elizabeth, New Jersey, and other sites. Soon, the organization will make the technology available over the Internet so that prospective retail employees can train from remote locations.

Performance TRAC is a technology used to teach retail skills. It contains a variety of modules that cover such areas as customer service, sales, monitoring inventory, maintaining appearance, and teamwork. Retail trainees use the software to work through a series of hypothetical retail situations.

In areas in which trainees are deficient, additional training is provided through other media, including CD-ROMs and videos. The NRF also provides a computerized test to determine retail skills and offer retail certification.

The retail skills center at the Jersey Gardens outlet mall in Elizabeth, New Jersey, is considered a "one-stop shopping" place for retail skills assessment, training, and job placement for would-be retail associates and a clearinghouse for potential retail employees. Retailers including the Gap and Burlington Coat Factory have hired graduates of the center.

It is part of an ongoing effort by the NRF to raise the skill levels of retail employees and assist retail members in finding qualified employees. The organization is pushing to have a national skill standard.

Source: *Women's Wear Daily.* November 3, 1999:20. Courtesy of Fairchild Publications, Inc.

College scholarships, $500 sign-on bonuses, free housing, and transportation were advertised as employers raced to staff their businesses.

Senior citizens, disabled persons, and non-English speakers have all been targeted by retailers that find the job market diminished. Citing a lack of bilingual ability, Tuesday Morning, a home furnishings retailer in Dallas, teaches Spanish to its executives and English to its warehouse employees. The company believes that better language skills will ultimately increase profits.[10] Programs like this not only aid recruitment efforts, but also internal and external public relations.

Human Resource Budgets

Staffing should be planned far in advance and based on an analysis of last year's performance and next year's expectations. A human resource budget must consider all fluctuations of retail sales on a yearly, monthly, weekly, and daily basis. With a budget, the use of executive search firms might not be as necessary when a sudden opening occurs. Luring executives from competing firms, or cutting staff when business takes a downturn, might also be avoided. Unfortunately many retailers do not hire enough entry-level, full-time people to provide for future growth.

Six Developmental Steps Six steps for developing a human resource budget are as follows:

1. *Forecast personnel needs.* The forecast should begin at the lowest operating level and continue through to the highest level in the organization. It should include the number of the people required and descriptions of each position.

2. *Inventory current employees.* A review of personnel records helps identify the skills and status of current personnel. This information helps identify the type of training needed if existing employees are promoted or transferred within the organization.

3. *Modify existing data.* The budget is affected by both internal and external factors. For example, the rate of employee turnover or the acquisition of one retailer by another alters personnel needs. The condition of the economy also changes personnel requirements.

4. *Review related factors.* Improved selection and training methods may lower employee attrition or promotions may result in other vacancies. Factors such as these are considered at this stage.

5. *Execution of the budget.* This should take place after approval and support of top management. Without adequate financing, facilities, and staff to carry it out, the plan will not succeed.

CYBERSCOOP

Visit discount retailer Bluefly at **www.bluefly.com.** Locate "about Bluefly" then click on "jobs at Bluefly." What's available this week? What special qualifications do you think an online retailer expects from its employees? What did you learn about the corporate culture of this retailer by visiting its site?

6. *Evaluation.* Assessment substantiates quantitative and qualitative aspects of human resource planning. Continuous monitoring and evaluation of the plan is essential.

Adherence to these procedures makes it more likely that a retail organization will function smoothly and cut down on high attrition.

Three Employment Tools Three employment tools help further determine needs once the budget is set. These tools help to match applicants to job requirements.

- *Job analysis.* A job analysis covers the specific employment needs of a company. The analysis focuses on what needs to be done and who can do it. The job analysis is accomplished through observation, questionnaires, and personal interviews. From the data gathered, a meaningful job description can be written.

- *Job description.* A job description is a summary of the basic tasks of a position including job duties, skills needed, and identification of an immediate supervisor. The section on job duties indicates what the employee does, how it is done, and why it is done. Through the job description, an employee becomes aware of performance expectations and the activities necessary for promotion. A job description also serves as an evaluative tool if standards are established for each task. Then employee performance can be compared to each standard.

- *Job specification.* A job specification identifies the personal qualifications necessary for the proper performance of a job. This is prepared from the information provided in a job description. The job specification indicates the education, experience, and personal attributes needed for each position. Only those who meet the desired qualifications should be considered for available positions.

With these steps and tools in mind, retailers are ready to go forth with the actual process of finding appropriate personnel and bringing them into the organization.

Human Resource Components

Recruiting, hiring, training, motivating, and evaluating are key components of human resource management.

Recruiting

In retailing, the sources of employees are almost as varied as the jobs. An electronic help wanted sign might attract the right kind of part-time employee to a local pizza shop, but it would probably not bring the right prospective fashion director to a department store. An Internet advertisement for a computer store may reach an information technology specialist, but not a potential sales associate. Regardless of level, the search method must be matched to the (1) job, (2) type of retail establishment, and (3) target market. This matching process cannot be stressed enough in an industry characterized by long hours, night and weekend work, part-time workers, low compensation, and a labor pool that often lacks experience and training.

Filling positions in retailing is critical because profit margins are small. Both money and time are wasted if recruiting is done in a haphazard manner. Methods of recruitment vary whether staff or management is sought.

Figure 9.3 These CVS and Harrod's advertisements appeared in *jobpostings* magazine and *Women's Wear Daily*. Both publications offer many job postings targeted to students like you.

Methods for Recruiting Staff Employees There are many ways employees can be recruited both within the store and outside it. The internal sources for staff employees which include sales associates, stock clerks, and basic office and information technology help are:

- *Current employees.* They are excellent candidates for transfers or promotion, often on short notice.
- *Past employees.* Former full-time or part-time help with good records are productive with minimal retraining. This option is useful when business cycles are erratic.
- *Employee recommendations.* Friends or relatives of employees who are looking for work and have the needed skills and training may be good risks.

The external sources for staff employees are:

- *Newspaper advertisements.* Advertisements work well when filling peak season needs.
- *Government employment agencies.* These are excellent places to post jobs for part-time or full-time entry level help.

- *Private employment agencies.* Of limited use for entry level employees, they have value in locating staff in technical areas, such as accounting and information technology.
- *Educational institutions.* Excellent sources for part-time or summer help are high schools and two-year or four-year colleges and universities. High schools that have DECA programs are particularly attuned to the needs of retailers. Postsecondary students from all majors are routinely sought. Business majors requiring internships or cooperative education experiences are particularly good candidates.
- *Unsolicited applicants.* Walk-in applicants often seek part-time or entry-level sales jobs.

Effective retail recruitment advertising brings information to prospective employees where they are most likely to read it. IKEA, profiled at the end of this unit, places handwritten advertisements in rest rooms to capture the attention of prospective employees.

Methods for Recruiting Managerial Employees The internal sources for managerial employees are similar to those used for recruiting staff positions, but differ in scope and intent. Promotion from within is one of the best methods for securing new executives and has always had support from human resource professionals. For example, Liz Claiborne, uses several resources to identify talented employees and cultivate their skills. Off-premises leadership development seminars, executive coaching, and guest speakers are used to spark interest and encourage employees to stay with the company.[11]

Often a participant in a company's management training program will leave to work in a number of management positions in other firms and then return, years later, to fill a vice presidential slot. Keeping in touch with former executives who left in good standing is always a good idea.

External sources for managerial employees include advertising and word of mouth, but take a different guise than those geared to staff personnel:

referrals The names of an informed person's acquaintances who might be potential employees.

- *Referrals.* The names of an informed person's acquaintances who might be potential employees are called **referrals**. Suppliers, customers, and even competitors may suggest individuals as prospective executives. Because the skills developed in one retail organization are easily transferable, there is opportunity for movement within the industry. At trade industry conferences retail executives have the opportunity to examine the job market, and network with other business leaders. Many conversations revolve around human resource needs.
- *Advertisements.* When seeking middle- and upper-level managers, retailers often advertise in metropolitan and trade papers such as the Sunday edition

of *The New York Times, Wall Street Journal, Daily News Record*, or *Women's Wear Daily.* Local newspapers and magazines are also used. Recruitment advertisements for CVS pharmacy and Harrod's are shown in Figure 9.3.

- *Executive search firms.* Some recruiters specialize in finding the right executives for their clients. Individuals or agencies who are paid to find managers or executives for a client company are called **headhunters**. Pirating from other retailers is one of their techniques.

- *College and university recruiting.* Educational institutions have long been primary sources for retail management trainees. Majors in the business disciplines, including marketing and retailing, are actively recruited. Merchandising students from programs in consumer science areas are prime candidates. Students from liberal arts curriculums who have excellent communication skills and problem solving abilities also are sought. Many retailers are involved in internship or cooperative education programs, which allow them to bring potential trainees into the company while they are still in school. Other retailers become guest lecturers in retailing classes or host field trips, exposing a new generation to the rewards of retail management.

- *Job fairs.* Colleges and independent agencies host job fairs at which scores of employers have the opportunity to meet students nearing the completion of undergraduate and graduate degrees (See Figure 9.4).

- *Unsolicited applicants.* Graduating seniors often send resumes to retailers in geographic areas where they hope to locate. Some retail managers who wish to relocate to another part of the country or the world also operate in this manner.

Figure 9.4 Many companies, such as IBM, send recruiters to conferences and job fairs in order to meet prospective employees. *© David H. Wells/CORBIS*

headhunters Individuals or agencies who are paid to find managers or executives for a client company.

Uses of Technology in Recruiting Technology intensifies the search process for both staff and management positions. Two examples illustrate this trend. Job search kiosks developed by Adecco, a Swiss temporary agency, have been placed in shopping malls and on college campuses. The company works with retail clients in the United States and Europe and expects to expand into Spain, Britain, Australia, and Canada. It places 2.5 million people in jobs annually.[12]

Using the Internet has proved successful for some retailers. Rite Aid and Blockbuster use Web site recruiting for both staff and management positions. Blockbuster claims it receives two to three thousand responses per month. Using its own Web site, or a link to the Career Mosaic career

CYBERSCOOP

Visit Eddie Bauer at **www.eddiebauer.com** and click on "career opportunities." Find any jobs that interest you? Are you qualified for a position? How would you apply?

development site, job seekers can apply online for positions with Rite Aid drug stores.[13] More information on using the Internet for job search is provided in Appendix A, Retail Career Directions.

Hiring

Careful selection and matching of potential employees to the existing openings will result in greater productivity, high company morale, and lower attrition.

To select the best applicants, employees evaluate and rank each one on the basis of predetermined criteria. Evaluation and selection techniques vary widely from one retailer to another. Many rely on the rapport that builds during personal interviews. Some rely mainly on applications and resumes. Others find interviews, testing, or simulated problem solving situations effective in the selection process. When the final choice is made, most firms use a combination of both objective and subjective measures.

Application Forms Almost all retailers require prospective employees to complete an application form which gathers preliminary information used for further screening of candidates. Application forms may be written or electronic. Either should contain only the type of questions that help employers distinguish between qualified applicants. It is a violation of the Equal Employment Opportunity Act to ask questions that could be discriminatory, such as those concerning race, religion, age, or sexual orientation. Even if no current openings match the applicant's skills, applications of good future prospects are often kept in the company's data base.

Resumes The resume reflects a person's organizational and communications skills, both important in retailing. Almost everyone who applies for full-time work, especially those who are looking for jobs that require customer contact, should be required to submit a resume. Although resumes are expected from executive management program candidates, they are not always used when evaluating staff personnel.

Interviews A job candidate may be interviewed several times before being hired. The initial interview for staff personnel usually takes place at the time the application is filled out. It is generally conducted by an employment interviewer and lasts about 15 to 20 minutes. There are several purposes of an interview:

- to obtain additional information from the applicant
- to verify the information on the application

- to eliminate applicants who do not seem to qualify for the jobs available
- to inform the applicant about the company

Candidates who are under serious consideration, particularly for such jobs as managers or management trainees, are invited to return for follow-up interviews. These are more formal and intense than initial interviews. Stress interviews may be used to see how a person reacts under pressure. A **stress interview** is a type of screening tool in which a panel of interviewers fire questions requiring quick, thoughtful answers and evidence of problem solving ability by the candidate.

Awareness of how people talk and behave during an interview may help in selecting, motivating, and managing them effectively. According to Lee J. Colan, a human resource consultant, interviewers should spend 80 percent of their time listening to prospective employees. Companies should prepare questions that will help identify candidates' ability to handle difficult situations.[14]

An interviewing technique using psycholinguistics allows the interviewer to understand the direct correlation between language and behavior patterns. In some respects everyone uses this technique to learn more about people. A defensive posture with arms tightly crossed does not indicate an open attitude when observed during an interview or in a personal relationship.

Testing Questions of discrimination gradually forced retailers to take a good look at their testing programs. In doing so, many made the decision to eliminate tests except for those directly related to skills such as math and computers, for example. Larger retail companies make use of psychological tests to predetermine aptitudes toward drug abuse or criminal activity. Small retailers rarely use extensive testing.

Reference Checks Toward the end of the selection process, the company checks references for the candidates it may wish to hire. A reference check can be conducted by mail, e-mail, telephone, or personal contact. Checking references—professional, educational, or personal—gives the employer another opportunity to verify information that was obtained through the application and the interview. Most people will not list a person or company as a reference if they suspect the respondent will speak of them in anything other than glowing terms. This fact alone takes some of the credibility out of references.

Physical Examinations Some retailers may require applicants for full-time jobs to take a physical examination. Physical examinations are always

stress interview A type of screening tool in which a panel of interviewers fire questions requiring quick, thoughtful answers and evidence of problem solving ability by the candidate.

required for those who handle food or drug products as part of their job. Drug testing is becoming more common and some retailers are requiring AIDS testing. Although applicants can refuse to take these tests, most people do not if they really want the job.

Final Selection Candidates who successfully pass all the steps in the selection process are hired. Human resource professionals do not make decisions lightly. They spend a great deal of time reviewing applications, resumes, and tests of the candidates who have made the final cut. Sometimes a group decision is made by all who interview the candidate.

The best selection process cannot always produce perfect employees. All human resource managers try to improve methodologies. Some candidates are asked to become involved in role playing exercises. **Role playing** is a training exercise in which individuals experience a situation through dramatization, by participating as actors. Usually this approach is limited to candidates for management positions. Whatever the system, objective criteria and testing, human resource management experience, and good personal judgment should go into the final decision.

role playing Training exercise in which individuals experience a situation through dramatization, by participating as actors.

Orientation and Training

Nothing is more anxiety producing than a new beginning. Remember freshman orientation or the move to a new town? Starting a new job produces the same feelings even for those who have worked before. A new organization means unfamiliar people, regulations, and duties. Even the most self-confident person needs to be eased into an organization and provided with proper training.

Orientation An orientation program should be offered to every new employee in a retail organization whether the new person is a full-time management trainee or a part-time sales associate. Familiarizing new workers with their roles, the company, its policies, and other employees are the objectives of orientation programs. Frequently company manuals, videos, and computer learning tools are used.

During its "On-Boarding" program, the Limited goes to great lengths to help new employees get settled at its Columbus, Ohio, headquarters. CEO Leslie Wexner greets all new recruits during their first day-and-a-half of meetings. The company also provides information and field trips to help acclimatize participants to the Columbus area. Seminars with key department heads are held and mentoring is encouraged. Since the turnover rate of buyers at Limited Brands is less than 10 percent, the program appears to be working.[15]

Goals and Scope of Training Training in all retail institutions has the same goal—to develop employees' ability to perform their jobs to the satisfaction of customers, management, and themselves. Training programs are not only for new employees, but should be made available on a continuous basis to all employees.

New employees are trained in the basic skills required by their jobs, but skills grow stale if not updated. Rapidly advancing technology has made it imperative to be on top of the knowledge tree in all retail sectors. Experienced personnel may need sessions on new computer systems, leadership training, team building, merchandising techniques, advanced selling, or customer service skills.

Initial Staff Training When new sales associates or support staff are hired they may spend a few hours of their first day on the job filling out various company and government forms and then attend orientation sessions. The next few days are spent learning retail systems. The amount of training provided depends on the complexity of the job.

New sales associates also are taught selling techniques, which may be followed by a day or two of on-the-job training. **On-the-job training (OJT)** involves instructing employees during regular working hours while they also are doing productive work and are being paid regular wages. Figure 9.1 illustrates a typical on-the-job training scene in a specialty store. Initial training techniques may include lectures, role playing, discussion, case studies, and in most large retail operations, self-paced computer learning modules.

Improvement of training programs and involvement of part-time as well as full-time employees benefits all retailers. High attrition of sales associates and other support staff could be lowered as a result.

Supervisory Training Often retail sales associates are promoted to supervisory positions. Some are experts in their job functions but not in human relations. Many find they are ill equipped to deal on a professional level with co-workers with whom they have socialized. All new supervisors should learn human relations skills. It is not easy to manage peers or people older than oneself, keep sales up, and motivate employees concurrently.

Management Training Programs Designed to develop managerial talent, formal training programs are commonly found in large retail organizations. College graduates enter a company as management trainees and progress from lower to higher level positions by interspersing study of policies and procedures with increasingly demanding work assignments. Learning to present merchandise effectively on the selling floor is an example of an appropriate task for a management trainee as shown in Figure 9.5.

Did You Know?

Ongoing training at JC Penney is done through distance leaning, a method of instruction delivered by Penney's satellite broadcast system. Special classes on topics such as hiring, motivating, and coaching typically reach 500 employees.
Source: *Women's Wear Daily.* May 13, 1998;15.

on-the-job training (OJT)
Instructing employees during regular working hours while they also are doing productive work and are being paid regular wages.

Figure 9.5 As part of her management training program, this assistant manager learns how to set up a selling floor and display merchandise.

line management Members of the management team who are directly connected to retail functions such as operations, finance, information technology, and merchandise management.

Training of line management tends to be more formal, longer, and in some respects more generalized. **Line management** are members of the management team who are directly related to retail functions such as operations, finance, information technology, or merchandising. These individuals will eventually fill middle- and upper-level management positions. New employees are usually exposed to all facets of the retail business before they select a specific track—usually in merchandising or operations. Many department stores train new managers in this way. Saks' management trainees learn specific merchandising functions first, including buying, planning, distributing goods, and working in the stores. Those that successfully complete the three-month program go on to be assistant buyers or planners or marketing analysts.[16]

Macy's executive training program is one of the best in the United States. The selection process for the merchandising training program is highly competitive. The process begins with 12 weeks of formal classroom training devoted to computer instruction, and the basics of merchandising, promotion, and retail math. It continues with a combination of classes and OJT. Each trainee has a mentor who acts in an advisory capacity. At six-month intervals after the formal training period, trainees' skill levels are assessed as their experience builds. Most trainees become full-fledged buyers in two to four years. The program has been heralded as the "Harvard" of retailing.[17]

In most stores executive trainees advance according to their abilities and the needs of the company, not by a predetermined schedule. Training programs require both effort and an investment of time on the part of trainees. For that reason, many who are unwilling to wait for the rewards leave in their first year. Many people who enter management from training programs move to positions with other retailers or other industries within a few years.

Training in small retail businesses is much more informal, since owners wear many hats. Entry-level employees can learn the retail business from a unique perspective if they choose to enter the industry in this way. The desire to become a generalist, rather than a specialist, must be strong in individuals who take this path. The intrinsic rewards can be great when learning many phases of a business concurrently. A sense of ownership, used here in a figurative sense, grows deeper in a small store than in a large organization. These advantages may be important for some individuals to consider.

Opportunities to participate in special training indicate to employees that the company cares. Programs take many forms and are held either on or off the premises. Sending branch store home electronics sales managers to annual home office product information sessions is a form of off-site continuous training. Seasonal visits made by department store sportswear buyers to resident buying office fashion trend presentations is another example, as is attending annual conventions of the National Retail Federation or any of its specialized seminars. The form may vary, but the important point is that employees have the opportunity to participate and learn.

Levi Strauss takes a global perspective on management training. The company has established a list of global leadership competencies and expects its managers to spend time working in its foreign operations as they progress on their career paths.[18] This policy is not an unusual expectation of retailers with international divisions.

The Internet offers tremendous potential for training at all levels. Through UNext.com, several major universities and businesses are working together to deliver graduate courses to corporate employees. The London School of Economics and Columbia University in New York are two of the schools that are developing programs that will help individuals learn advanced skills through UNext.com.[19]

Evaluation

The process of assessing an individuals progress on-the-job is called evaluation. Evaluation guarantees job security to those who meet predetermined standards and provides rewards to those who surpass those standards.

Evaluation Objectives Evaluations are intended to assess employees' performance in order to determine salary increases, promotions, or other rewards. Viewed as progress reports, evaluations also indicate areas in which improvement is needed. Ineffective people need to be reassigned or removed. In many retail stores much time is wasted tolerating repeated infractions of employees at all levels. However, firing an employee still ranks as one of the most unpleasant aspects of being an owner or manager.

Evaluation Methods Retailers use a number of different methods to evaluate employees:

■ *Performance records.* These are quantitative ways of measuring performance of sales associates and managers using criteria such as the total dollar sales,

Did You Know?

Retail companies employing less than 100 people comprise 98.4 percent of stores in the United States.
Retail Industry Indicators. Table IV.2: "Employment Size of Retail Firms, 1998." NRF Federation. August, 2001. (Source: U.S. Small Business Administration, Office of Advocacy.).

the total number of sales transactions, the units sold per transaction, the number of customer complaints, the number and dollar value of returns, the net sales per hour worked, and the number of days absent or late. Performance records are useful in identifying effective or ineffective salespeople and their managers.

■ *Management by objectives.* **Management by objectives (MBO)** is a process in which a superior and a subordinate jointly set measurable performance goals for the subordinate and then meet periodically to assess progress. Because managers are aware of their performance goals from the moment they start their jobs, this method encourages self-development and self-evaluation.

■ *Rating scales.* Scales are used to identify and list performance criteria. Ratings may be a simple satisfactory/unsatisfactory, or the scale may provide for a poor, fair, average, good, or excellent rating. Supervisors find that this method is a quick and easy way to rate their employees. On the other hand, it is often too subjective to be of real value. Good rating scales also require written explanation of the evaluation.

■ *Shopping reports.* These are used by retailers to monitor customer service standards and honesty. Outside evaluators are hired to come into stores as shoppers. Their evaluation is based on how they were treated as customers and their observation of the person under scrutiny.

Formal appraisals are usually done once or twice a year, but should be an ongoing process. The person being evaluated should be informed of a formal evaluation ahead of time. After the evaluation, feedback should be immediate. This avoids anxiety and promotes faith in the system.

Compensation

Payroll is the largest single expense item for most retailers. It reflects costs of salaries, wages, commissions, and fringe benefits. Because a good compensation package is so costly, retailers are constantly looking for ways to trim this enormous expense without losing good employees.

In most large retail stores close to 40 percent of all employees work part-time.[20] Most usually work no more than 20 hours a week, and some are paid little more than minimum wage. This dispels the legend of long hours but not of low pay, because many part-time employees receive no fringe benefits. Hiring part-timers is a major strategy among retailers to keep payroll costs under control. Part-time employment in retailing is charted in Table 9.1. The figures show the total percentage of part-time workers in retailing,

management by objectives (MBO) A process in which a superior and a subordinate jointly set measurable performance goals for the subordinate and then meet periodically to assess progress.

Table 9.1 Part-Time Employment in Retailing, 2000
(In Thousand of Employees and Percent)

	Total	Men	Women
Total Retail			
Employment**	21,159	10,334	10,824
Part-Time Retail			
Employment	7,375	2,726	4,649
Share of Total	34.9%	26.4%	43.0%
Voluntarily			
Part-Time	6,557	2,403	4,154
Share of Part-Time	88.9%	88.2%	89.4%
Involuntarily			
Part-Time	818	323	495
Share of Part-Time	11.1%	11.8%	10.6%

*Less than 35 hours per week
** The number of retail employees reported here is smaller than previous totals because the survey used to determine the part-time or full-time status of employees classifies some of the workers as unemployed.
Source: Derived from US Department of Labor, Bureau of Labor Statistics data. "Retail Industry Indicators," © NRF Foundation, August 2002.

employment by gender, and the breakdown of voluntary and involuntary part-time workers.

Characteristics of Compensation Packages

The best compensation packages directly relate rewards to contributions to the organization. A satisfactory retail compensation plan should be:

- Suitable for the functions being performed.
- Fair to the employee and the owner, whether sole proprietor or corporation.
- Easily calculated and understood.
- Designed to provide relatively steady income and incentive for exceptional performance.
- Related to performance without causing friction, such as fighting over customers for commission.

Because of the many different types of jobs in retailing, there are a number of compensation plans. Plans for sales associates in furniture stores will be different from those for visual merchandising directors in department stores. The following section looks at nonexecutive and executive compensation plans.

Table 9.2 Top Retail Executive Compensation*

Rank	CEO	Company*	Compensation+
1	Robert Tillman	Lowe's Companies	20,687,000
2	Richard Schulze	Best Buy	20,322,000
3	Warren Eisenberg	Bed Bath & Beyond	20,177,000
4	Robert Nardelli	Home Depot	13,789,000
5	H. Lee Scott	Wal-Mart Stores	11,613,000
6	Joseph Pichler	Kroger	11,396,000
7	R Lawrence	Montgomery Kohl's	10,399,000
8	Allen Questrom	JC Penney	8,054,000
9	Lawrence R. Johnston	Albertsons	7,518,000
10	Robert J. Ulrich	Target	6,610,000

* Limited to CEOs of companies in which retailing was principle activity.
+ Compensation includes salary, bonuses, stock holdings.

Source: Derived from Forbes "Big Bosses and Paychecks." April 23, 2002
Available:www.forbes.com/home/2002/4/25/ceos.html

Nonexecutive Compensation Plans

There are several basic salary and commission plans as well as other income enhancement measures used by retailers.

Straight Salary Plan Straight salary is a fixed amount of compensation for a specific work period such as an hour, day, week, month, or year. For the retailer, the straight salary plan has the advantages of easy administration and a high level of employer control. For the employee, the straight salary plan has a known level of financial security and stability. One disadvantage of this plan for the retailer is a high ratio of wage costs to sales.

Retailers typically use straight salary plans for almost all staff positions in nonsales areas of the company. Hourly wage plans are the most common form of remuneration for sales associates.

Straight Commission Plan Under this plan, sales associates receive a percentage of what they sell. Straight commission is usually offered for big ticket products such as automobiles, jewelry, computers, furniture, and appliances.

The major advantage of a straight commission plan is monetary incentive. It can result in problems for the retailer, because commission sales associates sometimes only service customers who indicate an interest in high commission products. Other problems for retailers who use this plan can be customer discontent due to high pressure selling tactics.

The greatest weakness for employees in the straight commission plan is financial instability. Although they can make phone calls, send e-mails, and write notes to prospective customers, retail salespeople cannot totally control who enters the store. They also cannot influence a downturn in the economy. Because of this, some straight commission plans include a drawing account that allows employees to be paid during slow times in the business cycle. A **drawing account** is monetary compensation available to commissioned salespeople that allows them to take a fixed sum of money at regular intervals against future commissions.

drawing account A regular monetary compensation available to commission salespeople that allows them to take a fixed sum of money at regular intervals against future commissions.

Salary Plus Commission Plan This plan combines the stability of the straight salary plan with the incentive of the straight commission plan. Generally, in the salary plus commission plan, the base salary constitutes the greatest share of the employee's total compensation; however, the employer does have the option of increasing the commission rate when additional monetary motivation is needed.

Quota Bonus Plan Similar to the salary plus commission plan, the incentive pay in the quota bonus plan begins only after a specified sales level has been reached. Quota bonus plans vary by department within the same store. Type of merchandise, selling season, gross margins, and volume may be considered when quotas are established.

Push Money Sales employees are motivated to sell in other ways. **Push money (PM)** is an incentive payment given to sales associates for selling certain items. As an example, a home electronics retailer may offer $25 to $50—beyond commission or bonus—to all sales associates who sell a slow-selling TV model. With PM, the salesperson, retailer, and manufacturer all benefit. Push money may be provided by the retailer or the manufacturer.

push money (PM) An incentive payment given to sales associates for selling certain items.

Executive Compensation Plans

Most retail executives are amply rewarded for their hard work and long hours. Buyers, for example, earn anywhere from $35,000 to $100,000 a year depending on length of time on the job, type of store, department, volume, and bonus plan. Some retail CEOs earn well over $1 million a year. Table

9.2 lists the salaries and bonuses of the 10 best-compensated U.S. retail executives. Store managers on salary are also rewarded with a yearly bonus based either on net sales or net profit. The figure depends on the amount of control they have over store operations and on the volume level of the store they manage. Owners of single stores usually take a salary each week or month and then, out of profits, award themselves a bonus at year end—if the year was profitable. Whether a sole proprietor or a corporate manager, executives in retailing are as well paid as executives in other industries.

Fringe Benefits

Fringe benefits add to the appeal of compensation packages. For retail employees in the United States compensation other than cash amounted to 20.6 percent of their gross incomes in 2000.[21] The tax free aspects of many fringe benefits add to their appeal and may contribute to high employee morale and level of performance. Low attrition also results when good fringe benefit packages are part of compensation packages. Basic fringe benefits such as health, accident, and life insurance are received by most employees. Pension and 401K plans, sick leave, and paid vacations are also common. Extended fringe benefits often address quality-of-life issues. Paid memberships in fitness clubs, on-site child care facilities, and tuition reimbursement plans are examples.

New perks are finding their way into benefits packages. Online grocery services have partnered with corporations to offer employee discounts on orders that are placed from home or office. Some even deliver to business parking lots. In periods when the job market is tight, benefit packages usually become more appealing.

Job Enrichment

The finest training in the world and monetary reward cannot guarantee a productive workforce. Constant effort on the part of management is needed to keep attrition down, wage–cost ratios in line, and sales productivity up. The best way to accomplish these three goals is through job enrichment programs that are positive motivators. **Job enrichment** is a way to improve an employee's efficiency and self-satisfaction by increasing the challenges, opportunities, and nonmonetary rewards provided by the company.

Job enrichment can take many forms, but it should fill the psychological void that exists when management offers only the usual monetary reward for expected performance. People should be encouraged to take initiative. Rewards should be given when extra steps that bring more profit to the

job enrichment A way to improve an employee's efficiency and self-satisfaction by increasing the challenges, opportunities, and nonmonetary rewards provided by the company.

company are taken. Programs should consider all individuals' needs for recognition, self-esteem, and fair treatment.

Motivational Programs   Blending both cash and noncash incentives is important when developing good motivational programs. Properly conceived motivational programs satisfy employees' needs for achievement and recognition. They also encourage team spirit and a sense of belonging. Cash may swell the bank account of a manager whose department achieved a great increase in sales. However, offering a meaningful awards dinner, extra time off, or a free vacation trip to the company's condo may help produce a more loyal employee.

Some companies offer employees the opportunity to suggest time or cost saving measures which may be rewarded with a monetary sum, gift, or preferred parking spot. This type of enrichment activity encourages employee input, and builds pride in the company.

Grievance Procedures   Providing a grievance process is another type of positive employee reinforcement program. A **grievance** is a complaint that is handled formally through fixed procedures. Employees perform much better when they know that they have someone who will not only listen to their problems, but who is in a position to help with solutions. Being able to air grievances without fear of reprisal empowers employees. Grapevine chatter loses credibility when formal grievance procedures are in place.

grievance A complaint that is handled formally through fixed procedures.

Retailers develop procedures that best suit their particular organizations. In small stores, bringing issues directly to owners may be most appropriate. Large, multistore retailers need more complex systems. Staff members first go to their immediate supervisors, who either solve the problem or take it to higher management.

In serious cases, it might be necessary for a representative from corporate headquarters to visit the store where the grievance occurred. If necessary the company may use an outside mediator. A **mediator** is an impartial evaluator hired to listen to both sides of a conflict and suggest solutions. All involved parties might be interviewed and recommendations of the mediator would be made to the appropriate line manager, who would then discuss the proposed resolution with the disgruntled employee. Other retailers use elected grievance committees to implement this process.

mediator Impartial evaluator hired to listen to both sides of a conflict and suggest solutions.

Perception of Compensation

Perceptions of compensation and other managerial issues differ depending on whether survey respondents are in the retail industry or not. One study showed that retailers rank competitiveness of pay and benefits in retailing

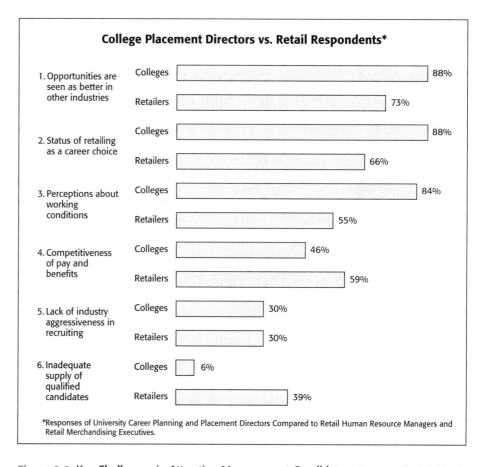

Figure 9.6 Key Challenges in Attracting Management Candidates *Courtesy of Fairchild Publications, Inc.*

much higher than do college placement directors. Also, there is disparity between how retailers and college placement directors view the recruitment of management personnel. Although only 6 percent of college placement directors felt there was an inadequate supply of qualified management candidates, 39 percent of retailers saw this as a significant problem. Conversely, 66 percent of retailers believed that the poor status of retailing as a career choice was an obstacle to recruitment, but 88 percent of college placement directors indicated problems in this area.[22] More data on this topic are graphed in Figure 9.6.

Human Resource Managers

In addition to overseeing the recruitment, selection. training, motivation, and evaluation of employees, human resource managers administer the menu of fringe benefits and plan job enrichment programs. Much detail, paperwork, and computer time is spent on these and other aspects of management.

Responsibilities

In addition to the administration of major human resource components identified earlier, human resource managers have many other responsibilities. For example, they constantly evaluate their benefits programs to make sure they have maximum appeal and minimum risk. Medical benefits have become one of the most costly benefits retailers extend, requiring most to pass on a portion of the cost to employees. Managers are responsible for sorting out these issues.

Human resource managers also monitor health and safety on the premises through standards set by a federal agency known as the Occupational Safety and Health Agency. Sexual harassment issues that may confront retailers are also handled by human resource personnel.

In small retail stores the human relations function may be handled by owners or designated employees; in small chains general managers may also take on human resource responsibilities. Human resource people may act as a liaison within the community, spearhead charitable functions, and even schedule field trips for college classes.

Competencies of Successful Managers

The consulting firm, Kurt Salmon Associates, has prepared a competency framework as part of a series of key initiatives for retail recruitment and management training. A summary of these competencies provides a fitting conclusion to this chapter. An effective manager should be:

- *Forward thinking.* Use insights and intuition to create future successes, and pursue innovations in markets, sourcing, products, services, technology and management.
- *Results oriented.* Develop and implement strategies, initiatives, and business plans to achieve objectives. Set high standards for customer service, product quality, and community involvement.
- *A risk taker.* Find courage to act when faced with obstacles. Show willingness to move beyond that which is customary.
- *Seek integrative solutions.* Collect and synthesize diverse information to maintain a broad perspective, understand how the various parts of the business operate, and maintain a supply chain focus.
- *Mentor-oriented.* Recruit and develop new people and delegate responsibility and authority appropriately.[23]

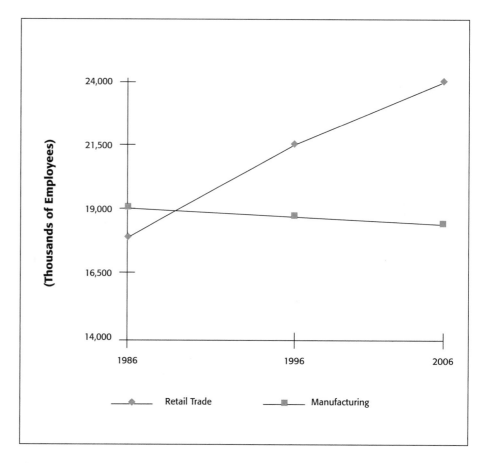

Figure 9.7 U.S. Employment Trends in Retailing and Manufacturing, 1998–2008.
Source: Derived from data in U.S. Department of Labor, Bureau of Labor Statistics, Monthly Labor Review, *November 1997. "Retail Industry Indicators" © NRF Foundation, August 2002.*

This is an ambitious framework, but well worth implementing. Figure 9.7 shows U.S. employment trends in retailing and manufacturing through 2008. The projected upward movement in the retail sector will benefit qualified, competent people who seek careers in the field. Retailers who plan well and develop their employees will thrive in the 21st century.

Summary

Success in retailing depends on the ability to serve customers. Therefore employees must be well selected and trained and fairly compensated. Profits and a positive company image are linked to effective human resource management.

Some contemporary challenges that retailers face include irregular demand for workers, the small labor pool, attracting competent employees, competition from other industries, government standards, union matters, retail image problems, internal theft, ethnic diversity, and quality-of-life issues.

A good human resource program starts with a six-step plan that includes a personnel forecast, inventory of current employees, accounting of factors that may affect employment needs, execution, and evaluation of the plan. Job analysis, job descriptions, and job specifications are important planning tools. Budgeting for people is as important as it is for merchandise.

Recruitment involves attracting qualified candidates in a variety of ways. The Internet, college recruitment, and job fairs are contemporary forms of employee solicitation. Advertising, search firms, word-of-mouth referrals, and electronic kiosks also are used. Recruitment techniques vary whether staff or management is sought.

The screening of new employees utilizes many tools including applications, resumes, interviews, skill tests, physical exams, drug screenings, and reference checks. Once hired, new employees must be given orientation and training. Continuous training of employees should be practiced by all retailers.

Compensation packages should include monetary and nonmonetary rewards, fringe benefits, and job enrichment programs. Employees need recognition and opportunities to build self-esteem on the job.

Human resource management in retailing is complex and diverse. Basic competencies of successful managers include the ability to think futuristically, be results-oriented, take risks, seek integrative solutions, and mentor new employees.

Questions for Review and Discussion

1. Discuss three major challenges that face human resource managers this decade. How are these challenges being met?
2. Referring to the six steps in developing a human resource budget, how would you "modify existing data" to help determine personnel needs?
3. Name at least three internal sources and three external sources that are useful in recruiting staff and managers.
4. Do you feel that orientation and training should be offered to every new employee, both full-time and part-time? Why or why not?
5. What markets do the retail skills centers sponsored by the NRF serve? Will they be successful?
6. How do job enrichment programs enhance regular compensation packages?

7. What are the five competencies retail managers should develop? Which of these do you believe is most important?

Endnotes

1. *Retail Industry Indicators.* "Non-Agricultural Employment by Industry, 2000." NRF Foundation. Washington, DC. 2000:17. Source: U.S. Department of Labor Statistics.

2. Ibid: 19.

3. Ibid. "Retail Employees by Occupation," 2000:22.

4. Ibid. "Retail Employees by Age, 2000." 23.

5. Ibid. "Women in the Retail Workforce, 2000." 25.

6. Kabachnick, Terri. "The Strategic Role of Human Resources." *Retailing Issues Newsletter.* Arthur Anderson/Center for Retailing Studies, Texas A&M University. Vol. II, No. 1. January, 1999:2.

7. "'Sales and Service Voluntary Partnership." Fact Sheet. National Retail Institute, National Retail Federation. 1998.

8. "Retail Skills Center at King of Prussia: The Next Generation of Retail Workers." Brochure. National Retail Institute. National Retail Federation. Washington, DC. 1998.

9. *Retail Industry Indicators.* "Sources of Inventory Shrinkage, 1999." NRF Foundation. Washington DC. 2001:43. Source: Center for Retailing Education and Research. College of Business Administration. University of Florida. 2000.

10. "Business Briefs." *Wall Street Journal.* June 8, 1999:A1.

11. "A Roadmap for Retail Training." *Women's Wear Daily.* May 6, 1998:10.

12. Lewis, Diane E. "Going Shopping for Help." *Boston Globe.* January 31, 1999:D4.

13. Ibid.

14. Williamson, Rusty. "Good Help Is Hard to Find and Keep." *Women's Wear Daily.* March 30, 2000:12.

15. Moin, David. "Retail's Quest for Talent." *Women's Wear Daily.* April 29, 1998: 11.

16. Ibid.

17. Ibid:12.

18. "A Roadmap for Retail Training." *Women's Wear Daily.* May 6, 1998:10.

19. McGeehan, Patrick. "UNext.com 4 More Schools Agree to Deals." *Wall Street Journal.* June 23.1999:B2.

20. "Part-Time Employment in Retailing, 1998." *Retail Industry Indicators.* National Retail Institute. National Retail Federation. Washington, DC, 1999:14. Source: Derived from US Department of Labor Statistics data.

21. Table III.15: "Compensation Paid to Retail Employees, 1999–2000." *Retail Industry Indicators.* NRF Foundation. Washington, DC. August, 2001:29. (Derived from U.S. Department of Labor, Bureau of Labor Statistics data.)

22. "A Roadmap for Retail Training." *Women's Wear Daily.* May 6, 1998:10.

23. "A Roadmap for Retail Training." *Women's Wear Daily.* May 6, 1998:10.

Chapter 10

Customer Behavior

Learning Objectives

After completing this chapter you should be able to:

- Discuss how individual and group variables shape retail shopping behavior.

- Relate how demographics and psychographics influence customer behavior.

- Describe societal factors that affect customer behavior.

- Identify the steps in the customer purchase decision-making process.

- Relate the three types of decision-making time frames to the four classifications of goods and services.

Figure 10.1 Customers come in all shapes, sizes, and ages. They may have similar interests or divergent tastes, but all equally challenge retailers.

Understanding customer behavior is a precursor to retailing excellence. At a recent National Retail Federation conference, a key presenter voiced the preference to refer to retail shoppers as customers, not consumers. Elliot Ettenberg, chairman and CEO of Bozell Retail, cited the root definitions of these terms. Consumer implies user, someone who acquires, but customer means a person to be dealt with. This mind-shift is necessary, he believes, if retailers are to successfully meet the needs of contemporary customers. This text acknowledges the nuance as an important paradigm shift and emphasizes the term.

Customers today have less predictable purchasing habits than ever before. It is more difficult to understand their motivations, priorities and lifestyles. In a customer behavior context, **lifestyles** describe the way people live, work, play, and spend their money. Society is more enlightened, media influence has intensified, and the World Wide Web has added a new dimension to shopping behavior. Great value is placed on instant communication, ethnicity as well as diversity, rapidly expanding technologies, and global outlooks.

Retailers serve people from varied backgrounds. Everyone does not want to look, think, eat, or dress alike—although cultural, peer, and family pressure surely play parts in product selection. Customer behavior involves a complex assortment of individual and group influences which will be studied from a number of vantage points.

lifestyles The way people live, work, play, and spend their money.

Individual and Group Influences on Customer Behavior

The fields of psychology and sociology provide insight into the complexities of human behavior. Within these disciplines is a wealth of information for retailers. Many influences constantly impinge on the decisions individuals make.

Individual Influences

Every purchase is based on individual needs or wants. Classic psychological theories attempt to categorize and explain human complexities. They involve need determination, physiological and psychological bases of behavior and personality.

Biogenic and Psychogenic Needs Human needs can be divided into two broad categories—biogenic and psychogenic. **Biogenic needs** are physiological needs for food, warmth, shelter, and sex. **Psychogenic needs** stem from the socialization process and involve intangible aspects, such as status, acquisition, or love. Both types affect behavior.

biogenic needs Physiological needs for food, warmth, shelter, and sex.

psychogenic needs Needs that stem from the socialization process and involve intangible aspects such as status, acquisitiveness, or love.

Three psychogenic needs, originally defined by James Baylor, provide more insight regarding human behavior:

- *Affectional:* The need to love and be loved; to form relationships.
- *Ego-bolstering:* The need to build ourselves up in our own minds or in the eyes of others, develop self-esteem, desire status.
- *Ego-defensive:* The need to protect ourselves, our families, and our fragile egos.[1]

Psychogenic needs are often the basis for advertising campaigns. Cologne, liquor, and cosmetic ads frequently play on affectional needs; insurance, personal and health care products on ego-defensive needs; designer clothing and high-performance automobiles on ego-bolstering needs.

Maslow's Hierarchy of Needs From the annals of human psychology, Dr. Abraham Maslow's **hierarchy of needs** states that people seek to satisfy needs in an ascending order of importance: biogenic, social, and psychogenic. Although not intended to predict shopping behavior, Maslow's theory helps retailers understand the buying motivations of customers. The hierarchy is illustrated in Figure 10.2. The theory provides a valuable frame of reference shown in the following contexts.

hierarchy of needs Maslow's theory that people seek to satisfy needs in this order: biological, social, psychological.

In the early years of retailing, trading posts sold basic goods such as fur skins for bodily warmth and axes for cutting down trees for shelter and heat. Satisfying fundamental human needs were most important to customers of this era.

Affluent individuals of the 1980s chose their Porsche automobiles and Rolex watches to fulfill the higher- level ego needs for self-esteem. Parents lavished possessions on their children in what some psychologists and sociologists claim was one of the greatest attempts in history to buy love, substituting a new bike or dollhouse for an evening of shared activities.

Today, customers may be somewhat less ostentatious, but many have discretionary incomes that equal or surpass those in the 1980s. Their self-esteem may emanate from more intrinsic than extrinsic sources.

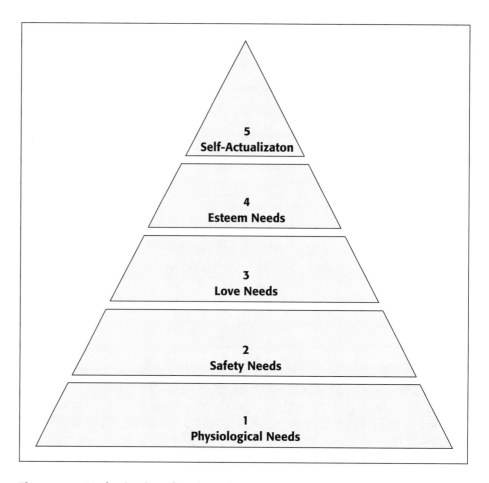

Figure 10.2 Maslow's Hierarchy of Needs *Source: Abraham H. Maslow, "A Theory of Human Motivation,"* Psychological Review *50 (July 1943): 370–396.*

self-actualization The desired result when a person sets out to become all that he or she is capable of becoming.

Those who achieve self-actualization care little for status merchandise as a means of achieving self-fulfillment. **Self-actualization** is the desired result when a person becomes all that he or she is capable of being. At this level, people feel secure and do not have the need to state their accomplishments through possessions. This group is the most difficult of all to serve. The search for self-actualization is reflected in the proliferation of products in the market today that encourage introspection, spirituality, and expansion of self and soul. The image of what individuals hope to become is closely allied with aspirational wants. **Aspirational wants** are those that relate to products and services that people perceive will help them achieve higher status in life. Ironically, most people never reach a truly self-actualized state.

aspirational wants Wants that relate to products and services that people perceive will help them achieve higher status in life.

Maslow's theory is useful for determining market segments and positioning products, but is not the only basis for retail strategy development. People have diverse backgrounds and complex psychological needs. How do we explain why people buy the most expensive computer equipment, yet drive used compact cars? What about those who live in lavishly furnished homes but seldom eat out in fine restaurants? It is necessary to probe the depths of the human psyche farther before the work of contemporary behavior experts is studied.

Personality Types Because shopping is a form of self-expression, understanding personality types is helpful to retailers. Although more complex than this, certain personalities respond to retail sales situations in different ways. For example, extroverts, who outwardly express their ideas, are more talkative and enjoy attention. Because of this they usually enter into lengthy discussions during sales presentations. As long as the sale is open they have the attention of the salesperson. Introverts are more emotionally contained and less loquacious. They respond negatively to high pressure tactics because they do not enjoy directed personal attention. Training sales associates to use selling techniques that consider different personality types can have a bearing on customer retention.

Shopping behavior may also be related to brain dominance. This supposition is discussed in this chapter's From the Field. Some may treat this theory lightly, but knowing which customers are left-brain or right-brain shoppers could be useful to retailers.

Group Influences

Our attitudes are also shaped by our interactions with others. Friends and family, peers, and professional associates affect our behavior—some to a greater degree than others.

Reference Groups An individual's self-image is developed from external as well as internal influences. Reference groups guide the decision-making process. **Reference groups** are social or professional associations with which a person identifies and looks to when forming opinions. Fraternities and sororities, business affiliations, country club and church memberships are examples of formal reference groups. Roommates and classmates and even spectators at a soccer game can be informal reference groups. The following examples show how reference groups influence individual purchases. Sara, following the custom of other young managers in her firm, chose a Honda Accord as her first car. Jay, after hearing his fraternity brothers rave about the latest release from the Dave Matthews Band, bought the CD. Society sets certain norms of behavior to which its members are pressured to conform. Very little is bought at retail that does not reflect social influences.

reference groups Social groups or professional associations with which a person identifies and looks to when forming opinions.

From the Field: The Polarity of Retail

"An unbelievable shift is taking place in retailing," states Bruce Dybvad, Design Forum's president of design and architecture. "Trips to most stores today are driven by need. Function, value, self-esteem, and fashion are just a sampling of those needs. This trend called 'retail polarity,' emerged in the late 1990s and is causing retailers to re-examine the changing needs of their customers and their shopping habits."

Retail polarity is another way to look at buying behavior—as left-brain and right-brain shopping. "Left-brain shoppers look for the low experience, low service, low cost shopping venture and usually go to stores like Wal-Mart, Trader Joe's, and the Internet. They look for the retail experience that offers functional, analytical, need-fulfilling, value-oriented experience," Dybvad continues.

"Right-brain shoppers purchase for creative and emotional reasons. They want the 'high-touch' or the 'WOW' experience. With price not a concern, right-brain shoppers usually frequent stores like Disney, Gander Mountain, REI, and FAO Schwarz, to name a few."

What else can we say about this new breed of shoppers? "Everyone shops with a left-brain and a right-brain perspective, and therefore, usually crosses from the left pole and the right pole, and back again. Those who cross seek two different retail experiences to meet an immediate need," adds Dybvad.

For instance, from a left-brain perspective, a shopper visits a warehouse club to purchase commodity prod-ucts or other discounted merchandise. They want a value-based shopping trip with good prices, having little or no concern about store atmosphere. Then, crossing over to the right-brain side, the shopper takes the money saved at the warehouse wholesaler to spend it more frivolously at an upscale department store on a higher priced product in a higher service, attentive and experiential environment. In each case, the motivator (low price/low service or high price/high service) moves the customer to the polar extreme. And it is because of this buying behavior that retailers today are finding it difficult to understand their customers.

Source: Excerpted from "The Polarity of Retailing." *Ideations.* Design Forum. Dayton, Ohio. Summer 1998.

The Family Family members exert more influence on buying behavior than any other group within a given culture or socioeconomic class. As family structure changes, so do retail strategies. Often it is difficult to determine who makes purchasing decisions.

Children are sophisticated, media-savvy, and often sway household purchasing decisions. Frequently teens in the family are the experts when buying a DVD player or even a new car. When a middle-aged adult is seen driving a Mitsubishi 3000 or a Chevrolet Camaro, it becomes apparent that a teenager has wielded some pressure on the family purchase.

Children have considerable clout in the marketplace. Through allowances and gifts, children have money to spend, and they often make purchases with little parental consultation. Products such as fashion apparel, lip gloss, movies, and games are frequently purchased by children aged 6 to 12. Their habits are more like teenagers who grew up in decades past than children. As a result, sales of classic products like Barbie dolls have declined. To preserve their market, Mattel has introduced the Barbie Fashion Designer CD-ROM to please the techno-tots.[2] A lifesize Barbie house is located inside select Toys "R" Us stores. It carries not only dolls but Barbie apparel for girls as illustrated in Figure 10.3. Retailers

Figure 10.3 Barbie is an icon for doll-lovers of all ages. Her two-storied house within Toys "R" Us features everything for the consumate collector. Apparel is one of the newer products to bear the Barbie label.

also address the needs of children and their parents by providing child-oriented shopping environments that include play, child care, and rest areas.

The stereotype of Americans as big spenders may be true. A study done on the savings habits of children in 11 countries substantiates this belief. Results showed that children in the United States saved only 20 percent of their allowances as compared to Japanese children who saved 62 percent.[3] These statistics reinforce cultural differences and the important role parents play in encouraging saving habits in their children.

Studying individual and group differences helps retailers understand the diverse needs of their customers. Many other factors influence customer behavior.

Factors Affecting Shopping Behavior

People make purchasing decisions on the basis of who they are, who they want to be, where and how they live, and how much they earn. Age, social class, and family makeup influence shopping behaviors. Special activities in which individuals choose to participate, unique combinations of interests they hold, and opinions they voice on a myriad of topics also affect their behavior. Demographic and psychographic factors often intertwine and present new avenues of customer understanding for retailers. A classification of people on the basis of their lifestyles, activities, interests, and opinions is called **psychographics**.

psychographics Classification of people on the basis of their lifestyles, activities, interests, and opinions.

Demographics

Introduced in Chapter 3, the following demographic trends contribute to the shaping of customer demand: (1) population growth and distribution, (2) family and household composition, (3) labor force participation rates, (4) educational attainment levels, (5) household income distribution, (6) age breakdowns, and (7) ethnic composition. This section presents enhanced coverage of certain demographic factors in relation to shopping behavior.

Age Age is a powerful determinant of customer behavior. It affects individual interests, tastes, purchasing ability, and investment behavior. Population distribution among different age groups is used to indicate where opportunity may exist for new retail institutions. Growing interest in the youth market precipitated research studies that are cited in the following two examples.

Research illuminated brand preferences of the teenage market. When asked to identify the "coolest" brands, Nike scored the highest.[4] It is not surprising that the brands identified in this study are those that appear on the racks and shelves of retailers targeting teens.

In another study, the shopping habits and attitudes of teenage females were compared with young women in their early twenties. The results produced valuable information for retailers. Although both groups like to shop, the younger women tended to spend more time in stores. They also shop for clothing more often, but are not as quality conscious as their older counterparts.[5] Provided with more insight, retailers can adjust their merchandise mixes and price levels to meet the needs of their young customers.

Social Class Based on the assumption that birds-of-a-feather-flock-together, social class theorists segment people into groups based on demographic data including income, occupation, and education. Social class designators like lower-upper, upper-middle, and lower-middle provide a framework, but do not accurately or adequately predict all customer behavior. A contemporary look at social class categories is shown in Table 10.1.

Table 10.1 U.S. Social Class Structure and Expected Retail Purchasing Behavior

Social Class	Approximate Percentage of Population	Membership & Occupation	Purchasing Values	Behavior
Upper Upper	1%	"Old Money"; Socially prominent aristocrats; professionals, and financiers	Live graciously & well; value philanthropy, civic involvement	Services; not Ostentatious
Lower Upper	5% to 10%	"Nouveau rich"; successful business entrepreneurs and professionals	Pursue upper upper; strive for success	Ostentatious; travel, status goods, cars, boats, vacations; second homes
Upper Middle	30% to 35%	College Educated Upwardly mobile, managerial & professional occupations	Child and Home Oriented; living the good life computers	Housing, good clothes, club memberships,
Lower Middle	30% to 35%	Non-managerial; trade & technical workers; supervisory positions; may be high hourly wage workers	Desire respectability, neat homes; want college education for children	Less expensive clothes, may have more $ in savings than upper-middle families; trucks, campers, beer
Upper Lower	9%	Less-skilled workers; live just above poverty level	Try to enjoy life, stay afloat	Big cars; TV for major entertainment including sports; go bowling
Lower Lower	7%	Unemployed & unskilled workers; live below poverty level; on welfare	Fatalistic & apathetic	Necessities only, low disposable income

Source: Adapted from R. P. Coleman, "The Continuing Significance of Social Class to Marketing," *Journal of Consumer Research*, December 1983:267.

Informed retailers study the similarities of each group before designing a retail mix. They also watch opinion leaders for clues to their behavior. **Opinion leaders** are trendsetters whose opinions are respected within a group. By acknowledging similar shopping tastes and habits, retailers have a better chance of attracting more customers and increasing market share.

opinion leaders Trendsetters whose opinions are respected within a group.

For example, members of the lower-middle class tend to be blue-collar workers who live in apartments or small homes in older neighborhoods. Spending money on children's needs, family vacations, movies, and sporting events such as bowling is typical of their social class. In contrast, upper-middle class individuals are more likely to hold middle-management positions and live in larger, suburban houses. Spending money on dining out, attending concerts, and escaping for the weekend describes their probable activities.

Household Composition The trend toward marriage at a later age, increasing numbers of single and divorced people, and multiple sequential marriages in the United States have created changes in household composition and family lifestyles. Working women wield significant economic power. Dual-income households have more discretionary dollars to spend for goods but less time available to shop for them. Firms that can provide quality, time-saving products and services to these customers will meet with success.

By examining the ways families evolve over time, retailers are better attuned to the needs of their customers. The family life cycle theory helps explain changes in the family constellation. Increasing numbers of single adults, single parent families, multiparent families, and nontraditional living arrangements have an impact on buying behavior.

The purchasing behavior of unmarried singles is radically different from single parents although both are technically single. Both may be apartment dwellers, but unmarried singles tend to spend money on car payments, home electronic equipment, clothes, and sporting goods. Singles with children focus on children's clothing, toys, medical and dental expenses. In most cases they spend less on entertainment and social pursuits. Family life cycle, which uses demographic information to help retailers understand more about their customers, is detailed in Table 10.2.

Psychographics

Humans are a complex species displaying many crossover tendencies in their behaviors. The person who skips lunch in order to take part in an aerobics class can be the same person who eats at a gourmet French restaurant that evening. It is impossible to pigeonhole such an individual. Segmentation methods that consider specific activities and interests people are involved in and the opinions they hold bring more understanding to these manifold issues. Two psychographic segmentation methods are VALS™ and clusters developed by Faith Popcorn.

VALS™ Segmentation Lifestyle categories have been developed by research companies like SRI International. Its eight Values and Lifestyles (VALS™) classifications describe how people perceive their lives and use their financial resources:

1. Actualizers—Possess the most resources; are open to new ideas and products, but leery of advertising.
2. Fulfilleds—Not interested in status; purchase goods for their homes; interested in education.

3. Achievers—Drawn to top-quality merchandise; read business and self-improvement publications.

4. Experiencers—Are fashion conscious; tend to be impulse buyers; listen to rock music.

5. Believers—Behave ethnocentrically; are resistant to change; watch TV frequently.

6. Strivers—Concerned with personal image; use credit extensively; watch TV more than they read.

7. Makers—Purchase value-oriented, basic merchandise; not interested in luxury goods; listen to the radio.

8. Strugglers—Use coupons and follow sales; read tabloids and believe advertising.[6]

Looking at smaller segments, rather than at mass markets is one way to avoid overgeneralizing that accompanies most social class and family life cycle theories. Clustering uses psychographics to create contemporary customer behavior identification tools.

Popcorn's Clusters Faith Popcorn, founder of a trend reporting and marketing research firm called The Brain Reserve, uses social and lifestyle tends to predict customer behavior. Highlights from her trend reports include:

1. Cocooning—The tendency for people to stay at home for work and play; focus on home-educating children, gardening; may change shopping habits because of fear of crime in traditional shopping areas.

2. EVEolution—Focuses on the growing power of women in business and as key purchasing agents in the marketplace.

3. Anchoring—Reflects the need to center one's life; seek higher planes of spirituality; prime market for angel paraphernalia, aromatherapy supplies, psychic seminars, and meditation tools.

4. Fantasy Adventure—Members seek new thrills; from intercultural foods to rock climbing as an escape from boredom or stressed lives. Virtual reality games and programs might also suit these customers.

5. EGOnomics—To counter what they perceive as a sterile, high-tech era, some people will seek products that encourage individuality. Tattoo parlors, eclectic apparel and home furnishings illustrate this trend.

6. Small Indulgences—Individuals purchase small things to promote happiness—a raspberry cream Godiva chocolate bar, lingerie, a scented candle, a moment of peace and quiet over a Dunkin' Donuts coffee.

7. 99 Lives—Overstressed individuals who want it all NOW comprise this group. Many people multitask and purchase anything that gives them an

Table 10.2 Family Life Cycle Categories and Retail Implications

Status	Characteristics	Implications for Retailors
Young & Single	Never married, independent, frequently in early stages of career; moderate discretionary income	Never marrieds living alone buy new cars, furniture, and small appliances geared toward a first apartment, career clothing, entertainment and electronic goods figure prominently.
Single, Living at Home	Never married or divorced, living in home of parents; high to low discretionary income, respectively	Never marrieds living with parents may enjoy ample discretionary income; they may purchase better cars, computers, vacations, and clothes than the Young & Single.
Single Heads of Households	Divorced or never married single people, often low discretionary income	Divorced singles may regress financially after the divorce. A Bloomingdale's shopper may turn to Kmart for personal and household needs. Homeowners may become apartment dwellers. The outlook for never married heads of household may be more bleak due to child support or alimony payments, reduced standards of living.
Newly Married	Independent, present and future oriented; good discretionary income; usually dual incomes	Setting up a new household is a priority, new furniture, appliances, and carpeting are important. Many couples save for or purchase starter homes. Many couples postpone or choose not to have children, thus making them prime targets for luxury goods and travel.
Not Married but Cohabitating	May be less future oriented than the newly married; usually dual incomes	Maintaining sense-of-self in the relationship may be more important than making joint purchases for the home. Clothing and entertainment expenditures are significant.
Homosexual partners	May function as traditional married or cohabitating partners, may have children in the household	Homosexual partners tend to behave as other families and are in various social classes; tend to reside in certain U.S. cities more than others.
Full Nest I (one or two incomes)	Present and future oriented, youngest child under 6 years old; moderate discretionary income	Child and family-oriented, these couples spend a good portion of their income for toys, education, family travel, and household necessities.

(Table 10.2 continued on page 291.)

extra moment in the day. Microwaveable foods, cellular phones, and shopping services please them.

8. Cashing Out—People—mostly women—who retreat from corporate lives to open their own businesses, and those that have strong entrepreneurial desires belong in this cluster. This trend may be related to the cocooning.

Table 10.2 Family Life Cycle Categories and Retail Implications *(Table 10.2 continued from page 290.)*

Status	Characteristics	Implications for Retailors
Full Nest II (two incomes usual)	Present and future oriented, youngest child over 6 years old; somewhat more discretionary income than Full Nest I	Needs of growing children still dominate with clothing and electronic goods gradually replacing the emphasis on toys. Saving for college expenses may become paramount at this point.
Full Nest III (two incomes usual)	Future oriented, may have some thoughts of retirement, may have youngest child living at home but most children are independent	New furniture is often purchased and decorating services are utilized, after most children have left the nest. Emphasis on travel as a couple with more dinners out. Couples married for the second or third time may see an increased durable and non-durable goods as well as educational expenditures in all Full Nest categories.
Empty Nest I (two incomes)	No children at home, may have thoughts of retirement; good dual income	Often very affluent, people in this category may tend to travel, join golf clubs, indulge their grandchildren and purchase future retirement homes. Situation may change if parental care becomes part of their responsibility in this and other categories.
Empty Nest II	Likely to be retired, though many may still be in the work force full or part time, present oriented; income fixed to ample	Health care products may become more important. More affluent empty nesters may spend their money on travel, leisure activities, and meals eaten out. Other less affluent retirees may be more restricted to purchases of basic necessities.
Sole Survivor I (spouse deceased)	Actively employed, present oriented, more likely to be female than male; good income	The employed sole survivor may experience a reflowering of ambition and expenditure patterns. Clothing, vacations, and leisure pursuits become joyful priorities.
Sole Survivor II (spouse deceased)	Retired, present oriented, some may experience a sense of futility; others retain vitality; income poor to adequate to ample	Some retired sole survivors tend to rely on long-time shopping habits rather than seek change. Others remain involved in activities for a longer time than past generations. Health care products and medicines may dominate spending. Many reside in nursing homes or with adult children, indicating distinct shifts of consumer behavior patterns.

Source: Cushman & Wakefield and Hanley & Baker.

9. Being Alive—Health and fitness buffs who may be vegetarians, focus on less strenuous forms of exercise such as Tai Chi and Yoga and celebrate longevity. Strong market for tofu, organic foods, herbal remedies, self-help tapes and books.

10. Down-Aging—Interested in anything that will cultivate eternal youthfulness, this group values retro 1950s clothing, furniture, and music.

CYBERSCOOP

Visit www.FAO.com and proceed to the Virtual Playroom. Select a toy and see how it operates. What Popcorn descriptor best fits customers who would particularly enjoy this shopping experience? Does FAO Schwarz target any specific ethnic groups?

Anti-aging cosmetics, hair-replacement products, and dermatological services are popular. Their strong need to play may be met at adult sports camps.[7]

Psychographic clusters such as these are always in a state of flux. Astute observers of customer behavior use their knowledge to identify target markets and tailor merchandise to customers.

Changing Societal Factors

Conflicting ideologies in world cultures gain acceptance, rejection, or adaptation. As examples, several religious movements are growing in popularity, safety is a growing concern, and attitudes toward affluence, or the lack of it, are changing. Customers' unprecedented need for speed of service is accelerating. These shifts presently influence the ways retailers address their customers. Faith Popcorn's descriptors have substance as the following sections illustrate.

Religious Influences Individuals have different perspectives on this sensitive aspect of society and culture. Although personal beliefs vary, evidence indicates that religious movements influence retail sales. For example, as the number of Muslims in the United States grows, so do sales of Islamic halal products. To be considered halal, meat must come from animals that have been blessed before being slaughtered by hand. Non-Muslim customers who develop a taste for halal foods perpetuate the trend in much the same way kosher foods have mainstreamed. New retail markets develop as a result.

Fundamentalist Christian groups brought pressure on retailers in the South and Mid-West to close their stores on Sundays. In the mid-1990s, Wal-Mart came under fire from employees who refused to work on the Christian Sabbath. One employee filed a discrimination suit which was settled out of court. The company now provides religious awareness training for managers in all of its stores, developed a computer-based manual identifying employees rights, and hired several trainers dedicated to the subject of religious harassment.[8]

Safety Concerns Crime has a negative influence on trade. Retailers are devising new ways of bringing products to customers safely. The Mall of America in Bloomington, Minnesota, imposed a weekend curfew on teenagers unaccompanied by parents after a rash of incidents—some involving shootings—precipitated the decision to tighten security. Many people were dismayed that urban crime had infiltrated the largest shopping center in the country. Mall management curtailed the activities of all youth as a way to deter organized teen gangs and other "mall rats" who had become too frisky. Tightening security, setting the curfew, and establishing civilian safety patrols contributed to a safer environment at the mall.

Providing safety and security for customers is reflected in other ways. Until recent years, crimes committed in retail parking lots were considered problems of society, not retailers. Sentiment shifted as several court cases have illustrated. Retailers are liable and have taken measures to ensure the safety of customers inside and outside of their stores. Car, cart, and foot patrols; better lighting, escort services, and camera surveillance all contribute to safer environments.

Other retailers and mall developers look for high-potential store locations that were formerly considered unsafe or otherwise undesirable. Projects in New York's Harlem support this trend. Research determined that a high number of Harlem residents shopped outside of their high-crime neighborhoods. Developers perceived unmet needs and opened Harlem USA and East Side Plaza, malls designed to encourage neighborhood shopping.

Changing attitudes toward safety and security are apparent as retailers seek new locations and customers. Several other growing concerns for safety in the wake of September 11 were addressed in Chapter 3.

Attitudes Toward Affluence The pressure of providing a living for families usually supersedes worry about whether the next pair of jeans purchased will be Tommy Hilfiger or FUBU. Yet much in the lives of customers revolves around the accumulation of wealth and the preoccupation with how to spend it. Families in which saving money, paring down one's existence, and being happy with less are becoming more common, but seem discordant with the media depiction of affluent contemporary life in industrialized societies.

In a want-driven, affluent society, it is important to understand the different lifestyles of people, because mass marketing techniques do not work as they did when most customers shared the same basic needs. Different segments interpret the "good life" in different ways. For example, outdoor enthusiasts on a limited budget who see themselves as weekend adventurers may shop for clothes and equipment at their local Wal-Mart. Those that seek traditional merchandise that is unconditionally guaranteed will turn to L.L.Bean. Technologically comfortable customers concerned with maintaining image will shop the Eddie Bauer Web site, but die-hard outdoor advocates may select their products through an Orvis or Cabella's catalog. Affluence—or the lack of it—affects lifestyle choices and purchasing decisions.

Did You Know?

To draw more children from affluent families to its ranks of loyal shoppers, FAO Schwarz offers "The Ultimate Sleepover Party." For a mere $17,500, fifteen kids can camp out in the store overnight. A portion of the fee is donated to charity.
Source: *Wall Street Journal*. Business Bulletin. November 12, 1998:1.

Table 10.3 Differences in Consumer Buying Habits in the U.S. and Emerging Markets			
Consumer Behavior	U.S.	Asia	Latin America
Consumers Enjoy Shopping Experience	Not as much	Yes	Yes
Shopping is more of a social occurrence	Not as much	Yes	Yes
Family is Involved in the shopping experience	Less	More	More
Mobility Factor	More	Less	Less
Time Constraint Factor	More	Less	Less

Perception of Time Many people in the United States today live life on fast-forward. They want wide choices, easy credit, good value for their money and above all, instant gratification. However perception of time as a life constricting factor varies somewhat in Asia and Latin America. Differences in this and other consumer buying habits are charted in Table 10.3.

Though time-saving services are valued by most customers, importance placed on the passage of time also varies by culture. Customer queues are a well-established aspect of British life. A **queue** is a British term for a line of people. Proper behavior is expected when lining up at bus stops, ticket, service, or check-out counters. Though lines may move slowly, obvious impatience is frowned upon. Customers must stay on queue and never merge or cut into an established line, or they risk the wrath of proper Brits.

The simple activity of getting through checkout lines fast is a priority of most time-starved customers. Toe tapping and finger drumming characterize people in a hurry. According to a U.S. study, 83 percent of women and 91 percent of men surveyed indicated that long lines were one reason they ceased shopping in a store.[9] Retailers respond to the need for speed in various ways. The policy of opening additional registers when more than three people are in line is practiced by some, while others have hastened transaction time by installing customer-controlled automatic checkout lanes. Upgraded product identification tags and handheld computers used to scan items while still in the shopping cart also are expected to speed transactions.

Stereotyping rarely works, which is why customer research is growing in importance. Psychographic profiles may vary by country, but all provide insight on customer behavior. Lifestyle changes provide new opportunities for retailers in areas they may not have considered a decade ago.

queue British term for a line of people.

Understanding Ethnic Markets

The size and composition of ethnic groups are changing as are the needs of customers. Ethnic markets present many opportunities for retailers that understand the importance of celebrating diversity. Those that segment their markets based on the special needs of ethnic groups are better able to serve their customers. In the United States, Hispanic, Asian, and African Americans are members of growing ethnic markets.

Targeting Hispanics Although the term Hispanic is used to describe a variety of Spanish-speaking peoples, care should be taken not to lump customer habits and lifestyles together. Hispanics from Mexico differ from their counterparts from Cuba, for example. Hispanic lifestyles are unique in several ways. As a whole, Hispanic families tend to value family relationships and camaraderie within their extended families more than other ethnic groups in the United States, or the population as a whole. Dressing for church and Sunday dinner is a custom still respected by Hispanic families, whereas it seems to be the exception to the rule in most communities in mainstream America. Spanish is the first language for many Hispanics living in the United States.

The following example illustrates how some Hispanic people have adopted mainstream American values. In the early 1990s, Tianguis was one of nine supermarkets in California developed by the Vons Companies to service the strong Hispanic population in the greater Los Angeles area. As the photos in Figure 10.4 show, Tianguis featured an in-house Tortilleria, bilingual advertising and signage, and enough ethnic delicacies to tempt Hispanic as well as other palates. By 1994, the company recognized that its customers wanted value and cost savings as much as they wanted their ethnic products. Tianguis became Expo supermarkets. The change in customer sentiment was attributed to a mainstreaming of taste. Hispanic customers were becoming more like than unlike other Americans. Concerns about pricing also paralleled those of non-Hispanic customers.

Findings of an ACNielsen study indicated that Hispanic households in the United States spend more on certain products than the market as a whole. They spend 67 percent more on carbonated soft drinks, 39 percent more on cereal, and 41 percent more on toilet paper. One reason for the significant figures is the larger size of Hispanic families. Although Hispanics comprise almost 12 percent of the U.S. population, only 2 percent of advertising dollars in the United States are directed to Hispanics.[10] These statistics indicate great potential for growth in retail markets that serve Hispanic customers.

Figure 10.4B. Tianguis featured an in-store Tortillaria, Taco bar, extensive Hispanic foods—including over 100 varieties of sausages and hot peppers, and Spanish signage.

Figure 10.4A. Tianguis facade and logo attracted the 95 percent Hispanic neighborhood in El Monte, California.

Figure 10.4C. By 1994, the company had refitted and renamed the store, Expo to appeal to growing consumer interest in value pricing. *Courtesy of Marilyn Lavin.*

Figure 10.4D. Expo's focus is on low pricing, English signage, and mainstream American merchandising. *Courtesy of Marilyn Lavin.*

Impact of Asian and African Americans The importance of Asian and African American shoppers in the marketplace cannot be underestimated. Numbers of Asians are growing, their household incomes are higher than other ethnic groups including Caucasians, and their buying power is significant. Gender differences surface when Asian consumers are studied. A survey done by Asia Market Intelligence examined the grocery shopping habits of men in 12 Asian markets. Results showed that 31 percent of the decision makers across all markets were male, compared with 10 percent in the West. The findings were attributed to the role Asian men play in the shopping experience. More men grocery shop with their families and make more spontaneous decisions on what goes into the shopping cart.[11] Cultural values remain strong as families emigrate to other countries. Many maintain their shopping habits long after they assimilate to another culture. Most supermarket advertisements in the United States target female shoppers. Replication of this study in Western markets may show that more promotions should be directed toward men in markets heavily populated by Asians.

Different shopping behaviors are also observed in African American markets. In a research study done by a University of Tennessee scholar, it was found that black female catalog shoppers valued certain service attributes, products, and pricing techniques more than mainstream white Americans. As examples, African Americans spend an average of 5 percent more than Caucasians at shopping malls but express increased dissatisfaction with customer service in stores. As a result many turn to catalog shopping. Certain items—such as hats, dolls, and toys—are purchased more frequently by African American women than mainstream white females. African American women are more price sensitive and spend less per year than mainstream white consumers. This may be due to the fact that fewer catalogs are directed to African Americans, and fewer of them are on company mailing lists. Two catalogs that target black consumers are *Essence By Mail* and *JC Penney Fashion Influences.*[12] Results of this study indicate that the African American market is underserved, and that it has great potential for retailers that make the effort to understand their customers.

Ethnic diversity within neighborhoods provides merchandising opportunities for retailers. For example, supermarkets might customize their broad assortments of food. At one Pathmark supermarket in New York, 18 feet of shelf space is used to display mango chutney and other condiments from Pakistan. Close by are Goya brand products popular with Hispanic shoppers. A large section is also devoted to Chinese, East Indian, and kosher foods.[13] Cultural differences in customer buying habits are apparent in large and small communities around the world. The need to discern differences in attitudes and shopping behaviors is important to retailers.

Customer Behavior Variables

Knowledge of patterns of expenditures, frequency and intensity of shopping expeditions, and different shopping situations add to retailers' knowledge of their clienteles.

Family Expenditures

Engel's Laws of Family Expenditures Theory developed by 19th-century German statistician offering basic view of how people spend their incomes on goods and services.

People shop for certain products and services more intensely at different stages of their lives. They shop differently because of income, regardless of age or circumstance. **Engel's Laws of Family Expenditures** is a theory developed by 19th-century German statistician Ernst Engel offering a basic view of how people spend their incomes on goods and services. He observed that:

1. As a family's income *increases,* the percentage of that income spent on food *decreases.*
2. As a family's income *increases,* the percentage of that income spent on clothing is *roughly constant.*
3. As a family's income *increases,* the percentage of that income spent on housing and household operations remains *roughly constant.* One exception to this is a decrease in the proportion spent on utility payments.
4. As a family's income *increases,* the percentage of that income spent on all other goods increases.

In all scenarios it should be stressed that the percentage of income, not the amount, changes. Generally, as family income increases, the actual money spent for all goods increases.

Classification of Goods and Services

Although Engel's Laws provide an understanding of the ebbs and flows of family finances, they do not indicate where, when, or in what manner they affect specific kinds of purchases. To help answer these questions, all goods and services have been broken down into four categories:

shopping goods High priced merchandise purchased after the buyer compares the offerings of more than one retailer.

big ticket Merchandise that is expensive such as cars or computers.

■ *Shopping goods.* High-priced merchandise usually purchased after the buyer compares the offerings of more than one retailer is called **shopping goods**. Important major personal and household purchases fall into this category. The decision to buy is premeditated, and most items under consideration are big ticket. **Big ticket** refers to merchandise that is expensive such as cars or computers. People usually comparison shop, seek out product information, and consult knowledgeable friends and relatives before making final decisions. Purchasing furniture, insurance, a cruise, or a diamond is a shopping experience. Figure 10.5 illustrates the time-consuming, thoughtful process of purchasing a diamond ring.

■ *Specialty goods.* Buying specialty goods is referred to as destination shopping. Products bearing name brands or with special features for which buyers will go out of their way to purchase are called **specialty goods**. Customers are less likely to settle for substitutes should the specific item they seek be unavailable. Possession of the merchandise desired is often more important than price. Insisting that you absolutely must have a pair of Puff Daddy's *Sean John* shoes or need to drive an hour for a loaf of Swedish rye bread are examples of specialty shopping. Brand and retailer preferences are strong when specialty shopping.

Figure 10.5 Big ticket items like diamonds are usually considered shopping goods. Finding the perfect stone takes time. Bellman Jewelers, a single-unit store in Manchester, New Hampshire, uses high-tech equipment to analyze diamonds, which in turn helps build customer confidence.

■ *Convenience goods.* Low-cost items that are purchased with minimum effort or time are called **convenience goods**. Products are purchased by habit with little preplanning. Picking up bread, soda, and the latest edition of *In Style* at 7-Eleven on the way home from work, or frequenting a dry cleaner because it is the closest one are examples that fit this category.

■ *Impulse goods.* Items that are purchased on the spur of the moment are called **impulse goods**. Picking up a single rose at a supermarket checkout or the sweater that looks appealing on your virtual model on the Lands' End Web site are examples. Virtually no forethought goes into an impulse purchase, but impulse does not necessarily mean low ticket. The availability of easy credit and our psychological needs to feel good about ourselves means expensive goods also fit this category. Whether our budget advises it or not, purchasing clothing or even an automobile on a whim is not unheard of, nor is taking off to a distant city for the weekend. Impulse purchases are a retailer's best friend. In-store visual merchandising encourages this behavioral tendency.

As these examples show, certain retailers regard income and life cycle factors less and base their segmentation strategies on shopping situations and behavioral aspects of customers.

Did You Know?

College professors from two major American universities found that impulse purchases account for 68 percent of goods bought on major shopping expeditions and 54 percent of merchandise bought on less significant shopping trips. Statistics remain the same whether or not a shopping list is used.
Source: *Wall Street Journal.* April 15, 1999:A1.

specialty goods Products bearing name brands or with special features for which buyers will go out of their way to purchase.

convenience goods Low-cost items purchased with a minimum of effort or time.

impulse goods Items that are purchased on the spur of the moment.

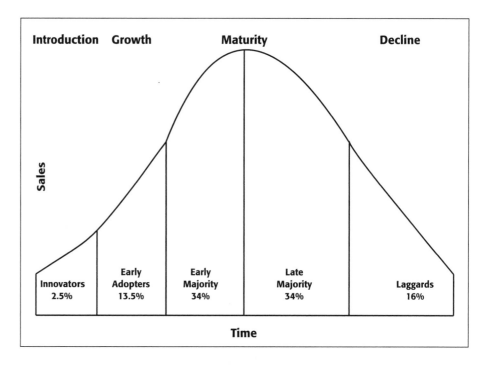

Figure 10.6 Adoption Categories and their Relationship to the Product Life Cycle
Source: Adopter Categories adapted from Diffusion of Innovations, *3rd Ed, by Everett M. Rogers.*
© 1995 by Everett M. Rogers, © 1962, 1971, 1983 by The Free Press, a division of Simon & Schuster.

Rate of Adoption

All customers do not plan to purchase items in the same stage of the product life cycle, introduced in Chapter 1. To be the first in the neighborhood to have a spa bath on their deck was important to some families. Others did not care if the trend ever reached their suburban retreat. They remained impervious to peer pressure and retail sales promotion techniques. Adopter categories break down customers into five major types: innovators, early adopters, early majority, late majority, and laggards. Most people fit into the two majority categories. Figure 10.6 describes when in the product life cycle individuals would be most likely to make a purchase. As examples, shoppers identified as early adopters would be first to adopt new trends such as retro hippie peasant blouses and skirts in the 2002 spring season. Laggards have probably not yet purchased a pair of cargo pants or an Abercrombie & Fitch shirt.

A new look at this model identifies a special group of early adopters, dubbed "technologically advanced families" (TAFs) by Yankee Group, a Boston research firm. TAFs are those families most likely to have purchased items such as computers, peripherals, and cellular phones. These customers recognize that they pay more at retail for cutting-edge products, but high prices do not deter them. They want the fun and time-saving advantages more than they want to practice deferred gratification. When prices go down, later in the product life cycle, the majority of shoppers will make purchases. Their need for up-to-the-moment technology is not as great. According to Yankee Group, TAFs comprise 16.2 percent of U.S. households. They are younger, well-educated, have high household incomes, and more children than average families in the United States.[14]

Shopping Frequency

Customers are shopping more frequently and visiting more retail stores. Results of a study done by Indiana University indicated that 94 percent of customers surveyed had shopped in a discount store at least once in the previous three months. Discount stores were closely followed by grocery stores, and drug stores ranked third in the same time period. Only 70 percent of respondents indicated that they had shopped in a department store in the previous three months.[15] Earlier studies had placed supermarkets first, followed by department stores.

The significance of these findings has far-reaching implications. Customer have changed. They do not want to pay top dollar for household consumable products and basic apparel. Many have turned away from department stores toward discount and drug stores. This tendency has helped fuel the closure of some weaker regional department store chains in the United States, and mergers and acquisitions of others. The increase in the number of stores visited may indicate an increased competitive environment and the tendency of more customers to comparison shop.

A wealth of knowledge regarding customer habits is available to retailers. Most large organizations employ outside market research agencies to feel the pulse of their customers. Smaller stores conduct more informal research, but are no less sensitive to the changing natures of their customers.

The Decision-Making Process

By studying the purchase decision-making process, retailers can develop strategies that lead to sales and diminish buyer's remorse. People go through the process at different speeds and may skip some steps, depending on the price or importance of the product. Different decision-making circumstances also affect the process.

Steps in the Decision-Making Process

Six steps in the decision-making process usually lead customers to purchase goods or services in the absence of any constraints, such as overpricing or poor quality.

1. *Stimulus.* The decision to buy is not unprovoked. A signal can come in a number of different ways, either from the external environment or from within. As examples, a Border's bookstore newspaper advertisement might alert readers to a new paperback. The whiff of coffee emanating from Starbucks could very well trigger the purchase of a pound of Colombian coffee beans. A casual stop at the Target Web site may act as a reminder of the entertainment unit you need for your dorm room. Walking by an oxygen bar in a shopping mall—illustrated in Figure 10.7—may remind you that you did not get enough sleep last night and that you need a jolt of pure O_2.

2. *Problem awareness.* An unfulfilled need or want demands resolution. Your ancient Toyota finally died and you must invest in a new vehicle. This is an example of an obvious crisis requiring action.

3. *Information search.* At this point customers seek facts and figures to expedite the decision making process. Collecting brochures, talking to opinion leaders, seeking out advertising materials, and/or going online to comparison shop is initiated during this stage. If you are looking for a CD burner to create your own music, you might first telephone home electronics stores in your area to compare prices. Then, you will undoubtedly shop the Internet to gather product information. Next, you will probably talk to knowledgeable friends before you move to the next stage of the decision-making process.

4. *Evaluation of alternatives.* Studying the information collected and ranking choices accordingly comprise the next phase of the process. Cost of product, ease of shopping, fast delivery, service policies, and reputation of the company are some of the factors that influence your decision.

5. *Purchase.* The decision is made. The scale has been tipped in favor of one particular good or service and the transaction is completed. Will that be cash, check, credit card, or electronic payment?

6. *Postpurchase behavior.* The shopping experience should be satisfying. Retailers strive to reinforce this in many ways. If the product proved inadequate, the first shopping experience will probably be the last.

More detail and innuendo exist in these steps, depending on the price and complexity of the purchase. Time frames are also important in the decision-making process.

Decision-Making Time Frames

Basically, customers engage in three types of purchase decisions: (1) extended, (2) limited, and (3) routine. All consider the degree of involvement experienced by customers and the time frame in which the steps leading up to the transaction occur.

Extended Decision Making When a customer goes through all six steps in the process, extended decision making occurs. Usually a major purchase is involved, such as a new home, a college education, or an automobile. Because of the expense and risk, much information is needed to properly evaluate the alternatives. Buying a personal computer is a complex decision and involves the extended decision-making process.

Limited Decision Making The main difference between the limited decision-making process and the extended process is the amount of time spent on each of the six steps. For example, if you were satisfied with your last two Chevrolet trucks and the service you received, you likely will go to the same dealer when you are in the market for a new truck. Your previous experience shortens the process of limited decision making.

Figure 10.7 Spotting O₂, an oxygen bar at the Desert Passage Mall in Las Vegas, may precipitate the need to partake in this unusual service.

CYBERSCOOP

Go to www.footlocker.com and click on your favorite sport to view footwear geared to your interests. See whether Footlocker has your size in the style of your choice. What type of decision making timeframe is involved in the purchase of a pair of shoes?

Routine Decision Making When customers buy products or services on a regular basis, routine decision making occurs. Going through the steps requires less conscious effort and customers may not shop extensively to check the available alternatives. Brand recognition and ease in shopping are important when making a routine purchase. Routine decision making is also affected by type of product. People do not put much effort into shopping for low-ticket items such as a loaf of bread. However, if an individual is brand conscious, Pepperidge Farm may be the only package that is seen as the customer races through a convenience store.

Shopping Classification Relationships The shopping category into which the product or service falls influences the decision-making process. Convenience goods are generally purchased routinely, but shopping goods require extended decision making. Specialty goods are often purchased with limited decision making, but the extended process is used when the product or service is expensive or being bought for the first time. Impulse goods are purchased so spontaneously that it appears the decision-making process is almost nonexistent. It does occur, but responses to stimuli may be deep in the subconscious. Color, odors, and textures may conjure up past experiences and urge us to buy. Even hunger may affect shopping habits as any starving college student who has gorged on a huge bag of chips while waiting at a checkout counter can attest.

Decision-making time frames are directly related to personal selling tactics, visual merchandising techniques, branding strategies, and price.

Postpurchase Implications

After parting with significant amounts of cash, many customers experience anxiety and need positive reinforcement from friends, family, and retailers. They want to feel confident that their purchase decision was a sound one.

Anxiety that occurs when people have mixed feelings or beliefs is called **cognitive dissonance.** First postulated by Leon Festinger in the late 1950s, cognitive dissonance comes from the field of psychology and is not from the realm of marketing research. However, the concept has much to do with retailing. Postpurchase dissonance is reduced when retailers support the purchase decision. A follow-up telephone call commenting on the customer's wise decision, a thank-you note, or a small gift strengthens the bond with the customer and encourages repeat business. Liberal return policies and postpurchase service options also strengthen the sale. Customers want to be assured that they have made the right decision and patronized the right retailer.

To paraphrase Shakespeare: a fickle and changeful thing is the customer ever. Customers may be an unpredictable lot, but retailers must accurately interpret customer demand if they are to be profitable.

> **cognitive dissonance** Anxiety that occurs when a person has mixed feelings or beliefs.

Summary

Group and individual influences converge as customers attempt to satisfy their shopping needs and retailers try to serve them. Demographic, psychological, and social influences affect human behavior in the marketplace. Needs and wants change with age, income, education, and membership in ethnic, business, or professional groups.

Because the market changes constantly, retailers must cultivate customer intelligence in other ways. VALS™ segments and Faith Popcorn's descriptive clusters offer a contemporary view of customers. Religious movements, attitudes towards safety and affluence, and membership in ethnic groups also affect customer behavior. As family income increases or decreases, percentages of income spent on most products and services will vary.

Items classified as convenience goods are purchased routinely. Anything classified as a specialty or shopping good requires a more lengthy decision-making process. Impulse purchases are made on the spur of the moment and may involve low- or high-priced items.

Certain types of shoppers tend to purchase goods and services in different stages of the product life cycle. The customer decision-making process traces the six steps by which people become aware of and informed about products and services for which they shop.

The three types of purchasing decisions are extended, limited, and routine. Each considers the degree of involvement and time invested by customers. Retailers use a number of techniques to reduce cognitive dissonance, that is, postpurchase anxiety or buyer's remorse.

Questions for Review and Discussion

1. What are three psychogenic needs? Find several retail advertisements that acknowledge these needs.
2. How is social class theory used to help retailers identify target markets? In what ways does it fail to provide adequate customer information?
3. How is family life cycle information useful to retailers? Where do you presently fit in the cycle? Is your shopping behavior similar to those presented in Table 10.2?
4. What are reference groups? Give an example of how a reference group has influenced a purchase you have made.
5. Choose two demographic trends that affect you. How do retailers use demographic information to reach customers? Name some specific retailers that answer your needs and wants.
6. How has growing popularity of religious movements affected retailers and customers? Is this an important aspect of your culture or lifestyle? If so, how does religion affect your shopping behavior?
7. How are retailers catering to the needs of ethnic markets? What is the degree of ethnic diversity in your city or town?
8. Define and differentiate among the following:
   a. convenience goods
   b. shopping goods
   c. specialty goods
   d. impulse goods

9. What are the six steps in the customer decision-making process?

10. Have you ever experienced cognitive dissonance? How did you feel? What can retailers do to counter the negative effects of cognitive dissonance?

Endnotes

1. Baylor, James. "Motivation, Cognition, Learning: Basic Factors on Consumer Behavior." *Journal of Marketing.* January, 1958.

2. Bannon, Lisa. "As Children Become More Sophisticated, Marketers Think Older." *Wall Street Journal.* October 13, 1998:1.

3. Wysocki Jr., Bernard. "Americans Take on Their Beloved Role as World's Spenders." *Wall Street Journal.* August 11,1998:1.

4. Parr, Karen. "Who, What and 'Y'." *Women's Wear Daily.* February 27, 1997: 9.

5. "Teens vs. Twentysomethings." *Women's Wear Daily.* April 23, 1998: 2.

6. Schiffman, Leon G. and Kanuk, Leslie Lazar. *Consumer Behavior.* 7th Edition, Prentice Hall, 2000:55. Adapted from SRI VALS™ Segments, SRI Consulting.

7. Popcorn, Faith. "Retailing in the 21st Century." Presentation. National Retail Federation Annual Conference. New York City. 1995., and *EVEolution, The Eight Truths of Marketing to Women.* Hyperion. New York. 2000: xix and xx.

8. Jacobs, Margaret A. "Workers' Religious Beliefs May Get New Attention." *Wall Street Journal.* August 22, 1995:B1.

9. Nelson, Emily. "Big Retailers Try to Speed Up Checkout Lines." *Wall Street Journal.* March 13, 2000:B1,6.

10. Wartzman, Rick. "A Push to Probe Buying Habits in Latino Homes." *Wall Street Journal.* August 5, 1999:B1, B4.

11. Lee, Louise. "Men in Asia Grocery Shop, Survey Finds." *Wall Street Journal.* February 19, 1999:B5A.

12. Young, Allison. "Clothing and Catalog Usage Variables and African American Attitudes Towards Afrocentric Apparel Catalogs." Paper presentation. American Collegiate Retailing Association Spring Meeting. Toronto. May, 2000.

13. Nones, Rachelle. "Ethnic Centers." *Supermarket News.* August 3, 1998:32.

14. Lourosa, Cristina. "Understanding the User." *Wall Street Journal.* June 15, 1998:R18.

15. "Consumers' Current Shopping Behavior." *Retail Technology in the Next Century.* Indiana University/KPMG. 1999:5.

Global Retail Profile

Kriss Cosmetics in Malaysia

In addition to learning about large global companies, it is important to understand what small entrepreneurs are doing. Sylyn Enterprise, Sdn. Bhd. of Malaysia and Silk Accent, Inc. of the United States joined forces in 1993, to determine the sales potential of a line of private label cosmetics. Both companies were formed to support the manufacturing and distribution of hand painted silk batik scarves in the U.S. fashion market. The companies intended to diversify their offerings to maximize opportunities in Malaysia and the United States. The companies set up a temporary site in a high traffic ground floor location at the City Point Shopping Center. It was the only large shopping mall in Alor Setar, a city in the northern state of Kedah. The cosmetic test market was scheduled for a one week period.

Kriss Cosmetics is a cosmetic marketing firm that was founded by Kriss Soterion in 1990. The company sells private label skin care and makeup products through a retail studio and an extensive direct marketing and personal contact network. The owner is a former Miss America contestant who used favorable publicity gained from that experience along with a degree in business to start her own company. She added a diploma from an esthetician school and a license to practice the trade to her credentials. Kriss is a commercial makeup artist who has a clientele ranging from major television networks to retail catalog companies. She has even applied makeup to the President of the United States to prepare him for television broadcasts.

Status of the Malaysian Market

Until the currency crisis in 1997–1998, and subsequent economic unrest, Malaysia was a growing economy with a burgeoning middle class. Young people in particular worked in jobs with upward mobility, earning more income than ever before. Mass communications brought advertising and product knowledge to Malaysians. Many young people study outside the country and return home with favorite products and fresh ideas for new businesses. The supply of goods has not kept up with the demand, and opportunities abound in most all merchandise categories.

On the other hand, Malaysia is a Muslim country and religious laws can diminish the need for certain items. As in all potential markets, some knowledge of the culture was needed before a new product or retail store could be launched. Several cultural and demographic factors were studied before the test market was held. Preliminary research indicated that the population is comprised of three distinct racial groups: the Malays who make up about 55 percent of the population; the Chinese who comprise about 35 percent; and the Indians who make up the remainder. This factor is of significance regarding responsiveness to cosmetics in general, the degree of fashion consciousness displayed by women, makeup color preferences, and amounts of money spent on personal care.

Traditional Malay women dress colorfully, yet very conservatively. Women wear the *baju kurung*, a two-piece dress that covers a woman's body from neck to ankle. This is topped by a head scarf that covers all hair when worn properly. Malaysian women often wear makeup, but less than women from non-Islamic countries. The skin tones of Malaysian women run the gamut from very fair to quite dark. Fairer skinned women are perceived as more beautiful than darker skinned women, particularly by younger generations.

Chinese women tend to be more fashion conscious in a western sense, dress less conservatively, tend to wear more makeup, and usually have very fair skin tones. Indian women tend to be darker skinned than the other two groups and need more specialized products.

These facts posed several questions to Kriss Cosmetics. First, based on the predominant religious beliefs, would the market be large enough to warrant investment? Second, would the products offend those of more devout religious persuasions? Third, would makeup colors be appropriate for women of all races? Finally, would the formulations be appropriate for women's particular skin care needs? The partners expected that test market results would answer these questions.

At lower to mid-range price points, Malaysian women do not have as much brand choice as women in the United States and other developed countries. Avon, sold through direct selling methods and retail stores, is the most widely sold skin care line in the country. Mary Kay products are also popular in the direct selling market. Global brands such as Revlon, Clinique, and Shiseido are available in department stores, but at much higher prices than Avon and Mary Kay. Competition at lower prices was limited. For these reasons the partnership chose to assess the responsiveness of Malaysian women to Kriss Cosmetics.

Test Market Overview

At the test market site, products were simply but attractively and hygienically displayed. Signage was in Malay and English and counter cards featured photographs of Kriss and information about the products and price lists in both languages. An area was set up to perform counter demonstrations for customers who wanted to either try out a new shade of lipstick or have a full makeover.

Some interesting differences in customer reactions to U.S. sales promotion techniques were noticed. At first Malay women tended to be a bit shy about approaching the counter and usually preferred the moral support of friends. Participants were usually young women between the ages of 16 and 22; many were college students. Once a customer consented to a full makeover, frequently a large, mixed-gender crowd gathered. Demonstrations of this type attracted people, whether or not attendees showed specific interest in purchasing the products.

Malaysian malls have their share of teenagers who pass the time socially in much the same way as they do in shopping centers around the world. This usually served as a means to get others involved in the demonstrations, as shyness diminished. The demonstrator was one of the few Caucasian women in Alor Setar, which may have added to the novelty of the promotion.

Extensive feedback on all aspects of the products was sought. Kriss Cosmetic packaging is simple. It features clean lines, light colors, and informative labeling. It looks therapeutic, like many of the back-to-basic lines in the United States. Results of the test market showed that Malay women perceived products as more upscale or desirable if the packaging was more ornate or flashy.

Attitudes towards the skin care preparations in the line also varied. Many of the younger customers preferred to delve right into the makeup products with little desire to prepare their faces properly before applying foundation, eye and lip color products. This illustrated the need to provide skin care information and training sessions for customers.

Color preferences were different than in the United States. Although a wide range of foundation colors was offered, it often was difficult to get a good match with women's skin tones. It was not a simple case of a foundation being too dark or too light. Proper match was often a function of the amount of yellow in the formulas. The demonstrator found that only black eyeliner sold well and that dark browns, blues, or greens were not valued—even for occasional dramatic looks. At the time of the study, neutral colors in eye makeup were favored by U.S. consumers, but many Malay women preferred blue tones on their eyelids. An obviously made-up look rather than a minimalist one enhanced their self image and made them feel that they were getting their money's worth. Lipsticks sold better than any other product, and the leading color was a rich, vibrant red. The partnership learned that market testing helps identify important product development directions.

Marketing Opportunities

As a result of the test market, several marketing opportunities were identified, including pricing, product, and promotional direction. Once a customer decided to make a purchase, price resistance to individual products did not seem to be a major factor. Younger women typically purchased a lipstick and perhaps an eye color. Older women usually invested in three basic skin care preparations, a foundation, and a color makeup item or two. A lipstick cost $5.00 and the three skin care items retailed for $25.00 in U.S. dollars. These prices reflected an average markup of 40 percent.

Shortly after the demonstration, the partnership was asked to conduct a makeup workshop for new female employees at a local bank. The invitation by the training director acknowledged the bank's awareness of the ways good grooming affects perceptions of customer service. From a marketing perspective it also presented a valuable opportunity to build favorable public relations in the community.

Based upon the encouraging response and product development knowledge gained, the partners explored developing a direct selling network as well as selling the products through company-owned retail shops. Although those plans did not reach fruition, the test market was a fascinating experiment in getting to know the Malaysian customer, ascertaining the market potential of the line, and determining the feasibility of retail distribution.

Profile Discussion Questions

1. Why did the Silk Accent/Sylyn partnership see potential in the skin care market in Malaysia?

2. What did preliminary research indicate about the ethnic mix in Malaysia that was of significance to the use of skin care and makeup products?

3. What product development and packaging issues surfaced as a result of the test market? How could the products be adapted to better meet the needs of the Malaysian customers?

4. How did Malaysian makeup color preferences differ from those in your home country?

5. Is there a place in the Malaysian skin care and makeup market for Kriss cosmetics? What could the company do next?

Global Retail Profile

IKEA, Sweden

With 143 company stores in 22 countries and 20 franchised stores in 13 countries, IKEA is the premier global retailer of Scandinavian designed furniture and home furnishings.[1] Annual sales for 2001 reached $9.6 billion.[2]

The IKEA name was registered in Sweden in 1943. The anagram stands for the initials of founder, Ingvar Kamprad, and the first letters of the farm, Elmtaryd, and the village, Agunnaryd, where he was born. As a child, Kamprad sold matches door-to-door in his hometown. It was not until 1951, that the company's first catalog was published. Modest by today's standards, it featured writing pens and home furnishings. In the mid-1950s, IKEA began designing and producing its own furniture, and introduced its self-assembly concept. Both aspects are still important parts of the company's brand equity.[3]

Mass appeal and popular pricing of IKEA products are captured in the company's mission statement, which it calls its *vision*. A portion of it states: "For IKEA, helping create a better everyday life means offering a wide range of home furnishings in IKEA stores. Home furnishings that combine good design, good function, and good quality with prices so low that as many people as possible can afford them." This statement also serves as the basis for IKEA's marketing strategy.[4]

Although founded in Sweden, the company's corporate headquarters, Inter IKEA Systems, is now located in The Netherlands. Overseeing product development, trading, and wholesale distribution, The IKEA Group division is located in Denmark. Individual retail stores are operated as franchises.

Global Multichannel Expansion

Thoughtful progression describes the pace and timing of IKEA's global expansion. After the debut of its first store in Almhult, Sweden, in 1958, IKEA's second store opened in Oslo, Norway, in 1963. The company opened a landmark store in Stockholm in 1965, which is inspired by the circular architecture of New York's Guggenheim Museum.

The first unit outside Scandinavia opened in Switzerland in 1973. IKEA has opened one or more stores every year since in Europe, the Middle East, Asia, and North America. IKEA has had stores in China(PRC) since 1998, and in 2001, opened its first store in Moscow. The company entered the U.S. market in 1985.[5] By 2002, the company operated 16 stores in the United States and 9 in Canada, with 9 more stores planned for North America by 2004.[6] It plans to open a store in Japan in 2005.

Europe is the stronghold of IKEA's revenue, with 80 percent of sales coming from this area in 2001. North America accounted for 17 percent and Asia 3 percent of sales. IKEA works with a network of 2,000 suppliers and maintains 14 distribution centers. About two-thirds of the merchandise purchased by IKEA comes from Europe, 29 percent in Asia, and only 4 percent from North America.[7]

A multichannel retailer, IKEA sends 110 million catalogs in 34 language versions annually. Comprehensive product coverage, and light, airy graphics exemplify IKEA catalogs. IKEA increased its exposure to world-wide customers when its Web site went online in 1997. Although direct e-commerce is not available on the Web site, customers can use an Internet order form that can be mailed or telephoned to the company. Online ordering is available in Sweden and Denmark. IKEA offers many customer services such as information on shipping, out-of-stock merchandise options, and return policies online. Complaints can be logged and assembly assistance can be arranged for customers who are not do-it-yourself oriented. Shoppers can apply for an IKEA credit card online and use the services of a design consultant. Store opening information and local store phone numbers are available.

Environmental impact is important to IKEA. The company practices energy and natural resource conservation in many ways. It prides itself on never using any more resources—such as wood—than is necessary to create its products. IKEA believes that by using minimal packaging materials, encouraging self-assembly of furniture, and using environmentally sound materials it is contributing to the well-being of the planet. It selects environmentally responsible suppliers and also prints its catalogs on recycled papers.

Human Resources

IKEA employs approximately 65,000 full and part-time people world-wide.[8] Maintaining a large staff requires careful human resource planning. The IKEA philosophy embraces clear objectives for the company and employees at recruitment, selection, and training levels.

Foremost in the company's recruitment goals is to find people who understand and exemplify the values of IKEA and its customers. IKEA expects its employees to treat one another and customers equally and with sensitivity. To show enthusiasm and take initiative on the job is also important, being cost-conscious is encouraged.

In exchange IKEA vows to be respectful of its employees, reward their efforts. and provide an environment where employees can learn new skills and choose from many career paths. The company promotes from within whenever possible.

Continuous professional development is provided to employees, primarily through on-the-job training and problem solving opportunities. Employees are expected to assume responsibility for their own progress and to share their knowledge and experience with fellow workers. IKEA emphasizes its intentions to provide a proper learning environment for its people. They are granted the freedom to make mistakes. Responsibility is given freely, as is the incentive to train others. Opportunity to review performance with immediate supervisors and other mentors is provided.

Managers are considered leaders at IKEA. They are expected to achieve department and company goals and serve as human resource managers in their stores. They are responsibile for recruiting, hiring and developing personnel.

Job opportunities at IKEA cover all functional areas of retailing and include some of the following:

- sales support/marketing
- stores/call center
- human resources
- information technology
- finance/operations
- distribution/supply chain

Prospective IKEA employees in the United States are encouraged to apply online at www.ikea-usa.com, or mail a resume to

IKEA North America

Att: Human Resources

496 W. Germantown Pike

Plymouth Meeting, Pennsylvania 19462

Well-designed products, good quality at low prices, and slow and steady international expansion summarize IKEA. For those who can easily access one, visiting the huge expanse of an IKEA store is an adventure. For those who cannot, a visit to the Web site will convey the Scandinavian flavor of the company and its products. IKEA's sensitivity to customers and its employees may prove to be one of its greatest strengths.

Profile Discussion Questions

1. What are the most important components of IKEA's brand equity? How do these qualities help the company achieve a competitive advantage?

2. Comment on the company's vision. How does it compare with the mission statements of other retailers you have studied? What makes IKEA's vision unique?

3. What kind of growth pattern does IKEA prefer as it expands globally? Compare its strategy to Wal-Mart's.

4. What does IKEA expect from its employees? What does the company offer in return? Do you believe these are realistic expectations?

5. What type of training does IKEA offer its managers? Contrast the company's approach to those of other management training programs with which you are familiar.

6. Review the range of job opportunities at IKEA by visiting its Web site at www.ikea-usa.com. What is available this week? How would you apply for a position?

Profile Endnotes

1. http://www.ikea-usa.com/about_ikea/facts&figuresfacts_all-world.asp Available: June 12,2002.

2. Ibid.

3. http://www.ikea-usa.com/about_ikea/timeline/years_1950.asp Available: June 12, 2002.

4. http://www.ikea-usa.com/about_ikea/our_vision/better.asp Available: June 12, 2002.

5. http://www.ikea-usa.com/about_ikea/timeline/fullstory.asp Available: June 12, 2002.

6. http://www.ikea.usa/ikea_near_you/near.asp Available: June 12, 2002.

7. http://www.ikea-usa.com/about_ikea/facts&figures/facts_figures.asp Available: June 12, 2002.

8. Ibid.

Store Location

and Planning

Chapter 11

Site Selection

Learning Objectives

After completing this chapter you should be able to:

- List the key factors involved in choosing a specific retail site.

- Explain what a trading area is and how it is determined.

- Discuss how optimum locations are selected using research and analytical techniques.

- Identify the principal types of traditional commercial locations that are significant to retailers

- Classify the various kinds of contemporary locations that are becoming more important to retailers.

- Compare the advantages and disadvantages of owning retail property as opposed to leasing it.

- Discuss how retail leasing costs are derived and what affects different rates.

Figure 11.1 Melrose Avenue in Hollywood hosts funky retailers that target hip customers. Residential areas border the string street and act as informal parking lots for the hordes of customers that frequent the area (See p. 330).

Retail expansion was rampant during the last half of the 20th century. In the early years of the 21st century, it has become more difficult to find new business sites that will provide a profitable return on investment. Oversaturation is the nemesis of most large retail organizations and one reason some retailers select other countries for new locations. Others develop new stores in sites previously considered unprofitable, unimportant, or undesirable.

As customers, we probably give little thought to how and why shopping centers and individual stores appear almost everywhere. Retailers that intend to grow domestically or globally evaluate potential business locations scientifically, using technology-driven tools and lifestyle, demographic, and geographic analysis.

Site selection criteria, common research practices, a survey of principal types of retail locations, and ownership/leasing information are presented in this chapter.

Criteria for Site Selection

Choice of location is perhaps the most important decision that retailers make. A good location allows easy access and attracts large numbers of customers. Even slight differences in location can have an impact on market share and profitability. Since many retail outlets have nearly identical product offerings, this point becomes more significant. Location represents a long-term investment; a poor location decision is extremely difficult to overcome. Matching retail offerings with potential customers in the right location is both an art and a science.

The specifics of the trading area are gathered in order to determine a customer profile. Many examples of demographic information, given in Chapters 3 and 10, are useful to consider in this context. Details such as whether residents are homeowners or renters, the market value of homes in the area, and levels of fashion consciousness provide a deeper look at customers.

In order to determine an appropriate site, retailers need information on city population dynamics, economic trends nationally and locally, the competition, and local media. Some knowledge of the history of the city or town, including its reason for existence, is also important. Criteria used when selecting a specific site include:

- *Pedestrian traffic.* The number of people who pass by a location is important to chart, but must be qualified as to shoppers and nonshoppers. Pedestrian traffic is monitored by time of day and the age and sex of people in transit. Checklists stating minimum requirements are often used in this context. For example, a video rental store in a small shopping center might determine that it needs 200 people entering the area hourly before considering opening a store. More on checklists is included in the section on research techniques. If a more qualitative study is sought, individuals could be questioned as to destination, shopping habits, and retail preferences.

- *Vehicular traffic.* An analysis of traffic patterns, congestion times, and road conditions is needed. This information is particularly important for retailers such as convenience stores, fast food restaurants, gasoline stations, video stores, and shopping centers.

- *Parking.* The number and quality of parking spots, their distance from the store or mall site, and the availability of employee parking should be evaluated. Size of parking lots should be judged not only on their ability to service customers on average shopping days, but also during peak traffic periods such as holidays. Convenient, inexpensive, and safe parking should be easily accessible for customers who will be driving to urban sites. Extremely large facilities plan for shuttle services to convey customers from their cars to the door. Some upscale stores and malls offer complimentary valet parking.

- *Infrastructure.* Both customer vehicles and delivery trucks require access from major highway networks to retail stores and malls. Many public highways are open to passenger car traffic but not to large commercial vehicles. Infrastructure analysis allows retailers to evaluate how public and private conveyances may affect their location. Physical facilities that support the economy in a specific area including highway systems, transportation, communication, public utilities, and other services, are part of the **infrastructure.** Stores in central business districts need proximity to mass transportation. Customers are occasionally perplexed when they see two identical fast food restaurants across the highway from one another. Most likely, traffic pattern studies have indicated commuting patterns that justify two units. When the highway is physically divided, the reasoning is more apparent. At that point infrastructure criteria are as important as vehicular traffic issues. Infrastructure decisions impact safety, customer convenience, and business efficiency. A few yards or meters can make all the difference in retail.

infrastructure Physical facilities that support the economy in a specific area including highway systems, transportation, communication, and other public services.

Figure 11.2 Even a small grocery store benefits from increased visibility provided by a corner location in a central business district.

Did You Know?

What business is located between a Dunkin' Donuts and a Carvel ice cream store in Williston Park, New York? You guessed it, the Inches-A-Weigh weight loss center.
Source: *Wall Street Journal.* January 7, 1999:A1.

■ *Placement and visibility.* The actual location on a street or in a shopping center needs to be carefully studied. Corner locations are important to high volume retailers. Although rent is higher for street corner sites, larger sales volumes justify the choice. Companies like Starbucks and Rite Aid seek corner spots as part of their location strategies. As illustrated in Figure 11.2, small retailers also benefit from corner locations. Some retail companies look for spots that are near compatible retailers. Their premise is that a grouping of strong retailers increases the draw of an area. For example, Bob's Stores, a retailer of casual men's and women's apparel, seeks sites near Marshall's, the off-price retailer. It is the cumulative attraction that benefits both retailers.

Macroenvironmental factors surrounding the selection of a mall are complex, but so are the microenvironmental decisions on specific store placement within the mall. For example, some chain stores seek spots directly adjacent to anchor stores. Others look to be near food courts in order to benefit from the increased traffic in those areas. Apparel stores prefer not to be next to food operations, and many retailers do not like corner locations in the "L" of a community shopping center. More on this topic is covered in the next chapter.

Research Methodology

Sophisticated marketing research methods have supplanted traditional head count methods, but the goal remains the same: retailers must determine who is presently shopping in their stores or who will be in the future. The immediate area surrounding the store or site is the first place to start gathering this information.

Trading Area Analysis

Usually mapping strategy starts with an analysis of the larger geographic area in contention for a new retail store or mall. Called **metropolitan statis-**

tical areas (MSA), these geographical areas have large, concentrated population centers that may cross county or state lines. Mass merchandisers often select MSAs based on population density. Specialty stores seek out smaller trading areas within the MSA as potential sites. A **trading area** is the geographic area from which a retailer draws its customers.

Types of Trading Areas The **primary trading area** is a geographic area that encompasses 50 to 80 percent of a store's potential customers. It also is referred to as the primary service area (PSA). It is the area closest to the store and possesses the highest density of customers in terms of population and per capita sales. Convenience stores draw well from this area, but poorly from the secondary trading area. The **secondary trading area** is a geographic area located just outside the primary trading area that contains an additional 20 to 25 percent of a store's potential customers. The **tertiary trading area** is a wide area located outside the primary and secondary trading areas, containing 5 to 25 percent of the store's potential customers. It is sometimes referred to as the *fringe* area. As examples, a discount store might have a primary trading area of two miles, a secondary trading area of four miles, and a tertiary trading area of eight miles. Potential customers are more dispersed in the secondary and tertiary areas. Different store types also impact the size of their trading areas. Furniture retailer IKEA may pull customers from a total 250 mile radius and a Starbucks from less than a mile in many of its locations.

Determining a Trading Radius When a trading radius is determined by using an existing or potential retail site as the locus, this is called **ring analysis**. Also known as the concentric circles method, this helps a retailer determine customer potential. Analysts study the area using one-, three-, and five-mile radius rings.[1] Ring analysis is commonly used but does not fully describe an area. Studying consumer drive-times in tandem with ring analysis is as important a measure.

More often a polygon method is used rather than the ring method. The **polygon method** is used when determining a trading area by considering natural and man-made phenomena that apportion the space into straight-sided geometric shapes. Polygon analysis, developed by Thiessen, departs from the contention that all customers are interspersed equally in the trading area. This method is useful when conservation land or a body of water exists within the site being studied. For example, a swamp consisting of several acres is not habitable. Therefore, equal dispersion population estimates using a purely concentric model would not be valid. The polygon method allows the swamp to be considered when analyzing the area. Information on competition, supply and demand, and other pertinent

metropolitan statistical area (MSA) Geographic areas with large, concentrated population centers that may cross county or state lines.

trading area Geographic area from which a retailer draws its customers.

primary trading area Geographic area that encompasses 50 to 80 percent of a store's potential customers; also referred to as the primary service area.

secondary trading area Geographic area located just outside the primary trading area, containing 20 to 25 percent of a store's potential customers.

tertiary trading area Wide area located outside the primary and secondary trading areas, containing 5 to 25 percent of the store's potential customers.

ring analysis Determining a trading radius by using an existing or potential retail site as the locus.

polygon method Determining a trading area by considering natural and man-made phenomena that apportion the space into straight-sided geometric shapes.

data regarding the trading area can be included when using either method. The importance of clèarly defining a trading area cannot be understated.

Retail Saturation

There are several methods used to determine the economic feasibility of new locations. Some consider the sales volume that could be expected from customers in a geographic area. More advanced measures consider the level of retail saturation in a market. The degree to which a trading area is overstored or understored indicates its level of **retail saturation**. Saturation reflects the amount of competition in the trading area.

The total amount of possible sales that can be realized in a trading area is called **sales potential**. The sales potential of a trading area is determined by studying the number of households and the average household income in a trading area. It is calculated by multiplying the number of households in an area by the average household income in the area.

To estimate a store's share of sales potential, the amount spent for different types of products is multiplied by total household income. Percentages derived from government or industry sources can be used for this purpose. Retailers also need to calculate the portion of the market that is not presently being served. Subtracting the actual sales from the potential sales of an area derives this figure.

An expansion of this method is called the Index of Retail Saturation (IRS). The **index of retail saturation (IRS)** is a measurement instrument that allows retailers to determine the degree of competition in a trading area. This quantitative measure uses refined sales potential figures along with retail square footage numbers to create a ratio that helps site selection specialists compare potential sites. The sales per square foot number can be applied to specific retail product lines such as shoe stores, drug stores, or home improvement centers. Sales potential figures are also tailored to the selected product line. The formula used to calculate IRS is shown conceptually in Table 11.1. Information of this kind can be used to help determine shopping center size and tenant mix.

Market Share Weighted Trade Areas One of the most sophisticated and most accurate measures employed by site selectors involves creating market share weighted trade areas. The technique involves taking the basic polygon approach two steps further. By adding components of market share and household income in a carefully constructed formula, much more detailed and accurate information on the trade area can be compiled.

---

retail saturation The degree to which a trading area is overstored or understored.

sales potential Total amount of possible sales that can be realized in a trading area.

index of retail saturation (IRS) Measurement instrument that allows retailers to determine the degree of competition in a trading area.

Table 11.1 Index of Retail Saturation

IRS = **Households in a trading area X Retail expenditures per household for product line**

Total square feet of selling space devoted to product line

Sources of Information

A number of secondary and primary sources of information are used to evaluate a potential retail site. Information that comes from previously published sources is considered **secondary data**. To answer specific questions pertinent to a site, primary data is used. Information compiled to address specific research issues is called **primary data**. Research techniques vary depending on whether an area is already developed or new. Most research begins with a survey of secondary data.

Using Secondary Data Retailers can obtain much existing data from the U.S. Census Bureau and other governmental agencies. Included in population data is information on age, gender, marital status, race, occupation, and educational backgrounds. Chambers of commerce, local municipalities, and trade associations are also respected sources of information. The International Council of Shopping Centers and the National Retail Federation, referenced frequently in this text, update a wealth of statistics annually. The *Survey of Buying Power* is published annually by *Sales & Marketing Management* magazine. Much of the data in this publication extends to the city level, making it particularly useful for specific site selection research. Retail sales trends by product lines, an effective buying income figure, and a useful buying power index are included in the publication. **Effective buying income (EBI)** is a statistic that measures the availability of personal disposable income in an area. The **buying power index (BPI)** is a weighted value that measures the purchasing ability of the households in a trading area. The higher the index, the more likely the area will be able to sustain retail sales. The formula used for calculating BPI is shown conceptually in Table 11.2.

Retailers also determine whether a population is expected to grow, decline, or remain constant. This information is directly correlated with sales.

Information on occupations and income levels of potential customers within the trading area assists retailers in placing the right kind of store in a particular locale. Tiffany would probably not find success locating on a college campus, but the Gap and Pizza Hut would.

Dwelling types are analyzed, as is the composition of homeowners versus apartment dwellers. Residential analysis will illuminate customer groups

secondary data Information that comes from previously published sources.

primary data Information compiled to address specific research issues.

effective buying income (EBI) Statistic that measures the availability of personal disposable income in a trading area.

buying power index (BPI) Weighted value that measures the purchasing ability of households in a trading area.

Table 11.2 Buying Power Index

BPI   =   Effective Buying Income of an area x .5, plus Retail Sales

of an area x .3, plus population of an area x .2

Weighted components are used to calculate the percentage of BPI,
retail sales, and population in a specific area of the United States.
The weights reflect the importance of each of the three components.

---

such as ethnic, religious, disabled, or aged that need specific kinds of merchandise.

Collecting Primary Data When fresh input is needed, primary data is sought. Administering exit interviews with a random group of customers at a mall is an example of primary research because it generates new information. Timely, detailed demographic data including family income, family size, age of respondent, number of children, educational background, occupation, and type of housing can be compared to secondary data published on the area. Interviewers might also record the amount spent during that particular visit to the mall. Finally, interviewers gather information regarding customers' attitudes toward the store and its competition.

All customers do not come directly from their homes to shopping areas; in fact, many shop near their place of work. Commuting patterns are determined by capturing zip code information at the point of sale, in-store surveys, or by using vehicle spotting techniques. Monitoring the license plates of automobiles in shopping center parking lots is a popular way to further define commuting habits, trading areas, and target markets.

Geographical Information Systems

geographical information systems (GIS) Technology that allows retailers to analyze potential sites on the basis of interrelated demographic, psychographic, and geographic data.

A look at other tools and site selection models illustrates the level of sophistication that technology brings to research. Technologies that allow retailers to analyze and map potential sites on the basis of interrelated demographic, psychographic, and geographic data are called **geographical information systems (GIS)**. Software programs, which enable retailers to learn more about customers than simply where they live, are readily available. Database development, discussed in Chapter 6, figures prominently in GIS. Approximately 50 percent of retailers use GIS, although growth is accelerating.[2] GIS makes many mapping applications possible. Users access information from a variety of databases and business documents, then superimpose it on a map. For example, a fast food chain with several locations in the same city could use GIS to determine the degree to which trading areas of each unit overlap. When two or more types of data are overlaid to more accurately define the drawing power of a specific site this is one form of **spatial analysis**. Spatial analysis also involves finding new information from old or incomplete data. The same fast food chain might want to determine potentially strong new sites. GIS can be used to point out cities that have high population density, types of housing in that city, and local transportation routes. By using spatial interaction models, retailers can learn more about how customers find their ways to their stores.

There are several methods used to determine the optimum site, ranging from the simple and inexpensive to the more complex and costly. Checklist and analog methods are considered fundamental, while regression analysis and use of gravity models are more substantive. Combining geographic information with descriptive consumer demographics can be very costly, but productive for site selectors. These methods and others are described in the following sections.

Checklists When using checklists, retailers establish a list of criteria that is measured against specific attributes of potential sites. Criteria are chosen arbitrarily based on the needs of the retailer and might include traffic counts and proximity to highways. Income levels, housing types, and age of residents in the trading area are other types of data that could be important to site selectors. This method is inexpensive to implement, but is somewhat subjective and lacks the rigor of more quantitative measures.[3]

Analog Method A method used for obtaining a sales forecast by comparing potential new sites with existing sites is called the **analog method**. By plotting customers' home addresses on a map, marketing analysts can determine how many sales dollars the store draws from each point. Taken in aggregate, this gives a picture of where the store's total sales volume comes from. By indicating a percentage of those sales dollars—typically 70 percent—the analyst establishes the store's trading area. Several software packages enable this relatively simple form of analysis to be done. This method also helps the retailer create a model to which new sites can be compared. The retailer cannot determine whether a new site will work without a good idea of what has worked in existing units and what can be expected in terms of sales.

Regression Analysis Multiple regression is a dominant method used to produce sales forecasts for new and existing stores. The statistical modeling method allows a retailer to include several variables in its analysis of a specific site. For example, square footage of the store, inventory turnover,

spatial analysis Overlaying two or more types of data to define the drawing power of a specific site more accurately.

analog method Method for obtaining a sales forecast by comparing potential new sites with existing sites.

and other characteristics of the trading area can be used in the calculations. This method provides a high degree of objectivity, although considerable expertise is needed to construct the model.[4]

Gravity Models Some retailers may ask the question, "What if we located a store here?" Others may want to determine the impact if a competitor opened a store nearby. Both scenarios suggest the need for **gravity models**, which are calculations used to identify customer drawing power of geographic areas. Supply and demand forms the basis for analysis using this method. Several types of pertinent data can be combined in order to measure customer tendencies more accurately. Gravity models are based on the assumption that two cities draw customers from the surrounding towns in direct proportion to the square footage, attraction, and number of retailers in those cities. Another element involved is the distance between the cities and the outlying population: the larger the city, the greater the draw; the farther the distance, the less intense the pull. The point at which influence of one city or the other shifts can be calculated, and this information can be used by researchers to predict customer patronage.

One classic method is Reilly's law of retail gravitation. A formula developed by William J. Reilly many decades ago remains the basis for contemporary site selection research.[5] One version uses the formula shown in Table 11.3 to determine the point at which two trading areas meet.

Models like these go beyond traditional trade area analysis because they acknowledge that customers cannot be defined only in terms of geographic boundaries. An example of a gravity model and other mapping techniques are included in the color insert. Newer versions utilize location and characteristics of customers and sites as well as competition in the area. For example, a site with excellent visibility, located on an interstate highway directly off the exit ramp may be the perfect spot for a home improvement store. Learning that the city has an above-average number of homeowners with moderate household incomes adds to the knowledge base. If customers in the area have a strong desire to purchase do-it-yourself supplies and there is no competition for their dollars in the area, this site would rank high.

Geodemographic Marketing Tools Retailers are recognizing opportunities in geographic regions they previously bypassed. **Geodemographics** uses computer-based methods to identify consumers in specific geographic locations. The neighborhoods classification technique blends demographics, psychographics, and geography, allowing marketers to identify specific customer groups. Next groups are pinpointed by region, state, city, zip code area, neighborhood, city block, and ultimately, specific address. The premise of geodemographics is based on the old adage, *birds of a feather flock to-*

gravity models Calculations used to identify customer drawing power of geographic areas.

geodemographics Computer-based method of identifying consumers in specific geographic locations.

Table 11.3 Retail Gravitation Formula

Trading area limit of City A in relation to City B	=	Miles between Cities A and B
		1 plus the square root
		of population of City A
		divided by population of City B

Source: Attributed to William J. Reilly, Methods for the *Study of Retail Relationships*, Monograph Number 4. University of Texas Press, Austin 1929:16.

CYBERSCOOP

For a fee, Claritas provides demographic information on any area in the United States. Go to its Website at: www.connect.claritas.com/learnmore/demographic.htm. Browse the site to discover the kinds of information that are useful to retailers and the formats in which data is available.

gether. Site selection researchers have a number of commercial geodemographic marketing tools at their disposal. Two of the more popular services include:

1. *Cluster-Plus*™ Donnelly Marketing information Services offers Cluster-Plus™, which displays 47 lifestyle classifications for any designated marketing area. Using cluster analysis, top-income, highly educated professionals to the lowest categories on the socioeconomic scale can be identified. **Cluster analysis** is a method used to group customers according to their attributes and behaviors. Using Cluster-Plus™ data, a study of an area might reveal that approximately 50 percent of the population falls into the category of young, mobile professionals who are homeowners with children. With these results, a developer could produce a tenant mix to appeal to a younger, more active clientele. As examples, toy and sporting goods stores would be appropriate. A totally different mix would be needed in an area that consists primarily of high-rise apartment buildings and few children.

cluster analysis Method used to group customers according to their attributes and behaviors.

2. *Prizm*® Another lifestyle segmentation service based on geodemographics is PRIZM®, owned by Claritas. PRIZM® is an acronym for Postal Residences in Zip Markets. Neighborhoods are assigned to one of 62 groups through factor and cluster analysis. Postal service zips, carrier routes, Census Bureau tracts, block groups, and Zip+4 areas are used in the process. PRIZM® clusters are based on dozens of key census variables, such as size of household and income, plus customer purchase records. The sales data provides "real life" behavioral verification for PRIZM® descriptors. Each represents a distinct neighborhood lifestyle and indicates predictable patterns of buying behavior. Clusters may have catchy names like Norma Rae-Ville, Furs and Station Wagons, or Shotguns and Pickups, but PRIZM® can identify target markets bearing characteristics of a particular cluster right down to a particular city block. Knowing that members of the Norma Rae-Ville cluster may be keen on canned hash but not on English muffins may be of considerable importance to retail developers.[6]

All of the techniques mentioned are in use, but the specific type of tool most frequently used differs considerably by type of retailer. Most people involved with site selection agree that despite the sophisticated measures now available, there is still an important place for instinct and experience.

Types of Retail Locations

Finding the optimal location is another consideration in the site selection process. Each geographic region or city consists a variety of commercial areas that house retail operations. As with all location decisions, there are benefits and disadvantages to each.

Commercial Areas

Although there are many hybrids, three types of commercial real estate form the core of options for retailers that are not shopping center affiliated. Shopping centers and malls are other forms of commercial districts. Because of their impact on retail trade, shopping centers are covered in a dedicated chapter.

free-standing stores Self-contained buildings that are usually located on the periphery of a shopping center or city. Free-standing buildings also exist in downtown areas or power nodes.

Free-Standing Stores A **free-standing store** is a self contained building usually located on the periphery of a shopping center or city. Free-standing buildings also exist in downtown areas. Easy parking, flexible hours, lower rent, and ease of one-stop shopping characterize units located on the outskirts. Toys "R" Us uses this strategy in most of its U.S. locations and many of its international sites.

power node Consists of a grouping of big box stores—including at least one power center—located at or near a major highway intersection.

Areas in which numerous free-standing stores are located are called power nodes. A **power node** consists of a grouping of big box stores—including at least one power center—located at or near a major highway intersection.[7] Shopping centers called *power centers* are discussed in the next chapter. The importance of power nodes accelerated in the 1990s, although the tendency of big-box retailers to locate in specific areas was noticed decades earlier. Big-box retailers include superstores, warehouse clubs, discount department stores, and category killers. The largest power node in the greater Toronto area is mapped in Figure 11.3.

Retailers dominating a city block may also be considered free-standing even though they may be located in busy downtown areas with limited parking and high rents. Macy's and Saks Fifth Avenue's New York City sites bear this distinction. Flagship stores of specialty retailers like Ralph Lauren are also free-standing. Some occupy opulent restored mansions and other ar-

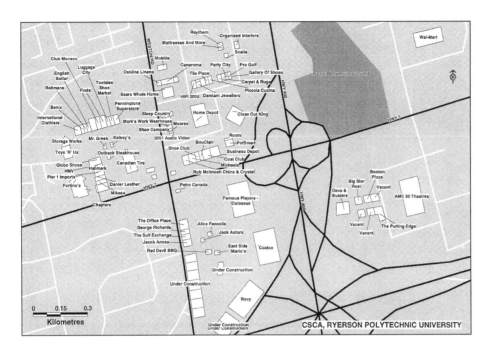

Figure 11.3 The largest power node in the greater Toronto area is near the intersection of highways 200 and 7 and nearby Weston Road. About 50 percent of the category killers in the area are U.S. retailers. *CSCA, Ryerson Polytechnic University.*

chitectural wonders. Because drawing clientele is expensive, small independent stores usually cannot afford free-standing locations such as these. Instead they develop sites in former homes and historic buildings, in tourist or smaller trading areas.

Central Business Districts **Central business districts** are downtown commercial areas in large and small cities where many businesses including retailers tend to congregate. They offer a broad range of specialty, convenience, department, and increasingly, discount stores. Usually within easy reach of financial and other commercial buildings, retailers in central business districts depend on foot traffic, private and public transportation to bring in business. **High streets** are busy retail thoroughfares where many retailers locate in the United Kingdom. They best compare to main streets in the United States where storefront retailers congregate. Downtown in the United States equates to *city centre* in the United Kingdom. Some high streets, like London's Bond Street and Sloane Street, have become magnets for designer and other luxury goods retailers. Bond Street is illustrated in Figure 11.4.

The popularity of central business districts in the United States vacillated in the last century. Downtown districts that faded in the 1970s experienced renewal in the 1980s and 1990s. Revitalization has created prime sites for

central business district Downtown commercial areas in large and small cities where many businesses including retailers tend to congregate.

high streets Busy thoroughfares where many retailers locate in the United Kingdom.

Figure 11.4 Bond Street is an attractive site for global retailers. Donna Karan and Ralph Lauren co-exist with Bulgari Jewelers, Dr. Marten shoes, and the Gap in this prime London location.

many retailers. Stores such as the Gap, Talbots, and Williams-Sonoma, operating originally as mall retailers, have opened in downtowns—large and small. Several reasons precipitated the move to city centers. Many customers perceive in-town shopping as slower paced compared to stressful mall visits. This perception varies greatly depending on the size of the city. Shoppers in New York, Hong Kong, or London might not agree. Retailers find rents in many downtown locations more palatable than in shopping centers. They also welcome city support for snow removal, outdoor electricity, and parking. Many target upper income families living in cities and those that prefer to avoid the redundancy of malls.

A new urban renewal movement draws retailers to refurbished downtowns in many parts of the United States. The South Beach section of Miami showcases restored art deco style hotels, restaurants, and retail stores in a section of the city that had been neglected for decades.

The mid-1990s witnessed discounters and large supermarkets vying for space in downtown areas of major metropolitan cities. Kmart opened in New York City on 34th Street near Penn Station in 1996. Now most discounters have a presence in urban areas. In 2002, Wal-Mart announced that it was opening a store in Dallas, a departure from its earlier small town location strategy.

Suburban centers are also drawing retailers back to the fold. Looking to service working class customers, TJX Company, parent of off-price retailer, T.J.Maxx, has opened several A.J.Wright stores in the suburbs of Boston. The locations are considered off limits to some shoppers because they were considered poorer sections of town in the past. The stores carry less expensive merchandise than the company's T.J.Maxx stores.

String Streets Retail thoroughfares located away from central business districts that retain thriving clusters of retail shops in or near residential neighborhoods are called **string streets**. Independent stores often find homes in these areas that may become a locus for innovative specialty retailing. Intermingled with national chains, these shopping areas retain unique characteristics that make them destination points for local residents and workers as well as tourists. Melrose Avenue in Hollywood, featured in Figure 11.1, and Spring and Wooster Streets in New York's SoHo are prime examples. At

string streets Retail thoroughfares located away from central business districts that retain thriving clusters of shops in or near residential neighborhoods.

Figure 11.5 Rodeo Drive is a string street bordering a residential district in Beverly Hills, California. Its fame as an upmarket shopping area inspired a similar street in Seoul, Korea to be named Rodeo-gil.

one time SoHo (the name comes from the area in New York City that is South of Houston Street) was home to art galleries and quirky shops that exuded a bohemian flavor. Between 1991 and 1998 rents increased from $35- to a high of $180-per-square-foot as scores of national and international retailers set up shop.[8]

Rodeo Drive is a notoriously pricey string street that celebrated its 25th anniversary in 1997. The Beverly Hills address is so popular that a street in Seoul, Korea was named in its honor. Stores on Rodeo-Gil are as trendy as those on its California counterpart. Gil means street in Korean. Both are illustrated in Figure 11.5.

Contemporary Retail Sites

A rash of new locations gained popularity in the last decade and continues to influence site selection decisions. Going where the customers are—even if that means to hospitals, museums, hotels, resort towns, train stations, subways, or airports—is changing the location strategies of many retailers.

Transportation Terminals Travelers to London's Heathrow Airport have enjoyed shopping while waiting for international flights for years, but airports as a sought-after retail site have been slower to evolve. Now large and small retailers have joined the foray, and duty free shops are no longer the major tenants.

British-based BAA plc is the developer of several airport locations including Heathrow and Gatwick Airports in England as well as Pittsburgh, Pennsylvania, Newark, New Jersey, and Portland, Oregon, in the United States. At some airport malls, the numbers of stores are rivaling those in more traditional locations. Pricing policies on products sold at airports is changing. Previously, customers paid excessive prices on most merchandise because retail vendors knew they held a captive audience. Now, goods are being sold at prices that are in line with off-site stores as the competition thickens.[9]

Watch retailer Fossil has several airport stores and is also considering opening units on cruise ships and at Universal Studios in California. According to one developer, airport stores earn in excess of $1000-per-square-foot as compared to regional mall stores that do between $200 to $300.[10] Airport retailing is becoming another conduit to customers worldwide. For this reason many international retailers select these sites. The From the Field in this chapter discusses the subtleties of airport retailing.

Not limited to airports, shopping centers play a major role in the popularity of Union Station in Washington, DC, and Grand Central Station in New York City. Not only can you board a train from these facilities, but you can also dine or shop while you wait. Underground transportation systems also provide opportunities to reach customers on the run. Retail shops are part of the British underground network, fondly called "the tube." Subway stops in major cities such as Montreal, Toronto, and Chicago also house vast retail offerings.

Tourist and Historic Sites Serving customers in resort areas who are usually relaxed and more attentive to retail temptations is the objective of some developers. Shopping sites that appeal to tourists exclusively have been well received. Rising from cactus-strewn land close to the Mexican border, Tubac, Arizona, is the location for a well-planned complex of gift shops, restaurants, antique stores, jewelry, and pottery specialists. The village exists primarily as a tourist stop for travelers heading for Tucson or Nogales. A performing arts center, art galleries, and the historical Presidio (fort) also draw traffic. Retail development in this area is shown in Figure 11.6.

Tourism's reach extends to hotels and resorts, many of which have installed retail shopping centers. In Hong Kong hotels, shopping malls are an integral part of the property. Casinos in Las Vegas and elsewhere link shopping facilities to their operations in increasing numbers. The Westin Boneventure in Los Angeles has a three-story mall that overlooks the hotel's atrium style reception area. The hotel caters to a significant number of

From the Field: Successful Airport Retail Requires Different Approach
by Edmund Mander

While airport retailing areas are beginning to look like malls, the resemblance ends there, say the people who develop, run, and study them.

"You can succeed wonderfully in airports, but come into it knowing you'll have to be flexible and adapt to that marketplace," warned Mark Pullman, executive director of Airport Retail Portfolio Group, a Chicago-based retail development and consulting firm.

Airport stores are far smaller than their mall counterparts—1,000-square-feet is considered large—and storage space is very limited. Therefore, retailers thinking of moving into airports should not be seduced by sales per square foot figures ($1,500 per square foot is not unheard of) alone, Pullman said. Instead, those in the business speak of sales per "Enplanement"—or passenger.

Most sales in airports are impulsive. Consequently, retailers have to be very picky about which merchandise to display to catch travelers' eyes. "Frontage is a lot more key," said Mark Knight, president of BAA Pittsburgh, Inc. "You have to be very good at marketing, be very impulse oriented."

Specialty stores will find that many of the items that are hot in their regular shops simply will not sell in the airport. A few retailers, such as Sunglass Hut and Tie Rack, who already sell very focused merchandise offerings from small spaces, are ready-made for airports, Pullman said.

Airports present other problems, too. Developers who add tenants expect to draw a lot more customers to their centers. But expanding an airport's retail offerings will not attract a single additional person to the airport, Pullman noted. Neither, after a certain point, will additional stores encourage passengers to spend more; they will give people more choice on how to spend the same amount of dollars.

This presents some conflicting interests between landlord and retailer: While airports and airlines want to make their passengers happy by providing them the largest number and variety of stores possible, that may not be in the interests of the retailers themselves.

This issue, according to observers, has arisen at Denver's new airport, which features a spectacular one-million-square-foot retail area. Because Continental Airlines decided not to make Denver a hub,

and Western Pacific went bankrupt, fewer passengers are using the airport than initially hoped, Pullman said. And passengers who are merely transferring to other flights at Denver have no access to that retail area, he noted.

Something Denver does have going for it is that its retail area was custom built. Many other terminals were not designed with retail in mind, and this can pose huge headaches when shopping areas are added later.

Stores open earlier and close later in airports, and deliveries are often restricted to the wee hours of the morning, noted Jeanne Raikoglo, senior manager of concessions development at Portland (Oregon) International Airport. Retailers who make the jump from mall or Main Street to the airport often stumble at first. "For some of them it's a struggle, because it's not an easy environment to operate in," She said. "There are tremendous rewards, but it does take some getting used to."

Source: SCT, January 1999:12. "Shopping Centers Today" (SCT) is published by the International Council of Shopping Centers, Inc., New York, New York and is reprinted with permission.

Japanese customers. This market is reflected in the tenant mix and signage in the mall.

Historical buildings as prime sites for retailing have always been popular in Europe. A retail complex stands on what once were 13th century warehouses in Lubeck, Germany. The interest in preserving antiquities is a more recent phenomenon in the United States. Some historical restoration areas have become retail destinations in themselves. Williamsburg, Virginia, for example, has much more to offer tourists than tours of historic homes and re-enactment's of colonial life. The city is a mecca for retail development.

Figure 11.6A and Figure 11.6B Tourist sites are popular locations for antique and jewelry stores, restaurants featuring local cuisine, art galleries, and cultural centers. Tubac lies half way between Tucson and the Mexican border—a perfect stop for road-weary travelers.

Did You Know?

Looking for high visibility, lawyers Lewis & Daggett located their office in the Four Seasons Town Centre in Greensboro, North Carolina. The firm's lease is written on a fixed-rent basis. According to Lewis, for a developer to charge percentage rent on the basis of legal settlements would be considered unethical.
Source: Bodamer, Dave. "Legal Tenants." *Shopping Centers Today*. April 2002: 24-25.

Hospitals Hospitals have grown and made their facilities more amenable to visitors, patients, and employees. Gift shops have gained visibility as a result. One study showed that more than 77 percent of hospital gift shops are located in the main lobby. More than two-thirds of gift shop customers are employees and about 20 percent are visitors, which goes against the common perception that most shoppers buy goods for patients they are visiting. The addition of services such as hair salons, better merchandising practices, and inventory management technology is expected to add to the productivity of these choice locations.[11]

Retailers are more committed than ever before to bring their goods where people congregate. Transportation facilities, tourist areas, hospitals, and even under or in office buildings can all be appropriate sites.

Owning and Leasing Considerations

Deciding whether to buy or lease a store, build from scratch, or acquire an existing property are other aspects of the site selection process. Negotiating the transaction requires time, expertise, and determination.

Buying Versus Leasing Property

There are advantages and disadvantages of purchasing as opposed to leasing property. Evaluating all possibilities is imperative before a place of business is chosen.

Owning the Premises By owning the premises, retailers benefit because they:

- Do not have to worry about a lease expiring or having to renegotiate a complex lease.
- Can alter or repair the store without landlord approval, as long as changes conform to local zoning laws.
- May be able to lease space to other retailers either as leased departments or stores themselves as space permits.
- Benefit from increases in real estate evaluation. In periods when real estate values appreciate, return on investment (ROI) on the property may outweigh ROI on the retail business.

On the other hand, there are negative aspects to owning since retailers:

- May tie up capital that might be better invested in inventory. In the case of small retailers, there may simply not be enough capital available to both purchase and stock a store.
- May not want to be a landlord or property manager.
- Have sole responsibility for paying tax and maintenance charges.
- May face decreases in property values in periods of economic downturn.

Leasing Retail Space By far the more common method of acquiring retail space, leasing may benefit retailers in several ways:

- The location available for lease may be in the highest traffic area—usually in a mall. A glimpse at the Eaton Center in Figure 11.7 emphasizes this point.
- Owners may lack capital for purchasing property; leasing may be the only alternative.
- The return on investment may be greater if available funds are invested in inventory rather than in real estate.
- The additional responsibilities of owning real estate are avoided, allowing the owner to concentrate on running the retail business.

Figure 11.7 Throngs of people visit Eaton Center in downtown Toronto. Shopping centers in high traffic areas are tempting locations for retailers that are prepared to lease space.

Retailers that lease space may face these drawbacks:

- Leases are complex, all-encompassing, and binding.
- Restrictions, policies, and procedures specified in a lease must be adhered to, although sometimes impractical or difficult to endure. Usually store hours, signage, and renovation are regulated in a lease.
- Because of high costs of space in prime locations, smaller retailers may have difficulty breaking even, let alone profiting.

Zoning Restrictions Whether a property is owned or leased, retailers are expected to adhere to local regulations. Zoning laws are designed to protect community image by restricting certain kinds of development, size of retail structures, or outside signage, for example. Other types of ordinances might involve hours of store operation or whether a commercial establishment is allowed to do business at a specific location.

Some zoning laws adversely affect retailers and appear to be unjust. A health club was located off a secondary road in a small industrial park behind a stand of trees. The facility could not be seen from the highway. After a complaint by a nearby residential property owner, the club was forced to remove its roadside sign that had been in place for several years. After heated discussion, the town zoning board ruled that the sign was illegal and could not be replaced. Despite appeals and the signing of petitions by local residents who supported the business, less than a year later the health club was out of business. Ironically, less than five hundred feet from the entrance to the industrial park, zoning laws differ, and an unattractive hand-painted sign promoting an in-home business still stands. The legal system is often slow to change even when positive community response supports it. Retailers contend with issues such as this quite often.

Negotiating with a Developer

Once the decision is made to lease a property, considerable time and effort go into negotiating the transaction with a property developer. A lease is a contract covering land, buildings, and/or selling space in which rights are described between lessor and lessee. There can be as many varieties of leases as there are stores in a shopping area. A typical lease runs 50 pages or more and covers everything from basic rental rates per square foot to escape clauses should either party choose to terminate the agreement before the lease expires. Several leasing technicalities deserve attention.

Bases for Establishing Rates Most retailers lease space on a square foot basis, assessed annually but paid in a variety of increments. Rent can be a fixed payment due monthly or annually, or it can be a fixed payment per square foot plus a percentage of sales above a certain volume designated by the lessor.

Retailers can negotiate with the developer or landlord to spread payments in proportion to typical retail sales cycles. Under this arrangement, retailers pay more rent in the busy months of November and December and less in the slower months of February and March. Others may negotiate for payments to be made in ascending increments over the period of time of the lease. This practice is very beneficial to new retailers that need time to establish themselves in the marketplace and build clienteles.

Derivation of Charges Cost per square foot is largely determined by type of location, dynamics of the trading area, the geographic area, and type of store. Size of organization also affects the ability to negotiate rental rates. Chains belonging to major holding companies like Limited Brands are in much better bargaining positions than small independent retailers.

In the case of mall stores, merchandise category and position within the mall affect rental costs. For example, fine jewelry stores are usually charged more rent than apparel retailers because jewelry stores are expected to generate higher volume.

Comparative regional leasing costs are difficult to identify because they vary greatly by city, region, and country. It is possible to lease space in a strip mall on the outskirts of a small city for approximately $10 to $12 per square foot. However, for retailers hoping to rent a store on posh Fifth Avenue in New York City, they can expect to pay as much as $1,000 per square foot.

Additional Leasing Costs In a typical retail lease, several other items are referred to as triple net charges. **Triple net** is a leasing term that describes a retailer's responsibility for paying insurance, utilities, and internal upkeep. The term gradually evolved to include other items, and developers appear to have different definitions of triple. Other additional charges can be flexible, depending on the retailer's ability to negotiate. They include:

- *Common area maintenance charges (CAM).* Charges assessed on retailers that fund general mall upkeep internally and externally are called **common area maintenance (CAM) charges.** Contributions for general mall upkeep, housekeeping, snow plowing, window washing, and outside refurbishment as deemed necessary by the developer are examples. Similar to "condo fees" in their intent, CAM charges are usually expressed in dollar amounts tied to the amount of square footage leased. The fees may range from $2 to $10 or more, depending on the property.

triple net Leasing term that describes a retailer's responsibility for paying insurance, utilities, and internal upkeep.

common area maintenance charges (CAM charges) Charges assessed on retailers that fund general mall upkeep internally and externally.

- *Promotional funds.* Sometimes called association charges, these fees are collected to fund shopping center activities such as fashion shows, special sale circulars, community activities, or the presence of Santa Claus.
- *Taxes and insurance.* These charges are usually prorated for each retailer on the basis of gross leasable area. **Gross leasable area (GLA)** is the amount of square footage available for lease in a shopping center, excluding common areas such as walkways, offices, and parking areas.
- *Utilities.* Although most large malls provide central heating, ventilation, and air conditioning (HVAC) as part of the lease, retailers are expected to pay their own electric and communications bills. In some circumstances even these areas are negotiable.

gross leasable area (GLA) The amount of square footage available for lease in a shopping center, excluding common areas such as walkways, offices, and parking areas.

Peripheral Locations Tracts of land on the periphery of a shopping center or other commercial site, often owned by the developer of the property, are called **outparcels**. Proper marketing and merchandising of adjacent land maximizes investment for developers. Most major retail companies have separate departments that handle peripheral land development.

outparcels Tracts of land on the periphery of a shopping center or other commercial site, often owned by the developer of the property.

In addition to shopping and living complexes, hotels are often partners in peripheral developments. Recreational and entertainment facilities might include theaters, ice skating rinks, and other sports facilities. Restaurants with a variety of themes and price points may enrich the retail mix. Office buildings, medical complexes, and financial institutions may also be included in the plan.

After the decision to launch a peripheral land project has been made and prime uses determined, other issues might arise. Easement agreements drawn up between the developer and key retailers have a tremendous impact on what the developer can and cannot do with the peripheral land. An agreement that allows limited use of land owned by someone else is called an **easement agreement**. For example, easement agreements might prohibit competing stores, limit parking to certain areas, or specify infrastructure improvements. The developer is placed in a crucial spot between the planner, retailers, and other businesses that want control over land development. Regardless of the many potential logistic and planning problems, land surrounding major developments is fertile soil for many retailers.

easement agreement Agreement that allows limited use of land owned by someone else.

Trends in Leasing and Property Acquisition

Many strategies are evident as retailers attempt to make property acquisition and management more effective. With costs of space rising in many areas, some retailers sublease their facilities to compatible businesses. In other circumstances, retailers practice multibrand strategies by sharing space, signage, and other resources. Still others are looking to shrink the sizes of new stores in order to reduce their leasing costs. Business-to-business use of the Internet for buying and leasing commercial property is expected to grow. This practice will reshape the ways retailers approach real estate transactions involving land, individual stores, and shopping centers.

Retailers testing new formats or locations favor short-term leasing. Shopping centers with available space benefit from temporary tenants in several ways. First, the positive psychological aspect of shopping in a mall that has no vacancies is apparent. Second, temporary tenants often become permanent if their experiment at the site has been successful. Third, retailers running seasonal businesses may benefit from a temporary site.

Another example illustrates how changes in the legal environment affect leasing decisions. U.S. bankruptcy legislation would make it harder for retailers to break leases if they are in Chapter 11 reorganization. A proposed bill, still pending in early 2002, would set deadlines of 180 days to declare which leases would be kept, and 120 days to determine which leases would be released for retailers that are under bankruptcy protection. Supporters of the bill, such as the International Council of Shopping Centers (ICSC) indicate that too many retailers use Chapter 11 unfairly. The ICSC believes some retailers file for reorganization only to be able to leave unprofitable locations. Detractors of the bill say that reorganization of retail companies would be much more difficult and would hurt retail companies with multiple locations. They contend that it would be difficult to adhere to the proposed time-frames if hundreds of stores were involved. The National Retail Federation is sympathetic to this position.[12]

Huge financial entities control most of the activity in large scale retail real estate transactions. A **real estate investment trust (REIT)** is a financial organization that masterminds large-scale real estate transactions. These organizations are involved in acquisitions of land and shopping centers. Many firms, like the developer Rouse, have evolved into REITs in order to control more aspects of the development business. REITS have great monetary power and marketing thrust.

The importance of using proper site selection methods and adequately analyzing trading areas should not be underestimated. Locations must be carefully planned since they contribute substantially to retail success. The next chapter examines shopping centers and malls as eminent retail sites.

Summary

Choosing appropriate locations is one of the more crucial decisions retailers make. Factors considered when selecting a site include pedestrian and vehicular traffic patterns, parking availability, infrastructure, placement,

CYBERSCOOP

To learn about geographical information systems and mapping software, go to www.esri.com. Browse the *Virtual Campus* and see what free GIS courses are offered this week. Next go to esribis.com/mapdata/free.htm and see what demographic and mapping samples are available. Other than retail applications, what else is GIS used for?

real estate investment trust (REIT) Financial organization that masterminds large scale retail real estate transactions.

and visibility. The three principal types of trading areas are primary, secondary, and tertiary.

Primary and secondary research helps determine the optimum location for a store or shopping center. Simple and advanced geographical information systems bring analytical tools to site selection research. Geodemographic marketing tools combine geographic, demographic, and lifestyle aspects for a more complete look at potential retail sites.

Principal types of commercial sites excluding malls are free-standing locations, central business districts, and string streets. Growing emphasis is placed on newer sites such as transportation terminals, tourist and historic areas, hotels, and hospitals.

There are several advantages and disadvantages of owning and leasing space. Leases include base rate per square foot plus a percentage of sales. In addition, costs including common area maintenance, promotion fees, taxes, insurance, and utilities are usually included in a lease.

Peripheral land surrounding a key location also is considered when developing retail and nonretail projects. In the future, more retail real estate transactions will be conducted using the Internet. In conclusion, the three classic principles of retailing remain: location, location, location.

Questions for Review and Discussion

1. How do infrastructure, placement, and visibility affect retail site selection decisions?
2. Define the terms primary trading area, secondary trading area, and tertiary trading area. How is sales potential calculated for a trading area?
3. How do retailers use geographical information systems during the site evaluation process?
4. What are the advantages and disadvantages of a central business district as a retail location?
5. What types of retailers prefer a free-standing location? Why?
6. Why are some retail companies aggressively seeking nontraditional locations such as airports and hotels? Why are these sites better able to attract international customers?
7. If you were going to open a store, would you choose to own or lease? Justify your decision?
8. How is a typical retail lease calculated? What additional costs are usually included?

Endnotes

1. Donelan, David. "Trade Area Analysis and the Site Selection Process." *Business Geographics.* September, 1997:16.

2. Hernandez, Tony. "Retail GIS: An International Perspective." Paper Presentation. American Collegiate Retailing Association Spring Conference. Toronto, Canada. May 5, 2000.

3. Hernandez, Tony and Bennison, David. "The Art and Science of Retail Location Decisions." *International Journal of Retail and Distribution Management.* Volume 28, No. 8. 2000: 360.

4. Ibid.

5. Reilly, William J. *Methods for the Study of Retail Relationships.* Monograph Number 4. University of Texas Press. Austin. 1929:16.

6. "The Right Answer." Brochure. Claritas, The Target Marketing Company. Alexandria, Virginia. 1986. Updated on www.connect.claritas.com. May 15, 2002.

7. Yeates, Maurice. *The GTA@Y2K: The Dynamics of Change in the Commercial Structure of the Greater Toronto Area.* Chapter 4, "Big-Boxes, Power Centres, and Power Nodes." Centre for the Study of Commercial Activity. Toronto. 1999: 45.

8. Edelson, Sharon. "Retail's Building Blocks." *Women's Wear Daily.* WWD/Global. January 1998:16.

9. Mander, Edmund. "New Tactics Help Airport Retailing Soar in United States." *Shopping Centers Today.* International Council of Shopping Centers. Volume 20, Issue 1. January 1999:1,12.

10. Edelson, Sharon. "Trains, Planes and Chains." *Women's Wear Daily.* July 14, 1997:8.

11. Donnellan, John. "Hospital Gift Shops as Retail Enterprises." Paper presented at the American Collegiate Retailing Association Spring Conference. Washington, DC. April, 1998.

12. Kopecki, Dawn. "Bill to Restrict Ailing Retailers on Lease Pacts." *Wall Street Journal.* March 23, 1999:B11A.

Chapter 12

Shopping Centers and Malls

Learning Objectives

After completing this chapter you should be able to:

- Describe eight basic types of shopping centers.
- Discuss the status of hybrid shopping center development.
- List several examples of centers that provide shoppertainment and acknowledge why they are successful.
- Document how older malls are adjusting to competition from newer facilities.
- Explain how developers work with their management teams to achieve profitability.

Figure 12.1a and 12.1b A&S was the anchor tenant at the original A&S Plaza in New York City. Later the name of the center was changed to the Manhattan Mall, and the A&S space became Stern's department store. The next tenant is likely to be a big box retailer or a collection of smaller specialty stores. Changes like this are inevitable as retail and consumer needs change. (See p. 353).

The type of retail site that has made the most impact on the way we live is the shopping center. There we look for entertainment, socialization, exercise, education, fast or fine dining, and escape in addition to sartorial sustenance.

Mallmania slowed in the early-1990s and has continued on a downward trajectory reflecting changes in the environment mentioned throughout this text. Despite the slowdown, approximately 12,000 new centers were built between 1990 and 1999 in the United States. There were 44,426 shopping centers in the United States at the end of the decade.[1]

Trends in mall development parallel the changing sentiments of customers, the need to revitalize older sites, and the effects of retail saturation. In some instances new construction is totally replacing outdated malls. In others, older structures are being converted to new retail formats. Some developers are entering overstored areas and instigating market share battles. Entertainment malls proliferate as developers recognize customers' desires to play as well as shop. Value centers evolve into value megamalls, as people continue to seek more for their money. Many developers combine trends to create hybrid malls.

Rates of shopping center growth vary by the state of the economy and geographic areas. Forty-five percent of the 130 shopping centers built in the United States in the fourth quarter of 2001 were constructed in the South. About 12 percent were attributed to the Northeast. New shopping center construction starts are graphed in Figure 12.2.

Mall management has shifted its emphasis in the last decade. Gone is the dependence on clichéd promotions to build traffic. Major shopping center developers are committed to building brand awareness of their properties through new products and services directed to their customers. These and other contemporary issues are explained in this chapter.

Classification of Shopping Centers and Malls

shopping center "A group of retail and other commercial establishments that is planned, developed, owned, and managed as a single property." (ICSC)

The first wave of shopping centers consisted of groups of free-standing stores in suburban locations where ample free parking was available. A **shopping center** is "a group of retail and other commercial establishments that is planned, developed, owned, and managed as a single property."[2] Early shop-

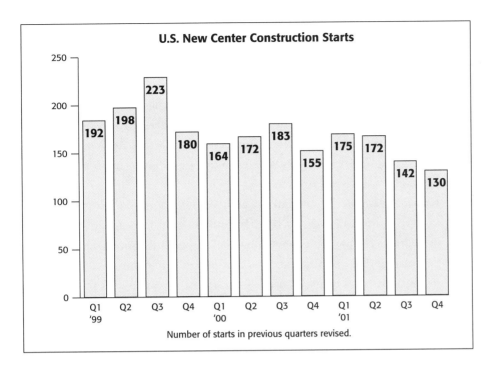

Figure 12.2 U.S. Shopping Center Construction Starts, 1999–2001. Source: "Eye on the Industry . . . U.S. Construction"—*ICSC Research Quarterly*, Vol. 9 No. 1—Spring 2002 (From F.W. Dodge, a unit of the McGraw-Hill Construction Information Group.)

ping centers were not covered by a central roof as are contemporary shopping malls. A **mall** is "a climate controlled structure in which retail stores are architecturally connected."[3] Shopping malls are planned for maximum accessibility, designed either horizontally or vertically, and positioned above or below the ground. A **strip center** is "an attached row of stores or service outlets managed as a coherent retail entity."[4] Not enclosed and climate controlled, a strip center is, therefore, a shopping center, not a mall. However, the terms shopping center and mall often are used interchangeably.

Shopping centers are described by concept, size, trading area, presence and type of anchor stores, and tenant mix. First, eight basic shopping centers are considered. Next, hybrid developments are examined. **Hybrid centers** are shopping areas that are of mixed composition, combining the qualities of two or more basic center configurations with contemporary twists. The evolution of shopping centers is no more complete than the evolution of store and nonstore forms of retailing.

mall "Climate controlled structure in which retail stores are architecturally connected." (ICSC)

strip center "An attached row of stores or service outlets managed as a coherent retail entity." (ICSC)

hybrid center Shopping areas that are of mixed composition, combining the qualities of two or more basic center configurations with contemporary twists.

Eight Shopping Center Types

Eight basic types of shopping centers are categorized by the International Council of Shopping Centers(ICSC) and summerized in Table 12.1.[5] They include:

CYBERSCOOP

The International Council of Shopping Centers maintains a Web site that provides a directory of major shopping centers. Although the service is for ICSC members, visitors to **www.icsc.org** can try a free query: What's new in Kalamazoo?

Did You Know?

Home run hero, Sammy Sosa owns a community shopping center in his hometown, San Pedro de Macoris in the Dominican Republic. It is called the 30-30 Plaza after his 30 home run, 30 stolen base record set in 1993.
Source: *Shopping Centers Today.* Volume 20, Issue 1. January 1999: 5.

neighborhood center Small strip center in a trading area that serves 5,000 to 40,000 people.

Community center Neighborhood center expanded to serve a trading area of 40,000 to 150,000 people.

regional center Center consisting of at least two anchor stores and 80 to 150 smaller stores, serving a minimum of 150,000 people.

anchor store Major mall tenant occupying a large, usually corner or end store.

superregional center Shopping center consisting of three or more anchor stores and as many as 350 specialty and service retailers.

theme/festival center Venues oriented toward entertainment as well as shopping; also called festival marketplace.

■ *Neighborhood centers.* A relatively small strip center in a trading area that serves 5,000 to 40,000 people is called a **neighborhood center**. Strip centers are constructed on main roads that carry substantial traffic in predominantly residential areas. The trading area covers a radius of about 3 miles. Main tenants are usually small supermarkets, drugstores, or convenience stores positioned next to 5 to 10 other small retailers. Usually development of neighborhood centers follows upturns in the housing market. New apartment complexes or a rise in single-family homes mean new opportunities for food and convenience retailers.

■ *Community centers.* A **community center** is a neighborhood center expanded to serve 40,000 to 150,000 people. It is anchored by large tenants such as supermarkets or discounters or both. The trading area is slightly larger than that of a neighborhood center and may extend 3 to 6 miles.

■ *Regional centers.* A center consisting of at least two anchor stores and 80 to 150 smaller stores, serving a minimum of 150,000 people is called a **regional center**. Major mall tenants occupying a large, usually corner or end stores, are called **anchor stores**. Regional centers draw customers up to a 15 mile radius. National chain stores are well represented. Centers are built either by developers that lease stores to retailers or by large retailers, such as May Department Stores or Sears, that operate anchor stores in the center. The number and types of stores are controlled in order to limit competition within the shopping center.

■ *Superregional centers.* A shopping center consisting of three or more anchor stores and as many as 350 specialty and service retailers is called a **superregional center**. It has more than two and a half times the gross leasable area of regional centers, and frequently includes hotels, office buildings, and recreation centers. Discounters are also common sights in centers that may cover 120 acres. Superregional centers often serve a population of one million or more, and draw from 25 miles. Draw is affected by competition in an area as discussed in the previous chapter.

■ *Theme/Festival centers.* A shopping venue oriented toward entertainment as well as shopping is called a **theme/festival center**. Socializing and dining are key pursuits for people who frequent these centers that are also called festival marketplaces. The Rouse Company of Columbia, Maryland, is the premier festival marketplace developer, having initiated the concept with its Faneuil Hall/Quincy Market project in Boston in 1976. Other Rouse sites include Harborplace in Baltimore, Union Station in St. Louis, Bayside in Miami, and Riverwalk in New Orleans. Most are located in historic districts, near seaports, or in revived downtown areas. Riverwalk on the Mississippi is illustrated in Figure 12.3.

■ *Fashion/Specialty centers.* An anchorless shopping center that focuses on a lifestyle cluster, unique merchandise, or specific price level is called a **fash-**

ion/specialty center. Featuring a cadre of retailers, these centers are suited to high traffic, bustling locations in urban or suburban areas. Specialty malls target people with refined fashion tastes, particular lifestyles, or those on vacation, to name only a few possibilities.

■ *Power centers*. A shopping centers that resembles an oversize strip mall and has as many as seven anchor stores, usually discounters or category killers, is known as a **power center**. Originating in the mid-1990s, power centers range from 300,000 to 600,000 square feet or more of gross leasable area. Although they resemble oversized strip malls or older regional malls, the similarity ends there. Big box retailers like Best Buy or Home Depot and discount operators are familiar tenants. The trading radius for a power center is 20 to 25 miles opposed to the 3 to 5 miles for most strip centers.

■ *Outlet centers*. The original intent of factory outlet stores to be a place for manufacturers to sell their excess stock has been surpassed by today's outlet malls. A shopping center composed mainly of stores owned by manufacturers is called an **outlet center**. Although manufacturers or their representatives still own the majority of stores in a factory outlet mall, customer focus and retail mix has changed radically.

Figure 12.3 Riverwalk in New Orleans is a theme/festival center developed by the Rouse Company. Located on the banks of the Mississippi River, the development encompasses almost two miles of waterfront.

Trends in Basic Shopping Centers

Demographics such as age and ethnic groups, lifestyles, and unifying themes set the tone for specialty center development. Outlet centers are in the throes of further evolution in the United States and other parts of the world. The following discussion illuminates trends and diversity in specialty and outlet centers

Specialty Centers As well as catering to refined fashion tastes, specialty malls are assuming a variety of different guises. Demographics are key in a specialty mall designed for children in Grand Rapids, Michigan. The development is the brainchild of a husband and wife team who named the mall Mackie's World, in memory of their son who died from a rare illness. The shopping center is totally tuned to tots, with child-oriented retail stores, car-shaped seats in the movie theater, and 50 types of peanut butter sandwiches served in the food court. From its main lobby vantage point, a scale model Tyrannosaurus rex welcomes families to the mall.

fashion/specialty center Anchorless shopping center that focuses on a lifestyle cluster, unique merchandise, or price level.

power center Shopping center that resembles an oversize strip mall with as many as seven anchor stores that are usually discounters or category killers.

outlet center Shopping center comprised mainly of stores owned by manufacturers.

Table 12.1 Comparison of Major Types of Shopping Centers

Type	Concept	SQ. FT. (Inc. Anchors)	Acreage	Primary Trade Area**
Neighborhood Center	Convenience	30,000 – 150,000	3 – 15	3 miles
Community Center	General Merchandise; Convenience	100,000 – 350,000	10- 40	3 – 6 miles
Regional Center	General Merchandise; Fashion (Mall, typically enclosed)	400,000 – 800,000	40 – 100	5 – 15 miles
Superregional Center	Similar to Regional Center but has more variety and assortment	800,000+	60 – 120	5 – 25 miles
Fashion/ Specialty Center	Higher end, fashion oriented	80,000 – 250,000	5 – 25	5 – 15 miles
Power Center	Category- dominant anchors; few small tenants	250,000 – 600,000	25 – 80	5 – 10 miles
Theme/ Festival Center	Leisure; tourist-oriented; retail and service	80,000 – 250,000	5 – 20	N/A
Outlet Center	Manufacturers' outlet stores	50,000 – 400,000	10 – 50	25 – 75 miles

Source: *ICSC Research Quarterly* V. 9, No. 2, Summer 2001:2

Ethnicity is the chief factor in the development of Koreatown Center, a specialty mall in Los Angeles, California. People of Asian and Latino heritage comprise the target market. H.K. Market, an Asian supermarket, is an anchor tenant. A food court features both Korean and American restaurants.[6]

A small strip center in Sedona, Arizona attracts customers interested in exploring their psychic selves. Sedona is known for the vortexes of energy that are said to emanate from the red rock geology and as a place for spiritual renewal. Here retailers sell books on meditation and self-study, crystals, new age music, and astrological artifacts. Visitors can have their auras cleansed or photographed, Tarot cards read, and futures told by individuals who provide these special services. Lifestyle and curiosity are the components that drive sales in this specialty mall.

Shopping centers with themes that are often theatrical, historical, or cultural bring new dimension to specialty malls. These highly stylized centers share common characteristics although locations and architecture can be quite diverse. The inspiration might be a foreign village, a historical setting, or a marine theme. Visiting the French Market in Columbus, Ohio, is like taking a stroll through New Orleans' French quarter or the left-bank of Paris. People live in apartments with wrought-iron balconies, and eat in small bistros like the one illustrated in Figure 12.4. Strolling the grounds of this pedestrian-only, mixed-use center is picturesque and safe.

Market selectivity and unique merchandise describe specialty malls. It is not the intent of specialty centers to fill all customer needs as most regional malls attempt to do.

Figure 12.4 The French Market outside Columbus, Ohio, is a mixed-use, theme center. Living, working, and retail areas carefully planned and contained in a pedestrian-only community. Buildings, complete with intentionally distressed architecture, imitate a quaint French village.

Outlet Centers The number of U.S. outlet centers has declined annually since 1996.[7] The drop in popularity can be attributed to several factors. Customers are more sophisticated and recognize good values when they find them. Not all merchandise in all outlet centers is significantly less expensive than that found in other retail centers. Competition has intensified across all retail formats and shopping centers. Finally, flagrant expansion of manufacturer's outlet chains diminished as companies close underperforming units. Numbers of U.S. outlet centers are charted in Figure 12.5.

Outlet centers that thrive answer more consumer needs than simply thrift. Once vacations meant going to lakes, mountains, or the seashore. Now getaway weekends spent at outlet malls vie with traditional leisure pursuits. Oulet stores in Freeport, Maine, are a destination for shoppers year round. During the peak summer season, hotels within a hundred mile radius of Freeport often are booked. The once quiet resort town, best known as the home of L.L.Bean, has become outlet city. Although development is monitored and most new stores fit the colonial flavor of Freeport, Main Street now evokes a much different image. What was once a typical small town center is a succession of free-standing stores and strip malls. Development has spilled over to many of the side streets. Stately homes have become fast food restaurants and the former library is now home to the Vermont Teddy Bear store. Though most businesses close at night,

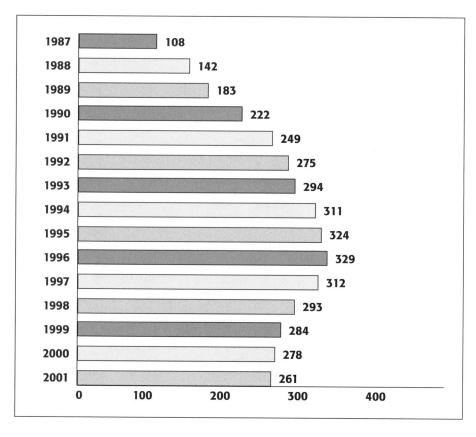

Figure 12.5 Number of U.S. Outlet Centers, 1987–2001 (as of December 31 of each year) *Source:* Outlet Stats, "2001 Numbers Show Who's Calling the Shots" by Linda Humphers—*Value Retail News*, May 2002:12. Produced by the International Council of Shopping Centers, Inc., New York, New York and the article is reprinted with permission.

L.L.Bean remains open 24-hours a day. At 11:00 p.m. it still does a brisk trade. Not all local residents are happy about the changes, despite the increase in real estate values and jobs. Most leave the area on weekends when heavy traffic snakes through the town that once housed shoe manufacturing and shipbuilding industries.

Outlet malls and customers in other parts of the world also experience resistance to change. Japanese shoppers were much slower than U.S. consumers to embrace outlet malls. In the past, Japanese taste for top quality items and distaste for anything labeled discount precluded their acceptance of outlet stores. Times have changed along with the economy and customers. Sawtucket is a planned community in a former industrial district in Yokohama, made to emulate the island of Nantucket. The development features restaurants and an outlet shopping mall near an established marina. Strong positive feelings toward American lifestyles hastened the adoption of outlet malls as did Japan's lingering recession. Tenants include J.Crew, Eddie Bauer, and Reebok. Store signs are in Japanese and English, but English versions are much larger. The developer, Mitsui Fudosan Co., does not expect the trend to last and plans to close the outlet stores when its lease on the property expires in 2008.[8] It remains to be seen if customers will agree with the intentions of the developer.

Hybrid Shopping Centers

Many variations on the eight basic types of shopping centers are evolving as lifestyles, business practices, competition, and economies change. Providing shopping experiences that satisfy several needs simultaneously is crucial to the success of newer formats. Mixed-use centers, vertical, and underground malls serve customers in a variety of locations worldwide. Discount malls cultivate customers who are price conscious, huge shopping arenas draw the multitudes, and shoppertainment malls bring out the need for hedonistic expression that exists in most of us.

Value Centers Most analysts feel that the general construction slowdown in U.S. mall development greatly affected power centers. When companies like Caldor, which went out of business in 1999, leave a power center, a considerable void is left to be filled by a shrinking number of retail stores. Value centers have evolved in an attempt to fill this gap. A **value center** is a cross between a power center and an outlet mall. Discounters, warehouse clubs, category killers, and scores of factory outlet stores comprise the tenancy. Very often targeted to a tourist market, these centers need a concentration of about 1.5 million customers to be successful.

value center A cross between a power center and an outlet center.

Megamalls Although there are not many examples of true megamalls, those that exist are noteworthy. A **megamall** is a mall of well over 1 million square feet, drawing from a trading area of over 100 miles and in some cases, several states or provinces. A megamall houses 400 to 800 stores, service businesses, restaurants, and entertainment facilities. Extensive acreage and tremendous draw is required, limiting the number of potential sites. The Mall of America, in Bloomington, Minnesota, and the West Edmonton Mall in Alberta, Canada, are examples. Both depend largely on tourists from all over the world.

megamall mixed-use mall of well over 1 million square feet, drawing from a trading area of over 100 miles and, in some cases, several states or provinces.

A **value megamall** is a large hybrid mall containing elements of power, value, and outlet centers, with added entertainment components. The conglomeration is considered the brainchild of The Mills Corp., developer of outlet centers throughout the United States. Ranging from 1 to 2 million square feet, value to customers is redefined by the intense retail mix in these centers. For example, national specialty chains and designer outlets may coexist with category killers, off-price stores, discounters, food, and

value megamall Large hybrid mall containing elements of power, value, and outlet centers, with added entertainment components.

Figure 12.6 The newest wing at Union Station in Washington, DC, houses specialty retailers, a gourmet restaurant on the perimeter, and upscale merchandising units in the center.

entertainment retailers. More of everything appears to be the main theme. Value mega-malls generate three times more volume than traditional malls. They are exerting great competitive pressure on older outlet centers.

Utah's Grand Salt Lake Mall was opened for Olympic crowds in 2002. The 1.5-million-square-foot value megamall, located near the airport, has 14 to 16 anchor stores on one level. Entertainment and restaurants are a big part of the center which was expected to draw 30 to 40 percent tourists.[9] Retailers were disappointed that retail sales did not live up to pre-Olympic predictions.

The Mills Corp. is also taking the concept global by opening value megamalls in Spain, and considering sites in Italy and Brazil.[10]

mixed-use center Shopping center with two or more uses, such as an office building with retail mall and residential areas.

Mixed-use Centers A shopping center with two or more uses, such as an office building with a retail mall and residential areas is called a **mixed-use center**. Many include a combination of shopping, living, working, transportation, and/or entertainment facilities. Some started as regional centers and grew by adding services and facilities. Some mixed-use centers are located in renovated public buildings; others are totally planned communities.

Union Station is the mixed-use complex featured in Figure 12.6. It houses the Amtrak terminal for Washington, DC, a theater complex, several restaurants and cafes, a huge food court, and 160,000 square feet of retail space. The restored, Beaux Arts decor made Union Station the perfect setting for two Presidential Inaugural Balls in the 1990s.[11]

Val d' Europe, located outside Disneyland Paris, is an example of a planned community. Although shopping areas will open much sooner, the town will not be complete until 2017. It will eventually house 50,000 residents and include office space and transportation systems. Buses will convey customers between the theme park, hotels, residences, and shopping centers. Traditional shopping areas as well as an outlet mall are planned for Val d' Europe. Nostalgia buffs will appreciate the buildings that resemble 19th century Paris architecture.[12]

Some theme/festival centers also are considered mixed-use centers. South Street Seaport in New York includes residential, office, and hotel space; the renovated Fulton Fish Market; a museum; and shops galore.

Vertical Malls A shopping center in a high-rise building, usually in an urban location, is called a **vertical mall**. The renovation of downtown areas, scarcity of land, and concentration of customers in urban areas paved the way for vertical malls. Trump Tower in New York, Water Tower Place in Chicago, and the Nordstrom-anchored San Francisco Centre are examples of vertical malls.

The benefits of high traffic, urban locations does not exempt vertical malls from problems. Merger and acquisition activity in the 1990s spurred changes at the eight-story Manhattan Mall in New York City. The center was originally called A&S Plaza when it opened in the late 1980s. Abraham and Straus (A&S) department store, the first anchor tenant, evolved into Stern's after Macy's and A&S merged in 1995. Poor performance necessitated the closing of this and other Stern's stores in 2001. Several plans under consideration at that time included transforming the vacated space into smaller specialty store units or leasing the space to a big box and other smaller retailers.[13] Earlier views of the Manhattan Mall anchor stores are shown in Figure 12.1.

Occasionally vertical malls use their height to parallel pricing strategy. Lot 10, a center in Kuala Lumpur, Malaysia, features lower-price retailers on the bottom levels. As customers ride the escalators to the upper floors, up go the prices. Look for Byblos, Hugo Boss, and Armani on the top floor. This Japanese-owned mall, anchored by the Isetan department store, is illustrated in Figure 12.7.

Where department stores have retrenched, vertical malls have blossomed bringing a fresh approach to urban retailing. Despite the high costs of real estate in select urban areas, most vertical malls appear to withstand the tests of time.

Underground Malls Some shopping centers resemble conventional malls, but bear the distinction of being located underground. Although they originated in cities such as Montreal and Toronto, where long, cold winters curtailed trade, there are other reasons for their existence. Shopping malls make sense at underground transportation stops. In several world cities, malls make shopping more convenient for subway commuters. Lack of available land and congested shopping areas also precipitates underground development.

Figure 12.7 The Lot 10 shopping mall in downtown Kuala Lumpur provides deluxe surroundings for seven stories of retailing, from budget to deluxe. On the mezzanine level is a French café—not easy to find in Malaysia.

vertical mall Shopping center in a high-rise building, usually in an urban location.

Figure 12.8a and 12.8b What is the Louvre doing in a retailing text? Under the plaza and the I.M. Pei sculpture is a shopping mall. Le Carousels du Louvre featuring global retailers including Virgin Records Megastore, The Body Shop, and Esprit.

Crystal City in Arlington, Virginia, is an underground center, where in theory, people need never see the light of day. Residents live in high-rise apartment buildings, and might take an elevator to the lower level in the morning, stop at an underground mall for breakfast, and scurry to work in other skyscrapers via underground tunnels. After work they can visit the extensive Crystal City Mall, do grocery shopping, stop at the dry cleaners, and have dinner before returning to their dwellings. This lifestyle may be extreme for some tastes, but it is possible in this mixed-use center.

In Norwich, England, the Castle Mall is located next to an historic castle. Conservationists insisted that the view of the castle not be compromised, so construction took place underground. A park over the mall preserves the beauty of the area. The Castle Mall is the only mall in Norwich, therefore important to the local economy.[14]

Climate, limited space in large cities, conservation and preservation issues in others have brought shopping centers underground. The move has not darkened the enthusiasm of customers. A shopping center is located under the famous Louvre museum in Paris that is illustrated in Figure 12.8.

Shoppertainment Complexes Just when we thought we had seen it all, shoppertainment burst onto the retail scene. Combining retail shopping with many forms of entertainment is called **shoppertainment**. Shoppertainment centers are designed to amuse customers, encourage longer stays, present new activities, and—as almost an afterthought—generate retail sales. They encourage the total retail experience. The following examples show how developers are addressing the needs of growing numbers of people who have little time to have fun or shop, so they do both concurrently.

shoppertainment Combining retail shopping with many forms of entertainment.

Successful at providing entertainment for its customers is the Forum Shops at Caesar's Palace in Las Vegas. The mall has expanded twice since it opened in 1992. The first addition in 1997 doubled its size and brought 35 more retailers including Diesel, Virgin Megastore, Emporio Armani, and Hugo Boss to trade beneath its vaulted, hand-painted blue sky.

It also features a replica of the Roman pantheon at its entrance on the famous Las Vegas strip. The complex also boasts a giant Trojan horse, an aquarium, plus animatronic sculptures.

Another 200,000 square feet of retail space will be added by 2004, bringing its size to 700,000 square feet.[15]

Can a shopping center successfully combine outdoor adventure, a zoo, food, and shopping? Food service giant, Ogden Corp. thinks so with its American Wilderness concept. The department store–sized unit in Ontario Mills Mall in California opened in 1997 and plans more locations in the United States and internationally. Included on site are five biomes which are planned areas that approximate wilderness terrain such as deserts,

Figure 12.9 Lotte World in Seoul, Korea, is a facility meant to dazzle, entertain, and fulfill customers shopping needs. It features an amusement park, skating rink, and special events throughout the year. *Courtesy of Jennifer Han*

forests, and seashores. Animals abound in a semicaged environment. Also included is a motion-simulator experience, lectures, and sensory exhibits where customers can touch starfish and smell the redwoods.[16] Customers are urged to eat and shop. The center draws locals and tourists, providing experiences that can be shared by families.

Sony opened its Metreon, billed as "an entertainment megaplex" in San Francisco in 1999. The extravaganza encompasses an entire city block and houses an IMAX theater as well as 15 cinemas. Restaurants, amusements, and retail stores round out the tenant mix. Microsoft's first retail unit is located in the Metreon, along with a Discovery Channel store and Sony's PlayStation video game venture. Competition from the Internet is a key factor in the decision of Sony and others to create huge shoppertainment complexes.[17]

Malls that appeal to multiple senses and needs are present throughout the world as several examples illustrate. Lotte World in Seoul, Korea is a multiuse shopping center that includes an amusement park, global as well as local retailers, and an ice rink as seen in Figure 12.9. The upscale center is so large that during a New Year's celebration a parade was held indoors.

In Norway, where the winters are long and cold, entertainment for those with chronic cases of cabin fever takes a different form. "Outdoor" cafes are set up inside malls so that customers can pretend they are sitting outside at a sidewalk bistro in mid-summer.[18] Climate obviously has a bearing on the kinds of experiences that are arranged for customers.

Whatever the setting, entertainment is an important concept in mall retailing. The need to experience the environment, to relax and have fun, may be as strong as the need to acquire material goods. When developers acknowledge these human needs and respond creatively the result is sales and profits.

Shopping Center Challenges and Strategies

When slick new centers enter established trading areas, competition flares. Some centers built in the late 1960s and early 1970s aged gracefully, others did not. This occurrence challenged retailers to form new strategies including renovation and reimaging. Customer fascination with old-fashioned lifestyles and downtowns sparked another direction for tired malls or undeveloped areas. Another technique used by retailers and developers as they adjust to pressures in the marketplace include breaking up older malls into freestanding or other configurations.

Town Center Development

New open-air shopping centers, or renovations of old ones, are called town centers. **Town centers** are retail urban villages located outdoors consisting of buildings with nostalgic architectural features or theme designs. Sometimes older malls are converted to open-air centers. In other instances brand new malls are constructed.

The stark reality of older, urban centers is softened when well-planned retail projects are implemented. Outside Chicago, the One Schaumburg Place power center opened in 1989. Several of the mall's original tenants were either struggling or had filed bankruptcy by the mid-1990s. This misfortune, as well as increased competition, put the mall in jeopardy. The project was transformed into a town center in 2000. It is expected to bring more excitement and lifestyle-focused retailing to customers. Tenants include Galyan's sporting goods, Gameworks, and a huge Starbucks Coffee and Wine Cafe.[19]

The Easton Center on the outskirts of Columbus, Ohio, is an example of a town center project that was developed from scratch. On land owned by Limited Brands, the complex covers more than 150 acres and is a tribute to the ingenuity of Leslie Wexner, CEO of Limited Brands, and Steiner Company, the developer. When strolling the traffic-controlled streets of the downtown center, one gets the impression of being on the set of the film, *The Truman Show*. Those who have seen the movie will agree that its setting evokes a near perfect community. Easton Center captures this perfection in a customer-friendly, enticing way. One phase of the construction includes many retail stores where customer participation is encouraged. Browsers can design their own teddy bears at Build-a-Bear or paint and fire pottery at Color Your World. Store facades are reminiscent of those in older downtowns—with the exception of a few superstores like Barnes & Noble and a Virgin Megastore. Later phases will add residential areas and a fashion mall anchored by Nordstrom. One of the downtown streets is illustrated in Figure 12.10.

Complexes like these rely heavily on architectural details to convey the village image. Walkways are often paved with cobblestones to capture a vintage allure. Building materials are carefully chosen to reflect the theme. Developers direct their efforts toward customers who are bored by the sameness syndrome in traditional shopping centers described earlier in this

Did You Know?

Moscow's famous department store, GUM, actually looks and operates more like a mall. Retailers from all over the world consign or lease space in the three-story, castle-like enclosure. GUM is the acronym for the Russian equivalent of State Universal Store.

town centers Retail urban villages located outdoors consisting of buildings with nostalgic architectural features or theme designs.

Figure 12.10 Easton Center is a planned town center on the outskirts of Columbus, Ohio. Hybrid centers such as this answer consumers' needs for shoppertainment, mixed-use, and a return to the nostalgia of downtown locations. *©2000 Copyright. Designed by Development Design Group, Inc., Photo by Walter Larimore.*

lifestyle center An outdoor shopping center encompassing several small retail strips and freestanding anchor stores in an appealing environment serving an upscale clientele.

demalling Breaking up older enclosed malls into open-concept clusters of stores.

text. Projects of this magnitude must achieve critical mass so that consumers will consider town centers first choices when selecting shopping venues.

Lifestyle Centers

Similar in intent to a town center, but less dependent on nostalgic downtown themes, lifestyle centers are also becoming destinations of choice for retailers and consumers in the twenty-first century. A **lifestyle center** is an outdoor shopping center encompassing several small retail strips and freestanding anchor stores in an appealing environment serving an upscale clientele. Designed for easy access, convenience, and the ultimate in ambiance, these centers primarily serve active, young, affluent families. Retailers such as Williams Sonoma, Pottery Barn, Restoration Hardware, The Cheesecake Factory, Ann Taylor Loft, as well as service and entertainment businesses might comprise the tenant mix.

The Shops at Dove Valley, a lifestyle center on the outskirts of Denver, Colorado, is scheduled to open in 2004. The center is located near an existing business park on a 30-acre site bisected by a stream. This natural attribute is considered in the placement of an attractive configuration of stores and service areas. The site is located directly off a major highway in close proximity to the Denver Broncos Football Training Center, a soccer complex, office park, technology center, and extensive residential complexes. The lack of competing malls in the area make this a highly desirable sight according to Nancy Adam, Vice President for real estate development for Greenwood Plaza Partners. The architectural rendering of the site plan and an artist's rendition of the planned center are illustrated in Figure 12.11.

Demalling

The term "malling" has often been used to describe the expansion of the shopping center movement. Now a new word has been coined: demalling. **Demalling** is breaking up older enclosed malls into open concept clusters of stores. Circumstances—usually aging—occasionally warrant the conversion of enclosed mall space to open concept shopping centers. The following examples illustrate this point.

Figure 12.11 Artists rendering of the architectural design and site plan of Dove Valley lifestyle center in Denver is exemplary of new trends in shopping centers. *Greenwood Plaza Partners, LLC*

One of the first climate-controlled malls in California was the Anaheim Plaza. By the 1980s newer malls outshone the aging structure. Its owner decided to turn it into an open concept center and the old mall was bulldozed.[20] To view this strategy with greater lucidity, the developer essentially removed the older department stores to make way for new discounters.

The 30-year-old, 100-store New Rochelle Mall in New York was razed to make way for a transformed mixed-use center. Reopened in 2001, the New Rochelle Center includes a transportation center, apartment and office complexes, and a strong entertainment component. An ice hockey rink, cinemas, an IMAX theater, and a hotel are part of the redevelopment. Local businesses are hoping the project will lend new life to the city.[21]

Demalling serves a valuable purpose in shopping center growth and redevelopment. However, some early outdoor centers have withstood several cycles of development as they morphed from clusters of stores to enclosed malls and back again to a collection of freestanding big box stores. Concepts are rarely finite.

Expansion

While some centers are contracting or reconfiguring, others are expanding. Some add new levels and extended parking while others construct entire wings designed to reach new markets.

The Somerset Collection—once too luxurious to be called a mere mall—is located in Troy, Michigan. Its average transaction was more than $400 per customer compared to about $45 per customer at most regional U.S. malls in the mid-1990s. The atmosphere was cultivated, quiet, with not a McDonald's in sight. The elite market was shrinking, however, and new tactics had to be implemented.

To reach an expanded market, the center added a new wing in the mid-1990s. In addition to Saks and Neiman Marcus, Hudson's and Nordstrom now anchor the mall. Although still upscale by most standards, newer specialty retailers appeal to a larger cross-section of customers. The new section is connected to the old by a moving skywalk that spans a major highway.[22]

Although the mall movement moved later and more slowly to other areas of the globe, many early centers also are ripe for renovation. The largest mall in the Middle East, the Al Ghurair Centre, is located in Dubai, United Arab Emirates. The mixed-use center combines shopping with office and apartment complexes. A massive renovation effort completed in 2000, tripled its size to approximately 800,000 square feet. One may not expect shopping centers of this size and grandeur in the Persian Gulf, but locals call it a "city within a city." Dubai is expected to grow dramatically in the next decade and can easily sustain a mall of this size.[23]

Expansion works best when centers are ripe for renovation due to age, when increased competition tips the balance, or when new viable markets initiate change.

Spatial Reconfiguration

Another area of mall development that is receiving attention is the layout and tenant allocation within centers. Faced with changing customer expectations and increasing competition—including the threat of online shopping—mall owners are reconsidering layout strategy. Some malls are positioning competing stores in clusters rather than interspersed throughout the mall, previously a common tactic. The rationale behind this shift is customer-driven. Many shoppers requested that malls situate all stores that carry children's products in the same general area, making it more convenient for parents and children. Some centers are catering to department store customers by positioning anchors in close proximity to each other. Other developers who were holdouts in encouraging discounters, now welcome stores such as Target as anchors.

Strategies used by developers to extend the lives of malls are both innovative and discordant. In one setting the outdoors is moved inside to create a new reality. In other circumstances, the outside shopping experience popular on the main streets of days past is revived. In some centers major renovation efforts are needed to keep up with burgeoning populations. The contrast in approaches indicates the complexity of shopping center development, the necessity to carefully interpret customer demand, and the ingenuity of those dedicated to building profitable businesses.

Shopping Center Management Trends

Mall management involves much more than collecting rents and seeing that the mall opens on time. Professionalism sets the tone for the shopping center industry as management assumes responsibility for marketing and productivity as well as operations. Developers are increasingly concerned about their brand equity and are promoting their names at every opportunity. These and many other issues affect shopping center operations.

Stronger Marketing Orientation

One of mall management's chief responsibilities is to plan and implement projects to increase sales of mall retailers. Motivation is strong because profit for the mall is made on percentage rent not on base rent. Therefore, if stores do well, the mall does well.

Marketing 15 years ago meant simply having a craft, car, or fashion show. Now the focus is on stronger promotions that involve most merchants and show measurable sales results. Mall loyalty programs, one-day sales, bonus bucks, birthday clubs, and programs that target specific lifestyle clusters are more effective.

Mall management maintains good relations with anchor stores while not being as involved in their marketing efforts, but works more directly with individual line stores. Mall managers receive weekly sales reports and can help retailers tailor promotions to help increase sales. Most malls offer customer service and sales training for store staffs. Adept at visual merchandising and other sales promotion strategies, they can also offer assistance in these areas.

Promoting Malls as Brands

As consolidation in the industry intensifies, developers are concerned with positioning their shopping centers competitively. Major mall developers are establishing their companies as brands as many retailers have done. Some are undertaking promotional campaigns to make their ownership status more visible to customers. Prime and Tanger outlet mall companies consistently use their corporate logo prominently on all properties in tandem with the mall's local name. Mall management is responsible for implementing programs that edify the differential advantage of each center.

Simon Property Group, the top developer in the United States, believes that customers want to know who owns the shopping centers that they patronize. The company embarked on a nationwide campaign to promote the Simon name as a brand in 1999. Using television and radio commercials, parking lot signs, new lettering on doors, and posters in its malls, the Simon brand was brandished wherever customers gathered.

These examples show the extent to which mall owners are promoting their brands as well as the brands of retailers that do business in their centers. It remains to be seen if consumers care whether or not their favorite shopping center bears a developer's brand name. It may hold true that location, tenant mix, shoppertainment potential, and need satisfaction remain the chief factors for selecting a mall.

Involvement in Re-leasing

If one mall store goes out of business, management can increase the rent when it releases the space to whatever tenant can pay the price. Or, it can increase the drawing power of the entire center by being more selective. Management, working on behalf of the developer, must have a successful re-leasing program in order to create an optimum tenant mix. Retailers that are not generating adequate revenues need to be replaced with others who will.

This process entails analyzing the existing retail mix, reclaiming some of the large older stores and subdividing others into more efficient retail operations. Recruiting innovative retailers is another objective. The role that supermarkets play as they assume new positions as anchor tenants in rejuvinated shopping centers is discussed in this chapter's From the Field.

Occasionally bumpbacks are used to create a semblance of unity when a large mall tenant moves out. Locating a smaller, usually temporary tenant, in the front portion of a space vacated by a larger retailer is called a **bumpback.** Bumpbacks utilize square footage only in the portion of a vacant site that faces out to the mall. Until a suitable replacement can be found, a smaller, temporary tenant moves in and the mall appears to be full.

The Rouse Company has been a forerunner in retenanting its properties. Finding new retailers to replace those that have gone out of business or otherwise vacated the premises is called **retenanting.** Rather than

bumpback Locating a smaller, usually temporary tenant, in the front portion of a space vacated by a much larger retailer.

From the Field: Industry Turns to Supermarket Anchors to Fill Big Boxes
By Karen M. Kroll

Like other shopping centers around the country, Knollwood Mall, in St. Louis Park, Minnesota, was left with an empty box in early 1998, after anchor Montgomery Ward closed as part of its bankruptcy filing. General Growth Properties, which owns and manages the center, was charged with filling about 90,000 square feet—nearly 20 percent of the center's leasable space. The replacement? A new Cub Food store opened in March, 1999, joining anchors T.J. Maxx and Kohl's department store.

Regional mall leasing staffs may find themselves inking a few more deals with supermarkets, say industry observers, although they agreed it may be too early to call this a trend. Retail consolidation is one contributing factor. "With the big department store chains contracting, which will continue, shopping centers are faced with filling huge boxes. They'll have to go to nontraditional uses." said Steve Claytor, president of retailing consulting group, MAS Marketing, Chicago. In addition to grocery stores, Claytor points to category killers such as Home Depot as potential anchors.

The move to nontraditional anchor tenants is especially likely to happen at centers such as Knollwood, that sit in a central location but could use a boost. Located in St. Louis Park, a first-ring Minneapolis suburb, Knollwood Mall was built in 1955 as a strip center, and was enclosed in 1980. The mall enjoys easy access from its location at the intersection of two heavily traveled thoroughfares. The demographic profile of the surrounding population is strong: Average household income is about $70,000, and 70 percent of adults have had at least some college education.

However, Knollwood has been caught in an increasingly competitive market. It is smaller than many regional malls, with 57 stores and just over 500,000 square feet. In addition, it's situated between two larger competitors: the 1.25-million-square-foot Southdale Center in Edina, and the 1-million-square-foot Ridgedale Center in Minnetonka.

Convenience has become a big selling point for the mall. Customers can get in and out quickly, and the strip center includes a dry cleaner, several take-out restaurants, a hair salon, and a Walgreens. Many customers visit the mall almost once a week, said Amy James, Knollwood's marketing director. "We're making it a place where people can get a lot done in one trip. Cub adds to that," she said.

Residents of St. Louis Park have been clamoring for additional grocery options. However, the stores that wanted to enter the market were hampered by a lack of available land. Locating Cub within Knollwood addresses both issues.

While grocery stores in larger US shopping centers appear few and far between today, they're a common sight in Europe and Australia, according to Tom Agan, a principal in the Atlanta office of retail consultants Kurt Salmon Associates. The same is true of Asia, said Anan Jain, professor and chair of the marketing department at the State University of New York at Buffalo. Both experts predict they'll become more popular in the United States.

Most agree that supermarkets won't work in every shopping center. For example, they may not co-anchor well in high-end fashion centers. However both the supermarket and center can benefit where the two are complementary. Agan said, "Some of the fun of the mall can spill over to the grocery store shopper, and some of the regular nature of the grocery store trip can spill over to the rest of the mall."

Source: *Shopping Centers Today*. Volume 20 Issue 2. February 1999:1.16.

---

abide by safe yet often boring stores, Rouse prides itself on luring offbeat and smaller independent retailers to its centers. Rouse believes a tenant mix must be adjusted to accommodate changes in trading area demographics.

retenanting Finding new retailers to replace those that have gone out of business or otherwise vacated the premises.

Presence of Service Tenants

Tenants that sell services rather than tangible products round out the retail mix in most 21st century shopping centers. Health clubs, hair and nail salons, photo studios, cellular phone service providers and a myriad of financial services are commonplace. They not only dilute the sameness syndrome but provide customers with more opportunities for one-stop shopping.

Simon Property Group set up a business division charged with bringing more services to its malls. Simon Brand Ventures added vacation timeshare, car rentals, and credit cards to the products offered to customers in many of its shopping centers.[24] It is expected that most malls will make a concerted effort to bring more service tenants to their facilities.

Management Training Programs

Participating in continuing education and professional development programs are ways in which managers advance their skills. Training programs conducted by trade associations provide certification in many areas of mall management. The International Council of Shopping Centers (ICSC) operates the University of Shopping Centers. Its curriculum covers a wide range of topics including retailing, finance, lease administration, development, design, architecture, construction, law, technology, marketing, management, and leasing. The ICSC also holds meetings annually at which industry trends and workshops are presented.

Programs such as these ensure that mall managers are well versed in the workings of shopping centers. The growing body of knowledge that helps managers cope successfully with change is equally important to possess.

Although the mall movement has slowed, it is far from over as new combinations of "shopportunities" present themselves. Customers may be fickle, value-conscious, status-oriented, or time-starved, but they are still drawn to malls. Entertainment is playing a more important role in shopping center development throughout the world. This trend is expected to continue well into the 21st century. Customers that are totally weary of traditional shopping centers can, of course, visit Internet malls.

Summary

Retail saturation affects mall development. Fewer malls are being built this decade, but those that are constructed will reach new heights. Facilities will not only serve customers' basic needs, but also provide satisfying life experiences.

Shopping centers come in eight basic forms including: neighborhood, community, regional, superregional, theme/festival, fashion/specialty, power, and outlet centers. Hybrid developments have taken on many new shapes, sizes, and characteristics. Some of these formats include: mega-malls, mixed-use centers, vertical and underground malls, and shoppertainment complexes.

Redevelopment of existing malls is an important issue. In order to compete with newer facilities, many of those built more than 20 years ago have been renovated. Others are becoming town centers, demalling, or expanding as market changes dictate.

Major developers and mall management companies throughout the world are organizations that give marketing high priority. Most are promoting their properties as brands. Developers are extending customer choices by providing innovative services in their shopping centers. Mall management also is involved with leasing and re-leasing, operations, finance, construction, and other business functions. All people involved value ongoing professional development.

Questions for Review and Discussion

1. How do the eight basic types of shopping centers differ in terms of size and draw?

2. What are the purposes of a mixed-use center? Give an example of one that you have visited or read about.

3. In what geographic areas do vertical malls thrive? What customer groups do they usually serve?

4. What trends in specialty malls seem in accord with changes in demographics and lifestyles?

5. What is the status of outlet malls in Japan? Why were Japanese shoppers slower to accept them?

6. Give an example of a mall that combines value, factory outlet shopping, and entertainment? Does this hybrid format appeal to you? Why or why not?

7. What happens to malls when they age? What strategies are developers using to make them more competitive?

8. Discuss how mall owners are branding their properties. Do you agree with this strategy? Why or why not?

Endnotes

1. www.icsc.org/srch/rsrch/census/chart. November, 2000.
2. Ibid.
3. www.icsc.org/srch/lib/shopcentdefs.html. October, 2000.
4. Ibid.
5. Ibid.
6. SCT Design Trends. "Koreatown Center Has Multicultural Appeal." Supplement to *Shopping Centers Today*, April, 2002:38.

7. Humphers, Linda. "Outlet Stats. 2001 Numbers Show Who's Calling the Shots." *Value Retail News.* May, 2002:12.

8. Ono, Yumiko. "Once-Proud Japanese Discover Outlet Malls." *Wall Street Journal.* December 30, 1998:B1,4.

9. Springer, Jon. "Grand Salt Lake to Add Value to Mix." *Shopping Centers Today.* February 1999:25,28.

10. Knight, Mary Beth. "A New Set of Values.*" Chain Store Age.* February 1999:143.

11. Union Station Fact Sheet. Washington, DC. 1998.

12. Mander, Edmund. "Disneyland Paris to Get Grown-up Fun—a Mall." *Shopping Centers Today.* November, 1998:35.

13. *SCTXtra.* "Stern's Leaving Manhattan Mall." *Shopping Centers Today.* International Council of Shopping Centers. September 25, 2000:1.

14. *Europe 2000.* Supplement. "Balancing Act." *Shopping Centers Today.* International Council of Shopping Centers. April, 1999:29.

15. "Forum Shops to get Another Expansion." *SCT Xtra.* Newsletter. Vol. 7. No. 17. April 29, 2002:1.

16. Bird, Laura. "Move Over Mall Rats, Wild Beasts Are Taking Your Turf." *Wall Street Journal.* July 8, 1997:B1.

17. Tran, Khanh T.L. "Sony Builds Big-Box Entertainment." *Wall Street Journal.* June 23, 1999:B12.

18. Mander, Edmund. "Polar Malls Offer Cold Comfort." *Shopping Centers Today.* July, 1999:1,63,65.

19. Hazel, Debra. "Suburban Power Center Takes Cue from City Streets." *Shopping Centers Today.* October 1998: 24.

20. Pacelle, Mitchell. "The Aging Shopping Mall Must Either Adapt or Die." *Wall Street Journal.* April 16, 1996: B1,16.

21. Ferguson, Stuart. "Town Bets on a Hollywood Happy Ending." *Wall Street Journal.* September 2, 1998: B10.

22. Edelson, Sharon. "Somerset's Bridge to New Customers." *Women's Wear Daily.* August 14, 1995: 12.

23. Warson, Albert. "Renovation Reguilding City of Gold's Downtown." *Shopping Centers Today.* International Council of Shopping Centers. April, 1999:10

24. Pacelle, Mitchell. "Simon DeBartolo Group to Invite Wide Variety of Firms Into Malls." *Wall Street Journal.* August 29, 1997: B3.

Chapter 13

Store Design and Visual Merchandising

Learning Objectives

After completing this chapter you should be able to:

- Summarize the components of store image.

- Evaluate how retail store design is planned and implemented.

- Discern how the elements of art and principles of design work are used in visual merchandising.

- Identify the options available to the visual merchandiser in both exterior and interior display.

- Detect why safety and security are considered part of store planning and design.

Figure 13.1 The invitation to enter Caché is apparent: faced-out merchandise, clear signage, and a welcoming facade (See p. 372.)

Striking window displays, tantalizing tables of sale merchandise, your favorite tunes playing in the background, nostalgic aromas, and big screen video are all elements of store design. The combination of things seen and unseen is the force that draws customers into a store. It also may be the reason they choose to not enter. Because many retailers carry the same or similar merchandise, retailers must create a differential advantage. One way to do that is to carefully consider the various components of store image.

Store planners create excitement through traffic flow, building materials, fixtures, electronics, lighting, sound, and scent. Visual merchandisers use these tools plus artistic expression when they work to make their stores compelling places to shop.

Activity in the retail environment affects store design. Customers are difficult to impress—largely due to stimulation from the media, intense retail competition, and changes in society. Mirroring the growing importance of technology in our lives, many stores of the 21st century are monuments to the electronic age. For example, Niketown in Atlanta features sleek black decor. Cash registers are barely visible in the well-engineered service desk consoles. Eight huge video screens welcome customers in a large rotunda area. Stock from the store's lower level is sent to the selling floor via Plexiglas pneumatic tubes. The space-age-techno meets power-sports theme is articulated well.

Store design is the result of contemporary social influences. Enter a specialty store filled with candles, herbs, and books on spirituality. Notice the astrological theme in the rich blue and gold decor. Inhale the patchouli incense and enjoy the music of a sitar. Changes in lifestyles have made it possible for retail stores like the one described to thrive.

There is a fine line between the architectural features of store design and the promotional aspect—visual merchandising. Because of this close relationship, both topics are covered in this chapter.

Store Image

store image A combination of concrete and esoteric factors that contribute to the total impression customers have of a retailer.

Retailers need distinct identity. **Store image** is the combination of concrete and esoteric factors that contributes to the total impression customers have of a retailer. The perceived image that retailers have of their stores should coincide with those experienced by customers. Store layout and design are important components of store image, but many other factors are involved:

- *Physical appearance of the store.* Interior and exterior architectural features, window displays, fixtures, and traffic patterns are physical aspects of the store.
- *Merchandise quality and pricing policy.* Merchandise may be high quality and high priced, low quality and low priced, or any combination of steps in between. All are valid images if the objectives of retailers and impressions of customers mesh.
- *Ambiance.* **Ambiance** is a mood evoked by the use of tangible and intangible store design tools. It is the feeling brought forth by something as simple as a scent in the air, such as "Sun-ripened Raspberry" or "Juniper Breeze" in Bath & Body Works stores. Ambiance also is affected by more complex factors such as subtle color variations in a carpet. Ambiance is one reason why customers return to a store—or Web site—again and again.
- *Employee attitude and appearance.* The impressions made by sales associates, greeters, and managers reflect store image. Customers respond to employees who are dressed appropriately and share similar physical characteristics with them. Apparel stores in which sales associates are dressed in store merchandise sell more merchandise. A sales associate dressed appropriately in Club Monaco clothing is shown in Figure 13.2. In contrast, individuals who have multiple body piercing or green spiked hair may not encourage sales in a conservative department store, but they would in Hot Topic.
- *Advertising.* The face that retailers put before the public is a powerful aspect of store image. One determinant of image is the use of white space in a print advertisement. **White space** is the portion of an advertisement that is not used for type or illustration. Usually, the more white space used in an advertisement, the more upscale the store. Conversely, the less white space used in an advertisement, the more likely the store is a discount operation. This concept is discussed in Chapter 17.
- *Services.* Retailers do not always compete on the basis of price, quality of merchandise, location, or physical features of their stores. Many customers return more often if they are assured of courteous, knowledgeable service and hassle-free transactions. Customer service and extended retail

Figure 13.2 Appearance of sales personnel is an attribute of store image recognized by Club Monaco. Sales associates are encouraged to dress in appropriate apparel—preferably that made by the company.

ambiance The mood evoked by the use of tangible and intangible store design tools.

white space The portion of an advertisement that is not used for type or illustration.

services such as free delivery or gift wrapping also contribute to store image.

Once retailers have found an image that works for them, they usually stay with it. However, some stores have successfully changed image in order to seek new markets or update their retail persona. Dunkin' Donuts is a franchise chain that sells coffee, donuts, and other baked goods from almost 5,000 stores in the United States and abroad. The company's image has changed appreciably in the 50 years it has been in business. When Dunkin' Donuts opened in 1950, products were served from luncheonette counters by wait-staff. The menu was limited to coffee and donuts, and the decor was simple and utilitarian. Most stores were in downtown areas. Fifty years later, Dunkin' Donuts stores are more colorful and inviting, counters are self-service, and the menu has expanded to sandwiches, bagels, and their famous Coolattas. Many units are freestanding and most provide cafe-style tables and chairs.

Among other factors, image changes reflect shifts in customer lifestyles, competition, and company goals. Consistency of image also is important, but retailers cannot ignore the forces of change.

Store Design Process

Store planners give stores their visual personality by thinking like customers. An honest answer to "What would make me interested in shopping here?" lends impetus to the process. The integration of all aspects of the retail store to achieve desired image, operational efficiency, and ultimately build traffic and sales are the anticipated outcomes of store design.

Objectives of Store Design

Generating sales is the principal motivation behind effective store planning. Specific objectives of store design address many factors including financial goals, operational efficiencies, aesthetic concerns, and competitive advantages. Three objectives are considered.

To Increase Sales and Profits The main objective of store design is to increase sales and profits, therefore all merchandise categories should be carefully evaluated. Retail store designers work with management to determine prime positions for best sellers, seasonal goods, special purchases, and slower moving merchandise. Stock turnover rates also influence placement of merchandise. All affect sales and profits.

To Increase Operational Efficiency One of the reasons most national chains adopt common storefronts and layouts is to present a consistent image. This practice also increases operational efficiency by carefully delineating space requirements for each product classification or department. Usually planograms are used to guarantee adherence to store layout and merchandise presentation standards. Developed by central headquarters, **planograms** are detailed scale drawings that illustrate precisely where each fixture and piece of merchandise is to be placed in a store. Less is likely to go wrong when established practices are followed by all stores in the chain.

ACNielsen company produces software that helps retailers interpret sales data in terms of specific facilities planning. The geodemographic-based planogram software called SPACEMAN can be used to allocate space in a cosmetics department based on the percentage of racial groups living in the area, for example.[1]

To Avert the Sameness Syndrome Many shoppers in regional malls go from one specialty shop to another without knowing the names of the particular retailers they visit. The redundancies in merchandise make it difficult to differentiate among stores—even though each company may believe it appeals to a different market segment. However, establishment of a distinct identity through store design helps overcome the sameness syndrome.

Mechanics of Store Design

Before creating a store design, retailers identify the target market, store image, merchandise assortment, and philosophy of selling. Once that is accomplished, theme, space allocation, and implementation costs are addressed.

Setting the Theme Theme is the subject of a written work or recurring melody in a piece of music. Applied to store design it is the story the store tells, the song it sings to customers. Look at the huge reptilian-leg pillars in front of the F.A.O. Schwarz toy store in Figure 13.3. It is easy to see that the theme is fun, fantasy, and adventure. In this case materials, color, and size communicate the message.

Configuring Space The next step is to establish a comprehensive plan for the building space, with input not only from designers and planners, but also from merchandisers and managers. Configuration of the store is dependent on planned sales and merchandising objectives. For example, Liz

planograms Detailed scale drawings that illustrate precisely where each fixture and piece of merchandise is to be placed in a store.

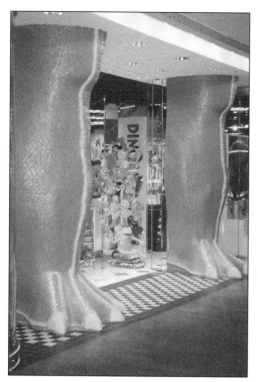

Figure 13.3 An exciting theme is particularly important for mall-based retailers that must differentiate themselves from their competitors. FAO Schwarz giant reptilian pillars encourage children of all ages to enter the store.

Claiborne is an important apparel resource for all department stores. Because sales volume is high and the business is profitable, choice square footage is dedicated to the company's merchandise. Return on investment relative to merchandise placement is important to retailers.

Seasonality also affects use of space. In many stores an important holiday, back-to-school period, or anticipated changes in the climate initiate new allocations of selling space. Several measures are used to help retailers determine the proper amount of floor space for merchandise categories or departments and are discussed later in the chapter.

Determining Costs In planning the store, costs must be anticipated. These cover architectural design, construction, and mechanical engineering systems; interior design, fixtures, and display elements; and all operational equipment. Planning and construction time schedules also affect cost estimates.

Store planners carefully consider financial issues. Construction costs rise every year. Retailers need to invest in stores that can compete successfully for many years. These two independent ideas often create discord. Designing a store requires constant evaluation of new techniques, styles, materials, methods of fabrication, and installation.

Details of the Physical Structure

Before the customer steps over the threshold, the store is selling. Every detail of the facade, display windows, parking areas, and entry canopies creates an impression. Much thought goes into this phase of store design.

The Invitation The exterior design of free-standing buildings or shopping centers welcomes customers first. Elements such as signage, window display, entrances, protection from weather, and distinctive character are combined in an arresting architectural form. At the same time, the form is influenced by the store's interior functional needs. The facade of Cache, a women's apparel shop shown in Figure 13.1, is in tune with its image. It invites the customer to enter.

Imaginative window displays also are an aspect of exterior design. Variations are based on location—whether in a central business district, shopping mall, or free-standing store—and depend on accepted standards of taste, use of materials, construction techniques, and security factors. They are commonly called the eyes of the store and when used well are important communicators of store image.

Floor Plans The basic guidelines for laying out a retail selling floor are (1) fully utilize all of the space available and (2) avoid sacrificing function for aesthetics. The ultimate goal of store layout plans is to maximize sales. There are two basic floor plan designs and several alternative arrangements:

Figure 13.4 Grid floor plans allow retailers like Costco Wholesale to maximize square footage and maintain low margins by displaying merchandise efficiently and inexpensively.

■ *Grid.* Stemming from a gridiron pattern such as a football field, grid floor plans are rigid spatial configurations. **Grid floor plans** are linear geometric floor arrangements with aisles and fixtures parallel or perpendicular to walls. Discounters, category killers, supermarkets, superstores, and drugstores are stores that use a grid floor plan. Maximum available square footage is allotted for merchandise placement. Costco Wholesale employs a grid layout as shown in Figure 13.4.

■ *Freeform.* Although freeform floor plans are less rigid, there is no less emphasis on traffic flow, placement of departments, merchandise, and fixtures. Less structured floor arrangements with emphasis on engineered traffic flow are called **freeform floor plans**. Upscale department stores, specialty stores, and others tend to use freeform layouts. A freeform floor plan for Lots of Toys, a virtual toy store is illustrated in Figure 13.5.

In addition to basic floor plans, several variations on grid and freeform designs are used by retailers. Racetrack, pathway, diagonal, and curved plans are some of the options available.

■ *Racetrack.* Racetrack floor plans encourage customers to shop the entire store. Floor arrangements in which elements of grid and freeform are combined to engineer customers around the entire store by means of oval shaped walkways are called **racetrack floor plans**. Walkways are designated by the materials used in their construction. Sears indicates their racetrack by using tile flooring, while other parts of the floor are carpeted. Saks Fifth Avenue uses wood parquet flooring to indicate the racetrack. Smaller stores can also benefit from this design. A racetrack circling a central cashier station provides excellent traffic flow while providing security.

■ *Pathway plans.* Particularly suited to large, one-level stores, pathway plans are good architectural organizers. **Pathway floor plans** engineer traffic from the front of the store to the rear and back again by means of designated

grid floor plans Linear geometric floor arrangements with aisles and fixtures parallel or perpendicular to walls.

freeform floor plans Less structured floor arrangements with emphasis on engineered traffic flow.

CYBERSCOOP

For a tour of a virtual reality toy store, go to **acadweb.snhu.edu/faculty/poloian_lynda**. Click on "Principles of Retailing" then follow your way to Chapter 13 and the Lots of Toys store. Does this retailer use a grid or freeform layout? What draws people into a store like this?

racetrack floor plans Floor arrangements in which elements of grid and freeform are combined to engineer customers around the entire store by means of oval shaped walkways.

pathway floor plans Engineer traffic from the front of the store to the rear and back again by means of designated walkways.

walkways. Stew Leonard's, a famous dairy store in Norwalk, Connecticut, uses a floor plan that resembles a roadway. The pathway actually winds its way through the entire store, like the famed yellow brick road in *Wizard of Oz*.

- *Diagonal plans*. For small, self-service stores, a diagonal plan is optimal. Aisles are placed at 45 degree angles to the side walls. The cashier is usually near the front, with sight lines to all areas of the store. Drug, video, and record stores sometimes use the diagonal plan since it maximizes visibility of many small items on display.

- *Curved plans*. For boutiques, salons, or other high-quality stores, curved plans create inviting environments for customers. Graceful curved walls or counters encourage traffic flow and enhance eye appeal. More costly to construct than angular or square plans, the results can be dramatic when a focal point such as a water fountain is placed in the center.

Traffic Flow Variables Traffic flow is closely related to type of floor plan, aisle width, lighting, merchandise and fixture placement, and other intangible factors. Traffic flow engineering refers to the methods used to draw customers efficiently through the store. It is based on several assumptions. First, given an equal opportunity to go left or right, 85 percent of customers will turn right and do so at a 45 degree angle. This may happen because approximately the same percentage of the population is right handed. Second, many customers enter a store to browse and are not on a shopping mission that would take them directly to a specific area of the store. Third, studies show that males and females have different shopping habits and preferences regarding store access routes. For example, men prefer to access mall stores directly from the parking lot. Women prefer to enter through the mall's general entrances before visiting specific stores.[2]

Whenever possible, traffic studies should be conducted to determine natural flow and frequently used areas. Floor plans must also accommodate nonmovable elements such as escalators, elevators, stairways, and entrances.

Space Allocation and Productivity Once a general floor plan has been determined, space must be allocated to each product classification. Square footage is not assigned equally to all merchandise categories. High-volume or high-margin goods deserve prime square footage, which is why jewelry, small leather goods, cosmetics, and fragrances frequently are positioned in high traffic, central areas in department stores. This information is used by planners as they allocate appropriate square footage to departments based on contribution to store sales.

Aisle width and adequate personal space are other details to be considered. In hardline departments, about four feet of space is allowed between racks or displays. In soft goods areas, width may be slightly less. Customers are uncomfortable if adequate space for viewing goods is not granted, and if they are forced to shop too close to other customers. Studies have shown that if a customer is brushed by a fellow shopper, he or she may choose to move on, rather than complete a purchase.

The positioning of sale merchandise varies according to the philosophy of the retailer. Some retailers believe that sale merchandise should be prominently positioned at the front of the store. Proponents of an opposite tactic want sale merchandise positioned at the rear of the store. They believe that customers should work a little harder to find sale items, and that they should be exposed to higher margin and perhaps newer merchandise as they work their way back to the sale rack.

In grocery stores frequently purchased items like milk are often located at the back of the store. Encouraging customers to make impulse purchases as they make their way to or from the milk is the objective.

Sales per square foot is the standard unit of measurement for productivity in most conventional stores used as examples throughout this text. However, sales per square meter is used in some foreign stores. Sales per linear foot is used to measure productivity in supermarkets that rely on shelf space for merchandise presentation.

Simple sales per square foot figures are helpful in making decisions on space allocations. Average sales per foot numbers vary greatly by type of store and merchandise category. For example, cosmetics departments generally earn greater sales per square foot than children's clothing departments. High-performing discount stores like Wal-Mart typically earn more dollars per square foot than other similar discounters, but less than most grocery stores. Many factors affect productivity, but comparing sales per square foot with retail industry averages is useful in the early stages of store

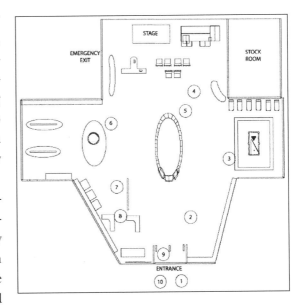

Figure 13.5 *Lots of Toys* Freeform Store Layout

1. Image is conveyed before the customer steps over the threshold. Appropriate signage, well chosen construction materials, and an arresting window display urge entry into Lots of Toys.

2. Eighty-five percent of the time, customers will turn right upon entering a store. Positioning hot sellers, like scooters, to the right of the entrance ensures high visibility.

3. Pool tables, dart boards, and arcade games are shown in a game room setting so that customers can relate to products in a lifestyle setting.

4. Entertainment is a key factor in store design today. Big screen video screen, playhouse, and theater-like setting encourage involvement with merchandise.

5. Motion-sensitive displays, like this centrally positioned electric train, are used to attract attention.

6. Interactive toys, such as radio-control cars, captivate young shoppers. They are placed within easy reach at child-sized display units.

7. The use of repetition as a display technique encourages impulse purchases as customers approach the check out area.

8. All customers expect easy access to checkout and customer service counters.

9. After passing through the radio frequency identification (RFID) security detection system, customers exit directly to the parking lot.

10. Thanks for shopping at Lots of Toys. Come back again!

layout planning. However, this method only considers sales, not contribution to gross margin or profitability. More sophisticated measures are used when more information is available.

The **space productivity index** is an advanced tool that is used to help retailers determine optimum merchandise placement. The index compares the proportion of a stores gross margin achieved by specific merchandise category to the proportion of selling space used for the merchandise. For example, a ratio of 1.0 indicates that the amount of square footage allocated to a department or merchandise category is in direct proportion to the contribution to gross margin it generates. A ratio below 1.0 indicates that the merchandise is not selling well and that space allocated to it should be decreased. A rating over 1.0 means that the merchandise category is performing better than average. This might indicate that the department should be enlarged, or at least monitored closely for possible change in the future.

When a store is adding a new merchandise category or opening for the first time, it is impossible to use past sales figures to allocate space. Most trade associations, including the National Retail Federation, publish data on existing retail stores that can be used as benchmarks for new ventures. Determination of return on investment relative to merchandise placement is an important productivity measure for retailers.

space productivity index Advanced tool used to help retailers determine optimum merchandise placement.

Tangibles and Intangibles of Store Design

Flexibility comprises the creative core of successful store designs. Tangible features include fixtures that are usually moveable. Concept shops and designer boutiques, constructed from modular wall units, are semipermanent, allowing for easy reconfiguring when the next important trend debuts. Intangible features are used to create atmosphere in a store. These include sound, lighting, and scent.

Selecting Fixtures Fixtures have traditionally been subdivided into wall systems and floor fixtures. Full-height perimeter partitions and high partitions placed between departments are called **wall systems.** High wall systems house many mechanical subsystems of the building: lighting, heating, ventilating, and air conditioning. A full-height partition is attractive and creates a strong surface for merchandise placement. However, wall systems obstruct the line of sight and make it more difficult for sales associates to serve customers effectively. High walls also create more security concerns.

wall systems Full-height perimeter partitions and high partitions placed between departments.

Slat wall is a building material often used on wall surfaces. Its tongue-in-groove construction simplifies merchandise display since a variety of hooks, shelves, and other hardware can be hung from the grooves. A disadvantage is that slat wall is sometimes overused, making it seem less exclusive to some observers.

Floor fixtures are display units designed to house and present merchandise. Included in this category are showcases, tables, gondolas, counters, platforms, pedestals, garment racks, and point-of-sale fixtures. **Gondolas** are moveable, bin-type display fixtures frequently used for promotional merchandise. Floor fixtures are generally prefabricated and prefinished. Most are relocated seasonally or as merchandise emphasis changes. The forms, materials, and colors of fixtures should be compatible with one another, the merchandise, and the store image. Fixtures can be either custom designed or selected from manufacturers' stock catalogs. Some are built of knockdown metal parts that allow for simple on-site fabrication.

Floor fixtures often are positioned on an angle to encourage traffic flow, create more effective display areas, and add harmony to the overall aesthetics of the store.

Creating Ambiance As important to store design as the floor plan itself is the creation of ambiance. The intangibles of store design such as lighting, sound, and aroma are used to create overall atmosphere. It is often the first expression of image perceived by customers. Walk into Blockbuster and what impresses you first? If you are like most customers, probably whatever video is playing on the big screen. The sounds and visual imagery are welcoming, pique interest, and ultimately encourage sales.

Lighting is a significant intangible element of store design. With the vast array of lighting options in today's market, care should be taken when deciding whether to light floors or individual displays. Track lighting is used in many specialty stores because it is flexible, creates spotlight effects on merchandise, and lends a theatrical flair to store design. **Track lighting** is display lighting that consists of moveable units mounted on vertical or horizontal tracks. For discount stores, overhead lighting is usually the choice. Long fluorescent tubes that cast consistent, bright light are installed in ceilings. Since intense light fatigues many customers, retailers should underlight rather than overlight, or risk defeating their purpose of encouraging sales. This chapter's From the Field illuminates the lighting design concepts of Niketown stores.

The aroma that permeates a store conveys image, and may influence the amount of time customers spend in the store. Some retailers pipe the aroma of branded fragrances into the vestibules of their stores. Shopping malls also introduce pleasant scents into their common areas. Scents of fresh brewed coffee and baked cinnamon buns not only draw customers to

Did You Know?

In an attempt to bolster holiday trade, a HyVee Food and Drug store in Omaha, Nebraska, displayed Barbie dolls and Tickle Me Elmos on top of frozen food cases. They also positioned a model train on top of the salad bar. What next, a Cadillac on display in the parking lot? HyVee did that, too!
Source: *Wall Street Journal.* November 19, 1997:B1.

floor fixtures Display units designed to house and present products.

gondolas Moveable, bin-type display fixtures frequently used for promotional merchandise.

track lighting Display lighting that consists of moveable units mounted on vertical or horizontal tracks.

From the Field: Sporting a New Look . . . Nike Tones Down Its Lighting Scheme
By Jenny Schnetzer

Niketown: It's a brash, in-your-face retail experience. And theatrical lighting has long been an important part of the mix. But for Nike's Miami store, it tapped Seattle-based Candela to tone things down a bit with an entirely different lighting design and a cool attitude.

According to Megan Strawn, lighting designer at Candela, the biggest problems with the previous Niketown stores were spotty lighting and intrusive light fixtures. In addition to implementing a more uniform lighting scheme, Strawn says, "Nike wanted to integrate the lighting into the architecture so that it wasn't about the lighting, it was more about the merchandise. "Nike also desired the flexibility to change the colors of the individual sport pavilions and re-aim the fixtures to wherever the merchandise is placed.

For the two-level, 18,000-square-foot Miami store, designers skipped the open ceilings and the dark, moody feel of traditional Niketowns

in favor of a lighter, cleaner and decidedly more architectural feel. The dark wood typically used in other stores is absent here, where lighter finishes prevail. Strawn says, "There was more thought put into what happens above your head. And though it's still an experience, it's not the *theatrical* experience that you get when you walk into other Niketowns."

One of the biggest changes in the lighting design was the use of metal halide lamps in lieu of the low-voltage lighting used in previous store designs. Besides a longer life and lower energy costs, the lamps offer greater flexibility. For example, Candela used light to delineate some of the different pavilions by putting colored gels on the uplight to give each pavilion its own color. So if Nike decided to change the color scheme, it could simply change the gels.

Despite the new look, some common elements prevail. Nike likes to mix its branding elements with local

flavor. So, Miami took cues from its Latin connection to emphasize a soccer theme. Graphics in the entryway, and throughout the store, depict soccer players in action.

And in Town Square, a gathering place in all Niketown stores, a media show runs Nike commercials, sports videos, etc. at 20 minute intervals on an 8-by-15-foot video screen. The main store lighting dims and the music changes to indicate the start of the next show.

The store's new look is evident immediately. In the circular entrance—called the "decompression chamber"—customers bask in a blue glow. Strawn says the entryway creates a transition for customers, taking them out of the Miami heat, letting them breath and preparing them for the Nike experience.

Source: *VM+SD* Magazine, November, 2000:41. ©ST Media Group International, Inc.

food courts or specialty stores, but also are uplifting and add to the general pleasure of the shopping experience. This translates to increased sales for retailers.

These are the tools of the trade. The fine line between science and art becomes more apparent as visually powerful merchandise presentations are created.

Visual Merchandising

The best music groups and the best stores have a lot in common. They both relate to the widest possible audience and attempt to convey messages to their ticket holders or customers. Both abilities contribute to their continuing popularity. Customers in concert halls or stores want action. They want assurances that they are seeing the best show around. When customers share favorable experiences with their peers and purchase CDs, this is the true measure of worth for performers. The same concept holds true for retailers. The store is their concert hall.

The impact of visual merchandising is profound. There are several reasons for this. Much of the merchandise in directly competing stores is virtually identical. Further, barring influences from advertising or loyalty programs, a customer's first contact may depend largely on whether a convenient parking spot can be found.

Finally, there is an overabundance of retail selling space in most developed countries, and an oversupply of goods. Because obstacles need to be overcome, visual merchandising assumes great importance. Stores that create engaging visual presentations in their stores encourage sales.

Visual merchandising is an art—integrating a pallet of color, signage, mannequins, fixtures, lighting, ambiance, and merchandise. Visual merchandising communicates store image to customers whether that image stresses service, quality, or prestige.

Merchandise Presentation

When a customer approaches a store or department, featured merchandise is the first thing they see, followed by displays on the back wall. Areas that show major sales potential are sometimes called thrust areas. **Thrust areas** are prime locations in stores used for the display of new, high-margin, or seasonal items. As sales escalated, placing DVD players in thrust areas was an expected practice. Placement of merchandise influences traffic patterns. Customers will gravitate to faced-out merchandise that is positioned around a racetrack or other high-traffic part of the store. **Faced-out** placement occurs when merchandise is displayed on fixtures so customers can see the product head-on. Fixtures called four-ways or quads often are used for this purpose. Cosmetic counters positioned at a slight angle, allow maximum exposure of products and encourage traffic flow.

Key areas in stores that are used for rotating displays or small temporary departments are called **swing areas**. What is a trim-a-tree shop in December may be a swimwear boutique in June. Swing areas capture attention and guide customers to other key areas of the store.

Customers want to be entertained, excited, and educated. Theatrical elements can be used to lead customers to the merchandise and to encourage purchases. Effective presentation uses repeated patterns, angles that make eyes focus on thrust areas, vibrant or soothing colors and incongruities. Visual merchandisers who create action see the results of their efforts in the store's increased sales. An aura of theater can be summoned in all kinds of retail stores, as illustrated throughout this text. Figure 13.6 illustrates a

thrust areas Prime locations in stores used for the display of new, high-margin, or seasonal items.

faced-out Placement that occurs when merchandise is displayed on fixtures so customers can see the product head-on.

swing areas Key areas in stores that are used for rotating displays or small temporary departments.

Figure 13.6 Even humble products can be displayed with theatrical flair like this end-cap profusion of radishes in a Carrefour hypermarket. End-caps are popular display formats in big box stores.

CYBERSCOOP

For a little sensory sampling, visit **www.cdnow.com** and hear a sound clip from your favorite CD. Does the addition of sound on a Web site affect your decision to make a purchase? Is the atmosphere created by online retailers comparable to the atmosphere in conventional stores?

Carrefour hypermarket display that brings visual excitement to simple vegetables.

Other senses, in addition to visual, should not be overlooked in merchandise presentation. For example, product information is communicated through touch. When Lord and Taylor positions its fuzzy cashmere sweaters in bins close to escalators, more than an attractive sale price is bringing customers to the registers.

Art Elements

Visual merchandising employs the same basic art elements as do all recognized art forms. The main difference is that visual merchandising creations are temporary in nature and have a commercial purpose rather than a purely aesthetic one. The success of any display is measured by the resulting sales. The artistic merit of the display itself is a qualitative measurement of image. Art elements refer to the building blocks of all art forms—line, texture, color, and weight. They are considered when creating displays.

■ *Line.* The merchandise itself inspires line and imparts special meaning to the customer. Straight lines produce feelings of precision, rigidity, and directness. Curved lines give feelings of flexibility and continuity. Horizontal lines represent calm, quiet, and restfulness, and may also give the impression of width. Diagonal lines indicate action and movement. Lines join together to form two and three dimensional shapes that may be of any geometric configuration.

■ *Texture.* Texture is the look or feel of an object's surface. Texture may be real or artificial. The element of texture is vital in a display, for it creates either harmony or contrast. Real texture is inherent in the merchandise itself; examples are the softness of silk or the coarseness of straw. The customer can easily detect real texture by touch. Using artificial texture makes something appear different from what it really is, such as when faux marble is sponged or painted on a table top.

■ *Color.* Color is a dramatic and powerful tool in displays and general store design. Color can be used to identify shops within the store, as a theme, to indicate a promotion or to provide impact for staple—but sometimes dull—merchandise. It can also be used to create a specific mood. Display artists first consider the colors of merchandise or packaging that is to be used. Then they build a color story that will provoke interest, but also one to which customers will relate. Colors have psychological overtones and personal associations. The primary colors—red, blue, and yellow—have the most shelf appeal which is why they are frequently seen in supermarket packaging. Blue is the most popular color in the United States, but not necessarily in all cultures. In some Hispanic cultures, lavender is a color of mourning, so retailers mounting a spring dress display might be wise to acknowledge this tradition. When illuminating merchandise, color theory can be used. Complementary colors, those that are opposites on the color wheel, provoke strong color contrasts. Red and green are complementary colors, for example. If a group of emerald green dresses is presented in a window display, putting red gels on track lights will make the green fabric appear more vibrant. Probably the most important element of visual merchandising, color is inherent in each piece of merchandise, prop and fixture. Visual merchandisers try to elicit psychological reactions from consumers through an understanding of color.

■ *Weight.* Every piece of merchandise has an actual weight and an optical weight. **Optical weight** is the amount an object appears to weigh rather than what it actually weighs. A foam pillow covered with dark fur may look heavy because of the texture and color, for example, but in reality it is very lightweight because of the materials. The optical weight of an object is more important in terms of visual merchandising and balance in a display. Shape, color, and texture will determine the optical weight of an object, and this will determine its placement in a display. Lighting can also affect the optical weight of an object.

optical weight The amount an object appears to weigh rather than what it actually weighs.

Design Principles

Design principles refer to the methods used to manage space in order to create unity within a work of art or advertisement. The perception that all items belong together is called **unity**. Principles of design—balance, repetition, proportion, contrast, dominance, and rhythm—have their place in visual merchandising. If elements all are properly coordinated, unity is achieved in the display. These principles also relate to two dimensional space and are important when creating effective advertising layouts.

unity The sense of wholeness that is achieved when elements are well integrated in artwork, advertising, or display.

■ *Balance.* Display artists choose either symmetrical or asymmetrical balance when building displays. In either case, the display is divided in half by an imaginary line that serves as a central axis. **Symmetrical balance** involves positioning items on either side of a center line so that they are equally weighted optically. Items can be centered horizontally or vertically. Symmetrical balance, also is called formal balance. Equal amounts are placed on each side of an imaginary line, not necessarily duplication of exact items in the display. Using asymmetrical balance, also called informal balance, the

symmetrical balance Positioning items on either side of a center line so that they are equally weighted optically.

Figure 13.7 The Great Wall of China window display uses the element of repetition to show the depth of assortment carried by a table-top specialty store.

asymmetrical balance Positioning items on either side of a center line so that they are not equally weighted optically.

items on either side of the imaginary line do not repeat each other. **Asymmetrical balance** is the positioning items on either side of a center line so that the are not equally weighted optically. They appear unified because they draw upon other design principles such as proportion or contrast to create weight.

■ *Repetition.* Repetition is the regular occurrence of an object throughout a display. Repetition may be accomplished through the use of color or form. The china display in Figure 13.7, illustrates that the same item duplicated several times may bring more recognition or meaning to viewers. Several mannequins positioned in a row create more impact than one. Using the same background in a series of windows can also create repetition. Repetition helps customers register a theme and reinforces purchasing behavior.

■ *Proportion.* Proportion acknowledges a proper relationship between objects and spaces in displays. Sometimes displays are purposely out of proportion. Oversized display elements create more attention than conventionally sized units. For example, Diesel uses over-sized custom shelving units that spell out D-I-E-S-E-L when viewed from the street. Unless you step back to recognize the retailer's intent, up close they appear as contemporary fixtures. A custom Diesel fixture is illustrated in Figure 13.8.

■ *Contrast.* Contrast occurs when tension is created between props and merchandise or between any of the elements of visual merchandising design. It must be dealt with carefully and skillfully. Contrast is used as an attention getter. For example, stark white modular furniture displayed against an ink black background uses color contrast to make the furniture stand out and arrest the eye of the customer.

■ *Dominance.* A focal point, or dominance, is necessary if a display is to be entirely successful. This is the main point to which customers' eyes are drawn. Dominance can be accomplished through unusual placement of merchandise, eye movement, use of color, or lighting.

■ *Rhythm.* Rhythm refers to the feeling of visual movement that brings the eye through all aspects of a display. It also transmits unity to the observer. Items in a display are positioned skillfully so that the eye is lead from one piece of merchandise to another. Eye flow is based on the assumption that most people in Western cultures read left to right. Since this is not the case in some Eastern cultures, rhythm is established by creating a right to left flow.

Although technically not a principle of design, motion is used by visual merchandisers to attract attention. It is most related to rhythm. Turntables in a window display, spinning pinwheels, jiggling signs, round-racks in perpetual motion—all are used to not only capture customers' attention, but keep it for a longer time. A window display at a French Connection store on London's Kings Road featured three rotating black and red circles behind three well-placed mannequins dressed in black. All sidewalk traffic stopped and stared.

Art elements and design principles are the aesthetic backbone of the visual merchandising trade. They are used in the creation of window displays. Often called the eyes of the stores, windows are used to attract attention, create interest in the items on display, and urge customers into the store to purchase merchandise.

Figure 13.8 Custom shelving units spell out D-I-E-S-E-L in oversized letters for all to see in or out of the store.

Window Displays

Window displays have only a few seconds to stop a passersby. For shoppers who are already in the store, an interior display has a bit more time in which to make its point.

Windows are not as common in contemporary shopping centers as they are in downtown sites. Most shopping malls are constructed with few or no outside windows; the emphasis is on interior display. Some anchor stores have outside windows, but it is not the norm for line stores. Windows project store image and indicate the character and the quality of merchandise carried. In order to bring customers into the store, windows should be warm and inviting.

Several different kinds and configurations of windows exist. This section will describe open and closed-back windows, glass storefronts, and shadow-boxes, which are some of the more popular types. Whether a store is free-standing, located on a downtown street, or in a shopping mall, these types can easily be discerned.

- *Open-back.* Open-back windows combine the window and the selling floor itself through physical and visual unity. They are used by smaller stores because they create the illusion of more interior space than really exists. Glass panels sometimes are used to permit the customer to see through

Figure 13.9 Shadowbox displays can be effective inside or outside a store. Jewelry is presented with a strong point of view in Neiman Marcus.

shadowboxes Small display windows located in-store or out, often used to display luxury items.

step format Display that begins at a low point on one side and climbs incrementally to a higher point in a diagonal arrangement.

the window into the store while providing some protection for the merchandise on display.

■ *Closed-back.* Closed-back windows are the favorite of creative display people because they are like a stage. Since the back of the window is partitioned off from the store, customer focus is totally on the merchandise. Proper lighting can turn a closed-back window into a magical display location.

■ *Glass storefronts.* Some merchants consider modern glass storefronts, through which customers see directly into a store, more valuable than open-back or closed-back windows. The entire store interior becomes visible, and the interaction of customers, merchandise, and salespeople produces a lively setting by day and night.

■ *Shadowboxes.* When the objective is to use little space but create a visual oasis, shadowboxes are used. **Shadowboxes** are small display windows located in-store or out, often used to display luxury items. Since they are closed off from distractions, shadowboxes are small but eye catching. A behind-the-counter shadowbox is illustrated in Figure 13.9.

In-store Displays

Window displays provide the initial attraction, but the store interior is where visual merchandising truly assists in selling. Increased emphasis on in-store display has prompted innovation on the part of visual merchandisers. Creative treatments make use of display arrangements and units; mannequins and forms; signage; and point-of-purchase displays.

Display Arrangements The elements and principles of design combine in several practical spatial arrangements including step and pyramid displays. End-cap displays are another format used to attract customers in supermarkets, discount stores, and other retail venues that use a grid floor plan. Special techniques are used to maximize vertical merchandising opportunities. The following arrangements can be used with almost any classification of merchandise and in many store settings.

■ *Step format.* A **step format** begins at a low point on one side and climbs incrementally to a higher point in a diagonal arrangement. With this format merchandise and props may be either symmetrically or asymmetrically balanced, depending on the impact desired.

■ *Pyramid format.* A pyramid display uses a three dimensional step arrangement. A **pyramid format** is a geometric display that follows the lines of a triangle, beginning at a broad base and progressing to an apex. Sometimes an additional prop or piece of merchandise is displayed on the apex. The pyramid format is illustrated in Figure 13.10.

■ *End-Caps.* End-caps are often used in stores that use a grid floor plan. These crucial merchandising areas can incorporate step or pyramid display elements to enhance merchandise presentation in supermarkets or category killers. Customers rarely resist special promotion or sale merchandise in these high-traffic areas.

■ *Striping.* Retailers practice this technique when they want to impress customers with their great depth of stock. Striping is most effective in stores that have high ceilings. **Striping** is the practice of displaying merchandise in vertical formats to bring attention to deep assortments carried by the retailer. It may be impossible for customers to reach baseball hats that are above eye level on a twenty foot "stripe," in The Sports Authority stores, but that isn't the intent. **Eye-level merchandising** utilizes the line of vision in an approximate 18 inch range of eye level for product placement. The point of striping is to show the vast assortment available, to warehouse stock, maximize store productivity, and to create visual excitement.

Display Units Constructed units that are used to display merchandise include platforms, ledges, environmental settings, and showcases.

■ *Platforms and islands.* Displays created in a prominent area using temporary or permanent low-rising units are called **platform or island displays**. Usually square, rectangular, or round in design, platforms are available commercially or can be constructed by the display department from wood and then covered with a variety of suitable materials. Islands tend to be more permanent and are placed near entrances to key departments, escalators, elevators, and other high traffic areas. Spotlights installed above these areas maximize visibility.

■ *Ledges.* Ledges are used in a different manner from other display areas for they are often found in locations that are above eye level. One type of ledge is found in main floor selling areas such as a central cosmetics area. These

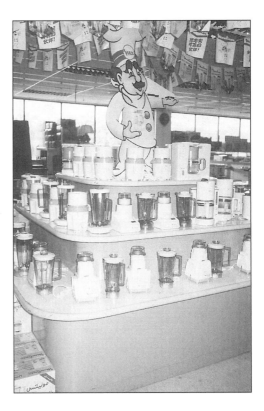

Figure 13.10 Small appliances work well on this tiered pyramid arrangement, topped with a decorative display prop for added impact.

pyramid format Geometric display that follows the lines of a triangle, beginning at a broad base and progressing to an apex.

striping The practice of displaying merchandise in vertical formats to bring attention to deep merchandise assortments carried by the retailer.

eye-level merchandising Utilizing the line of vision in an approximate 18-inch range of eye level.

platform or island displays Displays created in a prominent area using a temporary or stationary low rising units.

Figure 13.11 Showcases are used to display merchandise artfully and safely. Meat and other foods are the focal point in a traditional, Soviet-style supermarket in Bishkek, Kyrgyzstan. *Courtesy of Anthony Pizur.*

Did You Know?

In an attempt to bolster holiday trade, a HyVee Food and Drug store in Omaha, Nebraska displayed Barbie dolls and Tickle Me Elmo's on top of frozen food cases. They also positioned a model train on top of the salad bar. What next, a Cadillac on display in the parking lot? HyVee did that, too! Source: *Wall Street Journal.* November 19, 1997:B1.

environmental settings Simulated rooms with three walls used to display home furnishings and accessories in a coordinated group.

are normally trimmed according to the store's current promotion or for holidays. This type of ledge is usually visible from all four sides and must be designed accordingly. Other types of ledges may rest above traditional rack or shelving units or on staircase risers.

■ *Environmental settings.* Simulated rooms with three walls used to display home furnishings and accessories in a coordinated group are called **environmental settings.** Adding appropriate wall covers and carpets allows customers to see how furniture will look in their own homes. Some may cross-merchandise by introducing apparel-garbed mannequins to the scene.

■ *Showcases.* Showcases serve a triple purpose. First, they can be positioned to physically enclose space on the selling floor. Second, they can store merchandise directly on the floor. Third, they can be impressive pieces of furniture that contribute to store image. Cases should be simple and uncluttered and, as in all displays, the merchandise should dominate. Two-tiered showcases display meat in a Kyrgyzstan supermarket shown in Figure 13.11. In this situation, showcase housing protects the product and ensures freshness.

The key to a successful display—whether a series of windows, showcases, or room settings—is coordination and a unified presentation. Continuity of theme is necessary not only in the individual displays but also in related promotional materials and the store as a whole.

Mannequins and Forms Mannequins and forms are used by soft goods retailers and are chosen to complement store image. Customers should identify with them easily. Mannequins may be very human-like or distinctly abstract, depending on store image and target market. Some are constructed from advanced polymer and resin compounds, others are made from soft, pliable materials that allow more flexibility than older, more rigid types.

Forms include broomsticks, on which goods are displayed hanging from a horizontal bar, and wire sculptures that are used to present a variety of soft goods. Soft sculptures, some that look like large Cabbage Patch dolls, for example, are also used to display merchandise. An assortment of mannequins and forms is shown in the color insert.

Signage. The use of signs can help or hinder merchandising efforts. External signs do more than announce a retailer's presence. They might herald a seasonal sale as do those in Figure 13.12. Internal signs are used to draw attention to a specific department, special purchase, newly arrived merchandise, a sale or service areas.

Signage speaks its own language, judging by the aisle interrupters, danglers, and wobblers found in stores today. **Aisle interrupters** are signs, usually made from cardboard, that protrude into an aisle. **Danglers** are signs that are suspended from a shelf. **Wobblers** are signs on spring assemblies that jiggle to attract attention. These types of signs are popular in grocery and drug stores.[3] The principles of design are considered when creating signs because they also convey store image.

Self-Service Displays Simple display props or counter cards by cash registers have evolved into sophisticated point-of-purchase(POP) aids. POP display areas are expanding dramatically as manufacturers provide retailers with bigger, more complicated permanent displays. They do this to maintain a high level of brand awareness, for consistency, and to give them an edge on their competitors. The basic rule in POP design, however, is to put merchandise in as attractive a package as possible using as little space as possible.

ClipArt™ is a California-based company that produces pens positioned as fashion accessories. The line is merchandised according to themes that are easily recognized by customers. For example, some of the best-sellers are Moo (cow), Route 66 (highway sign) and pens in the Golf, Space, and Cities collections. Because of the unique nature of these products, the company supplies retailers with a variety of self-service display units. Custom fixtures, designed for department stores, are illustrated in Figure 13.13.

As discussed in Chapter 2, the use of interactive displays is growing among large retailers and shopping center operators. Interactive touchpoints have been integrated into the design of Total Com, a telecommunications retailer in Canada. Several computer stations have been set up as color-coded departments such as Business Solutions, Personal Solutions, and Entertainment and Discovery to encourage customers to learn more about services offered by Bell Canada. The systems convert to POS terminals once customers make product and service decisions. Programs are offered in both French and English and are easy to operate.[4] More technological elements like this will be integrated into store design.

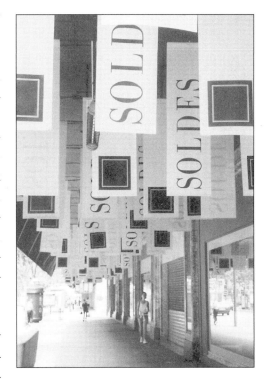

Figure 13.12 Dramatic exterior signs announce a semi-annual sale outside this Paris department store.

aisle interrupters Signs, usually made from cardboard, that protrude into an aisle.

danglers Signs that are suspended from a shelf.

wobblers Signs on spring assemblies that jiggle to attract attention.

Figure 13.13 Oversize pens draw attention and custom units provide self-service for ClipArt™ customers in a department store. ©*The M.I.I. Group 2002.*

Safety, Security, and Loss Prevention

Safety and store security is addressed as part of store design. Aesthetics sometimes have to be sacrificed in order to make the shopping environment a safe one for customers and a secure one in which to do business. Safety factors are important to acknowledge in the early planning stages of store design, and are equally significant to visual merchandisers. Sprinkler systems, access for disabled persons, stairwells, escalators, raised or lowered areas, and sensible material choices are all relevant to store design. Selecting and housing security systems is not the glamorous side of store design, but it is necessary. Some stores have incorporated security ports into their store design. Constructed from usual construction materials, ports can provide an unobtrusive area for electronic or human surveillance activities. Examples include two-way mirrors, decorative columns, or display props.

Video and Electronic Article Surveillance

Larger retailers usually use video cameras to monitor traffic flow, employees, and customers. Video surveillance systems are often housed in behind-the-scenes areas or a nook in the stockroom. Control centers allow security personnel to view various parts of the store on a continual basis. One is illustrated in Figure 13.14.

electronic article surveillance(EAS) Systems that use security apparatus, often located at store exits, to deter shoplifting.

Electronic article surveillance (EAS) devices are integral parts of most retailers security plans. **Electronic article surveillance (EAS)** is a system that uses security apparatus, often located at store exits, to deter shoplifting. The bulky, often unattractive equipment that houses the triggering devices has given way to a new breed of security apparatus designed to blend in or enhance store décor as well as provide a security function. Hidden in vases, pedestals, or even "watch mannequins," these new devices seem more like unique store fixtures than obtrusive security systems.

Dressing Room Security

Almost 39 percent of inventory shrinkage in men's and women's apparel stores is attributed to customer shoplifting.[5] A good part occurs in dressing rooms. Therefore all retailers that provide fitting rooms for their customers plan for the positioning of them. Hiring security guards or attendants is not financially feasible for many retailers. Fitting rooms should be located where they are in direct view of employees on the selling floor.

Other security techniques revolve around the type of fitting rooms incorporated into the floor plan. For example, many stores opt for the "barrel effect" when designing dressing rooms. Although privacy is granted, the customers' heads and feet can be seen while they are in the cubicles. Less than total seclusion reduces shrinkage. Other stores use fitting rooms that can be locked, while those that service large numbers of customers plan their banks of fitting rooms as modular units. In this way, some fitting rooms can be put out of service during slower periods. Dressing rooms should not be positioned near restrooms, because proximity encourages shoplifting.

Figure 13.14 Behind-the-scenes store planning includes banks of cameras for video surveillance in large retail stores.

The scope of store design and visual merchandising is all-encompassing. Coordinating visual display with advertising is an important aspect of promotion and is addressed in Chapter 17. Extensive planning, creativity, marketing knowledge, and technological assists go into the making of retail emporiums of this century.

Summary

Designing a store that welcomes customers is a goal of all retailers. Many factors contribute to store image including physical appearance of the store, merchandise, ambiance, employee attitude and appearance, advertising, and services rendered.

Objectives of store design, include increasing sales and profits, operational efficiency, and averting redundancies that plague many retailers. Creating a workable theme that conveys store image and allows it to stand out from the competition is important. Using space effectively and anticipating realistic costs are equally important.

The facade, including outdoor display windows, invites customers into a store. Once over the threshold, floor plans encourage traffic flow. Two basic floor plans are grid and freeform. The racetrack floor plan is a popular one used by many large retailers and is a combination of both basic plans. There are many variations on both themes. Methods of assigning space to individual departments vary but are based on profitability and return on investment.

Fixture design and placement are important in store planning. An amenable ambiance is created through the use of intangible aspects of design such as lighting, sound, and aromas.

Merchandise presentation is dependent upon proper knowledge and use of art elements and principles of design. Art elements include line, texture, color, and weight. The principles of design include balance, repetition, proportion, contrast, dominance, and rhythm. The goal for using the elements and principles is to create unity, the sense that everything works in the visual perception of the display.

Exterior window displays bring customers into the store; interior displays convince them to buy. Windows are of several kinds: open- and closed-back, glass storefronts, and shadowboxes.

Common display arrangements include step and pyramids. End-caps and the technique called striping are effective in-store display formats. In-store areas also utilize showcases, platforms and islands, ledges, and environmental settings. Mannequins, forms, and signage also project store image. Self-service displays are growing in importance as manufacturers and retailers partner to present easy access to merchandise. Safety and security systems also are part of store planning and design.

Questions for Review and Discussion

1. What are the key components of store image? Use these as criteria to evaluate stores in your area. What constitutes an effective store image?

2. What is the most important objective of store design?

3. Describe the two basic plans for a retail sales floor layout. Under what circumstances is each used? Give examples of retailers in your area that use each type.

4. What is space productivity? How is it measured? Do all categories of merchandise contribute to sales equally?

5. How does traffic flow in a store affect merchandise placement? What specific techniques do retailers use in thrust areas?

6. What is ambiance in store design? Give examples of retailers that use ambiance to enhance image.

7. Why is a display that uses asymmetrical display more visually exciting than one that uses symmetrical display?

From Abstract Forms to Super-Realistic Mannequins, Choice and Use Is Important to Retailers

CLOCKWISE FROM TOP LEFT

Dress forms used in an imaginative way draw customers into a small boutique in Nantucket.

Apparel hangers on metal forms are used to display menswear at Harry Rosen in Toronto.

Motion is conveyed through abstract torso forms designed by Toledo for Pucci International, a mannequin company in New York.

Torso forms are essential for retailers like GapBody.

CLOCKWISE FROM TOP LEFT
Repetition of headless mannequins calls attention to simple but powerful displays at H & M.

An unusual pose and position within the store accentuates designer merchandise at Prada.

The use of realistic mannequins with abstract heads is seen at Burberry.

Human features and the use of artwork contribute to the image of Catherine, a trendy designer boutique in New York's SoHo district.

The elongated, stylized faces of Pucci mannequins convey the fashion-forward appeal of men's and women's apparel at a Parisian department store.

LEFT
Total realism makes customers want to excuse themselves as they pass this mannequin by Adel Rootstein, New York.

BELOW
A mannequin is used to enhance the impact of fine wine in this lifestyle display in a Hout Brox department store in the Netherlands.

Retailers around the world draw customers into their stores using enticing signage, building façades, and window and interior displays.

SIGNAGE AND FAÇADE

CLOCKWISE FROM LEFT
Cartoon-like imagery and bold positioning trigger consumer awareness of this pub sign in Belgium.

Larger-than-life motorcycle emerges from the façade of a Harley Davidson Café in Las Vegas. Exaggerated size or quantity of display elements help encourage customer patronage.

Vibrant color and a bold sale announcement capture customers' attention before they step over the threshold of this H & M fashion apparel store in Amsterdam.

Red door, awnings, and initial letter in the logo help create a polished, inviting look for Talbots at The Summit in Birmingham, AL.

OVER THE THRESHOLD

ABOVE
Customers are drawn into this Belgian specialty store by an artistic, asymmetrical display of furniture.

LEFT
The 60-foot-high Ferris Wheel in the Times Square, New York Toys "R" Us store creates a jaw-dropping response in most customers who see it for the first time.

BELOW
Carrefour of France creates a relaxed environment by the use of back-lit translucent panels and inviting furniture in its optical shop.

Letting merchandise speak for itself through repetition works well when space is at a premium as in this souvenir boutique in Paris.

Large quantity of decorated wooden shoes attracts tourists to this window display in the Netherlands.

Sidewalk display of a few key apparel items lures customers into a quaint specialty store in Bruge, Belgium.

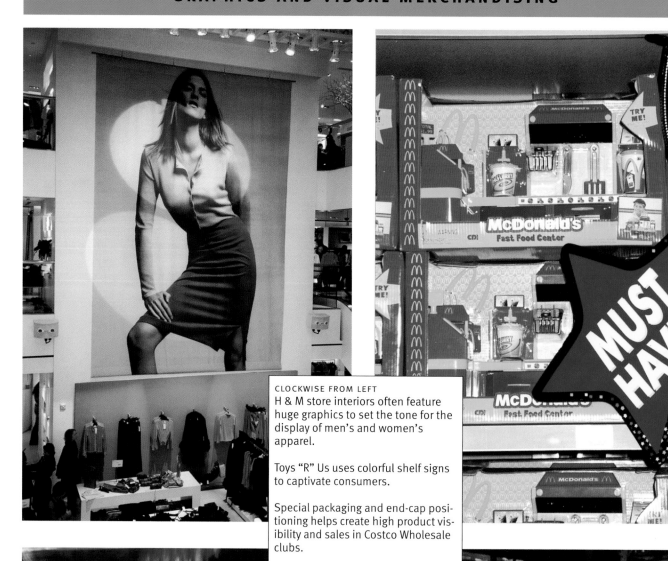

CLOCKWISE FROM LEFT
H & M store interiors often feature huge graphics to set the tone for the display of men's and women's apparel.

Toys "R" Us uses colorful shelf signs to captivate consumers.

Special packaging and end-cap positioning helps create high product visibility and sales in Costco Wholesale clubs.

Candy is displayed in a glass showcase at Fauchon, the epicurean retailer in Paris. The company name is imprinted on chocolates to enhance merchandise presentation and encourage purchase of a full assortment.

The Gravity Model is an old idea in spatial analysis. It is based on the principle that the probability of a given consumer visiting and purchasing at a given site is some function of the distance to that site, its "attractiveness," and the distance and attractiveness of competing sites.

The Gravity Model idea was further refined and made operational by Dr. David Huff of the University of Texas almost 40 years ago. The advent of powerful desktop computers has made it possible to apply the model.

The basic "Huff" formulation of the Gravity Model takes the following form:

$$P_{ij} = \frac{W_i / D_{ij}^{\alpha}}{\sum\limits_{i=1}^{n} \left(W_i / D_{ij}^{\alpha} \right)}$$

Where,
P_{ij} = the probability of consumer j shopping at store i.
W_i = a measure of the "attractiveness" of each store or site i.
D_{ij} = the distance from consumer j to store or site i.
a = an exponent applied to distance so that the probability of distant sites is dampened. It usually ranges between 1.5 and 2.

In practice, census polygons (e.g., block groups) are substituted for individual consumers. The calculated probability for each polygon is then multiplied by some data element in the polygon database (e.g., households and dollars spent on groceries). This measure can then be summarized to give an estimate of the total. Some measure of size, such as Gross Leasable Area (GLA), is often used as a surrogate for "attractiveness."

NOTE All Gravity Model inputs, exponents, trade area size, and results require detailed analysis by someone who is well-versed in the operation of such a model. Some calibration is always required to account for other factors such as "leakage" (when people don't buy all their groceries at supermarkets, some of that spending "leaks" to other trade areas such as convenience stores, farmer's markets, and mail-order).

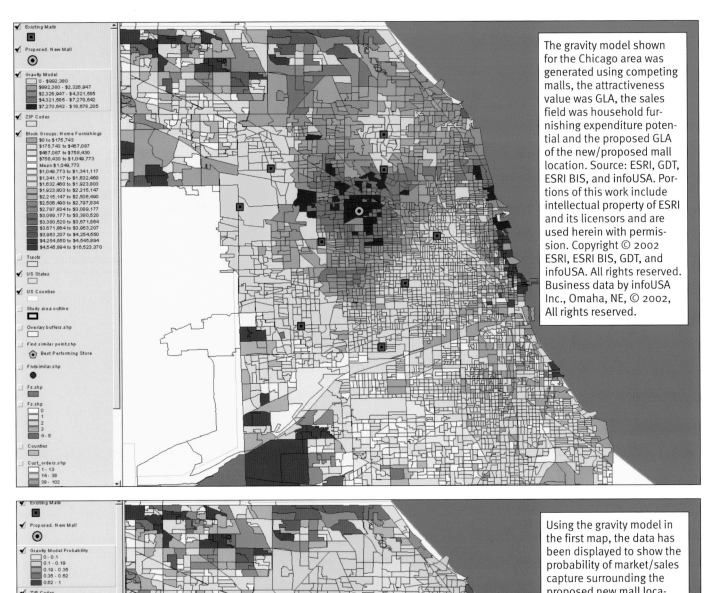

The gravity model shown for the Chicago area was generated using competing malls, the attractiveness value was GLA, the sales field was household furnishing expenditure potential and the proposed GLA of the new/proposed mall location. Source: ESRI, GDT, ESRI BIS, and infoUSA. Portions of this work include intellectual property of ESRI and its licensors and are used herein with permission. Copyright © 2002 ESRI, ESRI BIS, GDT, and infoUSA. All rights reserved. Business data by infoUSA Inc., Omaha, NE, © 2002, All rights reserved.

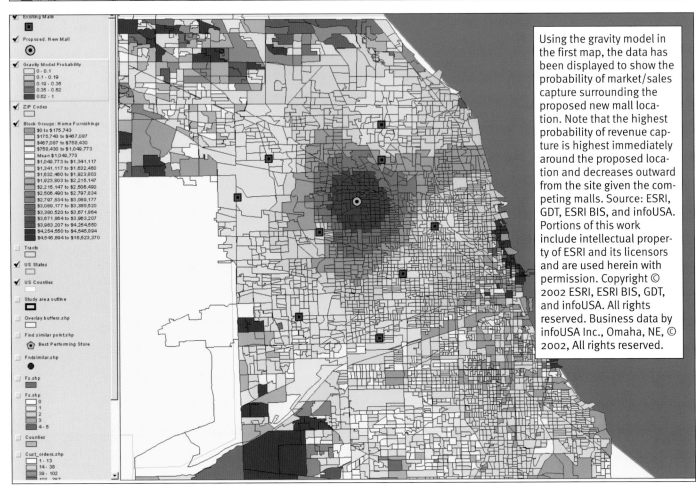

Using the gravity model in the first map, the data has been displayed to show the probability of market/sales capture surrounding the proposed new mall location. Note that the highest probability of revenue capture is highest immediately around the proposed location and decreases outward from the site given the competing malls. Source: ESRI, GDT, ESRI BIS, and infoUSA. Portions of this work include intellectual property of ESRI and its licensors and are used herein with permission. Copyright © 2002 ESRI, ESRI BIS, GDT, and infoUSA. All rights reserved. Business data by infoUSA Inc., Omaha, NE, © 2002, All rights reserved.

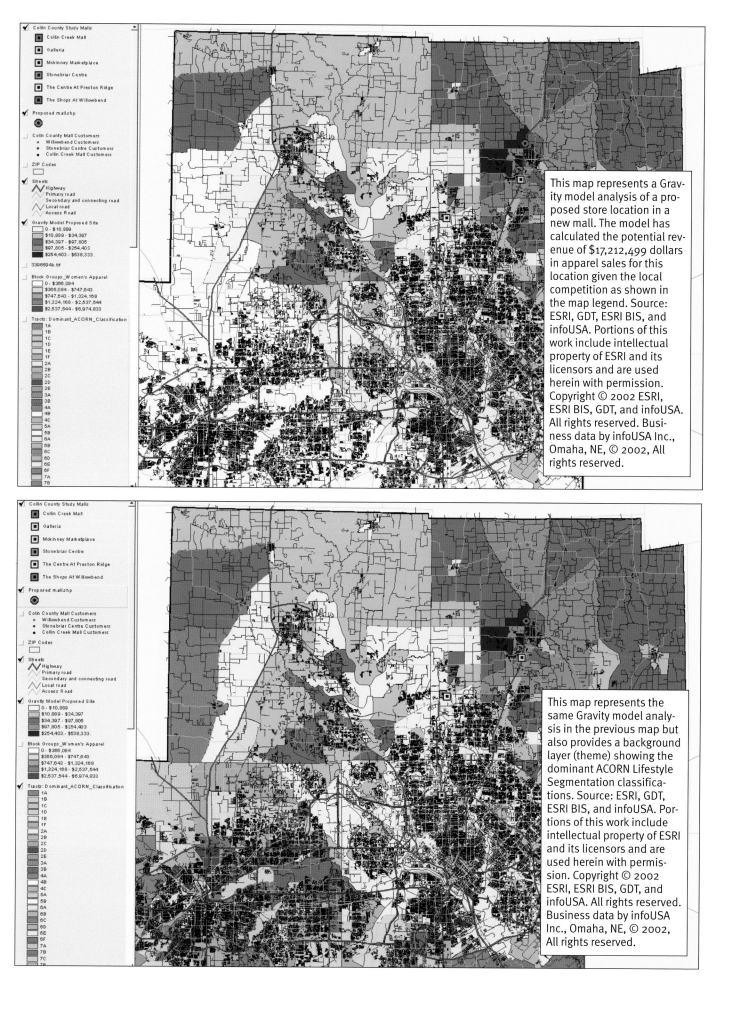

Map 1 legend:

Collin County Study Malls
- Collin Creek Mall
- Galleria
- Mckinney Marketplace
- Stonebriar Centre
- The Centre At Preston Ridge
- The Shops At Willowbend

Proposed mall.shp

Colin County Mall Customers
- Willowbend Customers
- Stonebriar Centre Customers
- Collin Creek Mall Customers

ZIP Codes

Streets
- Highway
- Primary road
- Secondary and connecting road
- Local road
- Access Road

Gravity Model Proposed Site
- 0 - $10,889
- $10,889 - $34,397
- $34,397 - $97,805
- $97,805 - $254,403
- $254,403 - $538,333.

3396594b.tif

Block Groups_Women's Apparel
- 0 - $366,084
- $366,084 - $747,643
- $747,643 - $1,324,168
- $1,324,168 - $2,537,544
- $2,537,544 - $6,974,833

Tracts: Dominant_ACORN_Classification
1A 1B 1C 1D 1E 1F 2A 2B 2C 2D 2E 3A 3B 4A 4B 4C 5A 5B 6A 6B 6C 6D 6E 6F 7A 7B

This map represents a Gravity model analysis of a proposed store location in a new mall. The model has calculated the potential revenue of $17,212,499 dollars in apparel sales for this location given the local competition as shown in the map legend. Source: ESRI, GDT, ESRI BIS, and infoUSA. Portions of this work include intellectual property of ESRI and its licensors and are used herein with permission. Copyright © 2002 ESRI, ESRI BIS, GDT, and infoUSA. All rights reserved. Business data by infoUSA Inc., Omaha, NE, © 2002, All rights reserved.

This map represents the same Gravity model analysis in the previous map but also provides a background layer (theme) showing the dominant ACORN Lifestyle Segmentation classifications. Source: ESRI, GDT, ESRI BIS, and infoUSA. Portions of this work include intellectual property of ESRI and its licensors and are used herein with permission. Copyright © 2002 ESRI, ESRI BIS, GDT, and infoUSA. All rights reserved. Business data by infoUSA Inc., Omaha, NE, © 2002, All rights reserved.

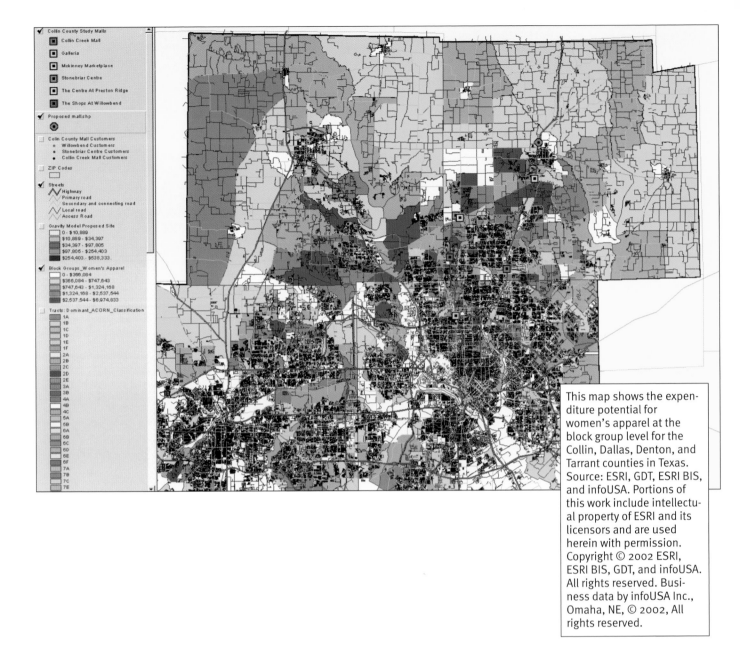

8. What is the difference between open-back and closed-back windows. When is each used? What is the main advantage of glass storefronts?

9. Explain how point-of-purchase (POP) displays have evolved in visual merchandising. Give an example of one that caught your eye in a store.

10. Why are safety and security store planning and visual merchandising issues? Explain what retailers are doing to discretely prevent shrinkage.

Endnotes

1. Garrison, Sue. "Inside Space: The New Frontier. ACNielsen Releases Its First Geodemographic Planogram. *Business Geographics.* January 1999:18.

2. Hall, Cynthia. Regional Vice President, Simon Property Group. Interview. Manchester, New Hampshire. October, 2001.

3. Ono. Yumiko. "'Wobblers' and 'Sidekicks' Clutter Stores, Irk Retailers." *Wall Street Journal.* September 8, 1998:B1.

4. Karas, Jenn. "Telecommunications Retailer Integrates Online Resources into Store Design." *Stores* September, 1998:82,88.

5. "Sources of Inventory Shrinkage, 1999." *Retail Industry Indicators 2001.* NRF Federation. August, 2001: 43.

Global Retail Profile

Tesco, United Kingdom

The number one food retailer in the United Kingdom, Tesco has responded to change in many positive ways. From humble market stall roots early in the 20th century, to become the world's largest online grocer by 2001.[1] Tesco operates 979 stores in 10 countries. Sales volume for the chain was $38 billion in 2001.[2]

Store Format and Location Strategies

The company operates several formats including:

1. Superstores—at 100,000 square feet, featuring food and general merchandise.
2. Supermarkets—at 50,000 square feet, primarily food with some scrambled merchandising.
3. Compact—less extensive product assortment, but similar to superstore concept in somewhat less space.
4. Metro—smaller inner-city stores, featuring lunch and snack areas
5. Express—petrol (gasoline) stations with convenience store sections, often including a bakery.

Operating from different size formats allows the company to tailor its merchandise mix to specific target markets and also accommodate different population densities. Tesco's Brent Cross store on the northern perimeter of London is typical of its supermarket format. This 48,000-square-foot store brings in 1.1 million pounds sterling (approximately $1.8 million) per week and is used as the principal example in this profile.[3]

Located directly off a major circular road north of London in an area called Neasden, the Brent Cross Tesco is a freestanding store. Directly across the highway is the Brent Cross Shopping Center anchored by Marks and Spencer and Fenwicks Department Store. Toys "R" Us is within view of the parking lot and competitor Safeway operates a huge superstore less than a mile away. Trade laws allow Tesco to stay open only 6 hours on Sundays. However, the store is open 24 hours, 5 days a week.

The intangibles—light, color, sound, aromas—play an important role in retail store design. Tesco supermarkets are invariably well-lighted and maintained. The aisles are wide. Fresh fish displays are masterfully arranged, and one can discern no fishy aroma, confirming strict cleanliness standards. No background music is played in the store.

Close to the front of the Brent Cross store, a display is devoted to men's packaged dress shirts, a selection of neckties, and other men's furnishings. Health and beauty aids, over-the-counter medications, in-store bakery and cafe, florist area, and large magazine section are similar to those found in most U.S. stores. However, magazines are prominently positioned on the right wall immediately inside the main entrance. This practice is different in U.S. stores, where reading material tends to be located closer to check-out aisles.

The Brent Cross store reflects a unique community link as well as a successful resolution of a zoning conflict. A recreation center is located adjacent to the Brent Cross store. The Neasden municipal council requested that Tesco build the center in exchange for the privilege of building its store on the site. This example shows the extent to which retailers must work with local officials to obtain the best possible locations.

Demographic studies of the Brent Cross area indicated a high socioeconomic base populated primarily by young single people living cosmopolitan lifestyles. Tesco also targets young families, older families, and older single adults. This store carries extensive kosher product lines to serve a large Jewish clientele.

Comparative Merchandising Techniques

One might argue that a supermarket is a supermarket wherever you are in the world. Although there are many similarities, much of the fun of studying retailing lies in discovering, understanding, and appreciating the differences found in other cultures.

An aisle of crisps (potato chips) attests to the universal desire for snack foods—no matter what they are called. *Fairy* brand dishwashing detergent is as common on Tesco shelves as *Palmolive* is on U.S. shelves. *Ariel* (owned by Proctor and Gamble) is a big selling laundry detergent in the United Kingdom. Although available in Mexico and in the Southwest United States, most Americans have never heard of the brand. Lemonade in the United Kingdom is more like Sprite, the lemon-flavored soda sold in other parts of the world. Kellogg's *Raisin Bran* is called *Sultana Bran* in the United Kingdom and some other countries.

Sometimes products may not differ, but methods of housing or displaying them do. Eggs, always merchandised from refrigerated units in the United States, are stocked on unrefrigerated shelving routinely in the United Kingdom. Also, many Brent Cross customers prefer selecting frozen foods from bin-type freezing units rather than from upright, glass door fronted models that are popular elsewhere. Milk is displayed in storage racks on wheels that are located near refrigerated floor registers. This is in contrast to vertical, refrigerated coolers that are stocked from the rear. Tesco brand mayonnaise is packaged not only in traditional glass containers, but in inverted plastic squeeze bottles bearing upside-down labels.

Many global brands are evident: Kellogg's, Nestle, Pepsi, Del Monte, and even Entenmann's baked goods. Close to 80 percent of products are Tesco branded and the Tesco label is represented in most product categories. Private label goods are often designated as *special value* items. A can of beans for 10 pence (about 16 cents) is a good deal in most currencies.

Heavier emphasis is placed on fresh produce rather than on canned or frozen fruits and vegetables due to customer habits of cooking from scratch. However, increased shelf space is allocated to prepared food sections, showing growing concern for convenience and time saving. Marinated meats, stuffed chickens, and microwavable meals are featured in the store.

Even though Tesco meat was not affected, the mad cow issue that began in 1996 caused interesting reverberations. Sales of beef went down after major media announcements regarding the possibility of disease-ridden meats in supermarkets. Eventually sales rose again, but not to the levels that existed before the crisis. Chicken and fish sales went up during this period and remained strong a year later. Prices on in-stock beef products were reduced astronomically in the early stages of the scare. This provoked a run on the market. Many customers remarked that they had eaten beef all their lives and would not be deterred by the frenzy. Because of the high demand, Tesco soon returned prices to their normal levels.

Customer Service Policies

Management implemented several programs and services in response to customer demand. Before customers enter the facility, Tesco's concern for them is apparent. They can choose from several different types of trolleys (shopping carts) depending on special needs or size of family. Special seating for one infant and one toddler, two infants, a disabled child, or a special unit for a disabled adult are available along with more traditional carts.

Tesco also prides itself in its *no quibble* refund policy, allowing for total customer satisfaction. In addition, the company practices *pricing integrity*. If by chance a customer is overcharged, Tesco will not only refund the purchase price of the item, but will also give the product to the customer at no charge. *Unbeatable value* is another incentive to shop at Tesco. Throughout the store, huge yellow and black signs indicate the store's policy to double the difference between its price and the competitor's price if the competitor is located within three miles of the Tesco store.

Queue reduction is practiced as new tills (registers, terminals) are opened when lines get too long. Bag packers are always on duty and restrooms are equipped with baby care panels providing diaper changing space and other amenities. These particular services may not seem unusual to most U.S. consumers, but for the typical U.K. shopper, these new standards are an improvement over customer service practices as recent as a decade ago. In 1986, shopping bags were not provided by Tesco, much less baggers. Restrooms were generally not available to the public and baby changing stations were nonexistent. However, during that era one could visit the nearby Safeway store and purchase a plastic shopping bag for an additional four pence. Times have changed for Tesco and its shoppers.

Competitive Strategies

Throughout this profile many specific visual and other techniques used by Tesco to differentiate itself from the competition are cited. Other ways the company reaches its customers are through loyalty and social responsibility programs.

Keeping demanding customers coming back for more is not an easy task for any retailer. Tesco uses microchip technology to build customer loyalty through its Clubcard program. Since 1995, customers have been able to enroll at no charge and earn one point for every pound spent in the store or at Tesco petrol stations that are located in the parking lots of many Tesco stores. Special store promotions are tied to the Clubcard so that customers can earn extra points. Ultimately, Clubcard points are turned into vouchers which can be used toward more shopping. The majority of customers at the Brent Cross store use Clubcards. Tesco requires users of its Web site to first enroll in the Clubcard program.

Use of the Clubcard reward system allows Tesco to build a database that is used to reach customers through direct marketing. Cards are scanned at the registers to capture, maintain, or update personal history and transaction activity. Information is centrally collected at the home office, but stores also have the ability to generate data for local use. Customers whose sales records indicate frequent baby related purchases are sent coupons for baby supplies. This is one example of Tesco's lifestyle promotions.

Tesco participates in several consumer awareness programs as part of its community outreach. One program stresses the company's concern for animal welfare by featuring RSPCA (Royal Society for the Prevention of Cruelty to Animals) monitored *freedom food*. Meat sold bearing the RSPCA seal is pledged to be from animals that are raised under humane standards. The company also does not perform product testing on animals and indicates this fact on the labels of products such as Tesco brand toiletries, cosmetics, and household cleaning products.

Its Charity of the Year program recognizes a different organization annually through staff-generated fundraising activities. Tesco employees have raised millions of pounds for charities such as Save the Children, the Muscular Dystrophy Association, and other local foundations. In 2002 more than 11,000 female employees participated in a Race for Life to raise money for cancer research.[4] Brochures explaining these activities are available for customers in all Tesco stores.

International Expansion

With headquarters in Cheshunt, England, Tesco operates in Poland, the Czech Republic, Slovakia, Hungary, Taiwan, Thailand, South Korea, the Republic of Ireland, as well as the United Kingdom. The stores in the former Eastern Bloc countries were acquired from Kmart when sluggish performance resulted in divestiture of its foreign-owned stores in the mid-1990s. As Kmart attempted to improve its standing in America, Tesco became the benefactor in Eastern Europe.

Tesco moved into Ireland in 1997, when it acquired Associated British Food. This purchase made Tesco the second largest food retailer in the Republic of Ireland.[5] This was not Tesco's first attempt to enter that market. In early 1986, the company sold an unprofitable division in Northern Ireland.[6] These experiences show that Tesco had tested the international waters and experimented with entry strategies for some time prior to its Eastern Europe acquisitions.

Tesco.com provides online shopping for growing numbers of customers. The online division delivers products by vans to customer's addresses from its supermarkets rather than from a central distribution center. To further extend its reach, Tesco bought 35 percent of Safeway supermarkets Web-based business in the United States.[7] The company hopes the Tesco formula will work as well in the United States as it has in the United Kingdom.

Food and general merchandise retailing are not the only items on Tesco's agenda. It has taken steps to enhance its apparel sales and has founded the Tesco Clothing division. Challenging business cycles and changing consumer needs kept Tesco alert in the late 1990s. The company now extends company mission over a greatly expanded international and electronic market and is actively engaged in developing strengths in new areas. With Wal-Mart and other significant competitors in the market, the next few years should be volatile ones for the U.K. supermarket industry.

Profile Discussion Questions

1. Explain the five store formats used by Tesco. Why does the company need this many different types?

2. Discuss how Tesco dealt with a legal situation affecting its Brent Cross location.

3. How do Tesco's attitudes toward customer service differ from supermarkets in your home country?

4. How does Tesco behave as a socially responsible retailer? Give examples of programs in which the company is involved.

5. Several merchandising and display examples were given in the profile. Which might work in supermarkets in your home country? Why?

6. What strategies should the company implement in order to maintain its number one supermarket status in the United Kingdom? How might the development of Tesco.com affect the companies performance?

Profile Notes

1. Hagerty, James R. and Hall, James. "British Supermarket Giant Cooks Up Plans to Go Global." *Wall Street Journal*. July 5, 2001:A9.

2. http://62.169.137.181/tesco/newinvestor/pubandresults /annandint/an2002/directors/sfs.htm Available: June 12, 2002.

3. Carson, Laura. Customer Service Manager. Tesco Supermarket. Brent Cross, England. Presentation to the American Collegiate Retailing Association. July, 1997.

4. http://www.tesco.com/corporateinfo Available: June 12, 2002.

5. Strassel, Kimberly A. "UK's Tesco to Buy Irish Groceries in $1 Billion Pact." *Wall Street Journal*. March 24, 1997:A14.

6. Harris, Derek. "Tesco May Expand in Europe and US." *The Times*. London. April 14, 1986.

7. Hagerty and Hall.

Global Retail Profile

Costco Wholesale Corporation, USA

Merging wholesale and retail audiences and bringing a diverse product mix at competitive prices to a select group of members is the mission of Costco. Costco Wholesale and Price Club—then a competitor—merged their operations in 1993. The company began trading under the Costco Wholesale name exclusively in 1999. The company had 345 warehouses worldwide and sales were $34 billion in 2001. Corporate headquarters is in Issaquah, Washington.[1]

To join Costco, individuals must work for one of many businesses, government agencies, or other widely recognized industries. Called Gold Star members, individuals or families pay $45 per year for the privilege of shopping at Costco. Documented businesses, nonprofits, government agencies, farmers, and ranchers pay the same fee. A category called executive membership offers extended services for members. For $100 per year, individuals can obtain discounts on mortgages and homeowners insurance, business loans, health insurance for small business owners, telecommunication services, and 2 percent rebates on warehouse or costco.com purchases.[2]

The Costco customer breakdown in a typical store is approximately 60 percent private customers and 40 percent businesses. Families who shop Costco tend to have household incomes in excess of $50,000, two cars, and two children. Bulk purchases, which characterize the typical warehouse club shopping experience, are not for everyone. However, the sales generated from private customers compared to businesses has shifted dramatically since the inception of the concept.

True to warehouse club tradition, Costco operates on a very low gross margin by retail standards, about 10 percent. Most of its warehouses report very low shrinkage due to tight inventory control and close monitoring of transactions at the point of sale and as customers exit the facility.[3]

Merchandise Assortment Policies

Merchandise assortments are broad and shallow with approximately 3,000 SKUs represented. About 60 percent of the inventory is rotated constantly, while 40 percent is staple merchandise. Full selections of merchandise in categories such as fresh meats, bakery goods, fine wines, canned goods, apparel for the family, automobile tires, health and beauty aids, books, computers, and frozen foods are carried.

Known as department 44, the company sponsors road shows which are roving groups of specialty merchandise ranging from bagels and gourmet coffees to oriental rugs, pianos, and artwork. These special events appear in Costco stores on a rotation basis. This permits new merchandise to be infused into the mix—sometimes for test marketing purposes. The road shows also add a bit of excitement to the shopping experience for shoppers.[4]

The *Kirkland* signature label is on products as diverse as candy and socks. *Simply Soda* is Costco's private label beverage and competes favorably with national brands. In 1999, the company launched a new line of Kirkland appliances, made by Whirlpool.[5]

International Operations

Costco operates worldwide, with warehouses the United States, Canada, Puerto Rico, Mexico, the United Kingdom, South Korea, Taiwan, and Japan. The company is looking toward future expansion in the Pacific Rim, notably in Malaysia, Indonesia, and Singapore. Also in contention are France, Spain, and South America. The Mexican operations are under joint venture with Controladoro Comercial Mexicana, and the South Korean with Shinsegae, a department store retailer. The company expects to have 500 stores worldwide by 2005.[6]

Costco opened its first club in London in 1993, through a unique partnership between Littlewoods of the United Kingdom, Carrefour of France, and Costco. A second store opened north of London the following year. United Kingdom stores follow the same concept as their U.S. counterparts with emphasis on food, apparel, housewares, and electronics priced 20 percent lower than conventional retailers. Well-known brands are included in the merchandise assortment. Membership fees are similar to those in the United States. Costco looks for 50,000 members in each store's trading area.

There were no other warehouse clubs in Canada when the company opened more than a decade ago, giving Costco a unique advantage. Its stores span the country from British Columbia to Newfoundland with the highest concentration in the provinces of Ontario and Quebec. Food sales make up slightly more than half of all sales in the Canadian stores, a figure that parallels the proportion in U.S. stores.[7]

The warehouse club format is in some ways much like the hypermarkets popular in Europe. It is quite possible that Costco hopes to capitalize on the preferences of European shoppers as it brings its concept to the world.

Store Layout and Design

Cavernous concrete block structures typify Costco stores. The grid floor plan is delineated by makeshift fixtures, mostly utilitarian metal shelving and piles of wooden pallets. The company does not use planograms as competitor Sam's Club does, but most units are designed in similar fashion.[8]

Impulse areas are located inside the entrance, featuring seasonal products and best buys heaped along side the main aisle. Near the front is the home electronic and computer areas, high volume categories for Costco. At what Costco calls a *surge* area near the loading docks at the rear of the store, rapidly turning merchandise such as soda and paper towels is stocked. This is in contrast to department and specialty store layout strategy where fast-moving products are usually put closer to the front of the store within easy reach of customers. Costco knows its customers will traverse the entire store during their shopping expeditions and will not take offense to this layout technique. Costco encourages front-to-back traffic flow in this manner.

Pharmacies, one of the top sales generators at Costco, are located near the front of stores, along with optical and hearing aid centers, snack bars, and photo shops.

The center core of the store is devoted to apparel, office products, candy and snacks, seasonal items, books, and tires. Prices too good to be true increase the compulsion to pick up a good buy right off the pallet display. Bakery, fresh meat, produce and prepared foods sections are at the back of the store. All foods are prepared and presented under extremely rigid health standards. Costco's goal is to be ahead of government requirements. Displayed on vertical shelving units, hard goods dominate one side of the store and canned goods, frozen foods, and health and beauty aids the other. Even new-age health products such as St. John's Wort have a prominent place at Costco. In all categories, care is given to present full-shelf displays, significant end-caps, and faced-out merchandise. Customer service kiosks facilitate the ordering of home improvement supplies. The kiosks also serve as a focal point in the well-merchandised, but vast interior.

Sales Promotion and Customer Service

Costco does not advertise extensively, but will to announce new store openings. The company sponsors charitable events and fundraising activities at the local community level. Exterior and interior signage is kept to a minimum. The bulk of sales promotion activities fall under member services. The company offers its *Costco Connection*, a monthly lifestyle magazine geared to small business owners and families. Tempting brochures with discount offers tout its travel agency. Members can shop online at the Costco.com.

Product demonstrators add color to in-store promotions on weekends when traffic is the heaviest. Sampling foods and beverages has become the custom for members who often joke about going to Costco for lunch.

Once a cash-or-check only domain, Costco introduced its own credit card in conjunction with American Express. Costco terminated its earlier partnership with Discover in 2000. It has introduced gas stations at about 14 percent of its warehouses and expects to roll out that concept to 70 percent of its U.S. units. Prices well below the going rate per gallon are for members only, and gas is dispensed only at warehouse locations.

The corporate culture is informal, executives are on a first-name basis and employees are among the best paid in the retail industry. With further global expansion plans, entry into underserved U.S. markets, new services for customers, and a growing clientele, the company is poised for growth. Costco's blend of wholesale and retail in an era where the two markets are merging will also contribute to its future successes.

Profile Discussion Questions

1. Compare the Costco wholesale membership club to the Carrefour hypermarket profiled in Unit I. What are the major similarities and differences?

2. Why does the company target wholesale as well as retail customers? How do the retail and wholesale functions differ?

3. How has Costco internationalized its operations? Explain the unique advantage the company had when it entered the Canadian market.

4. What store design and merchandise placement techniques used by Costco are contrary to those used by department and specialty stores?

5. How can Costco operate successfully on a 10 percent gross margin?

Profile Endnotes
1. Annual Report 2001. Costco Wholesale: 1.
2. "Discover the Benefits of Real Buying Power." Costco Wholesale Brochure. Seattle, Washington. 2001:3.
3. Loveless, Mike, Merchandise Manager, Costco, Seattle, WA and MacKay, Celia, Administrative Manager, Costco, Nashua, NH. Interview. Nashua, NH February, 2001.
4. Ibid.
5. Annual Report, 2000. Costco Wholesale: 2, 3
6. Loveless and MacKay.
7. Kim, Nancy. "Price Costco Enjoys Unique Position in Canada Market." *Puget Sound Business Journal.* July 19, 1996:v17n10:12.
8. Loveless and MacKay.

Marketing the

Merchandise

Chapter 14

Merchandise Planning and Buying

Learning Objectives

After completing this chapter you should be able to:

- List the sources of information that help retailers interpret consumer demand.

- Describe the steps in creating dollar and unit merchandising plans.

- Apply the basic stock method for determining inventory needs.

- Identify the members of a merchandising team and discuss their responsibilities.

- Explain the importance of vendor relationships.

- Identify trends in product development and sourcing.

Figure 14.1 Keeping up with trends is one of the chief objectives of retail buyers. Changes in the popularity of sports such as skateboarding can impact merchandise plans significantly.
AP/Worldwide Photos

Planning for sales requires a clear-cut plan of action. First, all retailers determine customer demand for their products. Next, budgets are formulated. Finally, details—including quantities, colors, styles, and models—are specified. Completing these tasks requires strong relationships with vendors, input from all levels of the organization, and information technology. Merchandising is at the heart of all retail activities and is the sum total of these steps and considerations. **Merchandising** means having the right goods at the right price in the right place at the right time. Not only does it involve the purchasing of goods at wholesale to be resold to retail customers, but it also reflects the actual positioning of goods on the selling floor for maximum exposure and appeal to customers.

Although general and divisional merchandise managers in large retail organizations set priorities and develop financial plans, retail buyers mastermind the actual purchasing of goods for resale. In small retail stores the owner may be responsible for all phases of the planning and buying process.

Standard operating procedures used in the merchandising planning process are dollar and unit planning. A **dollar plan** is a forecast used by retailers to determine how much they need to invest in new merchandise. A **unit plan** is a detailed list of all items being purchased by color, style, size, and price. This configuration constitutes an appropriate merchandise assortment.

Store policies dictate the kinds of goods or services the store will sell, the quality of products and the details of the merchandise mix. For example, Express is a well-known national fashion chain that limits its merchandise to apparel and accessories geared to fashion-conscious, young, middle-class women who want the latest in smart fashion at moderate prices. Target, the discount retailer, practices a much different kind of merchandising. In that store everything from pool supplies to notebook paper, food to fashion must be planned, purchased, and sold. Understanding merchandising objectives provides a frame of reference before the actual budgeting process commences.

Collecting information at the stock keeping unit level, enables buyers to compare actual figures to planned figures on a daily or hourly basis. A typical SKU for a home electronics item is illustrated in Figure 14.2. State-of-the-art retail management software provides sales, reorder, markdown,

merchandising The practice of having the right goods at the right price in the right place at the right time.

dollar plan A forecast used by retailers to determine how much they need to invest in new merchandise.

unit plan A detailed list of all items being purchased by color, style, size, and price.

gross margin, and sell-through data. **Sell through** is the percentage of stock sold in a store or department in a specific period of time.

When developing merchandise dollar and unit plans, store image, changing economies, and distribution practices are also acknowledged. Most important, the procedure begins and ends with customers. Translating their needs and wants into merchandise is at best a challenging task.

Sources of Customer Information

There are many sources of information used by retailers to learn more about their customers. Amassing as much data as possible and synthesizing that into workable plans is the goal. When interpreting customer demand, both in-store and out-of-store resources are used.

Figure 14.2 Numbers that indicate important merchandise information such as model, vendor, and department are called SKUs. They often accompany a universal product bar code such as this one located on a pricing sticker for a television set. *Reprinted with permission. Zebra Technologies International, Inc.*

sell through The percentage of stock sold in a store or department in a specific period of time.

In-Store Information

Carefully analyzing past and current sales is the usual starting point for retail merchandise planners. In addition, examining returned goods, credit, and loyalty program data also provides valuable information. Retailers also do research to determine specific customer spending habits.

- *Past and current sales.* Both past and present data are important when interpreting customer demand and estimating sales. Analyzing past sales lets the buyer know exactly which backpacks, in what colors, from which vendors were sold in a specific time period. Because all items do not have a history, selection of new items is much more subjective. Scanning devices instantly record a wide variety of information that is useful for capturing sales and inventory figures for planning purposes.

- *Returned goods and adjustments.* The unspoken message from customers who return goods is displeasure. Retailers may reject items, entire classifications of goods or vendors on the basis of heavy returns. Rates of returns varies by type of store. For example, customers return less then 1 percent, reflected as a share of sales, in grocery stores. In department and consumer electronics stores the percentage is almost 11 percent and in apparel specialty stores, the percentage ranges from about 6 percent in menswear stores to 11.5 percent in women's shops.[1] This information is useful to retailers planning new stores or classifications.

■ *Credit and loyalty program data.* Analysis of store credit and loyalty data results in two types of important information: records of purchases and customer profiles. Because credit sales make up a large proportion of total sales, transaction receipts are an excellent source of both quantitative and qualitative data. Loyalty card data provide similar information, not only regarding kinds and prices of merchandise purchased, but also customers' lifestyles and spending habits.

■ *Internal research.* Both customer inquiries and suggestions made by customers, salespeople, and staff offer additional input to merchandise planning. Many retailers use customer suggestion boxes, conduct exit interviews with shoppers, and utilize want slips. **Want slips** are notations gathered by sales associates regarding merchandise requested by customers but not carried by the store. Often computer tallies are used.

Out-of-Store Information

Moving out of the box is also important. Studying the competition, talking with vendors and buying offices, attending trade shows, reading trade and consumer publications are necessary. Expert opinions gleaned from consulting firms, external research, and testing laboratories are useful.

■ *Competition.* A great deal of useful information may be obtained by studying the competition, both in and out of the trading area. In any marketplace, one can be sure Federated and May Company are in each other's stores on a weekly—if not daily—basis. Small retailers who cannot afford costly market research can also learn by scouting similar stores in other market areas and visiting major stores in metropolitan areas for fresh ideas. Identifying hot items they may have overlooked is another motivation to shop the stores. Retailers also study the competition so they can avoid the same or similar merchandise. Analyzing the competition is not done to encourage me-too merchandising, but to have more ammunition on hand. It is an excellent research method whether the goal is to meet, beat, or avoid the competition.

■ *Vendors.* Although not unbiased, vendors and sales representatives contribute valuable information. Vendors know what is selling and the dynamics of demand in many geographic areas. Most vendors are reliable because lying to retail clients would not help build long-term relationships. However, their suggestions should be carefully considered in the light of one's own market conditions.

---

want slips Notations gathered by sales associates regarding merchandise requested by customers but not carried by the store.

Did You Know?

Several changes that will affect society in the third millennium that begins in 2999 have been predicted by Morgan Stanley Dean Witter: the end of obesity and cellulite; availability of no-wash clothes; today's extreme sports will be considered tame. Speculate on how these changes might affect merchandise assortments of the future.
Source: Ryan, Thomas J. "ShelfLife: Predicting Fashion's 3rd Millennium." *Women's Wear Daily.* July 6, 1999.

■ *Resident buying offices.* Resident buying offices, also called central market representatives, study trends for clients and send them a constant flow of information. **Resident buying offices** are companies that facilitate market coverage for retailers by acting as their eyes, ears, and legs in the marketplace. Most retailers belong to buying offices and use their services when preparing for and while on buying trips. A retailer in South Dakota may find it difficult to go to market more than once or twice a year, much less keep abreast of trend information and available resources. Buying offices provide valuable services to large and small retailers.

■ *Trade shows.* Two to four times annually, manufacturers who supply the retail industry hold huge business expositions. Held in major cities worldwide, trade shows bring together under one roof a variety of manufacturers and distributors showing their wares. The large International Gift Show held in Birmingham, England, literally covers acres and features seven huge showrooms geared to the various gift areas. Silverware and novelties are in one room, household items in another. A computer trade show is illustrated in Figure 14.3. Because so many manufacturers take booths at these events, retailers can compare and contrast offerings in the marketplace. They can also see what is new in their particular venue, enjoy one-stop-shopping, and place orders on the spot.

Figure 14.3 The World Trade Center in Taipei, Taiwan hosts many trade fairs including computer shows for retailers from around the world.

■ *Consumer publications.* Business strategists react to the President's State of the Union address, global economic conditions, reports of tariff reductions, fighting in Africa, and social upheaval in Chechnya. Daily newspapers are a great source of current data. Retailers in all locations, large and small, have this quick form of research available. Reading news magazines like *Time* or *Newsweek* and business periodicals such as *Forbes* or *Business Week* also contributes to a retailer's bank of knowledge.

resident buying office Companies that facilitate market coverage for retailers by acting as their eyes, ears, and legs in the marketplace.

■ *Trade publications.* Trade papers that are directed toward a business rather than a general consumer audience are another information resource. Fairchild Publications is one of the most respected sources of data for merchandise planning. Many retailers consider *Women's Wear Daily* and *Daily News Record* invaluable. In addition to offering all the latest industry news, the newspapers carry fashion trend and merchandise resource information. *Stores* and *Chain Store Age* are monthly trade magazines that also provide general retailing data and articles. *Supermarket News* and *Vending Times* carry articles specific to these fields.

■ *Consulting firms.* Business consultants concentrate on specific or general management issues. Firms from either group are helpful to retailers in the merchandise planning phase. Small retail companies might be wise to hire a consultant when planning their first merchandise budgets. Large retailers might use consulting firms when planning global expansion, upgrading technology, or when major merchandising changes are under consideration. Deloitte Touche Thomatsu, Kurt Salmon Associates, and PricewaterhouseCoopers, are three of the best-known large consulting firms. In smaller cities regional firms are helpful because they understand their markets so well.

■ *External research.* Conducting mail and telephone surveys are other ways to collect customer patronage information. Results of random surveys conducted with current and prospective customers are useful to retailers in pinpointing product preferences. Many companies use their Web sites to not only capture merchandise preference information, but also to develop their databases for future promotional purposes. Also helpful are focus groups, made up of representative customers from a store's clientele. **Focus groups** are panels of 5 to 15 people invited to discuss a product, service, or market situation. They consider a variety of business issues in an informal but controlled setting. For example, participants might be asked by a moderator to pass judgment on merchandising, customer service, or advertising effectiveness. National research organizations, such as ACNeilsen Company, use customer surveys to develop valuable information for the industry. Neilsen Reports may be purchased by retailers. **Neilson reports** are commercial reports providing information on market share, sales, and trends useful to retail planners.

■ *Testing laboratories.* The offer of quality is something that customers have the right to expect from retailers. To ensure the quality of the goods they offer for sale, some large retailers like Sears or JC Penney do extensive testing in their own laboratories. Retailers that do not have their own testing facilities can hire outside testing bureaus like Underwriters Laboratories, Inc. to test products for them. **Underwriters Laboratories, Inc.** is a are large, independent nonprofit testing groups whose trademarked UL mark means the product has been safely tested against national standards. Many vendors also seek product certification from publications such as *Consumer Reports*. Retailers like to purchase goods from vendors who have good reputations because they know how important this is to their customers. Manufacturers and other supply chain members also generate research studies that are provided to the retailers they service.

Gathering appropriate information for evaluating past and current conditions in and out of the store is only the first step in merchandise planning. Next the financial aspects of the process are addressed.

focus group Panel of 5 to 15 people invited to discuss a product, service, or market situation.

neilsen reports Commercial reports providing information on market share, sales, and trends useful to retail planners.

Underwriters Laboratories, Inc. Large, independent, nonprofit testing group whose trademarked UL mark means the product has been safety tested against national standards.

Six Month Merchandise Plan							
/____/ Total Store /____/ Department /____/ Classification	Department #_____			Classification #_____			
/__/ Spring, 20__ /__/ Fall, 20__	Feb. Aug.	Mar. Sept.	Apr. Oct.	May Nov.	June Dec.	July Jan.	Total
Net Sales							
Last year							
Plan							
Revision							
Actual							
Beginning of Month Stock (At Retail)							
Last year							
Plan							
Revision							
Actual							
Reductions (Markdowns + Shortages + Discounts)							
Last year							
Plan							
Revision							
Actual							
Purchases (At Retail)							
Last year							
Plan							
Revision							
Actual							
Purchases (At Cost)							
Last year							
Plan							
Revision							
Actual							

Figure 14.4 Six-month merchandising planning documents help retailers track key information. Sales from last year (LY) form the starting place for next season's projections.

The Dollar Merchandise Plan

Retailers plan sales differently depending on the type and size of store, merchandise, and inventory turnover. They plan long term and short term, by chain, division, store, department, classification and subclassification. Most work from two 6-month plans that are updated on a monthly basis. Line items are referenced in this section. Retailers are prepared to adjust their business on a daily basis if necessary. Seasonal operations may operate only for a 4-month period, but that time span must be carefully planned. Swimsuit shops in summer resort areas are examples. A 6-month plan worksheet is illustrated in Figure 14.4.

The dollar plan, is a forecast for buying and controlling the amount of goods purchased to meet customers' needs during a specific time period. The five major segments in any dollar merchandise plan are:

1. estimated sales
2. planned stock (inventory)
3. planned reductions
4. planned purchases
5. planned gross margin

Acknowledgment and management of these aspects are crucial to the success of large and small retailers.

Estimated Sales

Estimating future sales is the starting point in any budgeting process. At this stage, past year sales are analyzed and percentage changes are projected. In determining the percentage change several factors are considered. The state of the economy, specific retail growth indicators, changes in competition, and department square footage all affect the forecast. Retail trade associations are excellent sources of comparative sales figures and other statistics vital to the planning process. Whether the product is a fad or classic item, its place in the product life cycle also is considered.

Most retailers plan sales in dollars regardless of the economy. In an inflationary economy some retailers estimate sales first in units and then in dollars. This is done because future dollars will not always buy as many units as past or current dollars and the projected figures might represent an insufficient number of planned items. Once units are planned, dollar amounts can easily be estimated by building in a currency fluctuation factor. On the other hand, future dollars may buy more units than past or current dollars. When this happens, overstocking occurs.

Buyers who purchase in global markets monitor currency fluctuations. The deflation of the Indonesian rupiah during the Asian crisis illustrates the importance of this practice. In January 1998, 1 U.S. dollar would buy approximately 8,000 rupiah. Because of the monetary situation, American retail buyers of Indonesian furniture or apparel could then purchase much more than they could a year previously when 1 dollar would buy about 2,500 rupiah.

If a retailer is considering not planning a sales increase, it probably should not be in that business. However, there are exceptions to this rule. Departments and classifications vary greatly. For example, Beanie Babies had waned in popularity by early 2000. Retailers that were strong in that product line in past seasons did not drop the items, but they did not project increases in Beanie Baby business.

If future sales are not estimated accurately, too much or too little merchandise will be purchased. Money invested in inventory will be spent incorrectly. If this happens, the four steps that follow will not fall into place smoothly and the entire budget will be of little use.

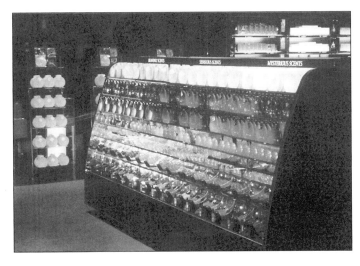

Figure 14.5 Imagine the detail involved when planning for many different scents and bath products. Merchandise categories like this present unique challenges to planners at Sephora.

Planned Stock

The second step in the budgeting process is to plan the correct amount of merchandise to meet sales expectations and inventory requirements. Changes in store locations or layout may affect plans. The addition of new stores, the closing of others or an enlarged selling floor can change inventory requirements radically. For example, during the 1990s retailers who specialized in the music business had to consider vast shifts in customer preferences and manufacturing trends as they planned their tape and CD assortments. In the early 1990s, vinyl record albums comprised about 10 percent of all music sales. By the mid-1990s tapes made up about 60 percent and CDs 40 percent. Because tapes and CDs took much less space than albums, inventory needs and space requirements changed. By the late 1990s the bulk of sales were in CDs with cassette tapes rapidly phasing out of the merchandise assortment. Sephora, the French cosmetics retailer, offers 365 different lipstick colors. Planning quantities of diverse colors and adequate space to display the merchandise presents unique merchandise planning challenges for this retailer (See Figure 14.5).

Stock plans help keep inventory investment at an acceptable level. Planners know that the end-of-month stock is just as important a figure as estimated sales. **End-of month (EOM) stock** refers to the dollar amount of stock remaining at the end of a month's selling period. Because standard practice one year may change the next, it is difficult to create the perfect

end of month (EOM) stock
Refers to the dollar amount of stock remaining at the end of a month's selling period.

plan. Several methods are useful to retailers depending on their specific needs and their type of store.

Two methods of stock planning that are most frequently used are the weeks-of-supply system and the basic stock method. The **weeks-of-supply method** is an inventory planning system in which stock on hand is kept at a level representing projected sales for a predetermined number of weeks. The **basic stock method** is an inventory planning system in which estimated sales for the month are added to a minimum stock to determine merchandise needs for the planning period. The method chosen depends on the type of merchandise, turnover, and other factors. However, the basic stock method has the most universal applications and is the method taught at National Retail Federation workshops. The mechanics of this method will be emphasized in this section. Smaller retailers may find using simpler stock-to-sales ratios adequate for their needs. A **stock-to-sales ratio (SSR)** reflects the relationship between goods on hand at the beginning of the month and merchandise sold during that time period, expressed in dollars or units.

weeks-of-supply method Inventory planning system in which stock on hand is kept at a level representing projected sales for a predetermined number of weeks.

basic stock method Inventory planning system in which estimated sales for the month are added to a minimum stock to determine merchandise needs for the planning period.

stock-to-sales ratio (SSR) The relationship between goods on hand at the beginning of the month and merchandise sold during that time period, expressed in dollars or units.

Weeks-of-Supply Method To determine the right amount of goods to have on hand, the weeks-of-supply method is one that is used. Sales are planned on an as-needed basis in specific situations. Optimal conditions exist when turnover rates are high and selling periods are short. Goods on hand might equal sales estimates for several weeks. This method is frequently used when planning fast-moving fashion merchandise or supermarket packaged goods.

The formula for calculating weeks of supply is:

$$\text{Weeks of Supply} = \frac{52}{\text{Turnover}}$$

Once calculated, the number is used to determine the amount of inventory needed to achieve sales goals. This is done by multiplying the planned sales figure by the weeks-of-supply number. The weeks-of-supply method is used when sales of a product are relatively stable over time. It would not be the best method to use for fads.

Stock-to-Sales Ratio The numerical relationship between current retail stock and sales is expressed as a stock-to-sales ratio. For example, if the stock for a particular classification of merchandise on November 1 is worth $50,000 at retail, and sales for November are $25,000, the stock-to-sales ratio is 2.

Another way the SSR is used is when planning for specific merchandise items. If a store is selling men's white shirts it may determine that it needs

25 shirts to sell 1. This ratio may seem high, but it is not. Because of many variants in sizing—neck, sleeve, and body cut—plus considerations for collar style and fabric type, large inventories are typical in this product classification. The store must be prepared for the next customer who may want a white oxford cloth shirt with a button-down collar and tapered body in size 17 1/2 with a 36" sleeve. And the customer has not yet mentioned brand name!

Basic Stock Method The basic stock method is useful for determining inventory levels for most types of merchandise, particularly staple goods. Merchandise that is routinely purchased is called **staple goods**.

staple goods Merchandise that is routinely purchased.

In spite of fluctuations in demand, the basic stock method helps retailers meet sales goals and avoid out-of-stock conditions. Stock levels at the beginning of each month equal the estimated sales for that month plus a cushion in case actual sales exceed estimated sales. If retailers provide a balanced merchandise assortment, it is less likely that customers will go elsewhere because they can't find the right size, color, or model. The cushion also acts as a regulatory mechanism by helping retailers maintain an optimum stock level. **Optimum stock level** means having the right amount of merchandise on hand to satisfy customer needs without being over- or understocked. Using this method also protects against stockouts if future shipments of merchandise are delayed or have to be returned to the vendor because of damage.

optimum stock level Having the right amount of merchandise on hand to satisfy customer needs without being over- or understocked.

There is a downside to using the basic stock method. Building in a cushion increases the inventory carried by a retailer. Because margins are small on some items, this could cut into profits if products don't sell as well as expected.

The basic stock method involves calculating inventory needs for each month based on two important dimensions—volume and time. "How much can you sell?" and "How fast can you sell it?" are the chief questions the basic stock method answers. Average sales per month reflects the volume portion of the equation. Average stock is a function of turnover and represents the time factor. Turnover rates translate to average days in inventory. For example, in a store with a 4.0 turnover, the inventory sells completely in about 90 days. This is a typical turn for department stores. A jewelry specialty store might operate on a turn of 2.0. This would mean that it takes approximately 180 days to achieve total sell-through of merchandise.

Once calculated, basic stock remains the same for each month of the planning period unless buyers choose to revise their plans. In an ideal merchandising world basic stock is the same as planned EOM stock. Formulas used when calculating basic stock are expressed in Table 14.1.

Table 14.1 Formulas for Calculating Basic Stock

Basic Stock = Average Stock − Average Sales per Month

Average Stock = Total Planned Sales
      Plus Prior Month's Sales ÷ Turnover

Average Monthly Sales = Total Planned Sales   Number of
            Plus Prior Month's Sales ÷ Months in Sale Period
                        Plus 1

Inventory Needs = Planned Sales for One Month + Basic Stock

Planned Reductions

Because reductions are inevitable, retailers build a planned figure into their merchandise budget. Markdowns, stock shrinkage resulting from customer or employee theft, discounts, and human error all contribute to the reductions category.

If a reasonable percentage of sales for reductions is not included when planning sales, retailers could lose sales, having underestimated needed stock. For example, if a retailer grants senior citizens' discounts every Tuesday, this reduction must be anticipated in advance.

Because these occurrences are common in retailing, a logical percentage for reductions, based on past performance and current trends for each merchandise group, must be used. Reductions are calculated by multiplying the reduction percentage by planned sales. Reduction percentages are charted by trade associations and can be used by retailers for comparative purposes, when adding new merchandise classifications or opening new stores.

Planned Purchases

The next step in the process includes adding planned sales, planned reductions, and the planned end-of-month (EOM) stock, and then subtracting planned beginning-of-month (BOM) stock. When planning far in advance of a selling season, you do not have merchandise on hand (OH).

Using the Planned Purchases Formula To see how the formula works, assume that you are the owner of a snow and skateboard shop that targets males and females between the ages of 14 and 26. Usually retailers plan per month, but you are planning snowboard sales for the winter season. Because of your choice Colorado location, favorable economy and demographics, you estimate that the shop should be able to sell a total of $200,000 worth of items. Your worksheet looks like this:

Planned Sales	$200,000
+ **Planned Reductions (10.4%)**	20,800
+ **Planned Ending Inventory (EOM)**	58,000
	278,800
– **Planned Beginning Inventory (BOM)**	83,000
= **Planned Purchases**	$195,800

It is important to note that when using the basic stock planning method, planned ending inventory (EOM) is the same as basic stock. If actual sales go as planned, you will be left with stock equivalent to the basic stock figure at the end of the selling period. Using the formula, planned purchases for the selling period amount to $195,800.

For a new store, department, or classification, there is no beginning inventory to subtract:

Planned Sales	$200,000
+ **Planned Reductions**	20,800
+ **Planned Ending Inventory (EOM)**	58,000
	$278,800
– **Planned Beginning Inventory (BOM)**	–
= **Planned Purchases**	$278,800

If the store had been new, the planned purchases figure for the month or season would be $278,800.

Calculating Open-to-Buy The amount of money a buyer has allocated for purchasing merchandise for a designated period of time is called **open-to-buy (OTB)**. The OTB figure should always be thought of as a guide, not an absolute.

> **open-to-buy (OTB)** Amount of money a buyer has allocated for purchasing merchandise for a designated period of time.

Planned purchases become the open-to-buy figure if there are no goods already on-order. Because retail buying is never nice and neat, often a buyer has already committed funds to merchandise on order but not yet received. The planned purchase and open-to-buy figure are also the same when the season or month being planned is not yet underway.

Once the selling period begins, the situation changes. Buyers must be able to calculate an open-to-buy figure at any time during a season or month. Goods already on order will affect OTB calculations. The following example again uses the skateboard store:

Planned Sales	$200,000
+ **Planned Reductions (10.4%)**	20,800
+ **Planned Ending Inventory (EOM)**	58,000
	278,800
– **Beginning Inventory (BOM)**	83,000
= **Planned Purchases**	195,800
– **Goods On Order (OO)**	30,000
= **Open-to-Buy**	165,800

To find the open-to-buy figure, it is necessary to estimate how much merchandise is needed, then determine how much of it is already available. The mid-month or mid-season open-to-buy figure is found by subtracting available goods from needed goods.

Converting Retail OTB to Cost Budgets are planned using retail dollars for all categories. The open-to-buy figure is also computed at retail, but actual purchases from vendors are made at cost. Conversion is necessary. If the markup is 55 percent, cost is 100 percent less 55 percent, or 45 percent. In the example given earlier, the open-to-buy figure at retail is converted to cost in this way:

$$45\% \times \$165,800 = \$74,610.$$

The open-to-buy figure is flexible. Conditions often change between the plan and its implementation. It is best to think of OTB as a monthly guide, not a yearly absolute.

Planned Gross Margin

The difference between the retail selling price and the cost of goods sold is called the gross margin. This concept was introduced in Chapter 4. Gross margin must cover the expenses of doing business and provide a reasonable profit. It is an extremely important figure that is calculated as follows:

$$\text{Gross Margin} = \text{Net Sales} - \text{Cost of Goods Sold}$$

If the initial price put on merchandise is not high enough, factors such as reductions or the rising costs of doing business, may result in a loss rather than a profit. On the other hand, if the initial price is too high, customers will not respond. In both scenarios profit will be affected. Gross margin also can be perceived as the cost of doing business plus a reasonable profit. Retail markup, which affects gross margin, is discussed in detail in Chapter 15.

The best way to plan sales is to use a calendar that offers some uniformity. The **4-5-4 calendar** is an adaptation of a conventional calendar used for retail planning and accounting. When preparing assortment plans and budgets, merchants compare planned sales to past sales for equal periods of time. On a regular monthly calendar this is not always possible because months may end or begin in the middle of a week. Using a 4-5-4 calendar, each season has the same number of weeks and days for two consecutive years. In the third year, the last season has an extra week in the last month, and so it is a 4–5–5 rather than a 4–5–4 quarter.

4-5-4 calendar Adaptation of a conventional calendar used for retail planning and accounting.

Table 14.2 Benefits of Planning by Classification

- Enables dollar sales and units to be planned well.

- Permits the development of a realistic open-to-buy figure.

- Allows buyers to evaluate each segment of their business in order to locate areas for future growth, greater profitability, and cost savings.

- Permits associates in each selling area to understand what merchandise is to be stocked and at what prices.

- Allows department sales managers and buyers to identify merchandise areas which have unmet or insufficient demand.

- Prevents duplication of merchandise.

- Encourages optimum timing for each classification on the selling floor.

- Presents the right colors, styles, prices, and models when customers want them.

- Calls attention to the most productive classifications.

- Assures coverage of each key merchandise area.

With many uncontrollable factors affecting profit, it would be disastrous to attempt to buy merchandise without advance planning. Once the merchandise budget is completed, buyers turn their attention to the actual assortment of products called a unit plan.

The Unit Plan

Whether buying fashion or basic goods, most retailers begin by breaking down the total inventory for a department into manageable units. For example, the classification *jackets* could include snap-front short coats and draw-string-waist anoraks. This classification might be part of an outerwear department. Some buyers start at the classification level and build up to the major category or department. Either way, dollars are allocated to specific groups of merchandise.

Classification Planning

With classification plans, dollars can be allocated to give the best possible return on investment. For example, if private label goods are selling better than designer brands, this is considered when determining stock levels. Without classification planning there is a greater chance of understocking one item and overstocking another. Benefits of planning by classification are highlighted in Table 14.2.

Planning by classification guarantees proper representation of items at planned prices, helps channel purchases to preferred vendors, and provides an opportunity for customers to experience the best the store has to offer. Some retailers choose to plan their inventories in even greater detail by using sub-classifications.

Sub-Classification Method Groups of merchandise in a classification that are defined more narrowly are called **sub-classifications**. To better understand the concept of classification management, consider the Payless Shoe Source system. The company breaks down its large shoe inventory into eight sub-classifications that include:

> **sub-classification** Groups of merchandise in a classification that are defined more narrowly.

- EASTSIDES: Fashionable shoes for X and Y generations.
- RUGGED OUTBACK: Rugged casual shoes for men, women and children; many in this group are boots.
- HIGHLIGHTS: Dress shoes for women and girls.
- PRO WINGS: Synthetic sneakers for the family.
- EAGLE: Leather sneakers for the family.
- COMFORT PLUS: Heavy-duty shoes for men and women; comfort is the priority.
- CHANDLERS: Dress shoes for men and boys.
- HONCHOS: Work boots for men; many with steel toes.

Payless, a national chain, sees merit in assorting its merchandise by use and lifestyle. Other retailers may select styling nuance or end use as criteria for sub-classification. For many, more detail equals better planning.

Model Stock Plans Also used to plan merchandise assortments are model stock plans. **Model stock plans** are lists that show specific stock levels needed for a selling period. The model stock method for planning inventory levels is used for staple as well as fashion goods because it takes into consideration the variations that occur not only from season to season but also within a season.

> **model stock plans** Lists that show specific stock levels needed for a selling period.

Three types of data are gathered:

- Specific information such as classifications, sub-classifications, prices, colors, and sizes.
- Important dates in the season for which model stocks are to be constructed.
- Sales estimates for the months preceding and following the date for which the model stock is set in units have to be calculated. The total is translated into dollars and then checked against the dollar plan.

In preparing a model stock list, the amount of goods needed in each classification is determined by past sales and current trends. There are additional factors that affect assortment planning.

Factors Affecting Merchandise Assortments

Keeping closer track of customer purchasing habits is another way retailers are modifying their unit plans. They are also changing their formats to better capitalize on changing demographics and the increasing demands placed on them by customers.

Retailers spend more time analyzing current customer behavior in order to prepare better merchandise assortments for the future. Learning whether the customer who purchased a home computer this year may be interested in new peripherals next year is a piece of information that has a direct effect on the buying process. Determining how inactive customers can be brought back into the fold is another way research can temper merchandise plans.

Stores are overhauling their physical plants to better meet the needs of customers. This is also true of their merchandise. Wal-Mart developed its Sam's Club and Toys "R" Us opened Kids "R" Us stores, necessitating new directions in structure and merchandising tactics. LL Bean opened LL Kids stores bringing greater assortment of children's apparel and other necessities to the market. Ann Taylor Loft stores, illustrated in Figure 14.6, presents merchandise at lower prices and at a more casual focus than its original Ann Taylor stores.

Figure 14.6 Ann Taylor established its Ann Taylor Loft stores in response to customers' demands for less expensive, more casual apparel, thus altering the company's merchandising strategy.

Proactive approaches like these are indicative of thoughtful strategic planning. Other retailers tend only to react to competitive pressures. Some try to be all things to all people instead of developing specific merchandising niches. It is possible to react to market conditions without trying to serve a broad market. Small retailers that sell limited but distinctive product assortments always will be welcome shopping destinations. Large or small, it is evident that all retailers must carefully analyze customers, determine need, then plan well in dollars and units to meet customer expectations.

The Merchandising Team

An efficient system of planning dollars and units is vital to profits. Equally important is the selection of merchandise. As retail purchasing agents, buyers are charged with many responsibilities including gathering market information, shopping the market, preparing detailed orders, negotiating terms and other related tasks. However, buyers are not the only members of the team responsible for implementing merchandise plans.

Responsibilities of Team Members

Titles may change from store to store, but the same functions are performed by all retailers. Starting from the lowest level of responsibility to the highest, key merchandising positions include:

Assistant Buyers Considered an entry-level position in many organizations, assistant buyers:

- provide merchandising and administrative support for buyers
- set up market trips for buyers
- monitor delivery of merchandise
- communicate with vendors via EDI systems
- provide product information to sales promotion departments
- may initiate markdowns
- report to buyers

Buyers Retail buyers take chief responsibility for the procurement of merchandise as they:

- gather and interpret customer information
- develop dollar and unit plans for their department or classification
- shop major and secondary markets, select and purchase merchandise
- negotiate terms of delivery
- arrange for cooperative advertising money, trade discounts, and markdown money
- cultivate and maintain vendor relationships
- communicate product information to department sales managers
- monitor competition
- report to divisional merchandise manager

Qualities of effective retail buyers are summarized in Table 14.3.

Table 14.3 Characteristics of an Effective Retail Buyer

■ The ability to handle pressure in a variety of forms including long hours on the job, frequent travel, achieving management's financial goals.

■ An eye for quality, taste and value—based on customers' preferences, not always your own.

■ Excellent human relations skills; the ability to deal favorably with many different personality types.

■ Sharp negotiating skills.

■ Superior math and computer skills.

■ The ability to read and interpret financial and merchandising reports.

■ The ability to be flexible and juggle many tasks at once.

■ An indefatigable nature.

■ A desire to maintain high ethical standards.

Divisional Merchandise Managers Overseeing multiple departments, usually in either soft or hard goods areas, divisional merchandise managers:

■ initiate financial planning

■ supervise higher-level buying functions for a major store division

■ give directional and trend input to buyers

■ work with information technology to utilize appropriate merchandise information systems

■ report to the general merchandise manager

General Merchandise Manager Controlling fiscal and merchandising decisions on a store, region, or chain-wide basis, depending on the size of the organization, the general merchandise manager:

■ initiates dollar and unit planning on a storewide basis

■ conducts strategic planning in the merchandising area

■ reports to vice president or president of company, depending on size of the organization

Responsibilities of Support Staff

Allocators Acting as a liaison between merchandising and distribution, allocators have become very important positions in large specialty chains, department stores, and discount operations. **Allocators** are individuals who support merchandise teams by providing detailed distribution information. Their duties include the following:

allocators Individuals who support merchandising teams by providing detailed distribution information.

- ensure that each store has the optimal assortment of merchandise to maximize sales, profits, and customer satisfaction
- make distribution recommendations to buyers based on their close monitoring of stock levels
- keep aware of regional and local needs and competition
- communicate merchandise information to stores

Allocators technically may work on the distribution side of the house, but their interaction with the buying team is imperative if the retail organization is to achieve a smooth flow of goods.

Merchandise Analysts Merchandise analysts perform additional functions in large organizations. Their responsibilities include:

- planning detailed stock levels by utilizing database and other computer-generated reports
- communicating information to other merchandising team members
- facilitating the distribution of goods to stores

Sources of Market Information

Earlier in the chapter several methods for gathering customer information were discussed. These serve as the underpinnings of a buyer's job. However, there is more work to be done. Sources of information need to be probed deeper. In this way retail buyers build confidence in their ability to make the correct choices.

Shopping the Market

Manufacturers show merchandise in major cities at specified times of the year in advance of a selling season. Scheduled seasonal showings of merchandise by manufacturers in market centers are called **market weeks**. Although different industries show their wares at different times, the objective remains the same—to provide the opportunity for buyers to see the best and the brightest new merchandise. In most cases, market week showings are held in manufacturers showrooms four to five times per year. Sometimes hotel suites are used, and, in the case of the designer fashion market, more elaborate arrangements are made.

Manufacturers' Showrooms Going directly to the market offers an opportunity for buyers to see many different lines of merchandise. Major manu-

market week Scheduled seasonal showings of merchandise by manufacturers in market centers.

facturers lease space in established market centers in major cities throughout the world. For example, major markets in the United States include New York City, Dallas, Los Angeles, and Chicago. The Atlanta Apparel Mart in Georgia, a 12-story facility housing numerous permanent and temporary showrooms, is shown in Figure 14.7. Shopping markets has several advantages to buyers who:

- identify new lines that appear stronger than lines presently carried
- determine which current resources have added new products to their lines
- comparison shop more vendors with ease
- make decisions based on seeing the big picture
- become more aware of significant trends in their industry
- give undivided attention to the task of purchasing products

Sales Representatives Sales representatives operate from permanent or temporary showrooms in major markets during market weeks. Some manufacturers also go on the road to meet with buyers in their stores. Some independent sales representatives operate without showrooms and travel limited geographic areas, calling on smaller retailers. Multiline sales reps carry a few to 25 or more lines of related merchandise. The biggest advantage to the retail buyer is convenience. A transaction in progress in a multiline showroom is illustrated in Figure 14.8.

Trade Shows Concurrently, or close to market weeks, trade shows are held several times per year in all merchandise categories. They are a major source of product information and serve as an arena for exchange for retail buyers. The role of the trade show in merchandise procurement has changed. In the past many retailer buyers would *leave paper* while attending a trade show. **Leave paper** is a slang expression for writing an order on the spot. Today, most buyers and small store owners peruse vendor booths collecting trend and preliminary planning information for later use.

Some of the important trade shows in the fashion industry include Premier Vision and Fashion Coterie, for buyers of upmarket women's apparel, and the Fashion Accessories Expo for buyers of jewelry, scarves, small leather goods, and other accessories. All are held in New York City. MAGIC is one of the most important of the menswear trade shows. Held in Las Vegas, its popularity has extended to the sale of womenswear.

Figure 14.7 During market weeks, thousands of buyers converge on the showrooms at the 12-story Atlanta Apparel Mart.

leave paper Slang industry expression for writing an order on the spot.

Figure 14.8 Shopping the market, retail buyers evaluate merchandise lines, identify trends, and weigh input from sales representatives before they write orders.

Most retailers concur that trade shows provide opportunities to find new resources that add spark to their merchandise assortments. With several hundred to more than 2,000 vendors represented, trade shows run 3 to 5 days and are held in all major cities of the world.

Resident Buying Offices

The nature and purpose of resident buying offices was explained earlier in this chapter. Detail on their structure, formats, and the services they provide retailers is covered in this section.

Organization Buying offices are set up so that staff members can work with their retail counterparts. Senior executives of buying offices are equivalent to vice presidents of merchandising in retail organizations. General and divisional merchandise managers are comparable on the next levels. Resident buyers are counterparts to store buyers. They are responsible for a department or single classification of merchandise and fully immerse themselves in the stores they serve. Retail image, target markets, company objectives, and geographic areas served are carefully studied so that buying offices can provide effective service.

Services Rendered The primary role of buying offices is market coverage. Resident buyers spend most of their time in the market visiting vendors. They gather information on trends, new resources, best sellers, prices, and delivery dates. The information is made available to store buyers through a variety of reports, hot sheets, vendor evaluations, catalogs, or via the Internet. Most buying offices are compensated on a percentage of sales.

Some buying offices are empowered to place merchandise orders for member stores. This practice allows stores located far from the market to test items immediately without traveling to the market.

Changes in attitudes, lifestyles, and patterns of consumption tend to move across the globe in uneven waves. Buyers may learn of advancing trends from a resident buyer and be better prepared when it reaches their markets.

Types of Buying Offices There are three basic kinds of resident buying offices:

■ *Independent firms.* Companies that represent a variety of noncompeting retail stores are the most common. The buying office and the stores are separate entities that work together for mutual gain. Frederick Atkins and the Doneger Group in New York City are examples of independent firms. The companies service hundreds of retail clients.

■ *Company owned or affiliated offices.* An office that serves only one company is another type. Sears and JC Penney each maintain their own buying offices. Divisions of holding companies that operate chains of retail companies are slightly different. Only the stores belonging to the corporation are served by the office. Federated Department Stores owns Bloomingdale's, Macy's, and Burdine's, among others. All stores use the services of Federated's buying offices around the world. Stores belonging to Target Corp. such as Mervyn's, Marshall Field's, and Daytons use the services of Associated Merchandising Corporation (AMC), the company it purchased in 1998.

■ *Specialty offices.* Smaller offices may focus on specific types of stores or merchandise classifications. For example, buying offices that serve only stores selling women's larger sizes fit this category.

Additional Sources of Buying Information

Effective buyers are aware of every inkling of a trend. One of the best ways to identify new opportunities is simply to watch people. Knowing what music men and women are listening to in London, what is being worn on the streets of Milan, or what fad replaced Japan's Pokemon will eventually affect sales in other global cities. Several examples illustrate how inspiration from films and input from trade associations and forecasting firms benefit retail buyers.

The now classic film *Titanic* influenced merchandising in many product categories. Replicas of the "Heart of the Ocean" necklace were sold in jewelry stores around the world. Madonna appeared at the Academy Awards in an icy, grey-blue gown wearing silvery makeup reminiscent of the fatal final scene in the film. Retailers did well selling reproductions of the whistle used by the character Rose to summon help. Influence was profound and affected merchandise planning in fashion, memorabilia, and jewelry stores. A Leonardo DiCaprio poster became one of the top sellers of all time. Retail buyers responsible for these categories had to plan quickly or revise plans due to the popularity of the film and its affect on customers.

Trade associations help retail members define their markets and forecast sales. They provide information on market share, customer preferences, and sales and merchandise trends. If the National Sporting Goods

CYBERSCOOP

A visit to *www.doneger.com* lists the many services provided by a resident buying office. Doneger has 800 clients, the majority of which are single-unit stores or small chains. See what the company has to offer.

Association reports that sales of sports equipment and footwear are relatively flat, this is of note to sporting goods retailers. An announcement like this could be attributed to the lack of emergence of a new sport to drive sales. Conversely, the skateboarding trend, which began a decade ago, is expected to impact sales for years to come. Information of this sort helps sporting goods retailers refine their merchandise plans.

Many manufacturers and retailers use the services of forecasting houses to clarify and detail trends that are occurring in the areas of style, direction, and color. Companies like Nigel French and Promostyl are international trend prognosticators. The Color Association of America and The Color Box are smaller, independent firms that deal primarily with color pallets and do their predictive research 18 to 24 months in advance of retail selling seasons. Although this type of research may seem most appropriate in the fashion industry it is not the only aspect of business that makes use of it. Car and appliance manufacturers, home furnishing and furniture retailers all use color forecasting.

Vendors also are good sources of information. Retailers' relationships with vendors are second in importance only to their links with their customers.

Vendor Relationships

Building key resource relationships helps increase bargaining power and gains many advantages for the store. To evaluate vendors, buyers consider the following factors: quality of merchandise, location and reputation of the firm, brand policy, terms of sale, return policies, sales and profit potential, and ethical business practices. The establishment of preferred vendor lists and the power wielded by large retailers on vendors have changed the way business is done.

Preferred Vendor Lists Giant retail companies demand that vendors do business on their premises and usually establish preferred vendor lists. Being on this list usually means that a manufacturer is able to communicate via EDI systems and has established a partnership program with the retailer. Retailers like Wal-Mart, Kmart, and the major specialty and department stores operate primarily on this basis.

Pressures in the Supply Chain The great power exerted by giant retailers in the supply chain has caused conflict between retailers and manufacturers. Although retail companies are large in terms of volume generated, most manufacturers are relatively small. Manufacturers have been forced to meet stringent criteria in order to do business with large retailers. For example, retailers may specify that goods must be shipped on hangers in certain cartons, labeled precisely, routed to the store in an exact manner, or documented according to detailed instructions. If manufacturers fail to comply exactly, retailers penalize them by increasing distribution costs or imposing chargebacks on the vendors. **Chargebacks** are financial penalties imposed on manufacturers by retailers. These fees are often reversed by the retailers, but in the meantime cause ill feelings in what should be a close and mutually beneficial relationship.

chargebacks Financial penalties imposed on manufacturers by retailers.

Pressure escalated in the mid-1990s as retailers faced sluggish sales in many soft goods areas and cut their resource lists. Heavy consolidations in the industry and erratic customer behavior also contributed to the malaise. Afraid of being removed from preferred vendor status, manufacturers found themselves in the uncomfortable position of acquiescing to retailers' demands or face losing their business. In addition to stiff logistics demands, retailers also increased pressure in other areas. Manufacturers were expected to share the risk in uncertain markets by providing guaranteed profit margins and increased remuneration should merchandise purchased not sell in their stores.

Key Trends in Merchandising and Sourcing

Retailers try to find the best products for their stores wherever advantageous buys can be made. Global sourcing, private labeling, licensing, and product development are all ways retailers can increase margins and profits this century.

Global Sourcing

Positive and negative aspects of global sourcing continue to challenge retailers this decade.

Advantages and Logistics Through importing, retailers are able to offer well-designed products that their competitors are less likely to have. Sound relationships with vendors and contractors need be established before exclusive production runs are feasible. Retailers are able to achieve higher markups on imports because they usually cost less to produce off-shore. This is true of most fashion apparel since it is labor intensive to produce. Today's emphasis on private labeling is another reason product developers turn to production facilities where they can find the most lucrative arrangements. A typical workroom located in a country where the labor rate is low is illustrated in Figure 14.9. When a good working relationship is established with

Figure 14.9 Jean company in Penang, Malaysia, is typical of production companies that dot Southeast Asia and other areas of the world where labor costs are low but quality is high.

foreign suppliers, lower inventory levels can be kept and initial markups on products can be higher.

Some countries, such as Italy, are known for their high quality and strong design work. Others in Asia are famous for the production of volume merchandise. Some parts of the world are important for specialty merchandise—Peru for sweaters and knits; Haiti and Africa for carved woodenware; and Indonesia for batik. Despite the shrinking globe, interesting materials are still undiscovered in parts of Africa, South America, and Asia. However, to find and develop them, buyers must have patience and time to work closely with small manufacturers or cottage industries.

Buying offices can be instrumental in planning foreign trips for retail buyers. Many have branches or affiliates in key international cities. Some large retail organizations such as Limited Brands have their buyers travel in groups accompanied by a merchandise manager, looking for fast-breaking, and they hope, profitable trends.

Overseas market representatives may not only facilitate entry into foreign markets, but they might also be a retailer's best link to the best providers of merchandise. Knowledge is power, in this case, and can affect a buyer's success in the marketplace. Local representatives can also make appropriate introductions and help arrange for exclusive merchandise. One of the most progressive buying offices abroad is AMC.

As well as being represented in foreign countries, retail buyers also should be knowledgeable about the quotas and tariffs discussed in Chapter 8, and international finance and shipping standards.

Ethical Conflicts Ethical issues that arise when doing business abroad also affect people who source products globally. Counterfeit goods, labor abuses, and even environmental issues bring challenges of a different nature.

Bogus goods are a universal problem that ultimately contribute to increased costs for vendors, retailers, and customers. In some cases, complete underground industries have cropped up, replicating Louis Vuitton handbags, Versace belts, or Prada leather goods. Often skilled workers are lured into the trade, working nights on fake goods after their legitimate day jobs in the fashion sector. According to one source, Italy leads the world in production of counterfeit goods, followed by Taiwan and

Korea.[2] Figure 14.10 shows a group of counterfeit T-shirts identified in Asia.

In Colombia, Calvin Klein experienced problems with counterfeit fragrances and packaging. South American officials seized more than 6,000 packages of fake CK One, Escape, Eternity, and Obsession—complete with printing plates and cartons. According to Colombian officials, the heist was part of on-going activities to apprehend a known counterfeiting ring in South America. The government estimated that the ring garnered $15 million in sales of bogus goods in one year.[3]

Respect for intellectual property rights, including trademarks and copyrights, is an area of concern to industry leaders worldwide. The problems won't subside, however, until the level of education regarding ethical issues rises, more monitoring programs are developed, and stiffer penalties are enacted. Customers must also recognize the impact purchasing counterfeit goods has on their own wallets.

Private Labeling

Because so many stores are selling the same merchandise to the same customers in the same market, private labeling has affected merchandising greatly. Private labeling occurs when a store contracts with a manufacturer to produce exclusive items. The items will bear the name developed by the retailer rather than the name of the manufacturer. This is a successful tactic when the store name or its invented brand carries an image of quality, fashion, or value. Private label goods account for the majority of sales in specialty stores such as Barneys New York, Diesel, and Talbots.

Private labels can achieve widespread recognition and loyalty. The Neiman Marcus' Red River food brand, Macy's INC (International Concepts) women's apparel label, and Sears' Canyon River Blues sportswear line are other examples of private labels demanded by their respective customers. Catchy brand names may emanate from anywhere in the world. Metrojaya department stores in Southeast Asia developed a label for its line of nautical-inspired sportswear called "Cape Cod Massachusetts."

Private labeling also is an important strategy for discounters. The top three U.S. discounters, Wal-Mart, Kmart, and Target, are using private labeling to position their stores as desirable destinations for exclusive merchandise and to increase their profits per unit. Brands are important in apparel, grocery, health and beauty aid, and general merchandise categories.[4] Candles topped the list of the fastest growing mass merchant private label

Figure 14.10 On the resort island of Langkawi, these counterfeit T-shirts were spotted at an outdoor market. Probably manufactured in nearby Thailand, they were not under license to the designers portrayed.

categories in the late 1990s, emphasizing their importance as a lifestyle merchandise category.

Licensing

In this brand-conscious world, product licensing has become the chief way major designers, sports teams, and entertainment businesses have expanded their brands worldwide. **Product licensing** is a contractual relationship between a designer, or other holder of rights to a brand, and a manufacturer to produce items under that name or brand. Ironically, when companies grow in this manner, they lose some control over the very thing that made them successful in the first place—their names. Fragrances and underwear bear the Calvin Klein logo, but all are manufactured by companies other than the CK parent. For example, fragrances are licensed to Unilever and underwear to Warnaco. Bill Blass has licenses in 40 product categories.[5]

A license is a legal contract between the holder of rights to a name or product and a manufacturer. Often holders are designers who license their names to other parties to produce and distribute merchandise to select retailers. This method has become a popular and profitable way for companies to extend their brand internationally. Designers such as Tommy Hilfiger, cartoon characters like Barney the Dinosaur, and sports heroes including Tiger Woods bring handsome profits to retailers that stock merchandise bearing their names.

The typical royalty fee paid to designers is between 5 and 7 percent. Because many customers are brand and status conscious, licensed goods are another avenue buyers consider in their assortment plans. If you are still unsure of the power—and extremes—of brand licensing, consider this example. Gucci has licensed a dog bed. Learn more about the pros and cons of licensing in this chapter's From the Field box.

Product Development

Taking the buying function a step further, dependence on global sourcing has spawned a new retail career position—product developers. **Product developers** generate ideas, design prototypes, and arrange for production of exclusive products for retailers. Product developers are very knowledgeable regarding material specification, textile performance standards, manufacturing procedures, and quality control. Many speak the languages of countries where they do business. In these areas, their expertise usually goes beyond that of buyers. Asia is one of the prime areas for product development, especially Taiwan, China, Sri Lanka, Thailand, Malaysia, and South Korea.

product licensing Contractual arrangement between a designer, or other holder of rights to a brand, and a manufacturer to produce items under the designer's name or brand.

product developer Generates ideas, designs prototypes, and arranges for production of exclusive products for retailers.

From the Field: To License or Not
By Dianne M. Pogoda

When does it make sense to license and when is it better to launch a product in-house? Apparel executives often wrestle with the question of whether they should keep full control over their brands or cede some of their authority to a company with expertise in the product field.

Industry experts agree the keys to making this decision are the strengths that exist between the licensor and licensee, and the nature of the product. "A company must capitalize on its core competencies," said Adele Kirk, manager of consumer marketing for Kurt Salmon Associates. "It needs to look at what it does and knows well, especially in terms of product development and sourcing."

If the company can reasonably produce a new product using its own resources, than taking the in-house route is probably the right decision, she said. If not, finding a licensing partner with the needed expertise is the way to proceed.

"When a company with a strong brand wants to launch a new product, it must throw a huge amount of resources behind it—human and financial," Kirk said. "It has to build a team of experienced people with expertise in the new area. Sometimes, you're better off going with someone who's already up and running." Kirk said critical factors in a successful licensing venture are back-end partnerships with companies that have a strong sourcing network, and a detailed cost-benefit analysis to determine the worth of the investment.

A frequently cited case of a misstep in doing a product in-house is Donna Karan's first attempt at marketing beauty products, which stumbled badly; the products finally were licensed to the Estée Lauder Co in 1997. "I'm sure [the in-house strategy] was motivated by a fear of giving up control over the product," said Sydney Brooks, a partner in the consulting firm Smart Co., adding that this is common. "The key in licensing is being in charge of the marketing strategy and having in-house staff devoted to working with the licensee to insure that the quality of the product, vision and the message getting to the consumer are consistent."

Fulton MacDonald, president of consulting firm International Business Development, said the biggest requirement in licensing is strong legal support to insure compliance with design direction and payment of royalties. "It's vitally important in licensing to make sure that the licensee has sufficient capital to produce, market, package, sell, and distribute the product adequately," he stresses. "The licensee must have a strong merchant-manager in charge of the licensed division who can properly interpret design direction from the licensor, which is probably the most important need, and there must be a close working relationship between licensor and licensee."

Specialists can execute a product much better than people not experienced in a specific area, MacDonald said, citing such areas as handbags, shoes, jewelry, cosmetics, luggage, furs, hats, and sleepwear as examples.

But when is it a better idea to launch a product in-house? MacDonald listed several criteria for taking this route:

- When the product application is an easy extension for the brand and its developer and/or designer.
- When the same channel of distribution is used.
- When there are compatible department or classifications.
- For a product that doesn't require special technical production skills—as do fine leather goods, furs, fragrances, jewelry, tailored clothing, bathing suits, undergarments and hosiery—or special marketing and sales skills—as do fragrances, jewelry, big-ticket tailored clothing, furs and gowns—for which the company is not suited.
- When there are similar production and selling cycles between the core business and the new launch. "Dresses, for example, are produced broad and shallow, with many different styles flowing into stores continuously," MacDonald said. "This is a different selling cycle from what exists for most sportswear, which is produced and sold narrow and deep."

Other reasons for manufacturing in-house are if the company has an exceptionally strong production management capability, and if the firm has sufficient resources—money and talent—to effectively manage and control a much-enlarged operating base.

Source: *Women's Wear Daily.* May 27, 1998:34. Courtesy of Fairchild Publications, Inc.

Micro-merchandising

micro-merchandising Practice of creating and manufacturing product lines or items targeted to a specific market.

Another technique retailers are using to counter mass merchandised assortments that are the scourge of many large stores is called micro-merchandising. **Micro-merchandising** is the practice of creating and manufacturing product lines or items targeted to a specific market. Many large retailers have been content with doing large sales volume at the expense of tailoring products to specific interest groups in different parts of the country. Micro-merchandising is making it easier to personalize assortments and increase sales. For example, Family Bargain shipped T-shirts to some of its 156 discount stores featuring slogans publicizing local events such as balloon races in Albuquerque, New Mexico, and the Extreme Games in Bear Mountain, California. Micro-merchandising is expected to improve sell-through, turnover, and build customer loyalty.[6]

Merchandising strategies are profoundly complex and encompass thinking globally and locally to provide customers with the merchandise they want in a timely fashion. The buyers job is not complete, however, until the details of the purchase have been negotiated and finalized.

CYBERSCOOP

Buyers have online options as they look for the best value for their retail customers. VIRTUAL-RAGS™ is an online wholesale sourcing service where buyers can search for specific items by category, size, minimum price, or country. Access the site at **www.virtualrags.com** to see what is available.

Finalizing the Purchase

After merchandise selections have been made, the next responsibility of retail buyers is to negotiate the terms of the wholesale transaction. The purchase terms may include some or all of the following: discounts, completion dates, shipping arrangements, point of transfer of title, prices, exclusivity agreements, cooperative advertising, return policy, markdown money, and reorder capabilities.

Time and Money Incentives

Cash Discounts Almost all lines of merchandise carried by a store are purchased with cash discount terms, commonly ranging from 2 to 8 percent. Consequently, obtaining cash discounts is of great importance to gross margin management.

Discounts are taken as a percentage of total purchase price and are offered in return for prompt payment. For example, under terms of 2/10 net 30, the first numeral designates the percentage discount rate, the second the time period. In this case, a 2 percent discount is offered if the bill is paid within 10 days of the invoice date. After 10 days the full amount of the invoice is due. Net 30 indicates that the retailer has 30 days from date of invoice to pay the bill in full, even if it chooses not to take advantage of the discount period. After that period, the company seeking payment can impose a finance charge on the outstanding balance.

Savvy retailers often use advanced or extra dating to extend their payment terms. This can be advantageous to retailers that purchase coats in June for an August, preseason sale but do not want to pay for those goods until they have had ample opportunity to be sold. For example, on terms of 8/10 net 30 X 60, the retailer would be entitled to deduct the 8 percent discount for approximately two months beyond the original remittal date.

Retailers also might ask for another early payment incentive called anticipation. **Anticipation** is an additional discount sometimes allowed when the invoice is paid before the expiration of the cash discount period. Anticipation is also deducted from the invoice price. There are other nuances to discounts based on invoice dating that extend credit to retailers as they juggle gross margins and cash flow. Although beyond the scope of this discussion, all are important in the negotiation process.

anticipation An additional discount sometimes allowed when the invoice is paid before the expiration date of the cash discount period.

The reality of discounting is sometimes quite different and the issue of ethical business practices is often raised. Early payment discounts offered are usually worked into the wholesale price. Even if a time-dependent discount is agreed upon, some retailers do not adhere to the terms. Large, powerful firms have been known to pay at will and still take their discounts, even if payment occurs six months later. This certainly puts cash flow pressure on manufacturers. Better partnership arrangements, based on mutual concern and respect, are alleviating this problem. However, disrespect of the discount period still exists in some sectors of the industry. Growing acknowledgment that all supply chain members are responsible for the satisfaction of customers should further combat this negative tendency.

Trade Discounts Deductions from an agreed price, usually granted by manufacturers to other supply chain members, are called **trade discounts**. Trade discounts are quoted in a series and commonly occur between manufacturers and wholesalers or other members of the supply chain. The amount of the discount is dependent on the market prices at the time of the sale, the size of the order, and the payment record of the retailer. An invoice might carry terms of "less 25 percent, less 10 percent, less 5 percent." This would mean that one company might pay 75 percent of invoice, or take a 25 percent discount. Another might be allowed an additional 10 percent, and a third company might receive another 5 percent off. However, large chains and department stores buy much larger quantities than some wholesalers and also secure trade discounts. The buying power of large retailers has changed the way business is done.

trade discount A deduction from an agreed price, usually granted by manufacturers to other supply chain members.

CYBERSCOOP

Nygard International is a manufacturer of women's moderate apparel and supplies products to Hudson Bay and Sears in Canada and Dillard's, Sears, and Macy's in the United States. Nygard uses a state-of-the art replenishment system to provide its retail accounts with speedy service. To learn more about the company go to **www.nygard.com.** What is its slogan?

completion date The date promised by the manufacturer for total receipt of goods by the retailer.

free on board (FOB) Term identifying the point from which the retailer assumes responsibility for goods and payment of transportation charges.

Shipping Terms and Title Issues Retailer buyers also discuss completion dates with vendors. A **completion date** is the date promised by the manufacturer for total receipt of goods by the retailer. Although all goods on the same order might not arrive on the same day, they must arrive by the completion date. Retailers can choose to cancel the order if goods do not arrive on time.

In addition, the mode of delivery—U.S. Postal Service, Federal Express, UPS, rail, truck, water, for example—should be specified. The party responsible for shipping charges must be articulated. **Free on board (FOB)** is the term identifying the point from which the retailer assumes responsibility for goods and payment of transportation charges. It usually indicates where title to the goods passes to the retailer. Usually, terms are FOB factory, meaning the retailer pays for transportation charges to the store or distribution center. FOB destination indicates that the manufacturer is picking up the shipping costs.

Because there are several alternatives for transfer of title, retailers assume different levels of responsibility under each. Retailers may take ownership of merchandise at various points in the purchase process: upon purchase, when the merchandise is loaded for delivery, when the shipment is received, or at the end of the billing cycle. Another possibility is that the retailer does not own the goods at all, but accepts them on consignment. In this arrangement, the seller retains ownership, requiring the retailer to pay only after the goods are sold. This might occur when the manufacturer needs the retailer as an account, when products are new and untested, or in the case of unusually high-priced merchandise such as furs or fine gems. As noted in the Chapter 8, this is common practice in Japan and other parts of the world.

Merchandising and Advertising Incentives

Other items open to negotiation before the purchase is officially complete include markdown money and cooperative advertising. Taking advantage of one or both options extends the retail gross margin.

markdown money Extra reimbursement allowed the retailer if a manufacturer's goods do not sell well.

Markdown Money In an attempt to share the risk, many buyers ask for and get markdown money from vendors. **Markdown money** is extra reimbursement allowed the retailer if a manufacturer's goods do not sell well. Some might negotiate to return to the vendor all items in an order that did not sell in the store after a specified time on the floor. But more are turning to markdown money as a way to receive cash for slow-moving merchandise. This may put pressure on the vendor, but create leverage for the retailer.

Cooperative Advertising Vendors often make advertising allowances available to the retailers they service. **Cooperative advertising** is a program under which retailers and manufacturers agree to share costs for retail advertising. Based on a percentage of sales—usually about 5 percent—funds accrue on an annual basis and can be used as a draw account for advertising expenses. For example, if a retailer chooses to run a newspaper ad, co-op funds can be used to pay 50 to 100 percent of the cost, provided criteria set by the manufacturer are met. Although sales promotion departments administer co-op programs, buyers are at the table with manufacturers. They are responsible for inquiring about co-op opportunities at the time they are negotiating the sale.

When selecting merchandise intended to meet the needs of customers and secure profits for retailers there are no guarantees. Retail merchandising teams can increase the odds and their gross margins by planning dollars wisely, being aware of worldwide trends, seeking input from a variety of professional resources, synthesizing that information into a workable assortment plan, and negotiating carefully. Buyers provide the vital artery between retailers and manufacturers. All are in business to satisfy their customers.

cooperative advertising Program under which retailers and manufacturers agree to share costs for retail advertising.

Summary

The retailer's primary function is to generate a profit by buying and selling merchandise. Inventory planning is the most critical issue faced by all retailers from the giant chains to the smallest shopkeepers.

Retailers begin the process by analyzing past and current information from both in-store and out-of-store sources. Accurately interpreting customer demand is crucial at this stage. Dollar planning requires consideration of sales, stock levels, reductions, purchases, and gross margin. Unit plans should be made for each classification of goods.

No formula guarantees having the optimum number of items on hand to meet the demands of the market. Adherence to a planning process and using methods like the weeks-of-supply method, stock-to-sales ratio, as well as basic stock and model stock plans reduces risk. Stock planning software from a number of resources makes merchandise planing more efficient.

The merchandising team is responsible for the creation and control of the merchandise budget and buying plan. Many sources of market information are available for retail buyers who are on the front line of the purchasing process. Buyers shop the market by attending trade shows and visiting manufacturers showrooms, multiline sales representatives, and buying offices.

Vendor relationships are important to cultivate and maintain. Global sourcing has become particularly important because of increased retail competition and the resulting need to develop exclusive products that are lass costly to manufacture. Product developers are taking buying to new levels as experts create and manufacture products where the best deals can be struck. Ethical issues such as counterfeiting should be addressed globally. Private labeling and product licensing continue to play important roles in merchandising. Merchandising is the lifeblood of all retail organizations.

Questions for Review and Discussion

1. What internal and external sources of information do retail buyers seek when planning their merchandise assortments?

2. Why is it necessary for retailers to plan sales in dollars and units? What steps are taken to create a dollar merchandise plan?

3. Give examples of a classification and a sub-classification. How do retailers use these concepts to merchandise their stores?

4. Describe the members of a merchandise team and explain their principal duties.

5. What are resident buying offices? How do they act as the eyes, ears, and legs of a retail buyer in the market?

6. What is the main purpose of a trade show? Explain how information acquired at a trade show is used by a buyer?

7. Why do many retailers source and develop products globally?

8. Why are vendor relationships important to retailers? What areas of friction exist between retailers and manufacturers?

9. What impact do private labeling and product licensing have on merchandise assortment planning? Discuss examples of private labeling and product licensing observed in retail stores in your market.

10. What characteristics should an effective retail buyer possess?

Endnotes

1. "Merchandise Returned for Refund, 1996." *Retail Industry Indicators*. National Retail Institute. National Retail Federation. Washington, DC May, 2000. Source: Center for Retailing Education and Research. College of business Administration. University of Florida, 1997: *National Retail Security Survey*.

2. Mueller, Tom. "Counterfeit Couture." *Conde Nast Traveler*. November 1997:54,56.

3. Owens, Jennifer. "Klein Fakes Seized." *Women's Wear Daily*. April 24, 1998: 7.

4. "PL Spurs Mass Market Share." *Discount Store News*. September 6, 1999:25,26.

5. Wilson, Eric. "Is Licensing Dead?" *Women's Wear Daily*. August 1, 2000:6-8.

6. Edelson, Sharon. "Micromerchandising: When Retailers Grow by Thinking Smaller." *Women's Wear Daily*. May 1, 1997:12.

Chapter 15

Pricing for Profit

Learning objectives

After completing this chapter you should be able to:

- Articulate how customer behavior and factors in the retail environment influence pricing objectives.

- Examine several passive, aggressive and neutral pricing methods used by retailers.

- Assess pricing strategies and techniques being used by retailers.

- Evaluate the use of markup and markdown as pricing tools.

- Explain the relationship between pricing and profitability.

Figure 15.1 Fifty percent off sales are part of most retailers promotional pricing strategies (See p. 450).

Many customers refuse to pay full retail prices. They shop at discount and off-price stores, membership warehouses, and category killers. At department and specialty stores, they wait for promotional prices. Telling friends where they got a great buy has become as important as relating the latest designer purchase for many. Yet some customers spend more to get better service, quality, or status.

Customers perceive price in many ways. Quality, value, ambiance, convenience, and services rendered by retailers all affect customers' interpretations of fair prices. Price comparisons between stores are made easily. In fact, the pricing policy of some stores is to beat competitor's prices at all costs. They encourage customers to shop around and will match competitors' prices, or in some cases, offer an additional bonus.

Pricing objectives are set before detailed pricing strategies and techniques are determined. Chances are few products will sell at the price first ticketed. Therefore, the management of markups and markdowns is strategically imperative to retailers. This chapter considers several aspects of pricing.

Pricing Objectives

Earning profits may be the ultimate goal of retailers, but the ways of achieving profitability vary. Some retailers strive to gain market share, some to reach specific sales volumes, and others to achieve high gross margins. Goals for department and specialty retailers are different from those of discount retailers. Some of the most common pricing objectives include:

- *Profit maximization.* Retailers that advocate this objective set prices that will assure them high profits. In theory this approach sounds admirable; in practice it is unrealistic in highly competitive markets.
- *Volume driven.* Firms intent on dominating a retail category may opt for volume-oriented sales goals. Best Buy's determination to erode Circuit City's market share illustrates this pricing objective. The rivalry between Wal-Mart and Kmart is illustrated in the competitively priced product in Figure 15.2.
- *Image driven.* Some retailers set pricing objectives that cement a specific image in the minds of their customers. A discounter like Dollar General has

made its name selling inexpensive, needed products to low-income markets. With prices on small leather goods starting at $250, Louis Vuitton has the opposite in mind. Both use pricing to communicate image.

■ *Status quo.* Some retail companies pride themselves on offering the same or similar prices over a period of time. For example, 99 cents stores or those where everything is $10 fit this category.

Retailers may change objectives as market demands require. Market share battles today may become image issues tomorrow.

Figure 15.2 Volume-driven pricing objectives are used by discounters like Kmart. The pricing technique, called odd-pricing, is also evident in this display of interior paints.

Factors Affecting Retail Pricing

Before choosing a retail pricing strategy, store executives consider several factors that may impact their decisions: customers, competition, government regulation, business design, and merchandising strategies.

Customer Lifestyles and Perceptions

Unless retailers know the economic status and lifestyles of their customers, they cannot make appropriate pricing decisions. For example, a factory worker earning $35,000 a year would spend money differently and have different tastes than a teacher earning the same salary. Not all customers buy with price as their first priority. Visual presentation of merchandise and store ambiance, also influence purchasing behavior. Image can be as important as price, or price can be more important than any other factor.

The worth that customers place on merchandise, which may be different from true value, is called **perceived value**. Many people pay a higher price in order to have Perdue chicken or Mrs. Fields cookies on their tables, and designer labels in their closets. Mrs. Fields cookies cost about one dollar per cookie; homemade cookies cost about ten cents each. Can the difference in price and quality be fully justified in terms of production and marketing costs? If not, are Mrs. Fields cookies better than homemade? How much better?

An interesting exercise is to ask a roomful of people to indicate what they would be willing to pay for a hotel room in a major city for one night

perceived value The worth that consumers place on merchandise, which may be different from true value.

CYBERSCOOP

Price comparisons are easy to do with shopping robots. Try out a "bot" at **www.PriceSCAN.com** or **www.mySimon.com** and see where you can find the best price on a new pair of in-line skates. Did you have many to choose from?

during the business week. The responses usually vary greatly, because everyone has a different idea of a suitable accommodation and how much it should cost. Many variables intercede. For example, a major chain such as Westin charges more than lesser-known hotels. Location plays a role, as do the services offered, time of year, length of stay, and whether any promotional offers are in effect. How we perceive a product or service largely determines what we are willing to pay for it.

Certain individuals can be very inflexible about price. People who insist that they have never paid more than $15 for hair styling and refuse to do so are not necessarily in the minority. Retailers need to consider customer behavior when they are considering raising prices.

Competition

The oversaturation of the marketplace has been discussed throughout this text. Too many retailers are chasing the same customers. To counter this trend, Target's signature division competes with discounters such as Wal-Mart or Kmart. Mervyn's, also owned by Target, is a mid-market department store and competes with Sears. All Target divisions operate in different price zones.

Large retailers have pressured smaller companies with limited resources. Small retailers have learned to compete in different ways. Some offer personalized service, others innovative merchandise concepts, or great depth in a single product category.

Retailers track comparative prices on a daily or weekly basis. Large retailers like Wal-Mart employ people whose sole responsibility is to collect pricing information from competitive stores. Those stores, catalogs, and Web sites that have the potential to become competitors are also closely monitored.

The wealth of information available on the Internet has made it easier for customers to comparison shop. Also, it is less expensive to purchase some products, such as books, stocks, newspapers, cars, golf clubs, and airline fares. For example, in a study done by an automobile research firm, 22 percent of shoppers paid the full sticker price on cars, but only 9 percent of shoppers who used the Internet to collect information paid that much.[1]

Because it is a powerful source of consumer research, the Internet is expected to continue its influence on retail pricing. The trend toward value pricing that began in the 1980s will only accelerate as more customers find electronic ways to continue the mission: never pay full price.

Government Regulation

In the 19th century, small retailers that were being hurt by larger firms with greater purchasing power needed to be protected. The Sherman Antitrust Act was passed in 1890 to prevent horizontal price fixing that might take place in any kind of business. The law, aimed at keeping competition open, makes it illegal for manufacturers, wholesalers, or retailers to fix prices. This chapter's From the Field describes a pricing conflict between independent shoe store owners and their supplier, Nine West.

Individual states have enacted a number of unfair trade practice laws in efforts to protect smaller retailers. Manufacturers are prevented from price discrimination in the sale of goods of like quality by the Robinson-Patman Act. The act does permit manufacturers to establish different prices based on sales volume differences. They must prove that specific price agreements do not hinder retail competition.

Business Design

Retailers have different operating philosophies, called business designs. Generally, retailers with high gross margins, such as jewelers, operate on a low-turnover basis. Retailers with high gross margins and high turnover include convenience stores and some vending machine operations. On the other hand, low-margin retailers, such as grocers or warehouse clubs, operate on a very high turnover basis. Average food retailers achieve net profits of 1 percent. Typical soft goods retailers earn net profit of 2 percent—10 percent or more for high achievers. Gross margin, and its relationship to the retailer's ability to turn a profit, is the final topic in this chapter. Discount and department store pricing policies vary as the following sections illustrate.

Discount Stores Today's discounters are different from their predecessors which sold a wide variety of lower-priced—and often lower-quality—merchandise. The philosophy of discounting is based on high-volume, low-margin sales.

Kmart has combined fashion appeal and attractive price points with its Jaclyn Smith sportswear collection. Kmart also features nationally branded jeans such as Gitano and Lee at competitive prices. Private label merchandise such as its Route 66 and B.E. (Basic Essentials) sportswear is priced lower than nationally branded goods. Other discounters keep demand high and prices low by adopting similar strategies.

Family Dollar is a store that sells general merchandise at competitive prices out of smaller stores than typical discount retailers. The company

From the Field: Treading a Contentious Line
By Melody Petersen

Peter Polites, owner of a Nine West store in New Jersey, slashed the price of a popular, smart-looking women's shoe, knowing he would attract many more customers—and still earn a smooth 60 percent [gross] profit on each pair. But Polites's sale irritated some managers at large department stores down the hall in the Mall at Short Hills. One Nordstrom manager, he said, walked into Mr. Polites's small store, picked some shoes off the shelf, looked at the prices, slammed them down and left without a word.

Mr. Polites said the Nordstrom manager later explained that the flats Mr. Polites had reduced to $49.99 from $60 were included on a confidential list of styles—known as the "off-limits list"—whose prices Nine West Group, Inc. rarely, if ever, lets stores markdown.

Mr. Polites's low prices also maddened executives at Nine West, the footwear giant that says it sells one out of every five pairs of shoes sold to women in the United States. Executives at Nine West called Mr. Polites and demanded that he end his sale. When Mr. Polites refused, he was told that in that case, Nine West could not ship him shoes. Mr. Polites taped his phone conversations with Nine West executives because, he said, he felt his store, which sells only Nine West shoes, was threatened.

He and two other owners of Nine West stores, who have fought with the company over other business issues before, say the incident helped them solve a puzzle they had been piecing together for years. The answer, according to information gathered by the three store owners, is that for years, Nine West and major department stores in the United States, which sell millions of pairs of the company's shoes, have worked together in an elaborate and secret system that almost guarantees that women, no matter how many stores they shop in, will always find the same prices for most Nine West styles.

The store owners say they talked to regulators at the Federal Trade Commission, which enforces the antitrust laws, about the pricing practices and gave them copies of the so-called off-limits list, as well as memos by Nine West employees and tapes of phone conversations with Nine West executives.

According to the store owners' information, the system works like this: Nine West and some department stores agree on minimum prices, Nine West employees patrol all stores to insure that prices are not lowered, if a department store finds another store charging prices below the minimum it complains to Nine West, and Nine West warns that shipments will be delayed or even ended if prices are too low.

If Nine West stopped enforcing the minimums and allowed stores to compete on price, women would almost surely find lower prices, saving as much as $10 or more on many styles. Nine West prices most of its shoes from $50 to $90 a pair.

So are Nine West's pricing practices illegal? That is not clear. Ken M. Peterson, a lawyer in Wichita, Kansas, who represented the three store owners, wrote a letter to Nine West saying he believed that its practices violated Federal antitrust laws, to which he received no response. And he warned his clients not to give in to company demands that they raise prices. If they did, Mr. Peterson said, they themselves could be found guilty of conspiring to fix minimum prices.

Herbert J. Hovencamp, a University of Iowa law professor, who is an antitrust expert, said it is illegal for a distributor and a company that sells its products to agree on minimum retail prices. It is, though, legal for a distributor to demand that its price list be followed, he said. The federal laws are technical and ambiguous, Mr. Hovencamp added, and they have been weakened over the years by court decisions. He said it was unclear whether Nine West and the department stores were breaking the law.

Several department store companies, including Nordstrom and Federated Department Stores, said they had strict policies prohibiting any agreements with a manufacturer or competitor on pricing. Dennis Broderick, general counsel for Federated, said he was not aware of any meetings between Federated and Nine West at which minimum prices might have been agreed on. He said that Nine West asks department stores to follow the price list, and that if they do, Nine West gives them financial incentives or discounts for expenses like advertising. Nine West sells hundreds of millions of dollars worth of shoes to department stores each year.

Source: *New York Times.* January 13, 1999:C1,2.

targets low-income families, stocking low-margin, high-turnover items. Flannel shirts for $5.00 and a 20-ounce squeeze bottle of Heinz ketchup for $1.00 are typical Family Dollar prices.[2]

Off-price discount retailers sell name-brand merchandise at lower prices than department stores. Services, ambiance, and assortments are limited. Turnover usually runs double that of traditional apparel stores. Prices are 20 to 60 percent less than those in department stores for the same merchandise. Part of the growth in off-price sales comes from the sharp increase in the number of outlets. The off-price chain T.J. Maxx sells predominantly first-quality, in-season merchandise at higher margins than traditional discounters. The company operated 701 T.J.Maxx and 589 Marshalls stores in 2002.[3]

Department Stores Department stores traditionally prioritized high gross margins. That focus has changed as the most aggressive department stores adapt to the methods of off-pricers. Department stores and others have been criticized for their policies of marking goods up at a higher than customary percentage in order to bring prices down for a sale or special purchase. Knowledgeable customers perceive this method of establishing prices as next of kin to a scam. Retailers insist it is a legitimate pricing technique. Both make strong points. Retailers know that all products in a group of merchandise will not sell at the same price. In fact, for typical fashion classifications, retailers are fortunate if 30 percent of their inventory sells at the full retail price. Due to a plethora of one-day sales, three-day sales, pre-holiday sales, and post-holiday clearance sales, its a wonder that anything sells at its original retail price. Usually another 30 percent of stock sells at a first markdown, and another third at a second markdown. The remainder sells well below wholesale costs of the merchandise. Retailers are most concerned with the average retail selling price, and if they have to mark up to mark down, they do. Customers are concerned that merchandise is overpriced. It is no surprise that many wait for goods to be marked down before considering a purchase. Pricing policies have created a strange tension between retailer and customer showing no retrenchment.

In a study conducted for *Women's Wear Daily* by International Communications Research, women polled were asked about their attitudes toward pricing. Most believed the initial prices on apparel were inflated before being marked down. The survey also confirmed that most women buy apparel when it is on sale, or use discount coupons when making purchases.[4] Throngs of customers traditionally shop during peak sale periods as illustrated in Figure 15.3.

Did You Know?

In a spot check of price scanning systems in major discount and department stores, 14 out of 100 items were scanned incorrectly. Overcharges were rung 12 times and undercharges twice. Boston passed the Consumer and Merchant Protection Act in 1998 which allows the city to impose fines on retailers that fail to pass scanner inspections.
Source: Mohl, Bruce. "Kmart, Macy's Cited on Pricing." *Boston Globe*. September 11, 1998:B2.

Figure 15.3 Storewide department store sale in Amsterdam convinces shoppers to come out in throngs. Pent up demand like this is considered as retailers determine pricing strategy.

Merchandising Strategies

Pricing is closely related to certain merchandising practices. Private label merchandise allows retailers to achieve higher profits. Bridge lines are another way retailers merchandise their stores based on specific price levels.

Private Label Retailers have developed their own lines of merchandise with their store label as a way of competing with stores selling national brands at discounted prices. Private labeling was discussed in Chapter 14. The primary reason for using private label programs is to increase gross margins. Economies of scale due to large production runs and increased control over the manufacturing process create savings. Retailers are then able to price private label goods lower for their customers. Private label pricing advantages are realized by retailers at all stages of the price/quality continuum. Costco Wholesale produces items under its Kirkland label, which are sold at prices that are considerably lower than those of nationally branded items. A display of private label shirts at Costco is shown in Figure 15.4. Barneys New York does extensive private label work under its store label. Fashion products are invariably well-made, of quality fabrics and fine styling details. They are not inexpensive but are well-received by Barneys upmarket clientele.

bridge line A line of apparel that is priced lower than designer fashions.

Bridge Lines Some groups of women's apparel are designed to fit a specific price zone. A line of apparel that is priced lower than designer fashion is called a **bridge line**. The bridge market falls between "better" and "designer" price zones in the industry. Donna Karan's DKNY line and designer Emanuel Ungaro's Emanuel line are examples. Some manufacturers produce lines intentionally for bridge selling such as Dana Buchman, manufactured by Liz Claiborne, and Ellen Tracy. Bridge lines have a price range several hundred dollars below the regular designer collections. If a Donna Karan jacket costs $1,000 dollars in her designer line, for example, one in the DKNY line might be priced at $400.

Other factors such as store location, quality, and fluctuation of wholesale prices or transportation costs also affect pricing. The complex nature of pricing lends itself to a profusion of possible practices.

Retail Pricing Practices

Many methods exist for determining retail prices. The method chosen depends on a variety of factors. New products are treated differently than products that have been in the market for several seasons or years. Customer demand plays a role, as does product availability. The level of competition and customer sensitivity to price also have an impact on pricing.

Figure 15.4 By manufacturing men's shirts under its Kirkland private label, Costco prices products significantly lower than comparable national brands.

Pricing methods fit into three categories: passive, aggressive and neutral. A **passive pricing** method is based on a retailer's differential advantage rather than on beating competitors prices. Location or unique merchandise might constitute a differential advantage. An **aggressive pricing** method is based on undercutting competitors prices rather than concentrating on the company's strengths. It can be very risky to implement. A **neutral pricing** method is based on adding a fair amount of money to the cost of products to cover overhead and profit. Products are priced independent of competition, as when a fixed margin is added to the cost of products.[5]

Different strategies and techniques based on these three ideologies are used by retailers. Two basic pricing strategies culled from marketing theory are skimming and penetration pricing. They are used during the introduction stage in the product life cycle and have important retail applications. Skimming is a passive method while penetration is a more aggressive technique. Several variations on each method are explained.

passive pricing Pricing method based on a retailer's differential advantage rather than beating competitors' prices.

aggressive pricing Pricing method based on undercutting competitors' prices rather than concentrating on the company's strengths.

neutral pricing Pricing method based on adding a fair amount of money to the cost of products to cover overhead and profit.

Passive Methods

Setting a high initial price on a product when competition is low is called **skimming**. This strategy is used in circumstances when:

- customers are insensitive to price
- there is little competition
- customers may know little about the costs of producing and marketing a product
- when the product is targeted toward a small market segment

skimming Setting a high initial price on a product when competition is low.

If sales volume builds and competition increases, prices may be adjusted downward. Advantages gained by using a skimming strategy include high margins and the development of a prestige image. Skimming can attract competition, however, and may endanger the life cycle of a product.

The progression of VCRs through the product life cycle is used to illustrate skimming. Prices were in excess of $800 when VCRs were first introduced in the early 1980s. Of course, innovators and early adopters who first purchased VCRs did not mind paying a high price to be the first to experience what was then advanced technology. They also could not easily compare VCRs, since they were produced by only one or two manufacturers and sold in few retail stores. Less knowledge about the merchandise made customers less sensitive to price. As VCRs gained customer acceptance, demand grew. More manufacturers entered the market and more retailers carried the product, intensifying the competition. Prices dropped appreciably by the mid-1980s, when units could be purchased for under $500. As VCRs reached the maturity stage of the cycle, competition was most intense, production costs had decreased, and price wars were common. Units sold for $199 or less. In the late 1980s and early 1990s, as customers began to replace older models or add extra units to their home entertainment centers, prices stayed competitive. As late maturity approached, VCRs could readily be purchased at stores for well under $100, and at flea markets for less than $50. As sales of DVD players grow, prices of VCRs will decline further. Two other passive models are noteworthy:

- *Differential pricing.* Using this method, prices are set based on past sales history. Research using vendors, retail sales associates, or customers can be used to learn whether a new product under contention should be priced more or less than a similar product that sold well last season.
- *Blind item pricing.* Products that are rare or not easily found in other stores may be candidates for blind pricing. Sometimes this method is used in conjunction with private labeling as retailers build their own brands on untested, but potentially sound, products. Those involved in the decision-making process determine the highest price customers could be expected to pay. Prices are treated as though they were in a test market. If the item doesn't sell in a respectable amount of time, the price is lowered until a more acceptable level is reached.

Aggressive Methods

penetration Setting a low initial price on a product when competition is high.

Setting a low initial price on a product when competition is high is called **penetration.** The goal is to generate demand for the product through mass

merchandising. This also lays the groundwork for repeat purchases. Penetration pricing is used when:

- customers are sensitive to price
- competition is intense
- large groups of initial users are sought
- market share growth is the object

Initial losses are expected when using
penetration pricing. The method is used
by supermarkets to introduce new food
products. After the initial period, prices
could be raised or lowered further depending on the reactions of customers and competitors.   Other   aggressive   measures
include:

Figure 15.5 Competition influences price at this service station on a busy Paris street, but grade of fuel, location, and fluctuations in wholesale prices are also factors.

- *Experience curve pricing*. Used by major discount retailers and category
  killers, this method depends on the retailers' ability to reduce prices consistently, for the duration of the products' stay on the selling floor. The philosophy is based on the vast purchasing power of giant companies, the
  volume they generate and the pressures they exert on vendors to reduce
  costs.
- *Matching the competition*. Circuit City, Kmart, and others advertise their policy to meet or beat competitors prices. Usually customers who challenge a
  specific price must provide proof such as an advertisement or a receipt before the retailer will adjust pricing. It is difficult to determine how many
  customers take advantage of these offers. However, it is certain that meet-
  the-competition policies keep prices more level and lower for customers.
  Gasoline prices are affected by competition and other factors illustrated in
  Figure 15.5. Customers may also be sensitive to changes in price per gallon
  or liter. For these reasons price wars may ensue when gas stations attempt to
  meet or beat competitors' prices.

When retailers determine price by adding a fixed percentage to the cost
of their merchandise, they are using a cost-plus method. This is considered a neutral pricing approach. The method allows them to cover expenses and make a profit. Fluctuating prices of competitors matter less
than negotiations with vendors to secure more advantageous buys at
wholesale. Most small independent retailers and some specialty stores use
this method.

Retail Pricing Techniques

Expressing the price in a way that initiates customer response more readily is a pricing objective of many retailers. Several techniques enable retailers to do this. Some are difficult to discern from straight promotional techniques. Others are related to customer psychology and merchandising strategies.

One Price Versus Flexible Pricing

one-price policy When all customers pay the same price and purchase an item under similar conditions.

When all customers pay the same price and purchase an item under similar conditions, a **one-price policy** is in use. Early department store retailer John Wanamaker was the first merchant to mark each piece of merchandise with its own price. This policy eliminated bargaining and led to the newer concept of unit pricing. The quotation of prices in terms of a standard unit of measurement such as pounds or kilograms is called **unit pricing**. This technique has been adopted by supermarkets. The exact cost per pound or pint is computed for every item in the grocery and dairy departments. Labels with unit prices are attached to shelves where merchandise is displayed.

unit pricing The quotation of prices in terms of a standard unit of measurement such as pounds or kilograms.

In contrast to the one price approach, flexible pricing often occurs in automobile showrooms, jewelry shops, and at flea markets. The setting of prices that are open to bargaining is called **flexible pricing**. To do so successfully, customers should be knowledgeable about the merchandise and the competitive market.

flexible pricing The setting of prices that are open to bargaining.

Psychological Pricing

Custom, habit, and repetition have contributed to many pricing techniques in use today. All capitalize on customers' perceptions of price, value, and sales and include several variations:

multiple pricing The offering of a discount for buying in quantities of more than one unit.

- *Multiple pricing.* Offering a discount for buying in quantities of more than one unit is called **multiple pricing**. When socks which are normally sold for $1.00 per pair sell for 6 pairs for $4.99, multiple pricing is in effect. Grocery stores offer lower prices on bulk packaging, often called family packs. Customers save several cents per pound when they buy 12 pork chops as opposed to the customary four.

twofers Retail slang for offering two products at one price.

- *Twofers.* Offering customers two products at a price less than what each costs separately is called a twofer. **Twofer** is retail slang for offering two products at one price. A retailer that advertises shoes for $20 per pair or two pair for $34.99 is using psychological pricing to encourage multiple sales.

With both bulk packaging and twofers, retailers achieve increases in unit sales, although profit per unit may be reduced.

■ *Odd pricing.* Selecting prices at points that are below even dollar values is another form of psychological pricing. The setting of prices that end in an odd number such as $9.99 rather than $10.00 is called **odd pricing**. For customers who have a budget of $1,000 for a big screen TV, a price of $999 has immediate drawing power. Retailers hope customers will sense a bargain. Consumers have been conditioned to expect that an odd ending signifies a promotional price, even though a retailer, for the sake of a cent or two, is achieving a full margin.

Promotional Pricing

The practice of setting prices below that which is usual or customary is called **promotional pricing.** Inducing customers to shop for specially priced items with the hope additional purchases will be made at regular prices is the intent. In this way total retail sales volume and profits increase. Using loss leaders, advertising branded merchandise with time-sensitive implications, and using couponing to drive sales, shows the close link between pricing tactics and promotion.

Loss Leaders Items that are priced below cost to increase store traffic are called **loss leaders.** They are restricted by minimum price laws in some states, but these laws are rarely enforced. Advertised loss leaders bring customers into the store. For this reason items priced in this way are also called traffic builders. When a photo shop offers 35-mm film for 97 cents a roll, it may not earn any profit on that item, but anticipates a significant increase in camera sales during the promotion. An apparent loss leader is featured in Figure 15.6.

Time-Sensitive Tactic When supermarkets price 12-packs of Coca-Cola at $2.99 for one week rather than selling it at the usual $3.99, a time-sensitive pricing tactic is being used. Some customers plan their entire weekly food shopping expeditions based on promotional prices. Since soda is promoted 35 out of 52 weeks per year, profits are securely built into the pricing structure. Coke, however, earns its biggest profits from vending machine sales. This raises the question of whether the company's promotional pricing is really large scale loss leader pricing.

Figure 15.6 Loss leader pricing is evident in this display of sale merchandise, or is it? The price of the shirts is in the Malaysian ringget, which was worth approximately 26 cents in 2001, a low price in any currency. However, the goods were purchased as closeout merchandise for 10 to 20 cents on the dollar, so the retailer is still making a profit.

odd pricing The setting of prices that end in an odd number, such as $9.99 rather than $10.00.

promotional pricing The practice of setting prices below that which is usual or customary.

loss leaders Items that are priced below cost to increase store traffic. Also called traffic builders.

Figure 15.7 Signage in a Tesco supermarket shows the importance of value pricing as a strategy to promote feature items such as apples.

bait and switch Unethical promotional pricing technique that attempts to lure customers into the store on false premises.

value pricing Providing the best quality for the lowest price as viewed by customers.

Couponing Coke's experience in Russia reinforces the loss leader impression. To keep prices low in the face of an unstable Russian economy, Coke uses extensive price promotions. During one, it issued 5 ruble coupons (22 cents) through print media to customers. In one Moscow supermarket, the regular price for a 2-liter bottle of Coke was 21.90 rubles (95 cents). With the coupon discount, the price is considered low by Moscow or U.S. standards. Experts have speculated that it will be a long time before Coke is profitable in Russia.[6]

Unethical Tactics An unethical promotional pricing technique that attempts to lure customers into the store on false premises is called **bait and switch**. For example, an appliance retailer might run an advertisement for a washing machine priced at $199. A customer visits the store expecting to see the advertised item, but instead is greeted by a sales associate who tells the customer that the $199 model is out of stock, but that $299 model would be perfect. If a $199 model never existed, and the intent is to deceive the customer, this is an unethical pricing policy. On the other hand, if the store is legitimately out of the product, a rain check could be offered. Also, it is not unethical to practice trade-up selling. In this way, the sales associate could show the $199 washer but point out the enhanced features of the more expensive model and let the customer decide on the appropriate machine.

Other types of promotional pricing techniques include percentage off sales, buy-one-get-one-free offers, or those that suggest customers purchase one item at full price and receive another at half off. A 50 percent off sale is illustrated in Figure 15.1.

Merchandise-Driven Techniques

Techniques that put merchandise policies at the center of pricing decisions are also used by retailers. Value pricing and price lining are examples.

Value Pricing Value pricing dominated the strategies of retailers and the preferences of customers in the 1990s. Providing the best quality for the lowest price as viewed by customers is called **value pricing**. Wal-Mart and Sears both offer every-day-low-pricing to their customers. Most discount and off-price stores apply the concept to their pricing policies. Supermarkets also practice value pricing as shown in Figure 15.7. True value can be had at any price and is not confined to low-price retailers.

Price Lining The practice of setting distinguishable price levels, according to store policy, is called **price lining**. Merchandise assortments are purchased specifically to meet price line standards. Before an order is placed, retail buyers must be convinced that customers will pay the asking price in order to cover expenses and make a profit. Store policy sets price lines for various merchandise categories.

price lining The practice of setting distinguishable price levels, according to store policy. Often part of a good-better-best approach.

If price lines are wisely established, they afford some range of choice for customers at various income levels. They should also be far enough apart to make differences of quality and style distinguishable. A customer who is prepared to pay $800 for a TV set may be interested in looking at TVs priced at $1,000 or $600, the next higher and next lower price levels. If TVs were offered at random prices, the retailer might find it more difficult to justify differences in price. Customers might lose confidence and not make a purchase. One of the advantages of limiting price lines is that past sales data can help plan future assortments more effectively. Another is that price lining allows a retailer to adopt a good-better-best merchandising strategy and in doing so may attract more customers.

Setting a price that customers view as fair, yet earn an equally fair return for the retailer is not easy. The establishment of markup and its management during the period of time merchandise is on the selling floor is an important part of retail operations.

Methods of Price Setting

Buyers go to market with the purpose of finding items that can be priced with confidence. There are several methods of determining prices, but the most common in retailing is the markup method.

Markup Method

Markup is the figure that covers fixed and variable costs of doing business plus a fair profit. It is the amount that is added to the wholesale cost of merchandise to determine the selling price. Markup is expressed as a percentage or dollar amount. A keystone markup, introduced earlier in the text, is calculated by doubling the cost of an item to determine its retail price. Expressed in another way, it is the same as a 50 percent markup on retail.

markup The figure that covers the fixed and variable costs of doing business.

markon The target or first markup placed on a retail product.

The terms markup and markon are frequently used interchangeably. Technically, **markon** refers to the target, or first, markup placed on a retail product. In its most basic form, the retail selling price is calculated like this:

Selling Price = Cost + Markup

Nothing is quite that simple in retail pricing. Several methods of manipulating the markup to better serve customers and profit motives are used.

Additional Markup Under certain circumstances, retailers may take an additional markup. An **additional markup** is a price increase taken after the original markup has been determined. Retailers may decide, after initial prices are set, that higher prices will make goods appear more attractive and desired. Or an item may become scarce, justifying a higher retail price. Occasionally, a retailer may adjust a price upward to meet the competition or because inventory costs have gone up. For example, cost of reorders may have increased.

additional markup Price increase taken after the original markup has been determined.

Markup Cancellation On occasion, goods are marked up additionally and then returned to their original price. When the additional price increase is removed and the original price is restored it is called a **markup cancellation**. It does not become a markdown until the price dips below the original retail price.

markup cancellation When an additional price increase is removed and the original price is restored.

Dimensions of Markup

There are three types of markup that all have a place in retail pricing and control. They are initial, maintained, and cumulative markups.

Initial Markup The difference between the gross delivered cost of merchandise and the original retail price for a single item or a total assortment of goods is called the **initial markup**. The gross delivered cost is the wholesale price of an item plus transportation charges. The formula for calculating initial markup is:

initial markup The difference between the gross delivered cost and the original retail price for a single item or total assortment of goods.

$$\text{Markup Percentage} = \frac{\$ \text{ Retail} - \$ \text{ Cost}}{\$ \text{ Retail}}$$

To illustrate, if the invoice cost of a shipment of athletic footwear reflects a cost of $59 per pair and the transportation cost is $1.00, the delivered cost is $60. If the buyer then places an original retail price of $100 on the article, its initial markup is $40, expressed as 40 percent. Applying the formula:

$$\text{Markup Percentage} = \frac{\$100 - \$60}{\$100} = \frac{\$40}{\$100} = 40\%$$

The initial markup may be placed on an entire shipment or on a single item. Markup percentage is based on retail not cost. Retailers prefer this approach because it accurately reflects the changes in retail prices of merchandise during a selling season.

Maintained Markup **Maintained markup** is calculated on a group of merchandise or a department at the time the goods are sold. To continue the example, let us assume that there were 500 pairs of shoes in the shipment of athletic shoes. Three hundred pairs sold in the first four weeks, then sales tapered off. The retailer decided to mark the goods down to $80 to promote sales. At that price the remaining shoes sold. The maintained markup takes into consideration the reduction in retail price.

Cumulative Markup After all goods have been sold or at the end of the selling season markup is calculated once again. The average markup for an entire department or classification after a selling period is called **cumulative markup**. A target percentage is determined by the merchandising divisions, after analyzing past records and considering the outlook for the coming period. Retailers use these figures for comparative purposes. Continuing the earlier example, assume that the athletic footwear retailer intends to reach a cumulative markup of 35 percent on sales for a season. The retailer understands that if less than 35 percent is achieved on some sneakers, it is necessary to take more than 35 percent on others. Cumulative markup is calculated for an entire department or classification.

Markup Calculations

Retailers use other formulas to calculate markups in special situations. One situation arises when original retail in dollars and desired initial markup in percent are known, but it is necessary to determine wholesale cost in dollars. As an example, the buyer for an accessory department is ready to buy silk scarves for a $90 price line. The initial markup goal is 50 percent. The buyer needs to determine the highest wholesale price that can be paid for scarves while still maintaining pricing policy.

Original retail price in dollars multiplied by the initial markup percentage gives the initial markup in dollars. This figure subtracted from original retail in dollars gives the cost in dollars. This relationship is expressed in these two formulas:

maintained markup Markup that is calculated on a group of merchandise or a department at the time the goods are sold.

cumulative markup The average markup for an entire department or classification after a given selling period.

Original Retail		Initial Markup		Initial Markup
(dollars)	x	(percentage)	=	(dollars)

Original Retail		Initial Markup		Cost
(dollars)	–	(dollars)	=	(dollars)

The original retail in dollars may also be multiplied by the percentage of original retail that represents cost of merchandise. The cost percentage of original retail is the complement of the initial markon percentage, namely 100 percent minus the initial markup percentage. Translating this into a formula, cost in dollars is found this way:

Original Retail		Initial Markup		Cost
(dollars)	x	100% (percentage)	=	(dollars)

Suppose the buyer is purchasing the $90 scarf price line and is aiming for a 50 percent cumulative markup. The required cost can be determined by the following calculation:

$90	x	.50	=	$45 Markup
$90	–	$45	=	$45 Cost

The following alternative method can be used:

$90	x	50%	=	$45 Cost

The buyer can afford to pay no more than $45 for a silk scarf to be retailed at $90, if an initial markup of 50 percent is to be obtained. This is easy to understand when a keystone markup is involved, but slightly more complicated when a markup of more or less than 50 percent is used. Pricing breakdown for the scarf used in the preceding examples is given in Table 15.1.

Markdowns

If markdowns are kept in check, they can be a useful merchandising tool for a retailer, because they facilitate the flow of goods. Reducing a price below its original level is called a **markdown**. However, markdowns should be taken only after a complete analysis of business has been made. Excessive markdowns keep the retailer from achieving a target gross margin. Markdown money as a negotiable aspect of merchandise planning was discussed in the previous chapter.

Typical markdown percentages vary by merchandise category and type of store. This is another figure that can be tracked internally and in the MOR for comparative purposes. Markdowns should help stores achieve their sales plans without hurting gross margins. They can be taken for a variety of reasons:

markdown Reducing a price below its original level.

Table 15.1 Pricing Breakdown for One 42″ Jacquard Hand-Painted Batik Scarf

Fixed and Variable Costs

CONTRACTOR'S MARGIN		
	$6.00	Fabric
	$ 5.00	Labor
	$1.50	Contracted Services
	$4.00	Overhead
	$3.50	Profit
	$2.00	Export Expenses
$22.00		CONTRACTED COST

WHOLESALE GROSS MARGIN		
	$ 3.00	Payroll
	$ 3.00	Rent
	$1.00	Utilities
	$1.00	Taxes and Insurance
	$2.00	Custom Fees, Tariffs, Shipping
	$10.00	Sales and advertising (Includes travel, and trade show expenses)
	$2.50	Profit
$44.50		WHOLESALE PRICE TO RETAIL STORES

RETAIL GROSS MARGIN*		
	$10.00	Payroll
	$10.00	Rent
	$5.00	Utilities
	$2.00	Taxes and Insurance
	$2.00	Advertising
	$5.00	Profit
	$10.00	Markdowns
	$1.00	Shipping
$90.00 to $100.00		RETAIL PRICE TO ULTIMATE CUSTOMERS

*Based on 50% to 60% initial markup on retail

- having a sale or special promotion
- stimulating customer traffic
- clearing stocks of out-of-season or obsolete merchandise
- moving slow-selling goods faster
- clearing stocks of damaged goods that vendors will not take back

The formula for calculating a markdown percentage is:

$$\text{Markdown Percentage} = \frac{\text{Markdown Dollars}}{\text{Original Retail Price}}$$

Calculating a markdown percentage can be a confusing issue for retailers and customers. Customers perception of the price on which a markdown is based may not be the retailer's reality. To the retailer, the markdown percentage is related to sales obtained. Therefore, the markdown formula looks more like this:

markdown cancellation Restoring a price to its pre-markdown level.

gross profit Net sales less the cost of goods sold. Retailers consider gross profit and gross margin the same thing.

operating profit The resulting number after the costs of doing business are deducted from gross margin.

$$\text{Markdown Percentage} = \frac{\text{Markdown Dollars}}{\text{Current Retail Price}}$$

When markdowns are taken in accord with a sale or special promotion effort, retailers use what is called a markdown cancellation. Restoring a price to its pre-markdown level is called a **markdown cancellation.**

Pricing and Profitability

Understanding how pricing decisions affect profit is complex, because retailers, accountants, and customers have slightly different perceptions of what profit is. Net sales less the cost of goods sold equals **gross profit**. The resulting number after the costs of doing business are deducted from gross profit is called **operating profit**. From a retailer's perspective gross margin and gross profit are the same. The definitions of operating profit and net profit also concur. The following formulas are used to calculate both types of profit:

Net Sales	–	Cost of Goods Sold	=	Gross Profit
Gross Profit	–	Expenses	=	Operating Profit

Management of the gross margin means planning markup and markdowns carefully, controlling expenses, and planning to produce profits. To the uneducated customer, gross margin dollars are pure profit to a retailer. This is, of course, not true. Net profit is calculated after all expenses of doing business have been considered. The average net profit of large retail organizations is about 2.5 percent.

Pricing strategies and techniques will help a retailer's journey to profitability, but they are not the only contributing factors. Management of many fixed and variable costs of doing business are equally important. Payroll, rent, costs of distribution, taxes, insurance, and promotion also intercede. Table 15.2, referenced earlier, shows the pricing breakdown for a hand-painted batik silk scarf. Manufactured in Malaysia, the scarves were distributed by Silk Accent, an American company, to specialty stores in the United States, South America, and the Caribbean. Figures show expenses incurred at manufacturing, wholesaling, and retailing levels. In the retail example, figures are based on a keystone markup method using a 5 percent operating profit model.

Achieving sales and profits in a booming economy is easy. Almost any pricing strategy will work in that circumstance. The real test comes when business cycles are down. Profit is a tenuous and fleeting element. Its place in a sinking retail ship is nonexistent. The next chapter relates other ways to strengthen profit through technologically advanced distribution systems and supply chain management.

Summary

Pricing objectives differ among retailers and may include volume, market share, image, or growth opportunities. Factors that retailers consider when deciding on a price strategy are customers, competition, government regulation, business design, and merchandising strategies. Perceived value is often the criterion for purchase decisions. The Internet is making it easier for customers to comparison shop.

There are three general methods for determining pricing practices. They are passive, aggressive, and neutral. Market saturation has led to retail market share battles. This has helped generate diverse pricing strategies. When choosing pricing techniques, one price or variable pricing, psychological, promotional, or merchandise-driven pricing are options for retailers.

After selecting methods and techniques, retailers calculate markup taking into consideration the cost of the item, operating costs, and profit goals. Markdowns are useful pricing tools when not taken in excess. They make it possible for retailers to sell merchandise, replenish inventory, and increase turnover.

Gross margin and gross profit are the same to retailers and are not to be confused with operating, or net, profit. Retail profits are difficult to achieve in good economic times and close to impossible to earn in bad times. Many fixed and variable expenses challenge retailers to run a tight ship. Well-chosen pricing strategies help retailers earn profits.

Questions for Review and Discussion

1. What are three major factors that impact retail pricing strategy?
2. How do the pricing policies of discount and department stores differ?
3. What are the important differences between passive, aggressive, and neutral methods of determining pricing policies?
4. In what circumstances are initial, maintained, and cumulative markup used by retailers?
5. Why does a retailer take markdowns? Explain the concept mark up to mark down.
6. How is gross profit calculated? What is its relationship to pricing?

7. Why are owners of small, independent Nine West stores concerned about alleged price fixing between the manufacturer and large department stores?

Endnotes

1. Wysocki Jr., Bernard. "The Internet is Opening Up a New Era of Pricing." The Outlook. *Wall Street Journal.* June 8, 1998:1.

2. Terhune, Chad. "In Modest Times, 'Dollar' Stores Remain Upbeat." *Wall Street Journal.* December 22, 2000:B1,4.

3. TJX Corp. Press Release "The TJX Companies, Inc. Announces Quarterly Common Stock Dividend." June 4, 2002. www.businesswire.com/webbox/bw.060402/221552588.htm Available: June 5, 2002.

4. Schneiderman, Ira P. and Friedman, Arthur. *Women's Wear Daily.* August 12, 1997:4.

5. Dickinson, Roger. "Pricing at Retail." Paper Presented at American Collegiate Retailing Association Spring Meeting. Dallas, Texas. April 9, 1992.

6. Deogun, Nikhil. "Aggressive Push Abroad Dilutes Coke's Strength as Big Markets Stumble." *Wall Street Journal.* February 8, 1999:A1, A8.

Chapter 16

Supply Chain Management

Learning Objectives

After completing this chapter you should be able to:

- Describe the three main areas of the supply chain and the activities that occur in each.
- State several reasons for the formation of strategic partnerships between retailers and other supply chain members.
- Detail the components of an efficient physical distribution system.
- Relate how supply chain members work together using technology-based systems.
- Identify the role played by business-to-business exchanges.
- Evaluate different types of inventory control methods and shrinkage deterrence systems.

Figure 16.1 Coca Cola is distributed to retailers worldwide. The movement of goods takes many forms not always anticipated by ultimate customers. (sculpture: Leuven, Belgium)

collaborative planning, forecasting, and replenishment (CPFR) Initiative to develop distribution efficiencies throughout the supply chain.

Twenty years ago it took many retailers 30 days to get merchandise from domestic manufacturers onto their selling floors. Today it takes about 24 hours. Supply chain efficiencies and strategic partnerships powered by information technology have made this possible. An industry-wide program referred to as CPFR forms the backbone of distribution practices. **Collaborative planning, forecasting, and replenishment (CPFR)** is an initiative to develop distribution efficiencies throughout the supply chain. CPFR is a contemporary term used to describe several aspects of quick response. Getting products on the selling floor as rapidly as possible is the goal of all retailers.

The distribution process is customer-centric. The supply chain responds to customer needs for better products delivered faster. No loyalty is given to retailers that do not fulfill customers' needs. If an activewear department does not have extra large sweatshirts in heather gray at the time customers want them—they'll go elsewhere. If a convenience store does not stock your favorite cola drink you'll opt for a competitor's brand. Take a break and look at an amusing form of beverage distribution in Figure 16.1.

Distribution includes all activities required to physically move the product through the supply chain from manufacturers to final customers. It includes transportation, warehousing, inventory management, and shrinkage control.

It takes cooperation from all members to track and move merchandise through the supply chain. Building strategic partnerships is crucial to the process. Business-to-business exchanges encourage cost efficiencies for retailers. **Business-to-business (B2B) exchanges** are Web-based businesses that facilitate purchasing and the development of partnerships between supply chain members. The roles and interdependencies of key retail supply chain members are discussed in this chapter.

business-to-business (B2B) exchanges Web-based businesses that facilitate purchasing and the development of partnerships between supply chain members.

Supply Chain Management

The composition of the supply chain, performance objectives, and ways supply chain management minimizes costs and maximizes services are considered in this section.

Supply Chain Membership

The supply chain is comprised of three main areas: production, distribution, and customer interface. This concept was introduced in Chapter 1. Production activities include product sourcing, manufacturing, and related activities. Distribution involves logistics such as transportation and warehousing. Supply chain members that are part of distribution include transportation companies, wholesalers, and distribution and fulfillment centers. At the point-of-sale (often called point-of-service), people, systems, equipment, and technologies that maximize customer satisfaction complete the supply chain.

Performance Objectives

All members of the supply chain must work in harmony to meet these objectives:

- on-time merchandise delivery
- complete shipments of orders
- accuracy of orders shipped
- equal accuracy of domestic and foreign sourced products
- customer satisfaction

To achieve these ends, retailers have turned to technology-based supply chain management systems. New methods address areas such as cost efficiency, best physical distribution practices, and greater use of information technology. **Physical distribution** is the process of transporting goods from producer to retailer. Several ways these performance objectives are met are discussed in the next section.

physical distribution The process of transporting goods from producer to retailer.

Supply Chain Lean Practices

The 1990s witnessed a reduction of participants in the retail marketing channel and several new practices designed to increase efficiency and save money. **Lean practices** are methods of doing business that facilitate cost reductions, timing efficiencies, and inventory turn increases in supply chain management. Several economies have been initiated including:

lean practices Methods of doing business that facilitate cost reductions, timing efficiencies, and inventory turn increases in supply chain management.

- *Cost savings.* Distribution costs can be reduced by determining the optimum number and location of warehouses, improving materials handling to speed deliveries, better inventory management, and by implementing quick response systems. A Saks distribution center designed to streamline

Figure 16.2 Saks distribution center in Alabama is designed to receive and ship 75,000 cartons per 16-hour day. It is the top capacity distribution center in the world based on processing volume per square foot.

cycle time The period of time that elapses between production of goods and order fulfillment.

just in time (JIT) Efficient logistical systems that allow for reduced inventory levels and timely distribution resulting in cost savings.

total quality management (TQM) Management systems that encourage team work and ownership of the production, distribution, or retailing process.

merchandise handling and save money is illustrated in Figure 16.2. Throughout the supply chain, cost savings are apparent in transportation and labor rates. Chains use their purchasing power to persuade vendors to make substantial contributions by packaging and pre-ticketing merchandise. In turn, these practices keep costs down. Carrying excessive inventories or warehouse space were luxuries of the past. Economies in both areas create savings for retailers.

■ *Shortened cycle times.* The period of time that elapses between production of goods and order fulfillment is called **cycle time**. For example, minimal cycle times for durable goods produced in the United States is 6 days. For nondurable goods that figure is 14 days. These figures include transit times between manufacturer, distribution center, and retailer. For example, department stores show substantially shorter cycle times than category killers.[1] Time spent in a holding facility is time not spent on the retail selling floor. The costs of storing merchandise until it is picked, packed, or sorted for delivery to individual stores is high. Contemporary systems strive to minimize or eliminate time spent in distribution centers. Consider your own experience with mail order or Internet purchases. If you expected your purchase within one week after placing an order, but delivery took a month, you would not be satisfied with the service. You might even stop buying from the retailer.

■ *Increased inventory turns.* Advanced information technology has improved distribution practices. Better distribution contributes to increased stock turns. The number of times inventory turns into sales annually is an important performance measurement tracked by all retailers.

■ *Upgraded management systems* Introduction or fine-tuning of just-in-time and total-quality management systems also encourages distribution efficiencies. **Just in time(JIT)** refers to efficient logistical systems that allow for reduced inventory levels and timely distribution resulting in cost savings. JIT systems are specific quick response applications. Using JIT systems, retailers stock minimum inventory, but rely on frequent shipment of goods. On-target forecasting is crucial to the success of this method. **Total quality management (TQM)** refers to management systems that encourage teamwork and ownership of the production, distribution, or retailing process. Achieving total-quality status means manufacturing and delivering the product in optimum condition. If products are damaged, or if the wrong sizes or colors are shipped, TQM goals are not met. When other variables are equal, retail buyers will buy from vendors that constantly deliver undamaged products the fastest.

■ *Strategic partnerships.* The importance of team work between channel members has never been greater. Both large and small retailers are forming fruitful working arrangements with other supply chain members. Strategic partnerships vary depending on size of business and degree of involvement and on available technology. For example, large retailers need more sophisticated information technology systems and distribution methods because of the volume of merchandise they ship and the number of stores and customers they service. Smaller retailers that are more involved with customers on a personal basis need finely-tuned merchandise assortments and flexibility. Both require on-time, accurate, cost-effective delivery. In the past, supply chain members were concerned primarily with performing their functions independently. Now, working together to achieve mutual goals is the goal of partnerships. To that end, business-to-business exchanges have become important facilitators in the supply chain.

CYBERSCOOP

To learn more about business-to-business exchanges, visit **www. worldwideretailex-change.org.** What kinds of products and services can be purchased? Find out how purchases made through business-to-business auctions lowers prices for consumers.

New distribution techniques and consolidation in the retail industry affect lean practices. Cross-docking and customer-direct shipments are operating methods designed to move goods faster by eliminating unnecessary stops in physical distribution systems. **Cross-docking** is the practice of moving goods in and out of a distribution center with minimal handling of merchandise. Cross-docking lets a company ship all pieces of a coordinated apparel group simultaneously rather than in small increments. Mass merchandisers have practiced this technique for some time, but specialty store chains have been slower to implement cross-docking. One that has done so is The Children's Place, a 400-store clothing chain for the young set. Seventy-five percent of all merchandise goes directly from a receiving dock to a shipping dock at the company's New Jersey distribution center in as little as 30 minutes. Less handling of merchandise cuts distribution costs and time for the company.[2] To move goods expediently, companies using cross-docking expect vendors to pack goods by SKU according to company specifications. Ways that cross-docking and business-to-business exchanges help retailers work more effectively are discussed in this chapter's From the Field.

cross-docking The practice of moving goods in and out of a distribution center with minimal handling of merchandise.

Consolidation in the retail industry also has affected the supply chain. Some retailers have merged with or acquired competitors, creating larger, more powerful companies. Others have taken on manufacturing and distribution responsibilities by vertically integrating their companies. Some

From the Field: B2B Exchanges Inspire Cross-Docking at Supervalue
by Deena M. Amato-McCoy

While trading exchanges like the World Wide Retail Exchange (WWRE) are already having an impact on the way retailers procure products from vendors, grocery wholesaler, Supervalu, is leveraging its relationship with those exchanges to promote cross-docking in its distribution centers.

Food exchanges are being seen as having an impact on the distribution center of the future as dialogue with suppliers gives retailers and wholesalers a clear, real-time view of demand and stock levels. Armed with that information, retailers and distributors can carry out cross-docking, thereby reducing inventory in distribution centers, while accelerating product introductions.

In cross-docking, products or pallets entering a distribution center are broken out of individual pallets or packages and reassigned to another shipment for immediate outbound delivery to stores, never having been stored in the distribution center. This practice allows retailers and wholesalers to reduce inventory and speed shipments to customers. It requires, however, careful tracking of pallets and packages. "By collaborating with our suppliers, we can get a better understanding of our demand issues," said Robert Borlik, senior vice president and CIO, Supervalue. "Collaboration has also lead to the more rapid introduction of new products and promotional items, and as a result, we now have to increase cross-docking of those items."

Eden Prairie, Minnesota-based Supervalue plans to expand its cross-docking efforts to include 25 percent of its products, while shipping 50 percent of its orders from the distribution center inventory and leaving 5 percent untouched as safety stock.

The wholesaler is a member of WWRE, a retail-focused business-to-business exchange where participants conduct food, nonfood, textile, and drugstore e-commerce transactions with vendors. The WWRE, whose membership now includes 53 of the world's largest retailers, can reduce the costs of net market services like auctions and group buying, and features cost-advantaged access to software tools for e-procurement, supply chain management, and product development.

Web-based exchanges allow users to monitor shipping status on a real-time basis. "We are responsible for making sure our suppliers deliver the right quantity and quality of products in a timely fashion," explained Borlik. "We needed better tools to do business more cost effectively, more productively, and cheaper. We joined WWRE because it focused on retailing, and its mission is to reduce the costs of doing business and acquisition of products. It made sense to us," he explained.

Emphasized Borlik," Whenever we cannot supply a [retail} member, it is considered a lost sale. So we try to tightly integrate to our suppliers and close any holes that could lead to a lost sale or order preprocessing, he added. "We are using the exchanges to tighten our supply chain, keep sales and reduce costs."

Source: *Retailtech.* January, 2001:49-50.

retailers have forced suppliers to change operating procedures because they control logistics.

Retail companies that control the supply chain are changing the way business is done. Limited Brands has its own procurement arm, Mast Industries, to source and distribute merchandise. This has cut down the number of supply chain members needed by the company. It also leases aircrafts to bring products to stores faster.

In the 1980s, Wal-Mart pioneered electronic links from its headquarters to its stores by way of satellite networks. The company introduced links with its vendors in the 1990s that allowed it to track sales and inventory in real-time. The great purchasing power of Wal-Mart pressures suppliers to adapt their business practices to Wal-Mart's.

Every time a customer tries to buy a product that is not available and buys a competitor's product, the retailer has lost a sale. The cost of that lost sale is profit the company would have made. By practicing best physical distribution practices through greater use of information technology, retailers can minimize these costs.

Physical Distribution and Logistics

Effective supply chain management requires careful physical distribution and logistics planning. Physical distribution operations include receiving, processing, storing, picking and packing, shipping, and stock replenishment. The selection of appropriate delivery networks, transportation scheduling, and traffic management are parts of logistics planning. Other concerns include import and export processing and the utilization of technology for decision making.

Domestic and international chains share three basic concerns:

■ managing great distance between stores
■ moving merchandise quickly from suppliers to customers
■ keeping distribution costs down

Smaller retailers share the latter two concerns. To deal with these problems, retailers need considerable merchandise and logistics information. They also need the opportunity to respond quickly to changing market conditions.

Efficient logistics allow geographic regions to specialize in products that best fit natural resources, climate, and other local characteristics. For example, avocado growing is concentrated in Florida and California, but world-class distribution systems deliver fresh fruits almost anywhere. Planning and distribution functions are important since both expedite the flow of merchandise to stores. Choice of transportation mode is equally important.

Transportation Providers

There are four principal means of transportation that are used to physically transport goods domestically or globally. They are air, sea, rail, and truck. The strengths and weaknesses of these modes are evaluated in Table 16.1.

Land Participants in land transportation include railroads and trucking companies. Fewer rail and more truck deliveries are the general rule in domestic transportation of retail goods. Larger trucks and specialized vehicles

---

Table 16.1 Strengths and Weaknesses of Major Transportation Modes

Mode	Strengths	Weaknesses
AIR	■ many locations served ■ fast delivery times ■ feasible for light weight, high-ticket or perishable merchandise	■ very high costs ■ limited variety of goods feasible to ship
SEA	■ very low cost ■ feasible to ship large quantities of goods ■ best when used in conjunction with intermodal systems	■ slow deliver times ■ limited ports served ■ not feasible for perishable items ■ limited scheduled sailings
RAIL	■ medium cost ■ able to transport containers ■ feasible to ship heavy, bulky products ■ often used in conjunction with intermodal systems	■ dependent on existing rail systems ■ low frequency of scheduled runs
TRUCK	■ extensive areas served; global made ■ flexibility of shipment scheduling ■ speedy, local delivery ■ multiproduct potential	■ high cost

---

handle all types of merchandise effectively. Stacktrains, however, are used by many transportation firms. These highspeed trains feature rail cars with two piggybacked freight containers per car.

The two major categories of truck transportation are line-haul and short-haul delivery. Moving goods long distances between cities and towns is called **line-haul**. Moving goods to customers locally is called **short-haul** delivery. Line-haul normally involves large trucks, usually tractor-trailers that deliver large quantities to major distribution centers. Logistics managers evaluate routes to find better ways to dispatch and reduce mileage.

Several small shipments are much more expensive than a single large one. In the independent trucking and rail industries, freight forwarders and consolidators bring together products manufactured by several small firms and transport them as one shipment to major retailers. **Freight forwarders** are firms that group shipments of several manufacturers into truckload, railroad, or container shipments. This service saves shippers and

line-haul Moving goods long distances between cities and towns.

short-haul Moving goods to customers locally.

freight forwarder Firms that group shipments of several manufacturers into truckload, railcar, or container shipments.

retailers considerable freight costs. Trucks are specialized vehicles with fittings so that apparel, for example, can be hung on racks. Shipping and delivery are more efficient when merchandise is consolidated and shipped appropriately.

Sea When time is not of the essence for delivery of goods produced overseas, containerships are the main carriers of cargo. **Containerships** are sailing vessels that are outfitted with large numbers of cargo holders that are roughly 40 feet long and shaped like a tractor-trailer bed. Costs are lower, ocean crossings are slower, but huge quantities of goods can be shipped at one time. Containerships carry retail products from and to major ports. Newer ships hold close to 5,000 containers and cross the Pacific in less than two weeks. The average cost to have a full container shipped from North Europe to the United States is approximately $1,000.[3]

Air Although it is the most expensive and the least utilized method of cargo transportation, air still reigns as the most safe and efficient mode for several product categories. Air transportation is cost-effective for small, lightweight merchandise classifications such as silk scarves. Jewelry and other high-ticket items also travel well by air. Much retail-bound merchandise is shipped via United Parcel Service, Federal Express, and government mail services—all of which maintain their own carriers. Partnerships have formed between government mail services and independent companies. The U.S. Postal Service and DHL Worldwide Express work together to provide two-day delivery service between certain U.S. and European cities. The German postal service, Deutsche Post AG, owns 25 percent of DHL International, the Brussels-based subsidiary of DHL Worldwide Express.[4] These examples indicate the growing number of alliances between public and private delivery services and the increase in global trade. Some large retail organizations own or lease their own aircraft.

Intermodal A high volume of imported merchandise creates a need for improved transportation logistics. Companies that integrate transportation by land, sea, and air command physical distribution channels. The practice of shipping goods via more than one transportation conveyance owned by the same company is called **intermodal**. Several transportation providers have the capability to move freight from Asia to all of North America using ship, train, and truck, for example. Sea-Land Service Inc., the largest U.S. shipping line, has intermodal capabilities. The company also has formed an alliance with the Danish Maersk shipping line giving the partnership greater presence in global trade routes.

Did You Know?

Billions of euros are lost annually because of inconsistent trucking restrictions. In Germany, trucks are not allowed to travel on holidays, and in Austria they are prohibited from Saturday night to Sunday night. The European Union is taking steps to harmonize trucking bans by restricting trucking on main roads only on Sundays between 7 A.M. and 10 P.M. Uniform policy should make retail logistics planning simpler.
Source: *Transportation & Distribution*. April,1998:16,19.

Did You Know?

By studying the cargo holds and bills of lading of containerships during August, retail researchers can learn what the following Christmas season's big sellers might be.
Source: *Wall Street Journal*. August 6, 1997:B1.

containerships Sailing vessels that are outfitted with large numbers of cargo holders that are roughly 40 feet long and shaped like a tractor-trailer bed.

intermodal The practice of shipping goods via more than one transportation conveyance owned by the same company.

Effects of Currency Devaluation on Distribution

The Asian currency crisis that began in 1998 serves as a good example of how economic malfunction affects distribution. The abrupt currency devaluation created traffic jams in shipping lanes as manufacturers and retailers tried to ship merchandise for the holiday selling season. Because of the high demand globally for low-cost products, containerships were at a premium. Major ports were overburdened.

The problem created nightmares for many businesses. One sporting equipment retailer complained that thousands of bicycles bound for the United States were detained in Asia because no ships on which to transport them were available. Some retailers arranged alternative transportation, others paid up to 50 percent more to secure sea passage for their merchandise. When goods are scarce, retail prices on goods that get delivered may be higher. Transportation costs account for 5 to 10 percent of the retail price of goods.[5]

Because of unprecedented demand, the trucking industry could not keep up with distribution once ships reached Long Beach, California—a key port of entry for cargo ships coming from the Pacific Rim. Under normal circumstances, once ships arrive, containers are stacked on trains and delivered to major U.S. cities. At that point trucks take over the distribution process. Because of the traffic conflagration in Long Beach, some retailers diverted their goods to trucks, rather than wait for train transportation.[6]

To address these problems, 13 sea and intermodal carriers operating on United States/Asia trade routes formed a trade policy group. Members drafted the Transpacific Stabilization Agreement(TSA) to help cope with rising shipping costs and inconsistent service. The agreement called for a surcharge of $100 per 40-foot container to be imposed on all shipments. This policy was intended to help recover costs incurred and provide uninterrupted service for shippers. Retail importers opposed the agreement saying charges were excessive since shipping costs had already been inflated due to excessive demand.[7] This example shows that the physical distribution process is complex and greatly affected by uncontrollable elements in the global environment.

Warehousing

Warehousing is the process of housing merchandise at various stages of the physical distribution process. Warehouses may be publicly or privately owned. Major retailers rely on a network of strategically placed warehouses called distribution centers. These are football field size facilities, fully automated for efficient handling of merchandise. Figure 16.3 illustrates an automated system at a supermarket distribution center. Major decisions regarding warehousing include number, location, size of centers, and level of customer service and technology required.

Optimization of Distribution Centers Whether a retailer utilizes one or more distribution centers depends on several factors. One distribution center per country or major trading area makes sense under certain circumstances. For example, when customers don't mind waiting for products, such as furniture or items in high demand, one central facility may be adequate. Companies that rely on products with high per-pound values, may find one warehouse to be the most cost effective. When the objective is to provide high order fulfillment rates, shipping from one distribution center may be simpler. Better inventory organization is possible when goods are stored in one facility. If a chain is not geographically dispersed, one center may be sufficient. It may also be best to have one facility if some aspects of manufacturing are done in the distribution center.

Category killers top the list of retailers that typically have three or more distribution centers in operation.[8] The shear size and scope of national and global mass merchandisers and specialty chains also indicates the need for multiple distribution facilities.

Figure 16.3 Automated storage and retrieval systems at Ralph's grocery distribution center in California, help service this large supermarket chain. Barcoded labels determine product placement in the warehouse. Founded by George Ralph in 1873, the chain is now owned by Kroger Supermarkets.

Customer Service Standards Customer service requirements in terms of turnaround time for delivery and minimum acceptable order fill-rates are guiding factors. **Turnaround time** is the time that passes between an action and the response to it such as the placement of an order and the receipt of it. **Fill-rates** refer to the ability of manufacturers or distributors to ship all goods ordered. It is expressed as a percentage. Less than a 100 percent fill-rate means sales are lost at retail. Location of warehouses can be a trade-off against additional transportation costs to reach customers from other stocking points. When these variables are known, turnaround time and fill-rates are known.

Efficient Warehouse Systems Computer models help determine efficient use of space. Using random storage, warehouse space is not assigned needlessly to products that do not need it during specific time periods. **Random storage** is a computer model for optimal use of storage space. Automated storage and retrieval systems reduce both aisle space and manpower required.

turnaround time The time that passes between an action and the response to it such as the placement of an order and the receipt of it.

fill-rates The ability of manufacturers or distributors to ship all goods ordered; expressed as a percentage.

random storage Computer model for optimal use of stock storage space.

automated storage and retrieval (ASR) Warehousing system that combines the use of computer control of stock records with mechanical handling.

Automated storage and retrieval (ASR) refers to warehousing systems that combine the use of computer control of stock records with mechanical handling. In the stock-holding area of a food distributor that uses ASR, one might see pet food next to paper towels and beverages next to cereal because it has been deemed more efficient. The capital cost of automation can be measured against labor savings, better inventory control, and better customer service.

Push-Pull Strategies Two methods of distributing goods to stores are used. A **push strategy** is used when a distribution center initiates shipments to a retailer in anticipation of sales. A **pull strategy** is used when a retailer initiates shipment from a distribution center in response to sales. The method selected depends on the type of goods carried, inventory turnover rates, type of store, and retailer preference. For example, grocery stores almost invariably use a pull method and specialty apparel chains mainly use a push method.

push strategy When a distribution center initiates shipments to a retailer in anticipation of sales.

pull strategy When a retailer initiates shipments from the distribution center in response to sales.

Effective physical distribution methods and logistics management methods depend heavily on technology and close supply chain relationships.

Supply Chain Decision Systems

An area in which information technology has made significant contribution to supply chain management is inventory control. Complete merchandise and financial control systems support all retail functions in large as well as many small retail stores. These systems make it possible for retailers to:

- Use electronic purchase orders.
- Print sales tickets.
- Hold purchase orders for invoice matches.
- Facilitate physical distribution of merchandise.
- Poll POS systems.
- Highlight slow-selling merchandise and initiate markdowns.
- Highlight transfers, reorders, fast sellers, and age of stock.
- Compile SKU, classification, and department reports.
- Integrate financial data.
- Extract historical sales data.
- Create online linkages with suppliers.

Retailers and vendors share information in order to provide more effective decision making and better service for customers. Many exchange data

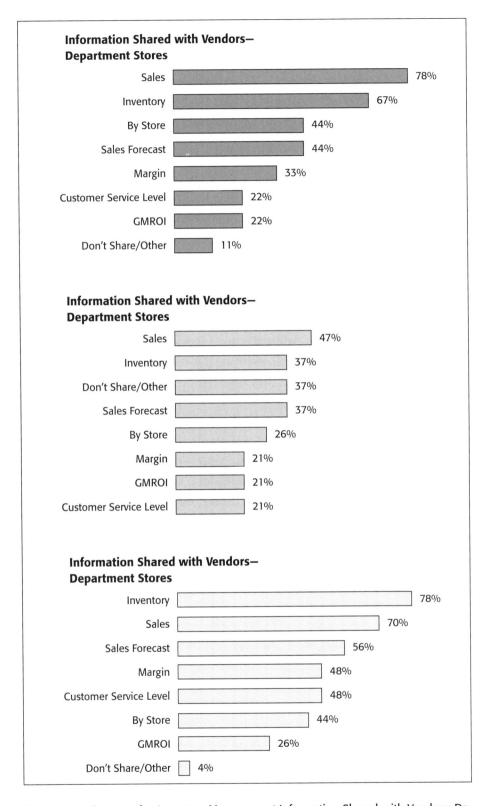

Figure 16.4 Comparative Inventory Management Information Shared with Vendors: Department Stores, Specialty Stores, and Home Centers *Source:* Reprinted by permission from *Chain Store Age* ("December, 2001"). Copyright Lebher-Friedman, Inc., 425 Park Avenue, New York, New York

Did You Know?

Bar codes have been around since 1974 when the first pack of gum was scanned. Demand for the current 12-digit bar code has reached crisis stage and starting in 2005, 13-digits will be implemented. Technology may be taxed to the max to make this change. And some thought the millennium computer bug would create havoc! Source: Murphy, Kate. "Bigger Bar Code Inches Up on Retailers." *New York Times.* August 12, 2002.

universal product code (UPC) Product identification information electronically encoded in a series of printed stripes found on most products.

barcoding Capture of information at point of sale by scanning the universal product code (UPC) with an electronic device.

advanced shipping notice Electronically generated document that alert receivers to impending shipments of goods.

regarding units and inventory, and increasingly supply chain members are sharing more sensitive financial information such as gross margin figures. Standardization of point of sale technology makes it easier for retailers to communicate sales information to manufacturers and other supply chain partners. Figure 16.4 shows the type and frequency of inventory management information shared between retailers and vendors across three types of retail organizations.

Retailers collect and analyze information in several ways. Internet technology is gradually outpacing other types of communication between supply chain members. Certain types of wireless technology also increase efficiencies for retailers and customers. Quick Response systems that incorporate CPFR information form the core of supply chain management. Finally, inventory counts take on new importance as retailers streamline procedures, increase accuracy, and reduce shrinkage.

Inventory control systems depend on two technologies—UPC and EDI. **Universal product codes (UPC)** are product identification information that are encoded in a series of printed stripes found on most products. The stripes and SKU numbers identify vendors, departments, classifications, and style numbers, for example. Barcoding is used for data entry. **Barcoding** is the capture of information at the point of service by scanning the UPC with an electronic device. Electronic data interchange (EDI), introduced in Chapter 1, is a computer-guided communications network between retailer, manufacturer, and other supply chain members. Inbound merchandise is marked with UPC codes that can be communicated via EDI systems. From this point advanced shipping notices can be prepared. **Advanced shipping notices (ASN)s** are electronically generated documents that alert receivers to impending shipments of goods.

Quick Response

In the past, high inventory levels of slow-selling goods significantly retarded the flow of goods. As a result, cash flows of both retailers and manufacturers were affected. When retail sales were sluggish, open-to-buy was not available for new merchandise to be purchased from manufacturers. Or retailers were forced to cancel orders already placed. A negative cycle of sales and replenishment ensued.

Quick response helps refine CPFR procedures, which benefits the entire supply chain. When QR was coined in the 1980s, its main objective was to increase the speed and accuracy of retailers' orders and manufacturers' shipments. What took weeks in cycle times takes days when QR is used. Other attributes of QR systems are these:

- QR systems increase turnover. The cost of carrying inventory drops when turnover increases, thus improving gross margin.
- QR integrates well with high customer service standards.
- QR demands a management philosophy that welcomes change within a retail organization.

Supply chain members that use QR have a vested interest in continuing to work together. Most retailers use QR systems and that figure is expected to continue to grow.

Internet-Based Technologies

Manufacturers and retailers seeking to make supply chain management more efficient have tapped into Internet technology. Apparel manufacturer Liz Claiborne, using intranet and extranet communication tools, keeps in touch with 250 mills, factories, and offices in Asia. In some countries, telecommunication systems may be more advanced than highway systems, making the extranet a logical alternative to tedious business travel.

Microsoft has developed a program called Value Chain Initiative that brings together scores of software, hardware, and logistics companies. The group's main objective is to develop a set of international standards to aid communication between supply chain members. Better communication allows companies to track merchandise shipments globally.

The computer language supporting inventory control and business-to-business functions is evolving rapidly from EDI to the more advanced XML technology used on the Internet. **Extensible markup language (XML)** is an electronic message format that integrates different forms of hardware and software and allows data sharing by many users. It is becoming the standard since it is more versatile, accurate, and easy to use than older formats such as hypertext markup language (HTML).

Because of the push to form strategic partnerships, compatible information technology systems are mandatory. As retailers replace old point-of-sale systems, new standards will ease the transition to better supply chain communication.

extensible markup language (XML) Electronic message format that integrates different forms of hardware, software, and applications.

Wireless Tools

State of the art wireless information technology tools provide retailers with a wealth of decision-making and customer service tools. Some are designed to make receiving, price management, and inventory control more accurate and efficient. Auto identification systems electronically capture

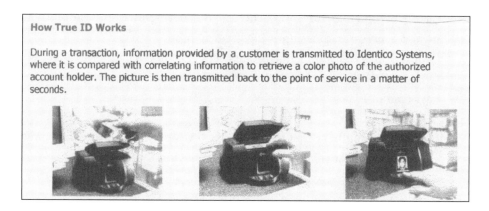

Figure 16.5 Electronic fraud detection devices, like this one produced by Identico Systems, significantly reduce the number of bad checks received by retailers. *Courtesy of Identico Systems.*

customer signatures—and even photographs—for credit and check verification transactions. A fraud prevention device that uses photo identification, marketed by Identico Systems, is illustrated in Figure 16.5. Self-scanners allow customers to check prices before getting to the checkout lane. Other tools, such as on-cart video, electronic shelf labels and signage, information kiosks, and electronic shoppers' assistants, provide better customer service.

Stores large and small benefit from wireless communications. The world's largest retail information network under one roof is in use at Macy's Herald Square flagship store in New York City. That system features technology from Symbol Technologies (formerly Telxon). For smaller retailers, such as specialty stores, boutiques, and kiosks, Symbol also provides wireless systems.[9] One of Symbol's handheld wireless image readers is illustrated in Figure 16.6. Other information technology improvements are expected to occur in vendor relations, inbound transportation, and purchase order management.

Inventory Management

Controlling the ebb and flow of inventory ensures that retailers will be able to satisfy customers' needs. The mechanics involve all activities that maintain the flow of goods. There are two basic inventory management systems, periodic and perpetual. Shrinkage significantly affects inventories and must be calculated and controlled.

periodic inventory Physical count of all merchandise on hand, usually taken annually or semi-annually.

perpetual inventory Ongoing measurement of merchandise in stock as purchases and sales occur.

Periodic and Perpetual Systems A **periodic inventory** is a physical count of all merchandise, usually taken annually or semi-annually. A **perpetual inventory** is an ongoing measurement of merchandise in stock as sales and purchases occur. The perpetual system provides retailers with several advantages including:

- increased revenues
- reduced out-of-stock positions
- reduced inventory levels
- identification of slow-selling goods
- reduced markdowns
- higher inventory turnover
- integrated dollar and unit plans
- balanced store inventories
- decreased store transfers[10]

Because a perpetual system is considered a book or estimation method, discrepancies can occur. For example, a scanner-based POS system used for inventory control can record actual sales, but it does not have the capability to record shoplifted items. Inventory can be charted by units or dollars in both perpetual and periodic systems.

Some retailers choose to outsource the physical inventory process. They do this to utilize the expertise of specialists in the field and provide objectivity. Washington Inventory Service (WIS), a third-party provider, stresses the advantages of unbiased inventory counts in its trade advertisement in Figure 16.7.

Figure 16.6 Wireless, handheld scanners from Symbol Technologies help streamline retail operations such as ordering, receiving, price control, and replenishment. *Photography copyright Symbol Technologies, Inc. Holtsville, N.Y.*

Shrinkage Deterrents Shoplifting, employee theft, damaged goods, and human error contribute to shrinkage rates. Shrinkage is determined by subtracting actual stock on hand from the book inventory. A comparison of the two counts will yield an inventory shrinkage rate.

Electronic article surveillance(EAS) originated in the mid-1960s, when cumbersome plastic-encased electronic devices were invented and used to help deter potential shoplifters. Most retailers feel that EAS is the most effective means of shrinkage control. This concept was discussed briefly in Chapter 13. The following examples show profoundly different ways that merchandise can be protected.

Knogo Corporation developed a hair-thin micromagnetic thread that is hidden on a small surface such as a price ticket or barcode sticker. Among the most creative and embarrassingly messy devices is a security tag from ColorTag Inc., containing a dye-filled capsule that breaks when tampered with, leaving a potential crook blue-handed! **Radio frequency identification (RFID)** is a technology that uses radio waves to detect the presence of security devices. RFID triggering devices can be hidden even

radio frequency identification (RFID) Technology that uses radio waves to detect the presence of security devices.

Figure 16.7 Trade advertisement for Washington Inventory Service (WIS) lists several ways retailers benefit from outsourcing periodic inventory counts. *Illustration © Bob Lynch*

Cyberscoop

To learn more about radio frequency identification (RFID), the technology behind leading retail security devices, visit Sensormatic Electronics' Web site at **www.sensormatic.com.**

in mannequins. One company makes Anne Droid, a mannequin with a concealed video camera behind its eyes and a microphone in its nose. Not limited to loss prevention, RFID technology has other retail applications. It is used to enable instant access to gas pumps and to hasten the video rental process.

Throughout the world, suppliers are dealing with the shrinkage problem by devising new deterrents. A United Kingdom company, Norprint Labeling Systems, combines hangtag and merchandise security essentials in one device. Its paper tags, incorporating product information and magnetic labels, are used by British retailers Selfridges department store and Boots drug store chain. Two garment label companies in South Africa have joined forces to produce sewn-in fabric labels incorporating Norprint's advanced technology. After a three-month test in a South African retail store, shrinkage rates decreased 85 percent.[11]

Devices such as these help keep shrinkage rates in check. Efficiencies elsewhere in the supply chain are veiled when inventory shortages run high.

Supply chain members cannot work in isolation as they bring products to customers. To provide an environment in which solid working partnerships can thrive, many factors must converge. As markets mature, and globalization intensifies, retailers become more competitive in their attempts to increase supply chain effectiveness. Technology-driven supply chain improvements continue to create differential advantages for retailers.

Summary

The goal of distribution from the standpoint of the retailer is to move products from manufacturers to customers in the most efficient way possible that is consistent with the level of service required by customers.

Industry lean practices address cost savings, timeliness of delivery, increased inventory turnover, upgraded management systems, and the formation of strategic partnerships. Technologically enhanced distribution methods, such as business-to-business exchanges, increase profits for retailers and other members of the supply chain.

The components of a physical distribution and logistics system include transportation, warehousing, inventory, and shrinkage control. Transportation systems include rail, air, truck, and sea. Intermodal companies combine two or more transportation methods for maximum efficiency. Crises in the global retail environment affect logistics management.

Warehousing involves the storage of goods in temporary facilities. Retailers operate with one or many distribution centers depending on their size, objectives, and product categories. Physical handling of goods is kept at a minimum in order to achieve cost effectiveness. Through cross-docking, replenishment cycles can be shortened.

Inventory control methods rely on the integration of information technology and partnerships between retailers and vendors. Quick response is the umbrella term for the marriage of EDI and UPC systems. Newer message formats such as XML are making supply chain communication more effective. Wireless communications networks are becoming increasingly important as retailers streamline operational and customer service systems. Controlling shrinkage, including employee theft and shoplifting, is an ongoing issue.

Understanding the service levels expected by all members of the supply chain is critical to the evolution of distribution methods.

Questions for Review and Discussion

1. In what businesses are members of the supply chain involved? Discuss the major performance objectives of supply chains.

2. What are lean practices? How do retailers benefit from increased distribution efficiency?

3. Why do supply chain members such as vendors and retailers form strategic partnerships? How widespread are business-to-business exchanges?

4. How does cross-docking make physical distribution more cost and time effective?

5. How do retailers evaluate transportation systems?

6. What is quick response (QR)? How do electronic data interchange (EDI) systems and XML formats facilitate the use of QR?

7. What are several ways radio frequency identification technology is used in controlling inventory shrinkage?

Endnotes

1. "Global Supply Chain Performance Trends." *Stores*/KPMG. Section 2. April 1998:S10.
2. Gentry, Connie Robbins. "Moving Boxes is Child's Play." *Chain Store Age.* February, 2001:90.
3. Machalaba, Daniel. "North Atlantic Shipping Firms Propose Pact to Allow Exchange of Market Data." *Wall Street Journal.* February 16, 1999:A3.
4. Blackmon, Douglas A. "Postal Service and DHL Join to Offer 2-Day Delivery Between US, Europe." *Wall Street Journal.* March 2, 1999:A6.

5. Mathews, Anna Wilde. "Holiday Imports From Asia Jam Shipping Lanes." *Wall Street Journal.* September 22, 1998:B1.

6. Ibid.

7. Chirls, Stuart. "TSA Plays Catch-Up With New Charges." *Women's Wear Daily.* April 28, 1998:15.

8. *Managing the Supply Chain.* "Distribution Centers." *Chain Store Age/* Garr Consulting. Section Two. October 1998:5.

9. www.symbol.com/about/telxon/telxon_products.html Available June 6, 2002

10. "Inventory Management Policies and Practices." Overview. Section Two. *Chain Store Age/*Arthur Anderson. December 1998:4A.

11. "Apparel Industry Utilizes Innovative Tagging Solutions." *Synergy.* Issue 7. Fall 1998:6.

Chapter 17

Retail Promotion

Learning Objectives

After completing this chapter you should be able to:

- Identify the elements of the retail promotional mix.
- State several methods used to formulate a promotional budget and ways to evaluate the results.
- Contrast the advantages and disadvantages of the major media.
- Identify several types of sales promotion activities.
- State why personal selling is a key promotional technique.
- Discern the importance of customer resource management.

Figure 17.1 Dominating the facade of Printemps department store in Paris, a billboard heralds the department store's semi-annual sale. (See p. 489).

Did You Know?

Promotions such as scratch-off coupons, roulette wheel spins, and rolling dice that appeal to customers' gaming instincts may produce greater response than more conventional methods.
Source: *Wall Street Journal.* January 22, 1998:A1.

promotional mix Advertising, sales promotion, publicity, public relations, personal selling, and customer service.

The finest products in the world go unsold if customers are unaware of them and the benefits they offer. The goals of retail promotion are to inform customers where, when, and how they may purchase merchandise, and to create a favorable impression in the customers' minds. Promotion, comes from the Latin word *promovere* meaning to move forward. It is in this context that the major media and other promotional tools are assessed in this chapter.

Advertising, sales promotion, publicity, public relations, personal selling, and customer service comprise the **promotional mix**. Most retailers spend between 1 and 5 percent of sales on the promotional mix. This estimate does not include personal selling costs which run approximately 8 to 10 percent of sales. Publicity is not directly paid for.

Retailers are concerned with tracking the results of their efforts. It is sometimes difficult to discern whether a promotion is effective or not. An aesthetically appealing full-page print ad, an online fashion show, or a seductive billboard may be pleasing to the eye but may not produce immediate sales. On the other hand, a simple flyer, jam-packed with savings on name-brand ski equipment, may prove effective if the merchandise sells out in three days.

The objectives of promotion open this chapter, followed by descriptions of the promotional mix, major advertising media, and sales promotion tools. The important roles personal selling and customer relationship management play also are featured.

Setting Objectives and Budgets

Promotion plays a vital role in retailing. It is the voice of the store. Few merchants can rely on their locations alone to build traffic. Communicating image and merchandise information to the public is necessary. This is done by carefully defining promotion objectives and setting a budget before planning the promotional mix.

Objectives of Retail Promotion

The true worth of a promotion is measured by how much merchandise it sells or how positively it reflects and reinforces retail image. Every promotion must:

- *Sell.* It can sell an idea, a service, an item, or the store. Promotion is deliberately planned and created to elicit a response. The reaction may be an immediate one, as when a person clicks on a Web site banner with the intention of ordering items. Or the impetus to indulge may be delayed. Seeing a giant butterfly flapping its wings on the Rainforest Cafe® facade may generate an emotional response of joy that encourages customers to return later for dinner.

- *Attract attention.* Promotions encourage customers to stop, look, listen, taste, touch, smell, or otherwise tune-in. Customers notice advertisements through their layout, illustration, or provocative headline. Listening stations in music stores invite customers to try out new releases. Most promotions have only a few seconds to capture customers' attention.

- *Educate customers.* Customers want to know how merchandise benefits them. In-store demonstrations show customers how to operate food processors, polish their cars, or prepare crab Rangoon. Facts necessary to make a buying decision—such as sizes, prices, options, fabrication, and colors—are presented clearly on retail Web sites. Fashion shows teach customers how to dress on the job or prepare for a new season. A fashion show staged by a Parisian department store in Birmingham, Alabama, is illustrated in Figure 17.2.

- *Present a differential advantage.* Uniqueness of location, fashion, price, or service should be clearly presented. Identifying a special reason to visit Best Buy rather than a competitor is one reason why the company uses promotions that focus on its low prices.

- *Reflect store image.* A way to test the strength of store image is to cover the logotype in a newspaper or magazine ad and see if the retailer sponsoring the promotion can still be recognized. Promotions that exude the style and personality of the retailer over time are more likely to be remembered and to produce sales.

Objectives may include increasing sales and profits, maintaining loyal customers, and attracting additional customers, but without adequate funding, these goals cannot be reached.

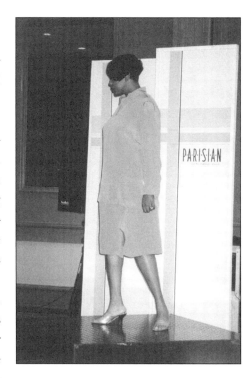

Figure 17.2 Fashion shows present product in an intimate and subtle sales promotion environment. Sponsored by Parisian department store, the special event presented seasonal trends and educated attendees regarding appropriate professional dress, fabrics, and accessories.

Promotion Budgets

The promotion budget takes objectives into consideration, then details the amount of funds needed to implement plans. The type and amount of media used has a direct bearing on promotion allowances and varies greatly by size of business. In small stores, when money is spent for advertising space and production owners feel that it is coming out of their pockets. It probably is. In large stores budgeting for advertising space, production expenses, and sales promotion materials are planned by key executives. There are several methods for setting budgets:

- *Unit-of-sales method.* The unit-of-sales method for establishing a budget is based on the number of sales rather than on dollar amounts. A fixed sum is set aside for each unit the merchant expects to sell. For instance, if it takes 10 cents worth of promotional materials or events to sell a bottle of perfume and the retailer plans to sell 15,000 bottles, the store must plan to spend 15,000 times 10 cents, or $1,500 on promotion. Because the amount of promotion needed to sell a particular unit must be known, the key to unit-of-sales planning is past experience. This method is effective for retailers of specialty goods like fine jewelry and rugs.
- *Percentage-of-sales method.* The percentage-of-sales method for establishing a budget is based on a percentage of past sales, anticipated sales or a combination of both. Past sales are the figures for the previous year or an average of several years. Anticipated sales are estimates. A combination of the two is preferred for establishing a budget during periods of fluctuating economic conditions. Large retailers spend lower, while smaller or newer retailers tend to spend higher percentages of sales.
- *Objective-and-task method.* The objective-and-task method relates the advertising budget to sales objectives for the coming year. This is considered the most accurate method. The merchant looks at the total marketing program and considers store image, size, location, and business conditions. The task method stipulates exactly how to meet the objectives. The level of advertising expenditure is directly related to what it will cost to do the job. This method is effective when a new retail business is opening.

Whichever method is selected, retailers then determine each month's percentage of annual sales. Promotional expenditures should coincide with or precede the sales curve. Next, department or classification allocations are identified. For example, if apparel accounts for 20 percent of sales, the department receives 20 percent of the promotion budget. Promotion budgets also need a degree of flexibility as market conditions change.

Components of the Promotion Mix

The major components of the retail **promotion mix** are advertising, sales promotion, publicity, public relations, personal selling, and customer service. Each is considered in turn. Advertising, sales promotion, publicity, and some public relations activities are dependent on media, which are communication methods used to deliver promotional messages to customers.

Promotional tools include signs and posters, sound and video systems, electronic kiosks, and displays. These are considered internal promotion. **Internal promotion** communicates ideas to customers inside the store. Major broadcast and print media are considered external promotion. **External promotion** communicates ideas to potential customers with the objective of bringing them into the store. Broadcast media includes radio and television. Print media such as newspapers, magazines, and magalogs are in this category. Electronic methods of communication are also considered external promotion.

Characteristics of national, trade, and retail advertising are distinguished first, followed by a discussion of product and institutional advertising.

internal promotion Communicating ideas to customers inside the store.

external promotion Communicating ideas to potential customers with the objective of bringing them into the store.

Advertising

Businesses use advertising to build their brands, generate traffic, sell merchandise, and maintain a favorable image in the eyes of customers. There are three major categories of advertising: national, trade, and retail. Companies use one or more of these types depending on their role in the supply chain and their objectives.

Categories of Advertising To encourage brand awareness and ultimately sales, national advertising is done. **National advertising** is advertising that is placed in major media by manufacturers and distributors, usually on a broad geographic basis. Local retail stores where customers can purchase popular brands are often listed in manufacturer's national magazine advertisements. Although not the main intent of the manufacturer, this form of advertising helps retailers by combining brand awareness and locus of sales. This technique is a form of cooperative advertising that is discussed later in this chapter. **Trade advertising** is business-to-business advertising used among supply chain members and not directed to final consumers. **Retail advertising** is advertising specifically directed to final consumers by retailers. Retail advertising differs in several ways from national and trade advertising:

national advertising Advertising placed in major media by manufacturers and distributors, usually on a broad geographic basis.

trade advertising Business-to-business advertising used among supply chain members and not directed to final customers.

retail advertising Advertising specifically directed to final customers by retailers.

■ *Trading area specific.* Retail advertising for most small businesses is usually confined to the territory from which the store draws its trade. Retailers with national or international distribution and Internet retailers draw customers from a larger trading area.

■ *Relationship to customers.* Because many retailers draw business from limited geographic areas, those retailers can direct advertising to succinct target markets. In this way they develop closer relationships with their customers.

■ *Reader interest.* When customers make their purchases in nearby stores, they tend to focus on local retail advertising more intently than national advertising. This tendency is particularly true for frequently purchased products such as groceries. For example, 64 percent of all grocery advertisements are placed in newspapers.[1]

■ *Response expectations.* Retail advertising induces customers to purchase items promptly.

■ *Use of price.* Because much retail advertising generates immediate response, price is a key element and usually is included in print advertisements.

product advertising Advertising that features specific merchandise and is designed to encourage timely sales.

institutional advertising Advertising designed to convey a positive image of the store rather than present specific merchandise.

Advertising can be broken down into two further classifications: product and institutional. Advertising that features specific merchandise and is designed to encourage timely sales is called **product advertising.** The two main types of product advertising are regular and promotional. Regular advertisements are those that feature merchandise at usual, nonsale retail prices. Frequently the items chosen are new or image enhancing. Some retailers focus on product, but do not specify styles or prices. Promotional advertising features merchandise at sale prices. Most retail advertising is promotional in nature. **Institutional advertising** is designed to convey a positive image of the store rather than present specific merchandise. Sometimes it is called idea or image advertising. Used by retailers to aim for long-range sales results as opposed to immediate sales, institutional advertisements concentrate on building the reputation of the store by focusing on unique qualities and services. Some advertisements attempt to build an image of fashion leadership. Others promote unique services, position the store as a community leader, or focus on the retailer's stance on social responsibility. In any case, marketing the total store or in some cases, shopping center, is as important as advertising specific items. All advertisements are institutional to the extent that they promote store image. An institutional advertisement is illustrated in Figure 17.3.

Major Advertising Media Advertising uses different forms of communication to reach groups of potential customers. Facts and benefits of a product, service, or store are presented to target markets through print media such as newspaper, magazine, yellow pages, or flyers. Broadcast media includes television and radio. Internet, videos, and CD-ROM formats fit the electronic media category. Outdoor billboards and transit advertising comprise special media categories, generally paid for by the retailer. The advantages and disadvantages of major media are compared next and are summarized in Table 17.1. Direct mail advertising was covered in Chapter 6 and is not detailed in this section.

1. *Newspapers.* The most common medium for retail promotion, newspaper advertising maintains its importance although some reports indicate a slowdown in use by retailers. According to the Newspaper Association of America, retail advertising accounts for approximately 50 percent of all newspaper advertising spending.[2] Newspapers offer a variety of editions. Daily, weekly, and Sunday versions are often available, as well as multipage advertising inserts.

   Newspapers provide other advantages to retail advertisers. They offer short lead times that allow retailers to submit advertisements close to publication. **Lead time** is the amount of time required between receipt of an advertisement and the appearance of it in print, broadcast, or electronic media. Although stores might pay premium price, the benefits of placing advertisements on short notice are noteworthy. If a late-breaking news story occurs, such as the results of a major sporting event or the Academy Awards telecast, retailers can react with appropriate advertisements. If a city is bogged down by heavy snow, rainfall, or heat, retailers can release ads for snow tires, umbrellas, or air conditioners. Merchandise test market results can be assessed swiftly through newspaper advertising. Retailers can tailor messages and request special placement to reach select target markets. For example, sports enthusiasts, entertainment buffs, and home and garden devotees read corresponding newspaper sections regularly. People rank newspapers high in terms of easily finding product information, prices, and money-saving offers.

   Some ethnic markets may not display the same demographic patterns or reading habits as mainstream populations. A research study comparing retail advertising in Spanish-language and English-language newspapers showed some significant differences. For example, retailers that advertised in *El Diario*, a Spanish newspaper published in New York City, featured products ranging from used clothing to expensive watches. Several advertised furniture and floor coverings, indicating that customers were intent on furnishing and improving their American homes. In contrast, other retailers advertised power generators. It was understood that customers usually shipped generators to their homelands, indicating a

lead time The amount of time required between receipt of an advertisement and the appearance of it in print, broadcast, or electronic media.

Figure 17.3 This institutional advertisement does not present specific products, but implies what being a member of Gold's Gym can do for consumers. *"Beach Barrel Ad" by Gold's Gym. Agency—JACK, Photography by Tom Nelson*.

more transient existence.[3] When markets with diverse incomes, tastes, lifestyles, or ethnicity are targeted it is more difficult to judge the effectiveness of newspaper advertising.

2. *Magazines.* Superior color reproduction and unlimited target marketing opportunities are reasons why magazines are used to reach customers. Magazines have the advantage of reaching specific age and interest groups. Many manufacturers and retailers advertise heavily in women's fashion magazines to reach key markets for apparel and cosmetics. In a typical fashion magazine such as *Vogue*, more than 70 percent of the pages are advertisements.

The use of magazines by retailers was limited in the past. Now discounters like Target and strong regional department stores like Macy's and The Bon Ton are turning to magazines to reach lucrative teen markets. Wal-Mart, Doc Marten, Benetton, and DKNY Jeans are examples of international retailers that are using this medium. All of these retailers and manufacturers have advertised in *Seventeen* magazine.[4]

Table 17.1 Comparison of Major Media Categories

Advantages	Disadvantages
Newspaper	
■ Low cost.	■ Inferior quality of reproduction and color compared to direct mail and magazines.
■ Short lead time needed by publisher.	
■ Flexible market coverage.	■ Wasted circulation. Some readers are not geographically or economically potential customers.
■ Recall potential.	
■ Format control. Photos or drawings in any style can be used to help convey image.	■ Short carryover time. Customers must act immediately
■ Immediacy of customer response.	
Magazines	
■ Geared to selected markets. Retailers can reach audiences based on interests, sex, age, or ethnic background.	■ High cost.
	■ Long lead time. (2 to 3 months needed by publisher.)
■ Long life.	
■ National or regional editions.	
■ Fine quality color and graphics.	
Direct Mail	
■ Can be personalized.	■ Long lead time to prepare.
■ Long life.	■ High cost of printing and mailing.
■ Less wasted circulation.	■ Considered "junk" mail by some customers.
■ Fine reproduction and color.	
■ Flexible size and scope.	
Radio	
■ Flexibility. Radio advertisements can be changed quickly.	■ No visual stimulus.
	■ Poor listener recall.
■ Coverage. Radio goes into most homes and automobiles.	■ Need for constant identification of brand, location, store name.
■ Immediacy and urgency can be stressed.	
■ Low cost to produce.	
■ Station formats encourage market segmentation.	
Television	
■ More dimensions than other media—motion, words, pictures, sound.	■ High total costs; production and air time.
	■ Poor viewer recall.
■ Glamour and prestige medium.	■ Zapping. Viewers have the tendency to change channels when a commercial comes on.
■ Large audience.	
Electronic	
■ Lower cost.	■ Unproven medium.
■ Highest socioeconomic markets accessed.	■ Graphics still being perfected.
■ On crest of new technology.	■ Limited customer access.

Many luxury goods retailers find magazine advertising the best way to build their brands. In Conde Nast UK, publishers of British *Vogue*, Louis Vuitton Moet Hennessy (LVMH) sponsored advertising pages were up 46 percent in 2000 over the previous year.[5]

Magazines are too expensive for local merchants with limited drawing power. The high costs of production and placement make magazines a medium of choice primarily for large retailers. However, many national

split run Practice of selling advertising space at reduced prices to regional advertisers.

magazines and newspapers have editions called split runs that extend regional retailers' advertising budgets. A **split run** is the practice of selling advertising space at reduced prices to regional advertisers. The publisher divides the national circulation into smaller sections, and merchants pay only for the geographic areas specified.

Magazines require long lead times before publication, usually two to three months. This limits retailers placement of product ads. Either brand or institutional ads or those featuring merchandise that will be in-store at the time the magazine reaches customers are run.

3. *Radio.* Radio is increasing its retail advertising revenues, but still has a long way to go before it commands the amount being spent on newspapers, television, and direct mail. Results of a study by Forrester Research indicated that spending on Internet advertising is expected to parallel spending on radio advertising by 2004.[6]

Radio is all around us and is capable of reaching very select markets based on customer preferences in music, talk, or news shows. This medium requires repetition of messages and key information within commercials. The opportunity to use drama verbally to create an intimate relationship with customers makes radio a creative and exciting medium for retailers.

4. *Television.* The impact of action, sound, and color is undeniable—TV is the medium for retail advertisers that want to maximize exposure for their stores and brands. Total television advertising outlays in 2000 were over $50 billion.[7] Buying national network or cable television time can be costly. Most people are awestruck when the annual Superbowl, multimillion dollar, 30-second spot rates are announced. Retail industry consolidation has created larger domestic and international companies that have the need and buying power to advertise via television. Once known for its mass market appeal, TV stations now are adept at segmenting their markets by age, gender, special hobbies, and interests. Because of its international presence, cable network CNN is a good choice for advertisers intent on reaching a global audience.

Retailers targeting a young audience weaned on television, have increased their television advertising. Cable networks like MTV make it possible to reach young customers on every continent. It is not surprising that global manufacturers/retailers like Tommy Hilfiger use this medium.

It is refreshing to note that even small retailers can benefit from television advertising in their local markets. Most cities have local-access cable stations and network affiliates whose rates are not prohibitive. Many encourage retailers to advertise by providing production assistance and offering cost-effective airtime packages.

5. *Electronic.* The many ways the Internet is changing the way customers shop and retailers do business were addressed in Chapter 7. However, read about Kmart's strategy in this chapter's From the Field.

   Technology has created other ways to reach shoppers. Travel agencies routinely give customers videos or CD-ROMs advertising vacation destinations. Room rates and airline schedules are displayed over the video images.

   Retailers targeting teenagers use video merchandising for in-store promotions, but in-store video is by no means limited to younger generations. As a means to inform, educate, and entertain, it is used to promote many products and services. A demonstration of a new garden tool, the qualities of a microfiber, and a fashion collection can be enhanced by the use of video, CD-ROM, or convenient Internet kiosks.

6. *Outdoor.* Designed to appeal to general audiences, billboards and signs are located along highways, in strategic metro areas near stores, or on stores themselves. An exterior billboard used to announce a sale is illustrated in Figure 17.1.

   Increasingly shopping centers are the venue of choice for interior billboards. Mall marketers see this as a revenue-generating strategy. This technique is illustrated in Figure 17.4.

   Another interesting outdoor development is phone booth advertising. Ads are on attractive back-lighted panels that increase illumination and safety for phone users inside the booths. In a similar vein, bus stop shelters and benches also provide advertising venues for captive audiences. Many companies are experimenting with electronic billboards. Messages can be changed easily and frequently when special materials that accept digital imagery are used.

7. *Transit.* Transit advertising exploits commuters' boredom in order to gain readership. Advertisements are seen in and around transportation terminals and within trains, buses, and taxis. Taxi Grams, positioned in full view of cab riders, are crawling red lights carrying 20 word messages in repeated bursts of advertising. Advertising messages on buses have almost become an art form. They serve as a means to reach international customers and travelers as seen by the Gap broadside on a double-decker London bus and one suspended over a moving airport walkway in Figure 17.5.

In addition to print, broadcast, and electronic media, manufacturers and retailers are using product placement as a way to increase brand exposure. A Dunkin' Donuts coffee cup, American Eagle sportswear, or a BMW automobile spotted in films are examples.

From the Field: It's official: BlueLight.com becomes Kmart.com

In a 180-degree turn from an earlier strategy that separated Kmart Corp.'s web operation from its stores with a different name, BlueLight.com, in hopes of attracting a different customer online, Kmart this week changed its web site's name to Kmart.com to strengthen ties to its stores. The e-commerce site also now features more information on Kmart stories, such as a dedicated area on the home page that features promotions and sales; and an expanded inventory of nationally known brands such as Disney apparel and Pentax cameras. Kmart is kicking off the relaunch of its web site with a promotion offering customers 10% off purchases of $99 or more.

The name change follows consumer research that the company says shows shoppers "overwhelmingly preferred" the Kmart.com name to BlueLight.com. "As we build a new Kmart we feel it is important to demonstrate a unified brand message across all of our consumer touch points," says Richard Blunck, Kmart senior vice president and CEO of BlueLightcom. "We are responding to our customers who have a very strong affinity to Kmart and what it represents—exclusive brands, value and convenience."

Though the web site's name is changing, there are no immediate plans to change the name of Blue-Light.com, the wholly-owned Kmart subsidiary that operates the web site, or the name of its BlueLight Unlimited Internet Service. Consumers are able to access the shopping site through www.Kmart.com or www.BlueLight.com.

The name change linking the site closer to the stores is an interesting twist on a common strategy in which retailers use established store presence to bolster a still-developing online presence. "It's a reverse of that situation here, in that the company is using its online operation to bolster what's going on in the stores," says Mary Brett Whitfield, senior analyst at consultants Retail Forward Inc. "It is trying to tie the site more into the stores in featuring 'This week in Kmart stores' more prominently on the site to drive traffic into stores, as store traffic has dropped precipitously."

Kmart, in the process of repositioning itself in the marketplace after filing Chapter 11 bankruptcy in January, is closing 13% of its stores this year.

Source: *InternetRetailer.com*. July 19, 2002

---

media mix Specific configuration of media chosen by an advertiser for a campaign.

reach The number of actual readers, listeners, or viewers in an audience.

coverage The geographic area in which an advertising message potentially is seen or heard.

Media Selection For retail advertising to generate sales, the message must reach the correct target market. The specific configuration of media chosen by an advertiser for a campaign is called the **media mix**. There is no one successful formula for selecting media, because stores, markets, and customers differ. Media availability and circulation also vary. Questions the retailer should consider before making media mix decisions are:

- Which media can best reach the greatest number of and best targeted people at the time the retailer wants to reach them?
- Which media or combination of media can the retailer afford?
- If one medium does not reach a large share of the market, what other medium will? At what cost?
- Will a greater expenditure in the present media generate a bigger dollar share of the market?
- Will a greater expenditure in additional media in the same market area bring extra business? At what cost?

A sound principle for buying media is to avoid spreading advertising dollars too thinly. Instead of using a number of media, retailers should make a maximum impression in one medium before considering others. In the assessment of each medium, reach and coverage are important considerations. **Reach** is the number of actual readers, listeners, or viewers in an audience. **Coverage** is the geographic area in which an advertising message potentially is seen or heard.

An interesting option for retailers is the media buying service. A **media buying service** is an organization of media specialists that buys blocks of advertising time and space on behalf of a group of businesses. In contrast, an advertising agency media department generally buys time and space to advertise a client's products or store. Media buying services wield considerable clout and may make media buys more cost effective for retailers.

Cooperative Advertising Supply chain members sometimes share the costs of advertising with retailers. There are several benefits to retailers of cooperative advertising that include cost savings, the ability to run larger or more frequent advertisements, and the opportunity for more exposure in the marketplace. Disadvantages include the need for the retailer to comply with the vendor's advertising design and placement criteria. The vendor's advertising philosophy may not be totally compatible with the store's. In addition, securing cooperative agreements, administering accounts, and maintaining standards set forth by vendors is time-consuming. Arrangements for cooperative advertising are either vertical or horizontal. **Vertical cooperative advertising** is advertising for which a manufacturer or other supply chain member agrees to share costs with a retailer. Cooperative agreements are based on a percentage of business—usually around 5 percent—transacted by a retailer and vendor annually. Retailers may use funds from the cooperative account to pay all or part of an advertisement. Agreements vary, but are usually done on a 50/50 share between vendor and store. Retailers are reimbursed after the advertisements have been printed or aired. Invoices or documents from the media, such as tearsheets, are required as proof that the advertisements appeared. A **tearsheet** is a page torn from a publication and sent to an advertiser, vendor, or agency to prove that the advertisement has run. The manufacturer sometimes supplies materials, such as artwork and advertising copy containing open space for the retailer's name. **Horizontal cooperative advertising** is joint advertising by a group of businesses, usually at the same level of the supply chain, done to increase traffic or interest in a product or special event. Shopping centers often sponsor promotions

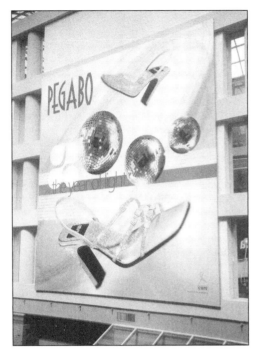

Figure 17.4 Part of a campaign designed to promote fashion leadership, Pegabo, a division of Canada-based Aldo shoes, uses billboard advertisements within the Eaton Centre in Toronto.

media buying service Organization of media specialists that buys blocks of advertising time and space on behalf of a group of businesses.

vertical cooperative advertising Advertising for which a manufacturer or other supply chain member agrees to share costs with a retailer.

tearsheet Page torn from a publication and sent to an advertiser, vendor, or agency to prove that the advertisement has run.

horizontal cooperative advertising Joint advertising by a group of businesses usually at the same level of the supply chain; done to increase traffic or interest in a product or event.

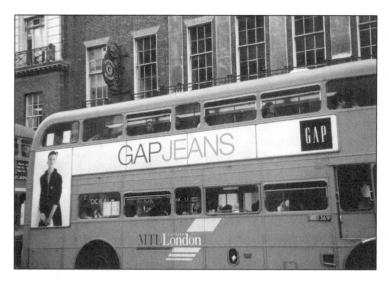

Figure 17.5a Transit advertising reaches a broad spectrum of customers around the world. The broadside of a double-decker London bus makes the perfect surface for the Gap's message.

Figure 17.5b Constant traffic on moving walkways in a major airport provides a captive audience.

with local businesses to draw people to the center. When a ski resort teams with local restaurants and retail shops to promote a big weekend, it is horizontal cooperative advertising.

Small merchants are often unaware of cooperative funds and do not know how to apply for them. Manufacturers often encourage large retailers but not small merchants to use joint advertising, partly because it is more costly to administer programs that involve many small merchants. The Robinson-Patman Act, however, requires vendors to give the same promotion allowance to all retailers on a proportionate basis. Therefore, if a vendor gives a large department store chain a 5 percent advertising allowance, all other retailers are entitled to the same arrangements. Retailers benefit because cooperative advertising helps increase their profits.

Measuring Advertising Results Not every advertisement has an immediate and measurable response. Measurement is related to whether the advertisement was designed to sell the store image or products. Through institutional advertising a retailer creates and maintains its personality long term. However, the results of institutional advertising cannot be quantitatively measured. Long-term goals of institutional advertising include:

- Gaining respect for the store from its customers, suppliers, and stockholders.
- Increasing sales and profits over time.

Whether the price in a product advertisement is regular or promotional affects customer reaction. Regular product advertising creates and maintains store reputation through its merchandise. Response is measured over a period of a week or a season, not necessarily the day after the advertising appears. Sale, clearance, and special purchase advertising are all promotional. Planned for immediate response, promotional advertising is measured the next day or the next week, depending on the length of the event.

Response varies depending on store location, time of year, and intensity of campaign. Factors that contribute to the success or failure of a campaign can include weather change, the economic climate, or an unexpected occurrence in the news. The announcement of an outbreak of foot-and-mouth disease in Europe will curtail the best promotions of beef or lamb in supermarkets, for example. Circumstances like these are taken into account when measuring advertising results.

Retail Sales Promotion

The list of sales promotion activities is as vast as the imaginations of retailers. Promotion techniques change with the retailer, market, competition, and stage in the product life cycle. Some retailers offer loyalty programs, gifts, prizes, or even print messages in the sky to get attention. Most utilize some of the following retail sales promotion techniques: special events, coupons, sampling, contests, giveaways, demonstrations, and premiums.

Like advertising, sales promotion helps retailers attract and retain customers. Although attention is piqued by various forms of visual merchandising and advertising, customers may not take action unless their interest is turned into desire. This is difficult to do when product differentiation is not apparent or when customers are price sensitive. By careful selection and use of promotional activities sales are stimulated.

Today, little difference exists between sales promotion activities in department stores and those in discount stores or even those on the Internet. A look at several techniques suggests the diversity and ingenuity of retail sales promotion.

vertical cooperative advertising Advertising for which a manufacturer or other supply chain member agrees to share costs with a retailer.

tearsheet Page torn from a publication and sent to an advertiser, vendor, or agency to prove that the advertisement has run.

horizontal cooperative advertising Joint advertising by a group of businesses usually at the same level of the supply chain; done to increase traffic or interest in a product or event.

Did You Know?

Every August, Macy's flagship store in New York City hosts Tap-O-Mania, a special event geared to thousands of would-be Rockettes. The event draws tap dancers from around the world who range from 2 to 89 years old.
Source: *American Way*. July 15,1997:23.

1. *Special Events:* Fashion shows, art exhibits, parades, marathons, and celebrity appearances generate great enthusiasm. Special events promote the store as an institution whether they are held on-site or off. Probably the best-known example of a retailer-sponsored special event is the annual Macy's Thanksgiving Day parade, viewed on television by people from coast to coast. Most viewers have never visited Macy's Herald Square store. This parade has helped make Macy's name synonymous with the best in retailing and draws customers to its stores across the country. As illustrated in Figure 17.6 animated animal orchestras—lead by Leonard Bearnstein—are used to bring unique entertainment and traffic to shopping centers. Special events draw crowds and are considered worthwhile by most retailers even though it is almost impossible to measure direct return on investment.

2. *Coupons:* Individuals clip coupons from magazines, newspapers, and direct mail pieces. They print them from Web sites, pick them up at supermarkets, or find them on product packages. They use them to get price reductions on specific items. The redemption of coupons waned in popularity in the 1990s, and this trend continues as customers embrace other forms of money-saving incentives. Industry estimates indicate that only a small percentage of manufacturers' coupons are redeemed annually. Some supermarkets and home improvement centers encourage coupon exchange between customers by providing bins or bulletin boards for this purpose. Most supermarkets have on-site electronic devices that dispense coupons based on purchases customers are in the process of making. Receiving a 75-cents-off coupon for kitty litter after purchasing a supply of canned cat food is not unusual.

   Some retailers are using coupons to stimulate sales on their Web sites. Barnes & Noble Booksellers offered $5 coupons exclusively for online use in a joint promotion with American Express. Coupons were enclosed with credit card holders monthly statements. Coldwater Creek encloses similar coupons with its apparel catalogs for use only on its Web site.

   CompUSA found that response to a promotion for personal digital assistant and cell phone accessories was encouraging. The company delivered coupons to two million owners via their wireless devices.[8] Couponing is an established institution, but it changes with the needs and shopping habits of customers.

3. *Sampling:* Placing products in customers' hands for trial use is called sampling. Manufacturers of products such as cereal, detergents, and health and beauty aids promote trial use of their products by mailing introductory-sized samples to households. Sampling of this nature encourages trips to retail stores since coupons are often included in the pitch.

4. *Contests/Sweepstakes:* Contests and sweepstakes are similar in intent, but in a contest the customer must demonstrate some skill in order to win, while participation is all that is required to win a sweepstakes. Both are used to attract and keep customers by encouraging participation.

5. *Giveaways:* Pens, calendars, and T-shirts, bearing the names of retailers often are given away to shoppers. Because freebie Frisbees are visible reminders of the store, sales promotion continues long after the event.

6. *Demonstrations:* In-store product demonstrations attract potential purchasers. Customers whose senses are aroused in a store by the smell of perfume, taste of pizza, or feel of facial tissues often purchase the item on impulse. Cosmeticians draw interest when demonstrating how to apply new makeup. The smell of nachos being prepared in a warehouse club causes many nonusers to try a package. When combined with sampling and couponing, most customers cannot resist a product they may not have noticed previously.

7. *Premiums:* Desirable items are offered to customers at substantially reduced prices or, in some instances, for free. The idea behind giving premiums is to generate immediate sales. A special edition toy or trading card that a seven-year-old can take home after lunch is often the deciding factor in selecting one fast food restaurant over another. When both parent and child are happy, repeat business is the result.

Cosmetic companies consistently use similar gift-with-purchase techniques. Many customers time their purchases to coincide with premium offers and may spend more than they intended during the promotion.

Figure 17.6 An orchestra made up of speaking, instrument playing animated creatures is sure to draw attention in a shopping mall setting. Retailers benefit from sales promotion events like this.

CYBERSCOOP

Are you a coupon clipper? If so, join the cyber set. A trip to **www.valuepage.com** will alert you to savings, rebates, and free samples. Find out what retailers near you participate. Any good deals on music this week?

Publicity

Nonpaid news or editorial comment about ideas, products, services, or stores is called **publicity**. Some retailers hire specialists or use staff publicists to get their names and messages in the public eye. To enhance a store's image, publicity must be current, credible, and newsworthy. It also helps if the story is dramatic and has human interest. The value of nonpaid publicity is priceless.

publicity Nonpaid news or editorial comment about ideas, products services, or stores.

Public Relations

Promotional activities that enhance retail image and support charitable foundations or important social causes are called **public relations**. Goodwill generated by participating in fundraising activities for organizations that fight devastating diseases go a long way to help a worthy cause and position the retailer as a caring member of the industry. For example, Macy's and co-sponsoring vendors gave customers discount cards, good on many products, for a $5 donation toward breast cancer research.

Other Promotion Techniques

Other paid forms of promotion include endorsement advertising and slotting fees. Both elicit mixed emotions from consumers, but provide benefits to retailers.

Celebrity Endorsement

For many customers, being able to identify with a favorite sports hero, musician, actor, or model may increase the propensity to purchase. Since many circumstances and motivations affect consumer behavior, it is difficult to gauge the effectiveness of celebrity endorsement advertising. If tennis ace Venus Williams touts Reeboks, or golfer Tiger Woods extols the virtues of Nike, does it mean more sales for retailers that carry these brands? Some are concerned that the person chosen may be detrimental to an advertising campaign if that person behaves in their public life in such a way that detracts from the manufacturer's or retailer's brand image. Most are betting on the fact that endorsement works and pay $20,000 to $250,000 per advertisement to celebrities that are willing to lend their image to products.[9]

Some retailers believe that the success of celebrity endorsement may depend upon the degree to which customers can relate to the celebrity. Christian Bagnoud, director of marketing for H & M says this about celebrity endorsement: "It's more about attitude and personality—someone the customer can associate with. Plus, since this is not their job to do advertising, it catches people's attention."[10]

Pay-to-Play Strategies

The supermarket industry historically has charged manufacturers for select shelf locations. Called *slotting fees*, this concept has spread to other retail institutions. For example, record stores charge music distributors listening-post fees to secure placement on the devices for CDs they want to promote. As competition for key locations continues, expect to see more evidence of this tactic.

Advertising and sales promotion take various shapes and forms, but all must be carefully planned and evaluated. The only form of sales promotion that interacts with customers face-to-face is personal selling.

Personal Selling

Employees who work with customers individually, or communicate with them on the phone or Internet greatly affect retail business. Managers, sales associates, gift-wrap clerks, door greeters, personal shoppers, and customer service experts are expected to extend gracious service to customers they hope will visit the store again and again.

Personal selling can be viewed as both a form of sales promotion and as a service. Good sales people expedite sales. They also direct their attention to shoppers who might become loyal customers. Customer service bridges the gap between the immediate sale and long-term satisfaction.

The selling floor can be the key to productivity and profit for retailers that consider personal selling part of their promotional mix. As you learned in Chapter 9, retailers must plan for and compensate employees with the same gusto they use to manage other retail functions. These details are not reiterated, but training and evaluating sales associates, qualities attributed to effective sales personnel, and selling techniques are covered in this section.

Training the Sales Force Sales people are expected to exert a positive influence on the behavior of customers. In many retail establishments, titles such as sales associate, sales consultant, or fashion representative are given to those who sell. These may help with orientation to the job, but title alone does not make an expert salesperson. The key is good training. Training should look beyond the basics. To the customer, salespeople *are* the store.

As part of its training efforts, Filene's, a division of May company, uses what it calls a "Friendliness Program." The 15-hour training program urges sales associates to polish their salesmanship techniques. They are asked to focus on greeting customers promptly, smiling at them, suggesting multiple purchases, thanking them for their patronage, and using the customer's name whenever appropriate.

Some retailers use computer-based learning modules so that sales associates can learn basic selling skills in self-paced study. Others use videos to nurture the development of skills. Still others combine these techniques with detailed training manuals. Researchers from Michigan State University noted the positive correlation between learning and performance of new sales associates. Results of their study indicated that higher levels of learning led to better performance on the selling floor.[11]

Many retailers use professional shopping services to spot-check associates' skills by staging sales and returns. Professional shoppers compile detailed reports on the improvised transactions that are shared with managers and salespersons.

Profile of a Retail Salesperson A salesperson's appearance, product knowledge, and selling techniques should match customers' expectations and taste levels. One trait common to all successful salespeople is enthusiasm for the store and its merchandise. Qualities of an ideal retail salesperson are listed in Table 17.2.

Successful salespeople can earn an excellent living. They often have regular customers and take care of them by calling when new merchandise arrives, ordering items not in stock, making personal deliveries, and helping family or friends select gifts.

Because selling can be a very satisfying and financially rewarding job, some people elect to make sales their career. Others see it as the first step to becoming a buyer or merchandise manager. Still others hope one day to open their own businesses. What better way is there to learn the intricacies of a particular market than to sell to it?

Once they have seen retail customers' reactions to merchandise first-hand, some sales associates take their talents to other firms in the supply chain. Many work for sales representatives or in manufacturers' showrooms. When sitting on the other side of the counter, speaking to retail buyers, they speak with authority.

Steps in the Selling Process The seven steps in the retail selling process are: (1) customer approach, (2) need determination, (3) presentation of merchandise, (4) overcoming objections, (5) closing the sale, (6) suggestion selling and (7) postsale follow-up.

1. *Customer Approach.* Approaches will vary, but most retailers agree that all customers should be recognized when they enter a store or department. In the past, when a salesperson asked, "May I help you?" most customers automatically responded, "No, I'm just looking." It would be considered pushy and offensive to some customers if a salesperson continued to pursue the question. A more contemporary approach is a greeting: "Hello, how are you today?" or "Good morning, please look around, I'm here to help you if you have any questions." Regardless of the exact words, the greeting should make the customer feel welcome and should show a friendly interest in being of service. Sales personnel should be prompt in approaching customers, even if only to indicate awareness of their presence. Nothing is more discouraging to retailers

---

Table 17.2 Qualities of an Ideal Salesperson

- High level of product knowledge.

- Enthusiasm for the selling process and the products or services to be sold.

- Excellent oral communication skills, including the knowledge of when to talk and when to listen.

- Good business etiquette; including prompt, friendly attention to customers.

- Positive attitude and the ability to handle rejection.

- Adaptable to different customer types.

- Credible, sincere attitude.

- Appropriate appearance; careful grooming aimed at the target market.

---

and customers as when customers wait in vain and end up as walkout statistics.

2. *Need determination.* To determine customers' needs, the salesperson must have a good understanding of human behavior. Underlying reasons may exist for the purchase of a Razor™ scooter. Is one being considered for urban transportation, childhood memory revitalization, or a gift for a favorite child? Even direct questions may not bring out the real reasons. A combination of observation and questions, plus the ability to empathize, helps determine customers' true needs.

3. *Merchandise presentation.* Sales personnel should not confuse customers. Faced with too many items to choose from, many customers become overwhelmed. If a decision is not made from three products presented, removing one item appearing less desirable to the customer may help bring the sale to closure.

4. *Overcoming objections.* Most customers have some sales resistance and ask questions that demand answers before they agree to purchase. Some customers have genuine objections. Salespeople with in-depth product knowledge can deal with these more easily than with ambiguous objections such as, "I'm not sure my spouse will like it" or "I really like it, but I don't feel like trying it on." These are only excuses. Objections can be met head-on and cast aside if the salesperson:

- does not argue with the customer

- anticipates the objections when presenting the merchandise and answers them before they can be raised

- shows respect for customers' opinions even while disagreeing with them

- offers tactful answers

- does not belittle the competition

5. *Closing the sale.* Some salespeople seem to know instinctively when the time is right to conclude a transaction. They realize that when a customer keeps coming back to the same item, it is time to ask: "Will you charge this, or would you prefer to use your ATM card or pay cash?" Salespeople know that once objections have been overcome, it is time to close. They can direct customers to this conclusion by physical maneuvers such as moving toward the register or even starting to wrap the merchandise. Talking too long after an appropriate closure point can delay or lose the sale. If the steps in selling are followed, the closing happens naturally. The more experience a person has, the easier this becomes.

6. *Suggestion selling.* A sale does not always end with the purchase of the one item the customer has originally requested. Customers can be led into multiple purchases by creative promotions and personal selling. For instance, before completing the transaction, the salesperson might suggest a few new CDs and disc cleaner to go with a new player. All retailers are interested in increasing sales volume in all classifications, yet many create barriers to multiple sales through their organizational structure and store layout. When a salesperson is not allowed to cross department lines in order to add aerobic footwear or hand weights to a workout outfit, it is unfortunate. Momentum is lost if merchandise is not readily available. An obvious way of practicing suggestion selling in apparel stores is to bring additional merchandise into the fitting room. Busy shoppers with limited time not only appreciate suggestion selling, they expect it.

7. *Postsale follow-up.* Even though the salesperson has devoted a great deal of time to the selling process, every potential customer does not make a purchase. Regardless of the outcome, the customer should be left with a feeling of goodwill and a desire to return to the store. Sincerity and a pleasant manner are prerequisites for success in selling. This is especially true at the conclusion of a sale. The memory of a smile and a friendly good-bye will often be the reason customers elect to return to one store instead of another. Some upscale stores follow up a sale with a personal note to the customer.

Sales associates are on the front line of customer service. They are a much more than a conduit to a sales terminal.

Customer Resource Management

customer resource management (CRM) Planning and implementation of strategies designed to serve the customer in an efficient and satisfying manner.

Customer service has grown in importance in the last two decades. This sales support area has gained more importance and respect since being designated customer resource management. **Customer relationship manage-**

ment (CRM) includes the planning and implementation of strategies designed to serve the customer in an efficient and satisfying manner. Customer oriented programs are intended to generate return on investment for the retailer. Retailers deliver several types of customer services including:

- services that enhance their merchandise
- services that promote their image
- services that are sold
- services that expedite the selling process
- service that precipitates return visits by customers

In order to meet the increasing demands of customers, retailers offer wide varieties of services. An appliance retailer that services products instore and maintains high standards may succeed despite the lower prices on products at a nearby discount store that does not provide repair services. Some retailers offer personal shopping services or a high degree of customer counseling and interaction. Astute specialty stores go well beyond basic selling skills and delivery of amenities to work with customers to determine and satisfy their needs. All realize the necessity of including service as a promotional technique.

Service Goals and Policies

Retailers must decide which service policies meet their needs. Services take many forms including:

- *Service enhancement.* Providing body-scanning technology to make online apparel shopping easier, offering liberal credit to customers who would rather not defer purchases, or delivering a new car to a customer at home are examples of services that go beyond simple product purchases.
- *Increasing convenience.* Examples might be in-store restaurants, banks, or film developing facilities. Nordstrom expects to offer checking accounts and money market accounts through its department stores. The company also anticipates offering these services on its Internet site to encourage online sales and build traffic for its traditional stores.[12] Drive-up food service and prescription windows are services that ease customers' hectic lifestyles.
- *Creating a desired image.* Some retailers have created a competitive advantage by offering an array of outstanding services. In contrast, other stores might intentionally offer few services if self-service and low prices foster the desired image.

Georgiou is a specialty store chain with over 65 stores in the United States. The company is headquartered in San Francisco and designs of fine quality women's apparel are produced under the *Georgiou Studio* label in Cyprus. Styling is fashion-forward, fabrications and construction are superior, but prices are less than comparable bridge apparel lines. Georgiou's true differential advantage is in the attention given to each customer and the indefatigable energy its managers and sales associates bring to the sales process. If a customer chooses to try on 25 items before making a selection, the task does not faze them. If many different sizes need to be fetched before the fit is just right, this is handled efficiently, and not treated as an imposition. Every effort is made to determine a customer's tastes, meet her expectations, and if possible bring the shopping experience to a higher level. Customers and associates feel they have made new friends before the sale is complete. To cultivate attributes and skills like these is the goal of many retailers. Customer service in action at a Georgiou store is illustrated in Figure 17.7.

With goals in mind, retailers must consider other factors: type and size of store, location, type of goods and services sold, service levels of competitors, and financial resources. Economic conditions also affect the type and extent of services rendered.

Credit Programs

Mostly all retailers offer the convenience of cashless shopping and deferred payments—credit. Credit is a way of life for so many people that retailers only need to decide what types of credit to offer. Three types of basic credit plans exist:

- *Regular or open account:* This plan allows customers who hold a store's own charge card to buy merchandise from that retailer and to pay within a specific time period without charges or interest. Usually this is within 30 days of the billing date. Some retailers extend the due date to 60 or 90 days to promote special events or identify a competitive advantage. Beyond the due date, a finance charge is assessed if payment in full is not received. Retailers generally reduce both credit costs and risks by limiting open accounts to customers who have established records of good credit.
- *Installment credit:* Installment credit is used by customers buying large ticket items such as computers, automobiles, furniture, and appliances. The installment credit plan allows consumers to pay the total purchase price plus interest charges in equal installment payments over a specified time period, usually monthly. Retailers sometimes request down payments on installment purchases, but some ask for none, rather than loose a sale.

Installment credit agreements are legal contracts between retailers and customers. Installment credit plans administered by third-party financial institutions are common in the retail industry.

■ *Revolving credit:* Probably the most frequently used type of account, this system incorporates some of the features of the regular account and the installment plan. Several variations of revolving credit plans are used but the most common is the option term plan which provides customers with two payment options. Customers can either pay the full amount of the bill before the due date and avoid finance charges or they can make a minimum payment and be assessed finance charges on the unpaid balance. Customers are assigned credit limits and may make purchases up to this limit as long as they continue to pay an agreed-upon minimum payment each month.

Figure 17.7 Top-shelf customer service is delivered by specialty stores like Georgiou. Managers and associates take special care with packaging details, and make an earnest effort to develop a relationship with customers.

Different types of credit cards include:

■ *Universal credit cards:* These include bank cards such as Visa or MasterCard; travel and entertainment cards such as American Express and Diners Club.

■ *In-house charge cards:* These bear the retailer's name and are handled by store credit departments or third-party firms. Increasingly retail companies also are offering Visa or Mastercard to their customers, co-branded with the store name.

■ *Business sponsored credit cards:* Gasoline company or airline sponsored credit cards are used routinely. Some are backed by university alumni organizations or other special interest groups.

The uses and abuses of credit are an evolving retail saga. Outstanding consumer debt figures are closely monitored by retailers, since the dynamics of this aspect of the economy affect sales.

Imaginative ways to obtain and use credit are available on the Internet. Shopping sites geared to teenagers allow parents to establish a credit limit for their children. Using their own credit cards, parents set up accounts with pre-established balances for their teenagers. Once assigned passwords, teens can shop on the sites. Parents can monitor balances using their own passwords.[13] Practices like this encourage customers who may be ineligible

CYBERSCOOP

Go to the Best Buy Web site at **www.bestbuy.com.** Is it easy to set up a credit account with the company? How long does the company give you before it invokes a finance charge on your purchase? Under what circumstances is this policy a good deal for the customer?

for regular credit cards to participate in e-retailing, and, one hopes, learn responsible personal credit management.

Common Retail Services

Many retailers offer gift wrapping, bridal and other gift registries, alterations, delivery, and rest areas in the store. Some offer amenities like valet parking, coat checking, or complimentary refreshments. Others provide necessities such as strollers and wheelchairs. Some typical customer services include:

- *Delivery.* Delivery must be geared to the market, the merchandise, and the method of distribution the retailer employs. Customers who shop in an urban flagship store and use public transportation cannot possibly take a new microwave oven home with them. Those who drive to a nearby regional mall and buy the same microwave oven in one of the company's branch stores can easily transport the product. The fact that not all customers require delivery becomes a major determinant when retailers make a decision concerning the extent of their delivery services. Stores that sell major appliances and furniture must offer delivery, as must catalog and Internet merchants. Few retailers offer free delivery unless it is used as an occasional special promotion. Return policies of catalog and Internet retailers tend to be more liberal in this respect.
- *Alterations and repairs.* Alterations to apparel are offered by many retailers, as a supplement to sales or as revenue-generating services. Retailers usually charge for repairs of durable merchandise they have sold, such as home electronics and computers, unless products are under warranty by manufacturers. Repair service can be in-store or done by independent firms.
- *Returns/Complaints.* All retailers have a system for handling customer complaints and returned merchandise. How a retailer handles customer complaints or returns can be more important to the customer than the solution. Willingness to listen and help goes a long way in retaining the goodwill of distressed customers. Some companies have established corrective action teams that are empowered to cut through red tape to reach solutions to customer problems in a rapid, positive manner.

According to several consumer behavior studies, people who have had a particularly good retail experience will tell 3 or 4 people. People who have had a particularly horrible experience will tell 10 or 12. Despite these illuminating statistics, more customers actually leave a store's patronage due to indifference than outright poor treatment.

Retailers can overcome this sense of indifference by responding to customer needs in a variety of ways. They can institute suggestion boxes, feedback cards, and instant messaging on Internet sites. Training associates well in human relations skills and initiating customer advisory panels also are helpful. Retailers also can use 800-number hot lines and interactive Web sites to their advantage.

To maintain and grow their markets, retailers must recognize and serve the most important aspect of their business, their customers. Retailing during the 21st century is characterized as much by the provision of services as by the sale of products. Competitive advantages are gained by technological measures, but profitable sales also depend upon effective customer resource management. Service should always be delivered in a prompt, competent, and caring manner.

Summary

The primary purpose of retail promotion is to sell something: merchandise, services, or the store as a wonderful place to shop. The retail promotion mix consists of (1) advertising, (2) sales promotion, (3) direct mail, (4) publicity, (5) public relations, (6) personal selling, and (7) customer services.

Internal promotion tools include methods of communication used inside the store. External promotion methods entice customers into the store. Retail advertising differs from national and trade advertising although all are valuable to retailers or other supply chain members. Two broad classifications of advertising are product and institutional.

Retailers formulate promotion plans and budgets that will return a projected sales volume for the money invested. Budgets may be established on the basis of the unit-of-sales method, the percentage-of-sales method, or the objective-and-task method. Retailers measure promotion results.

The media mix is the unique combination of promotional vehicles used by retailers. Major media categories include print, broadcast, and electronic. Cooperative advertising may be vertical or horizontal. Both methods imply strong relationships between supply chain members.

Sales promotion activities depend to a great extent on target market, type of store or service, merchandise, and the competition. They include a variety of activities such as special events, couponing, sampling, contests, sweepstakes, giveaways, demonstrations, and premiums.

Personal selling is an important form of promotion in many retail stores. Salespeople must be adequately trained in the seven steps of the selling process.

Customer resource management involves both customer services and income-producing services. There is a fine line between the two. Customer services include credit plans and the handling of returns and complaints. Valet parking, child-care facilities, bridal and gift registries, and personal shopping services are some of the special services retailers offer customers. Included in the income-producing category are alterations, shoe and jewelry repair, fur storage, gift wrapping, on-premises restaurants, beauty salons, and banking. The many faces of retail promotion may change in the years ahead, but one thing is certain: effective customer relationship management is imperative to retailers.

Questions for Review and Discussion

1. Is sales the only objective of retail promotion?

2. Describe the three major promotion budgeting methods. Which type works best?

3. What is advertising and how does it differ from other types of promotion? How does retail advertising differ from national and trade advertising?

4. In what circumstances are institutional advertising, regular product advertising, and promotional product advertising used? Give examples of each.

5. What is meant by the term *media mix*? What are the choices available to a retailer? How does a retailer determine which medium will be emphasized?

6. What is the difference between vertical and horizontal cooperative advertising?

7. What are socially conscious retailers doing to encourage positive public relations activities in your community?

8. What five personal qualities should ideal retail salespersons possess? Justify your choices.

9. Identify the seven steps in the retail selling process. Which stage is most crucial to the successful completion of the selling process? Why?

10. What role does customer relationship management play in successful retail companies?

Endnotes

1. *1999 Newspaper Advertising Planbook.* Newspaper Association of America: 5. (Source: 1997 NAA/ASNE Media Usage Study conducted by Clark, Martire & Bartolomeo Inc.)

2. White, Erin. "Newspaper Firms Face Drop in Retail Ads." *Wall Street Journal.* September 20, 2000:B8.

3. Lavin, Marilyn. "Retail Advertising in the Spanish-Language Press: Evidence from El Diario/La Prensa." Paper. American Collegiate Retailing Association Conference. New York. January, 1994:10.

4. Lockwood, Lisa. "A Hot Time on the Teen Scene." *Women's Wear Daily*. May 29, 1998:13,15.

5. Ball, Deborah. "Luxury-Goods Groups Splurge on Ads; Magazine Publishers Reap the Benefits." *Wall Street Journal*. January 30, 2001:B9A.

6. Dreazen, Yochi. "Net Is Expected to Rival Radio in Ad Spending by 2004." *Wall Street Journal*. August 12, 1999:B11.

7. "Total Meqasured Ad Spending in 2000." *Advertising Age Ad Age Dataplace. Source: Competitive Media Reporting*. Available Online: www.adageglobal.com. April 18, 2001.

8. Blank, Christine. "1,000 Redeem Wireless Coupons During CompUSA Experiment." *iMarketing*. Volume 3, No. 14. April 9, 2001:1.

9. Lockwood, Lisa and Socha, Miles. "The Star Pitch: Does It Work?" *Women's Wear Daily*. December 22, 2000:16.

10. Ibid:17.

11. Curry, Nettavia D. and Good, Linda K. "Factors Influencing Training Effectiveness for New Retail Sales Associates." Paper. American Collegiate Retailing Association Conference. Detroit. April, 1994:12.

12. Murray, Matt. "Retailers Use Legal Wrinkle to Link Sales, Bank Services." *Wall Street Journal*. February 8, 1999:B1.

13. Quick, Rebecca. "New Web Sites Let Kids Shop, Like, Without Credit Cards." *Wall Street Journal*. June, 1999.

Global Retail Profile

Gymboree, USA

Founded as a children's play program by Joan Barnes, a San Francisco mom, Gymboree is now a branded retailer committed to international expansion. In 1976, it launched its Play and Music Program, that is a franchised business that provides interactive learning experiences and fun for newborns to 4-year-olds and their parents. The California-based company opened retail stores in 1986, carrying Gymboree brand merchandise exclusively.[1] The company went public in 1993 and recorded sales of over $500 million in 2001.[2]

International expansion began in 1995. The majority of Gymboree's 577 stores are in the United States, with growing numbers in Canada, the United Kingdom, and Ireland. Because profits don't have to be shared, the company prefers to solely own international stores rather than own them through joint ventures. There are 460 franchised playsites in the United States and 21 in other countries.[3] The company also owned several Zutopia stores which it sold to Wet Seal in 2001.[4]

Gymboree learned that tenant requirements differ around the world. In London, for example, much longer leases are granted to retailers than in the United States. Also giving *key money* is the norm in many areas. That refers to the practice of paying significant sums for a property in advance of signing a lease. Occupancy costs are much higher at Gymboree's international sites than they are in the United States. In Canada it costs 25 percent more to open a store; in the United Kingdom about 50 percent more.[5]

In the United States, Gap Kids and Baby Gap are considered key competitors. Next, primarily a retailer of men's and women's apparel and home furnishings, and Mothercare are major competitors in the U.K. Please Mum is considered competition in the Canadian market.

Customer Service and Merchandising Practices

Customer service tactics vary widely in global markets according to Gary White, former Gymboree president and CEO. In Dublin, sales associates originally were asked to greet customers in typical American fashion by saying, "How are you?" Customers were somewhat offended at this approach which they considered too informal for Ireland. Despite the false start, the store has one of the highest sales volumes in the company. Stroller gridlock occurs frequently in the aisles due to the heavy store traffic.

In Britain, the company observed that customers do not like to be greeted from a distance, and prefer that a sales associate not offer a cheery "hi" from across the sales floor.

The company discovered that parents like American-designed products. Baseball-themed merchandise sells well in Britain, even though the sport is not played extensively. Early research showed that British customers prefer traditional, low key colors, and do not particularly like purple. They like red, but it must be a bright, "American" red. Gymboree's merchandise is very colorful, and the company chose to present lively hues rather than toned-down versions for the British market.

Research showed that nationalism and holiday timing affects merchandising plans. There is a 40 percent tariff imposed on imported children's clothing in Australia. White mentioned that if looking at this country for future locations, this fact would need to be considered. This kind of protectionism could affect expansion plans, merchandise strategies, and pricing.

Boxing Day is celebrated the day after Christmas in Canada. This is a huge sale day that is planned for well in advance, since customers expect that everything in the store is on sale. Merchants must remove all items that are not on sale from the selling floor or risk the wrath of customers.[6]

To spiff up sluggish U.S. sales, Gymboree hired consulting company, Technology Strategy(TSI) to assist in 1998. Its mathematical models are used to determine probabilities of success based on past experiences. The models are also used to indicate weaknesses in the plan in time to correct merchandise assortments. Two years after implementation, the company realized a sevenfold return on investment. This type of risk assessment tool does not replace the intuitive element in fashion merchandising, but it does help reduce risk of decisions based on past performance. Gymboree also uses TSI's gross margin model to test pricing and markdown strategies. TSI systems use mathematical algorithms to determine the most appropriate markdown strategy for various items.[7] Advanced systems such as TCI's should facilitate global expansion plans and contribute significantly to a healthy cash flow.

To make it easier for parents to choose children's outfits, Gymboree has instituted a new merchandising strategy. Called *Matchmatics*, the customer-friendly system indicates which items are designed to go together.[8]

Pricing and Promotional Differences

The company's experience also reinforces different visual merchandising practices recognized by other global retailers and customers. Throughout most of Europe, customers expect price tags to be prominently displayed in window displays. Gymboree revised its signage requirements to accommodate this preference.

True to tradition and the experience of U.S. customers, the company promotes more aggressively in the United States than in the United Kingdom. Two major sale periods in January and late June are adhered to in Britain, but in the United States, promotions occur much more frequently. In the United Kingdom customers are used to paying full price for merchandise at other times of the year; in the United States this is rarely the case. In line with this practice, U.S. stores take markdowns on a regular basis; therefore the company must incorporate this into their pricing policy. In the United Kingdom, markdowns do not affect pricing as radically.

According to Lisa Harper, vice chairman of the board and CEO, Gymboree operates on two guiding principles, "revere the customer and protect the brand, the essence of your company."[9] Customers in vastly different parts of the globe purchase Gymboree products and participate in its interactive children's program. Superior merchandise management systems are in use. With these strengths and Harper's strong sentiments, Gymboree should achieve its goal of becoming a global brand.

Profile Discussion Questions

1. What entry strategy does Gymboree prefer to use when opening stores internationally? Why? How does this practice contrast with

the expansion strategy for its Play and Music Program?

2. What retailers does Gymboree include in its list of competitors? Are you familiar with other retailers that could be competitors?

3. How do color preferences between the United States and Britain differ? How does the company use this information in determining its merchandise assortment?

4. How is Gymboree using mathematical models to streamline its merchandise management systems?

5. How has the company adapted operational strategies in its international stores?

Profile Endnotes

1. http://www.gymboree.com/our_company/cs_home.jsp? Available: June 12, 2002.

2. http://www.gymboree.com/(our_company) Available June 12, 2002.

3. http://www.gymboree.com (FAQ) Available June 12, 2002.

4. http://www.gymboree.com (press release) Available August 24, 2001.

5. White, Gary. Former president and CEO, Gymboree. Presentation. Global Retail Symposium. University of Arizona. Tucson. March 5, 1998.

6. Ibid.

7. Power, Denise. "Math Beats Markdowns, Boosts Margins at Gymboree." *Women's Wear Daily.* May 24, 2000:13.

8. Harper, Lisa. "Who's Minding the Future." Presentation. National Retail Federation Annual Conference and Expo. New York. January 15, 2002.

9. Ibid.

Global Retail Profile

Gap, USA

Magic the dog appears in Old Navy TV advertisements and graces the pages of its Web site. A dozen khaki-clad models swing dance across the TV screen, rapper LL Cool J's image dominates a super screen in Tokyo, a young guitarist dabbles with a new riff wearing Easy Fit Jeans and actors Dennis Hopper and Christina Ricci play chess in a subtle but provocative TV spot. All have been part of Gap's global advertising campaigns.

Based in San Francisco, Gap is part of the retail family that includes Banana Republic, Old Navy, and several Gap derivatives such as GapKids, BabyGap, GapBody, Gap Outlet stores, and their companion Web sites. Capitalizing on casual, updated classics for men, women, and children, the company built global brand awareness by focusing on a simple concept and consistently good quality products.

Founded in 1969 by Donald and Doris Fisher, the team based their original venture on the growing popularity of jeans in that era. Although their store originally carried the omnipresent Levi brand, they started private labeling their products in 1973. The company went public in 1976.[1]

Gap Divisions

The company operates more than 4,000 stores in the United States, Canada, France, the United Kingdom, Japan, and Germany. The more upmarket Banana Republic division, acquired in 1983, features rugged yet refined sportswear for some-what older customers. The company operates 425 stores in the United States and 16 in Canada. Banana Republic had been an independent safari and travel apparel chain and catalog prior to the acquisition.[2]

The fastest growing member of the organization is Old Navy which operates with 30 percent lower prices than Gap on sportswear for young men and women and for children. Several years ago Fisher expressed faith in the company's expansion plans: "While all our divisions have the capacity to expand overseas, we think Old Navy has the best possibilities."[3] The company lived up to its founder's prediction in 2001 when it opened its first stores in Canada. The company has more than 850 stores in the Old Navy division.[4]

Gap opened its first overseas store in London in 1987, soon followed with stores located in Wales and Scotland. By 2001, Gap had more than 200 stores in the United Kingdom, 59 in France, and 19 in Germany.[5]

In its quest to become a global retailer, Gap modified its store location procedures in the United Kingdom. High occupancy rates caused the company to lease space on the second floor or basement level in some locations.[6]

Early in its history in France, Gap had an international trademark dispute that exemplified how red tape issues distress international retailers. In 1983, a Swiss manufacturing company, Big Star SA, registered its brand name, *Gap Star*, for its jeans and sportswear lines. The brand enjoyed a loyal following in France and other European countries. Although Gap had registered its name in France in 1978, it had only run a leased department in Galeries Lafayette in Paris since 1991. At that time, it had not opened freestanding units. Big Star wanted to prevent Gap from using its name in France and the Benelux countries. Gap won its suit, but not without an outlay of considerable time and money.[7]

Gap opened two shops in Japan in 1995, one in Sukiyabashi Hankyu, a department store in Tokyo's Ginza, and one in Takashimaya, a department store in a shopping center located in Tamagawa, outside Tokyo. Both in-store shops incorporated the Gap, GapKids, and BabyGap. At that time, casual apparel was not widely sold in shops on the glitzy Ginza. The Gap bucked this tradition when it brought its casual merchandise mix to this important shopping district in Japan. Its first freestanding flagship store opened in Shibuya, Tokyo in 1996.[8] By 2002 there were 156 stores in Japan.[9]

Marketing Strategies

Constantly on the cutting edge of creative and aggressive marketing, Gap has entered into licensing and private label development programs. It has an agreement with the National Basketball Association (NBA) to design and sell children's apparel featuring the NBA team logos. Wanting to enter the personal care arena, soaps, lotions, gels, and hair care products were designed under the GapScents label. Gap also experimented with intimate apparel—panties, bras, sleepwear, etc.—in its regular Gap stores.

These slow but steady market tests precipitated the launch of a new venture. GapBody lingerie shops designed to compete with Victoria's Secret were opened in 1998.[10] Merchandise is geared to Gap shoppers who prefer a more tailored approach to intimate apparel than the frills and outright sexiness of Victoria's Secret.

Gap's Global Advertising

From "Fall into the Gap," to the Easy-Fit Jeans campaign to heart-touching childrenswear advertisements, the Gap is master of exciting imagery and brand promotion. In the late 1990s the company deluged media markets with progressive promotions, designed for its current multi-age markets.

With its customary all-white background, the company released subtle *Sleigh Bell* television spots for BabyGap during a Christmas season. One commercial featured an unusually appealing baby in a tiny sleigh. Backed by traditional holiday music, the simple message captivated all viewers. The concept was also featured in a series of magazine advertisements designed to generate more promotional mileage. Many other ads using the same general format followed.

Popular Easy-Fit Jeans™, the bread and butter of Gap business, were advertised using a succession of young celebrities from music and entertainment industries. Musician Peter Berg was featured on TV ads as well as on giant billboards in New York City and Los Angeles. The second wave of the jeans' campaign featured a new crew of rockers such as Aerosmith, hip hoppers, and country music stars. Their print images extended to street kiosks and double-decker buses in the United Kingdom.

Gap identifies with its growing legions of aging baby boomers and senior citizens. Stars such as Lena Horne, with her ageless dignity, and singer Johnny Mathis also were featured in Gap TV commercials during the company's *Individuals of Style* campaign.

Gap's major promotion in 1998–1999 engendered a whole new market for what had been a staple of the 1960s—khaki pants. Khaki sales had slowed in stores, but a fresh commitment to sales promotion changed Gap's position. Watching young people dancing to Louis Prima swing music from the 1930s and 1940s captured the interest of customers of all generations. Combining unexpected images and music created another success story for the company.

According to Michael McCadden, former executive vice president of Gap, Inc. Direct, all Gap advertising is global. He believes there is no need to tailor advertising for each country since music, MTV, and youth are universal.[11]

Strategic Directions

Despite the creativity and audience appeal of its advertising, by the Christmas season in 1999, sales of khakis were down. Retailers cannot usually sustain sales of one particular style for multiple seasons since most fashion items have a more limited shelf life. New competition also intruded on Gap and Banana Republic divisions with the growing excitement generated by retailers like Zara from Spain and Hennes & Mauritz (H&M) from Sweden. As Target and Wal-Mart upgraded their fashion images, they added to the competitive stew for Old Navy. These factors necessitated a change in strategic direction.

Gap attempted to revitalize its business through artful promotions, Web site and store development, and cost-saving tactics. The company was back to a pure denim focus by 2001 when its spring advertising campaign featured models in jeans cavorting to the music of Handel's *Hallelujah Chorus*.[12] The classic denim theme continued in the fall when everything from denim handbags to apparel was promoted heavily.

One of the most popular apparel retailers online, Gap's Web sites are simple and effective. Images translate well in cyberspace. Old Navy's site is colorful, hip, and youth-oriented, befitting its target market. These strengths have consistently kept Gap at the top of Internet hit lists. In addition, the company brought GapMaternity.com online in 2000. This was the first time in its history that Gap created an exclusive Web presence for a new concept rather than a brick-and-mortar store.

Gap and Old Navy divisions introduced in-house credit cards in 2001, extending the policy initiated by Banana Republic. Magic, the Old Navy mascot, inspired the introduction of Old Navy dog supply departments complete with canine accessories, spiffy collars and beds.[13]

As another cost-saving measure, part of the company's corporate headquarters moved to New Mexico in 2001.[14] It was expected that the company would eventually close underperforming stores in order to improve revenue streams.

Despite the efforts to create compelling advertising, manipulate its merchandise mix, and otherwise gain momentum, by mid-2002, the company had suffered through more than two years of declining sales and profits. Several possible reasons for Gap's problems include lessening of quality standards, increased competition, and lack of focus on its target customer. Some believed apparel selections had become too trendy for the tastes of aging Generation X customers.

Millard "Mickey" Drexler, CEO, resigned his position in May 2002, raising speculation on who and what would lead Gap back to profitibility. The company's sales reached $13.8 billion in 2001.[15]

Profile Discussion Questions

1. What is unique about the history of the Gap? Describe the various divisions of the company and the target markets for each.

2. When and where did the Gap first become an international retailer? What is the status of the company's global operations today?

3. Discuss the trademark dispute that the Gap encountered when it first did business in France. Do you think Big Star was justified in its request that the Gap not use its name in Big Star's territory?

4. What global promotional tactics does the Gap use?

5. What is the significance of the Gap's decision to use celebrities of various ages and interests in its advertising campaigns?

Profile Endnotes

1. http://www.gapinc.com/about/ataglance/milestones.htm Available: September 23, 2002.

2. http://www.gapinc.com/about/realestate/storecount.htm (as of August 3, 2001) Available: September 23, 2002.

3. Cohen, Bud. "Gap Plans Aggressive Expansion of Old Navy Discount Division." *Daily News Record.* May 25, 1995:3.

4. Gapinc Website: (storecount). Available September 23, 2002.

5. Ibid

6. Palmieri, Jean. "Gap Sees Old Navy Evolving Into Its Biggest Division." *Daily News Record.* October 4, 1994:3.

7. D'Aulnay, Sophie. "Gap Fights for Name in the French Courts." *Women's Wear Daily.* June 25, 1993:11.

8. Hirano, Koji. "Gap to Open 2 Japan Shops in September." *Women's Wear Daily.* August 2, 1995:5.

9. Gapinc Website: (storecount). Available September 23, 2002.

10. Gapinc Website: (milestones). Available: September 23, 2002.

11. McCadden, Michael. "Developing Global Brand Identity." Presentation. Global Retail Symposium. University of Arizona. March, 1999.

12. Gapinc Website: (highlights). Available: August 23, 2001.

13. Gapinc Website: (milestones). Available: August 23, 2001

14. Williamson, Rusty. "Gap's New Mexico Maneuver." *Women's Wear Daily.* May 9, 2001:2.

15. "Triversity Top 100 Specialty Stores." *Stores.* August, 2001:S5. Gapinc Web site: (financials and media.) Available: June 12, 2002.

Retail Career Directions

Learning Objectives:

After completing this appendix you should be able to:

- Identify retail career options.
- Discern why a technological background is important for a career in retailing.
- List the benefits of work experience programs.
- Describe the personal characteristics important for success in retail management.
- Discern the important components of a resume and the interview process.
- Develop a self-marketing plan for your job search.

If you enjoy diversity, new challenges, a fast pace, geographic and career mobility, retailing *could* be the field for you. If you also enjoy being with people, being creative, helping others to make decisions and are comfortable with information technology, retailing is *probably* for you. Even if you want a 9 to 5 desk job where the functions at 10 o'clock each day are exactly like the functions at the same time the previous day, retailing *may* still be for you. In any case, before making a decision, investigate all of the career options in retailing.

The opportunities in this dynamic industry are enormous, and demand for qualified employees is growing and changing. For example, Sears is very much aware of the shrinking pool of traditionally aged retail workers and the growing demand for help. Bill Donahue, vice president of recruitment, believes that the 14 percent growth rate for employment projected for retail by 2008 will challenge the company to find new recruitment sources. The company uses several online job recruiters, including Monster.com, but finds that most prospective employees come from the Sears Web site.[1] This challenge and similar tendencies are voiced by many retailers.

CYBERSCOOP

To find colleges and universities in the United States and beyond that offer undergraduate and graduate programs in retailing, go to **www.acraretail.org.** Is your school listed?

Management positions in retailing match and may even surpass salaries and benefits in other industries. Yet retailing suffers from a public perception that this is not so. The industry has not always been successful in conveying the fact that people with ability can advance from entry level to executive ranks in 10 years or less and achieve major compensation. Yet this is true.

Now more industry human resource managers are promoting retailing as a worthwhile and rewarding career is happening on many campuses. They recognize the importance of partnering with educators on fertile recruitment ground. The aim is to overcome the lingering negative image that hinders recruitment of many college graduates to retailing.

Many colleges and universities offer retailing courses as an integral part of curricula leading to bachelor's, master's, and doctoral degrees. Many also sponsor one or more retail executive seminars annually. The American Collegiate Retailing Association, a professional organization composed of educators from the United States and several other countries, lists schools that offer retail programs on its Web site.

When thinking about a career in retailing you must consider your own qualifications as well as job opportunities. You should look into the various managerial positions open to you as an employee and also at ownership possibilities. Wherever you start, it is important to think about the directions that emanate from your first job. Where can you expect to be in 5 years, in 10 years? Which retail companies are growing? What functional areas provide the best opportunities? What skills do you need? The following material will help you find answers to these questions as you learn how to prepare for a career search.

Retail Career Options

Retailing offers many career opportunities: in stores, with e-retailers, and in service businesses. Retailers are found globally in every size and type. There are careers for those who want to be in business for themselves and careers for those who prefer to work in large corporate organizations.

Experience is transferable from one business format to another because the basic functions are the same. The retail options are endless.

Opportunities with Retail Stores

Store retailers include every type of operation from superstore to drive-through pharmacy. Some retailers are large corporations in which functions are divided by specialty. On the other hand, many sole proprietors manage their stores, performing all the functions themselves.

Employees are needed for merchandising and real estate activities; in operations, promotion, human resources, and credit management; and for designing inventory management systems or private label merchandise. From CEOs to sales associates, traditional retailers recruit people with a variety of skills. Merchants who sell services, such as fast-food chains, travel agencies, hotels, and rental stores, also require personnel. Despite downsizing and retail consolidation, many new retail sales jobs are predicted in the United States in the early 2000s. This demand indicates an increase at the executive level also because more salespeople mean that more managers are needed.

Opportunities with Nonstore Retailers

A nonstore retailer is one who does not sell through a traditional location. Career opportunities also are available in direct marketing and selling operations, with vending machine companies and e-retail divisions of multichannel firms. For example, Amway gives generous rewards to its consultants who reach certain sales quotas through direct sales. Vending companies offer new ownership and/or franchise opportunities to those who are interested in dispensing everything from food to video games. L.L. Bean, one of the country's most successful retailers has forged links with colleges and universities for locating management trainees with bachelor's degrees for its catalog and other operations. Part-time jobs for students are available in stores, telemarketing firms, and distribution centers.

Technology has had a great impact on retailing as it has on every other industry. Distribution centers are automated and inventory is tracked by computer. Payrolls, credit systems, databases, accounting, and financial controls are powered by information technology. Multimedia online shows promote the latest fashions. Systems experts, programmers, analysts, technicians, designers, and Webmasters are part of the retail career spiral. At all levels of retail distribution technological expertise has never been more important.

Preparing for Your Retail Career

To embark on a retail career, enthusiasts should explore several formal and informal avenues to gain intimate knowledge of retailing. Work experience programs, management training programs, and promotion from within that includes on-the-job training are several ways in which this can be accomplished.

CYBERSCOOP
Federated Department Stores maintains a Web site that provides information for college students contemplating a career in retailing. Go to **www.retailology.com** and see what Federated has for you.

interns Students in a formal training program that allows them to learn on the job by working closely with professionals.

attrition Reduction of employees within an organization due to resignation, retirement, or death.

cooperative education An educational methodology that features alternate periods of formal study and work experience as a requirement for graduation.

Work Experience Programs

Internships, cooperative education programs, and part-time employment are three ways that individuals can sample the retail industry before committing to a career. Work experience programs help motivated students get the jump on competition for the best jobs.

Internships Many colleges and universities offer students an opportunity to sample careers while still in school. As interns, individuals work in selected jobs in their chosen field. **Interns** are students in formal training programs that encourage learning on the job while working closely with professionals. Students may work part-time during a semester, full-time for an entire semester or summer, or in other combinations. Internships may be paid or unpaid. In either case, college credit is usually earned because the internship is treated as a learning experience.

A typical retail internship may take place on a department store selling floor or in a merchandise office. One student may run the temporary Christmas decoration shop in one of the Bloomingdale's branch stores. Another may act as the assistant buyer in Debenham's department store in London. A third may be a fashion representative for a specialty chain store such as Express. Others may learn from the owner how to completely merchandise a local hardware store or set up a Web page for a small vintage clothing business.

The value of an internship varies because training is only as good as the trainer, the motivation and maturity of the student, and the demands of the academic institution. Most interns follow a syllabus and complete various assignments while employed.

A good internship often precipitates a retail career since many retailers hire previous interns as management trainees. Employers like to hire from this group, because its members are familiar with both the company image and retail procedures. There are few surprises for the new management trainee who has had previous experience with his or her employer. Attrition is much lower, training is easier, and advancement is faster. **Attrition** is the reduction of employees within an organization due to resignation, retirement, or death. Depending on their experience, some former interns start in management positions.

Cooperative Education Although the terms are often used interchangeably, there are differences between internships and cooperative education. **Cooperative education** is an educational methodology that employs alternate periods of formal study and work experience as a requirement for graduation. The major difference is in the number of work experiences. Students may have as few as two work periods in a two-year community college or a graduate program or as many as five in a five-year bachelor's degree program. Because students usually return to the same employer, it is possible to move from the lowest level during the first work term to a full-fledged managerial position by graduation. Cooperative education is an educational methodology practiced in over 1,000 colleges and universities in the United States, Canada, United Kingdom, Australia, Europe, Japan, and other countries committed to the philosophy.

Part-Time and Temporary Jobs Even if a college or university has no formal work program, students may still begin their retailing careers while in school. Many of the most successful retail executives began working part-time in stores while in high school and continued working part-time and summers through college. They committed to a career in the field long before receiving their degrees.

Long hours and low pay are typical when starting out in retailing. Those that accommodate these inconveniences and continue to pursue retail careers are excellent candidates for success.

Management Training Programs

Most large retail institutions have formal management training programs. Whether in merchandising or store operations, these programs offer college graduates a route to junior executive positions. Recruitment, training, and developing selection criteria are important to the task.

Recruitment Major retailers around the world recruit on selected college and university campuses annually. They also invite graduating students from all colleges to send their resumes.

Competition for slots in these programs is fierce, and it is not unusual for 800 students to be interviewed for 80 openings. Applicants who have had experience have a much better chance of being selected and of surviving the grueling first years.

Training Most training programs produce both merchandising and operations executives. Trainees tend to move ahead as quickly as their interests and skills develop. Programs usually combine intense work experience with structured seminars and study using computer modules, videotapes, CD-ROMs, and/or training manuals.

Management training programs vary in length from several months to two years, depending on the company. Focus of training programs also differs. Results of a study done by MOHR Learning, the largest retail training provider in the United States, indicated that training in management skills outranked all other areas in importance—including customer relations and technology skills.[2]

Starting salaries also vary according to the experience and educational background of the candidate and the geographic location of the employer. Most companies conduct periodic reviews of trainees and award salary increases based on merit. Starting salaries for management trainees in major retailing companies usually range from $25,000 to $35,000 per year. Although retailing salaries are somewhat low at the beginning, salaries for middle and upper management employees become comparable to, if not higher than, those in other fields. After five years of experience it is possible for executives to double their salaries.

Qualification for Selection Recruiters differ on the academic degrees they prefer for candidates seeking entry into their management trainee programs. Some seek general business majors or those specializing in marketing, management, retailing, fashion merchandising, finance, and information technology. Others recruit liberal arts graduates. Most admit that they favor a business major over a humanities major, if all else is equal. Some recruiters will accept two-year program graduates. Candidates with an MBA are viewed favorably because of the increasing importance of strategic planning, quantitative analysis, and information technology, areas in which those with advanced degrees are more adept.

Recruiters agree on the basic qualities they seek in candidates for the executive training program. Generally, individuals should be outgoing, effective communicators, and sincerely interested in retailing. They must have intelligence and demonstrated leadership skills. Candidates with high levels of energy and the ability to think on their feet do best. Candidates should also be mature, assertive, and able to make decisions. They must have above-average technological skills and analytical abilities. Some previous experience is expected.

Promotion from Within Although executive training programs offer the fastest route to management positions, there are other alternatives. Selling has been a starting point for many executives in retailing. From sales associate, individuals have moved to assistant department manager, group manager, assistant buyer, and even store manager. Some retailers have special training programs for company personnel who show management potential. These programs generally take longer than executive training programs.

Because everyone who applies cannot possibly be selected for a firm's management training program, the sales route, although slower, is an alternative road to a top management job. Often a good person who is passed over by executive placement recruiters, and who is willing to start in sales, proves to be a more valuable executive in the long run than some individuals in the training program. Radio Shack is a retail company that practices promotion from within extensively.

Many specialty store chains offer management positions in which employees have a great deal of responsibility ranging from supervising the staff to merchandising duties to total store operation. Besides store management, specialty chains also offer positions for district managers, regional managers, and training directors.

At the Gap, management trainees go through several steps on their career path. Advancement is based on performance on the job, not the amount of time that has been spent in each position. The first promotion for a management trainee at the Gap is to assistant manager, next to store manager. At that point, some individuals have the opportunity to become training store managers and assume the responsibility for teaching other managers on their way up the career ladder. Ultimately, Gap managers can become area managers, district managers, and regional managers. At this level their responsibility for overseeing several to many stores grows incrementally.

The impressions of a college graduate managing an Express store are related in the From the Field box. Her insight on the learning process and the importance of developing patience while waiting for promotion is valuable to those considering a retail career.

Qualities of Successful Retail Managers

Managers trained in management skills, finance, and strategic planning are in demand. These areas should be balanced by an understanding of marketing and an appreciation of the creative demands of merchandise- or service-oriented businesses. Because of this, a very special kind of person is needed.

A profile of a successful retail manager includes the following qualities and abilities:

- *Problem solving:* To analyze facts and data used in planning, managing, and controlling.
- *Creativity:* To bring imaginative ideas to merchandising and operations and be first in recognizing trends.
- *Confidence:* To take action, seize opportunities, and make quick, confident decisions in the ever-changing retail world.
- *Leadership:* To show initiative, help everyone work together to run a business smoothly.

From the Field: **Management Training at Express**
By Sara Bilodeau, Sales Manager

Years ago when I took a part-time job in retailing for the summer, never did I imagine that it would have such an impact on my life. After that summer, I returned to school as a sophomore and changed my major from Hotel/Restaurant Management to Retailing. I feel it was the right choice. People say you either love retailing or you hate it. I love it, but trust me, I have my days—and sometimes even weeks—when things do not go smoothly. I have learned the stresses of working retail, such as the long hours, understaffed stores, and rude customers. On the other side, there are the great clothes, cutting-edge fashion tips, valued co-workers, wonderful customers, and the opportunity to learn skills and gain responsibility.

I began my career in retailing as a sales associate and quickly was promoted to assistant manager. Fortunately, I was taking business classes and was able to use the information and tools to help me do my job better. Often I heard students say that they felt that what they were learning in the classroom was going to be useless once they got a job. I am very grateful that I did benefit from my education. Money well spent!

Upon graduation I accepted a job with one of the top divisions of the Limited. College classes and my internship prepared me well for my career. I was promoted to my position as partner (assistant manager) at a high-volume Express store within four months. I worked closely with the store manager by performing operations such as opening and closing the store, executing inventories, shipments, and transfers, and managing the register. I coordinated in-store contests and special promotions, re-merchandised the store, and assisted with hiring sales associates. All managers offer customer service by assisting customers on the sales floor. I was content with this position at the time, but aspired to bigger things. The pay was not high but adequate for my needs. The experience I gained made up for what was missing in my paycheck.

After two years as partner in three stores within my division, I was promoted to sales manager (store manager) in one of the lower-volume Express stores. Finally my own store and a raise! Within a few months I was promoted to a higher-volume store. I've been a manager for two years and my skills continue to develop. Finding and keeping good personnel and dealing with the problems that come with staffing a store with young part-time workers are challenges I routinely face. I still work long hours, but I've learned that to develop good managers you have to learn to delegate responsibility. Every day is different. One afternoon, a price tag hanging close to a display light unexpectedly caught fire and burned a pair of jeans. Mall security and the local fire department responded immediately, and no real damage was done, but the event certainly reinforced the point that managers have to be ready to react to most anything.

When I graduated from college, I had realistic expectations. I did not expect a set schedule and a high salary. I knew I would receive both eventually, but the first few years is when the most blood, sweat, and tears are shed. When I look to the future, I'm not always sure what I see myself doing, but that is all right. The training, knowledge, and experience that I have gained are enough to allow me to do whatever I choose in the retail industry. I know I will be successful because a positive attitude works miracles. Believing is achieving. At one point, I didn't believe that I could be successful. It took a wise professor to point out that I could. For this I am ever grateful. Self-doubt is what blocks the road to success. Do not let yourself or others put up roadblocks. Whatever you want can be yours.

- *Flexibility:* To be receptive to changing trends in styles and attitudes, and be adaptable to the everyday surprises in retailing.
- *Energy:* To handle the stress of the fast-paced, demanding job of retail managers.
- *Communication skills:* To practice excellent written and oral communication skills.
- *Human relations skills:* To relate well with others in a business setting. The human side of the marketplace is often neglected in the rush for profits. Yet profits are sometimes lost because of this neglect.

- *Ability to function under pressure:* To handle multiple tasks and make decisions effectively and expediently.
- *Optimistic attitude:* To maintain an optimistic outlook at all times and act as an inspiration to others.

Because managers frequently give verbal instructions to those who work for them and send written reports—including e-mails—to those for whom they work, the importance of developing good verbal and writing habits is stressed. Students often tend to ignore the professor who emphasizes the need for communications skills in business. Listen well, future retailers; few lessons are more important. Although possession of these and other qualities does not guarantee success, a retail manager has much less chance to succeed without them.

Many retailing students aspire to one day open their own stores. All of the qualities needed by a retail executive hold true for an entrepreneur. In some areas emphasis shifts, and some new traits are added. Sole proprietors must perform multiple tasks concurrently. When you own your own store, you can never say, "That's not my department." Ownership brings an even greater sense of involvement to an entrepreneur both professionally and personally. Knowing that you may be responsible for generating not only your own salary but that of your employees, lends a new meaning to the word *responsibility.* Being a store owner can be all-consuming. It becomes your whole life. There are advantages and disadvantages to working in this kind of environment that are discussed in the Small Business Focus in Appendix B.

The Career Search

Whatever the career choice, planning is essential when identifying jobs and employers. Without a plan graduates can easily end up in the wrong occupation, in the wrong location, and with the wrong firm. They must begin their search with goals in mind, a self-analysis, and a self-marketing plan. Before setting your own goals, ask yourself four questions about the career field you are considering:

1. Does it have a future? Consider trends in the retail environment such as technology, economics, social change, and competition.
2. Will it be financially rewarding?
3. Does it have growth potential to accommodate a large number of new recruits in the future?
4. Do you absolutely love it?

If retailing is your choice, then the answer to all four questions must be yes—in spite of the mergers, acquisitions, bankruptcies, and growth pains of the past decade. As you start your strategic career search, look at the growth potential in the industry. This is more important than the door through which you enter an industry or company. No one wants a dead-end job, but because too many people think only of the starting salary and job title, some miss the best opportunities. Thinking about your goals helps you stay on target as you develop, learn, and implement skills in your entry-level position.

Make an honest appraisal of your interests, abilities, and weaknesses. Do they fit the picture you are painting of your future? If not, you must reappraise your goals before going any further. They have to be realistic in terms of who you are, your interests, and your aptitudes. Part of self-analysis is determining what knowledge or skills you have acquired through your educational and work experiences and judging how this knowledge will transfer to your desired career path.

Set goals and relate them to who you are, what you desire, and how your capabilities and interests relate to the world of work. Then you will be at one step ahead of the competition. Most candidates only seek a job. They do not think about the long-range implications of planning for a career.

Career Search Preliminaries

Now the real work begins. Seek information on companies that interest you through research, interviews, and networking.

Seeking Information and Encouragement Explore the Internet, write or call companies and ask about jobs, the company, and future opportunities. Telephone or e-mail executives you know and ask if you can take a few minutes of their time for an informational interview. An **informational interview** is an informal meeting between executive and person seeking information on an industry, company, and career opportunities. Many people are flattered to be asked, and if you do this in a polite way, you may get an appointment. Talk to family friends, alumni of your college, and summer or part-time employers. Armed with information you will be better prepared to present yourself to potential employers.

Informational interview Informal meeting between executive and person seeking information on an industry, company, and career opportunities.

Turn to faculty, friends, relatives, and others to learn about employment opportunities and to let people know you are in the job market. Not surprising, the greatest number of positions are found by personal referral. Creating an organized and effective group of acquaintances who may help build business contacts is called **networking**. It is an excellent preliminary strategy that often leads to employment. A good tip when networking is

networking Creating an organized and effective group of acquaintances who help build business contacts.

Table A.1 Popular Internet Job-Search Web sites

Web site	Key Attributes
www.monster.com	■ *My Monster* resume design and storage facilities
	■ Leading global network
	■ Variety of positions in many industries
www.classifieds.yahoo.com	■ Multitude of listings by key word and location
	■ Retail specific category available
www.careerbuilder.com	■ Over 400,000 jobs listed
	■ Strong retail representation
	■ Interview tips
	■ International options
www.retailjobmart.com	■ Easy to navigate
	■ Listings from entry level to senior management

never to leave one contact without getting the names of one or two more people. Because they know the first contact, they will be receptive to the idea of seeing you. This method can help build a wonderful resource file of potential employers. Attending job fairs is another way to build your list of prospective employers.

You can obtain lists of employers from such sources as the College Placement Council, chambers of commerce, directories from professional associations, and references like Standard & Poor's register, Moody's manuals, and the Dun & Bradstreet directories. Specialized career publications such as *Job Postings* magazine are often available from career development offices. The yellow pages and the Internet are also valuable resources. In fact Web sites have become a primary means of alerting prospective employees about opportunities within a company. The Direct Marketing Association publishes on its Web site an annual listing of companies that provide paid summer internships. Material such as this may often pave the way to full-time positions as well. Popular Internet job-search Websites are listed and evaluated in Table A.1.

Seek out someone who can offer encouragement and support during the job search. It is helpful to have a friend, adviser, or approachable faculty member to report to weekly and discuss progress or frustration. Consider offering the same support to a friend or colleague who is also seeking a position in retailing.

Anticipating the Expense Try to plan for the necessary monetary investment in the job search. If you are not at home during the day you will need e-mail, a pager, and/or a telephone answering machine. Other costs may include transportation, interview clothing, postage, and resume printing charges. A part-time job may serve as a bridging position to allow time for job-search activities. Depending on the circumstances, one creative approach to job hunting is to offer to work free for a time as an intern.

Developing a Plan of Attack

Usually the greater number of contacts and interviews you have, the greater numbers of job offers you will receive. College placement offices offer on-campus interviews, help with your resume, employer lists, alumni lists, job openings, and Internet access.

Direct mailings and e-mails are useful in a long-distance job search. All letters should be addressed to an individual, and a cover letter should always be sent with a resume. A long-distance search should involve visits to the area of interest, subscriptions to the major newspaper, and inquiries to colleges that might offer reciprocal placement services.

Creative approaches to the career search include placing a position-wanted ad in newspapers or on the Internet, distributing cards at professional meetings, or developing a one-of-a-kind resume. Cold calls or walk-ins involve dropping in on companies to try to make contacts where you have been unable to get an interview or get the name of a contact person. Sometimes getting attention is the best way to get a foot in the door.

Career Search Tools

Three basic tools are essential in getting the first job: (1) resumes, (2) letters, and (3) interviews. All three must be approached from a marketing point of view. The marketing concept should be your guide, just as it would be if you were selling a product or a service instead of yourself.

resume A brief history of education and experience that job applicants prepare for prospective employers to review.

The Resume A **resume** is a brief history of education and experience that job applicants prepare for prospective employers to review. Two formats that can be followed when preparing a resume are chronological and functional. Chronological resumes list past experiences in order, beginning with your current position, then working back in time. Functional resumes stress competencies and experiences gained on the job which are not reflected on a timeline. There is no overall consensus as to what constitutes the perfect resume. However, keep in mind that employers spend less than 20 seconds scanning a resume to determine if a candidate is worth further consideration. Therefore, be certain your resume is organized, attractive, brief, concise, complete, truthful, and clearly written with no misspellings. A good resume opens interview doors.

The heading gives identifying information including name, address, phone number, and e-mail contact. The job or career objective may be a brief statement of short and long range goals. An option is a qualifications summary, a statement that indicates how your skills relate to your desired objective.

In giving your educational background, work backward from your most recent degree. Include your degree, major, minor, honors, date of graduation, and the name of your school. Courses are optional. Consider not including your grade point average unless requested. Some companies may have a cutoff of 3.5 and your very respectable 3.4 might eliminate you as a candidate.

In giving work experience, work backward from your most recent job. Summer employment, part-time jobs, volunteer work, internships, and so on should be included. Use action verbs to describe your duties and responsibilities.

Your interests and activities indicate that you are a well-rounded person. Highlight the activities and identify interests that closely relate to your career goals or the needs of the employer. Personal background need not be included on a resume, particularly because it is illegal for a potential employer to ask questions about age, marital status, health, or disabilities.

On your resume you need write only "References furnished upon request." Request permission from faculty or employers who know you well to use their names as references. Keep their names, affiliations, addresses, and contact information readily available. A good resume in itself does not guarantee that you will get the job, but a bad one can easily prevent you from being considered.

The Internet provides boundless opportunities for job searching, but you will find that some Web sites are easier than others to navigate, especially for new prospects. If you use the Internet to apply for a position, sending your resume through cyberspace requires advance planning and a different format. Special protocol should be followed. Resumes must be scanable, preferably set up in html programming style. They should include fewer graphic accessories—such as bullets, underpinnings, and elaborate columns—than conventional resumes to ensure delivery in an intact state. A universal type font should be selected in a size no smaller than 12 point. A one-page format is preferred, with contact information at the top.

Letters Effective letters are as important in the job search as an effective resume. The following is a list of letters you should consider as part of your personal marketing campaign.

1. *Letter of application* Employers read the letter before they read the enclosed resume. Make sure it is good. To maintain control of the process, you might end the letter with a sentence such as: "I will be calling you within ten days in order to follow up this mailing and see if an interview might be arranged."

2. *Letter of appreciation* It is never wrong to say thank you after an interview. Such a letter shows that you are considerate and displays common business courtesy.

3. *Letter seeking additional information*

4. *Letter inquiring about status*

5. *Letter accepting a position*

6. *Letter rejecting an offer of employment*

The Interview If a good resume opens the interview door, a poor interview can quickly slam it shut, so be prepared. You will be judged on your grooming, the way you express yourself, your maturity, and personality. This is the time to sell yourself. A good first interview leads to a second interview, and often the second interview leads to the job you want.

Interviews may be one-on-one, where the job candidate meets with only one human resource manager or other executive at a time. Sometimes panel interviews are conducted where applicants face a barrage of questions and problem solving situations generated by three or four company executives. Sometimes group interviews are conducted during informal meals or other events. In this scenario, the social skills and of prospective employees are evaluated as well as their levels of assertiveness.

Projections: Where the Jobs Will Be

Demand should be strong for specialty store executives, and opportunities for people in discount and off-price chains may be greater than in traditional department stores. Specialty chains, like the many divisions of the Limited, have clearly defined, exciting career paths, as well as good compensation packages including bonus incentive plans. They have the allure and ability to attract high-ranking graduates.

Department stores will continue to do an effective job of recruitment and of initial training. After the initial training stages, however, department stores lose a disturbing number of recruits to other firms in or out of the industry. In an effort to retain young people, some stores move them up too rapidly. Meaningful training programs and ongoing support are important for recruits to identify in all retail organizations.

There will also be excellent job prospects with direct marketing firms and in the food/supermarket industry. As firms embrace multichannel retailing, opportunities in e-commerce divisions indicate another avenue of growth for skilled individuals. Some global retailers actively recruit foreign students studying in the United States. The tactic is to identify and train qualified management candidates before they graduate and return to their home countries to work for that retailer. These examples are only some of the possibilities in a rapidly evolving industry. Whatever the setting, retailing should be valued as an exciting and rewarding profession. Discover this for yourself.

Notes

1. Conrad, Andree. "Converting Customers to Staffers." *Women's Wear Daily*. October 25, 2000:14.

2. MOHR Learning. "Management Skills Now Top Focus of Retail Training; Benchmark Survey Tracks Industry Training Trends." Press Release. January 15, 2001. Available: http://www.mohrlearning.com

Small Business Focus

Profile of an Entrepreneur

Susan Bates, Owner, The Cooperage

Every year many people answer the call of the entrepreneur within: "I want to open my own store." Many single-unit, sole proprietor businesses do not exist beyond their first anniversaries, yet others succeed beyond their owner's expectations. What are the crucial factors that tip the scale? A close look at a gift shop with an unusual flair for antiques, wholesome products, and an ambiance that many customers believe restores their soul, may provide insight. Owner Susan Bates has nurtured her business since 1989, operating from an historic building in Townsend Harbor, Massachusetts, illustrated in Figure B.1.

Bringing a dose of reality to individuals contemplating store ownership, this profile examines Susan's penchant for retailing, her early experience, and the pleasures and pitfalls derived from her chosen path. Competitive advantages, business strategies, visual merchandising practices, customer service techniques, and her personal measures of success are addressed.

Figure B.1 Housed in a centuries old building, The Cooperage welcomes customers into a world of herbs, flowers, antiques, and country-inspired gifts.

Getting Started

When you ask Bates how she started her business, she fondly refers to "Mary" and

Figure B.2 Well-preserved architectural details, like this center chimney, create focal points for the artful display of merchandise.

"Clover." Not friends in retailing or even business mentors, the pair were sheep given to her by her daughter's teacher. With a $200 investment, she opened an in-home business in the early 1980s. Wool products, courtesy of Mary and Clover, and dried flower arrangements from her farm were her first product lines.

An art and English major in college, Bates worked as a journalist for several newspapers after graduation. She had no formal business training. When she began her small venture, she says she, "learned fast, the hard way, on the job." Bates was "always an artist," and had created floral arrangements since she was a child. Once, she admits, she stole flowers from a neighbor and resold them to him! Her art has found a special conduit in the arrangements that presently grace her store.

Picking the Location

Always observant and ready to scout potential store sites, Bates noticed that a building owned by the Society for the Preservation of New England Antiquities (SPNEA) and maintained by the Townsend Historical Society was underutilized. She wrote to the local society and proposed a retail venture that would be in character with the historic district. The property had been a cooperage, a factory where wooden barrels were manufactured in the 1700s.

"When people come into my store, they appear to be on a treasure hunt," says Bates. A meandering pathway winds its way around a center chimney in the rustic saltbox style structure. The chimney makes a compelling backdrop for the display of merchandise as shown in Figure B.2. The unconventional floor plan would not be the choice of a major chain, but works very well for The Cooperage. Bates believes the atypical configuration encourages customers to browse. The melange of potpourri, pottery, hand-dipped candles, exotic apparel, antique furniture, garden supplies, books with a past life, fresh and dried herbs and flowers fill the store with unexpected scents and textures, tantalizing the customer. Classical music plays in the background, sales associates are always gracious. Sustaining the store image is the most important part of her job, according to Bates. She expects that her employees will not make personal phone calls while in the store and will never chew gum. The ambiance reflects the many aspects of store image controlled carefully, but never obviously by Bates.

Defining the Market

The Cooperage's target market is predominantly women who come from the surrounding towns. However, Bates has some customers from Boston—about an hour's drive away—who call to place special orders. She also gets a wealth of customers from all over New England during fall foliage season.

Most merchandise at The Cooperage is purchased at wholesale from established vendors. Some antiques are placed on consignment. She usually purchases items that reflect her personal taste, but also buys specific colors for customers once she is aware of their preferences. She has experimented with stocking what she calls "mass" items, which admittedly sell well. However, she will not compromise the unique image of the store with too many mainstream products. Many items are made by Bates or by a coterie of craftspeople from the area. An old quilt salvaged from an attic may take on a new life as a Christmas stocking or decorative pillow. Baskets found at yard sales or antique auctions may become the base for one of her famous dried herb and floral arrangements. Eclectic items typical of The Cooperage are shown in Figure B.3.

Figure B.3 Appealing merchandise is sourced from local craftspeople, antique shows, trade fairs, and exotic locales.

Global Sourcing

Bates engaged in global sourcing when she traveled to Nepal and discovered a wealth of textile products, handmade jewelry, and other gift items that have been infused into her merchandise mix. Immersing herself in the culture, she developed close personal relationships with several of the business contacts she met on her buying trips. She is sensitive to the poverty and political instability in which many Nepalese live and has established the Nepalese and Tibetan Resource Fund. Using proceeds derived from the sale of select items located in a special corner of the store, the fund helps finance education in the United States for Nepalese children.

As well as philanthropic inclinations, Bates has highly refined human relation skills. Her customers are her friends, and she appears to enjoy passing the time of day with them as much as selling her merchandise. She says she has met wonderful women and has heard their inspiring and tragic stories. Customers feel comfortable sharing their lives with her. Bates is a brilliant conversationalist and enjoys discussing wildlife, history, gardening, and retailing. This intimate atmosphere, of course, ensures that plenty of

Figure B.4 Susan Bates, owner, places great importance on her relationships with her customers whom she welcomes into a stress-free environment rich with merchandise.

goods will move off the shelves. According to Bates, "The customer is always right, if you want the customer to be your customer forever." An incident illustrates that her policy is not always practical to implement. A customer wanted to return an antique butter dish that had broken quite a while after she had purchased it. Bates nicely pointed out that she couldn't be responsible for breakage under those circumstances and that she could not take back the broken item. The customer never returned, but Bates felt justified in applying common sense to her decision.

Operating the Business

Countless hours are spent running the store, buying merchandise, supervising two or three part-time salespeople, producing many of the products sold in the store, and servicing customers as illustrated in Figure B.4. It is not unusual to see The Cooperage lights burning long after the store has closed for the night. During the busy fall and holiday season, the store is open seven days a week. During the winter, hours of operation are reduced.

Bates operates on a keystone markup system. If the market will not bear a 50 percent markup on retail, she prices selected items lower. In general, The Cooperage offers a competitive price range on most products, with very few high-end items in stock. Inventory is kept manually, although Bates is considering installing a computer system. She admits she intentionally runs a low-tech environment.

Hesitant to divulge annual revenue, Bates measures success by the personal fulfillment she feels doing a job she loves. Financial success means being able to live comfortably, travel a bit, put two children through college, and for the first time, purchase a new car of her choosing. Above all, she says, "I have realized my special gifts through this business."

Glossary

4-5-4 calendar Adaptation of a conventional calendar used for retail planning and accounting.

807 programs Caribbean initiative programs offering low taxation on goods and other incentives that encourage manufacturing in selected countries.

acquisition The buying of one company by another, in either a friendly or hostile manner; this practice is also called a *buyout* or *takeover*.

additional markup Price increase taken after the original markup has been determined.

advanced shipping notice Electronically generated document that alerts receivers to impending shipments of goods.

aggressive pricing Pricing method based on undercutting competitors' prices rather than concentrating on the company's strengths.

aisle interrupters Signs, usually made from cardboard, that protrude into an aisle.

allocators Individuals who support merchandising teams by providing detailed distribution information.

ambiance Mood evoked by the use of tangible and intangible store design tools.

analog method Method for obtaining a sales forecast by comparing potential new sites with existing sites.

anchor store Major mall tenant occupying a large, usually corner or end store.

anticipation An additional discount sometimes allowed when the invoice is paid before the expiration date of the cash discount period.

aspirational wants Wants that relate to products and services that people perceive will help them achieve higher status in life.

Association of Southeast Asian Nations (ASEAN) Trade alliance set up in 1967, with U.S. backing to benefit countries including Brunei, Indonesia, Malaysia, the Philippines, Singapore, Thailand, and later, Vietnam.

asymmetrical balance Positioning items on either side of a center line so that they are not equally weighted optically.

attrition Reduction of employees within an organization due to resignation, retirement, or death.

automated storage and retrieval (ASR) Warehousing system that combines the use of computer control of stock records with mechanical handling.

avatar An animated graphic form that portrays a human.

baby boomers The 76 million Americans born between 1946 and 1964.

bait and switch Unethical promotional pricing technique that attempts to lure customers into the store on false premises.

balance of trade The difference between a country's imports and exports over a period of time, such as a year.

bankruptcy Legal declaration to inform public of financial insolvency of a company.

banners Advertising graphics that appear on Web site homepages.

bar coding Capture of information at point of sale by scanning the universal product code (UPC) with an electronic device.

basic stock method Inventory planning system in which estimated sales for the month are added to a minimum stock to determine merchandise needs for the planning period.

big box stores Term used to identify a broad spectrum of discount and discount-like retailers that operate out of large, utilitarian stores.

big-ticket Merchandise that is expensive such as cars or computers.

biogenic needs Physiological needs for food, warmth, shelter, and sex.

branch stores Satellite stores within a department store group; usually located in the suburbs or cities remote from the main store.

brand equity The level of consumer recognition a brand, label, or store has in the marketplace.

branded concept shops Store-within-a-store formats featuring internationally known mega-brand merchandise such as Nautica, Tommy Hilfiger, or Liz Claiborne.

branding The process of developing, building, and maintaining a name in the marketplace.

bribe Payment made to an individual, company, or government in order to secure special business privileges.

bridge line A line of apparel that is priced lower than designer fashions.

browser Software that allows users to travel through cyberspace to search for information or go directly to a site.

bumpback Locating a smaller, usually temporary tenant, in the front portion of a space vacated by a much larger retailer.

business-to-business (B2B) exchanges Web-based businesses that facilitate purchasing and the development of partnerships between supply chain members.

buying power The amount of money a family has available for purchases after taxes.

buying power index (BPI) Weighted value that measures the purchasing ability of households in a trading area.

carryover The amount of time between a person's receipt of a catalog or advertisement and the actual sale.

category killers Specialty superstores that focus on limited merchandise classifications and great breadth and depth of assortments.

cause marketing The practice of staging promotions that benefit charitable organizations or communities and also secure positive public relations for the sponsoring retailer.

caveat emptor "Let the buyer beware." Latin expression applied to merchandise sold without a warranty or return option.

central business district Downtown commercial areas in large and small cities where many businesses including retailers tend to congregate.

chargebacks Financial penalties imposed on manufacturers by retailers.

classification A group of related lines carried by a retailer.

cluster analysis Method used to group customers according to their attributes and behaviors.

co-branding Retail partnership that is formed when two separate retailers (brands) join forces to reach more customers more effectively thus increasing sales for both parties.

cognitive dissonance Anxiety that occurs when a person has mixed feelings or beliefs.

collaborative planning, forecasting, and replenishment (CPFR) Initiative to develop distribution efficiencies throughout the supply chain.

collection shops Boutiques in department stores or stand-alone specialty stores that feature top-of-the-line merchandise by international designers such as Prada or Georgio Armani.

common area maintenance charges (CAM charges) Charges assessed on retailers that fund general mall upkeep internally and externally.

community center Neighborhood center expanded to serve a trading area of 40,000 to 150,000 people.

completion date The date promised by the manufacturer for total receipt of goods by the retailer.

concept shops Select in-store areas featuring merchandise that has high brand recognition. A format used by retailers to expand on a broad scale without the high overhead costs of chain expansion.

concession Independently owned and operated departments that cross all product and service lines, and are less dependent on special levels of management expertise than leased departments.

consultative selling In-home or in-office selling by specialists whose expertise is valued by the customer.

consumer cooperative Stores in which consumers own a stake, receive lower prices on merchandise, and may participate in profit sharing.

consumer price index Economic indicator that measures changes in the cost of living due to inflation.

containerships Sailing vessels that are outfitted with large numbers of cargo holders that are roughly 40-feet long and shaped like a tractor-trailer bed.

convenience goods Low-cost items purchased with a minimum of effort or time.

cooperative advertising Program under which retailers and manufacturers agree to share costs for retail advertising.

cooperative education An educational methodology that features alternate periods of formal study and work experience as a requirement for graduation.

corporate chain A string of 25 or more stores with identical or similar formats under central ownership.

coverage The geographic area in which an advertising message potentially is seen or heard.

cross-docking The practice of moving goods in and out of a distribution center with minimal handling of merchandise.

cross-merchandising The practice of allocating the same merchandise to two or more areas of the store instead of one.

cross-promotion Practice of using multimedia to promote retail Web sites.

cumulative markup The average markup for an entire department or classification after a given selling period.

customer resource management (CRM) Planning and implementation of strategies designed to serve the customer in an efficient and satisfying manner.

cycle time The period of time that elapses between production of goods and order fulfillment.

danglers Signs that are suspended from a shelf.

data mining Probing a database for pertinent information that can be used to target future offers to customers.

database marketing The process of gathering, maintaining, and using demographic, psychographic, and behavioral data on customers.

debit cards Plastic cards with electronic capabilities that allow purchase prices to be instantly deducted from customers' bank accounts.

deep discounter Discount store that operates on much lower gross margins than conventional or other discount retailers.

demalling Breaking up older enclosed malls into open-concept clusters of stores.

demographics Statistics on human populations including age, gender, ethnic origin, education, income, occupation, type of housing, and other descriptors.

department/specialty store Limited-line department store that usually focuses on upmarket soft lines.

department stores Retail stores organized into separate departments for purposes of selling a wide variety of soft goods, such as apparel for men, women, and children, and hard goods, such as furniture.

destination stores Stores that have drawing power because they offer unique merchandise or strong brand identification.

devaluation Reduction in the international exchange value of a currency.

developing countries Countries moving out of third world or emerging nation status.

differential advantage Unique characteristics of a business that may give it a superior position in the marketplace.

diffusion lines Groups of merchandise that are produced and sold at lower prices than designer collections.

direct marketing Any direct communication to a consumer or business recipient that is designed to generate a response in the form of an order, new lead, or store traffic.

direct selling The practice of selling to consumers through one-on-one situations or parties usually held in homes or work places.

discretionary income The amount of money available for nonessential purchases after taxes and basic expenses for food, clothing, and shelter have been paid.

discounters Retailers that buy and sell at low prices and depend on high volume and low overhead to be profitable.

disposable income The amount of money available for purchases after taxes are deducted.

diversification Acquiring or developing stores that are not directly related to a company's core business

divestiture The selling of one retail company to another.

dollar plan A forecast used by retailers to determine how much they need to invest in new merchandise.

domestic retailers Retail organizations that do business only in their home countries.

drawing account A regular monetary compensation available to commission salespeople that allows them to take a fixed sum of money at regular intervals against future commissions.

due diligence Evaluating of financial and other details in-depth before a merger or acquisition can occur.

easement agreement Agreement that allows limited use of land owned by someone else.

e-commerce All-encompassing term for business conducted on the Web.

Economic and Monetary Union (EMU) System set up to facilitate the adoption and use of the euro for participating EU members.

economies of scale Savings achieved through producing or purchasing large quantities of goods.

effective buying income (EBI) Statistic that measures the availability of personal disposable income in a trading area.

electronic article surveillance (EAS) Systems that use security apparatus, often located at store exits, to deter shoplifting.

electronic cash (e-cash) cards Smart cards that load and hold cash values in any currency via an ATM or telephone.

electronic data interchange (EDI) Computer-guided communications network between retailer, manufacturer, and other supply chain members.

electronic fund transfers (EFT) Computerized systems that process financial transactions, exchanges, or information.

electronic kiosks Small display units in stores or other locations that use computers and other devices to generate sales or provide extended customer services.

encryption codes Computer programs that prevent hackers from committing crimes such as fraud and unauthorized access of personal information.

end-caps Display areas located at the ends of shopping aisles.

end-of-month (EOM) stock Refers to the dollar amount of stock remaining at the end of a month's selling period.

Engel's Laws of Family Expenditures Theory developed by 19th-century German statistician offering basic view of how people spend their incomes on goods and services.

environmental settings Simulated rooms with three walls used to display home furnishings and accessories in a coordinated group.

e-retailing The practice of performing retail activities on the Web.

ethnocentric Viewing individual countries in narrow focus; the attitude that one's own country or culture is superior.

euro Common currency used by EU countries.

European Central Bank (ECB) Financial institution that administers the euro currency policy for the EU.

European Union (EU) One of the largest trading blocs in the world, its fifteen member nations include Austria, Belgium, Denmark, Finland, France, Germany, Greece, Ireland, Italy, Luxembourg, the Netherlands, Portugal, Spain, Sweden, and the United Kingdom.

extensible markup language (XML) Electronic message format that integrates different forms of hardware, software, and applications.

external promotion Communicating ideas to potential customers with the objective of bringing them into the store.

extranet Secured computer links between business partners such as retailers and suppliers.

eye-level merchandising Utilizing the line of vision in an approximate 18-inch range of eye level.

faced-out Placement that occurs when merchandise is displayed on fixtures so customers can see the product head-on.

factory outlets Company-owned stores that sell manufacturers' overruns, seconds, irregulars, and sample products.

fashion/specialty center Anchorless shopping center that focuses on a lifestyle cluster, unique merchandise, or price level.

fill-rates The ability of manufacturers or distributors to ship all goods ordered; expressed as a percentage.

flagship store The main store in a retail group, usually located in a city and often on the site of the original store.

flexible pricing The setting of prices that are open to bargaining.

floor fixtures Display units designed to house and present products.

focus group Panel of 5 to 15 people invited to discuss a product, service, or market situation.

franchise A contractual arrangement in which an independent franchisee agrees to purchase and operate a business according to the franchisor's specifications.

free on board (FOB) Term identifying the point from which the retailer assumes responsibility for goods and payment of transportation charges.

freeform floor plans Less structured floor arrangements with emphasis on engineered traffic flow.

freestanding stores Self-contained buildings that are usually located on the periphery of a shopping center or city. Freestanding buildings also exist in downtown areas or power nodes.

free trade The conduct of business without boundaries or taxation.

freight forwarder Firms that group shipments of several manufacturers into truckload, railcar, or container shipments.

generation X Children of early baby boomers, usually those born between 1965 and the late 1970s.

generation Y Persons born between the 1977 and 1994 that include contemporary young adults, teens, and younger school-age children.

generic goods Products that do not bear highly recognizable manufacturers' or retailers' labels and are cheaper than comparable brand-name goods.

geocentric Viewing the world as a whole—the locus for ideas and decision making.

geodemographics Computer-based method of identifying consumers in specific geographic locations.

geographical information systems (GIS) Technology that allows retailers to analyze potential sites on the basis of interrelated demographic, psychographic, and geographic data.

global retailers Retail organizations that do business in their home countries and in more than one other trading bloc.

goals Statements that indicate general company aims or end results.

gondolas Moveable, bin-type display fixtures frequently used for promotional merchandise.

government-owned store A store owned and operated by local, state, or federal government.

gravity models Calculations used to identify customer drawing power of geographic areas.

grid floor plans Linear geometric floor arrangements with aisles and fixtures parallel or perpendicular to walls.

grievance A complaint that is handled formally through fixed procedures.

gross domestic product (GDP) Total retail value of all goods and services produced by a country during a specific time period.

gross leasable area (GLA) The amount of square footage available for lease in a shopping center, excluding common areas such as walkways, offices, and parking areas.

gross margin The difference between net sales and the cost of merchandise sold, expressed as a percentage.

gross profit Net sales less the cost of goods sold. Retailers consider gross profit and gross margin the same thing.

harmonization Bringing tax rates across several countries into equilibrium.

hackers Individuals who break into computer systems with criminal intent.

hard lines Products such as furniture, home electronics, computers, home improvement goods, toys, housewares, books, and automotive supplies.

headhunters Individuals or agencies who are paid to find managers or executives for a client company.

hierarchy of needs Maslow's theory that people seek to satisfy needs in this order: biological, social, psychological.

high streets Busy thoroughfares where many retailers locate in the United Kingdom.

homepage The first screen image that comes up when users enter a Web site.

horizontal cooperative advertising Joint advertising by a group of businesses usually at the same level of the supply chain; done to increase traffic or interest in a product or event.

hostile takeover Ownership change that occurs when one company purchases large quantities of outstanding stock in another company giving controlling interest to the acquiring company.

hybrid center Shopping areas that are of mixed composition, combining the qualities of two or more basic center configurations with contemporary twists.

hyperlinks Web facilitators that allow a user to go from one site to another with a click of the mouse.

hypermarkets Stores of over 150,000 square feet,

70 percent of which is devoted to general merchandise and 30 percent to food products.

import snobbery The tendency for people to believe that better, more desirable products come from other countries.

impulse goods Items that are purchased on the spur of the moment.

independent retailer Single store, multi-unit operation, or service business owned by an individual, partnership, or family.

index of retail saturation (IRS) Measurement instrument that allows retailers to determine the degree of competition in a trading area.

industrialized countries Countries that have reached full production capabilities and have well-developed infrastructures and technologies.

inflation The abnormal increase in the volume of money and credit in a country resulting in a substantial and continuing rise in price levels.

infomercials Television commercials that combine detailed product information, demonstration, and excitement with a sales pitch.

information technology (IT) The umbrella term for computer-based decision-support systems that are used to provide more efficiency in retail operations.

information interview Informal meeting between executive and person seeking information on an industry, company, and career opportunities.

infrastructure Physical facilities that support the economy in a specific area, including highway systems, transportation, communication, and other public services.

initial markup The difference between the gross delivered cost and the original retail price for a single item or total assortment of goods.

institutional advertising Advertising designed to convey a positive image of the store rather than present specific merchandise.

intermodal The practice of shipping goods via more than one transportation conveyance owned by the same company.

internal promotion Communicating ideas to customers inside the store.

international retailers Retail organizations that operate in their home countries and within their own trading bloc or one other trading bloc.

Internet Computer lines and linkages that provide world access to information and commerce.

Internet service provider (ISP) National or regional companies that provide access to the Internet.

interns Students in a formal training program that allows them to learn on the job by working closely with professionals.

intranets Internal computer communication systems within a business or institution.

job enrichment A way to improve an employee's efficiency and self-satisfaction by increasing the challenges, opportunities, and nonmonetary rewards provided by the company.

just in time (JIT) Efficient logistical systems that allow for reduced inventory levels and timely distribution resulting in cost savings.

keystone markup A keystone markup constitutes a 50 percent markup on retail price.

keystoning The practice of doubling the cost of a product in order to determine its initial retail price.

lead time The amount of time required between receipt of an advertisement and the appearance of it in print, broadcast, or electronic media.

lean practices Methods of doing business that facilitate cost reductions, timing efficiencies, and inventory turn increases in supply chain management.

leased departments Departments that are owned and operated by a company other than the host store.

leave paper Slang industry expression for writing an order on the spot.

leveraged buyout Purchases in which the acquiring company borrows large sums of money, using the yet-to-be-owned assets as collateral, in order to finance the deal.

lifestyle center An outdoor shopping center encompassing several small retail strips and free-standing anchor stores in an appealing environment serving an upscale clientele.

lifestyles The way people live, work, play, and spend their money.

line haul Moving goods long distances between cities and towns.

line management Members of the management team who are directly connected to retail functions such as operations, finance, information technology, and merchandise management.

loss leaders Items that are priced below cost to increase store traffic. Also called traffic builders.

magalog A combination magazine and catalog published by a retailer and distributed in stores or by direct mail.

maintained markup Markup that is calculated on a group of merchandise or a department at the time the goods are sold.

mall "Climate controlled structure in which retail stores are architecturally connected." (ICSC)

management by objectives (MBO) A process in which a superior and a subordinate jointly set measurable job objectives for the subordinate and then meet periodically to assess progress.

manufacturer's representative Independent business person who works in a specific territory selling related but noncompeting products to more than one account.

markdown Reducing a price below its original level.

markdown cancellation Restoring a price to its premarkdown level.

markdown money Extra reimbursement allowed the retailer if a manufacturer's goods do not sell well.

market share The proportion of industry-wide product sales earned by one company.

market week Scheduled seasonal showings of merchandise by manufacturers in market centers.

marketing A set of business activities that includes product, price, promotion, and distribution. Most marketers also include people.

marketing channel The route taken by a product as it travels from producer to final consumer.

marketing concept The philosophy that guides a company in creating its marketing mix so as to satisfy its customers and, as result, make a profit.

marketing mix The unique blend of product, price, promotion, people, and distribution practices that is intended to reach and satisfy a target market.

markon The target or first markup placed on a retail product.

markup The figure that covers the fixed and variable costs of doing business.

markup cancellation When an additional price increase is removed and the original price is restored.

mass merchandisers Large format chain stores with broad geographic coverage that carry large assortments of general merchandise.

master franchise Ownership arrangement in which one company buys the rights to operate in a large region of a country, setting up scores of stores.

mature retail companies Large, well-developed retailers that have the financial and managerial expertise to consider global expansion.

m-commerce Business conducted on the Web using wireless devices such as cell phones or palm-held personal digital assistants.

media buying service Organization of media specialists that buys blocks of advertising time and space on behalf of a group of businesses.

media mix Specific configuration of media chosen by an advertiser for a campaign.

mediator Impartial evaluator hired to listen to both sides of a conflict and suggest solutions.

megamall Mixed-use mall of well over a million square feet, drawing from a trading area of over 100 miles and, in some cases, several states or provinces.

merchandise assortment All the goods in a store, defined in terms of breadth and depth of stock.

merchandising The practice of having the right goods at the right price in the right place at the right time.

MERCOSUR Trade agreement to promote free trade among several South American countries, including Argentina, Brazil, Paraguay, and Uruguay. Associate members are Chile and Bolivia.

merger The pooling of resources by two or more companies so as to become one.

metropolitan statistical area (MSA) Geographic areas with large, concentrated population centers that may cross county or state lines.

micro-merchandising Practice of creating and manufacturing product lines or items targeted to a specific market.

ministries of trade Government offices able to assist businesses with importing and exporting activities.

mission statement A brief paragraph that concisely describes a business and its reason for existence.

mixed-use center Shopping center with two or more uses, such as an office building with retail mall and residential areas.

model stock plans Lists that show specific stock levels needed for a selling period.

multichannel retailing The practice of trading through two or more methods of distribution concurrently.

multilevel marketing Direct selling by firms that are set up in a pyramid-style hierarchy. Salespeople pay commission on sales they generate to the leader who has recruited them.

multinational company Company that conducts manufacturing, service and/or retail business in its home country as well as in many other countries.

multiple pricing The offering of a discount for buying in quantities of more than one unit.

multi-unit department store Department store organization consisting of a flagship store and two or more stores.

national advertising Advertising placed in major media by manufacturers and distributors, usually on a broad geographic basis.

neighborhood center Small strip center in a trading area that serves 5,000 to 40,000 people.

Neilsen reports Commercial reports providing information on market share, sales, and trends useful to retail planners.

networking Creating an organized and effective group of acquaintances who help build business contacts.

neutral pricing Pricing method based on adding a fair amount of money to the cost of products to cover overhead and profit.

nonstore retailers Retailers that sell through means other than traditional storefronts.

North American Free Trade Agreement (NAFTA) Trade alliance that promotes free trade between the United States, Canada, and Mexico.

objectives Specific intentions stated by a company.

odd pricing The setting of prices that end in an odd number, such as $9.99 rather than $10.00.

off-price retailers Specialty discount stores that sell branded products at 20 to 60 percent less than traditional specialty or department stores.

on-the-job (OJT) training Instructing employees during regular working hours while they also are doing productive work and are being paid regular wages.

one-price policy When all customers pay the same price and purchase an item under similar conditions.

open-to-buy (OTB) Amount of money a buyer has allocated for purchasing merchandise for a designated period of time.

operating profit The resulting number after the costs of doing business are deducted from gross margin.

opinion leaders Trendsetters whose opinions are respected within a group.

optical weight The amount an object appears to weigh rather than what it actually weighs.

optimum stock level Having the right amount of merchandise on hand to satisfy customer needs without being overstocked or understocked.

outlet center Shopping center comprised mainly of stores owned by manufacturers.

outparcels Tracts of land on the periphery of a shopping center or other commercial site, often owned by the developer of the property.

outshopping The practice of purchasing goods from retailers that are located outside a customer's usual shopping territory.

party plan In-home or in-office selling to groups hosted by a customer.

passive pricing Pricing method based on a retailer's differential advantage rather than beating competitors' prices.

pathway floor plans Engineered traffic from the front of the store to the rear and back again by means of designated walkways.

penetration Setting a low initial price on a product when competition is high.

perceived value The worth that consumers place on merchandise, which may be different from true value.

periodic inventory Physical count of all merchandise on hand, usually taken annually or semiannually.

perpetual inventory Ongoing measurement of merchandise in stock as purchases and sales occur.

physical distribution The process of transporting goods from producer to retailer.

piracy Luring personnel from other firms.

planograms Detailed scale drawings that illustrate precisely where each fixture and piece of merchandise is to be placed in a store.

platform or island displays Displays created in a prominent area using a temporary or stationary low-rising units.

point of impulse (POI) Updated version of point of sale (POS) that more accurately records consumer behavior where and when it occurs.

point-of-purchase (POP) displays Fixtures or special racks and printed materials positioned close to customer interface areas in stores.

polygon method Determining a trading area by considering natural and man-made phenomena that apportion the space into straight-sided geometric shapes.

population density The number of people per square milie or kilometer in a specific geographic area.

portal sites Digital doorways to information stored in cyberspace.

positioning The perception a customer has of a store (or product) in relation to others.

power center Shopping center that resembles an oversize strip mall with as many as seven anchor stores that are usually discounters or category killers.

power node Consists of a grouping of big box stores—including one power center—located at or near a major highway intersection.

preferred trading partner (PTP) Countries that engage in trade freely with all other countries that have been approved by the World Trade Organization. Formerly referred to as "most favored nations."

preferred vendor lists Prescreened manufacturers that are chosen to do business with large retail companies. The practice often closes out smaller vendors.

price gouging The tactic of marking up retail products unreasonably high.

price lining The practice of setting distinguishable price levels, according to store policy. Often part of a good-better-best approach.

primary data Information compiled to address specific research issues.

primary trading area Geographic area that encompasses 50 to 80 percent of a store's potential customers; also referred to as the primary service area.

prime rate The interest rate charged by the Federal Reserve bank to commercial lending institutions.

private label Merchandise that is manufactured to store specifications and bears the retailer's name or other names created by the retailer.

product advertising Advertising that features specific merchandise and is designed to encourage timely sales.

product developer Generates ideas, designs prototypes, and arranges for production of exclusive products for retailers.

product licensing Contractual arrangement between a designer, or other holder of rights to a brand, and a manufacturer to produce items under the designer's name or brand.

product life cycle The process of tracing the existence of a product in the marketplace by examining the stages through which it passes and the time spent in each stage.

product line Group of closely related items produced by a manufacturer.

promotional pricing The practice of setting prices below that which is usual or customary.

promotional mix Advertising, sales promotion, publicity, public relations, personal selling, and customer service.

protectionism Government policy that protects domestic producers by placing restrictions on foreign producers of the same goods.

psychogenic needs Needs that stem from the socialization process and involve intangible aspects such as status, acquisitiveness, or love.

psychographics Classification of people on the basis of their lifestyles, activities, interests, and opinions.

public relations Promotional activities that enhance retail image and support charitable foundations or social causes.

publicity Nonpaid news or editorial comment about ideas, products services, or stores.

pull strategy When a retailer initiates shipments from the distribution center in response to sales.

push money (PM) An incentive payment given to sales associates for selling certain items.

push strategy When a distribution center initiates shipments to a retailer in anticipation of sales.

pyramid format Geometric display that follows the lines of a triangle, beginning at a broad base and progressing to an apex.

queue British term for a line of people.

quick response (QR) The umbrella term for integrated supply chain distribution systems that allow rapid replenishment of merchandise.

quota Limitations imposed on the quantities of products imported from other countries.

racetrack floor plans Floor arrangements in which elements of grid and freeform are combined to engineer customers around the entire store by means of oval shaped walkways.

radio frequency identification (RFID) Technology that uses radio waves to detect the presence of security devices.

random storage Computer model for optimal use of stock storage space.

reach The number of actual readers, listeners, or viewers in an audience.

real estate investment trust (REIT) Financial organization that masterminds large-scale retail real estate transactions.

recession Period of time in which there is less money in the economy than there previously was.

referrals The names of an informed person's acquaintances who might be potential employees.

reference groups Social groups or professional associations with which a person identifies and looks to when forming opinions.

regional center Center consisting of at least two anchor stores and 80 to 150 smaller stores, serving a minimum of 150,000 people.

resident buying office Companies that facilitate market coverage for retailers by acting as their eyes, ears, and legs in the marketplace.

resume A brief history of education and experience that job applicants prepare for prospective employers to review.

retail advertising Advertising specifically directed to final customers by retailers.

retail holding company Huge conglomerate comprised of many individual companies doing business under a variety of names.

retail mix Various activities in which retailers are engaged as they attempt to satisfy customers.

retail saturation The degree to which a trading area is overstored or understored.

retailers Businesses or individuals that sell more than 50 percent of their goods and/or services to final customers.

retailing The selling of goods or services directly to the final customer.

retenanting Finding new retailers to replace those that have gone out of business or otherwise vacated the premises.

ring analysis Determining a trading radius by using an existing or potential retail site as the locus.

role playing Training exercise in which individuals experience a situation through dramatization, by participating as actors.

sales potential Total amount of possible sales that can be realized in a trading area.

sameness syndrome The tendency of some retailers to offer the same or similar merchandise or services as their competitors.

scrambled merchandising Carrying products unrelated to a store's traditional or expected merchandise mix.

search engines Companies that provide the mode of transportation to specific Web sites on the Internet through complex electronic directories.

secondary data Information that comes from previously published sources.

secondary trading area Geographic area located just outside the primary trading area, containing 20 to 25 percent of a store's potential customers.

secure electronic transmission (SET) protocol Software that makes transmission between buyers and sellers safer.

self-actualization The desired result when a person sets out to become all that he or she is capable of becoming.

sell through The percentage of stock sold in a store or department in a specific period of time.

shadowboxes Small display windows located in-store or out, often used to display luxury items.

shoppertainment Combining retail shopping with many forms of entertainment.

shopping carts Special software features that allow online shoppers to collect several products and park them electronically until they are ready to purchase the items.

shopping center "A group of retail and other commercial establishments that is planned, developed, owned, and managed as a single property." (ICSC)

shopping goods High-priced merchandise purchased after the buyer compares the offerings of more than one retailer.

short-haul Moving goods to customers locally.

shurfers Name coined to designate surfers on the Internet who choose to shop.

situation analysis The process of determining the strengths and weaknesses of a company, specific business plan, or proposed strategy.

skimming Setting a high initial price on a product when competition is low.

smart cards Plastic cards with advanced microchip technologies that permit more sophisticated financial and nonfinancial services to be rendered.

soft lines Products such as apparel, accessories, linens, and bedding.

sourcing The identification and utilization of resources for the manufacturing of goods.

space productivity index Advanced tool used to help retailers determine optimum merchandise placement.

spam Unsolicited mail and advertisements on the Web.

spatial analysis Overlaying two or more types of data to define the drawing power of a specific site more accurately.

specialty goods Products bearing name brands or with special features for which buyers will go out of their way to purchase.

specialty stores Retail outlets that maintain large selections of limited lines of merchandise.

split run Practice of selling advertising space at reduced prices to regional advertisers.

standardization Establishment of uniform and monetary systems across several countries.

staple goods Merchandise that is routinely purchased.

step format Display that begins at a low point on one side and climbs incrementally to a higher point in a diagonal arrangement.

stock keeping unit (SKU) A multidigit number that indicates style, vendor, department, and other pertinent information for each unit of merchandise. (SKU is pronouced "skew.")

stock-to-sales ratio (SSR) The relationship between goods on hand at the beginning of the month and merchandise sold during that time period, expressed in dollars or units.

store image A combination of concrete and esoteric factors that contribute to the total impression customers have of a retailer.

strategic planning Process of gathering and analyzing information from a variety of internal and external sources for the purpose of reducing risk before specific business plans are executed.

strategies Action plans that prescribe tactics used by a company to reach common goals and objectives.

stress interview A type of screening tool in which a panel of interviewers fire questions requiring quick, thoughtful answers and evidence of problem solving ability by the candidate.

string streets Retail thoroughfares located away from central business districts that retain thriving clusters of shops in or near residential neighborhoods.

strip center "An attached row of stores or service outlets managed as a coherent retail entity." (ICSC)

striping The practice of displaying merchandise in vertical formats to bring attention to deep merchandise assortments carried by the retailer.

sub-classification Groups of merchandise in a classification that are defined more narrowly.

superette Small grocery store that is larger than a mom-and-pop store but smaller than a supermarket.

supermarkets Self-service food and grocery stores of under 100,000 square feet that carry some nonfood items but do not have extensive specialty departments.

superregional center Shopping center consisting of three or more anchor stores and as many as 350 specialty and service retailers.

superstores Huge retail stores, usually over 150,000 square feet, that combine general merchandise, and often food, under one roof.

supply chain Various participants in the marketing channel including manufacturers, suppliers, distributors, and retailers.

swing areas Key areas in stores that are used for rotating displays or small temporary departments.

S.W.O.T. analysis Lists a company's strengths, weaknesses, opportunities, and threats and is used to help determine future direction.

symmetrical balance Positioning items on either side of a center line so that they are equally weighted optically.

target market A group of people with similar characteristics and needs whom a company wishes to reach.

tariff A duty or tax imposed by a government on an import.

tearsheet Page torn from a publication and sent to an advertiser, vendor, or agency to prove that the advertisement has run.

tertiary trading area Wide area located outside the primary and secondary trading areas, containing 5 to 25 percent of the store's potential customers.

theme/festival center Venues oriented toward entertainment as well as shopping; also called *festival marketplace.*

thrust areas Prime locations in stores used for the display of new, high-margin, or seasonal items.

total quality management (TQM) Management systems that encourage team work and ownership of the production, distribution, or retailing process.

town centers Retail urban villages located outdoors consisting of buildings with nostalgic architectural features or theme designs.

track lighting Display lighting that consists of moveable units mounted on vertical or horizontal tracks.

trade advertising Business-to-business advertising used among supply chain members and not directed to final customers.

trade discount A deduction from an agreed price, usually granted by manufacturers to other supply chain members.

trade embargo Restriction set on the importation of goods by a government.

trade sanctions Penalties imposed on one country by another in an attempt to curb unfair trade practices.

trading area Geographic area from which a retailer draws its customers.

trading bloc Major geographic trading area such as Europe, North America, or the Pacific Rim countries in Asia.

triple net Leasing term that describes a retailer's responsibility for paying insurance, utilities, and internal upkeep.

turnaround time The time that passes between an action and the response to it such as the placement of an order and the receipt of it.

turnkey operation A methodically planned retail store or service that is completely ready to begin operation.

turnover The number of times inventory is sold and replenished in a year. Also referred to as *turn* or *stock turn*. (Note: Some European retailers use the word *turnover* to refer to annual sales volume.)

twofers Retail slang for offering two products at one price.

Underwriters Laboratories Inc. Large, independent, nonprofit testing group whose UL mark means the product has been safety tested against national standards.

unit plan A detailed list of all items being purchased by color, style, size, and price.

unit pricing The quotation of prices in terms of a standard unit of measurement such as pounds or kilograms.

unity The sense of wholeness that is achieved when elements are well integrated in artwork, advertising, or display.

universal product code (UPC) Product identification information electronically encoded in a series of printed stripes found on most products.

universal resource locator (URL) The unique address, called a *domain name,* given to each Web site.

utility Ability of a product to satisfy consumer's needs and wants. Four basic utilities include: time, place, form, and possession.

value-added tax (VAT) Tax on the value levied at each stage of processing for a raw material or of production and distribution for a commodity or retail product. The tax used in EU countries, similar to a sales tax in the United States.

value center A cross between a power center and an outlet center.

value megamall Large hybrid mall containing elements of power, value, and outlet centers, with added entertainment components.

value pricing Providing the best quality for the lowest price as viewed by customers.

vendors Direct suppliers of merchandise and business products for retail sale or use. Also referred to as *resources.*

vertical cooperative advertising Advertising for which a manufacturer or other supply chain member agrees to share costs with a retailer.

vertical integration When two or more supply chain members are owned by the same company.

vertical mall Shopping center in a high-rise building, usually in an urban location.

very small aperture terminal (VSAT) Satellite communication system that is linked to a computer network without using telephone lines.

video datacasting Technology that uses television airwaves to send Internet data.

wall systems Full-height perimeter partitions and high partitions placed between departments.

want slips Notations gathered by sales associates regarding merchandise requested by customers but not carried by the store.

warehouse clubs Large format, bare-bones retail stores that sell a broad assortment of merchandise to small businesses as well as families and individuals.

Web site Specific location of a business, organization, or person on the World Wide Web.

weeks-of-supply method Inventory planning system in which stock on hand is kept at a level representing projected sales for a predetermined number of weeks.

wheel of retailing Theory that describes a cyclical pattern of retail evolution consisting of three phases: entry, trading-up, and vulnerability.

white space The portion of an advertisement that is not used for type or illustration.

wobblers Signs on spring assemblies that jiggle to attract attention.

World Trade Organization (WTO) International governing body composed of representatives from approximately 140 countries that grants PTP status, regulates trade, and settles disputes among members.

World Wide Web Totally integrated informational and commercial electronic services accessible via global computer links and wireless technology.

Company Index

A&P, 128
A&W All American Food Restaurants, 130–131
Abercrombie and Fitch, 164, 299
Abraham and Straus (A&S), 147, 353
ACNielsen Company, 294, 408
Adam, Nancy, 358
Adecco, 261
Advanced Research Projects Agency (ARPA), 185–186
AEON Group, 140
Agan, Tom, 363
"Age of McFashion," 115
Ahold USA Retail, 128
Airport Retail Portfolio Group, 333
A.J. Wright stores, 330
Albertson's, 44, 127, 128
Alcas Corporation, 171
Alexander McQueen, 139
Al Ghurair Centre, 360
Allied Domecq PLC, 140
Allied Stores Corporation, 147–148
Alloy.com, 193
Amazon.com, 194, 196, 244–247
American Collegiate Retailing Association, 518
American Eagle Outfitters, 196, 198
American Express, 495, 504
American Fare (Kmart's), 129
American Greetings, 93, 204
American Stores, 127
Americans with Disabilities Act (ADA), 76, 79
America Online (AOL), 186, 196, 245
Ames Department Stores, 13
Amoskeag Manufacturing Company, 25–26
Amway, 172, 519
Anaheim Plaza, 359
Ann Taylor Loft, 358, 419
Arden B., 82
Argos, 125
Armani, 14, 353, 355
ARPANET, 186
Art Mart, 146
Ask Jeeves, 186
Associated Merchandising Corporation (AMC), 425, 428
Association of Southeast Asian Nations (ASEAN), 214–215
Atlanta Apparel Mart, 423

Auchan, 45, 129, 237
AutoZone, 116
Ayamas, 140

Baby Gap, 138, 509, 512, 513
Bagnoud, Christian, 497
Bali brand, 139
Banana Republic, 138, 512–514
Barnes & Noble Booksellers, 50, 82, 116, 122, 191, 245, 357, 495
Barnes, Joan, 509
Barneys New York, 140, 151–152, 429, 444
Barney the Dinosaur, 430
Baskin-Robbins ice cream, 140
Bates, Susan, 533–536
Bath & Body Works, 152
Bayside center, 346
B. Dalton bookstores, 90
B.E. (Basic Essentials) sportswear, 441
Bell Canada, 388
Bellman's Jewelers, 193
Ben & Jerry's, 189
Benetton, 488
Berg, Peter, 513
Bernstein, Leonard, 495
Bertelsmann, 245
Best Buy, 108, 116, 122, 347, 504
Big Lots, 116
Big Star SA, 512–513
Bill Blass, 430
Blischok, Thom, 39
Blockbuster video, 90–91, 261
Bloomingdale's, 49, 93, 109–110, 115, 147, 164, 425
Bluefly.com, 196, 258
Blunck, Richard, 490
Bob's Stores, 320
Body Shop, The, 59, 236
Bon Ton, The, 488
Bookpages, Ltd., 245
Boots drug stores, 237, 476
Borders Books, 122, 205, 245
Borders Group, 116
Brain Reserve, The, 289
Brimfield Antique Market, 16
British Retail Consortium (BRC), 235
Broadway stores, 147
Broderick, Dennis, 442

Subject Index